THE
WAY OF THE
SHIP

THE WAY OF THE SHIP

AMERICA'S MARITIME HISTORY REENVISIONED, 1600–2000

Alex Roland

W. Jeffrey Bolster

Alexander Keyssar

John Wiley & Sons, Inc.

This book is printed on acid-free paper. ♾

Published by John Wiley & Sons, Inc., Hoboken, New Jersey
Published simultaneously in Canada

Wiley Bicentennial Logo: Richard J. Pacifico

Design and composition by Navta Associates, Inc.

Limit of Liability/Disclaimer of Warranty: While the publisher and the author have used their best efforts in preparing this book, they make no representations or warranties with respect to the accuracy or completeness of the contents of this book and specifically disclaim any implied warranties of merchantability or fitness for a particular purpose. No warranty may be created or extended by sales representatives or written sales materials. The advice and strategies contained herein may not be suitable for your situation. You should consult with a professional where appropriate. Neither the publisher nor the author shall be liable for any loss of profit or any other commercial damages, including but not limited to special, incidental, consequential, or other damages.

For general information about our other products and services, please contact our Customer Care Department within the United States at (800) 762-2974, outside the United States at (317) 572-3993 or fax (317) 572-4002.

Wiley also publishes its books in a variety of electronic formats. Some content that appears in print may not be available in electronic books. For more information about Wiley products, visit our web site at www.wiley.com.

Library of Congress Cataloging-in-Publication Data

Roland, Alex, date.
  The way of the ship : America's maritime history reenvisioned / Alex Roland, W. Jeffrey Bolster, Alexander Keyssar.
    p. cm.
  Includes bibliographical references and index.
  ISBN 978-0-470-13600-3 (cloth)
  1. Merchant marine—United States—History. 2. Merchant mariners—United States—History. 3. Shipping—United States—History. 4. Navigation—United States—History. 5. United States—History, Naval. I. Bolster, W. Jeffrey. II. Keyssar, Alexander. III. Title.
  HE745.R54 2007
  387.50973—dc22
                                2007039348

Printed in the United States of America

10 9 8 7 6 5 4 3 2 1

To
Eliot Lumbard

CONTENTS

PART II

A World within Themselves: The Golden Age and the Rise of Inland Shipping, 1783–1861

PART III

Maritime Industry and Labor in the Gilded Age, 1861–1914

ACKNOWLEDGMENTS

This book was sponsored by the American Maritime History Project, Inc. (AMHPI), a New York, not-for-profit corporation conceived and organized by Eliot Lumbard. The authors are indebted to the AMHPI board of directors: Virgil R. Allen, Commander, U.S. Coast Guard (Ret.); Charles Dana Gibson; Albert J. Herberger, Vice Admiral, USN (Ret.); Captain Warren G. Leback; Dr. Gary A. Lombardo; Eliot H. Lumbard, Esq. (Chair); Dr. Warren F. Mazek; David A. O'Neil* (Vice-Chair); Thomas J. Patterson, Rear Admiral, USMS (Ret.); Ellsworth L. Peterson; Anthony P. Romano Jr., (Treasurer); George J. Ryan; Carl J. Seiberlich, Rear Admiral, USN (Ret.)*; Fred S. Sherman; and James H. Yocum. The authors also recognize the contributions of the AMHPI advisory committee: James H. Ackerman, Esq.*; Peter A. Aron; Dr. George B. Billy (Secretary); Frank O. Braynard; Dr. Jane P. Brickman; Dr. Charles R. Cushing; Jose Femenia; Donald W. Forster; Reginald M. Hayden Jr., Esq.; John Hightower; Edward V. Kelly; Robert H. Keifer; Adolph B. Kurz,*; Guy E. C. Maitland, Esq.; Dr. Karen E. Markoe; John Maxtone-Graham; Lauren S. McCready, Rear Admiral, USMS (Ret.); Captain Arthur R. Moore; Dr. Janet F. Palmer; Charles M. Renick, Captain, USMS (Ret.); George R. Searle; James T. Shirley, Jr., Esq.; Brian D. Starer, Esq.; Joseph D. Stewart, Vice Admiral, USMS; Eric Y. Wallischeck, Captain, USMS; and Thomas Wilcox.

---

*deceased

The research and writing of the book were supported by the generous contributions of the Project's benefactors: James H. Ackerman (Evalyn M. Bauer Foundation); Bunis S. Acuff; Alexander & Baldwin Foundation (Matson Navigation Co.); Myles J. Ambrose; American Bureau of Shipping; American Merchant Marine Veterans, National Headquarters, Cape Coral, FL; American Merchant Marine Veterans, Edwin J. O'Hara Chapter, New York, NY; American Merchant Marine Veterans, Dennis A. Roland Chapter, Midland Park, NJ; American Merchant Marine Veterans, Puget Sound Chapter, Seattle, WA; John O. Arntzen; Peter A. Aron (J. Aron Charitable Foundation, Inc.); Cecil S. Ashdown; William F. Bachmaier; James H. Baker; Samuel Bassini; William E. Berks; Dr. George J. Billy; Eugene C. Bonacci; Bruce and Christine Bowen; Roland A. Bowling; Donald C. Brett; Dr. Jane P. and John M. Brickman; Philip C. Calian; Harry Carl; Bernard J. Carpenter; The Chubb Corporation; John F. Clair; Albert B. Clarke; Thomas J. Clossey; Philip J. Comba; Sidney A. Cooley; August W. Cordes Jr.; Robert E. Crabtree Sr.; Susan M. Cropper; David and Ama Davies; Dr. B. G. Davis; Stephen E. Davis; Henry G. Dircks; Edward M. Donaher; Matthew M. Drag; John Dziekan; Fernando and Mary Ebhardt; James A. Fairfield; Harry Fisher; Donald W. Forster (Marine and Industrial Power, Inc.; Charles F. French; George Gans; Charles Dana Gibson; Alvin Golden; John R. Graham; Rodney Gregory; John F. Hatley; Peter S. Herrick; High Seas Mariners Chapter, Willow Grove, PA; Moses W. Hirschkowitz; Richard A. Hoffman; Russell H. Holm; Andrew A. Hunter; Harold D. Hunter; Niels W. Johnsen (International Shipholding Corporation); Edgar Arnold Johnston; Neil E. Jones; Robert H. Kiefer; Thomas A. King; Daniel Kowalyk; Arthur and Alice Kramer Foundation; Paul L. Krinsky; Dorothy Kurz; Edythe J. Layne; Walter Leander; Thomas J. and Cheryl Linter; V. J. Longhi Associates; Franklyn R. Lozier; Henry Luce Foundation; Eliot H. Lumbard; John A. Lumbard; Bruce N. Macdonald; Guy E. Clay Maitland; Herbert J. Maletz; Marine Society of the City of New York; Masters, Mates & Pilots; Lauren S. McCready; Thomas F. McEvily Jr.; Roberta I. McGalliard; William E. Meagher; Constantino J. Meccarello; Mark M. Miller; James J. Moore (National Maritime Historical Society); Richard G. Morris; David A. O'Neil (Seaworthy Systems, Inc.); Robert M. Pennoyer; Ellsworth L. and Carla Peterson Charitable Foundation (and the Fred J. Peterson Foundation, Inc., Peterson Builders, Inc.); Lawrence W. Pierce; Richard W. Quinn Sr.; Paul W. Reinhardt; Charles M. Renick; Robert W. Reutti; Cy Lloyd (Rosie) Roberts; Fred G. Roebuck Jr.;

Anthony P. Romano Jr.; George J. Ryan; George R. Searle; Carl B. Shaw; Fred S. Sherman; James T. Shirley Jr.; Enoch C. Silva; Leroy J. Smith; Lester Stoveken; SUNY Maritime College Alumni Association; Robert W. Sweet; Theodore H. Teplow; Theodore A. Tribolati (Gibbs & Cox, Inc.); Walter A. Turchick; Harold R. Tyler; USMMA Alumni Association, Northern New Jersey Chapter; William D. Walsh; Delmore Washington Sr.; Hugh L. Webster; Women's Propeller Club, Port of New York; William R. Woody; and Dorothy Zelinsky.

The staff of the U.S. Merchant Marine Academy at Kings Point, New York, has been consistently supportive and helpful. Academy Superintendent Vice Admiral Joseph D. Stewart has taken a personal interest in the project and followed its development closely. Professor Warren Mazek, who was the academic dean during most of the project, has been equally involved and helpful. Dr. George Billy and his entire staff at the USMMA Library have gone far beyond the call of duty in finding materials and making the entire resources of the library available to the authors. Many other members of the USMMA faculty and staff have likewise given freely of their time and facilities to make the authors feel at home and to help us understand the complexities of the maritime enterprise.

Above and beyond the credits that are given in the text to the owners of the images used as illustrations, special thanks must be accorded John Stobart for his extraordinary generosity in allowing his paintings to be used on the front and back dust covers of the book and in the two color inserts. Widely recognized as America's most celebrated marine artist, Mr. Stobart has captured both contemporary and historical maritime life with an unparalleled vibrance and accuracy that bring the words in this book to life.

The authors accumulated many professional debts in the course of researching, writing, and revising this text. David Sicilia and Raymond Ashley were original members of the authorial team. While both had to leave the project short of completing their sections, they nonetheless contributed to the conceptualization of the book. David Sicilia also completed twenty-four oral history interviews, which have been transcribed and archived with the records of the American Maritime History Project at the U.S. Merchant Marine Academy at Kings Point, New York. Jeffrey T. Coster assisted David Sicilia in the preparation of an extensive database, which is also archived at Kings Point.

Each author individually accumulated his own debts in the course of research. Alex Roland wishes to thank the staff of the Perkins Library system at Duke University for unstinting assistance in obtaining materials and offering research advice. Sebastian Lukasik assisted with research on, and drafted sections of, Parts II and V. Blair Hayworth prepared a preliminary reconnaissance of materials on maritime history in the libraries of the North Carolina Triangle Research Libraries Network. Andrea Franzius labored heroically to compile data on the collective history of the world's ports. Charles Franzen helped in the preparation of the appendices and the graphs derived from them. Dr. Martin Reuss provided access to the rich holdings of the History Office of the U.S. Army Corps of Engineers and shared his intimate knowledge of the corps' library holdings. In addition to reading early drafts of the text, Captain Arthur R. Moore and Charles Dana Gibson welcomed Alex Roland into their homes and shared their extensive knowledge and understanding of American maritime history. Through the generous offices of George Ryan, president of the Lake Carriers' Association and the Interlake Steamship Company, Captain Timothy Dayton welcomed Alex Roland aboard the *Mesabi Miner* in May of 2000 for an illuminating trip from Lorain, Ohio, to Taconite Harbor, Minnesota. Bill Kooiman and the staff of the J. Porter Shaw Library of the San Francisco National Historical Park educated Roland on their rich holdings of materials on the California gold rush. The many repositories that provided generous assistance with obtaining illustrations are recognized in the captions. Liz Roland read the entire manuscript in search of errors and inconsistencies.

W. Jeffrey Bolster, the author of Part I, would like to thank Dr. William B. Leavenworth for research assistance, especially with material on the colonial coasting trade. Dr. Neill DePaoli also worked effectively as a research assistant for many sections of Part I, as did Joshua Minty, who tracked down material on Florida and Louisiana. J. William Harris read the manuscript carefully and helpfully, and Molly Bolster provided levelheaded encouragement. Much of Part I was written at Syddansk Universitet (the University of Southern Denmark), in Odense, Denmark, where the author spent a year as the Fulbright Chair in American Studies. He thanks his Danish American Studies colleagues for their hospitality and intellectual companionship.

Alexander Keyssar would like to thank Nicole Tunks, Jessica Kinloch, and Allyson Kelley for their assistance on the research for this project.

In addition to Liz Roland, many others read all or part of the manuscript, some more than once. Eliot Lumbard read multiple drafts of the entire manuscript and provided more counsel than the authors could well absorb. Captain Warren Leback read the entire manuscript twice and provided exhaustive, detailed, often documented suggestions that reflected his distinguished perspective as a former administrator of the U.S. Maritime Administration and his legendary conscientiousness. George Ryan read the entire manuscript in revised draft and in page proofs and provided many helpful suggestions. Hana Lane, Dr. Arthur Donovan, and Salvatore Mercogliano also read the penultimate draft of the complete manuscript and provided helpful insights and observations. Charles R. Cushing provided enormously helpful recommendations and clarifications on Part IV and Part V, as did Anthony Romano and Donald Yearwood. Dr. George Billy brought his historian's eye to bear on various drafts as the project proceeded.

Hana Lane and her staff at John Wiley & Sons were more than professional and competent. They embraced this project with enthusiasm and commitment, repeatedly making interventions that made this a better book than it would have been otherwise. John Lane contributed not only original illustrations for the text but also hospitality and the invaluable insights from a career as an artist and a sailor.

In spite of all the help we have received, the authors take full responsibility for any errors of omission or commission that remain.

THE
WAY OF THE
SHIP

INTRODUCTION

WATER TRANSPORT HAS BEEN THE LEAST EXPENSIVE MEANS OF moving cargo and passengers throughout most of America's history. This book tells its story.

The United States is the world's largest trading nation. The dollar value of its imports and exports is greater than that of any other country. Ninety-five percent of the cargo tonnage that enters and leaves the United States comes and goes by ship. Never before, however, has U.S.-flagged oceanic shipping been such a small percentage of world shipping. Never in the nation's history has shipping been so invisible to Americans. Shipping has so far receded from public consciousness in the United States that it is now difficult to recall that the country began as a group of maritime provinces hugging the Atlantic coast of North America and depending on ships for their way of life, for life itself.

Perhaps the greatest irony in the history of shipping in America is the central theme of this book: most Americans think of shipping as an oceanic enterprise, as indeed it was during the colonial period. But for most of U.S. history, shipping on coastal and inland waters has exceeded oceanic shipping in both volume and value. America is a brown-water nation, with a blue-water consciousness. Beginning early in the nineteenth century, Americans began trading more with themselves than they did with the rest of the world. And all of this shipping was

1

protected from foreign competition by cabotage laws (the exclusion of foreign vessels from shipping between American ports) adopted early in the Republic. The quintessential depiction of shipping in the United States during that time is not Richard Henry Dana's *Two Years before the Mast* but Mark Twain's *Life on the Mississippi*.

Only in 1994 did the nation's oceanic shipping resume the preponderance over domestic shipping that it had enjoyed in the colonial era, thanks in large measure to the globalization that the megaships of the late twentieth century had fostered and exploited. The goal of this book is to retell the story of shipping in American history, revising the canonical account of the rise and fall of the American merchant marine. We substitute a tale that is no less stirring, although one that better fits the evidence. Based on a global perspective, and relying on the crucial contributions of coastal and inland shipping, it illuminates the defining ironies that have beset the way of the ship.

The heart of the maritime enterprise is, and always has been, commercial shipping, the transport of passengers and goods from port to port by water. Today this comprises a vast web of activities and infrastructure. Ships entering and leaving American ports require aids to navigation; resupply of fuel, food, and water; local pilots and agents; shore workers to load and unload; admiralty lawyers; insurers; and more. Intermodal cargo passes seamlessly between ships, trucks, railroads, and even airplanes; petroleum often flows directly from ship to pipeline at offshore platforms. Megaships a quarter of a mile long load and unload their cargoes in hours, not days, contributing to just-in-time inventory systems that have become a hallmark of the globalized economy. Ships seldom linger in port long enough for their crews to put ashore. The pace of shipping, especially oceanic shipping, continues to accelerate in the early twenty-first century, even as the ships themselves recede from public view and consciousness.

This book explains how the United States moved from the ships, barks, and pinnaces that brought Europeans to North America in the age of discovery to the megaships that sail the world's oceans today and the coastal and river craft that ply America's brown waters. It primarily illuminates the changing nature of cargo and passenger ships, riverboats and barges. It covers only tangentially naval vessels, military transports, fishing and whaling vessels, and special-purpose work boats such as dredges and research vessels. It covers shipbuilding and port activities to the extent (often considerable) that they shaped the carriage of people and cargo. The American merchant marine looms large in the story, though this is not their story. Rather it is the story of waterborne commerce in American history, of the ways in which that form of transportation fueled the material and economic expansion of the United States and its antecedent colonies, even while it slowly receded from public consciousness.

Invisible though shipping became in America, it nonetheless has played a critical role in American history. Its story is one of risk, determination (often in wartime), and innovation, for shipping constantly changed its stripes. Through the story run iconic ships like the *Mayflower*, *Clermont* (not its real name), *Savannah*, *Flying Cloud*, *Alabama*, *J. Pierpont Morgan*, *United States*, *Sea-Land McLean*, and *Exxon Valdez*; gritty ports that waxed and waned, like Salem, Boston, New Orleans, Philadelphia, New York, Buffalo, Chicago, Detroit, St. Louis, San Francisco, Honolulu, and Houston; people such as Elias Haskett Derby, Robert Fulton, Henry Shreve, Donald McKay, Matthew Fontaine Maury, Cornelius Vanderbilt, Andrew Carnegie, Robert Dollar, and Malcom McLean.

This book stitches these disparate entities together with five analytical threads. First, and foremost, is *economics*. Shipping is and always has been a commercial activity. America's oceanic shipping operates in a competitive market that has driven the rise and fall of shipping empires and business models. American brown-water shipping competed for passengers and cargoes with other forms of transportation as the country spread across the North American continent and overseas.

The economics of shipping goes hand in hand with government *policy*, the second analytical thread running through this volume. The cabotage laws that limit transport between American ports to American ships have done more to shape the history of shipping in this country than any other factor. America's search for a structure of subsidies to sustain its oceanic merchant marine dominated the nineteenth and twentieth centuries.

Labor forms the third thread running through this history. The harsh and dangerous life of the seaman was meliorated somewhat in the nineteenth and twentieth centuries by legislative reform and improved technology. But maritime labor in the United States has always been a house divided, seeking but never achieving the one big union that might find the proper balance between wages and working conditions.

The *military* forms the fourth thread of the story, actually three threads spun into one. As the naval theorist Alfred Thayer Mahan made clear, the sole purpose of a navy is to protect shipping. So naval history shadows maritime history. Additionally, in wartime, commercial shipping has often been pressed into military service, carrying to foreign shores the troops and supplies that allowed the United States to project its military power overseas. And naval architecture is a unified field of ship design and construction encompassing both naval and commercial vessels. It therefore serves as a conduit for technological innovation to flow between the two.

Finally, *technology* shaped shipping. Ships are, after all, complex technological artifacts, the largest movable structures built by humans. The United States has spawned some transcendent maritime technology, such as the clipper ships of the nineteenth century and the container ships of the late twentieth century. But shipping sails in an international marketplace that assimilates and normalizes technological innovation. Keeping up with the pace of maritime innovation has been a constant challenge throughout American history.

In the book that follows, these five threads weave together a single story of shipping in the making of America. Over the centuries, and sometimes year to year, the changes have been colossal: during the colonial era stubby square-riggers made shipping a leading sector of the American economy. In the midtwentieth century a drab aluminum box, the container, and the ships that evolved to handle it transformed the global economy and the consumption patterns of everyone in America. Shipping has at times been glamorous—a means of connecting America to Europe or Asia, and connecting East Coast to West Coast with clipper ships or five-star liners. At other times it has been mundane and ignored, a taken-for-granted but vital cog in the wheel of commerce. The mainstays of the U.S. economy continue to move by water, even though few Americans know port from starboard, or a ship from a boat. At one time the maritime trades were, after agriculture, the second largest employer of American labor; today only a minuscule percentage of Americans work in the shipping industry. Though shipping is no longer as salient in people's lives as it was when Richard Henry Dana and Mark Twain transformed working on the water into unforgettable American literature, it is still an indispensable component of the world's largest economy.

The American merchant marine has a story of its own, and quite a different one. Domestic shipping along America's coasts and inland waterways carries the bulk cargo that sustains the economy. But American-flagged oceanic shipping has experienced more or less steady decline, not just since the Civil War, as the canonical account of American maritime history suggests, but since the days of the early Republic. There were two flowerings of American oceanic shipping in the periods surrounding the two world wars. And some companies invented and sustained business models that allowed them to compete successfully in the international shipping market. But the threads running through this book—economics, policy, labor, war, and technology—reveal both the clarity of the long-term trend and the reasons for its trajectory. It turns out that the history of American shipping is less like that of Great Britain, to which it has often been compared, and more like that of Germany, a nation focused as much on river traffic into the European continent as on overseas shipping. This book does not address the question of whether the United States needs an oceanic merchant marine, but it does explain why the one it has is so disproportionate to the nation's economy and its place in the world. Nor does this book take a position on the merits of cabotage, which sustains a domestic merchant marine. It does show how important shipping has been in American history over the past four hundred years.

The way of the ship in the midst of the sea has captivated people's imaginations since biblical times. As deeply rooted and traditional as any enterprise in America, it is nevertheless a way of life and labor that will continue to evolve, as it always has, with an eye on the future. By then, new histories will be required. But for now, the story of American shipping deserves the reenvisioning it receives here.

PART I

WHEN SHIPPING WAS KING

Colonial Shipping and
the Making of America,
1600–1783

1

THE COLONIES
AND THE SEA

ISAAC ALLERTON WAS NOT A TYPICAL PILGRIM, ALTHOUGH HE loved the Lord as much as any of the Separatists who disembarked from the *Mayflower* in the blustery winter of 1620, and he sacrificed willingly for his domineering faith. Allerton served a term as deputy governor of the infant colony at Plymouth, and later became its commercial agent. Commerce meant controversy, however, in the cosmos of the Pilgrims. Most remained leery of its threatening potential to corrupt their godly society. Allerton, on the other hand, one of the first merchant shipowners and coastal traders based in English America, sensed the potential of the market. Ten years in Holland had opened his eyes to commercial possibilities in shipping so ably exploited by the Dutch, and despite most Englishmen's contempt for Dutch ways, he had assimilated sufficient Dutch culture and language to give him an edge in the world of international trade. Parting ways with Governor William Bradford and other Pilgrim leaders, Allerton eventually left Plymouth, taking up residence in New Haven and New Amsterdam, all the while crisscrossing the Atlantic to London, and trading in Barbados, Dutch Curaçao, eastern Maine, and Delaware Bay. By the time he died in 1659, the renegade Pilgrim had not only prospered, but had committed himself to the way of the ship, a path significantly more influential in the development of America than the Pilgrims' utopian communalism.[1]

During Allerton's decades in America, shipwrights between New Amsterdam and Cape Elizabeth, Maine, launched an impressive stream of vessels, modest in size compared to many European merchant ships, but capable nevertheless of coastal and ocean voyages. Even before the Restoration Parliament passed navigation acts to encourage and regulate English shipping, cargo vessels owned and built in American colonies began to appear in Fayal, Madeira, Barbados, London, and other ports. Some Englishmen in America clearly saw more opportunity on the Atlantic frontier than on the continent stretching westward.

As early as 1669 Sir Josiah Child, the renowned political economist, fretted that nothing was more prejudicial and dangerous to the "Mother Kingdom than the increase of Shipping in her Colonies, Plantations, or Provinces." His concern was not simply an increase in the number of colonially built hulls. Ships, after all, were only extensions of the men who operated them. As he perceived it, the threat to an empire dominated from London was the animating spirit behind Atlantic shipping, the willingness to take risks in the quest for economic development, and the fact that such a spirit might establish roots beyond the reach of authorities in Whitehall.[2]

By the time Child wrote, a new world was taking shape on the western edge of the Atlantic. Part of it was English, a loose assembly of colonies ranging from semitropical plantations to raucous fishing camps and pious communities of religious zealots. Binding them together was a shared sense of "Englishness," in addition to a fleet of seaworthy little ships that linked far-flung corners of empire, and the palpable energy of men bent on economic advancement. Shipping, as Child sensed, was not simply a means of transportation or a type of investment during the seventeenth century. Appearing traditional, it was actually a metaphor for forward-looking commercial energy that was leaving the past in its wake.

Shipowners and operators in the early modern age, including colonial American ones, were at the heart of several world-changing phenomena—the unification of the Atlantic world and the seismic shift in economic activity that has come to be known as the Commercial Revolution. For the first time, Europe, Africa, and America became linked, albeit loosely, into a unified commodity and labor market. This required hundreds of thousands of voyages, increasing numbers of which began or ended in the British American colonies that became the United States. And ultimately that nation, or at least many of the white people in it, became the greatest beneficiary of early modern Atlantic commerce. During the seventeenth and eighteenth centuries the long-term rate of economic growth in the thirteen mainland colonies exceeded, perhaps even doubled, that of Great Britain. By the time shots were fired at Lexington and Concord, per capita gross domestic product in what would become the United States was substantially higher than it had been one hundred years before, higher than that of every other country in the world, and higher than it would be for the foreseeable future. "Nowhere," note two leading economic historians, "was that rise to 'wealth and greatness' more rapid than in the colonies of British America." Predicated on abundant land and the exploitation of resources and labor, this remarkable development became possible because of overseas trade and shipping.[3]

The bluff-bowed ketches, sloops, and ships so visible in colonial seaports figure prominently in historians' calculations of early American economic growth, but they have rarely been credited with carrying the

Small, locally built sailing vessels, such as this bluff-bowed ketch, were a mainstay of colonial economic development. Such ships carried news, goods, and passengers from port to port among the colonies, connecting them commercially and socially before they finally connected politically.

freight of colonial American history as they should. Simply put, colonially owned and operated shipping contributed as much as any other single factor to the economic rise and political cohesion of the thirteen British mainland colonies. Obviously, without the land itself and salable commodities, or the robustly growing population and emergence of new political and cultural values, there would be no story to tell. But shipping was the only piece of the puzzle that was simultaneously a vital economic activity *and* a means of integrating thirteen disparate colonies into one relatively cohesive nation. The first colonial newspaper was the *Boston News-Letter* in 1704. New Yorkers could not read a local newspaper before 1725; Virginians not before 1736. By then coastal vessels had been sailing between Virginia and New England for more than a century, promoting intercolonial communication. Southern planters would have had much less in common with Yankee merchants and lawyers on the eve of the American Revolution had northern shippers not been freighting southern plantation staples for generations, creating mutual profits, mutual interests, and mutual trust. While it is impossible to imagine colonial America without abundant land and resources, profitable commodities, and its signature institution—slavery—none of those crucial factors, each of whose legacy remains prominent today, had the orchestrating effect of locally owned shipping during the colonial period.

Locally owned shipping made a vital difference. Had shipping services necessary for commercial development been provided by vessels from England or Europe, the North American colonies would have remained economically and politically subordinate to Great Britain for considerably longer, and the colonial standard of living would have been substantially lower. Locally owned shipping plowed profits back into the colonies, creating spin-offs and multipliers like insurance, shipbuilding, and chandlery services. *Shipbuilding* was unquestionably the colonies' most profitable export manufacturing industry, and significant numbers of American-built ships were added to the British fleet virtually every year before the Revolution. Meanwhile, maritime work became the second largest occupation in colonial America, exceeded only by agriculture. Colonial men not only made a living at sea, they shaped their personal and class identities in the distinctive world of the ship, while women in maritime communities developed independence through the absence of men. Living within a day's walk of the ocean, and knowing mariners or frequently seeing them, many residents in seventeenth-century and early-eighteenth-century British America lived in a maritime society.[4]

This part of the book explores the origins of colonial American shipping, its development under the protective tent of the British Navigation Acts and provincial legislation, and its reconfiguration during the American Revolution. While many Americans in the seventeenth and eighteenth centuries did not support unregulated economic growth, much less the social stratification that profits from shipping created, every resident was affected by commercialization and the trajectory away from economic isolation made possible by shipping.

2

RICHARD HAKLUYT'S MARITIME PLANTATIONS

THE FIRST TWO GENERATIONS OF COLONIAL AMERICAN merchants understood themselves as bit players on the remote western periphery of the European economy. Their remarkable success needs to be understood, initially at least, in the context of the European commercial revolution occurring between 1550 and 1650, when the Atlantic, including its western coast, was drawn securely into the orbit of European capitalism. Colonial American shipping was launched at a propitious moment, during an era of English commercial ascendancy.[1]

Until about 1550, exporting woolen broadcloth to northern Europe had been the sheet anchor of English commerce. As the broadcloth trade faltered in midcentury, however, English merchant companies pioneered new import and reexport trades with the East Indies, Russia, and the Mediterranean. English commerce was increasingly carried in English vessels, to the exclusion of foreigners. Truculent English seamen also developed a knack for privateering. Most scholars agree that English companies ultimately muscled their way into control of Mediterranean commerce because of their aggressive and well-organized business organizations in London, and their superior ships, which were often well armed. Success in the landlocked Mediterranean became a springboard for what Robert Brenner calls "the rise of English commercial power throughout the world during the following century."[2]

The embryonic shipping enterprises taking shape on the coast of New England during the first half of the seventeenth century were thus born to a robust parent. English merchant ship tonnage more than doubled between 1550 and 1630. By 1650, when ships from New England were becoming a presence on Atlantic sea lanes, the previously dominant maritime powers of Europe were in decline. Italians no longer controlled Mediterranean commerce, Germans (the Hansa merchants) no longer dominated northern European trading, and the merchant navies of Spain and Portugal were a spent force. Economic energy in Europe had shifted to the northern Netherlands, and to England. Innovative banking, expansive shipbuilding, and aggressiveness—both in privateering and in control over markets and routes—propelled Dutch and English success. While Dutch shippers would dominate world trade from 1585 to 1740, English merchants gained an ever larger slice of the Atlantic pie. By 1700 English shipping, including its colonial American branch, was thoroughly invested in Atlantic commerce, more so than the competition from any other northern European nation.[3]

No individual did more to promote the settlement of North America, and to extol its commercial possibilities, than Richard Hakluyt, the younger of two promoters with the same name. He believed passionately that the government should encourage economic development for the mutual benefit of the Crown and enterprising Englishmen. His "Discourse of Western Planting," published in 1584, envisioned English plantations in America as a means to "inlarge Revenewes of the Crowne very mightely and inriche all sortes of subjects ingenerally." Overpopulation and unemployment in England, according to Hakluyt, would drive the kingdom to its knees unless an outlet could be found for "lustie youthes." Ignoring the fact that North America was already inhabited by indigenous people, Hakluyt wrote breezily of converting Native Americans to the "gospell of Christe" and claimed that their "gentle and amyable nature" would make them content to serve ambitious Englishmen who were eager to establish plantations. Like most of his contemporaries, Hakluyt thoroughly misjudged the Indians. More than most contemporaries, however, he envisioned individual Englishmen's destiny linked to maritime commerce and American plantations. Hard work and entrepreneurship in colonies brimming with resources would guarantee what he called England's "honor glorye and force," and would boost individuals' fortunes and self-confidence, allowing them to "finde themselves" and "be raised again."[4]

Hakluyt was a dreamer, far ahead of his time. He wrote during an era when military adventurers like Sir Humphrey Gilbert and Sir Walter Raleigh were voyaging to America. They were followed by explorers like Bartholomew Gosnold, who made landfall on the southern coast of Maine in the summer of 1602, and then coasted southward to Cape Cod and the Elizabeth Islands before returning to England; and Martin Pring, who made a similar summer voyage to New England with two ships in 1603. Publicists essential to the eventual settling of North America, those Elizabethan voyagers were light-years apart from the first generations of New England–based shipowners in mental outlook and life experience. While more than one such adventurer brought home a lading of fish, furs, or sassafras (thought to be a cure for the "French pox," as the English called syphilis), voyages of exploration were distinct enterprises from the creation of a merchant marine.[5]

The story of American shipping rightly begins with locally owned and operated coasting voyages during the early seventeenth century. "Fly-by-night traders," "temporary settlers," and "almost to a man outcasts from the respectable world of the English middle class" is how the historian Bernard Bailyn assessed the first generation of English merchants in New England. Gaining a foothold before the Puritan migration to Boston in 1630, men like John Oldham and Thomas Weston were too poor and transient to own oceangoing ships. Men on the make, they bought and resold goods that moved in English ships to the Pilgrims' village at Plymouth, or to fishing camps like those on Maine's Damariscove Island. That first generation, however, relied on their own shallops and ketches to collect furs, fish, and other American commodities, and to transport English goods up and down the coast. John Oldham knew the coast from Connecticut to Maine as well as any Englishman in the 1620s. "A mad Jack in his mood," as a contemporary called him, he was probably the most ambitious and successful Englishman in New England before Isaac Allerton or the Puritan merchants of the 1640s. Profane and self-confident, he had little in common with Pilgrims or Puritans. He antagonized them by trucking indiscriminately between Indians, fishermen, traders, and religious settlers.[6] His devilishly independent group of coast-wise trading colleagues, along with a few of the Pilgrim Fathers, was the charter generation of American shipowners and operators. They deserve attention not only as the transitional group between explorers like Pring and Gosnold and the entrenched Puritan merchants who followed them, but also as coastal shippers, a group long ignored in colonial American shipping histories. Their success, modest as it was, fulfilled Richard Hakluyt's vision of what enterprising English seafarers could accomplish on the coast of America. And their values and decisions regarding shipping prefigured those of subsequent settlers. Living in the midst of abundant natural resources that they perceived as commodities, and unwilling to divorce themselves from European technology and consumer goods, despite their distance from Europe, that first generation turned to boats as the means of making markets in the wilderness. Maritime commerce was not an end in itself, but a method of acquiring and distributing the exports and imports that made possible English life, even in remote plantations.

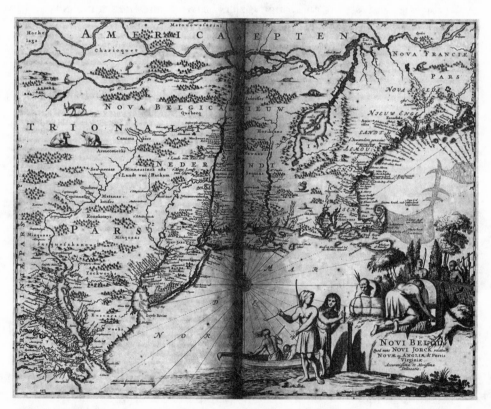

John Ogilby surveyed what he called New Belgium from the sea, looking to the northwest and capturing the coast of North America from the mouth of the Chesapeake Bay to the far reaches of what he called New England. This map, from his 1671 book *America: Being the Latest and Most Accurate Description of the New World*, shows a keen appreciation for the river systems that provided access to the interior.

This first generation of coastal shipping entrepreneurs shared the coast with native boatmen whose vessels and maritime traditions were significantly different. As early as 1524 Giovanni da Verrazzano had commented that indigenous people in Narragansett Bay "make their barges from the trunk of a single tree hollowed out in which 14–15 men will go comfortably, the short oar broad at one end working it solely with the strength of arms at sea without any peril with as much speed as it pleases them." English seamen later marveled at other native canoes for their extraordinarily light construction and versatility. "Their boats," wrote Martin Pring in 1603,

> were in proportion like a Wherrie of the River Thames, seventeene foot long and foure foot broad, and made of the Barke of a Birch-tree, farre exceeding in bignesse those of England: it was sowed together with strong and tough Oziers or twigs, and the seames covered over with Rozen or Turpentine. . . . And though it carried nine men standing upright, yet it weighed not at the most above sixtie pounds in weight, a thing almost incredible in regard of the large-nesse and capacitie thereof.[7]

The birchbark canoe was the crowning technological achievement of the native people residing in the northeast of America. Capable of voyages in protected coastal waters, it was admirably suited to traffic on rivers and lakes, and to portages that connected those waters.

Native peoples from the Hudson River east to Newfoundland routinely traveled to offshore islands, and moved along the coast in dugout and birchbark boats. Archaeological and ethnographic evidence indicates that they harpooned whales and swordfish from canoes, and caught cod and other fish. As English traders, fishermen, and settlers learned, natives also waged war from the water, using canoes to transport warriors. English newcomers thus assessed native nautical traditions with a mixture of respect and contempt. The first Indian the Puritans met at Cape Cod, for instance, was a notoriously skilled boat handler. He had just paddled alone, in winter, approximately one hundred miles from Monhegan Island on the coast of Maine.[8]

Although they lacked the technology to build plank-on-frame vessels, natives appropriated European boats almost from the moment of contact, and quickly learned to operate them. In the spring of 1602, long before the permanent English settlement of New England, John Brereton and his shipmates "came to an anker" in southern Maine, "where six Indians, in a Baske [Basque] shallop with mast and saile, an iron grapple, and a kettle of copper, came boldly aboord us." Numerous accounts during the next few decades relate how coastal natives attacked the English in canoes, occasionally seizing shallops or longboats, and burning ships.[9]

Yet English attacks and diseases rapidly overwhelmed many coastal Indians, and by 1637 (the year of the Pequot War) Long Island Sound had become an English lake. The sound lacked the fog, the harbors, and the escape routes that would continue to give native mariners an edge along the Maine coast. The last significant marine attack by natives against the English in southern New England occurred in 1634 when Indians killed John Oldham and his crew during a trading voyage to Block Island. They seized his vessel and were sailing toward the mainland when they were intercepted, evidence that coastal natives had learned to operate European sailing vessels by the 1630s.[10] But their grisly attack on one of New England's maverick traders, and the English settlers' retaliatory savagery in the Pequot War shortly thereafter, was an important turning point. It marked the end of the first generation of fly-by-night traders, and the end of Indian attacks by water south of Cape Cod. From then on devout Protestants rather than profane adventurers or Indians would control the southern New England coasts.

Native mariners continued to use boats for a variety of purposes. Some became accomplished sea fighters in European vessels, or whalemen and merchant seamen. Indians in Maine successfully attacked colonial fishermen until 1724. Samuel Hicks of Piscataqua volunteered that year to chase "the heavily armed Indian Pyrat who goes in a Marblehead Sconer with a great Gun that chases Everything and has taken Many and has driven the Fishermen from the Sea."[11]

Natives stopped their coastal attacks in 1724, but their birchbark canoes remained a presence on Maine shores well into the nineteenth century, where they were used by descendants of indigenous people for fishing and seasonal migration. Meanwhile settlers and their children borrowed dugout canoe technology, and "canoes" were often listed in inventories of decedents' goods. But cultural and technological exchange only went so far. Generally relegated to roles as workers aboard ship, natives ultimately exerted little collective influence on the commercial maritime culture that took root in New England. Richard Hakluyt had been right: not only would entrepreneurial Englishmen's maritime plantations prosper, they would also need to pay little heed to the Indians.

3

JOHN WINTHROP'S GODLY SOCIETY BY THE SEA

AMERICAN COLONIZATION AND LOCALLY OWNED SHIPPING emerged when influential Englishmen were reconceptualizing commercial activity and enthusiastically endorsing trade for the first time. This new openness to trade had profound implications for the development of American shipping. A continent rich in resources, an abundance of ship-building timber, numerous fine harbors, and technical comprehension of navigation were insufficient alone to build a powerful commercial sector and shipping network. The Chinese empire had all of those assets during the fifteenth century, as did Spain's Latin American colonies during the seventeenth and eighteenth centuries, yet in neither place did commercial shipping flourish. The Dutch republics during the seventeenth century, on the other hand, despite lacking many of those assets, due to their worship of trade nevertheless created one of the most remunerative merchant fleets the world had ever seen. And around 1600 some English gentlemen were beginning to self-consciously emulate them.

Only twenty-five years earlier Tudor society had still been "confused about the ethics of increased mercantile activity," notes the historian Carole Shammas, "and skeptical about its ultimate profitability to the public." The gentry were still *landed* gentry, unconvinced that foreign trade could be crucial to prosperity for themselves or the kingdom. Its function, they thought, was to dispose of England's surplus products, notably woolen broadcloth, and to import the few necessary commodities unavailable at home.[1]

Outmoded ideas often exist in tandem with innovative practices. At the end of the sixteenth century, as conservative gentlemen talked longingly of the need to restore religious and social coherence to a kingdom in flux, commercial contacts abroad were increasing. So were the numbers of English ships and seamen. Meanwhile, a growing population, increased agricultural productivity, innovative business arrangements, and the ramifications of overseas trade inexorably nurtured a market connecting every hamlet in the kingdom. As Joyce Appleby has summarized so ably:

> A new commercial network had been laid over the English country-side, bringing all but the most isolated areas into a unified economy. The glamorous foreign trades were integrated into the bread and butter commerce of everyday life. Rural shopkeepers began stocking the luxuries that the rich once went to London to purchase. Most important to the reconceptualization of human behavior, many of the new trade linkages were made by quite ordinary men—not the great merchants or landed magnates, but cattle drovers and cheese-mongers, peddlers and teamsters. These small fry created what economists call a commercial infrastructure. Because of the exigent distractions of civil unrest in the seventeenth century, the old system of economic regulation associated with the Tudors quite simply broke down.[2]

Yet commerce still appeared threatening to social critics who embraced stability. In *The King's Prophecie*, published in 1603, Joseph Hall lambasted "the greedy Merchant" whose ambitious voyages would "Raise by excessive rate his private store, And to enrich himself make thousands poore." Conservatives looked to arable land and fat cows as the most trustworthy path to sustenance, and they believed in economic regulation as a necessary prop for social stability. By the time John Winthrop led the Puritan migration to Massachusetts, ballasted with such outmoded ideas, Dutch citizens had come to realize that profit and social stability need not be mutually exclusive: cozy farms and a godly society could coexist with navigation, commercial fisheries, shipbuilding, and overseas commerce. The Dutch sense that fortune rested in every body of water on which they could float a craft propelled Holland to prosperity during the age of Rembrandt. A similar orientation would soon work wonders in New England.[3]

English willingness to head in the direction pioneered by Dutch shippers became evident during the 1604 session of the House of Commons. Two bills passed with great fanfare. One was titled "For all merchants to have free liberty of Trade into all Countries, as is used in all other Nations"; the other "For the Enlargement of Trade for his Majesty's Subjects into Foreign Countries." The accompanying report claimed that monopolies held by chartered merchant companies limited "the size of the merchant community and the volume of goods traded." Other Englishmen wanted a piece of the action. Within a few years pamphleteers were making a similar case. *England's Way to Wealth*, published by Tobias Gentleman in 1614; *The Trade's Increase*, published by Robert Kayll in 1615; and Thomas Mun's *Discourse on Trade* in 1621 all demonstrated a new fascination with mercantile activity. Each lauded the Netherlands' commercial success despite that nation's limited resource base, and Mun even foreshadowed Adam Smith by arguing that profits would accrue not only to merchants, but to artisans and others developing commodities for export.[4]

Governor John Winthrop did not want his Puritan Boston to become the Amsterdam of America, although he authorized construction of a 30-ton bark called the *Blessing of the Bay* within a year of his arrival.* Heavily constructed, with a single deck, the *Blessing of the Bay* had two masts, both square-rigged. She was launched at Medford in 1631, and soon embarked on a coasting voyage to Dutch Long Island. Governor Winthrop envisioned the vessel as necessary for communication among towns and plantations spread out in New England, and as useful for collecting furs and fish that would be exported from Boston.[5] A shipowner by circumstance, he was leery regarding commercialization's threat. He sought a society based on charity, mercy, and godliness, one in which naturally ordained ranks of people would live together quietly in a Bible Commonwealth, depending on one another. Such a society would flourish best, in his estimation, with a regulated economy in which the magistrates established wages, prices, and interest rates. It was his bad fortune

---

*Tonnage poses vexing problems for maritime historians. A "30-ton bark" was most likely a small merchant sailing ship of indeterminate rigging with a nominal cargo capacity of 3,000 cubic feet. But the tonnage of a ship may be measured in many ways. (See the glossary.) Historians and even original documents are notoriously vague on the nature of the ship's tonnage they are reporting, and this work cannot always discern what its sources leave unclear. Unless otherwise indicated, most references to tonnage may be assumed to be gross tonnage, a measure of the cargo-carrying volume of a merchant ship divided by 100.

The *Virginia* shown here in an artist's rendering, was the first vessel built in Maine by Europeans. The 30-ton pinnace was constructed at Sagadahoc in 1607 by "Master Digby of London," assisted by the craftsmen and workers who set up the short-lived colony.

to try to build such a society with English people accustomed to the profit motive, especially in a land brimming with economic opportunities.[6]

Possibilities for profit by trading coastwise had appeared very early, even before Winthrop arrived. In 1625 the Pilgrim colony at Plymouth decided to ship surplus corn to an English settlement at the Kennebec River, near what is today Bath, Maine. Their only two boats, however, were shallops, open craft built for fishing, propelled either by oars or fore-and-aft sails. The sole shipwright in the colony had recently died, but several men laid a deck over one of the shallops, and after sailing the corn to Maine, returned with seven hundred pounds of beaver pelts. The success of this voyage inspired the Pilgrims to lengthen and deck the larger of their two shallops, creating a more suitable vessel for coastal trading. Fur, not corn, was the commodity of choice, and Pilgrim entrepreneurs moved quickly to establish trade houses far to the east and west. Direct coastal connections with trading posts in Maine on the sites of what are now Castine and Augusta challenged skippers from Plymouth to navigate the Kennebec River's swift currents and the fog-shrouded Penobscot Bay. Meanwhile, from their post at the head of Buzzards Bay (where the Cape Cod Canal now slices the cape from the mainland), Pilgrim traders sailed west in the wake of John Oldham, and up the Connecticut River to Windsor, north of Hartford.[7]

The Plymouth settlers dominated the fur trade in New England for a decade, relying on their tiny fleet of little coasters to collect pelts from hundreds of miles away for export from Plymouth to London. But Plymouth never developed into an important commercial site. "Hoodwinckte" by their merchant associates in London, as William Bradford put it, the Pilgrims watched the profits flow into other pockets, and they virtually gave up on commerce altogether, becoming a colony of husbandmen. Their experience, however, was not typical.[8]

Boatbuilding, shipbuilding, and shipping ventures began very early in New England, in a variety of locales, and generally persisted because maritime entrepreneurship held out the promise of profit and capital accumulation. Although craftsmen as well as ironwork, sails, and cordage had to be shipped across the Atlantic, shipbuilding and shipping flourished. Old-growth timber was abundant, as was entrepreneurial energy in what was still a tiny population. An English merchant stated in 1638 that there were already one hundred New England vessels trading commodities abroad. This may have been an exaggeration, but incontrovertible evidence indicates that at least ten ships, several barks, and numerous shallops were built in Massachusetts, Maine, and New Hampshire before 1640. Shipyards existed at Pemaquid, Richmond Island, York, Kittery, Strawbery Banke (Portsmouth, New Hampshire), Salem, Marblehead, Mystick, Charlestown, Boston, and Dorchester. Locally built shallops fished near shore. Larger vessels plied the coast of New England, or sailed to the Caribbean or England.[9]

The *Richmond*, a bark of 30 tons, was launched from Richmond Island (near Cape Elizabeth, Maine) in the spring of 1637. Like the *Blessing of the Bay*, she was probably square-sterned and two-masted, with a single deck, and perhaps a raised cabin aft. Vessels like these, while tiny by later standards, were heavily built: massive scantlings were the best insurance against stranding. A 30-ton bark of that era would have been approximately 35 feet on deck, with a depth of hold of about 9 feet. She probably carried one square sail on each mast, in addition to a jib.[10] The *Richmond* had been partially financed by capital raised in England by Robert Trelawney, the absentee patentholder of the Richmond Island fishing station. A talented émigré shipwright oversaw her construction. She sailed for England in 1639 laden with six thousand pipe staves, worth about fifty pounds sterling in Boston. Trelawney's resident manager of the Richmond Island station, John Winter, had a 10 percent interest in the voyage. Apparently a ship like this could pay for herself with just a few voyages: the cost to build a similar vessel on Cape Ann in 1641 was only £45 13s. The *Richmond* was a pioneer, one of the first colonially built vessels to cross the Atlantic with trade goods. The coastal and West Indian trades, however, were the arena that colonial shippers would soon dominate. As early as February 1638, Governor Winthrop noted in his journal that "Mr. Pierce, in the Salem ship, the Desire, returned from the West Indies after seven months. He had been at Providence, and brought some cotton, and tobacco, and negroes, etc., from thence, and salt from Tertugos. Dry fish and strong liquors are the only commodities for those ports."[11] The *Desire* had been built in Salem, Massachusetts, where she was owned and manned, and she inaugurated what would become several centuries of profitable voyages by New England vessels to the Caribbean.

Technological improvements in ship design and construction were rare during the seventeenth and eighteenth centuries. Ships remained small, with little ability to sail close to the wind, and builders did not experiment much with hull form. In 1641, a few years after completing the 120-ton *Desire*, her builder launched a 300-ton ship in Salem. Such a vessel would have been relatively large for the next 150 years. While ships of up to 400 tons were occasionally built in New England during the colonial period, most transatlantic cargo ships were considerably smaller, in the 150-ton range; vessels in the West India trade were smaller yet. A seventeenth-century ship like the *Desire* typically had three masts, in addition to a raked bowsprit angling steeply upward. The main and foremasts crossed only two yards, with square sails, while the mizzenmast was lateen-rigged, like the Arab dhows emulated earlier by Spanish and Portuguese mariners. Sails were baggy compared to the cotton canvas ones that were in use by the early nineteenth century. During the colonial era, virtually all sailcloth was made of flax. Less pliable and harder to handle than cotton duck, it also did not retain its shape as well.[12]

The outbreak of the English Civil War in 1642, hard on the heels of what one historian labeled "the first depression in American history," provided an important impetus to New England shipping. By 1641 the colony of Massachusetts Bay was home to about ten thousand Englishmen and Englishwomen, whose financial straits were worsening every day. The civil war brewing in England between radical Puritans and supporters of the king had halted the flow of immigrants, and their money, to Boston. Newcomers' cash had been a mainstay of the Massachusetts Bay economy during its first decade, because new arrivals paid locals for food, cattle, and lodging in the process of getting settled. As the immigrant stream slowed to a trickle, prices for cattle and corn fell precipitously. English captains no longer had much incentive for destinations in New England, for the fares of passengers had been their chief moneymaker. Massachusetts as a whole confronted a catastrophic balance of payments problem. Unless the magistrates could find a financial solution to keep the colony afloat, the pious "city on a hill" envisioned by Governor John Winthrop would collapse.[13]

"The general fear of want of foreign commodities, now our money was gone," wrote Winthrop in February 1641, "set us on work to provide shipping of our own." Boston's leading men faced daunting problems as they looked into the maw of economic development: insufficient capital, little expertise with domestic manufacturing, lack of comprehensive experience organizing overseas trading ventures, and a merchant fleet that, while growing, was by no means large. Shipping would become the most important piece of their economic package, but its promotion by the government was actually just part of the overall promotion of a diversified economy.[14]

Cultivating sources of business information and reliable agents overseas was just as important as government support and a supply of stout ships. Information from England indicated that wood products were in demand in Spain and the wine islands of the eastern Atlantic, and in 1640 George Story shipped eighty-five hundred clapboards for sale in Malaga. Whether from Story's contact or another source, news reached Boston that a seller's market for wheat existed in Spain and the islands. Massachusetts had a surfeit of wheat, and in 1641 the General Court of Massachusetts encouraged the outfitting of a grain ship, which seems to have sailed in the spring of 1642. Six more ships laden with barrel staves and food sailed later that year, although it is not clear if they were locally owned. In 1643, however, Puritan merchants dispatched five locally owned ships to Fayal, Bilbao, Madeira, and Malaga carrying Massachusetts farmers' agricultural and forest surplus—

peas, wheat, corn, and wood. This trade in livestock, grain, fish, and timber products with Iberia, the wine islands, and the Caribbean saved Boston. Virtually overnight the Puritan capital assumed a position as the Amsterdam of America, "the chiefe place for shipping and Merchandize."[15]

The rapid development of New England's shipping industry was a reflection of colonials' sense that commercial markets were a rising tide that could lift all boats, that economic regulation often hindered economic development, and that many men could achieve a degree of self-sufficiency and independence if allowed to channel their industriousness into landownership and commercial pursuits. Predisposed to relative economic freedom, Englishmen and Englishwomen in Massachusetts took it for granted that they would improve their economic circumstances if possible. Governor Winthrop's reservations about the pursuit of profit withered on the vine. Unwilling to revert to a primitive standard of living lacking English consumer goods and manufactured items, settlers realized that the amenities they desired would have to be purchased. Although there were exceptions, the general pattern was that cattle, wheat, fish, and most timber products were not worth transporting to markets in England. New England, moreover, lacked a valuable agricultural staple, like sugar or tobacco. Entrepreneurial members of the first generation thus became commercial middlemen, negotiating their way to modest profits in multiple transactions, often indirectly. Seeking cash or bills of exchange that would be honored in London, these up-and-coming merchants had to provide many services.

Maritime commerce was the heart of the system. Merchants during the 1640s and 1650s were importers, exporters, wholesalers, retailers, moneylenders, and owners of vessels or shares of vessels, traders on their own account, commission agents for other merchants, processors, organizers, distributors, and market pioneers. None of them specialized in shipping alone as they sought a viable business model in a volatile market. American shipping began as one part of a linked series of diversified enterprises pursued by men who wished to make a profit, driven by a desire to elevate their standard of living and their personal status.

During the 1640s Boston became the preeminent port in America, and it would remain the most important port and largest town in British America for the remainder of the seventeenth century. By 1650 its commercial hinterland stretched from the outskirts of New Amsterdam on Long Island Sound to central Maine, and reached inland to the market towns of Hartford and Springfield. It became the funnel through which the wood, fish, and agricultural surplus of New England's villages flowed. "Who ever would send any thing to any Towne in New England," John Eliot noted in 1650, should send it to Boston or Charlestown (across the river), "for they are the haven Townes for all New England and speedy meanes of conveyance to all places is there to be had." Boston, and to a lesser extent Charlestown, were centers for business information and contacts. Capital was more readily available there than anywhere else. Farmers with produce to sell looked to Boston, as did entrepreneurs and investors.[16]

Boston was also the focal point for the distribution of goods from England, as it offered outfitting and provisioning services unobtainable elsewhere. What had been a beachfront camp in 1630 was a bustling town of about three thousand people in 1650, the first full-service seaport in English America. Its inhabitants included not only up-and-coming merchants, eager to cultivate ties with businessmen in England, but shipwrights, boatbuilders, sailmakers, blacksmiths, innkeepers, brewers, butchers, and shopkeepers. A sea-weary shipmaster knew that he could refresh his crew and outfit his vessel for its return voyage in Boston, in addition to selling his cargo or consignment. By 1650 twenty to twenty-five ships were arriving annually from England. By 1660 Boston-bound ships carried the imported manufactures for virtually all of New England. In the space of two decades Boston merchants had relegated other ports, including New Haven, Newport, and Strawbery Banke (Portsmouth, New Hampshire) to roles as minor centers for the collection of local goods, or, as in the case of Strawbery Banke's mast and timber trade, export centers for one commodity. No other place in seventeenth-century British America was as *commercial* as Boston.

The historian Bernard Bailyn astutely emphasized the significance of Boston as a commercial center by comparing the nature of New England's business communities circa 1660. Coastal port merchants in Connecticut and Rhode Island, he noted, were clearly subordinate to Bostonians and to the Dutch in New Amsterdam. Prominent men in the Connecticut River ports were really quasi-merchants who, while sending local produce to southern colonies or the Caribbean, considered themselves first and foremost landed squires in the English rural tradition. Portsmouth, New Hampshire, and Milford, Connecticut, had "men devoted entirely to trade, but their interests did not dominate the affairs of their towns."

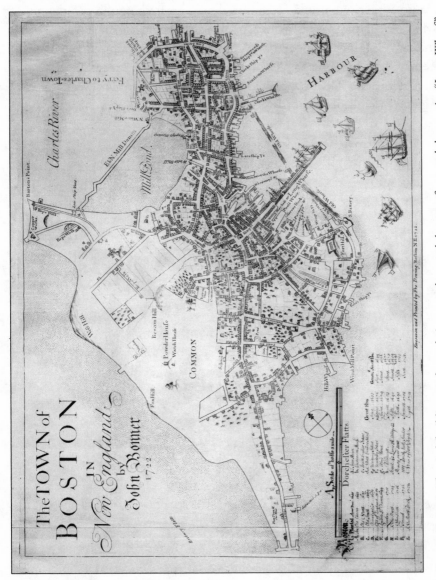

Boston in 1722. The city's buildings and population crowd around the waterfront and the massive "Long Wharf" that stretches into the harbor. The ships collected there run the gamut from small coastal vessels to a large, ocean-going man-of-war.

Salem and Charlestown were the only other ports prominent in the Atlantic carrying trades, but merchants there were eclipsed by bigger men in Boston who were commercial to the core. The capital city's wharves, warehouses, and stone-paved streets gave it an air of solidity. Decades of buoyant prosperity boosted property values, encouraging the population growth and productivity that made it British America's primary port for a century. Trappings of Governor Winthrop's Puritan imprint remained for generations, but after the restoration of King Charles II in 1660 merchants' acquisitive values permeated New England society as never before. The genie was out of the bottle.[17]

4

CODFISH, TIMBER, AND PROFIT

BUSINESSMEN GENERALLY PREFER A SITUATION IN WHICH AT least a significant part of their operation is predictable, regular, and stable. For those in the shipping business during the seventeenth century, controlling a slice of the transatlantic delivery of profitable commodities like sugar and tobacco was about as predictable as possible. Those trades, however, were controlled by London merchants with ample credit and connections, and were dominated by large ships. Londoners had better access to information on the changing nature of tobacco and sugar markets in Europe, a distinct advantage. Moreover, substantial planters in the Chesapeake and the Caribbean retained London merchants as agents. Rather than selling their crops in the field or on the wharf in America, they shipped the sugar or tobacco to their London agents to sell on commission. After 1660, as Ralph Davis notes, "the main task for English transatlantic shipping was the carriage to Europe of sugar from the West Indies and tobacco from Virginia and Maryland." In 1686, for instance, 275 ships arrived in London, Bristol, and Liverpool from the West Indies; 154 ships arrived in those ports from North America. Upstart New Englanders lacked credit, connections, and the economy of scale that big ships allowed. They never effectively broke into transatlantic carriage of tobacco and sugar before the American Revolution. On the other hand, they came to dominate the American coastal trade and the lucrative West Indian trade precisely because smaller vessels were more suitable to those routes and because they had better access to the commercial information that made those trades profitable.[1]

One of New England merchants' dilemmas was that they lacked a regional commodity that could be transported in regionally operated vessels. The diversification of New England's shipping, and merchants' spin-offs into processing, packaging, insuring, and other commercial operations, had very positive implications for the region's economic development in the long run. That outcome was somewhat serendipitous: merchant captains risking their lives and capital were interested more in short-term personal profits than in long-term economic development.

Catching, processing, and shipping codfish came to provide some of the predictability sought by New England merchants. By the eve of the American Revolution, dried codfish was the fourth most valuable export from the thirteen mainland British North American colonies. Only tobacco, grain, and rice surpassed it in value. Dried cod became part of the suite of maritime enterprises that propelled American shippers to prominence and wealth. The fishery promoted shipbuilding, trained seamen, instigated lines of credit in London, allowed regional merchants to accumulate capital, and fostered contacts in markets outside of England itself. Until the English Civil War, however, there was no New England–based cod fishery, despite common knowledge that the banks and ledges northeast of Cape Cod were among the best fishing grounds in the world.[2]

Englishmen from the West Country (Cornwall, Devon, Dorset) had been fishing in Newfoundland for a century, but the harsh Newfoundland climate precluded agriculture. Few permanent settlements took root. The fishery remained seasonal. English fishing merchants contracted with servants to work a season, staked them to victuals and equipment, and paid them when they returned to England at the end of the season with their fish. Newfoundland held few attractions, other than the wages to be earned in the fishery. As a result, the servants generally performed their duty. Free Englishmen who took the trouble to emigrate to New England, however, were much more likely to be attracted to the possibility of landownership and independence than to the dangerous and grueling work of hand-lining cod. Seventeenth-century English society prized economic independence, and Englishmen in America naturally gravitated toward an arrangement where they could work for themselves.[3]

With the exception of the settlement at Pemaquid, Maine, the many attempts during the 1620s and 1630s to organize a New England–based commercial fishery all failed, despite legislative incentives and land grants. Few of the Puritan migrants from the south and east of England had the skills or commercial contacts to make the fishery succeed. Men from the West Country who understood the fishery were generally Anglican or blasphemous, or both—not the sort of folk readily welcomed by the Puritans. And the business method of hiring servants for a fixed seasonal wage simply did not work in Massachusetts or southern Maine, where alternative opportunities abounded. From 1631 to 1634 Isaac Allerton managed servant fishermen in Marblehead, but the fishery did not thrive. John Winter oversaw servant fishermen at the Richmond Island plantation but complained bitterly in 1639 that despite the high wages, "Our men as their tymes Comes out do go away."[4]

The real problem was not fishermen's desire for land, or the Puritans' distaste for hard-drinking, hard-swearing fishermen. The actual business of fishing was complicated. It involved arranging credit to procure supplies, as well as catching, processing, storing, shipping, and marketing large volumes of dried fish. "Competing with the highly skilled and well-capitalized fisheries of western Europe for markets and with the developing rural economy of the Bay Colony itself for labor and capital," the historian Daniel Vickers explains, "was not going to be easy."[5]

The English Civil War gave colonial merchants the break they needed, as war-torn English maritime enterprises faltered. The number of West Country fishing boats working on the coast of Newfoundland fell from 340 in 1634, before the war, to fewer than 200 by 1652. Those that had worked the coast of New England disappeared entirely. These disruptions to production raised the price of cod in southern Europe as the supply dwindled. All of this provided New England merchants the incentive to try fishing again, and during the next several decades the region's output of dried cod steadily rose. Initially carried to Spain, Portugal, and the Atlantic islands in English ships, cod was soon being exported in prodigious amounts in American bottoms to Catholic markets in southern Europe and to the Caribbean plantation islands, where an increasingly large population of enslaved workers needed to be fed. Between 1645 and 1675 New England's total output of cod rose between 5 and 6 percent each year, increasing from about twelve thousand to sixty thousand quintals. (One quintal was 112 pounds of dried cod.) As Vickers, the preeminent historian of the early New England fisheries explains, "For the men it employed, the profits it earned, the vessels and provisions it consumed, and the shipping business it fostered, the [fishing] industry was without question the first leading sector in New England's remarkable history of economic development. It is hard to imagine how the carrying trades would have succeeded in Massachusetts without fish to ship, and equally hard to explain the colony's successful industrialization during the nineteenth century without the profits cleared in overseas shipping."[6]

By the restoration of Charles II in 1660, dried cod and distant islands provided the commodity and the markets that New England merchants needed to develop a merchant marine with staying power. London merchants, of course, initially dominated the shipment of manufactured goods to Boston, the export of New Englanders' fish to the wine islands, and return voyages from the islands to both London and the colonies. Colonials soon insinuated themselves, individually and in partnerships, into the legs that began or ended in New England. Small ships and mixed cargoes were a formula for success in island markets, whose small populations could absorb only limited quantities of any commodity. Outbound New Englanders carried fish, barrel staves and other wood products, and some agricultural surpluses. On the homeward voyage they loaded wine, fruit, and salt. Markets in the Caribbean islands operated similarly: on return voyages from the West Indies, Yankee ships carried rum, sugar, molasses, cotton, and some dyestuffs. "The sale of goods," note the historians John J. McCusker and Russell R. Menard, "was matched as an earner of credits in the colonial balance of payments by the sale of the invisibles in the current account—freighting, insurance, short-term credit and other commercial services."[7]

This business, moreover, promoted the American coastal trade. To assemble just the right cargoes for fragile island economies, New England merchants dispatched coasters laden with local products and imports. They traded for wheat in the Middle Colonies, tobacco in Virginia, rice in South Carolina, and tar and turpentine in North Carolina. They had to create contacts with agents in every one of these regions, and it became common for family members or other trusted representatives to settle in Charleston, South Carolina; Bridgetown, Barbados; or Madeira to make transactions flow as smoothly as possible. Meanwhile, merchants on the New England coast built wharves and warehouses, added tonnage to the fleet every year, hired seamen and other labor, and provided markets for the products of New England's farmers, woodcutters, and fishermen.

By 1660 two significantly different forms of maritime plantations had taken shape in English America, in addition to the Dutch model in New Netherland. The Dutch colony, including Manhattan, western Long Island, and the Hudson River valley, had fewer than a thousand inhabitants in 1631, only twenty-five hundred in 1645, and only nine thousand by 1664. The tiny population, and a centralized economy, retarded commercial development. While Dutch shipwrights launched six small vessels ("jagts") from New Amsterdam during the early 1630s, shipbuilding never flourished. Most tonnage servicing the colony, both before and after 1638, when the Dutch West India Company lost its monopoly on trade, came from the Old World. Documents reveal that Governor Peter Stuyvesant had a sloop built in New Amsterdam in 1652, but that the colony was unable to complete another in 1657. It is an irony of history that while the Dutch had become Europe's most accomplished mariners during the late sixteenth and early seventeenth centuries, New Amsterdam under the Dutch never rivaled Boston as a major port, or New England as a shipbuilding center.[8]

In the West Indies and the Chesapeake Bay, sugar and tobacco plantations specialized in one crop, and virtually all production was geared toward distant markets. Those plantations and ships were peas in the pod of commercial capitalism, separate yet dependent on each other. No other part of the seventeenth- and eighteenth-century global economy relied as heavily on shipping as did New World plantations. Ships imported supplies, labor, managers, and food, and exported the staple crops. Many of those ships, however, were based in London or other English seaports. While American sugar and tobacco plantations would require an increasing number of English ships and an increasing percentage of the English fleet during the century following 1660, colonial merchants themselves never got a significant slice of that pie before the American Revolution other than providing provisions to plantations.[9]

Settlers on Chesapeake Bay, moreover, did not encourage indigenous shipping. Several small coasters were built during the first seven years of the Virginia Company's existence, but the colony was almost devoid of boats shortly thereafter. In 1622 the company sent twenty-five ship carpenters to Virginia to build small craft, but most sickened and died, and little came of the ambitious plan. When the tobacco boom commenced in the 1620s, Virginians were more than content to let metropolitan-based shipping supply the colony and export its valuable crop, and to let New

Englanders pursue some coastal trading. Dugout canoes and other small craft connected the widely scattered plantations, allowing Virginians to cross the bay from eastern to western shores, but no coastal trading fleet developed during the early decades of Chesapeake settlement as it did in New England because virtually all commercial energy was channeled into tobacco cultivation.[10]

A different variety of plantation took root in New England and ultimately thrived in provinces from Pennsylvania to Nova Scotia. It balanced market production with self-sufficiency. Farms and workshops became inexorably oriented to the waterfront, where merchants who were determined to situate themselves in the growing Atlantic economy played the few cards that they held. Marketing food, livestock, fish, and timber, those northern merchants also built and sold ships, provided commercial services, and added as much value as possible to raw products through processing. Rapidly dominating American coastal and Caribbean voyages, they became indispensable players in a complicated pan-Atlantic trading system, simultaneously acting as customers and competitors of their English counterparts. Driven by financial speculation and the desire for profit, fueled by the exploitation of labor and natural resources, and regulated in beneficial ways by encouraging governments, by 1660 New England's commercial shipping had become the basis of an American merchant marine and a linchpin of the British American economy.

5

AN INFANT
INDUSTRY

PROMINENT SEVENTEENTH-CENTURY ENGLISHMEN INCREASINGLY believed that the public interest was served by promotion of private enterprise. Government became a staunch friend of commerce, and policy at the imperial, provincial, and local levels fostered the development of colonial American shipping. New England's autonomous towns and provincial governments demonstrated both the flexibility and the willingness to involve themselves in economic life, including shipping. By midcentury, as the historian Margaret Ellen Newell explains, New England's "colonists all but abandoned most traditional forms of socioeconomic regulation that circumscribed market behavior in favor of policies that facilitated it. First in response to a serious economic depression, but then as a matter of course, provincial and local governments assumed the responsibility for promoting economic development."[1] They provided economic encouragement for certain industries (including shipbuilding) through land grants and bounties, put teeth into laws that would protect commercial interests, eased restrictions on credit, and boosted international trade by removing restrictions on interest rates for bills of exchange. Governments also made sure that courts existed to ensure civil justice. They registered land sales and officiated over deeds and titles. Experimenting briefly with wage and production controls, they soon ignored such regulations, essentially encouraging free-market transactions. Commerce was thus free to flourish in a relatively unfettered way. Shipowners were direct beneficiaries.[2]

Seventeenth-century New England governments rarely owned or operated economic enterprises. Rather, explains Newell, they "provided a variety of incentives to private individuals who engaged in commercial and processing activities deemed in the public interest, appealing to individuals' desire for profit and commitment to the public good." In 1640, for instance, the town of Boston provided a sixty-acre waterfront lot to jump-start shipbuilding. The following year the Massachusetts General Court passed a law to encourage fishing and shipbuilding. Lawmakers agreed to pay substitute laborers "to plant and reap . . . in the season of the year" over the next seven years for fishermen, mariners, and shipwrights "at the public charge of the commonwealth." It is doubtful that this actually happened, but the intent to promote maritime commerce was clear. Whether making iron, erecting water-powered sawmills, dispatching voyages to New Amsterdam, or building ships, the provincial government's goal was to foster local control of productive business. The result was an economic infrastructure of considerable complexity and staying power, in which maritime trades had a prominent role. Local and provincial incentives to economic development were the first of several forms of government assistance that benefited the American merchant marine in its infancy.[3]

English governments had long regulated and encouraged the merchant marine, regarding it as essential to the security, if not the commerce, of the kingdom. The English coasting trade, for example, had been protected by cabotage laws since 1563, meaning it was closed to foreign ships. A century later, when Oliver Cromwell's Commonwealth Parliament ruled the land, and when English colonies in America were still fledglings, Dutch shippers in their ubiquitous *flytes* dominated large sectors of Atlantic commerce. Flytes, or "flutes" as the English called them, were large, simply rigged, inexpensively built ships with a tonnage-per-man ratio far superior to that of competitors. They were the most efficient bulk carriers of their day, and Dutch shippers dominated much of Europe's trade with England. By the outbreak of the English Civil War, whose tumults promised to provide considerable advantages to Dutch carriers, Dutchmen had edged English carriers off remunerative Baltic routes. They had also established a firm foothold in American colonial commerce, despite an English law of 1624 declaring that no one could import "any Tobacco whatsover in any forraine bottom."[4]

The Commonwealth Navigation Ordinance of 1651, England's first Navigation Act, challenged Dutch supremacy on the sea by insisting that goods carried into England would arrive in English bottoms and that Englishmen would earn the profits from carriage. Overly ambitious and impossible to enforce, it was nullified by the restoration of King Charles II in 1660, then replaced within a few months by a more effective act. Colonial shippers would live under variations of that act until the American Revolution. The goal of the act was a virtually closed system. Dutch carriers would be excluded, but colonial shippers would gain a privileged place. In fact, colonial shipbuilding made it considerably easier for England to exclude Dutch competitors. In 1686 half of the ships entering London from New England were colonially built and owned, and many of those bottoms were sold in England.[5]

The principle stipulations of the Navigation Act pertaining to American colonials were that all cargoes moving to or from England or its colonial possessions would be carried in ships owned and built by English people, and that captains and three-quarters of the crew were to be English. "As far as the Navigation Acts were concerned," note McCusker and Menard, "the colonies were a simple extension of the metropolis, the equivalent of new counties, somewhere west of Cornwall. All the laws explicitly recognized the right of English colonists to participate on equal terms with the residents of England in the trade of the empire." Certain commodities produced in English plantations were to be exported *only* to England or Ireland or other English possessions. These so-called enumerated articles included tobacco, sugar, ginger, indigo, and other dyewood—the principal colonial products, except for New Englanders' salt fish, which could still be shipped directly to Catholic markets in southern Europe. The coasting trade, including voyages between English provinces, was entirely limited to English ships, which of course included colonial ones. Successive parliaments tinkered with the Navigation Acts for decades, closing loopholes and tightening restrictions, but the essentials of the system were put into place between 1651 and 1673, when the Plantation Duties Act was passed. That act tacitly recognized colonial shippers as a force to be reckoned with. Hoping to dissuade New Englanders from competing with English carriers by "reexporting" valuable commodities from plantation colonies to their own ports, and thence to England, it imposed duties on goods sent from one colony to another. Smuggling certainly occurred, but in general smuggling to evade the Navigation Acts diminished with the passage of time.[6]

The Navigation Acts reflected political leaders' mercantilist assumptions that overseas trade could be harnessed in the service of the state. But "the increase of shipping and encouragement of the navigation of this nation," as the preamble to the acts put it, was not pursued purely for the sake of economic growth. Parliament consisted of more landed aristocrats and country gentlemen than merchants. Many of them did not think primarily in terms of commerce. All, however, shared a concern for national security, and they supported the merchant marine—a "nursery for seamen"—as a valuable auxiliary to the Royal Navy. While no unified set of economic theories, policies, and laws existed during the seventeenth and eighteenth centuries that can be dignified with the label "mercantilism," English governments acted in an implicitly mercantilist fashion, bolstering the shipping industry and encouraging the development of a colonial maritime system. Not only could overseas trade be taxed, a desirable feature in the eyes of the Crown, but the whole system was seen to strengthen the nation's strategic and economic position. Ships and seamen were the mainspring of the entire mechanism.[7]

From the perspective of the western side of the Atlantic, however, it remains to be asked how the Navigation Acts affected colonials. Procedures for enforcement were notoriously lax to begin with, and colonials essentially ignored both the act of 1651 and its successor in 1660. Conducting business on their own terms for more than a generation while the English government was distracted by civil war, colonists had cultivated a culture of rule-flouting independence. Colonial shippers thus continued to carry enumerated colonial commodities directly to the European continent and to trade with Dutch merchants in New Amsterdam, in addition to their "legitimate" commerce with the wine islands and the Caribbean. The bottom line was that, when evading the law, risks were minimal compared with potential returns.

Not until November 1673 were royal officials charged with enforcing the Navigation Acts even appointed to the colonies—and then only to Maryland, Virginia, and the Carolinas. The Plantation Duties Act that year referred to "great hurt and diminution of your Majesty's customs" because of colonial evasions. Although by 1678 His Majesty's customs collectors and surveyors were situated in all of the mainland colonies, they encountered considerable resistance and foot-dragging, especially in the rather autonomous New England provinces. Edward Randolph, in charge of enforcement in New England, apparently exaggerated when he claimed that evasions were costing the Crown one hundred thousand pounds each year, but noncompliance was obviously routine. The first two generations of magistrates in Massachusetts acted as though the province was a sovereign state, and colonials had grown accustomed to pursuing profits wherever possible, despite the letter of the law. But with time, the mechanisms for enforcement became more difficult to evade, and risks increased. Fulminate as they might against the Navigation Acts, colonial merchants ultimately channeled their commerce into legitimate trades. They flippantly disregarded the law less and less each decade after the 1660s. And from the early eighteenth century until the American Revolution, virtually all colonial trade operated within the navigation system, even though smuggling was on the rise again by the 1740s.[8]

Although English policy after 1651 essentially sought to maintain the colonies in a position subservient to the mother country, the Navigation Acts helped colonial shipping and the entire colonial economy more than they hindered it. "The costs imposed on the colonies by the restrictions on trade were small," note McCusker and Menard, "certainly less than 3 percent of colonial income, perhaps less than 1 percent. Furthermore, whatever the costs of membership in the British Empire, they were largely offset by the benefits: naval protection; access to a large free-trading area; easy credit and cheap manufactures; and restricted foreign competition."[9] Protectionist and exclusionary in nature, the British Navigation Acts nurtured the fledgling American shipping industry.

The imperial government also sought to assist shippers by eradicating organized piracy around the turn of the eighteenth century. Using naval squadrons and the hangman's noose, and leaving rotting corpses dangling on gibbets to make an impression on sailors considering a pirate's life, the British government asserted that it would no longer tolerate impediments to shipping by freebooting buccaneers. "It was the decline in piracy and privateering, permitting ships to reduce both manpower and armament," according to Douglass C. North, "which contributed most" to the decline in labor costs at sea prior to 1800. Diminishing threats of piracy also lowered insurance costs. North has demonstrated effectively that increased productivity in ocean transportation during the seventeenth and eighteenth centuries was "basically a function of the growing security of shipping." But during the heyday of piracy many merchant shipowners in Boston and New York were profoundly ambivalent about the pirates' impact. Far from clamoring for their extermination, merchants acknowledged that piracy—especially sea robberies committed against strangers in distant waters—was an important source of both specie and capital in their maritime economies.[10]

For more than a century before the crackdown on pirates by the Lords of the Admiralty and Royal Navy, most English governments had employed private sea warriors to fight on behalf of the nation. Queen Elizabeth profited personally from Francis Drake's notorious expeditions against Spanish settlements in South America during the 1570s, and other well-placed officials were in cahoots with pirates (called "privateers" when they had a commission) until the end of King William's War in 1697. Colonials in seaport towns had more intimate relations with pirates. Riotous Port Royal, Jamaica, was notorious as a safe haven, but so were staid Boston and New York. During the latter part of the seventeenth century, American shipping—and seaport economies in general— were energized by the sea robbers' loot.

Chronically hobbled by their lack of specie, colonial economies responded vigorously to the infusion of coin that occurred in the wake of a pirate's arrival in port. During the sack of Vera Cruz in 1683, buccaneers seized 960,000 pieces of eight, many of which apparently were soon spent in Boston. Shopkeepers, tavern owners, ship carpenters, and merchants all felt the ripple, and while everyone knew that piracy was illegal, officials' connivance was often taken for granted. New York's customs collector "selectively admitted pirates and their vessels into the harbor" between 1674 and 1681, according to one historian. His openness to piracy paled in comparison to that of Governor Benjamin Fletcher, who arrived in New York in 1692. The pirates' friend and promoter, Governor Fletcher virtually ignored laws regarding piracy. He preferred to boost the local economy and become personally wealthy, giving royal commissions to privateers, encouraging merchants to outfit their voyages, and watching as councilors like William Nicholl and Nicholas

Bayard grew rich through dealing with buccaneers. Numerous New York merchants used money laundered from pirates to buy real estate, ships, and wharves. It was common knowledge that Colonel Frederick Philipse, a prominent member of the city council, helped outfit the pirate base at Madagascar during the 1690s as an investment. According to the historian Cathy Matson, Philipse and another merchant named Thomas Marston "supplied Madagascar pirates with essentials such as clothing, liquor, guns and ammunition," profiting handsomely when their captains flamboyantly delivered the cash, slaves, and East Indian wares procured there back to New York.[11]

No other governor welcomed pirates so openly as Benjamin Fletcher, but many officials felt pressure from the commercial sector to at least wink and look the other way. A Bostonian writing to Parliament in 1700 sought to explain that those exercising "a due and vigorous execution of the Law against Pyrats or illegal Traders" would be "hardly safe in their Persons or Estates" because they would "incense the People against them." Seeking to suppress piracy in New York in 1699, Governor Bellomont lamented that prominent merchants hated him. "They say I have ruined the town by hindering the privateers (for so they call pirates) from bringing in £100,000 since my coming."[12]

By the early eighteenth century, however, the British government sought to purge the world's sea lanes of pirates. This signaled a new phase in imperial economic maturity and, according to the historian Robert Ritchie, a new insistence by the government that it should monopolize violence. The Lords of the Admiralty hanged Captain William Kidd in London in 1701. Kidd had once owned a fine mansion in New York, been the favorite of royal officials, and navigated across the line between legitimate commerce and piracy. His execution indicated a new modus operandi by the admiralty. A royal naval squadron, with assistance from two Virginian ships dispatched by Governor Alexander Spotswood, killed Edward Teach, also known as Blackbeard, in 1718. Around the Atlantic, vice admiralty courts condemned and executed pirates, "pushing them off" in large numbers. Boston had its share of executions, and for years seamen passing the islands of Nix's Mate and Bird Island in Boston harbor could stare at rusty chains on the gibbets where pirates had been hanged. By 1730 the organized European piracy that had been a corollary of colonial maritime expansion was finished, making Atlantic sea lanes less flamboyant, but safer and more predictable places for legitimate commerce. Meanwhile, that commerce had been bolstered substantially with the proceeds of piracy, and prominent merchants like the Boston shipping magnate Richard Wharton had been referred to (in 1679) as being "a great undertaker for pirates."[13]

6

THE SHIPPING BUSINESS IN 1700

SHIPPING REMAINED A RISKY, IF SOMETIMES PROFITABLE, enterprise at the turn of the eighteenth century. Pirates, privateers, and financial uncertainty compounded the perils of the sea. Although King William's War had finished in 1697, Queen Anne's War (also known as the War of Spanish Succession) would break out in 1702, not ending until the Peace of Utrecht in 1713. These conflicts were a mixed blessing for colonial shipping. War brought government contracts to some shipowners, raised freights, and provided the possibility of privateering profits, in addition to new tonnage via captures. But it also unleashed enemy privateers, increasing the odds that vessels and skilled mariners would be lost. Meanwhile, the pervasive shortage of specie continued to restrict business opportunities. The historian Bernard Bailyn observed long ago that the colonies still lacked banks and other financial institutions, making it difficult to invest profits in securities or to maintain cash reserves. There were no shipowning companies yet, and few stable or enduring partnerships; as a result, investment in shipping remained personal, ad hoc, and individual. Given these limitations, it is all the more remarkable that by 1698 Boston had become the third most important center of shipping in the British Empire—and one of the most important in the entire Atlantic world.[1]

Living on a teardrop-shaped peninsula jutting into the bay, Bostonians aggressively built, owned, and operated ships. Destinations, commissions, captains' reputations, and freights were on the tips of many residents' tongues, for not only did approximately one in every four adult males own shares in a seagoing vessel, but some eight hundred mariners called Boston home. Major English ports such as Yarmouth, Liverpool, and Hull harbored less tonnage than the Puritan capital, and only London itself and the western port of Bristol surpassed Boston in their number of vessels and aggregate tonnage in 1698. Moreover, virtually all of Massachusetts's fleet had been built in New England. During the years between 1697 and 1714, Boston's shipyards produced an average of 1,568 tons of new shipping per year. The colony's entire seagoing fleet in 1698 (excluding lighters, barges, and coastal fishing boats) consisted of 171 vessels aggregating 8,453 tons. Massachusetts had become a maritime metropolis, a commercial center on the American frontier. "There are more good vessels belonging to the town of Boston," noted Lord Bellomont in 1700, "than to all Scotland and Ireland."[2]

How had this happened in such a short time, and how did Bostonians' commercial fleet compare to that of other colonies? Answering those questions necessitates a tour of British North America in 1700, and an assessment of American shippers' business practices.

The British mainland colonies, whose white and black population numbered a quarter of a million at the turn of the century, remained a series of isolated regions rather than a continuous coastal settlement. The two most populous areas were the longest settled: Chesapeake Bay and its environs, and the coast and river valleys of southern and central New England. Separate hearths radiated out from New York City and Philadelphia. Smaller clusters existed in tidewater North Carolina, around Albermarle and Pamlico Sounds, and in South Carolina's Charleston and Port Royal. Each region depended on maritime commerce for its survival, but the nature of each region's involvement in shipping varied widely.

New York was the only port in America remotely comparable to Boston, a result of its Dutch legacy and emphasis on commerce. After the bloodless English conquest in 1664, local merchants were forced to reorient their trade to conform to the Navigation Acts, but they maintained important contacts in Amsterdam, and they continued to provision Caribbean plantations, especially in the Dutch and Danish West Indies. During this era when commercial information moved at the same speed as cargoes, trusted business contacts were essential to commercial survival.

It was natural that New York merchants under the English flag and English laws maintain the ties they had developed when New Amsterdam was a Dutch trading outpost. But New York's fleet was not huge. In 1687 Governor Thomas Dongan noted about thirty-two vessels there, averaging 46 tons burthen. Only nine or ten, owned by the most notable merchants, were "sturdy ocean going ships" ranging from 80 to 100 tons. By 1700 Lord Bellomont reported that New Yorkers owned 124 vessels, but only 6 of them were over 100 tons. Small locally owned vessels handled regional freights and coastwise trade, but without sizable Dutch and English ships New Yorkers would have been out of the loop of transatlantic commerce. New York had a much more productive hinterland than Boston, however, at least potentially, and Manhattan merchants had already begun to capitalize on their location in the breadbasket of colonial America. Foreshadowing important future developments, New York passed a Flour Regulation Act in 1678, and exports of grain and flour were already flowing to the West Indies, southern Europe, and other American provinces by 1700. Nevertheless, the dominance of the port of New York was still far in the future.[3]

Philadelphia had been settled for less than twenty years in 1700, and although ships and boats were being built immediately at Chester, Wilmington, Marcus Hook, and other spots on the Delaware River, William Penn's colony of eighteen thousand people (of whom two thousand lived in the capital city) was not yet a major commercial center. Early Philadelphians, like the first generation in Boston, immediately began shipping timber and grain to the Caribbean, Newfoundland, other American provinces, and southern Europe (including the wine islands). But none of these trades or markets proved particularly profitable for Philadelphians, especially as the Caribbean market was flooded with competitors from New York and New England. "As a consequence," note McCusker and Menard, "Philadelphia's export trade grew hardly at all in the thirty years after 1690."[4]

South Carolina's merchants coped with even more of a frontier situation in 1700 as they struggled to establish an economic base for the colony's six thousand people. The province's entire fleet consisted of about a half dozen oceangoing vessels in that year, of which the largest was only fifty tons. During the next twenty years, approximately thirty vessels were launched from the colony, most of them small sloops. Shipbuilding and ownership actually declined after 1720. As South Carolina's plantation economy developed, and exports of rice and naval stores increased, English ships dominated the commerce. Pettiaugers and sloops, most of which were manned and commanded by slaves, remained locally important in colonial South Carolina's tidewater economy. But mercantile pursuits revolving around ship operation were always secondary to planting. South Carolina's indigenous merchants never controlled a significant merchant fleet.[5]

Chesapeake ports and merchants ultimately would become more involved in shipping than those in South Carolina, but at the turn of the century this was not evident. Tobacco was king, and the tobacco trade was not conducive to the growth of a Chesapeake fleet. "Certain trades between the Americas and Europe," Jacob Price observes, "were in law and fact essentially bilateral trades." Unlike the much more complicated trading orchestrated from Boston, ships to and from the Chesapeake always carried manufactures like textiles and metalware into the bay, and tobacco out. While such a trade conceivably could be managed effectively from either end, English and Scottish merchants had an edge in marketing tobacco, as well as better access to credit and cheaper marine insurance. Scots factors resident in the Chesapeake arranged most tobacco shipments, and acted as storekeepers as well. But neither they nor the Chesapeake planters possessed coasters, much less oceangoing ships. Virginia's seventy thousand inhabitants owned only twenty-seven vessels in 1698, besides canoes and skiffs. In Maryland, the situation was similar. Only 17 percent of the vessels entering the colony's ports between 1689 and 1693 were owned there: Englishmen dominated the transatlantic trade, and New Englanders provided more coastal shipping services than Marylanders themselves.[6]

New England's shipping success, and the advantages of a decentralized free-market approach to economic growth, come into sharp focus when the commerce of Spanish Florida and French Louisiana are compared with that of the British North American colonies. Despite good harbors, abundant timber, and access to commodities worth shipping, neither Florida (which was settled by Spaniards and slaves between the 1560s and 1763), nor Louisiana (which was colonized by French residents and slaves between 1698 and 1763), ever developed a locally controlled fleet.

Fires, droughts, hurricanes, and attacks by Native Americans and European rivals troubled Spanish Florida for virtually all of its 190-year existence. The population of Spanish St. Augustine was only about five hundred in 1600, rising to a high point of about thirty-one hundred in 1763. That population included Indians, Africans, mestizos, people of color, and Spaniards. Supply ships from Spain annually freighted livestock, wine, salted meat, flour, sweets, spices, metalware, and ceramics to Florida. Spanish merchantmen from Havana, Cuba, frequently augmented those supplies. But retail trade during the sixteenth century and the first half of the seventeenth century was controlled by the governor of La Florida, directly or indirectly. The governor and treasury officials benefited tremendously, even as residents were forced to purchase overpriced goods, often of shoddy quality. By the eighteenth century, Spanish officials still served the colony poorly, and resident Floridians had not yet developed profitable commercial enterprises. Beginning in 1735 English traders from South Carolina filled the void, and within fifteen years English coastal traders from New York, Charleston, and Maryland were illicitly—but profitably—shipping foodstuffs and other goods there, filling a niche that Floridians had left open for more than 150 years. The Treaty of Paris officially put Florida into the orbit of British colonial coasters when it forced Spain to cede the colony to Great Britain in 1763. Even then, as in 1700, no local shipping had taken root.[7]

French settlers' paltry attempts to build a shipping sector in Louisiana did not fare much better. By 1723, after twenty-five years of settlement, the French had outposts in Mobile and Fort Toulouse, Alabama; Natchitoches, Baton Rouge, and New Orleans, Louisiana; and Natchez and Fort Pierce, Mississippi—all of which were loosely referred to as "Louisiana." As late as 1731, however, the total population was only about five thousand, of whom three thousand were slaves. During the late 1730s, led by a substantial planter named Joseph Villars DuBreuil, French Louisianans tried to develop a shipbuilding industry in New Orleans. Several vessels were constructed, but the ultimate objective of a locally controlled fleet never came to fruition. Insufficient capitalization, a lack of skilled ship carpenters, and shortages of hardware and rigging thwarted DuBreuil's efforts. Compounding the problem of a small population, the colony's economic affairs were always monopolized: first by the French Crown, then by a private monopolist named Antoine Crozat, then by the Company of the West or Company of the Indies, and finally—from 1731 to 1762—by the French Crown again. Each of these monopolists engaged its own vessels to service the colony, undermining private merchants' initiatives to invest. After sixty-five years of colonization, no indigenous merchant marine existed in Louisiana, and local settlers relied on French merchantmen and the occasional smuggler from Charleston.[8]

A tour of ports in the western North Atlantic circa 1700 would have revealed New Englanders' dominance in colonial American shipping. Bernard and Lotte Bailyn's pioneering work studying the Massachusetts Register of Shipping over the period from 1697 to 1714 provides unparalleled insight into the shipping business centered in Boston. With a population of about seven thousand, Boston was not only the number one port in British America, but the largest town. Small vessels predominated: the average was 49.4 tons. Sloops, single-masted vessels, were still the favored rig, comprising about 43 percent of the fleet. Brigantines and ketches, two-masted vessels, accounted for 29.3 percent, and three-masted ships and barks, 26.9 percent. The Bailyns' analysis of the register, however, reveals considerably more insight into the nature of shipping circa 1700.[9]

This was a locally owned fleet in which, for the most part, townsmen invested in vessels from their own town. Boston's oceangoing shipping was largely owned by Boston residents. The considerably smaller fleets based in Cambridge, Gloucester, Plymouth, Sandwich, and other towns were entirely owned by residents of those or adjacent communities. Overall, Massachusetts residents owned 91 percent of the tonnage registered there. Local capitalization meant local control.[10]

Small partnerships were the norm. The average vessel in Massachusetts was owned by 3.4 individuals. A few vessels in Boston and Salem were owned by one person, but for the most part shareholding among acquaintances was the preferred method: 332 people making 587 separate investments owned Massachusetts's fleet of 171 vessels in 1698. There were no companies or shipping firms at that time, although some men owned considerably more tonnage than the average shareholder. Most investors were small-scale. About two-thirds of the total pool had invested only once. Another fifty-eight made two investments in ships. That left fifty investors, all of whom had shares in three or more vessels, as the primary shipowners in Massachusetts in 1698. Even among this group individualism prevailed. Partnerships were "extremely fluid, formed to finance individual vessels," note the Bailyns. "Thus the leading investor, Samuel Lille, joined with others in the ownership of 18 vessels, but in no two cases did he invest with exactly the same group."[11]

Locally controlled and individualistic, vessel ownership in New England was neither oligarchic nor egalitarian. With small investors predominating, it is obvious that shares were widely dispersed throughout maritime communities, a far cry from patterns prevailing in Europe where shipping assets were more likely to be controlled by a merchant elite. Yet simultaneously with dispersed ownership in Massachusetts, a few major investors held a disproportionate share of the fleet. Five men, among them Samuel Lillie and Andrew Belcher, controlled 17.6 percent of Massachusetts's tonnage in 1698. Forming partnerships with kinsmen and trusted associates, they took more risks than most investors, and it is reasonable to speculate that they exerted more influence than most on the selection of markets, cargoes, and captains. From the broadest perspective, it is obvious that shipping was a choice investment among people with capital at their disposal. Ownership of New England's shipping assets was thus simultaneously widely dispersed among many towns and individuals, while being concentrated in the hands of a few wealthy Bostonians.[12]

The term "wealthy" needs to be understood in context of the era. "The opportunities for amassing great wealth . . . in the seventeenth-century port towns," notes Gary B. Nash, were rather limited, "so the fortunes of even the handful of affluent merchants and landowners were hardly a match for the wealth of a prospering London entrepreneur." Limited credit, the hazards of the sea, the way business news traveled at a snail's pace, volatile market conditions, and the lack of production of "large marketable surpluses" in seaport hinterlands all restricted the profitability of colonial merchants. Samuel Lillie, for instance, who owned more tonnage than any man in North America, would not have been considered rich in London.[13]

A few New Englanders outside of Boston also figured prominently in shipping at this time, none more so than

One of the colonial shipping barons, William Pepperrell Jr. of Kittery, Maine (then part of Massachusetts), is pictured here in his most famous role, that of leader of the British expedition that captured Fortress Louisbourg, Nova Scotia, in 1745 during King George's War. He went on to expand his father's shipbuilding and fishing business into one of the most successful mercantile houses in New England.

William Pepperrell Sr., of Kittery, Maine. Sufficient documentation exists to allow reconstruction of his creation of a substantial shipping business. Born about 1647 in Devonshire, England, Pepperrell apparently first saw America as a fisherman, probably a servant fisherman in Newfoundland. By the mid-1670s he had migrated south to the Isles of Shoals, a rocky outpost of islands offshore of the boundary between Maine and New Hampshire. The Shoals were fishermen's terrain, and by the time Pepperrell left the islands a few years later to settle in Kittery, across the Piscataqua River from Portsmouth, New Hampshire, he owned shares in a shallop and possibly in a sloop as well. These were prized possessions for what he hoped would be a path to financial independence. Pepperrell was no longer working for others, but had others working for him. In 1680 he married Margery Bray of Kittery Point, daughter of a local shipbuilder and landowner. This union seems to have helped Pepperrell's business. Over the next several decades John Bray built a number of vessels for his up-and-coming son-in-law.[14]

Pepperrell had fished with his eyes and ears open, studying the business as best he could while wearing a fisherman's apron and boots. Once he amassed sufficient capital, he took advantage of his experience as a Newfoundland fisherman and commenced coastal voyaging to trade with English fishing stations and settlements in Newfoundland. This seems to have occurred shortly after his move to Kittery in 1680. Pepperrell was no longer first and foremost a fisherman, but a businessman. Within a decade (but quite possibly earlier) he expanded his trade to Virginia and the West Indies, procuring supplies that could be sold to advantage in Newfoundland or New England. The first confirmed southerly voyage of a Pepperrell-owned vessel took place in 1693. That year, he sent two or three merchantmen to Maryland, Virginia, North Carolina, and Barbados. He soon included Antigua in his West Indies voyages. Three years later he jacked up his costs and risks, as well as his potential for profit, by venturing a transatlantic voyage to the Canary Islands. By then he had spent twenty years in New England. He had progressed from fishing for wages to owning a fishing shallop, and then to assembling a fleet of coasters, one of which he appears to have owned jointly with his son. In its foundation on fishing, its reliance on coasting, and its family orientation, Pepperrell's shipping business mirrored that of New England shipping as a whole in the late seventeenth century. Its impressive success, of course, made it atypical.[15]

By the turn of the eighteenth century, Pepperrell owned at least seven vessels, some outright, and some in partnership with other merchants and his two sons. His partners included Samuel Lillie, Boston's largest shipowner, Andrew Belcher, Boston's second most prominent shipowner, and lesser merchants from Boston and the Piscataqua region. The largest vessel in Pepperrell's fleet was a ninety-ton brigantine named for his sons, the *William and Andrew*.

Cognizant of the danger of having "all his eggs in one basket," Pepperrell diversified his holdings by investing shipping profits in real estate. Between 1689 and 1715 he acquired approximately two thousand acres of property: fifteen hundred acres of Kittery Point waterfront, in addition to parcels in York, Saco, and Damariscotta. This provided extensive tracts of timber, along with fields and grazing land. Integrating his business vertically, he began to oversee production of timber products such as barrel and cask staves, shingles, masts, and spars, some of which would be exported on, or traded from, his own vessels. His purchases also included a sawmill in York.[16]

Business success enhanced Pepperrell's social status and political position. Until the American Revolution voters uniformly elected "the better sort" to positions of power. The assumptions of the day were that cultural, political, and economic authority would naturally reside in the same individuals. As Pepperrell became financially more distinguished because of his mercantile success, townsmen honored him with the responsibility of leadership. In 1693 Kittery residents chose him as one of the town's selectmen. A year later, Maine's provincial council appointed him to the York County Court of Common Pleas. In 1696 he began nine years of presiding over Kittery's annual town meeting. He was also Kittery's representative to the general court in Boston, a justice of the peace, and county treasurer. Honorific posts that reflected his fellow citizens' trust and required his attention, these were also positions that fostered ties with northern New England's political and mercantile elite. Pepperrell was able to serve the community and himself simultaneously, something expected of officeholders in eighteenth-century America.[17]

Pepperrell's success notwithstanding, this was a tumultuous era for shipowners, as the rags-to-riches-to-rags story of Samuel Lillie illustrates. The son of a recent immigrant cooper in Boston, Lillie emerged from relative obscurity to become a shipping titan in Boston during King William's War. He was, according to the Bailyns, "easily the biggest

ship-owner in the western hemisphere." Before his spectacular bankruptcy at age forty, he "owned outright 42 of the 108 vessels in which he
was concerned, representing close to 2,500 tons." But, failing to maintain
ample cash, which was the norm in an economy where exchange of goods
generally sufficed in lieu of cash payment, Lillie watched in horror as
creditors began hounding him for immediate payment in 1707. The ripple began when two other shipowning merchants, Edward Bromfield and
Francis Burroughs, took him to court. As news spread that Lillie could
not pay his bills, a swarm of creditors demanded immediate payment.
Boston's largest shipping magnate not only was forced to liquidate his
fleet but also had to flee the province to avoid imprisonment for debt.
Lillie later tried to reenter American trade from London, but he never
succeeded, and he died many years later a poor man. Excessive risk-
taking and mismanagement may have been at the heart of his collapse,
but, as historians have noted, the business climate at the war-torn turn
of the century was anything but stable. Other prominent shipowning
Bostonians also failed, including Sir Charles Hobby and Louis Boucher.
They could not weather a system in which debtor's prison played a more
prominent role than banks, comprehensive insurance, and circulating
money.[18]

During the decade that followed the end of Queen Anne's War in
1713, William Pepperrell's business grew significantly in volume without
much change in its particulars. Already sixty-six years old in 1713, he had
long since involved his two sons. With Andrew Pepperrell's untimely
death in 1714, William Jr. assumed an increasingly significant role.
William Sr. and Jr. continued to dispatch the bulk of their cargoes to
Newfoundland, Antigua, Barbados, and North Carolina. They sent New
England timber products and fish to the West Indies in exchange for
rum, molasses, and sugar. They sent cargoes collected coastwise in the
West Indies and in America to Newfoundland for European luxury
goods, including silks, wines, and brandy. The Pepperrells had sufficient
connections that they used Newfoundland as a trade emporium, trafficking there in textiles, cutlery, ironware, clothing, boots, shoes, marine supplies, passengers, money, and bills of exchange, all of which had been
brought from England. They continued to rely on North Carolinian
naval stores as one foundation of their commercial system. In exchange,
they provided Carolinian merchants with rum, molasses, sugar, salt, and
textiles.[19]

William Pepperrell Sr. took advantage of his roots in Devonshire and established a modest trade with West Country outports such as Topsham and Exeter, even as he traded directly with Londoners. English merchants sent their own vessels to the Piscataqua laden with manufactures such as textiles and clothing, in return for which Pepperrell sent naval stores and fish. The Pepperrell fleet continued to expand as father and son purchased brigantines, schooners, sloops, and one pink, most of which they owned outright.[20]

Remaining active in business almost until his death at age eighty-seven, Pepperrell Sr. displayed characteristics that would distinguish many other shipping entrepreneurs in American history. Most importantly, perhaps, he demonstrated remarkable adaptiveness as commercial conditions changed in the 1720s and 1730s. To begin with, the Pepperrells cut back on direct trade with Newfoundland, which had launched the family fortune. Their ships now touched at Newfoundland ports only as part of transatlantic triangular voyages.

This change was a response to several factors: a decline in their North Carolina trade, an increasingly unwieldy business, and the English Crown's discouragement of both permanent settlement in Newfoundland and Newfoundlanders' trade with New England. As the Carolina trade atrophied, the Pepperrells lost a major source of goods that had been at the heart of their cargoes bound for Newfoundland. By 1730, responding to what they perceived as an unfavorable change in naval stores policy by the Crown, and to seriously declining profits, they discontinued trade with North Carolina altogether. They also dramatically reduced trade with Antigua, as the market there became too unstable for their tastes. However, they maintained strong commercial ties with Barbados. In a new twist, father and son expanded their West Indies trade to French possessions, particularly Martinique and Guadeloupe. This shift was part of a regional trend, encouraged by the actions of England's Privy Council. In 1728 the council "declared that English ships could not be seized for trading with French colonies" as long as they followed the Acts of Trade and Navigation. The French West Indies, long familiar to New England merchants with an appetite for smuggling, were henceforth a legal and cheaper source of rum and molasses than the British West Indies.[21]

By the time Pepperrell Sr. died in 1734, his namesake son was carrying on the business, and carrying it well. When Pepperrell Jr. died in 1759, he reputedly owned more tonnage than any other man in British North America. Unlike the star-crossed Samuel Lillie, however, who had been in that exalted position half a century earlier, Pepperrell Jr. avoided irredeemable debt and stayed ahead of the curve as business conditions changed in peace and war.

7

THE ECLIPSE OF BOSTON

QUEEN ANNE'S WAR ENDED WITH THE TREATY OF UTRECHT IN 1713, initiating a quarter century of peace during which the geographic shape, population density, and consumer appetites of the British North American colonies changed significantly. Scattered settlements grouped around several geographic centers were replaced by a continuous chain of British subjects and slaves stretching from southern Maine to Pamlico Sound in North Carolina. South of that, expanding population centers were to be found in both Carolinas, and in Georgia, which, as the most recent colony, was not settled until 1733. The colonists' ongoing emphasis on material improvement (for those sufficiently willing or able to prosper) nurtured an increasingly complex society stratified by wealth and status. The combination of abundant resources and the settlers' energetic "improvement" pushed the British North American colonies to become the most commercial society in the Atlantic world, despite the troubling lack of currency and banks. No competing value—whether religious faith, martial honor, a willingness to perpetuate the agricultural status quo, or an emphasis on family and cooperation—was more prevalent in the organization of colonial life than the desire for economic security. Commerce remained the preferred path for risk-takers bent on financial improvement, and shipping allowed this commercial society to function.[1]

While some economically marginal white workers in the crooked lanes of urban seaports faced deepening poverty during the eighteenth century, many colonists found upward social mobility, even affluence, in ways previously unimaginable. By 1740 the thirteen mainland colonies' white population numbered about three-quarters of a million. As eager to demonstrate refinement in their lives as they were to improve their land, Americans nurtured the consumer revolution gaining steam in Britain. Fashionable broadcloth, timely books, quality metalware, lambskin gloves, and Wedgwood dishes: all this and more flowed westward across the Atlantic to make life easier or to mark colonial consumers as people of taste and distinction. Meanwhile, European appetites for American tobacco, salt fish, rice, grain, and flour remained strong, sometimes insatiable. In this dynamo of eighteenth-century population growth and commodity flows, shipping continued to expand.[2]

As the eighteenth century unfolded, American shipping's initial story—one of phenomenal growth concentrated in New England—was not to be repeated. During the half century before the American Revolution, the industry changed its stripes. Not only did the center of gravity of American shipping move from Boston to the ascendant ports of New York and Philadelphia, but merchants in the major seaports changed the ways they did business. Innovations and adaptations in the shipping community were more common than many historians have recognized. Careful comparison of separate case studies of individual seaports clearly establishes that mideighteenth-century shipping was organized in significantly different ways from that of the seventeenth century.[3]

In New York and Philadelphia, for instance, the jack-of-all-trades merchant once prevalent was replaced by men or firms who specialized—some in dry goods, others in foodstuffs or even in specific kinds of foodstuffs. Simultaneously, as the economic historian Thomas Doerflinger discovered, "a relatively small group of Philadelphia firms provided a large proportion of the shipping services for the city." Although this concentration of tonnage in the hands of a few was a significant departure from the relatively widespread ownership of vessels in late-seventeenth-century Boston, it did not signal the elaboration of a self-contained merchant elite. Commerce remained volatile. In Boston, New York, and Philadelphia large numbers of small-scale traders vied for a share of business, even as the ranks of great men changed, with some ascending and others declining. Maritime commerce had the potential to create great wealth, but during the eighteenth century it was never a closed system or club. Part of its dynamism stemmed from the relative ease of entry, and the potential for catastrophe, faced by all players.[4]

Decentralization was another hallmark of the eighteenth-century maritime industry. Entrepreneurs in minor ports began to compete effectively in certain types of shipping. Even in the Chesapeake Bay, whose seventeenth-century shipping had been controlled by English interests, outport merchants came to control some commerce. Over the long run, American shipping would distinguish itself more by the kinds of adaptation visible during the eighteenth century than by the explosive growth characteristic of its seventeenth-century origins.

The growing American population was at once a source of production and consumption, and the colonial economy surged between 1700 and 1740.[5] The robust economic growth so evident during the eighteenth century was not uniformly distributed. Boston, whose population was still approximately twice that of New York or Philadelphia in 1735, declined from being the largest city in British America, and the most active port, to third in rank by 1772. Changes in American demography and in the nature of American business explain that reordering. It was set in motion, however, by the uneven burdens of war.

The quarter century of seaborne war and campaigns against the French preceding the Peace of Utrecht hit Boston hard. Substantial troop levies and a high rate of death at sea swelled poor rolls with the families of the missing men. The numbers of widows and orphans rose. Taxes and wartime inflation rose, too, as substantial issues of paper money depreciated real wages. While some merchants and artisans in the Puritan city profited, economic stagnation was more the norm, and Boston's registered tonnage declined. In 1708 a customs officer explained "the warr hath extreamly impoverished them, so that the trade is now one third of what it was." Four years later the governor picked up that refrain. Massachusetts's subjects, he noted, were "much impoverished and enfeebled by the heavy and almost insupportable charge of a long calamitous war which has chiefly lyen upon this Province."[6] The shock of war, compounded by a series of destructive fires, reduced Boston to a crowded and poverty-stricken city by midcentury. Though still a major port, it would never again dominate American shipping as it had in the age of the Puritans.

Philadelphia, on the other hand, was barely affected by the turn-of-the-century wars. The recently founded Quaker seaport contributed little in the way of manpower or tax money to either King William's War or Queen Anne's War. Sidestepping both the ruinous inflation and rising poverty that had become the norm in Boston, Philadelphia prospered. At the turn of the century its population was only about one-third that of Boston, but both population and shipping tonnage were growing. By 1760 the City of Brotherly Love had become the preeminent port in the British colonies.[7]

New York City fared better than Boston in the wars from 1689 to 1713, but its shipping industry did not remain as unscathed as that of Philadelphia. "In King William's War," Gary B. Nash has noted, "New York benefited as one of the main suppliers of foodstuffs for the British fleet operating in the Caribbean and gained additionally from the opening of a foodstuffs trade with the Spanish colonies in the West Indies. The town's fleet almost quadrupled, growing from about 35 vessels just before the outbreak of war in 1689 to 124 ships in 1700." Queen Anne's War, however, hit New York hard. Not only did the French navy and French privateers deprive New York merchants of one-quarter of their shipping, but Spain imposed new regulations to prevent colonial Americans from trading in the Caribbean. These events triggered a downward economic spiral. During the first decade of the eighteenth century, even though shipping was the backbone of New York's economy, British imports and local exports plummeted. Only four ships per quarter departed with exports from 1701 to 1704, and most of the vessels entering the port were English, rather than locally owned.[8]

Business conditions, then as now, were affected by external events over which merchants had no control, such as war and political decrees, in addition to population growth and mercantile innovation. Rising population did not always trigger expansion of shipping. During the 1720s, for instance, New York City's population grew by about 20 percent, but construction of new tonnage lagged far behind. Not until the 1740s, during the War of Jenkins' Ear and King George's War, would New York's fleet really grow. Only 53 vessels were registered in the city in 1738, but by 1749 the fleet had mushroomed to 157 vessels aggregating more than 6,400 registered tons.[9]

To some extent, the maturation of the shipping industry in New York between the 1730s and the 1760s was marked by eminent merchants' success at wresting part of the lucrative transatlantic trades away from British mercantile houses. As well-to-do consumers developed appetites for

This representation of the New York–Long Island ferry station around 1717 shows the wide range of maritime activity. A square-bowed ferryboat, its sail furled, is about to put ashore on Manhattan with a load of cattle, while a Royal Navy cutter fires a salute in midchannel. Long Island is in the distance.

luxury goods such as perfumes, coaches, silks, and snuff—only available from England or the Continent—New York's most successful merchants edged into that trade. Coasting and Caribbean commerce allowed many newcomers to flourish, and the number of small-fry and middling merchants continued to grow, from about one hundred circa 1715 to two hundred several decades later, to nearly three hundred by 1760, when about one hundred other merchants were sufficiently well-off to qualify as "eminent."[10]

As in Philadelphia at midcentury, specialization among New York merchants became more common. Eminent merchants gave up multiple retailing operations, preferring instead to import larger quantities of fewer goods. Most of the tea consumed in New York by the 1750s, for instance, was being imported by only a handful of specialist merchants. Specialization allowed the successful to secure prosperous niches. Some merchants, both eminent and aspiring ones, remained jacks-of-all-trades, juggling flour, sugar, peltry, flaxseed, dye plants, metalwares, and fish, but it is fair to say that the historical literature has paid too much attention to colonial merchants' diversification and insufficient attention to specialization. Part of specialization was the consolidation of vessel ownership, at least among prominent merchants who increasingly owned ships with only two or three partners. And by 1764, 10 percent of the New York vessels outbound to Britain and southern Europe were solely owned.[11]

Merchants in Boston remained more conservative. Although a few were exclusively wholesalers of dry goods, or limited to the coastal trade, virtually all of the approximately 425 merchants active there in 1760 diversified their investments as much as possible.[12] Individual entrepreneurs in the Puritan city adapted as circumstances changed. Thomas Hancock, who, according to an envious contemporary, "had raised a great estate with such rapidity, that it was commonly believed he had purchased a valuable diamond for a small sum, and sold it at its full price," held shares in about fifteen ships between 1732 and 1738. Trading with Newfoundland and southern Europe, and exporting codfish and whale oil, he had transformed a modest book-importing business into a major wholesaling, retailing, and shipping enterprise. Noteworthy, according to his biographer, is that when his oil trade with Newfoundland and London dried up around 1738, Hancock "suddenly scrapped many of the exchange devices that had served him well, and started to build up new connections with the outside world." He sold most of his tonnage in 1739 to increase his liquidity, then turned from dabbling in smuggling to smuggling Dutch paper and West Indian molasses on a grand scale, meanwhile changing the agent with whom he did business in London. King George's War provided the opportunity for profiteering on a scale theretofore unimaginable, and by the end of the war in 1748, when he was again a shipowner, Hancock was one of the three highest taxpayers in all the British mainland colonies.[13]

Successful or not, colonial merchants had no choice but to adapt. Whether specializing or diversifying their business, they had to juggle remittances, vessels, credit, and contacts just to stay afloat. They also had to contend with the Acts of Trade, a legal nicety that some found inconvenient or downright unprofitable. Smuggling expanded after the Molasses Act of 1733, even though it never accounted for a huge volume of the American colonials' trade. Smuggling clearly deprived the king of customs revenue and, according to theorists of empire, sacrificed "the Interests of the Commonweal." Customs officers knew that American merchants imported foreign goods disguised as British ones, or imported foreign goods surreptitiously, pretending to arrive in ballast after having offloaded in a secluded spot. Many customs officials colluded with this illicit commerce, including Benjamin Barons, a notorious friend of the mercantile community who also happened to be Boston's collector of customs during the late 1750s and early 1760s. New York merchants, like those in Boston, rarely feared that their contraband goods would be seized, because obliging officials looked the other way rather than condemning cargoes for the Crown.[14]

War at sea affected the business climate for virtually one of every two years during the eighteenth century, and no colonial merchant was immune from high insurance premiums driven up by war or the likelihood that his ship might be seized by foreign belligerents. In no other century between the seventeenth and the twenty-first were maritime commerce and war so intimately related. This included an upsurge in privateering, the outfitting of privately owned armed vessels with legal authorization to intercept cargo ships of enemy nations. From 1739 to 1748, during the War of Jenkins' Ear and King George's War, American colonials organized at least 466 privateering voyages, providing approximately 36,000 berths for seamen. They captured at least 829 foreign vessels worth hundreds of thousands of pounds sterling. Newport, Rhode Island, the fifth largest city in colonial British America at the time, outfitted fully a quarter of these privateering voyages. New York City merchants were close behind, with about 23 percent. Boston, Philadelphia, Charleston, and various Caribbean ports accounted for the remainder. Privateering attracted considerable capital, and vast numbers of men. More Americans served on privateers than in the three major British expeditions of those wars: the attack on Cartagena in 1741, the siege of Louisbourg in 1745, and the assault on Quebec in 1746. Shortages of seamen became the norm, for there were insufficient sailors to man the Royal Navy, the swarms of privateers, and the merchant fleet.[15]

The real impact of privateering is hard to gauge, although it is obvious that the impact of war at sea boosted marine insurance costs and sailors' wages, which in turn raised freight rates and the overall cost of shipping. Colonial commerce was always a gamble, but never more so than when outfitting privateers. Windfall profits were common enough: a group of shareholders in New York privateers averaged 140 percent on their investment. But at least one-quarter of the British colonial privateers failed to make any captures, and the unluckiest of the unlucky were captured or killed. Major merchants like Godfrey Malbone of Rhode Island lost considerable capital. Patriotism and an exaggerated sense of honor do not suffice to explain investments in privateers. Many colonial merchants were adventurous by nature, risk-taking men for whom privateering was the ultimate speculation. Its popularity was not simply a result of widespread imperial warfare, but a reflection of American shipowners' willingness—even their need—to take risks in that roller-coaster precorporate business environment.[16]

The eighteenth century was the heyday of minor ports, and middling merchants in many smaller towns thrived in ways unheard of during the seventeenth century, and that had been superseded by the middle of the nineteenth century. This was a geographically widespread phenomenon, ranging from New England to the Chesapeake. As Boston stagnated commercially, a number of coastal and river ports in New England captured relative market share in the region's shipping business. Merchants in towns like Norwich, Connecticut; Newburyport, Massachusetts; South Berwick, Maine; and Exeter, New Hampshire, garnered increasingly large slices of coastal and West Indian trade as well as occasional transatlantic ventures. For about a century, from roughly 1715 to 1815, warehouses sprouted along the shores of modest harbors and rivers, and shipwrights in these out-of-the-way towns built substantial schooners and square-riggers. "The emergence of these secondary ports," notes Christine Heyrman, "sustained the vitality of New England's economy over the later colonial period as Boston, the old center of its trade, suffered eclipse by New York and Philadelphia."[17]

Southern ports, including Norfolk, Annapolis, and Charleston, also became modest players in the shipping business. Local merchants began to buy, build, and outfit ships. Emulating the Bostonians who controlled the lion's share of their coastal trade during the seventeenth century, a handful of merchants in these southern towns developed commercial connections both overseas and in other British North American colonies. Chesapeake merchants specialized not in tobacco but in general trade and the grain trade, emulating successful merchants in Philadelphia. Tobacco remained king of the Chesapeake economy in 1773, as it had in 1733. But during those intervening forty years, it fell from comprising 77 percent of Virginia's exports to only 61 percent. Export of wood and wood products, grain and grain products, iron, peas, beans, and ships filled the void, providing opportunities for locally based merchants to get a foothold in shipping. Tobacco had precluded such chances because mercantilist regulations insisted it be shipped directly to Britain, and metropolitan tobacco merchants retained their lock on shipping and marketing. Rising grain exports, on the other hand, boosted the fortunes of small ports, like Oxford, Maryland, and its prominent merchant-planter families.[18]

Export diversification and locally based shipping grew hand in hand in the Upper South. Both contributed to the urbanization of the tidewater region. As long as Virginia and Maryland remained resolutely tobacco-growing provinces, towns languished. When it became possible, however, to profit from other exports, towns grew with the development of shipping services. Norfolk, Baltimore, and Chestertown, among others, were midwifed by shipping. Assessing the Upper South, McCusker and Menard point out that "the relatively small trade in foodstuffs on the region's periphery had induced a much greater degree of urbanization and an economy more developed and less 'colonial' than that of the plantation belt."[19]

If eighteenth-century American shipping was more specialized, more decentralized, and more influenced by the exigencies of war than it had been during the seventeenth century, it was categorically not more triangular. The notion of colonial commerce being structured along "triangular trade" has had a perverse staying power, perhaps because it is simultaneously a graphic image and a catchy phrase. In defense of the concept, the term describes the ultimate nature of major commodity flows in the seventeenth- and eighteenth-century Atlantic world: New England foodstuffs fed Caribbean slaves, who produced sugar consumed by English workers, who manufactured the goods purchased by New England farmers. But—and this is an important caveat—a single vessel rarely sailed all three legs of the triangle. To assume otherwise is to seriously distort the actual operation of colonial shipping. Gary M. Walton and James F. Shepherd tracked hundreds of colonial vessels from New England and the Middle Atlantic ports destined for Barbados and Jamaica, and followed them outbound from the islands. "Only a few," they note, "departed to Great Britain." The majority returned to North American colonies. During an age in which carrying goods and marketing them was tightly bound together, merchants found a degree of security in "specialized routes or shuttle patterns" instead of "multilateral or triangular patterns of trade."[20]

New England's slave triangle is a special case, carved indelibly into American history and the American psyche by Rhode Island skippers. The slave triangle was never a major component of New England's colonial shipping, but its memory has endured all out of proportion to its role in the regional economy because of its abrogation of human rights. As Walton and Shepherd explain, "of the annual average of 107,285 tons that cleared New England between 1768 and 1772, only 1,023 tons were destined for Africa—less than 1 percent of the total. This route was even less significant to the middle colonies."[21]

But the New England slave trade was colonial America's true triangular trade. From 1725 to 1807 Rhode Island merchants engaged continuously in the African slave trade. During those years at least 934 vessels departed the colony for West Africa, transporting approximately 106,000 unwilling captives across the Atlantic to the Caribbean or mainland ports. Ships outbound from Newport carried locally distilled rum to West Africa. They exchanged Rhode Island rum with African merchants for slaves, who were transported to the Caribbean and exchanged for molasses that would be shipped to Rhode Island distilleries. For Newport merchants, African slave dealers, and captives crowded in the hellish 'tween decks, this triangular trade mattered.[22]

Shipping people to America (slaves, servants, and free immigrants) was big business in the eighteenth century. Between 1700 and 1775 more than twice as many African and European people arrived in the British mainland colonies (approximately 586,000) as had lived there in 1700 (approximately 250,000). Almost half of the new arrivals were Africans. While some colonial merchants established themselves as slave traders, notably in Charleston and New York in addition to Rhode Island, the lion's share of the transatlantic slave trade destined for North America was managed by firms in England. English slave traders averaged about 10 percent profit during the eighteenth century, an attractive rate of return. The trade was complex, however, and sufficiently capital-intensive that most colonial merchants chose not to get involved. Of the approximately nine million Africans shipped to the Americas, fewer than 250,000 (less than 2.7 percent) arrived on vessels owned in the thirteen colonies or new republic.[23]

Colonial shippers corralled more of the emerging traffic in voluntary immigrants. That trade changed significantly from its rather sporadic and haphazard origins in the seventeenth century, becoming both profitable and specialized. Less is known, actually, about the business of importing free immigrants to British North America during the eighteenth century than about the slave trade. The beginning of German mass migration to North America between 1683 and 1775, however, has been reconstructed remarkably well by Marianne S. Wokeck. About 111,000 German-speaking people arrived in the colonies during those years, most of whom traveled down the Rhine River to depart from Rotterdam or Amsterdam. A port call in England was mandatory according to the Acts of Trade, so ships employed in this increasingly specialized business left Holland for a British port, and then proceeded to America, usually to Philadelphia. "In the early years of the German trade in emigrants," writes Wokeck, "most vessels were chartered in London, although later a substantial portion of passenger ships were Philadelphia built, owned, and operated." Merchants in the Dutch ports of embarkation, whether Dutch or British, needed contacts with merchants in London or Philadelphia to arrange appropriate ship charters, and to deal with provisioning and paperwork."[24]

Philadelphia merchants like Alexander and Charles Stedman, and Thomas Penrose, who became adept at the German immigrant business, frequently dispatched provision ships to Europe. Their agents then hired carpenters to modify the vessels for immigrants on the return voyage. During the peak of German migration, between 1749 and 1755, Philadelphia's share of the tonnage built and registered for that trade more than doubled. Not surprisingly, this complicated business, which involved knowledge of German markets for goods and laborers, as well as legal registration requirements for immigrants, became cornered by a few large firms that specialized in it.[25]

Whether shipping immigrants, slaves, dry goods, or provisions, merchants played prominent roles in the economic development of the British American mainland colonies. No scholar has done more to recover their "vigorous spirit of enterprise" than Thomas M. Doerflinger, chronicler of Philadelphia's merchant community. Doerflinger depicts the merchants as living in a world in flux whose essence consisted of "commercial credit, social mobility, risk, and innovation." This was an arena where "risk and opportunity fed on each other in a symbiotic relationship," not one for the faint of heart. Easily available credit allowed virtually any man to try his hand as a merchant.

But one man's opportunity was another man's brutal competition: this very ease of entry made trade extremely hazardous for the established wholesaler. Many other factors . . . compounded the risk of failure in the relatively primitive economy of the Delaware Valley. The high cost of labor and capital, the distant and easily glutted nature of export markets, the volatility of foreign exchange markets, the scarcity of specie for domestic exchange, the frequency of wars, and the small size of many merchants' estates—all gave rise to a high rate of bankruptcy.

Colonial shipping often has been portrayed as an essentially unchanging business. In reality it was anything but static. "Because risk was so deeply embedded in their everyday operations," Doerflinger concludes, "merchants were favorably disposed toward innovation."[26]

8

COASTAL COMMERCE IN COLONIAL AMERICA

ONE OF THE LEAST UNDERSTOOD ASPECTS OF THE ROLE OF shipping in the making of America is the extent of coastal and inland waters trading, and its implications. From the 1620s and 1630s, when immigrant coastal trading mavericks like John Oldham and a few Dutch skippers in New Amsterdam were the first resident vessel operators in America, to the eve of the American Revolution, when the annual value of commodities carried by coasters approximated £715,000, coasters were imperative to overall economic functioning. They were also an important source of jobs and occupational pride for the men who ran them, and an essential unifying mechanism for the thirteen disparate colonies. "In fact," note McCusker and Menard, "it can be argued that no such thing as a 'colonial economy' developed until nearly the end of the era, after the coastwise trade had performed its work of integration." Yet coasters have rarely gotten their due. The contempt in Governor Andros's comment in 1674 that New York City was "poore, unsettled & without Trade, except a few coasters" was essentially matched by that of President Thomas Jefferson, who wrote in 1808 that coastwise trade "may be of some trifling advantage to individuals . . . but it is not a farthing's benefit to the nation at large." Merchants knew better.[1]

Residents in Boston, the first urban center in British America, relied on short-haul maritime transportation almost immediately, as did other

settlers. The Shawmut Peninsula on which Bostonians settled was virtually treeless, a real drawback for people who cooked and heated with
wood. "We at Boston were almost readye to breake up for want of wood,"
Governor Winthrop wrote during the winter of 1637–1638. Lighters
saved the day, bringing firewood, as well as marsh grass for fodder and
roof thatch, from the mainland and surrounding islands.[2]

Lighters were simple barges, useful for a host of tasks. Settlers at Plymouth had built one during the summer of 1624. Farmers understood
them as floating equivalents of wheelbarrows, necessary implements in the
agrarian routine. They were also essential for moving cargo between
anchored ships and the shore in places without deepwater wharves, and
thus a vital link in the development of shipping in early America. Edward
Colcord and Richard Morris of Dover, New Hampshire, acknowledged
that fact in 1639 when they agreed with Stephen Greensmith to deliver
five thousand clapboards "within a cable's length of the usual riding place
of ships just at the waters side at Pascatt [Piscataqua] rivers mouth & to
fynd a boat or lighter to help put them on board."[3] About twenty lighters
were employed year round during the 1680s in the town of Salem; other
minor seaports from Delaware Bay to Kittery, Maine, must have had
similar fleets. Harbor lighterage was a variant of the boat work common
to all male settlers along the shore. But landsmen lightering hay or firewood were by no means coastal traders.[4]

Coasting was distinct, a business separate from international seafaring
and mundane boat work. By the 1640s or 1650s coasters in New England
were regularly stitching together tiny villages and outports with the
region's major market towns, Boston and Salem. One hallmark of coasting, then, from its beginning, was decentralization. Operating out of
small ports like Norwalk, Connecticut, or Perth Amboy, New Jersey,
seventeenth-century coasters made the business of shipping viable in a
host of small towns.

Serving as small vessel brokers, outport merchants kept sloops and
ketches (and later, schooners) shuttling locally produced and locally
owned goods to regional mercantile centers. Rarely did Boston vessels
nose into smaller New England ports: Boston merchants depended on
outport merchants to collect cargoes for export. Moreover, some coastal
commerce was extremely local—literally within one customs district.
Vessels transporting goods within the same customs district were not
recorded in the Naval Officer's reports. Yet in the Portsmouth, New

Hampshire, district, at least, the Pepperrell daybook and loose receipts indicate the existence of this distinctly internal trade. Fishing vessels and small coasters carrying merchantable commodities moved between places such as Kittery and Wells, contiguous towns within the customs district, generating merchants' receipts for credits earned but never being noted in the official paper trail. This movement of commodities within a given customs district almost certainly existed elsewhere as well. Small-scale coasting helped build a vibrant economy.[5]

Coasting was a homegrown business in other ways. Virtually all coastal traders in colonial America were resident in the colonies. The Acts of Trade required that shipmasters arriving and departing in British colonial ports be subjects of the British Crown, and that they operate only British-built vessels. This protectionist legislation excluded Dutch, Spanish, and other foreigners from coasting in British North America. Conducted for the most part in modest vessels, and consisting generally of locally assembled mixed cargoes, coasting did not provide sufficient financial incentive for nonresident merchants. As it expanded—and it expanded mightily during the colonial period—American colonials took all the risks and accrued all the benefits. The benefits were legion: freights, insurance, and commissions on handling cargoes, as well as revenues from vessel charters and vessel sales. Coasting, moreover, was the maritime path of self-advancement for men of modest means who wished to try their hands in business. Its innumerable opportunities allowed those short on capital or credit to launch a commercial career. While New Englanders ultimately controlled the bulk of the colonies' coastal trade, some coasting vessels were built and operated in each of the thirteen colonies.

Coasting began in boats and shallops, but as the century wore on coastermen acquired larger sloops, barks, and two-masted ketches, capable, seaworthy boats that could fish a season on the banks or traffic with the Caribbean as well as freight a lading between Maine and New York. Tiny craft still mattered, though, right to the end of the century. Between March 1694 and December 1695 small coasting boats (less than 15 tons) moved a great deal of lumber out of New Hampshire's Piscataqua customs district to Boston: 1,674,800 feet of boards, planks, and joists, not counting staves and other wood products.[6]

Vessels in the coasting trade got significantly larger as time passed. In 1692 a 15-ton shallop was typical of the coasters entering or clearing in Portsmouth. Just a few years later vessels so small did not warrant a full entry in the Naval Officer's records: they were noted separately as "coasting sloops and other small open vessels loaden with lumber, &c." As early as the 1720s, the average size was closer to 45 tons. By 1752 vessels of less than 25 tons had largely disappeared from the New Hampshire customs records. The average coaster entering or clearing from Portsmouth in 1751 was 49.3 tons. The same was true in Philadelphia at midcentury: coasters averaged 52 tons, while vessels engaged in West Indies trade were 76 tons and transatlantic ships about 150 tons.[7]

Sufficiently reliable data simply does not exist to allow precise analysis of the colonial coasting trade, even though by 1770 forty-two colonial customs districts existed, each of which generated paperwork. They ranged from Newfoundland to the fledgling East and West Florida districts of St. Augustine, Pensacola, and Mobile. Bermuda was its own district, as was the Bahamas. Most statistical studies of the colonial coastal trade thus define "coastwise" as the region covered by those districts, which excluded, of course, the West Indies proper. Contemporary mariners, who had no way of knowing that thirteen of the mainland colonies would become a distinct political unit in the future, understood it that way, too. Unfortunately, complete chronological records do not exist for any single district. The Naval Office Shipping Lists and various special customs records provide snapshots of commodities carried by coasters, and of coastal entries and clearances as a percentage of total entries and clearances for given ports in given years. ("Naval Officer" was the official title of the customs officer keeping track of vessels and cargos, inbound and outbound.) Those records are rife with substantial gaps. Comparative figures and statistics can be mustered to indicate some patterns, including the growth of the colonial coastal trade, but economic historians are still struggling to reconstruct the exact magnitude of coasting in the colonial economy. One thing is clear: coasting constantly reinvented itself to accommodate changing economic patterns and local demands.[8]

Coastal trading merchants in New Hampshire and Massachusetts diversified their business in several significant ways during the eighteenth century. Coastal trading expanded as would be expected in a maturing economy. Larger vessels made more stops in the mid-Atlantic provinces and in the South, distributing imports from Europe, and collecting and distributing locally produced goods. As colonists added more value to commodities through artisanal labor and industrial refinement, colonially manufactured goods began to supplant some of the old imports. Locally made bricks, ironware, and pottery began to travel along the coast stowed next to flour, molasses, rum, and pork. During the early and mid-seventeenth century, New Englanders had imported European iron and tools. But by 1744 colonial manufacturers were shipping their own products. Records show that merchants in New Hampshire could import iron from Pennsylvania and export "5 dozen axes here made" to North Carolina, whose lumber merchants in turn sent naval stores, including pitch, to shipyards in New Hampshire. When craftsmen in New Hampshire began to produce fine furniture and everyday shoes for export, Virginians sent black walnut timber to Portsmouth by coaster, and Carolinians sent hides and skins. Coasting accelerated regional economic development.[9]

Southern commodities such as wood, rice, tar, and even the occasional barrel of oranges moved primarily in vessels built and owned in New England. Between 1725 and 1751, for example, of the 162 sloops that traded in the port of Roanoke, North Carolina, only 24 (15 percent) were built in North Carolina. But 90 of them (56 percent) were built in New England. Rising populations and increasingly sophisticated internal economies promoted more coastwise trade, even if most of it continued to be dominated by New England merchants and traders.[10]

Coasters distributed imports from overseas throughout the colonies, collected cargoes for export, and exchanged surpluses produced within the thirteen colonies. Nevertheless, regional variations existed. A midcentury example of how New Englanders organized coasting voyages is instructional. In 1746 one of William Pepperrell's captains, Nahum Ward, entered Portsmouth, New Hampshire, from North Carolina in April with hogs' fat, hides, corn, black walnut timber, deer skins, pitch, tar, and tobacco. Twenty-four days later he cleared for Louisbourg, Nova Scotia, with pine boards, shingles, clapboards, corn, oxen, sheep, poultry, pitch, and turpentine. Most of the North Carolina imports had stayed in the Portsmouth region or been shipped elsewhere. Meanwhile, the cargo for Louisbourg had been assembled from both locally produced commodities and others imported from the Carolinas.[11]

In Salem, Massachusetts, however, during the same decade, a different pattern emerged. Coasters arriving at or clearing from Salem during the seventeenth century primarily had serviced the small towns and fishing centers down east on the coast of Maine. By the 1740s this business simply did not exist. "The new banks fishery," explains Daniel Vickers, "which had replaced the older Maine shore fishery, required fewer coasting services, since it provisioned itself and freighted its own fish. Several outports—namely Newbury, Gloucester and Marblehead—had developed into marketing centers in their own right, and traders there could deal directly with Boston or even in foreign markets without ever calling in to Salem." Simultaneously, however, merchants and traders with coasting tonnage in Salem discovered that the regional economy demanded more and more "regular transport inside Massachusetts Bay. Accordingly, by the middle of the eighteenth century, the short haul coasting business attracted more Salem residents than ever."[12]

Massachusetts had become a food importing region earlier in the century, and by midcentury the colony's traders were importing considerable amounts of flour, grain, rice, and meat, primarily to feed urban dwellers. Eight of the commonwealth's most populous towns were on the coast, and small sloops and schooners, including those from Salem, made a living transshipping foodstuffs that had been brought from the mid-Atlantic breadbasket to Boston or Salem. A few Salem coasters continued to trade on longer coastwise voyages, as well, seeking markets in Philadelphia, North Carolina, and Nova Scotia. Salem's coastwise trade thus intensified regionally even as it expanded geographically during the eighteenth century. New York City's coasting trade developed in a similar fashion, intensifying regionally in Long Island Sound, the Jersey Shore, and the Hudson River, while also expanding in long-distance coasting voyages.[13]

In Philadelphia the coastal trade operated in a somewhat different fashion. Commerce from Philadelphia to points north and east was generally dominated by New Englanders, who ran small vessels back and forth in the provisions trade that kept Yankees fed. "Since over half of the vessels sent to the Delaware from northern ports were consigned to the master of the ship," Thomas Doerflinger explains, "Philadelphia traders did not even pick up a commission for handling the vessel. The cargoes, too, were normally owned by the New England merchants." Philadelphia traders were restricted to making a profit, then, solely through their commissions for "assembling the outward cargoes of flour, bar iron, and other goods and selling the inward shipments of rum, fish, whale oil, and candles."[14]

In coastal trade to the southward, on the other hand, Philadelphians had much more control. They owned 50 percent of the tonnage, sold the insurance, marketed the bills of exchange, and arranged for transshipment to Europe of the southern commodities collected by their coasters. Sloops and schooners outbound from Philadelphia carried European manufactures south, in addition to locally produced manufactures, New England rum, Caribbean products, and—to South Carolina—regionally grown meat and flour. In South Carolina they traded for indigo and rice; in North Carolina for naval stores; and in Virginia and Maryland for tobacco and grain. Southbound coasters based in Philadelphia thus promoted the entrepôt function of that port, helping to solidify local merchants' dominant position in late colonial commerce.[15]

While certain commodities, such as lumber, dried fish, furs, and flaxseed were collected by coasters primarily for international export, trade within the thirteen colonies intensified considerably during the eighteenth century. By the early 1770s the British North American population was sufficiently large and sophisticated that much interregional trade existed solely to distribute dry goods and manufactures within the substantial market that the colonies themselves provided. Coasting merchants added value to commodities by delivering them to places with better markets. New Englanders shipped locally distilled rum, lumber products, pickled fish, and spermacetti candles to other Americans. Merchants in Baltimore, Philadelphia, and New York shipped grain and flour northward to remedy Yankees' food deficit. North Carolinians shipped naval stores consumed by boatwrights and shipbuilders in New York, Philadelphia, and New England.[16]

American coastal traders were sufficiently astute to reorient the commerce of Newfoundland and Nova Scotia from England to the mainland colonies, notably Boston, during the eighteenth century. The Newfoundland fisheries were then a linchpin in the Atlantic economy. Fishing on that great rock of an island had begun as a seasonal enterprise, with boats and fishermen coming from the West Country of England and returning each year. Over time, Newfoundland became more permanently settled, thanks largely to New England merchants like the Pepperrells and Thomas Hancock, who insinuated themselves into the local economy, providing supplies (including reexports from England), buying fish and whale products, dealing in bills of exchange, and establishing networks of credit. Colonial coastal traders effectively edged out British merchants, prospering in the Newfoundland trade. A similar process occurred in Nova Scotia, which became a separate colony in 1749. Given the magnitude of trade in Atlantic Canada—approximately £150,000 of commodity exports annually by 1772—this was no small accomplishment. By the time shots were fired at Lexington and Concord, Newfoundland and Nova Scotia were snugly in the orbit of colonial coasting, economically part of what some historians have called "greater New England." With the Revolution and resulting political settlement, those provinces began a slow reorientation away from New England's coasters.[17]

Changes in the nature of Virginia's coastwise trade are illustrative of several other important patterns in coasting as the eighteenth century progressed. Virginians themselves were not especially involved in the business of shipping. They controlled only about 10 percent of the tonnage carrying the province's coastal commerce from 1737 to 1742, and again from 1760 to 1769, years for which data is available. New Englanders controlled most of the tonnage, especially in the early years. But the volume of Virginia's domestic trade expanded rapidly from the 1730s to the 1760s, with an average annual rate of growth half again as much as the province's population growth. Corn exports to other provinces rose by a factor of 3.2, from 42,361 bushels to 136,632. Wheat exports increased from 10,224 bushels to 38,506, or 3.8 times. These amounts were not huge, and even when all other commodities moving coastwise were accounted for, the total value of Virginia's annual coasting between 1760 and 1769 probably did not exceed £50,000. Nevertheless, two things are noteworthy about this commerce. One is that Virginia's shift from tobacco monoculture toward mixed cereals materially assisted American shipping. The ratio in Virginia of the value of tobacco exports to grain exports (both deep-sea and coastwise) fell from 14:1 to 3:1 between the 1737–1742 period and the 1760s. This was good news for American shippers. Acreage planted in tobacco was primarily serviced by English ships. Acreage planted in corn, wheat, or peas was likely to be serviced by colonial coasters, or by American merchants in the transatlantic food trade. The destination of Virginia's coastal exports and origin of its imports changed during those years too, as Philadelphians, New Yorkers, and Rhode Islanders cut into Massachusetts's market share in coasting. "Both absolutely and relatively to Massachusetts, these three colonies were minimal markets for Virginia during the 1730's," notes David C. Klingaman. "Within three decades, however they were absorbing approximately one half of Virginia's coastwise exports," and providing most imports. During a thirty-year period in the late colonial era, it is fair to say that Virginia's coastal commerce not only expanded significantly, following agricultural diversification, but also began to flow in new channels.[18]

In addition to the bread, flour, rum, molasses, and corn, which together comprised 50 percent of the value of coastwise cargoes, colonial coasters also carried two low-value commodities, firewood and hay.[19] Without them urban economies would have ground to a standstill. While the records of this traffic are minimal, its importance cannot be underestimated. Coasters have always carried energy for Americans. During the last century oil has been the commodity of note; in much of the late nineteenth and early twentieth centuries, coal moved north from Chesapeake and Delaware bays to Portland, Portsmouth, Boston, Providence, New London, New York City, and other urban areas. Before that, however, lowly firewood boats and hay barges kept urbanites supplied with the fuel that heated their houses and shops, and the food for the animals that propelled machines and wagons. The Naval Office Shipping Lists note that the 20-ton sloop *Endeavour* arrived in Portsmouth from Hampton, New Hampshire, on September 17, 1692, loaded with hay. Most of the hay consumed in Portsmouth, however, arrived by Piscataqua River gundalows, sailing barges whose movements were never recorded. Early energy transportation is one of the many unwritten stories in American history.[20]

Among all towns in colonial America, Boston suffered the worst fuel shortages. During the seventeenth century wood boats plied the coast of Massachusetts Bay, but by the middle of the eighteenth century they ranged as far afield as Maine. "As a small vessel with three hands and carrying thirty cords of wood could make only fifteen trips annually," explained the historian Carl Bridenbaugh, "supplying firewood to sixteen thousand people the year round was a large and formidable operation. Besides, the charcoal needed by blacksmiths and braziers and for heating artisans' shops consumed large amounts of fuel." But Boston's problems were not unique. New Yorkers were consuming more than twenty thousand cords of wood annually by 1761, virtually all of which arrived by boat. As early as the 1730s Newport, Rhode Island, was entirely dependent on fuel shipped by coaster. Philadelphia and Charleston did not face the severe shortages of wood common farther north, but as in the other towns, most of their fuel arrived by water.[21]

The problem persisted after the Revolution, continuing to provide an opportunity for woodcutters and coasters. When an Englishman named Alexander Baring visited Massachusetts seaports in 1796, he was flabbergasted to discover that firewood was "dearer than it was in France and

Germany" on account of "a total want of any system of preservation of forests." As had been the case for fifty years, woodsmen harvested hardwood along Maine's innumerable natural harbors and shipped it westward in a fleet of lowly coasters that shuttled regularly to towns in Massachusetts.[22] As late as 1802 a writer describing towns on Cape Cod, where most men worked in the cod fishery, noted that "Orleans' only vessels are three coasters which bring firewood and lumber from the district of Maine, and one Boston packet." Virtually every coastal town of any size was serviced by coasters loaded with cordwood and hay. Commerce in fuel is yet another example of "invisible earnings" in the colonial coasting business, whose importance generally has been ignored.[23]

Coasting's importance in the economy varied by region, as can be seen by assessments of both value and tonnage. Expert interpretations still contain discrepancies, however, because of the nature of the data. Take the case of New England at the end of the colonial period. Reliable figures indicate that the average annual value of commodity exports overseas from New England for the years 1768–1772 was £439,101. Fish was New England's most valuable export, followed by livestock, wood products, whale products, potash, grain, and rum. Similar records are not available for coasting. By combing the secondary literature, however, McCusker and Menard have built a case about the magnitude of coasting in New England on the eve of the Revolution. Shepherd and Williamson, they note, estimated the value of commodities shipped coastwise in New England vessels as £304,000 annually, about 69 percent of the value of overseas exports. Once the invisible earnings are added, such as freight revenues and the sale of vessels, the figure becomes higher yet. Add the shipments of firewood and hay, and it grows yet again. While no one can identify with precision the exact value of coasting to New England, or to the colonial economy as a whole, it was substantial. Surpluses were being earned in each of the thirteen colonies through coasting.[24]

In the Middle Colonies, according to Shepherd and Williamson, coasting amounted to about 40 percent of the value of exports; in the Lower South, 17 percent, and in the Upper South, where tobacco still dominated the late colonial economy, only about 8 percent. Altogether, throughout the thirteen colonies, "the estimated total value of exports in the coastal trade averaged about 25% of the commodity exports to overseas areas" between 1768 and 1772. In terms of tonnage entered and cleared, however, coasting looms even larger. Coasters represented about

46 percent of the tonnage of international commerce in those years. This differential existed because commodities shipped coastwise were often less valuable per ton, and because coasters were more likely to sail in ballast (without cargo) or partially in ballast, than were deepwater ships.[25]

During the late colonial period the three major seaports—Boston, New York, and Philadelphia—employed significantly different amounts of tonnage in coasting. The figures are revealing. During 1765–1766, clearances (departures) coastwise from the port of Boston totaled 12,800 registered tons, or 46 percent of the tons cleared. In Philadelphia 14,600 tons cleared coastwise, approximately 37 percent of that port's tonnage cleared. New York City was far behind, in both actual tonnage and coasting as a percentage of clearances: only 3,000 tons cleared coastwise, 15.3 percent of the port's clearances. In 1772 Boston still cleared twice as much tonnage coastwise as did New York: 24,500 tons compared to 11,900. Philadelphia was between the two, with 15,100 tons cleared coastwise, 33.7 percent of all clearances. As Boston lost its ranking as the colonies' primary seaport, it sustained its dominant position in the coasting business. Moreover, even though most of the value of colonial American goods shipped was in overseas trading, coastal trading provided more jobs for officers and seamen, and allowed more entrepreneurs access to commercial opportunities, simply because of the tonnage involved.[26]

The colonial coastal trade differed significantly from that of the early republic because the thirteen colonies never had a uniform commercial policy. Intercolonial commercial squabbles bedeviled coastal traders for years. During the 1690s, for instance, a New Hampshire law prohibited the coastal lumber trade with Boston, as the leading men of the province hoped to channel its timber exports into the deep-sea shipping controlled by them and their cronies. Marginal traders in small boats had been content to freight New Hampshire timber to Boston markets, and the new law limited their opportunities. Provincial governments in Massachusetts and New Hampshire squabbled more than once over coasters. In 1720 officials in New Hampshire heard irate testimony regarding the "heavy burdens" that "oppress us very greatly," because Massachusetts was laying "a tunnage of 2s per tun on all our coasting vessels."[27]

Similar intercolonial commercial warfare broke out in greater New York during the late seventeenth century, to the bane of coasters. New York City had been known for free trade until 1668. Thereafter, regulations gave commercial privileges to city residents while imposing discriminatory port fees on traders from New Jersey and Long Island. New Jersey retaliated in 1676, declaring Perth Amboy a "free port." With no duties on commodities, merchants in Perth Amboy hoped to corral grain and livestock for export from the surrounding region, cutting out competitors in New York City. The competition persisted for a few years, until New York's governor, Edmund Andros, insisted that New Jersey traders follow the law and collect import duties. Ultimately, prominent city merchants influenced the royal governor and New York City's mayor and city council to enforce a mercantilist monopoly on exports. Ignoring the demands of small traders, who preferred free trade and regional cooperation, the eminent men systematically subordinated the interests of New Jersey, Long Island, and Connecticut to those of New York City. They scored a major victory in 1684 when it became illegal to bolt and pack flour for export anywhere in the region except in Manhattan. Lesser traders had to be content to corner a piece of the carrying trade that delivered grain harvests to New York City for milling and export.[28]

Coasters thus confronted a maddening, provincially based, minimercantilist system. Facing hazards of the sea and vagaries of the market, they also sailed with the knowledge that provincial officials could tax them, exclude them, or impose embargoes on the shipment of certain commodities. While most eighteenth-century merchants believed that imperial mercantilist policies operated to their benefit, coasters began to critique the logic behind them. The notion of free trade, which would gather momentum in many quarters as the colonies moved toward Revolution, was first congenial to lesser traders in the coasting business.[29]

Although coasters were generally hardheaded men with more of an eye on mundane freights than on philosophical matters, they helped consolidate an intercolonial identity, promoting the "Americanization" of Connecticut Yankees, Virginians, New Yorkers, and Carolinians. Commercial contacts were part of this, as was coasters' dissemination of provincial newspapers. "In the American colonies, first from Boston to Philadelphia, and later from Halifax to Charleston and the West Indies," notes the historian Charles E. Clark, "steadily increasing numbers of weekly (and occasionally semi-weekly) newspapers were enriching the conversation and trade of each seaport while, at the same time, contributing to a growing sense of American community and identity." The number of American newspapers rose from three to almost twenty between 1720 and 1760, not including the short-lived ones and the German-language papers in

Pennsylvania. While the term "American" was not used until the Revolution, it appears that as early as 1740 newspaper readers were becoming more intrigued with what were referred to as their "neighboring provinces." News of those provinces moved by coaster, as did the newspapers that increasingly bound American colonials together with a shared sense of what it meant to be a freeborn Briton in the mainland colonies.[30]

By the end of the colonial period it was already clear that America would prosper by trading with itself. Coasters promoted regional economic specialization in agriculture, manufacturing, and resource extraction. They promoted major ports' function as entrepôts. They accelerated social mobility, providing a venue for ambitious traders without other means to promote themselves in the world of commerce. While deep-sea shipping remained more important than coasting in the economy as a whole, colonists' trading with each other was clearly a significant piece of Americans' maritime activity on the eve of the Revolution.

9

THE SAILOR'S LIFE

VIRTUALLY THE ONLY ROUTES TO RICHES IN COLONIAL AMERICA were land speculation, plantation slavery, and maritime commerce, and some of the wealthiest men in British North America were merchant shipowners. Conversely, many of the poorest white American men in the colonies were seamen. Probate inventories, tax records, and other indicators of wealth consistently show seamen among the most impoverished workers in seaports such as Boston, New York, and Philadelphia, and even in lesser ports like Providence. Not all seamen were eternally poor: some were able to acquire a competence over the course of a life's work and, after spending some years before the mast, rise to a mate's or captain's berth, especially in smaller outports like Salem, Newburyport, and Norwalk. But others remained propertyless wage workers for their entire lives, living at or near subsistence. In a society notable for its preponderance of the "middling sort," merchants' conspicuous wealth and mariners' grinding poverty represented atypical extremes. The gap between the wealthiest colonials (many of them merchant shipowners) and the poorest colonials (many of them merchant seamen) was real, and it has rightfully structured much of what we know about maritime labor relations in colonial British America. But it is not the entire story.

Mariners were the largest occupational group among workingmen in major colonial seaports. In a society where many people owned productive resources, and waged work was less common than it would be in the future, maritime work was the primary employment of men working for wages. In Boston between 1685 and 1725, 40 to 50 percent of male laborers were seamen. Seafaring wages were steady throughout that period, but taxes rose, and consumers lost purchasing power because of inflation, so the prospects of accumulating a respectable competence were rather slim for mariners. Probate inventories reveal the relative wealth of Bostonians in that era, and it is no surprise that mariners were the most numerous group in the poorest 30 percent of decedents who left inventories. While some mariners in Boston owned real estate during the seventeenth century, there was a long-range "decline of mariners in the real estate market beginning in 1710," according to the historian Gary B. Nash.[1] The Boston men whose labor made it possible for ships to sail did not reap much of the reward.

During the late seventeenth and early eighteenth centuries the cost of labor, including victuals, was about 41 percent of a colonial shipowner's expense for an average voyage. The capital outlay, including original purchase of the ship and its maintenance, was only about 14 percent, while insurance, port fees, and other costs represented about 45 percent. During the century from 1675 to 1775 the actual cost of shipping commodities fell substantially. Economists normally express this as the cost to ship one ton of a commodity (such as wheat, whale oil, or rum) one mile (called a ton-mile). During the same century, average seafaring wages remained steady, despite significant fluctuations in wartime. Meanwhile, the costs of shipbuilding and victualing crews rose. Taken as a whole, it appears that while capital expenditures and the cost of provisions rose, the overall cost of shipping commodities fell, in large part because seamen did not get raises to compensate for inflation. Shipowners benefited from a favorable price-to-wage ratio, and increases in productivity and capital accumulation came at mariners' expense.[2]

Mariners fared better in times of war. At Boston in 1746 during King George's War, their pay skyrocketed to ninety shillings a month, but by 1754 it was back down to forty-two shillings. Similar patterns prevailed in Philadelphia. During the Seven Years' War sailors commanded as much as five pounds per month, but by the end of the war in 1763, pay had fallen to a more typical range of three to three and a half pounds per month. In both ports food prices rose as wages fell, so mariners' real wages fell even more than these comparisons indicate. And in Philadelphia, when mariners' pay declined after the Seven Years' War, captains were able to maintain the higher wages they had commanded during the peak war years, further distancing themselves from the men they commanded.[3]

The greatest extremes between merchants and seamen were in the big cities. Between 1750 and 1800, as Philadelphia became the largest seaport in British America, one of every five of its male workers was a mariner. "There are not less than a thousand Seamen here at this time," noted a custom house officer in 1770. The historian Billy G. Smith substantiated that comment recently when he determined that there were probably between eleven hundred and twelve hundred seamen in Philadelphia at that time. Seafarers were the largest occupational group in the city, although many other laborers were also engaged in the commercial sector of the economy, working as porters, draymen, flatmen, shallopmen, and carters. Most lived near subsistence, accumulating little property and experiencing little upward social mobility. Smith's investigations suggest that while these men moved back and forth between work at sea and work on shore, they rarely were able to break out of their role as dependent wage workers despite living in a society that praised financial independence as a masculine virtue.[4] Other than slaves, who occupied the lowest rung on the socioeconomic ladder, career seamen in big seaports faced some of the grimmest prospects for advancement in colonial America.

It is easy, however, to forget how parochial the labor market was at that time. Place mattered a great deal in the way one got a job aboard ship, in one's relations with shipmates, and in the ultimate nature of a maritime career path. This is not to say that seamen from smaller ports such as Providence, Newburyport, or Annapolis were well paid as men before the mast, which is how they referred to nonofficers. It is to suggest, however, that in the numerous small seaports from which much of the colonies' trade originated, seafaring was not just a dead-end job consigning a man to a lifetime of intermittent work at low wages.

The best studied of the smaller ports, by far, is Salem, Massachusetts. Daniel Vickers's superb work on Salem demonstrates that most foremast hands in the eighteenth century were young men from coastal towns who spent part of each year at sea and part ashore (whether at home or in a distant port) working as riggers, boatmen, or laborers. Thirty percent of Salem's young men who went to sea never saw their thirtieth birthday. Shortened by tropical diseases, shipwrecks, or accidents, their brief lives were somber reminders of the very real dangers associated with seafaring under sail. Meanwhile, sailors sufficiently lucky to stay alive were not earning enough as deckhands to pay for a household and family. In their communities, however, shipping out as a hand before the mast was seen as a normal part of growing up, a stage of life through which young men from coastal towns were expected to pass. To persist as a common sailor into middle age would be stigmatizing. Such men were poverty-stricken failures, dependent on others at an age when a man should have been independent. Such older, dependent men existed, but they were not the norm. Most deckhands who survived their apprenticeship were promoted to higher-paying and more responsible positions. Between 1745 and 1759, Vickers explains, 49 percent of the common seamen in Salem became mates of vessels, and 27 percent became captains. If the figures are recalculated after excluding those who died, the percentages are considerably higher: 70 percent of Salem's sailors became mates, and 39 percent became captains. And if the figures are recalculated to include modest coasters as well as deep-sea ships, the percentage of men rising to a mate's or captain's job would be higher yet. Mates and captains, generally not wealthy, nevertheless were able to support a household and family. Only about 25 percent of Salem's ship captains prospered sufficiently to become "Esquires," "merchants," or "gentlemen." "Salem shipmasters," Vickers explains, "were precisely what their title implied: workingmen who had risen to become masters of their trade. Within the professional seafaring families that predominated on the Salem waterfront, such a career pattern—from youthful dependency to adult mastery and independence—would have been a reasonable expectation."[5]

Going to sea from Salem in the eighteenth century—and, by extension, from similarly sized colonial seaports—was thus not the same as going to sea from Philadelphia or New York. Much of what passes for common knowledge about promotion, punishment, privileges, and pay in the world of the ship at that time has been based on admiralty court proceedings from major urban seaports. It has tended to emphasize lurid, violent aspects of seafaring under sail, and to accentuate the notion that most voyages were structured around class antagonism.[6] Ships were occasionally violent workplaces where officers hazed men and resorted to physical and psychological abuse, either from maliciousness or from a genuine sense that they were following owners' instructions. Many shipowners issued instructions to captains making it clear that quick passages were more important than sailors' concerns about hard usage and poor victuals. Admiralty law existed, for the most part, to foster commerce, and it gave captains considerable latitude to discipline sailors.

That said, most voyages were not violent, and most colonial American seamen did not expect to remain common sailors for their entire lives, pawns in a universe dominated entirely by class. Moreover, in voyages originating from outports, kin relationships and the ubiquity of gossip-mongers structured shipboard relationships. "When ship-owners selected their masters," Vickers explains, "when masters chose their crews, and when master and crew slipped over the horizon on their voyages abroad, they carried with them an inheritance of obligations, resentments, family secrets, and fond memories that could well cut against the grain of economic exigency, and masters and men alike knew well that whatever they did to one another away would soon be known at home."[7]

Seafaring skills provided many African Americans with an occupational identity and a sense of self during the age of sail. In the eighteenth and nineteenth centuries, the maritime industries employed many blacks, both slave and free, offering at least some of them limited social mobility.

In 1740 the ranks of deep-sea maritime labor throughout British America were largely white, but by 1803 black men (mostly free) filled about 18 percent of American seamen's jobs. During the second half of the eighteenth century African American men found jobs in increasingly large numbers aboard American ships. Seafaring became an occupation of opportunity for slaves and recent freedmen.

Providing wages for men with few alternatives, seafaring also was a pipeline to freedom for slaves on the lam, and a means through which widely dispersed black people could communicate with others. Actively part of the maritime culture shared by all seamen, African Americans were at times outsiders within it. "That culture created an ambiguous world," writes one chronicler, "in which black men simultaneously could assert themselves within their occupation and find with white sailors common ground transcending race, while also being subject to vicious racist acts."[8]

Despite such tensions and complications, during the generation after the American Revolution shipowners relied on black labor, and free black Americans in northern seaport cities (where about half of the nation's free blacks resided) relied on seafaring wages to provide crucial support for families, churches, and benevolent societies. American shipping and free black society expanded simultaneously, and inextricably, during the late colonial and early national eras. Unlikely to be promoted, black seamen were, on average, older than their white shipmates before the mast, and many seamen of color were prominent figures in free black communities then angling for respectability.[9]

After agricultural work, seafaring was the second most common occupation for men in colonial America. While merchants clearly accrued profits at the expense of poorly paid sailors, seafaring in colonial society has too often been colored as an exotic form of work, dominated by violence and class strife. In reality it was more normative, more matter-of-fact even, and more racially integrated than has been recognized. A deep-sea proletariat did exist in the most downtrodden neighborhoods of America's largest seaports. But in most shorefront communities, seafaring was seen as a stage of life, a way for a young white man or a black man to earn wages and a stepping-stone by which moderately competent white men would advance in their trade.

10

WAR AND TRANSFORMATION

BOUND BY THE ACTS OF TRADE NOT TO SAIL BEYOND CAPE Horn and the Cape of Good Hope, American merchants in the colonial era confined their activities to five areas in the Atlantic besides their own coasting: Great Britain, Ireland, the West Indies, Africa, and southern Europe—which included the "wine islands" of Madeira, the Canaries, and the Azores. Even without the entire globe at their disposal, possibilities for profit were considerable. Shipping had become a leading sector in the colonial American economy. By the end of the colonial period, earnings from shipping services amounted to more than the value of every commodity export from the thirteen colonies except tobacco. Known as "invisible earnings" because they did not appear in customhouse ledgers, shipping services were nevertheless one of America's major contributions to the Atlantic economy. From Baltimore northward, shipping was king.[1]

Striking improvements in shipping productivity occurred during the colonial era, some of which were attributable to the initiatives of merchants. The "costs of transporting and distributing commodities from producer to consumer were large relative to the initial costs of production," note Shepherd and Walton, whose work has dominated discussions of colonial shipping efficiency. Modest improvements in transportation efficiency thus translated into increases in overall economic productivity, even without improvements in production.[2]

Technological improvement, however, was not part of this equation. Ships themselves did not get appreciably bigger, faster, or more efficient between 1675 and 1775. Refinements in rigging were modest: individual sails remained quite small, sailcloth was still flax, standing rigging was still hemp, and royals (the fourth square sail above the deck) were virtually unknown. Jibs and staysails, while more common in 1775 than in 1675, remained relatively unimportant in ships' overall sailplan, compared, for example, to their role in 1850. Average ship speeds for colonial vessels outbound to the West Indies were 1.67 knots, 1.97 knots, 1.60 knots, and 1.80 knots for the periods 1686–1688, 1715–1719, 1742–1748, and 1764–1765. "On the return run," according to Shepherd and Walton, "they were 1.31, 2.09, 1.59 and 1.50 for the same respective dates." Clearly, sailing times were steady for virtually a century. So were sailors' wages, explaining why seamen remained among the poorest of colonial inhabitants. The cost of victualing crews actually rose. So did that of ships. Including interest and maintenance expenses, ship costs per ton almost doubled from 1675 to 1775. Nevertheless, freight rates of major commodities such as sugar, tobacco, flour, whale oil, and wine fell substantially, "at least 0.08 percent per year for the 100-year period preceding the Revolution." The dramatic decrease in these rates stemmed from a variety of efficiencies. Interest rates fell. Manning requirements per ton declined. Insurance rates also declined, in part (as with manning) because of reduced risks associated with piracy. Costs associated with packaging and inventory also apparently declined, as merchants created efficiencies through trial and error with containers and storage facilities. Time in port was reduced, sometimes by half— something dear to every ship operator. "The general growth of a more systematic market economy," observe Shepherd and Walton, "was a main factor in reducing port time." All of these factors together contributed to commercial expansion.[3]

Shipping services were a crucial piece in the colonies' balance of payments, along with major exports such as tobacco, flour, rice, and dried fish. While the southern colonies did not have a deficit in their trade with Great Britain, thanks to profits from tobacco and rice, New England and the Middle Colonies had substantial deficits. The mainland colonies' West Indies trade in commodities did not help: it was virtually even in terms of debits and credits. Taken as a whole, from 1768 to 1772 the overseas commodity exchanges of the thirteen colonies were incurring an annual deficit of more than £1.1 million.[4]

"Most of the deficit was made up," McCusker and Menard explain, "through the provision of shipping and other commercial services and through the sale of ships." Ships built for sale abroad were earning approximately £140,000 each year right before the Revolution. Freights provided even more revenue: approximately £600,000 each year. And estimates are that commercial services, which included insurance and interest on loans, among other things, provided £220,000 per year. These revenue streams from shipping totaled £960,000, virtually enough to compensate for the trade deficits.[5]

McCusker and Menard, the premier economic historians of colonial America, have calculated the contribution of external trade to the overall economic activity of the thirteen colonies. Their assessment is worth quoting at length. "Shepherd and Walton," they say,

> place the average annual per capita value of commodity exports from the thirteen continental colonies to all overseas areas (including the West Indies) between 1768 and 1772 at £1.40 sterling. Assuming total incomes per capita to have been between £11.00 and £12.50, exports contributed from 11 to 13 percent of the whole. If we include the value of ships sold abroad (£140,000) and an estimate of the invisible earnings (£820,000), per capita income from foreign trade rises to £1.75 and exports contributed 14 to 16 percent of total income. If we further add the value of commodity exports in the coastal trades (£715,000), the per capita figure reaches £2.10, 17 to 19 percent of the total. This seems a substantial share of colonial income. It would be slightly higher were a reliable estimate of invisible earnings in the coastal trade available.[6]

As the colonial period progressed, Americans accumulated the capital and business expertise that allowed them to take over a large share of the transatlantic commerce once dominated by merchants in the mother country. Americans increasingly organized and owned ships carrying grain to Europe, a seriously expanding business in the middle of the eighteenth century. They kept up their trade with the West Indies and southern Europe, even as they cut into the dry goods business that had been the bread and butter of merchants in London and Bristol. Shortly before the Revolution, colonials owned 60 percent of the vessels outbound from the port of New York to Great Britain. A handful of American merchants even acquired a piece of the lucrative tobacco and sugar trades, business that British merchants had once thought well beyond the reach of colonial traders.[7]

In Philadelphia, at least, successful merchants' earnings outstripped those of competitors in other ports at the close of the colonial period, and the distribution of wealth was becoming more unequal. As the imperial political crisis intensified during the 1760s and 1770s, merchants nevertheless expected shipping to remain profitable, and they plowed profits back into the fleet. "The share of shipping entering the port that was owned by the consignee—usually a local firm," Doerflinger points out, "increased from forty-six percent in 1766 to seventy-five percent in 1775."[8]

British merchants took offense as colonially owned shipping expanded. They found officials in Lord Grenville's government quite receptive to their complaints, for Grenville was determined to close the loopholes in the Navigation Acts through which much colonial trade flowed, loopholes that had allowed colonials to avoid duties for years. Beginning in 1763 with the Sugar Act, Parliament began a series of reforms designed to generate revenue at the expense of colonial merchants. The merchants, in turn, with their allies in colonial legislatures, began to reassess their relationship with Britain.[9]

Merchants, however, were by no means united in the discussions that preceded revolution, and, once the war had actually begun, the mercantile interest fractured. In Newburyport, Massachusetts, virtually the entire merchant community joined the patriot cause, but this was rare. In Philadelphia support for the Revolution was lukewarm at best, and by no means were Philadelphians—unlike some Bostonians—propelled to independence by commercial considerations. In both cities the merchant community split into at least three groups along political lines. Of 287 Philadelphia merchants in 1774, 84 were patriots while 60 remained loyal to the king. The preferences of the remaining 143 are unknown. Among Boston's 280 merchants whose sympathies could be ascertained, about 60 remained neutral, 113 were committed Loyalists, and 107 threw their support to the patriot cause. In Boston, dry goods merchants doing business with London were Loyalists almost to a man, whereas traders with southern Europe and smugglers routinely doing business with Holland became patriots. "Well aware of the profits that might be gained from trade outside the empire," notes John Tyler, Boston's "smugglers seized the initiative in pushing the rest of the business community toward gradual recognition of the economic necessity of revolution." In Annapolis, the much smaller merchant community split in a similar fashion, some sympathizing with the Tories and others with the Whigs. In the confusion of revolution, no single course remained clear for businessmen.[10]

Shipping interests emerged from the chaos and uncertainty of the American Revolution in extraordinarily diverse circumstances. A few individuals prospered mightily, none more so than Robert Morris of Philadelphia, who managed his own affairs while overseeing the military business of the Continental Congress. Lesser fortunes were made as well, in Philadelphia and elsewhere, but bankruptcies were legion. Comparing the changing nature of the shipping business during the war in Annapolis, Newburyport, and Philadelphia illuminates again how colonial American shipping was defined by risk, how innovation remained the key to success even as it often led to failure, and how the composition of the merchant class was anything but steady.

Annapolis had never been a major seaport in colonial America, but during the late colonial period it underwent a significant commercial expansion. Merchants capitalized on the growth of the Chesapeake region's grain trade and modest urbanization to retail increasingly large volumes of expensive English goods. Meanwhile, capital accumulation by Annapolis firms such as Wallace, Davidson and Johnson allowed them to break into the transatlantic tobacco trade between 1771 and 1776. These up-and-comers secured a market share previously controlled by British middlemen. Commercial prospects seemed bright in Annapolis despite the imperial crisis. But the war completely disrupted these budding prospects. In the short run it was not a disaster for merchants in Annapolis because the city became an administrative center for the American war effort. Merchants possessed the hands-on experience necessary to oversee complicated logistics, and half of the nineteen active merchants in town took government jobs feeding the army and navy, housing soldiers, and transshipping arms, ammunition, and supplies. Within a decade of the peace, however, merchants in Baltimore and Alexandria had eclipsed those in Annapolis. Local firms never recovered from the postwar depression, and Annapolis evolved into a quiet market town and government center devoted more to agricultural modernization than to commercial expansion. Its imposing brick town houses from the colonial era testified to its fleeting role as a profitable seaport.[11]

The war affected Newburyport, the easternmost port in Massachusetts, somewhat differently. As Benjamin W. Labaree has so ably explained, the merchants prominent in the late colonial and revolutionary periods lost their fortunes during the war or in the depression immediately thereafter. Those who invested in privateers incurred significant losses. Some merchants decamped for greener pastures. William Hazen, Leonard Jarvis, and John Bromfield went no farther than Boston, but others moved as far afield as New York or even Ohio. By 1783 the stock of ships for those who remained was old and worn out. Salt cod, formerly the mainstay of their export business, was barely available because Massachusetts's fishing fleet had disintegrated during the war. Trade with the British West Indies was no longer legal. As a result, Massachusetts's exports in 1786 were only one-quarter of those in 1774. Merchants there, as in other states, had been paid by the government for their services during the war with paper currency that depreciated to a fraction of its face value. By the time Newburyport's overseas commerce had begun to revive under the stimulus of "neutral trade" during the Napoleonic Wars in the 1790s, "a new group of merchants, unrelated to the earlier generation," dominated the port. In 1785 Nathaniel Tracy was unquestionably the wealthiest man in town. Five years later the town forgave him all taxes on account of his poverty. Each of his former business associates and well-to-do neighbors had a similar tale. Unlike Annapolis, Newburyport did not cease functioning as a seaport shortly after the war. But the volatility and unpredictability of the business climate during the Revolution caused virtually 100 percent turnover among its merchant group.[12]

While conditions in Philadelphia, the new nation's largest seaport, were significantly different than those in minor ports like Annapolis and Newburyport, its merchants also endured a wide variety of experiences during the war. No uniform or stable commercial plan worked in the rapidly changing conditions of the wartime city, and the men who survived to conduct business after the war were the lucky, the politically favored, and the innovative.

With the outbreak of war, it became impossible to clear British goods for the colonies, despite colonials' desires for consumer goods and war matériel. Saint Eustatius in the Caribbean, a Dutch freeport, became the crossroads for English goods destined for the colonies, at least until February of 1781 when the British navy captured the island and closed its lucrative multinational bazaar. Although His Majesty's navy also blockaded Delaware Bay, merchants arranged for goods in several ways. Blockade runners dashed into the mouth of Delaware Bay, and then offloaded in small ports, whence cargoes could be transported to Philadelphia by shallop. Occasionally, fast vessels with favorable conditions made it all the way to the city's wharves, at least before the British army occupied the city in September of 1777. Other goods arrived in Boston and came overland to Philadelphia. Despite the threat of impounded cargoes and ships, merchants managed to import considerable amounts of sugar, rum, cloth, wine, and tea. Prices—and profits—on these roundabout routes rose considerably, in part because of the shift in interstate transportation from coasting vessels to wagons. "Nothing was more damaging to the economy," notes Doerflinger, "than the wrenching shift of the interstate transport system from coastwise maritime trade to inland carriage." In 1773, 294 coasters had entered Philadelphia, but in 1781 and 1782 the annual average was only eleven arrivals. Bulky cargoes that had been moved easily by small crews relying on wind and tide were considerably more expensive to move by wagon. And overland carriage strained Americans' wartime supply of draft animals and teamsters, even as it eradicated a formerly profitable sector of the shipping business.[13]

The turmoil created by the blockade, the occupation, the eradication of coasting, the virtual eradication of the grain trade for several years (as hungry armies consumed local supplies), the Continental Army's logistical needs, and the introduction of unstable paper currency provided hurdles for most traders and great opportunities for a few. Robert Morris and William Bingham were two Philadelphia merchants who, while working for the Continental Congress's Secret Committee of Trade and the Marine Committee, managed to make themselves uncommonly wealthy. "There were exceptional commercial opportunities in 1776 and 1777 because of the huge differences in commodity prices in various parts of the Atlantic world," notes Doerflinger. "These differentials arose from the formidable barriers to trade, which inhibited the normal process of price adjustment through commerce. The members of the Morris group possessed extraordinary advantages in breaking through these barriers." Political connections clearly helped a handful of merchants get ahead dramatically during the war. The scarcity of shipping also contributed to the enrichment of a few key players by

Robert Morris, known as the "Financier of the Revolution," was a Philadelphia merchant and shipowner who turned his financial skills to funding the American Revolution. He built up an enormous personal fortune running privateers during the war and selling supplies to the government, even while serving on the government's Marine Committee and as its superintendent of finance.

minimizing competition in the dry goods business. During peacetime the norm had been for many merchants to receive goods on credit upon the arrival of a single ship. Blockade runners, on the other hand, typically arrived with cargoes consigned only to the owners of the ship, who—with astronomical profits in the offing—had no incentive to rent a square inch of their cargo hold to competitors.[14]

Peace brought a short-lived boom to Philadelphia in the mid-1780s, followed by a depression even deeper than that of Newburyport. Bankruptcies felled established merchants and start-up traders, immigrants who had only recently tried their hand at commerce, as well as some of the Quaker city's oldest commercial families. "In addition to restructuring the mercantile elite," explains Doerflinger, "the convulsions of the 1780s transformed the general character of the merchant community by making it far more unstable and anonymous. There were at least 50 percent more merchants in the city after the war than before, and they came and went more freely." In Philadelphia and Newburyport, as elsewhere, the Revolution's destruction of established political elites allowed a new group, including many merchants, access to political office.[15]

It is thus simply not accurate to talk about a "merchant aristocracy" during and immediately after the American Revolution in either small ports like Newburyport or major ones like Philadelphia. The Revolution had been disastrous for many individual merchants and the shipping industry as a whole. While some great fortunes were made, and while some men improved their circumstances, market volatility and business adversity kept anything like a genteel and self-perpetuating aristocracy from forming, despite the desires of many Federalist politicians and men of commerce. By the time of President George Washington's inauguration, however, it was clear in hindsight that the northern colonies of what became the new United States had been one of the most profoundly maritime societies in the world. Their commitment of human energy and financial capital to shipping had been essential to their remarkable political economy, and to a creation of wealth, infrastructure, and innovation unparalleled elsewhere.

PART II

A WORLD WITHIN THEMSELVES

The Golden Age and the Rise of Inland Shipping, 1783–1861

11

A TALE OF
TWO PORTS

SALEM WAS DECLINING, NEW ORLEANS RISING. IN THE FIRST two-thirds of the nineteenth century, the crossing trajectories of these two ports mirrored the transformation of American shipping. In 1800 Salem still sent its ships all over the world, dispatching dozens of vessels to international destinations and to other American ports. New Orleans passed in that year from Spanish to French hands, a minor pawn in a deal that Napoleon hoped would undergird a French empire in America. By 1840 Joseph Peabody, Salem's last great shipping magnate, was four years from his death, and the trade with the Indies that had made him wealthy and spread the town's reach around the world would die with him. New Orleans, now securely in American hands, had become the fourth busiest port in the world, receiving more than fifteen hundred river steamboats a year and a comparable number of flatboats.[1] When Reconstruction formally closed the books on the Civil War, Salem's maritime past was a distant memory. New Orleans was poised to transship the vast agricultural bonanza of the American heartland to ports in the United States and abroad.

Canonically, geography explains these mirror histories. Salem declined as larger commercial vessels outgrew her small, shallow harbor. In contrast, New Orleans exploited its strategic location near the mouth of the Mississippi, the largest river in North America, the fourth longest river in the world when combined with its feeder, the Missouri River. Certainly this explains part of the differing fortunes of these two seaports. But many other forces were at work as well. Policy, economics, technology, war, and labor all contributed. To understand the fates of Salem and New Orleans is to understand the transformation of the American shipping industry in the first half of the nineteenth century.

Politically, the United States repeatedly sacrificed its maritime industry to other international priorities, even while it passed legislation that protected domestic shipping from international competition. Economically, the nation embraced tariff policies that shaped international shipping and helped to bring on civil war, even while capital investment shifted from maritime commerce to other, more lucrative fields and the balance of American shipping shifted from international to domestic. Technologically, steam propulsion launched a revolution in ship design that opened up the inland waterways and undercut America's competitive advantage in wooden ship construction. Militarily, the Civil War permanently disrupted many shipping patterns, and naval technology moved decisively away from commercial ship design. Maritime labor fled the shrinking marketplace of Salem, while immigrants flooded New Orleans and other U.S. cities, contributing to the polyglot crews on American ships evoked so memorably in *Moby Dick*. Salem and New Orleans witnessed all these trends, one powerless to stop the current, the other swept along by events.

The maritime world unfolding before the new American republic in 1783 presented a riot of danger and opportunity. For the first time ever, the former colonists' ships found themselves without the protection of the Royal Navy. The Americans had cobbled together several ad hoc fleets during the Revolution, but nothing that could protect their commerce from predation by the pirates who infested the Caribbean and the Mediterranean. Nor could American shipping protect itself from the warships of France and Britain as those two countries engaged in commercial war at sea, paying little attention to America's claims of neutral rights. Between 1783 and 1812 the United States lost hundreds of commercial vessels to pirates and combatants, driving some shipowners into bankruptcy and stressing the capital resources of the others. Economic doldrums in the first decade of independence only worsened the plight of shipping. In the first ten years of the Republic, real per capita exports per year declined 30 percent.[2]

In spite of these risks, American shipping flourished. Unshackled from the British Navigation Acts, merchants looked overseas for markets and trade, primarily in Europe and Asia. A comparative abundance of timber in the United States favored American shipbuilding and held down the capital costs of shipowners. Britain compounded the advantage by boycotting American-built ships, handicapping herself to spite her former colony. Demand blossomed when Britain and France went to war in 1793, driving French commercial vessels from the sea lanes and diverting Britain's ships to support of herself and her allies in the continental conflict against France. Americans took up most of the slack, more than compensating for their losses to seizure by the combatants.

In the years between the Revolutionary War and the War of 1812, Salem fell under the sway of Elias Haskett Derby, the young republic's first millionaire. Descended from the "codfish aristocracy" that had brought Salem its first fortunes, Derby grew up in his father's lucrative shipping business, built around trade with Europe and the Caribbean.[3]

Ordered by Elias Haskett Derby during the American Revolution, the 300-ton, 22-gun *Grand Turk* went to sea in 1781. After a successful career as a privateer during the Revolution, the ship helped pioneer oceanic trade between New England and Asia, making three lucrative and historic trips to the western Pacific in the years immediately following the Revolution.

Accounting for 144 of the 458 prizes that Salem privateers captured during the Revolution, Derby emerged from war with a $1 million profit and was looking for an investment.[4] With Caribbean trade cut off, or at least curtailed, he began to think globally, inspired perhaps by his wartime experience. Expanding his fleet to six vessels averaging less than 400 tons each, he tried Russia and Europe before finding real success in the Indian Ocean. A famous voyage in 1786 by his largest ship, the 300-ton, 22-gun *Grand Turk*, helped open the Chinese market to American shipping and whetted his appetite for trade in the Indian Ocean. His son, Elias Haskett Jr., set sail the following year for Mauritius, where he stayed for three years and established trading patterns with Bombay, Madras, and Calcutta.[5] By the time the younger Derby returned to Salem in 1790, his venture had netted the shipping dynasty another $100,000.[6] In time, Salem would come to dominate the cotton trade with India, leaving the tea trade with China to Boston.[7] Derby sent his 560-ton *Grand Turk II* to Calcutta in 1792; when it returned the following year it paid $24,369.42 in duties, the largest single payment received by the U.S. Customs Service until that time.[8]

Shipping dynasties such as those of the Derbys and their in-laws, the Crowninshields, led Salem in the decades surrounding the turn of the nineteenth century to an unprecedented prosperity. The town boasted 9,031 tons of ships in 1791, 24,682 tons in 1800, and 43,570 tons in 1807.[9] Some two hundred ships called Salem home in that year.[10] The merchant princes amassed fleets numbering more than a hundred American-built ships and found cargoes to suit the markets available to them. Success came from the efficiency of the shipping operations and the dexterity of the supercargoes, such as Elias Haskett Jr., in adapting to local markets.[11] Supercargoes were agents of the shippers, empowered to sell the cargo for the best price they could get and use the proceeds to buy return cargo. Some of the early shipping magnates built, owned, and operated their vessels, and owned their cargoes as well, sometimes in family dynasties like the Derbys and the Crowninshields. Those operating from Salem made it the country's sixth largest city in 1789.[12] When "King Derby" died in 1799, his family pier and mansion dominated the Salem waterfront just as his ships carried little Salem's reputation around the world.

New Orleans at the time could hardly have offered a starker contrast. Made the capital of the French crown colony of Louisiana in 1722, the city had been envisioned as the anchor of a "river empire" in the New World. The St. Lawrence valley, the Great Lakes, and the Mississippi valley circumscribed the British colonies in North America, confining them largely to the area east of the Appalachians. The French plan for New Orleans was geostrategic, not economic. Perhaps for this reason, the port failed to flourish commercially in its first four decades. Wheat and flour, lead, copper, and especially furs moved down the greater Mississippi river system, making New Orleans self-sufficient in food and a net exporter of surplus produce.[13] Rice and corn cultivation in Lower Louisiana added to exports in the 1730s.[14] But as a port, New Orleans could not then compete with Havana or ports such as Fort-de-France, Martinique, in the French West Indies. It was farther from France and the supply of goods from the hinterland was subject to vagaries of river flow and Indian attack. Furthermore, its location a hundred miles up river from the Gulf of Mexico made it a tough port in the age of sail. The mouth of the waterway was hard to locate, and once a ship entered its twisting course, the ascent could be slowed by forests blocking the winds and by driftwood speeding downstream with the current. In one extreme case in 1729, a ship took forty-seven days to reach New Orleans from the mouth of the Mississippi.[15] Little wonder then that the French agreed to cede Louisiana to Spain at the end of the Seven Years' War in 1763.

In the Treaty of Paris, Spain received the vast territory west of the Mississippi, plus the Island of New Orleans, the territory east of the Mississippi below the network of lakes, bayous, and rivers below Lake Pontchartrain. In the same settlement, Britain received the trans-Appalachian region east of the Mississippi, plus the right of navigation of the river.[16] A struggle ensued to exploit the vast potential of the Mississippi River valley. Britain's model proved more fruitful than Spain's.

Like the French, the Spanish tended to view Louisiana and New Orleans in geostrategic and mercantilist terms.[17] They wanted to control British expansion in the New World, and they wanted trade with the territory to complement their larger American empire. There was no market in Spain for the colony's agricultural products and fur, but Spain's mercantile policy, the *comercio libre*, precluded Louisiana from trading with its natural economic counterparts in the French West Indies.[18] In addition to a vigorous smuggling trade, British and later American merchants took the lead in supplying the majority of the food for New Orleans throughout the city's tenure in Spanish hands.[19] In the process, they cleared the way for the establishment of an Anglo-American ascendancy in the city that endured in spite of the Spanish administrators' efforts to suppress it. As more and more land in the Mississippi and Ohio valleys was brought under cultivation by American settlers, New Orleans experienced an erosion of the fur trade and its replacement by another, more valuable commerce in the vast agricultural potential of the West.

In 1784, after the American Revolution, Spain closed the Mississippi to navigation by all foreign vessels. Three years later, however, she relented and opened the river to American vessels as far south as New Orleans. By the 1790s the flow of river craft conveying such commodities as flour, meat, butter, and tobacco from the North American heartland to the port had become steady and defining, in spite of the stiff duties imposed on American produce and the assorted forms of harassment to which American traders and flatboat crews were often subjected by Spanish authorities. The final, and greatest, spur to American commercial activity was provided by the Treaty of San Lorenzo del Escorial (October 1795), which recognized the American right to navigate the Mississippi free of all restrictions, and gave American traders the right to deposit their goods in and around New Orleans duty-free for transshipment from the port.[20] Trade in foodstuffs between New Orleans and the upper Mississippi became the centerpiece of the city's economic life, setting a pattern that would define it until the 1840s, when cotton, tobacco, and sugar replaced agricultural products as the major commodities passing through the city.[21]

In 1799, when Salem was at the height of its power, New Orleans was struggling to escape its past as a pawn of empire and realize its commercial potential as the gateway to an American heartland. That year witnessed $1 million in goods pass across the city's docks en route from the upper valley to transshipment abroad. Three years later, just before Spain's revocation of the American right of deposit and closure of the Mississippi to American shipping, the value of those goods reached $2 million. Flour dominated the traffic, followed by corn, pork, lard, tallow, and whiskey, headed primarily to French and Spanish possessions in the West Indies. Export of these commodities required 31,000 tons of shipping in 1802.[22] The economic potential of New Orleans was manifest, but its future was still in doubt.

12

ROBERT LIVINGSTON AND THE ART OF THE DEAL

AFTER FOUR YEARS OF UNSUCCESSFUL EXPERIENCE WITH THE Articles of Confederation, the new American republic rewrote its constitution in 1787, creating a reinvented government that took office in 1789. Its first legislation established a tariff that gave American shipping an overwhelming advantage in American ports. Within two years, the total value of U.S. foreign waterborne commerce had reached $48 million. More importantly for the American shipping industry, 55 percent of it sailed in U.S. ships. That number rose to 90 percent by 1795 and 92 percent by 1807.[1] Not until the Civil War would that percentage sink below half.[2] The tariff served its purpose, both in protecting infant industries and in promoting American shipping abroad. But that foreign commerce would prove to be less important than the founding fathers had imagined. One reason was geography.

America is a nation of rivers. The network of its natural inland waterways leaves few locales far from water. Along the East Coast, where the thirteen original colonies clung to the edge of the North American continent, many of those rivers flowed east from the Appalachian backbone, winding their way to the Atlantic and thus to oceanic trade. Among the longest of the eastern rivers were the Connecticut, Delaware, Potomac, Roanoke, and Susquehanna. All were avenues of commerce carrying goods and people to and from the sea and feeding major cities on their

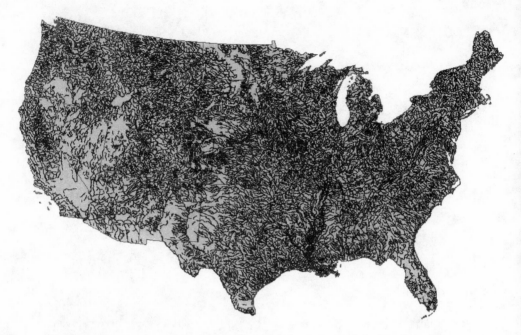

The United States is a nation of rivers. As Americans penetrated the North American continent, they traveled up the rivers and sent the products of their labors back down to market.

banks. Some of the longest, such as the Altamaha-Coosa, Pee Dee–Yadkin, and Santee-Wateree-Catawba never realized such commercial significance; they were less easily navigable or their shores less densely populated. For just the opposite reasons, some shorter rivers, such as the Cape Fear, the Hudson, and the James achieved importance out of proportion to their lengths. The growing American population settled along these rivers and used them for travel, communication, and commerce. As the number of inhabitants in the western states and territories swelled from 109,368 in 1790 to 386,413 in 1800 and 1,078,315 in 1810, settlements along the rivers grew apace.[3]

As expanding oceanic shipping in the late eighteenth and early nineteenth centuries fed the growth of ports along these rivers, two lines of development took wing. Campaigns were launched to make the rivers more navigable. Obstructions were cleared. Channels were dredged. And, most importantly, canals were dug to carry waterborne traffic ever farther inland, beyond the shoals and falls that marked the natural limits to navigation. On the Potomac River, for example, George Washington formed a company in 1785 to connect the broad, flat river at the new nation's capital with the navigable waters above Great Falls. Five canals skirting around rapids in the river sufficed for a while to float products of the army's arsenal at Harper's Ferry, Virginia, to the sea.

The second influence of expanding oceanic commerce on American rivers was what one observer in the 1790s called "steamboat mania."[4] In barns and workshops, in cities and on farms, crackpots and geniuses schemed to acquire or replicate James Watt's famous engine and mount it on a boat. There it was projected to drive all manner of propulsive machinery, from poles and paddles to fins and screw propellers. Some engines were to drive water in a jet behind the boat. The dream, of course, was to turn America's rivers into two-way streets, carrying goods and passengers both upstream and down. It was to open the American hinterland to waterborne commerce.

John Fitch invented a boat that steamed against the current of the Delaware River in 1787 and provided regular commercial service by 1790. James Rumsey invented a boat for George Washington's Potomac Canal, but it never went into service. In spite of the very limited capabilities of their respective inventions, both men sought and received monopolies from state and local governments for steamboat service on their rivers. The biggest prize was Virginia, for its territorial claims extended to the Mississippi River. "Our expectations of extensive profits," Fitch told his backers, "were built on the exclusive rights to navigate the Western Waters."[5]

The undeveloped lands on the western slopes of the Appalachians, which came into the possession of the United States after the Revolution, began to fill with settlers, speculators, and schemers soon after the war. Some of these settlers looked backward to the Atlantic coast and conceived their link with civilization to be through canals and rivers draining east. Others looked to the equally dense waterways draining west. The Cumberland, Green, Kanawha, Licking, Ohio, Ohio-Allegheny, Tennessee, and Tennessee–French Broad all flowed down the western slopes of the Alleghenies. All drained into the Mississippi. All finally passed New Orleans on their way to the sea.

Of course the Mississippi also carried the waters of the vast Louisiana Territory, which stretched north into Canada and as far west as the Rocky Mountains. Trappers and traders had worked these lands for centuries.

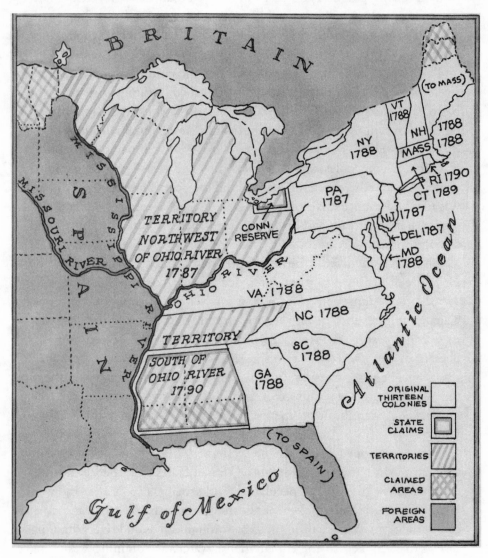

As with many of the original thirteen colonies, Virginia claimed territory over the Appalachian Mountains and beyond, as far as the western rivers. By 1790, only Virginia still claimed a western boundary on the Mississippi, where steamboat visionaries set their sights.

The traffic from their commerce was bound to grow. It was even possible to imagine settlement of them. The Mississippi, in short, was a growth enterprise, and New Orleans was the gate through which its riches would flow. Fitch believed it would become "the largest city in North America."[6]

It was little wonder, then, that Americans grew alarmed when Spain ceded the Louisiana Territory to Napoleon on October 1, 1800. Did Bonaparte have imperial designs in North America? Would he claim exclusive rights to the Mississippi? Might he try to control river traffic by closing New Orleans to American shipping? These concerns turned to crisis in 1802, when Spain revoked the right of Americans to deposit goods in New Orleans. Napoleon clearly was behind this move. Shipping on the Mississippi was in jeopardy.

President Thomas Jefferson turned to the U.S. ambassador in France. Robert Livingston had taken up his duties earlier that year, a reward for shifting his party allegiance over the course of the 1790s from Federalist to Jeffersonian Democratic-Republican. Descended from the landholding aristocracy of upstate New York, Livingston had helped draft the Declaration of Independence, had administered the oath of office to President George Washington, and had served as chancellor of New York from 1772 to 1801.[7] Jefferson directed this seasoned politician to stop the so-called retrocession of Louisiana from Spain to France, if it had not already taken place. If it had, Livingston was to make an offer to buy New Orleans.

He took his case to the appropriate French minister, the wily and adroit Charles-Maurice Talleyrand. As foreign minister in 1798, Talleyrand had precipitated the Quasi-War between France and the United States by demanding an outrageous bribe from American emissaries attempting to negotiate a treaty respecting the neutrality of American ships in France's war with Britain. Talleyrand had resigned over the issue but was back in power when Livingston approached him, in the company of special envoy James Monroe, to bargain for New Orleans. Talleyrand deflected their offer and kept them in limbo until Napoleon came to a decision about North America. Thwarted in Haiti by yellow fever and the revolutionary François-Dominique Toussaint-Loverture, threatened by Livingston and Monroe with an American rapproachment to Britain, and worried that Britain would seize the Louisiana Territory in the hostilities that were about to resume, Napoleon unexpectedly offered the Americans not just

New Orleans but the entire Louisiana Territory. Authorized by Congress to pay $2 million for New Orleans and by Secretary of State James Madison to go as high as $9.375 million to get Florida in the bargain, Livingston and Monroe agreed, without authority, to pay $15 million for the 828,000 square miles offered by France, less than three cents an acre.[8] Congress was left to wrestle with the constitutionality of the move. Jefferson, although something of a strict constructionist himself, readily jettisoned his principles and embraced the bargain. This, the largest real estate deal ever, changed not only American history in general, but maritime history in particular.

The United States would not be a coastal nation trading with the world through Atlantic seaports, as in the heyday of Salem, but a great continental empire, trading primarily with itself. Beginning as early as 1820, and continuing with interruptions only during the world wars of the twentieth century, American domestic waterborne commerce exceeded oceanic commerce, sometimes by multiples of three and four.[9] Along its coasts and up and down its rivers, Americans traded with one another in the world's largest maritime market, made possible by geography, internal improvements, and the boldness of Robert Livingston. In time, the Louisiana Purchase would fuel the enthusiasm of Americans for their "manifest destiny" of acquiring a swath of North America from "sea to shining sea." A series of acquisitions in the 1840s would add to the nation even more territory than the Louisiana Purchase and would make it a two-ocean maritime power. But the greatest impact of the purchase was on domestic, not international, shipping. Commerce on the great western waterway would make the United States a brown-water maritime state more than a blue-water nation.

While engaged in the negotiations with Talleyrand, Livingston also embarked on another deal that would change the course of American history. By chance he met in Paris and took an instant liking to a thirty-six-year-old American expatriate, a failed painter, canal developer, inventor, submariner, and schemer. Robert Fulton had been living in England and France for more than fourteen years, getting by mostly on charm, charisma, and the largesse of a series of benefactors, waiting for the main chance. The historian James Flexner says he was an "inventor in search of an invention."[10] Livingston, it turned out, was the main chance. Fulton had dabbled briefly in steamboats. Livingston had dabbled more deeply still, financing a boat in the United States designed in part by his

brother-in-law, John Stevens, and built to Livingston's ever-shifting specifications by Nicholas Roosevelt. Livingston had more money than engineering talent, and his boat failed to materialize in time to secure a
twenty-year monopoly on the Hudson River voted him by the New York
legislature. But he was sure he could renew the grant if he could produce
a steamboat. Fulton was just as sure that he could deliver the boat if
Livingston could extend the monopoly.

Of course, Fulton was sure that he could do most anything. His current scheme to achieve fame and fortune was to build submarines for
Napoleon, with which he promised to attack the British blockading fleet
in the English Channel and win for all humanity "freedom of the seas."[11]
In spite of this dubious enterprise, he had enough bona fide credentials to
convince Livingston that he could really deliver a steamboat. In London
in 1793 he had met and befriended James Rumsey, who was in Europe
looking to finance his steamboat developments. Fulton designed his own
boat at this time and began conducting experiments on models. He
allowed himself to be caught up in Britain's canal enthusiasm and wrote a
tract on the topic, *A Treatise on the Improvement of Canal Navigation*
(1796), that featured a whole system of shipping built around narrow
canals, trains of boats, and inclined planes to move the boats to different
elevations. He had, in short, a primitive notion of intermodal shipping
based on steamboats and an appreciation for the potential of inland
waterways. He also had connections with some of the most influential
lights of European science and engineering, including Richard
Cartwright, John Dalton, and Charles Stanhope in Britain, and Pierre-
Simon LaPlace, Gaspard Monge, and the Perrier and Montgolfier brothers in France. Livingston appears to have been impressed by Fulton's
connections, his persuasiveness, and his capacity to combine scientific
theory with empirical engineering practice. The strengths of the two men
seemed to complement one another; their weaknesses—Livingston's technical failings and Fulton's dreaminess—were canceled. Livingston was to
Fulton what the businessman and financier Matthew Boulton was to
James Watt.

Though Fulton and Livingston never entirely trusted each other, they
signed a contract on October 10, 1802. Fulton would patent and build a
demonstration boat in England, which would then serve as the basis
for a boat to be built in New York to satisfy Livingston's claim on the
Hudson River monopoly. The two men would invest equally and share

profits equally; Livingston was to put up his money immediately, Fulton two years later. By January of 1803 the partners had decided to make their first demonstration in France. In the French style, Fulton sent to the Conservatoire des Arts et Métiers a description of his plan, in which he revealed for the first time where his true ambitions lay. He intended his steamboat to tow a train of linked barges on inland waters, a plan reminiscent of his 1796 treatise on canals. This system he planned "to put in practice on the long rivers of North America."[12] The Hudson was not one of America's long rivers. The Mississippi was. Three months before his partner Robert Livingston began negotiating for the Louisiana Purchase, Robert Fulton already had his heart set on his homeland's greatest river system.

13

ROBERT FULTON AND THE ART OF STEAMING

FOUR YEARS WOULD PASS BEFORE FULTON MADE GOOD ON HIS contract with Livingston. The inventor built a demonstration boat in France in the summer of 1803, using an engine constructed by the famous Perrier brothers, who had earlier built the submarine that Fulton was attempting to sell to Napoleon. Fulton would have preferred a Watt engine from England, but deteriorating relations between Britain and France under the fragile Peace of Amiens precluded export of such an important technology. His 1803 steamboat moved successfully against the current of the Seine River before breaking up and sinking under the weight of its engine. Fulton declined to rebuild it, preferring instead to pursue what he still believed was the main chance, the sale of torpedo devices to the French government. These were designed to undermine, literally and figuratively, what he depicted as Britain's tyrannical hegemony of the sea.

Failing to win the favor he sought in France (Napoleon called him a charlatan before belatedly concluding that his schemes might have made possible an invasion of England), the peripatetic inventor entertained overtures from London to turn coat and work for Britannia. Knowing that his contract with Livingston depended upon a Watt engine and an export license, Fulton renounced Revolutionary France and freedom of the seas to accept English pounds and the favor of William Pitt the

Younger. He never convinced the British that his various schemes for torpedo war posed a serious threat to Britain or anyone else, but the Pitt government nonetheless felt more comfortable with him scheming on their behalf than on Napoleon's. They allowed Boulton to build an engine for him, but they withheld an export license. Content to stay in England after Livingston had stepped down as ambassador and returned to the United States to await his partner, Fulton nonetheless came to realize that the British would never award him the remuneration he sought. Pitt's government sent him on two separate expeditions, in 1804 and 1805, to attack the invasion fleet that Napoleon was gathering in Boulogne. Both times his floating torpedoes failed. Three weeks after the second raid, Admiral Horatio Nelson defeated a combined French and Spanish fleet at the battle of Trafalgar. France's naval threat to Britain evaporated, and with it the need to string Fulton along any further. Britain awarded him a settlement that amounted to little more than expenses he had already incurred and allowed him to export his prized Watt engine to the United States. Fulton followed the engine in October 1806, having spent almost half of his forty years in Europe.

Even then, he went not to New York, where Livingston and his engine awaited him, but to Washington, where he hoped to interest his own government in the torpedo inventions he had hatched in Europe. Not until 1807 did he finally turn his attention to the Livingston steamboat. Mounting his Watt engine on a hull of his own design, he displayed the self-confidence that had sustained him through twenty years of virtually unmitigated failure. On August 17, 1807, barely a week after his first test of the craft, Fulton launched an inaugural voyage from Greenwich Village in New York City to Clermont, the sprawling Livingston estate 110 miles up the Hudson River. The *North River Steamboat* sputtered to a halt shortly after setting off, but Fulton had it running again within half an hour. Steaming through the night, looking for all the world, as one alarmed observer put it, like the devil on a floating sawmill, the *North River* docked at Clermont (from which the boat would soon take its popular name) at one o'clock the next afternoon, after a journey of twenty-four hours. The following day it covered the forty miles to Albany in eight hours, cutting by more than half the average sailing time.[1] Family tradition has it that Livingston took the occasion to announce the engagement of Fulton to Harriett Livingston, a distant cousin and the sister-in-law of

North River by Robert Fulton. Fulton sketched the enlarged North River in 1808, representing it well north of New York City on the Hudson River, not far from the Livingston estate of Clermont, from which it derived its popular name.

the chancellor's own daughter.[2] The story is apocryphal, but it represents a larger truth: the steamboat, and Robert Fulton, had arrived.

The success of the *North River* was no fluke. For all his failed projects and shameless self-promotion, Fulton was a determined, accomplished, and informed engineer. His years in Europe had been spent in the company of some of the best scientific and technical minds of the age. He had absorbed the pragmatic engineering style of the British industrial revolution and the rational applied science of the French Enlightenment. He knew personally, or at least knew of the work of, almost every significant steamboat inventor before him, incorporating their many contributions in a vessel that could boast not a single original component.[3] Fulton's value added, as he was at pains to claim, was proportion, a sense of how the various components should fit together in a successful vessel. He even built a model of his first steamboat, the French craft of 1803, and constructed a modest towing tank in which to measure its performance. Though his predictions of the full-scale vessel's speed through the water proved to be hopelessly inflated (he predicted sixteen miles per hour and achieved five), he nonetheless displayed the kind of careful attention to design that was lacking in the work of John Fitch. Each of the twenty-one steamboats that Fulton finally built in America incorporated improvements gleaned from his previous experience. Fulton, in short, was systematic in his pursuit of this new technology, while Fitch was serendipitous. This, says the historian James Flexner, is why Fulton made "steamboats come true."[4] After the maiden voyage of the *North River*, steamboats were never again absent from American waters.

But more than technical success fueled the steamboat craze that swept America in the wake of the *North River*. Fitch's boat of 1787 had sailed faster than Fulton's and traveled more miles in its one year of service, 1790, than the *North River* did in 1807. The difference was revenue. Fitch's *Steamboat* never turned a profit. Fulton reported to Livingston that the *North River* returned 5 percent on capital in its first season; he expected a profit of $8,000 to $10,000 in future years, after the bugs were eliminated. A new boat costing $15,000, he predicted, would produce revenue of $10,000 a year.[5] Profits such as these reflected the particular market in which *North River* competed, a monopoly of steamboat carriage of mostly passenger traffic on the Hudson River. But Fulton saw no reason why the same business model could not work in other venues. With returns on investment like these, there would be no shortage of capital.

Protected by Livingston's monopoly on the Hudson and in New York harbor, and by two patents that Fulton took out with the federal government, the partners experienced ever-widening success. They put more boats in service on the Hudson. They inaugurated ferry service in New York harbor, employing a new catamaran design by Fulton that placed the ship's paddles in the center of the boat. So successful was this service that a grateful New York named for Fulton the street connecting the Manhattan docks of his New Jersey ferry across the Hudson and his Brooklyn ferry across the East River. Fulton proposed continuous service from Canada to Savannah, Georgia, with overland transportation to provide portage across points of land such as New Brunswick, New Jersey, to Trenton, and Philadelphia to the Chesapeake, that offered no protected water route. (Practical oceangoing steamboats were still years away.)[6] Though this particular scheme failed to catch on, it showed Fulton's fertile imagination. He foresaw intermodal transportation and the Intracoastal Waterway down the eastern shore of the Middle Atlantic states.

Fulton even attempted to export his invention. He signed contracts with both Russia and India for river steamboats, though nothing much came of either plan. Nor did this American success gain much purchase in Europe. Especially on the Continent, conditions were not yet ripe for steamboats. Most of the Continent's inland waterways paralleled roads that provided faster transport, especially for passengers. Europe in general, and Britain in particular, had denuded its woods for ships and fuel, leaving nothing like the forests that lined America's inland waterways and provided ready fuel for the inefficient engines of the early steam age. And labor in Europe was comparatively plentiful and cheap, while Americans constantly sought labor-saving technologies. Not until the steamship became a truly seaworthy craft in the 1830s would Europeans begin to take it seriously. Until then, it was better suited to the crazy quilt of rivers that blankets the eastern and midwestern United States.

Fulton's keenest ambition for expansion, the one he had identified in his first discussions with Livingston in France, was the Mississippi. "Everything is completely proved for the Mississippi," he had told the chancellor after testing his first steamboat in France in 1803, "and the object is immense."[7] The "puny" rivers of the East, as the *Cincinnati Gazette* depicted them in 1815, paled beside the great river systems beyond the Appalachian Mountains, the rivers that all found their way to the Mississippi and thence to New Orleans.[8] Even before he built the

North River Steamboat, Fulton had projected $30,000 in annual profits on the Hudson compared with $500,000 on the Mississippi.[9]

In spite of such expectations, the partners were slow to launch their Mississippi venture, perhaps because the Hudson instilled in them a debilitating taste for monopoly. They first sought an exclusive right to steam navigation on the Mississippi, to match their hold on the Hudson. But in this new, wide-open territory they had none of the political purchase that Livingston brought to bear on the New York legislature. States and territories in the Mississippi valley refused their entreaties. Only New Orleans Territory agreed to a deal, and that only for the portion of the lower Mississippi it controlled. Still, that was enough to lure the entrepreneurs west. Fulton sent Nicholas Roosevelt, Livingston's partner in his initial steamboat scheme, to Pittsburgh in 1809. There, on the banks of the Monongahela River, Roosevelt built an eastern-style steamboat on Fulton's Hudson model, aptly named the *New Orleans.* Setting out on September 27, 1811, the ship made its way to the Ohio, demonstrated its ability to sail upstream briefly at Louisville before shooting the rapids there, and arrived in New Orleans on January 12, 1812, the first steamboat to dock in its namesake city. There it was greeted by Edmund Livingston, the newly arrived agent of the eastern combine.[10] This former mayor of New York City had fled his native state in the wake of financial scandal, seeking to restore his fortune and his reputation in the West.[11] The Fulton-Livingston syndicate looked for all the world like an industrial juggernaut that would come to dominate the western rivers the same way it controlled the Hudson.

But such was not to be. One problem to which Fulton had not yet turned his considerable ingenuity was the difference between the eastern and western rivers. Because they were bigger and drained more territory, the western rivers tended to carry more silt and debris. They were shallower and more clogged than a river like the Hudson, and they needed a steamboat suited to their distinctive characteristics. The *New Orleans* that Roosevelt took south in 1811 never returned farther north than Natchez, in part because that city marked the upper reaches of the monopoly granted by the New Orleans Territory, but also because it was not powerful enough to fight the strong currents all the way back to Pittsburgh. That challenge called for a shallow-draft vessel (more like a flatboat than the sleek craft Fulton designed for the Hudson) and an engine more powerful than any that Fulton had yet employed. Ironically, such an engine would be pioneered by John Stevens, Livingston's brother-in-law, erstwhile partner, and current competitor. Stevens had worked for years to develop a high-pressure steam engine for the New York market, where it was not needed. He had a leg up when the western rivers placed a premium on this technology.

Stevens contended with the Fulton-Livingston forces over more than just design. He also led the opposition to the Fulton-Livingston monopolies, not just on the Hudson but wherever they tried to expand them. The monopolists were vulnerable on two counts. First, Fulton's two national patents could not bear close scrutiny. Fitch and many others had demonstrated prior art, and Fulton's claims for the originality of his "proportions" fell before countless other combinations of hull and machinery that arose in competition. The city of Albany, for example, sponsored two steamboats that entered service to New York City in violation of the Fulton-Livingston monopoly. Rather than seeking a restraining order in federal court based on his patent, Fulton used Livingston's political power in the New York legislature. The monopolists were authorized to seize and destroy the Albany boats without ever testing their claims before the bar.[12]

Stevens's other claim against the Fulton-Livingston monopoly was that national patents trump state monopoly. Armed with his own patents for steamboat designs, including high-pressure engines, he challenged the New York monopoly under the commerce clause of the federal Constitution. Not until 1824 would the Supreme Court finally uphold the position taken by him. In the famous case of *Gibbons v. Ogden*, the Court ruled that state and territorial monopolies of the kind held by Livingston and Fulton in New York and Louisiana violated the constitutional right of the federal government to control interstate commerce. The ruling applied even to waters confined entirely within a single state, such as the Hudson, because vessels from other states could not be blocked from carrying goods and passengers from their own states into the protected waterway. Once Stevens's position became the law of the land, coastal and inland shipping were forever freed from the shackles that Livingston and Fulton had tried to clamp upon them.

For the remainder of their lifetimes, the two monopolists fought competitors in and out of court. Livingston claimed shortly before his death in 1813 that endless litigation had robbed him of the profits from steamboating and the satisfaction of the technical achievement.[13] Fulton, scrappier and more accustomed to struggle, complained less. Ensconced in a palatial mansion in New York City, he spent his wife's inherited wealth and his own steamboat riches with the abandon of those who have known poverty. He indulged himself, supported friends and business associates generously, and sustained a team of attorneys led by the corpulent and able Thomas Addis Emmet. Tragically and ironically, his premature death came on the very night of his greatest legal triumph in a New Jersey court-room, when he caught pneumonia rescuing his lawyer, who had fallen through the ice on the Hudson River as the pair walked to the ferry.

In this 1883 statue by Howard Roberts, a young, handsome Robert Fulton contemplates a model of his creation. Though the subject is idealized, even romanticized, the sculpture nonetheless captures the research and planning (the scrolls at his feet) that went into his work and his use of ship models to test his ideas.

Fulton's contribution to American maritime history was significant and indelible. Yet in the minds of many he sullied his reputation by embracing an outdated form of monopoly that retarded the development of steam-powered shipping on coastal and inland waters. Fulton would claim in his own defense that monopolies were an established and proven method of rewarding invention. In the absence, or at least immaturity, of a national patent system in the early republic, they were necessary to compensate innovators like himself for the years of privation that went into new developments. He would also point to the steady improvement in the boats he developed over the years. He was not impeding development but spurring it.

His detractors claimed that monopolies restrained trade, slowed innovation, and enriched the few at the expense of the many. Livingston's monopoly of steam navigation on the Hudson was a piece of favoritism accorded by the New York legislature to one of its princes. A commoner like John Fitch had far more trouble winning his monopolies and less success at maintaining them. In fact, Livingston had Fitch's New York monopoly revoked in favor of his own. Competition would have benefited the customer and spurred innovation. Albany's first steamships had been just as good as Fulton's. Removing them from the river served private interests at the expense of the public.

Monopolies of water transit were especially unwelcome on the Mississippi and its tributaries. The settlers who braved the western territories were often refugees from the systems of privilege and power that ruled the seaboard states and they saw the Fulton-Livingston monopoly on the lower Mississippi as representing exactly the kind of eastern politics they had sought to escape. They often associated such practices with "the traders and Jew bankers of Philadelphia, Baltimore, New York and Boston," as one writer characterized them in the *Pittsburgh Commonwealth* in 1815.[14] They displayed even less respect for the New Orleans monopoly than Fulton's competitors had shown in New York for his Hudson rights, and Fulton had far greater difficulty enforcing his claims at a distance than he did in and about New York.

By the time the hated Fulton-Livingston monopolies were defeated—in 1819 in New Orleans and 1824 for the nation at large—Fulton and Livingston were dead. But their impact lived on. In 1820 commerce on America's inland and coastal waterways exceeded overseas shipping for the first time. The locus of American maritime history had shifted from blue water to brown. The heyday of American oceanic shipping was about to dawn, but it would prove to be the last florescence of a waning enterprise. Not until the late twentieth century would international shipping regain the relative preponderance in American waterborne commerce that it had enjoyed throughout the colonial era. The way of the ship in America had turned inward.

14

THE WAR OF 1812

THE OPENING OF AMERICA'S INLAND WATERS WAS ACCOMPANIED by armed conflict on the high seas. The fighting reflected and accelerated the country's inward turn. The United States fought nominally to protect the principle of free trade. But when all was said and done, the young republic revealed a willingness to sacrifice its oceanic shipping interests in the pursuit of larger national goals, a tendency that was to recur throughout the nineteenth and twentieth centuries. These contests also spurred the United States to create a navy and begin a century-long search for a viable naval policy. Finally, the wars reflected and exacerbated the regional tensions manifest in the West's distaste for the Fulton-Livingston monopoly.

Two apparently unrelated events in 1793 had a profound impact on American shipping. Eli Whitney introduced the cotton gin, rivaling Robert Fulton's steamboat as the most transformative technology of the early republic. The ensuing rise of King Cotton captured the southern economy, transformed American trading patterns, brought European specie into the American economy, and accelerated the centrifugal forces of American regionalism. Also in 1793, Britain joined the First Coalition against the newly declared French republic. Britain and France were to remain almost constantly at war for the next twenty-two years, locked in a classic struggle between a whale and an elephant, a sea power and a land power. This was the struggle in which Robert Fulton sided first with the French against British tyranny of the seas and then accepted British pounds to war against the tyranny of Emperor Napoleon. His duplicity in the conflict mirrored not just his mercenary ambition but also his native land's ambivalence toward the warring parties in Europe.

Unlike Fulton, the United States first took up arms against France. Responding to new British Orders in Council passed after the commencement of hostilities with France and the capture of American merchantmen by French privateers, the U.S. Congress debated a naval bill in 1794. The Federalists, representing a mercantilist and industrial Northeast, sought protection of their commerce and coasts. Their targets were the French and the Barbary pirates. They were willing to overlook British depredations against American shipping because 90 percent of U.S. trade was still with Britain. Jeffersonian Republicans, on the other hand, tended more toward isolationism and resented perceived British support for Indian attacks on Americans in the West. A compromise Navy Act of May 27, 1794, authorized the construction of six frigates to protect American shipping from Barbary pirates on the southwest Mediterranean coast.[1] The ships would ultimately prove to be far more successful than the compromise national policy that brought them into existence.

Late in 1794 the Americans came to terms with Britain in Jay's Treaty of Amity, Commerce, and Navigation, settling temporarily the right of U.S. vessels to trade with European states. A comparable attempt to settle with France produced the notorious XYZ affair, the bribery scandal that temporarily drove Talleyrand from office. "Millions for defense, but not one cent for tribute," cried out the American people in a triumph of jingoism over common sense. Stampeded by the uproar, Congress authorized a Navy Department on April 30, 1798. The following month it authorized the seizure of French ships. The Quasi-War with France was under way.

After heroic but inconclusive engagements between French and American men-of-war, coupled with disastrous shipping losses on both sides from commerce raiding and privateering, the two nations settled in September 1800, just as Napoleon was recovering the Louisiana Territory from Spain and Robert Livingston was jumping the Federalist ship to join the Jefferson bandwagon. Criticized by the Hamiltonian wing of his own Federalist Party for not leading the country into a formal war with France, President John Adams lost his bid for reelection, ceding the White House

to Thomas Jefferson and the Democratic-Republican coalition of south-
erners and westerners.

Once in office, Jefferson had even more trouble than his predecessor in
protecting American maritime interests. He dispatched American warships into a two-year war with Tripoli under the same banner that had
flown over the Quasi-War with France: no tribute. Other maritime states
such as Britain and France simply paid tribute to the Barbary pirates; it
was cheaper than fighting them and it damaged the commerce of competitors who could not afford to pay. But Americans, newly independent,
lacking a single ship of the line, and buffeted already in the Anglo-French
commerce war, felt they had to demonstrate that they could not be
pushed around. Again the fledgling navy scored some heroic triumphs.
These provided naval folklore and tradition but hardly deterred the Barbary states from continuing depredations. Jefferson finally settled for a
negotiated peace with the dey of Tripoli and subsequently paid tribute to
other Barbary states, national slogans to the contrary notwithstanding.
Suspicious that a blue-water navy served the mercantile interests of the
Northeast at the expense of southern and western citizens, Jefferson
mothballed the new frigates and sponsored a gunboat navy to protect
American coasts from invasion.

Neither these actions nor Jay's Treaty deterred the British from preying
on American vessels on the high seas. In spite of American protests,
Britain executed its Orders in Council, seizing American ships that carried
cargoes for France and removing alleged deserters from the Royal Navy.
The United States tolerated these assaults on its sovereignty because profits were so high. With French commercial vessels blockaded by Britain
and British commercial vessels devoted to the war effort, American ships
flourished in the Atlantic carrying trade. Business dropped off during the
Peace of Amiens (1801–1803), but then so too did the depredations. The
European war was better for American shipping than the Peace of
Amiens.[2]

The tension in American policy between profit and principle reached
the breaking point with the *Chesapeake-Leopard* crisis in the spring of
1807. A British frigate fired upon and boarded an American vessel off
Hampton Roads in search of deserters, killing some of the crew. At Jefferson's behest, Congress imposed an embargo on all American oceanic shipping. The hope was that the removal of American products from the
international market would injure Britain more than any other state and

bring about the cessation of British interference with American shipping. As Albert Gallatin and others warned, neither the 1807 act nor the two succeeding amendments had any such effect. The embargo actually stimulated American industry and coastal and inland shipping, but it devastated small Atlantic ports that had insufficient resources to sustain their infrastructure in the absence of overseas commerce.[3] William Gray of Salem, a prominent shipowner who had succeeded Elias Haskett Derby as the wealthiest and most powerful merchant prince of that storied town, supported Jefferson in principle and thereby won the vitriolic enmity of his townsmen. When Jefferson finally repealed the embargo on his last day in office, March 4, 1809, Gray decamped to Boston, harbinger of a sea change in the locus of America's major ports. Salem was wounded by the embargo, but it survived to experience a last great florescence. Other small ports east of Cape Cod did not survive.[4] The embargo inflicted little pain on Britain and practically none on France.

In the new administration of James Madison, Congress replaced the embargo with two nonintercourse acts. The second invited both Britain and France to respect neutral shipping, promising to trade with whichever country accepted the terms and not with the other. Napoleon immediately embraced the offer, setting the United States and Britain on the road to war. Madison welcomed the risk, in part because his Democratic-Republican Party had come under the sway of "War Hawks," such as Henry Clay of Kentucky and John C. Calhoun of South Carolina, imperialists who were intoxicated with the Louisiana Purchase and anxious to add Canada and Spanish Florida to the growing American empire. Northeastern Federalists tried in vain to alter the collision course with Britain, for the end of the embargo had brought a resumption of shipping prosperity. Though the United States had lost some eighteen hundred ships to the British, the French, and their allies by 1810, booming business more than covered the losses. The Federalists preferred a bigger navy to protect their interests.[5]

A flagrant case of British impressment from an American merchant ship off New York harbor in May 1811 fueled a war fever that did not abate until the chauvinists got their way. James Madison's war message, sent to Congress on June 1, 1812, cited impressment, neutral rights, and Indian attacks in the West. Congress responded with the closest war vote in American history, 79 to 49 in the House and 19 to 13 in the Senate. The legislators split along party lines, but most from Pennsylvania and the

South and West voted for war, while the majority from the North and East voted no.[6] In response, Sir John Borlase Warren, commander of the Royal Navy's newly established North American station, recommended concentrated operations against the southern United States and forbearance toward the Northeast.[7] New Orleans, in particular, became a prime target of British war plans. In spite of this emphasis, the weight of war fell most heavily on the maritime centers between Baltimore, Maryland, and Eastport, Maine.

For its part, the United States launched an impetuous, poorly planned, and comically inept invasion of Canada. It achieved nothing and lost Detroit. Thereafter, the country was thrown onto the defensive, achieving its greatest successes in lake warfare that foiled Britain's own schemes for overland invasion. But along the coasts, Jefferson's gunboats proved powerless to interrupt British depredations on American shipping and projections of power ashore. In spite of the incomparable sailing qualities of its 1790s frigates, the American oceangoing navy was essentially bottled up in port with the merchant marine. Only privateers had any sustained success on the high seas, capturing or destroying as much British commerce as the United States lost to British seizures. The young United States experienced the first flight from its flag, as some American shippers took on Portuguese registry. Thus began a pattern of foreign registry that would bedevil the country for the next two centuries.[8]

Finally, popular pressure at home convinced both governments to settle. A peace treaty was signed on Christmas Eve 1814, though news of the settlement arrived too late to stop the battle of New Orleans. Ironically, the assault on New Orleans, the capstone of Britain's southern strategy in the war, failed when Andrew Jackson and an ad hoc army of western irregulars defeated British veterans of the famous Peninsular War against Napoleon's forces in Spain. The victory would propel Jackson and the southern and western coalition into the White House in 1828. It would also immortalize another heroic participant, Henry Shreve, who took up the frontier battle against the Fulton-Livingston combine when the war was over.

The War of 1812 achieved one American goal: Britain and other nations thereafter took the United States more seriously. But this stature was bought dearly, and shipping paid the largest price. The net freight earnings of the U.S. oceanic carrying trade fell from $40.8 million in 1811 to $2.6 million in 1814.[9] Even the coastal trade suffered from the

British blockade. Only shipping on the inland waters escaped the British navy, contributing to a trend that was being accelerated by steamboats. U.S. gross tons in foreign trade fell by 40 percent between 1810 and 1820, while the coastal and inland trade increased by 45 percent. The coastal and inland trade was actually greater in 1820 than the foreign trade, a pattern that would continue almost to the end of the twentieth century, excepting only the periods surrounding the world wars.[10] Forced by the exigencies of war to be more self-sufficient and to trade more with itself, the United States developed synapses of waterborne communication that survived the peace and continued to spread, even as oceanic trade resumed in the years after 1815 and whaling and fishing prospered.

Desperate after the war to restore its oceanic shipping, Congress wrote into law the same principle that guided the tariff of 1789: protectionism. The Navigation Act of 1817, modeled on its British namesake, imposed trade penalties on nations that restricted the freedom of American vessels. In general this had the positive effect of spawning bilateral agreements with many states to the mutual advantage of both parties. But the most far-reaching provision of the 1817 act was to restrict coastal and inland shipping in the United States to American vessels. This policy, called cabotage, was pursued by most, but not all, maritime states. Its adoption by the United States marked a turning point in American history. Forces of geography, politics, war, technology, and economics were already driving the nation to trade and commune with itself via its coastal and inland waterways. Cabotage ensured that this commerce and travel would sail on American ships. A domestic American merchant marine was assured.

The Navigation Act of 1817 crowned the tumultuous experience of American foreign shipping during the wars of the French Revolution and Napoleon. Some Americans, such as William Gray, grew wealthy in war; others were ruined. The Northeast suffered most, the South and West least. Coastwise trade recovered quickly; movement on the inland waterways grew during and after the war. Transfers at New Orleans, for example, rose from an estimated 60,000 tons in 1812 to 77,200 in 1815.[11] Salem, in contrast, ended the war with only fifty-seven ships, a fourth of the fleet's size in 1812.[12] Other small ports fared even worse. Some New England shipowners converted their merchantmen to whalers; by 1829 the whaling fleet had grown from insignificance to 57,284 tons, about one-tenth the registered merchant fleet. Other merchants shifted capital from ocean shipping to manufacturing and the coastal trade. Massachusetts, in Samuel Eliot Morison's memorable phrase, turned "from wharf to waterfall," from shipping to manufacturing.[13] Innovative New Englanders, including some from Salem, would find new business models for oceanic trade, but the prosperity of the 1790s would never return.[14]

15

HENRY SHREVE AND THE TAMING OF THE RIVER

BETWEEN THE WAR OF 1812 AND THE CIVIL WAR, THE UNITED States experienced a transportation revolution.[1] It came in three realms of transportation: rivers, canals, and railroads, all of which shaped America's maritime history. Ironically, the dominant maritime commerce of the period, coastal trade, flourished amid all of this change. The revolution contributed to a trifurcation of the new nation into distinct regions with separate economic and political profiles, which exacerbated the tensions separating the old North and the old South, impelling rather than retarding the approach of war.

Robert Livingston and Robert Fulton had begun the process of opening America's rivers to commerce, but the conquest that Fulton had in mind from the outset, the Mississippi, eluded them. They created two companies for the purpose. They sponsored Nicholas Roosevelt's historic trip from Pittsburgh to New Orleans in 1811–1812. And they won and defended a monopoly of steam navigation in New Orleans Territory. But they never gained the purchase on the Mississippi that Livingston's political influence won them on the Hudson. Both men died before the War of 1812 ended. Their companies in the West fought a losing battle for several more years against a growing and aggressive competition that openly flaunted their monopoly claims on the lower reaches of the river. When they finally lost that monopoly in 1819, their chances of playing a major role all but disappeared.

The man who would come to be associated with opening the Mississippi offered a striking contrast to Fulton and Livingston. Uneducated, unconnected, unprivileged, innocent of political power, and devoid of capital, Henry M. Shreve represented a new breed of American, a Jacksonian "common man" who invented himself even as he invented the tools and techniques to tame the Mississippi River. He triumphed over Livingston, the patrician, and Fulton, the patrician manqué, by dint of practical adaptation to the physical realities of the Mississippi and the economics of inland shipping. The eastern model of comparatively deep-draft steam vessels powered by low-pressure engines carrying passengers and general cargoes up and down river to and from coastal cities simply did not work on the shallow but powerful western rivers. It took an experienced and imaginative westerner to figure out what would.

Shreve was born in Mount Pleasant, New Jersey, in 1785, the fourth son and eighth child of a bumbling Quaker who threw over his religion to cast his lot with George Washington in the Revolutionary War. Though relieved for incompetence in 1781, Israel Shreve retained the personal affection of Washington, who rented him a piece of property just south of Pittsburgh, at the juncture of the Monongahela and Youghiogheny rivers.[2] Israel Shreve was no better at farming than soldiering, and only Washington's indulgence and generosity kept him on his farm until the two men died on the same day in 1799. Shreve's family finally inherited the farm, but young Henry, like Robert Fulton before him, appears to have been chastened by growing up in financial straits. He emerges in the historical record at age twenty-one, owner of his own 35-ton keelboat, a large flatboat, generally with tapered ends, capable of moving upstream. Employing a crew of ten, Shreve loaded his boat with its first cargo, probably nails, hardware, and glassware, for which Pittsburgh was already noted.[3] These he floated down the Ohio River and then up the Mississippi to St. Louis, where he traded them for furs. In the days of keelboats, moving upstream on the inland waterway entailed pushing or pulling the boat against the current by hand. It was slow, painstaking, exhausting work, and many flatboaters and keelboaters simply took a load downriver and sold or scrapped the boat there rather than work it back upstream against the current. This was what Nicholas Roosevelt had done with the *New Orleans*, restricting it after its maiden voyage to service in the lower Mississippi. Not so Shreve. Taking on his load of furs at St. Louis, he floated down the Mississippi to Cairo, Illinois, and then back up the Ohio to Pittsburgh. Thence he shipped overland to Philadelphia, shortcutting the normal route to New Orleans for transshipment on an oceangoing vessel to the East. He made this innovative trade pay for three seasons before declining profits convinced him that the future was on the Mississippi.

In May 1810 Shreve took a new 35-ton keelboat and crew of twelve up the Mississippi beyond St. Louis to a lead-mining area near the mouth of the Fever River (modern-day Galena, Illinois). Reaching in just two weeks territory hitherto monopolized by the British entering from Canada, he and his crew bartered with the local Indians for about six weeks, amassing 60 tons of lead, more than his keelboat could carry. Building one additional boat and buying another from the Indians, he navigated his flotilla all the way to New Orleans, where he sold his lead and put it on a ship bound for Philadelphia. He broke up his makeshift fleet of boats for wood and sailed with his cargo for Philadelphia, returning home overland from there with a profit of $11,000.

Leaving others to exploit the trading possibilities he had opened on the upper Mississippi, Shreve spent the next four years running a 95-ton keelboat between Pittsburgh and New Orleans. The experience impressed upon him the inadequacies of animal power in moving upriver. When drifting downstream, sail, oars, and rudder were usually enough for a skillful pilot to steer the boat around the bars and snags that caught the novice or the unwary. But even a following wind failed to drive the boats against the current. Crew members would push against the bottom with "setting poles." Where the water was deep enough near shore, the crew would literally pull the boat along using a *cordelle*, a thousand-foot rope. Alternatively, they might tie the cordelle to a tree upstream and pull or winch the boat to it, a technique called "warping." With deep water near shore, the crew might also "bushwhack" the boat, grabbing the limbs of trees and bushes and walking the boat forward by pulling on them.[4] Aside from tedium and exhaustion, these techniques exposed the men to Indians and pirates along the shores. Between 1811 and 1814 these various hazards to navigation produced a one-in-three chance that the crew would not return from such a voyage.[5]

Returning to Pittsburgh from his first voyage to New Orleans, Shreve saw Nicholas Roosevelt building the *New Orleans* in 1811. Though

Shreve sailed three more keelboats to Louisiana, he had seen his future and the future of the Mississippi. Roosevelt's historic boat remained trapped in the lower Mississippi, lacking the power in its engines to steam against the river's currents. This was one of the many innovations that Shreve and others would address in the search for a steamship suited to the western rivers. In 1814 he purchased a one-fifth share in a steamboat being built at Brownsville, Pennsylvania, on the Monongahela River, by Daniel French, a mechanic and inventor driven west by the Fulton-Livingston monopoly on the Hudson. French's first western boat, the *Comet*, had proven, like the *New Orleans*, unable to return up the Mississippi. Shreve, a veteran of the western rivers, helped French design a second boat, the *Enterprise*, equal to the task. They competed against three boats then under construction in Pittsburgh for the Fulton-Livingston Mississippi Steamboat Navigation Company. On his last keelboat voyage downriver in 1814, Shreve retained the services of Abner L. Duncan, a prominent New Orleans attorney. For an advanced retainer of $500 and the prospect of $1,500 if he won the case, Duncan was prepared to take on Edmund Livingston and the legal monopoly he defended.

But then the War of 1812 intervened. Fighting during its first two years had made little impact in the West, but 1814 witnessed a British plan to attack in the Gulf. Andrew Jackson repelled an assault on Mobile, Alabama, and captured Pensacola, Florida, in November. In the same month, Shreve returned to Pittsburgh from New Orleans with intentions to steam south in the *Enterprise* with a shipment of ordnance. He reached New Orleans on December 14, just as British general Sir Edward Packenham landed a few miles south of the city with almost ten thousand veterans of the Peninsular War against Napoleon. Jackson commandeered the *Enterprise* and directed Shreve to carry troops and supplies to the defensive lines he was erecting south of the city, hazardous trips that Shreve capped with a daring run past British artillery positions on the night of January 3–4, 1815, to resupply Fort St. Philip, an outpost halfway between New Orleans and the coast. Returning with boat and crew intact, Shreve volunteered to join Jackson's ragtag army of western volunteers. Assigned to an artillery battery covering the river road on the extreme right of the American line, he served one of the twenty-four-pounders (cannons firing a twenty-four-pound ball) that drove back the column of General John Keane. In the celebration and self-congratulations that ensued, undiminished by the news that the war was already over when the battle of New Orleans was fought, Shreve found himself a local and regional hero.

That status strengthened his hand when the showdown with Edmund Livingston dawned. On the day that Shreve planned to take the *Enterprise* back upriver in May 1815, Livingston had the boat impounded for violating the Louisiana monopoly. Shreve and Duncan promptly posted and jumped bail, taking the boat upriver to a hero's welcome in St. Louis. The difficult ascent under power, which taxed to capacity the craft's engines, and the exceptional flooding conditions that carried his deep-draft vessels over the treacherously shallow waters, convinced Shreve that regular passage on the river called for a radically new design.[6]

The *Washington*, a 400-ton boat with a high-pressure engine, was entirely Shreve's design. Its boilers rode on deck, freeing more of the hold for cargo space. The stern wheel of the *Enterprise* gave way to side paddle wheels. The deep-draft design imported to the western rivers by Fulton and other eastern entrepreneurs surrendered to the flat bottom and shallow draft reminiscent of the indigenous flatboats with which Shreve was familiar. For the first time, the superstructure rose up two decks, providing the silhouette that would soon become standard on the Mississippi.[7]

Shreve sailed on June 3, 1816, to take his revolutionary but untested vessel on a combined maiden voyage and shakedown cruise to New Orleans. It turned out to be a historic voyage. Though plagued with minor mechanical problems in the first two days, Shreve pressed on to the vicinity of Marietta, where a boiler exploded, killing six passengers and three crewmen and injuring Shreve and five others. Shaken but undeterred, Shreve put into Louisville for repairs. Resuming the voyage on September 24, he reached New Orleans on October 7, where he and his revolutionary vessel were promptly arrested for violating the Fulton-Livingston monopoly. Crowds gathered to protest the jailing of the previous year's hero, threatening to riot until Shreve himself appealed for calm. He was released without having to post bond, whereupon he and Duncan countersued for damages. A friendly local jury had no difficulty in choosing between their local hero and the eastern monopolists.

Shreve resisted a personal offer from the Fulton-Livingston forces to join their camp. Instead, he took the *Washington* north to Shippingport, just downriver from Louisville, winning credit in many minds for establishing the feasibility of upriver travel, even though two boats designed by Fulton had also made the return voyage. The following year, a suit filed against Shreve in U.S. district court in New Orleans by the Fulton-Livingston interests was dismissed on the ground that neither the plaintiffs nor defendant were residents of Louisiana. This ruling dodged the issue of the Louisiana monopoly, but it was widely interpreted in the West as a victory for Shreve and free navigation of the Mississippi. Steamboat construction boomed on the river and other operators defied the monopoly. Recognizing force majeure, the Fulton-Livingston executors withdrew their monopoly claims in 1819, five years before *Gibbons v. Ogden* established the preeminent power of the federal government to regulate interstate commerce. The right to free navigation of inland waterways was thus established in the West de facto before it became the law of the land.

Between 1818 and 1827 Shreve remained a leader in the wave of steamboat activity that swept the Mississippi and its tributaries. To his growing fleet of boats, he added in 1825 the *George Washington,* successor to his innovative *Washington.* It featured twin engines, allowing the paddle wheels on either side of the vessel to be turned independently, offering greater maneuverability and efficiency. The bottom grew flatter and shallower. The superstructure rose to three decks of luxuriously appointed cabins where fine food and drink turned these workhorses into the

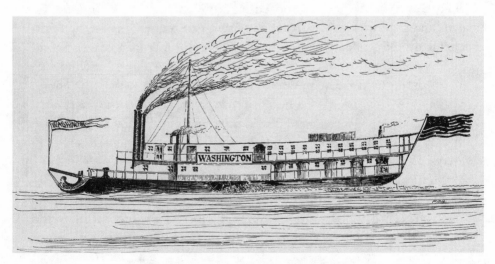

Henry Shreve's *George Washington* (1825) marked a transformation from his earlier *Washington,* the first steamboat to navigate back up the Mississippi, from New Orleans to Louisville. While about the same length and displacement as the earlier vessel, the *George Washington* featured side paddle wheels and a shallower draft, adaptations to navigation on the western rivers.

famous "floating palaces" of American legend. Concentrating on both passengers and general cargo, these river queens would compete through the nineteenth century in speed and elegance. The races between the best of them entered Mississippi folklore, and the bursting boilers resulting from the competition would finally stimulate government intervention and regulation in the 1830s.[8] But for those races to take place, the Mississippi itself had to be made safer for navigation. And once again, Henry Shreve showed the way.

As early as 1821 Shreve had drafted plans for a "snag boat" to clear the "snags," "sawyers," and "planters," uprooted trees embedded in the rivers and often entangled with one another. In 1824 Secretary of War John C. Calhoun directed the U.S. Army Corps of Engineers to solicit advice and proposals for clearing the rivers. Shreve missed the first round of attempts, but when those failed, Calhoun in 1826 appointed him superintendent of Western River Improvements. In spite of his Jacksonian aversion to working for the administration of President John Quincy Adams, he assumed the post on January 2, 1827. Launching his first snag boat, the *Heliopolis*, at New Albany, Indiana, in April 1829, Shreve—now an employee of the Jackson administration—moved methodically down the Mississippi River, clearing snags from the mouth of the Missouri to Baton Rouge. The government then authorized a second boat, the *Archimedes*, for working shallower waters. In 1832 Shreve accepted a renewed appointment and the challenge of clearing the "Great Raft," a mass of wood completely blocking the Red River for 160 to 200 miles above Natchitoches. Constricting commerce on the river and contributing to periodic floods, the raft was retarding the economic development of the entire river valley. It took Shreve six years, including almost a year and a half of suspended funding, to complete the job. He finished his last great undertaking in May 1839.

Martin Van Buren's defeat in the election of 1840 ended Shreve's government service. Removed from office the following September, he retired to his farm, Gallatin Place, just outside St. Louis. With enormous irony and characteristic prescience, he spent his declining years promoting a railroad from St. Louis to the West Coast. He died in 1851, to be buried on a bluff overlooking the Mississippi River, which he had done so much to develop.

Shreve was a legend in his own time, and his stature has grown with a generous, even adulatory historiography. He did not single-handedly open the Mississippi River. Nor did he design the prototypical Mississippi

Henry Shreve contributed as much as any individual to opening the Mississippi River to navigation. He helped win the battle of New Orleans, introduced innovative steamboats, and developed techniques to remove obstructions from the Mississippi and its tributaries.

steamboat. Nor did he clear the western rivers by himself. He did, however, make significant contributions in all these fields. And his personal heroics and achievements gave stature and dignity to an emerging American type, the Jacksonian "common man." He stood up to the eastern patricians, adapted existing technologies to the peculiarities of the western rivers, and did it all without much education, capital, or political influence. In his time, the western rivers became thoroughfares of American commerce and avenues of settlement and development within the vast and fertile lands drained by the Mississippi and its tributaries.

The flow of goods up and down those rivers is the best evidence of the contributions of Shreve and his fellow river mariners. Freight arrivals at New Orleans swelled from 94,600 tons in 1816 to 193,300 in 1826, 437,100 in 1836, and 971,700 in 1846; they passed 2 million tons for the first time in 1860. Improvements in steam navigation accounted for much of this increase, but, even more surprising in some ways, keelboats and flatboats continued to prosper as well; keelboat arrivals in New Orleans went from 1,287 in 1816 to a peak of 2,792 in the commercial year 1846–1847. All the while improved technology, the clearing of rivers, and more skillful rivermen improved shipping efficiency. The productivity of steamboats improved between 1815 and 1860 more steeply than any other form of transportation in the nineteenth century, allowing the boats to reduce upstream cabin fares from $125 before 1820 to $15 in the decade before 1860. Flatboats experienced comparable economies, aided by the savings in steaming crews upstream after they had delivered a boat to New Orleans. And statistics such as these fail to capture much of the Mississippi River traffic diverted to southern ports on the way south. By 1849 western river steamboats were carrying 3.32 billion freight ton-miles and 1.1 billion passenger miles, both about 30 percent more than all the railroads in the United States carried a decade later.[9] This activity turned New Orleans into the fifth busiest port in the United States and one of the busiest in the world. If it fell short of the stature that John Fitch and Robert Fulton had imagined when they dreamed of monopolizing this traffic, it nonetheless outshone once mighty Salem, which had declined to a shadow of its former self.

16

DeWitt Clinton
and the
Canal Craze

DEWITT CLINTON, A DOWNSTATE NEW YORK PATRICIAN TO
compare with Robert Livingston, came within one state (Pennsylvania) of
being elected president of the United States. But it was as a champion for
the Erie Canal, mockingly called "Clinton's Big Ditch," that he achieved
lasting fame. He took up a torch handed him personally by Robert Fulton and carried it farther than even the ambitious and optimistic Fulton
had envisioned. By demonstrating the potential of canals to promote
commerce, Clinton set off a decade of "canal fever" in the United States
that permanently altered the physical, economic, and maritime landscape.

Born to privilege and society in New York City, Clinton married into
wealth. These advantages he combined with tireless ambition, hard work,
education, and an imposing physical presence magnified by a handsome
face atop a six-foot-three-inch frame. Were it not for an imperious, sometimes condescending style and a boundless capacity to irritate, Clinton
might have ridden these assets to the White House. As it was, he won
election to the New York state senate, the U.S. Senate, the lieutenant governorship of New York, and the mayoralty of New York City. When he
lost that office in 1815 after losing his presidential bid to James Madison
in 1812, Clinton needed to rejuvenate his flagging political fortunes. He
embraced a canal project with a long history in New York and ripening
prospects in the United States.

Robert Fulton had been among the first to bring European enthusiasm for canals to the United States. His 1796 book on the subject, *A Treatise on the Improvement of Canal Navigation,* had been followed by a letter to George Washington proposing a series of canals connecting Philadelphia to Lake Erie. Nothing came of that proposal, but Fulton renewed his advocacy for canals with inclined planes when he was appointed, along with Robert Livingston, to the New York Board of Canal Commissioners in 1811.[1] Clinton, the dominant member of the board, was perhaps returning the favor of being appointed in 1810 an incorporator of the Ohio Steamboat Navigation Company, one of the Fulton-Livingston business ventures on the western rivers.[2] Fulton called a canal connecting Albany and Buffalo "a sublime national work, which will secure wealth and happiness to millions," and revised his 1796 treatise under the new title *Advantages of the Proposed Canal from Lake Erie to the Hudson River.*[3] The War of 1812 interrupted the commission's work, and Fulton died three days after the Treaty of Ghent arrived in the United States and two days before the Senate ratified it. Unable to champion his cherished inclined planes, he could not stop the new canal from using the more traditional locks, eighty-two of them, to raise vessels the 620 feet up from the Hudson River to Lake Erie.

When DeWitt Clinton revived the plan in 1815, there were only about one hundred miles of canals in the United States. Still, support seemed to be growing. Secretary of the Treasury Albert Gallatin had advocated canals in his famous 1808 report to the Senate on internal improvement.[4] Even Thomas Jefferson, a staunch advocate of limited government, had endorsed the concept. Clinton successfully lobbied the U.S. Congress for a federal appropriation to support the project, but President Madison vetoed it on his last day in office. Throughout the first half of the nineteenth century, the problem of "internal improvements" vexed the new republic. Before 1850 state and private investors provided most of the funding for development of the nation's transportation infrastructure. But many viewed the western territories differently, feeling that they needed the support of the federal government to realize their economic potential. Congress declared the Mississippi River to be a "national public highway" in 1811, and an editorial in the *Kentucky Gazette* in 1816 claimed that "the western waters are our canals." As the transportation revolution gained steam, so to speak, toward the middle of the nineteenth century, the federal government would assume a larger role in internal improvements generally and the development of inland waterways specifically.[5] But this trend offered cold comfort to DeWitt Clinton in 1817.

Still, by the time of Madison's veto, Clinton's political fortunes had completely reversed. He rode the canal issue to election as governor in 1816. With preliminary work on the canal already under way, the New York legislature on April 15, 1817, appropriated $7.6 million for its construction. Within weeks, Clinton was inaugurated governor, allowing him to dig the ceremonial first shovelful of dirt on the Fourth of July.

The first section of the Erie Canal opened in 1819. Immediately it began generating revenue that helped complete all 364 miles of the project. In the year of its opening, 1825, the canal generated half a million dollars in revenue, exceeding the cost of debt service by $100,000. The following year income rose to three-quarters of a million. Freight rates from Buffalo to New York City fell by an order of magnitude; by 1857–1860 they had dropped from 19.12 cents per ton-mile to .81 cents. The volume of canal traffic from the western states swelled from 54,219 tons in 1836 to more than a million in 1851 to almost 2 million in 1860.[6] In 1835 the New York legislature authorized a $4 million loan to enlarge the canal.

The immediate and unqualified success of the Erie Canal sparked a canal boom in the United States. During the 1830s, two thousand miles of canals would be built. None exceeded the ambition, the length, or the cost of Pennsylvania's Main Line. Worried that the Erie Canal would siphon traffic and business from Philadelphia, the city's merchants convinced the state to fund a canal connecting them with Pittsburgh. At a cost of more than $10 million, Pennsylvania completed a 395-mile canal linking its two largest cities. Even with 174 locks rising and falling 2,200 feet up one side of the Appalachian Mountains and down the other, the route still required a portage train to carry specially designed canal boats up and down inclined planes over the peak. Not content with this money-losing folly, Pennsylvania built a total of 772 miles of canals. It had 162 more under construction when it defaulted on its debts in the depression of 1839–1843. The contrast between New York's experience and Pennsylvania's highlighted the importance of geography in the transportation revolution. The natural plain followed by the Erie Canal across New York, the result of a break in the Appalachians, gave that state a particularly advantageous route from the Great Lakes to the tidewater.

Ohio did better than Pennsylvania. Amid many canal projects in the 1830s, it completed two that tied the Great Lakes to the Mississippi River system. The 308-mile Ohio and Erie Canal connected the Ohio River to Lake Erie at Cleveland in 1833. The Miami and Erie Canal connected Cincinnati to Dayton in 1832 and reached Toledo on Lake Erie in 1845.[7] The merchants of Cincinnati, Dayton, and other Ohio cities now had two routes to the sea, north through Lake Erie and the Erie Canal, and south through the Mississippi River system. The state thrived in the resulting commerce.

Not so Indiana. Its Mammoth Internal Improvement Bill of 1836 committed the state to invest millions in canals, roads, and railroads. It had to abandon the plan in the depression of 1839, but $9 million of its $13 million debt in 1841 can be traced directly to this spending.[8] Even then it continued the Wabash and Erie Canal, a 450-mile project costing $8 million, to replicate the connections that Ohio had made between Lake Erie and the Ohio River. The canal aided the development of northern Indiana, but it never came close to recovering its construction costs. The Illinois and Michigan Canal did somewhat better for Chicago, connecting that Lake Michigan port to the Mississippi via the Illinois River. But it took more than twenty years to complete and the real transportation advantages it offered were soon challenged by the railroads.[9]

In general, the canal craze of the 1830s produced more losers than winners. Canals usually exceeded their predicted costs, both of construction and maintenance. They were vulnerable to floods, and traffic moved through them with a speed inversely proportional to the number of locks. Most importantly, many, like the Illinois and Michigan Canal, soon found themselves competing with railroads. The country built five thousand miles of railroads in the 1840s, and twice that many the following decade.[10] There were surely successes other than the Erie and Ohio canals. The Delaware and Hudson, for example, connected the anthracite coal regions of northeastern Pennsylvania to the Hudson River. It paid dividends of 8 percent or better throughout the 1840s and by 1855 was reporting net profits at 18 percent on capital.[11] Even George Washington's old dream of a canal connecting Georgetown in the District of Columbia to Cumberland, Maryland, came to fruition in the Chesapeake and Ohio Canal, which remained in service into the twentieth century. But these were the exceptions to the general pattern of the canal age. The canals

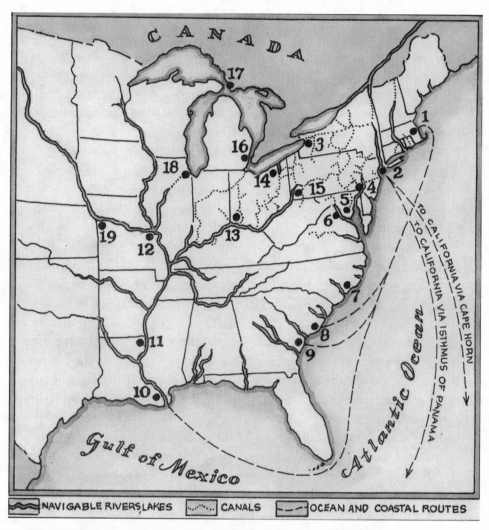

Rivers and canals connected many of the major cities in the eastern half of the United States in the first half of the nineteenth century. 1: Boston, 2: New York City, 3: Buffalo, 4: Philadelphia, 5: Baltimore, 6: Washington, D.C., 7: Wilmington, NC, 8: Charleston, 9: Savannah, 10: New Orleans, 11: Vicksburg, 12: St. Louis, 13: Cincinnati, 14: Cleveland, 15: Pittsburgh, 16: Detroit, 17: Sault Ste. Marie, 18: Chicago, 19: Independence.

contributed to the development of the antebellum United States, but seldom did they recover their costs.

The real impact of the canals is best measured not in their return on investment but rather in their transformation of the American economy. By reducing transportation costs, canals opened up new areas in the West to market forces. Steamboats and canals actually lowered transfer costs in their time more than the railroads would in subsequent decades.[12] Investments in towns, warehouses, and housing followed the waterways. Labor was drawn both from ports of immigration in the East and from subsistence farms in the West. Market orientation replaced pioneer self-sufficiency.[13]

At first, the canals served mostly local and regional interests. In their first decades of operation, both the Erie and Main Line canals, for example, brought produce from the western part of their respective states to the East Coast. In time, however, they shifted the entire pattern of trade within the United States. The old triangulation of 1789–1812 had bound the South and West together. In general, foodstuffs from the West, much of it coming down the Mississippi River, had allowed the South to specialize in its most lucrative crop, plantation cotton. The South exported its cotton to Britain or to the emerging textile mills of the Northeast. Imports to both the South and the West came primarily from the North, though the West had less surplus wealth and greater transportation costs to overcome, whether imports came up the Mississippi or over the Appalachians.

But the canals of the 1820s and 1830s reoriented the West to markets in the East. Extractive products—minerals and foodstuffs—could move to eastern markets more quickly and economically, and the income could buy more finished products for the prosperous farms and emerging towns and cities. The commercial relationship between North and South remained the same, but the West loosened its ties to the South and grew synapses with the North—in commerce, capital, and politics. As cotton grew to be king, the South dominated the influx of wealth that drove the American economy, but it simultaneously became more isolated commercially and politically from its regional counterparts in the North and West.

The most immediate loser was New Orleans. By 1840 it had become the fifth largest port in America, but it did not continue growth toward John's Fitch's prophecy of its being number one. By 1845 half the produce of the West was going down the Mississippi, but half was going directly east.[14] In 1855 traffic on the Erie Canal was estimated to be worth $204 million, while receipts on downriver traffic at New Orleans in 1860 amounted to $185 million.[15] Much of the downriver traffic on the Mississippi was being siphoned off to southern markets, but much of the volume through New Orleans was southern cotton. In 1819–1820, western products accounted for 58 percent of the value of receipts at New Orleans; by 1849–1850 they made up only 51 percent. By 1852, even before the full impact of the railroad was felt, shipments to New Orleans of almost all products from the Ohio valley had begun to decline. By 1860, concludes the historian George Taylor, "the canals and railroads had almost completely substituted direct trade across the Appalachians for the old indirect route via New Orleans and the sea."[16]

The big winner—in addition to the Great Lakes and Midwest regions—was New York City. The Erie Canal secured that metropolis's hold on the title of the country's largest city and largest trading center. Across its docks passed the immigrants who would take the inland waterways west and swell the growing number of cities stimulated by canals. Buffalo, Cleveland, Toledo, Cincinnati, Milwaukee, and Chicago grew up at nodes in the inland water transportation network, opening up the Great Lakes and increasing the incentives to connect them by still more canals. Even before the railroad cemented the pattern, the Erie Canal established New York City as America's great entrepot and its primary link with the overseas world.

But the canal craze was short-lived. It had run its course by the end of the 1830s. No new construction was undertaken after 1840.[17] The depression following the economic crisis of 1839 explains part of the downturn, but those hard economic times only served to illuminate the failure of most canals to recover their capital costs. On the surface it appears that the railroads hastened the demise of the canal, but the railroad boom did not really come until the 1850s. It simply reinforced patterns that were already clear by 1840.[18] Passengers and high-value cargo would gravitate to the fastest means of transportation, even at greater cost. Railroads cost more per mile to build and operate, but trains moved much faster than canal traffic. Poor migrants headed west and bulk cargo headed east would continue to use the canals; other traffic would shift to railroads, which often followed the canal routes already carved across the landscape.

Canals in particular, and inland waterways in general, came to specialize in bulk cargo. Between 1823 and 1848, for example, 95 percent of the
lead shipped east from Missouri passed through New Orleans.[19] The
canal connecting Lake Superior and Lake Michigan at Sault Ste. Marie,
constructed in 1853–1865, went on to be the busiest in the world, carrying ore and grain from the northern- and westernmost Great Lake to
points east.[20] The Welland Canal, connecting Lakes Ontario and Erie,
opened in 1829.

For all that river and canal traffic opened up the West to market forces,
the coastal trade remained the most voluminous. The coasting trade in
1852 more than doubled that on canals. It was five times the amount of
commerce on lakes and rivers in the previous year. An 1853 estimate of
domestic commerce placed the coasting trade at larger in volume and
value than canal and railway commerce combined. An inland corridor
down the East Coast, envisioned by Fulton and sketched out in Albert
Gallatin's plan for internal improvements in 1808, came into being, providing sheltered passage from New London, Connecticut, to Wilmington, North Carolina. But the volume of traffic it attracted never rivaled
the coastwise shipping that had been following the oceanic route from
port to port since colonial times.[21] It did, however, make its own modest
contribution to the great sea change in American shipping that took place
in the early republic.

Beginning in 1820 America traded with itself more than it traded with
the rest of the world. In 1830 world trade again exceeded domestic, but
thereafter, with the two exceptions of the world wars of the twentieth century, the United States traded with itself more than others. In the decade
1841 to 1850 the annual per capita value of American exports fell from
$22.83 to $11.27. The real gross domestic product was growing at about
1.3 percent per annum, and real per capita GDP in 1840 was probably 60
percent higher than at the turn of the century.[22] But Americans sold to
each other more and to foreigners less. In his report for 1847–1848
Secretary of the Treasury R. J. Walker estimated that "the value of our
products exceeds three thousand millions of dollars. . . . Of this
$3,000,000,000 only about $150,000,000 are exported abroad, leaving
$2,850,000,000 at home, of which at least $500,000,000 are annually
interchanged between the several states of the Union." In other words,
one-sixth of U.S. gross domestic product was circulating at home in interstate commerce while only 5 percent of it went overseas. Another estimate

in 1851–1852 put the value of internal commerce at $1.46 billion; $157 million moved on the Great Lakes, $170 million on rivers, $594 million, on canals, and $540 million on railroads.[23] As the historian Gordon S. Wood has remarked, taking a line from the nineteenth-century author Fanny Wright, Americans in this period found "a world within themselves."[24]

America was going to develop more like Germany than Britain. International trade would never be as great a percentage of total trade in the United States as it was in its mother country. In 1820 the nation had 1 percent of the world's population and 1.8 percent of its gross domestic product. It exported about 2 percent of GDP, compared with a world average of 1 percent. In other words, the United States in 1820 was already a relatively wealthy nation per capita, exporting about twice as much of its produce as the average. In 1870 it had 3.2 percent of the world's population and 8.9 percent of its GDP. It was growing quickly in size and even more quickly in wealth, both absolute and per capita. But in 1870 it exported only 2.5 percent of its GDP, while the rest of the world exported 5 percent. International trade had multiplied five times in that half century, but U.S. foreign trade as a percent of GDP had increased only 25 percent.[25] The explanation for this apparent anomaly is that Americans were trading with the richest market in the world— themselves. In a remarkable and fleeting historical conjunction, the West provided the foodstuffs and the South provided the cash crop that supported the industrialization of the North and the development of the American system of manufacture.[26] These three sections drove each other toward economic development and interdependence and political rupture.

17

RUSHING TO SAN FRANCISCO

BEFORE THAT RUPTURE CAME, THE ADMINISTRATION OF JAMES K. Polk (1845–1849) witnessed the greatest accretion of territory ever experienced by the United States, including all of what came to be known as the West Coast. The annexation of the Republic of Texas in 1845, the settlement of the Oregon Territory boundary dispute with Britain in 1846, and the Mexican Cession at the end of the Mexican War added more than 1.2 million square miles to the United States.[1] Polk's successor added the modest 29,670 square miles of the Gadsden Purchase, essentially completing the boundaries of the contiguous forty-eight United States. These acquisitions gave the nation more than 2,000 miles of coastline on the Pacific Ocean and added 367 miles of Texas coastline on the Gulf of Mexico. To Americans at the time, this consummation of their dominion from sea to sea appeared to be nothing more or less than their "manifest destiny."

Like many Americans, Polk learned about California from Richard Henry Dana's *Two Years before the Mast* (1840). In addition to educating his countrymen about the shipboard life he had experienced sailing from Boston to San Francisco, Dana also told of the surprising destination he encountered at the end of his five-month voyage around Cape Horn:

> a country embracing four or five hundred miles of sea-coast, with several good harbors; with fine forests in the north; the waters filled

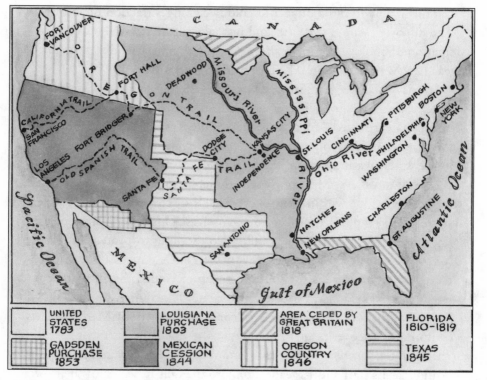

In the years when James K. Polk was president (1845–1849), the United States added more territory than it had with the Louisiana Purchase. The great swath of land would offer multiple paths to the West Coast when the California gold rush began in earnest in 1849.

with fish, and the plains covered with thousands of herds of cattle; blessed with a climate than which there can be no better in the world; free from all manner of diseases, whether epidemic or endemic; and with a soil in which corn yields from seventy to eighty fold. In the hands of an enterprising people, what a country this might be![2]

Americans, Native Americans, and Mexicans sparsely populated this vast new territory. Dana's enticing description notwithstanding, it would likely have filled up but slowly with more Americans had it not been for a chance discovery on January 24, 1848. Just nine days before the signing of the Treaty of Guadalupe Hidalgo, ending the Mexican War, James Marshall was inspecting a sawmill he had just built for Johann Sutter on the South Fork of the American River in the Sacramento valley of

California. He found a nugget of gold, weighing a fraction of an ounce. The discovery would turn the land just taken from Mexico into the destination of choice for Americans on the make, and it would turn America's new West Coast into a hub of maritime activity.

In view of the "gold rush" that followed this seminal discovery in America's new territory, it is remarkable how slowly the news spread. California had attracted American settlers while it was still a Mexican territory, and more than once those settlers had reported gold for the taking in the waters washing out of the Sierra Nevada into the Sacramento and San Joaquin valleys. Most of these early reports failed to pan out, as the saying went. But within days of Marshall's discovery, his own workers started drifting off to prospect for themselves. This time, instead of drying up, the reports of success multiplied. Seeking to protect his claim, Marshall soon negotiated a lease with the Native Americans occupying the territory around his site, but the governor voided the entrepreneur's attempt to stake a claim to the territory newly acquired by the United States. For the time being, it was first come, first served. By March 1, news of multiple discoveries in the mountains reached the pages of the *San Francisco Californian*. Within three months, the *Californian* ceased publication, as its staff and its readers took to the hills in search of their own fortunes. By then, news of the discovery had found its way to Monterey, the territorial capital. But not until the end of 1848 did it finally have an impact on the East Coast. At the end of August 1848, Lieutenant Lucien Loeser departed Monterey bound for Washington bearing a report on the gold discovery from Colonel Richard Mason (drafted by his adjutant, William Tecumseh Sherman), part of the army of occupation of California. With the report Mason sent 230 ounces of gold. Loeser used four relay ships, transfering in Peru, Panama, and Jamaica, just to get to New Orleans. From there he could finally send word ahead by telegraph. (Samuel Morse's new invention did not yet stretch to the West Coast.) Relying on Loeser's telegram and other official reports, President Polk reported the California gold discovery to Congress on December 5, 1848, more than eleven months after the event. Over long distances, people and most news still traveled at the speed of the best ship available.

More than Polk's message to Congress, the 230 ounces of gold that Loeser finally delivered to Washington in late November or early December ignited "gold fever" in the East.[3] By the end of the year, the rush was on. Fortune hunters all over the eastern United States scrambled to book the fastest transport to the West Coast. They were racing not only each other but also South Americans, Australians, Chinese, and other inhabitants of the Pacific rim. Many of these foreign gold rushers had learned of the discovery before the Americans, because they were closer by ship to the West Coast than Americans on the East Coast. That fact shaped the calculation of eastern Americans plotting their journey west. In spite of fantastic broadsides and newspaper advertisements promising steam-powered balloons that could fly the prospectors to California, only three routes and modes of transport warranted much confidence. All three, even the overland route, entailed shipping.

The most economical route followed one of the multiple trails from the Mississippi River valley, across the Great Plains, over the Rocky Mountains, through the Great Basin, and up again over the Sierra Nevada for the descent into California. Of course, most forty-niners took the Oregon/California Trail directly to the gold fields of northern California, but some took the Santa Fe Trail to Los Angeles, in hopes of catching a ship north to San Francisco. Some small number actually set out from east of the Mississippi River, but most departed from St. Louis or ports on the Missouri or Arkansas rivers. Most reached those points of departure by boat. Thomas Swain, for example, left his native Buffalo, New York, in mid-April 1849, traversing Lakes Erie, Huron, and Michigan by steamer. From Chicago he traveled south through the Illinois Canal, the Illinois River, and the Mississippi to St. Louis. There he boarded yet another steamer to travel up the Missouri River to Independence, arriving on May 2. This circuitous but reasonably comfortable journey carried him the 987 miles (as the crow flies) from Buffalo to Independence in slightly more than two weeks.[4] The arduous and dangerous trek to the Sacramento River over the California Trail would cover 1,449 miles but take 190 days, more than six months, creeping west at two miles per hour.[5] Travelers by such overland routes had to pay hundreds of dollars to outfit themselves for the journey, but they could recover much of their investment by selling their wagons and draft animals when they arrived in California.

Those who could afford the fastest available transportation booked one of the clipper ships racing from New York to San Francisco. Passage could cost as much as $400 on the speediest and most prestigious ships, but for that price one might reach San Francisco in less than four months. Many captains, including the legendary Robert "Bully" Waterman, had made their reputations and their fortunes pressing the crews of clipper ships to

SS *Sea Witch*. The fastest (and most expensive) route to California in 1849 was by clipper ship around Cape Horn. Donald McKay's *Sea Witch* made the trip in less than a hundred days three times in her career, though not until the 1850s, when the gold rush and the heyday of the clippers were both on the wane.

make record runs to San Francisco and other ports around the world. Waterman once sailed Donald McKay's famous *Sea Witch* from China to New York in seventy-five days at speeds as high as sixteen knots.[6]

When Nathaniel and George Griswold commissioned the famed New York shipbuilder William Webb to build the super-clipper *Challenge* for the California trade in 1848, even before the gold rush, they lured Bully Waterman from retirement with the promise of $10,000 for a ninety-day passage. Adverse weather and a novice crew denied Waterman his bonus; it took 108 days in spite of the brutalities that Bully inflicted on his hapless seamen.[7] Not until the 1850s would the *Sea Witch* and other clippers make the passage in less than a hundred days; the *Sea Witch* accomplished that feat three times in her illustrious career.[8] Those who could not afford the fare on a clipper ship might book passage on a more modest and roomy vessel. But the cheaper the fare, the slower the passage. Conventional vessels sailing directly took five to eight months to reach California, longer in many cases than the overland route.

No matter the vessel, the ocean passage from New York to San Francisco traversed thirteen thousand to sixteen thousand miles. To escape the Gulf Stream and prevailing winds along the East Coast, these sailing ships would stand out far into the Atlantic, sometimes sighting the African Coast or the Azores before heading to a South American port such as Rio de Janeiro for resupply. Then all would brave the treacherous Cape Horn. The most daring captains, such as Bully Waterman, opted for the risky shortcut through the Straits of Magellan. Working their way up the west coast of South America, most ships would then tack out into the Pacific as far west as the Hawaiian Islands before laying for San Francisco.[9] As in the Atlantic, this detour actually sped the trip by sparing the vessel the adverse coastal tides and winds on the U.S. West Coast. In the Southern Hemisphere, those prevailing tides and winds favored the route from east to west. Matthew Fontaine Maury, the famous "pathfinder of the seas" (of whom more later), published his *Wind and Current Charts* and *Sailing Directions* just in time to help the forty-niners sail west, though not all captains were well enough informed to take advantage of the 13,328-mile route that he recommended.[10]

Yet a third option for passage to California materialized just in time to serve the forty-niners. British oceangoing steamships had pioneered passage across the Isthmus of Panama in the 1840s to service their diplomatic and commercial interests on the west coast of South America. One fleet of vessels carried passengers, cargo, and mail across the Atlantic and Caribbean, and another fleet picked them up on the Pacific shore after they had crossed the Isthmus of Panama by inland water routes and overland packing. When the United States came into possession of California and the other western territories acquired during the Polk administration, it quickly appreciated the need for packet messenger service to its new West Coast. The Mail Act of 1848 authorized contracts to support packet mail service for both naval and civilian activities on the Pacific. The big winner was James Aspinwall, a principal partner in New York's largest import-export firm.[11] With government contract in hand and partners in line, he formed the Pacific Mail Steamship Company (PMSS) and ordered three new vessels (*California, Panama, Oregon*), two of them to be built by William Webb. The *California* was ready first. It departed New York on October 6, 1848, to round the cape and take up its duties in Panama City on the west coast of the isthmian route pioneered by the British. The *California* would become the first steam vessel to enter San

SS *California*. Before the California gold rush ended, oceangoing steamships offered a faster route to the West Coast than most clipper ships. Sailing through the Golden Gate in February 1849, the *California* became the first steamship to reach San Francisco. For want of coal, the vessel became marooned there, while her crew deserted for the gold fields.

Francisco Bay following the discovery of gold. Meanwhile, Aspinwall also patched together steamship service from the East and Gulf coasts to the Caribbean side of the isthmus and passage across the isthmus itself, both for mail and for any passengers who had the fortitude, the courage, and the $200–$500 fare.[12]

Jessie Frémont, the wife of the California adventurer and explorer John Frémont and daughter of Senator Thomas Hart Benton, became one of the first Americans to take advantage of this new route to the West. Seeking to join her husband, who had made an ill-advised and disastrous overland passage in the winter of 1848–1849, Jessie boarded the PMSC ship *Crescent City* in New York on March 15, 1849, bound for Chagres, the Atlantic port of the isthmian route. Following a three-day, fifty-mile passage by small boat up the Chagres River, Jessie and her daughter debarked at Gorgona, where they transferred to mules for the twenty-one-mile trek to Panama City. There they encountered the other travelers who had survived Chagres fever and the other hazards of the isthmian passage to get in line for a ship to San Francisco. The Frémont name and the Benton connection moved Jessie and her daughter to the head of the line for a berth on the PMSS's *Panama*. After a stop in San Diego, they reached San Francisco on June 4, 1849, just eighty-one days after leaving New York.[13] Not even the fastest clipper ship could have delivered them sooner. Indeed, the gold rush would prove to be the last hurrah of the clipper. Sailing vessels would ply the routes between the East and West coasts of the United States into the twentieth century, but never again would they be the fastest way to carry passengers or high-value cargo. The transcontinental railroad completed after the Civil War only sealed the fate of the clipper, which had already been determined by the arrival of steamship.

By late 1849 travelers rushing to the gold fields across the Isthmus of Panama encountered passengers and cargo returning east.[14] Many of the passengers were early rushers who had failed to discover the riches that had lured them. But traveling with them in some cases was gold, in enormous quantities, a cargo so precious that it warranted the fastest transportation available. The historian John Haskell Kemble has calculated that 335 passengers traveled from New York to San Francisco via the Panama route in 1848, meeting no returnees. In 1849, 4,624 followed that route west, encountering 1,629 headed home. In 1850, 11,229 sailed toward their dreams via Panama; 7,770 returned, some with gold and some with disillusionment. In 1849, more than $4 million in gold crossed the isthmus headed east; the following year that number jumped to $26.6 million.[15] In all, California's hills disgorged more that $600 million in the precious metal;[16] most of that went east by ship, most by the isthmian route.

By 1852 travelers favoring the speed of the isthmian route could choose a second option. The cunning and indefatigable "Commodore" Cornelius Vanderbilt led a team of investors developing a second trans-isthmian passage, this one across Nicaragua. Having made his first fortune challenging Robert Fulton's monopoly of steam navigation in New York harbor, and having sold off his maritime empire to invest in railroads, Vanderbilt now sought to experiment with intermodal transportation. As a principal stockholder of the American Atlantic and Pacific Ship Canal Company, he secured an arrangement with the government of Nicaragua to cross the isthmus via the San Juan River and Lake Nicaragua, with a small overland leg of eighteen miles. Though the total distance of this route was more than three times longer than the Panama route, the overland portage was shorter. Furthermore, the Nicaraguan route cut 374 miles (7 percent) off the New York–San Francisco distance of 5,245 miles. Vanderbilt's company, which was seeking to wrest the mail contract from the Pacific Mail Steamship Company, announced the initiation of service in 1852, though it was not until the following year that it could carry passengers across the isthmus. Thus began a fare war with the PMSS, and with other contenders who entered the fray, that lasted until 1860, when Vanderbilt accepted cooptation by the PMSS, conceding that firm's dominance of the isthmian route.[17] Ironically, a short transcontinental railroad connecting the Atlantic and Pacific water routes across Panama had helped to seal the victory for the PMSS. After the Civil War, transcontinental railroads across the United States would cut into the mail and passenger service across the isthmus and raise the premium on an isthmian canal.

Meanwhile, ships piled up in San Francisco harbor in the first frantic years of the gold rush. In the year leading up to April 1, 1848, only four cargo vessels arrived at San Francisco from the East Coast. In 1849, 777 vessels sailed from the East Coast for the same destination.[18] The crews of these ships promptly abandoned most of them on arrival, heading to the hills in search of gold, and officers who tried to hold them faced violence and even death from sailors besotted with gold fever. The population of San Francisco rose from 870 in 1849 to 35,000 in 1850.[19] Even the *California*, the pride of the PMSS and the first steam vessel to enter San Francisco harbor, lost its crew to the gold fields when there proved to be no stocks of coal on hand to refill its bunkers.[20] In October 1849, 348 ships were counted among the "forest of masts" sighted and photographed in Yerba Buena Cove, 635 in April 1850.[21]

This photo captures some of the hundreds of vessels that were abandoned in Yerba Buena Cove, off San Francisco, while their crews fled to the gold fields. While some resumed sailing when the gold fever subsided, many ships never escaped the cove, where they were consumed by fire or finally plowed under the expanding waterfront.

At its peak, the influx delivered 1,147 vessels in 1852, the first year when clearances began to match arrivals.[22] The historian H. W. Brands likens San Francisco harbor to a maritime black hole, sucking in ships and allowing none to escape.[23] Only when failed prospectors straggled back out of the hills in 1852 and 1853 did some of the abandoned ships finally take sail again. Others were converted to floating (or beached) hotels and warehouses, never to return to sea.

As ships and people crowded into San Francisco, all the perils and promises of a boom city presented themselves.[24] Fire was the greatest danger. Six blazes swept the city between Christmas Eve 1849 and the most disastrous fire on May 3, 1851.[25] Each conflagration escalated the reckless inflation that beset San Francisco's economy, leading many enterprising forty-niners to realize that wealth often came sooner and easier to those who provisioned and serviced the miners than to the miners themselves. The whaling ship *Niantic* illustrates the pattern. When Captain Henry Cleaveland learned of the discovery of gold during a port visit at Paita, Peru, he set sail for Panama. There, in May 1849, he embarked 249 passengers, people variously describing themselves as bonnet manufacturer, barber, lawyer, dentist, jeweler, coppersmith, gentleman, minister of the gospel, physician, engineer, silversmith, saddler, school master, tinner, bootmaker, moulder, piano maker (three of them!), "counter jumper," editor, druggist, hatter, grocer, bookseller, student, and more—all bound for the gold fields.[26] This cross section of America paid $150 to $250 apiece for the sixty-two-day passage to San Francisco, arriving on July 5. Hauled ashore to be used as a storeship, the *Niantic* earned her owners monthly rents of $20,000 before being destroyed in the fire of May 3, 1851.[27]

Demand also sparked the birth of a local shipping industry. Small, shallow-draft schooners were designed and built locally to carry prospectors up the Sacramento and San Joaquin rivers and their tributaries to the gold fields. Coastal schooners were designed and built to carry lumber and other supplies from newly acquired coastal ports such as Seattle, Washington, and Portland, Oregon. Each time San Francisco burned, the demand for lumber spiked, both to rebuild the city and to build the coasting vessels that would carry the lumber and other supplies south. It was not long before enterprising shippers connected the old transpacific trade with China and other parts of Asia to the booming metropolis that was springing up in California. As gold fever subsided in the years leading up to the Civil War, many maritime entrepreneurs turned their gaze across the Pacific Ocean.

18

STEAM, SPEED, SCHEDULE: A BUSINESS MODEL FOR THE GOLDEN AGE

WHILE AMERICAN SHIPPING EVOLVED IN THE 1840S TO connect the country's two coasts, another segment of the shipping industry made an equally challenging bid for a share of the North Atlantic trade. In the 1840s, steam propulsion began to seriously compete with sail on the high seas. It held out the prospect of liner service between the United States and Europe, the unfulfilled dream of an earlier generation that had provided sailing packet service on the North Atlantic.

Following the War of 1812, American shippers sought to regain the share of oceanic traffic that they had enjoyed during the wars of the French Revolution and Napoleon. Shipowners such as the Derbys of Salem, many of them grown wealthy in privateering during the war, continued to prosper afterward, in part because the cost advantage bestowed by the superiority of American shipbuilding helped them compete for international cargoes. In the old fashion, they outfitted vessels, identified cargoes, and conducted their own trading in foreign ports. From the Caribbean to Asia and the Mediterranean, they sailed profitably and relatively securely under the umbrella of the Pax Britannica.

Ironically, they had more trouble trading with Europe, not because of the shipping competition but because of a mismatch in cargoes. The growth of the American population and economy spurred a ready market for European manufactured and luxury goods, but the United States at first had insufficient exports of interest to European markets. Tobacco and rice had some appeal in Europe, and cotton was beginning its climb to export preeminence. But American imports outran European demand for these commodities, creating an imbalance in transatlantic cargoes. The asymmetry was compounded by the volume of passenger traffic headed to America. The nation experienced a wave of European immigration that would swell to flood proportions in the 1840s and later in the nineteenth century.

American ships held an advantage in the cargo traffic, because most of the European imports were sought in northern ports, while most of the exports came from southern ports. The cabotage law of 1817 ensured that only American vessels could take advantage of the three-port voyage that picked up cotton or tobacco in a southern port such as Charleston, sailed to New York to add fast freight and passengers, and then sailed for Liverpool. The return voyage carried passengers and cargo to New York and then continued south with a combination of European and northern goods and passengers. For these reasons, among others, 90 percent of American overseas trade sailed in American vessels by 1838.[1]

Early on, in 1817, four New York textile merchants, Quakers all, introduced a far-reaching innovation that would dominate North Atlantic shipping for twenty years. They proposed to provide regular, scheduled service to Liverpool. Two facts of shipping had always argued against such a service. First, vagaries of wind made sailing times unpredictable. Even the best skipper could sail only as quickly as the wind would allow. Second, promising to depart on schedule burdened the shipowner with the risk of sailing empty, or only partially full. The Salem model had called upon the supercargo to fill the hold and thus maximize the return on operating costs. To make scheduled lines work, the New York Quakers would have to take business from other shippers.[2]

Their hook was speed; their target the packets of mail that crossed the Atlantic in the quixotic rhythms of tramp shipping. By promising to depart on schedule and arrive at their destination quickly, they hoped to capture the mail trade and additionally draw in other commerce, passengers, and fast freight willing to pay a premium for relatively speedy passage. Their instrument was the packet ship, an evolving American design greatly refined during the War of 1812. Originally associated with

Baltimore and put into service in the coastal trade, the packet ship sacrificed carrying capacity for speed. Since the medieval cog, blunt of bow and bulbous of hull, commercial Atlantic sailing vessels had favored carrying capacity and seaworthiness over aesthetics and speed. The Baltimore clipper trimmed that traditional shape by narrowing the bows and beam, raking the gunnels, flattening the keel, and adding sail.[3] Refinements cascaded through the American shipbuilding industry during the War of 1812, when privateers bid up ships that could outrun British commercial vessels and warships. By the time the New York Quakers undertook to place such ships on the transatlantic trade, the Baltimore packet ship was well on its way to becoming the legendary American clipper.

The *Courier*, the first of four ships inaugurating service on the Old Line, departed New York on January 5, 1818. It carried seven passengers, a small mail packet, and a cargo of apples, flour, ashes, and cotton. The distinctive black ball on its sails soon led to the company's better-known appellation, Black Ball Line. Averaging twenty-two to twenty-five days for

The Black Ball packet *Columbia* was designed by William H. Webb to provide scheduled service between New York and Europe. The distinctive black ball, from which the company derived its unofficial name, appears on the fore lower topsail.

an easterly passage, and thirty-three to forty-eight days coming back, the Black Ball ships soon began to draw passengers and cargo from other lines.[4] Offering twelve round trips annually, the line began to fill its ships, launching a sixty-year run of sailing on schedule.

For twenty years or more American packets dominated the North Atlantic routes between Europe and North America. America's natural advantages in forest products, its experience in shipbuilding and design, its cabotage laws, and its national infatuation with speed all contributed. The natural competitor, steam, was evolving rapidly on inland and coastal waters, but the awkward paddle wheels and the bulky and inefficient engines with their prodigious appetites for fuel were not well suited to oceanic voyages. In 1819 the Savannah Steamship Company commissioned the *Savannah*, a hybrid steam-sailing vessel that succeeded in

A Model of SS *Savannah* (1819). Originally designed as a sailing packet, the *Savannah* was converted to a combination steam/sail vessel. It was the first steamship to cross the Atlantic, but the technology of oceanic steam navigation was insufficiently mature to yield a commercial success.

crossing the Atlantic, mostly under sail, but never won commercial acceptance. The experiment appeared to have deterred others for almost two decades.

Finally, the British, not the Americans, took the next initiative in North Atlantic shipping. The British admiralty, the agent for overseas postal service, called for bids in 1838 to provide steamship mail service to North America. Among the respondents was Samuel Cunard, a merchant shipowner from Halifax, Nova Scotia, who had failed in an 1831 attempt to provide steamship service between Canada and Britain.[5]

Born in 1787, four years after his Loyalist parents emigrated from the newly independent United States, Cunard apprenticed in the shipping industry across the Gulf of Maine in Boston. Returning home to join his father's business, he soon displayed the commercial acumen that was to make his name synonymous with Atlantic passenger service. Arriving in London to press his case for the mail steamship subsidy, he teamed with John Napier, a shipbuilder of stature to rival his own. Their partnership won the mail contract for Cunard's British and North American Royal Mail Steam Packet Company. For a subsidy of £60,000 a year for seven years, Cunard's line promised to provide steamship service twice a month from Liverpool to Halifax and Halifax to Boston. Each ship was to have 400 horsepower, 200 feet of length, and 1,120 tons displacement, characteristics that made them useful for military service on demand.[6]

"I want a plain and comfortable boat," Cunard told Napier, "but not the least unnecessary expense for show."[7] This philosophy governed his early decades in the North Atlantic trade, giving way only later to the opulent luxury that he adopted from the American competitors he vanquished. The other pillar of his business style, a preference for safety and reliability over speed and panache, marked his entire career in shipping. Cunard played tortoise to American hares. He was a businessman, not an adventurer or innovator. He watched more daring competitors come and go.

Service began when the *Britannia* left Liverpool four days late, on July 4, 1840. The citizens of Boston, expecting the vessel on July 14, grew anxious when she failed to appear. The city had a lot riding on Cunard's venture. Having lost its maritime preeminence to New York, the once great colonial port had offered free docks and tax exemptions to become Cunard's western terminus, and the eventual appearance of the *Britannia* late on the night of July 18 occasioned great relief and genuine celebration. The transit time of fourteen and a half days cut two-thirds of the time off the passage of the most recent sailing packet to arrive from Britain. If the American sailing packets had made speed the desideratum of oceanic shipping, Cunard's steamship had just trumped their hold on the market. Boston's dignitaries turned out en masse for the ensuing "Cunard Festival" to toast their Halifax benefactor and his "floating palace." All concerned had reason to hope that this marked the beginning of a new age in Atlantic shipping.[8]

Over the next seven years, the Cunard Line set the standard for reliable, safe, comfortable passage between Europe and America. But it was rough going for a while. Cunard experienced early problems with cash flow as he tried to get his four vessels into service and attract enough business to cover capital costs and expenses. The line ran at a loss of £15,355 in its first nine months, prompting Cunard to ask that his subsidy be doubled. The government raised his subsidy to £80,000, not the £120,000 he requested, not enough to save him from his creditors. In the spring of 1842 he had to sneak aboard one of his own vessels to escape creditors on the docks in Liverpool trying to serve him with a writ. He won an additional £10,000 subsidy in 1843, helping him achieve a hard-won solvency. The most serious competition came from the British and American Steam Navigation Company, the brainchild of the American expatriate Junius Smith. Begun in 1835, the company achieved some prominence in 1840 with the launching of SS *President*, the largest steamship afloat at 2,000 tons and twice the size of the Cunard ships. But on its second voyage in March 1841, the ship was lost with all 136 people aboard in a North Atlantic storm, victim apparently of the wooden hull failing at the keel under the weight of machinery in heavy seas. In their first eight years of operation, Cunard steamships suffered nine groundings and at least two collisions, but not a single passenger fatality. Even when the *Columbia* grounded and sank on the Devil's Limb, southwest of Halifax and a mile and a half offshore, all the passengers survived. In fact, the Cunard Line never lost a passenger in the nineteenth century, a record that contributed to its steadily growing popularity. As competition from the sailing packets dropped away, Cunard sailed into a monopoly that allowed him to raise rates to whatever the market would bear.

All along, Cunard knew that the Americans would eventually challenge him. "The Americans will be alive to every thing," he warned his partner in 1847.

I do not apprehend any serious injury from the French—their Ships were built for Men of war and will be strong and heavy and not fast. The American ships will be different. They will introduce all our improvements, together with their own. We shall also have national prejudices to contend with, so that every attention will be required to meet them.[9]

The expected challenge came in the form of Edward Knight Collins. A native of Cape Cod, just 378 miles across the Gulf of Maine from Halifax, Collins made his fortune running sailing packets to New Orleans and Liverpool. A victim of Cunard's success, he lobbied forcefully but in vain for a U.S. government subsidy to match the British. Unpersuaded in 1841, the U.S. government came around in 1845 after just eight months of Cunard Line operations, when Cunard monopolized speedy service between Europe and America. The first contract, to an unknown novice, had little impact beyond moving Cunard to build newer ships and extend his service to New York. In 1847 the U.S. government upped the ante, offering an annual $385,000 mail contract for the express purpose of challenging the Cunard Line. Collins won the contract.

With characteristic flare and extravagance, Collins set about building the fastest, most luxurious liners in the world. He raised $3 million in private capital to recreate in steam the "splendid extravagance" that had marked his aptly named Dramatic Line packet sailing vessels. Surpassing the contract requirements for 2,000-ton vessels, he built four ships of 2,800 tons driven by engines of 814 horsepower. In addition to design and operating innovations of the kind that Cunard had expected from the Americans, the Collins ships featured opulent interiors and furnishings, heated by steam and complemented by fine dining and services.

As the showdown approached between the staid and reliable Cunard vessels and the fast and opulent Collins ships, both magnates worried that one or both would be wrecked by additional competition. In 1849, before any Collins ship had sailed, the two companies struck a secret deal to set passenger and cargo rates and to split revenues, two-thirds to Cunard and one-third to Collins. Not yet a violation of either country's laws, this cartel nonetheless flew in the face of the war of words between the two shipowners. It especially confounded Collins's promises to "drive the Cunarders off the sea."[10] In practice, only trivial amounts of money changed hands, but the arrangement allowed both companies to sustain high fees. Shippers and passengers absorbed the cost of chicanery.[11]

The speedy and luxurious Collins vessels soon captured the bulk of the high-end transatlantic trade, displacing Cunard and restoring America to the commanding position it had enjoyed in the sailing packet era from 1820 to 1840. But Collins's vessels were also the most expensive in service, both to build and to operate. The wooden hulls were tortured by the powerful engines, requiring unplanned maintenance and repairs. The ships established transatlantic speed records in both directions, beating out the Cunard vessels by a full day in passage each way, but they ran an average loss of $17,000 per round trip, pushing the Collins enterprise toward the same bankruptcy that had threatened Cunard in his first years. Like Cunard, Collins returned to his government for increased subsidy, characteristically raising the rhetorical and political bar several notches. His supporters declared a "third war with England" and Collins sailed one of his ships up the Potomac River to treat more than two thousand

Edward Knight Collins built the *Arctic* (pictured here) and other luxurious transatlantic liners in the middle of the nineteenth century to challenge the dominant Cunard Line. Cunard never lost a passenger in the nineteenth century, but the *Arctic* went down in September 1854 with most of her passengers, including Collins's wife and two of his three daughters. The Collins Line folded two years later.

Washington dignitaries to enough free food and drink to induce passage of an $858,000 yearly subsidy, more than twice the original contract price. This provided some relief for the stressed company but not enough to offer a sustainable business model of transatlantic liner operation.

Compounding the company's woes, the *Arctic*, one of the company's fastest vessels, struck a French steamer on September 27, 1854, while pressing for New York at full speed of thirteen knots in a dense fog. When it became clear that the ship could not be saved, the crew abandoned the passengers to their fate and took to the boats. Only 23 of the 281 passengers survived, compared with 61 of the 153 crew members, including 4 of the top 5 officers. The company's reputation for reckless pursuit of speed was now alloyed with a shameful lack of integrity and courage. Criticism was muted by the sad fact that Collins lost his wife and two of his three daughters in the tragedy.

The insurance settlement from the *Arctic* helped the Collins Line through its financial crisis. Then business picked up during the Crimean War, when Cunard ships were called into government service in keeping with their subsidy contract. But when Collins's *Pacific* disappeared without a trace on a Liverpool–New York run early in 1856, with the loss of 186 persons, the company could not recover. Congress cut its subsidy and then withdrew it altogether, unwilling to underwrite what some saw as a luxury service for wealthy passengers. The ships were sold at auction for a fraction of their cost, the company folded, and Collins retired from shipping, never to recoup his fortune. Though other American companies would provide liner service in the North Atlantic after Collins, the demise of his company marked the last serious challenge to Cunard in the nineteenth century. As the historian Stephen Fox has put it, "the American national will in effect conceded the Atlantic Ocean to the British. The contest was over."[12] America had failed to find a business model to sustain this prestigious branch of maritime activity.

Nor did America play a major role in the other North Atlantic traffic that loomed large in the nation's history. The Cunard and Collins ships catered to wealthy passengers who could pay up to $120 for a one-way passage across the Atlantic. Their ships had little space for steerage passengers, those poor European émigrés looking for cheap passage to a better life in America. The sailing packets carried unconscionable numbers of these people cramped in poorly ventilated spaces below decks, blanketed in the stench of vomit and human excrement. The voyages dragged out for weeks; death from dysentery or cholera was not unusual. The U.S. government finally intervened in 1819 with legislation to limit overcrowding. But enforcement was poor and conditions remained abominable.

Enoch Train of Boston provided some relief when he inaugurated inexpensive sailing packet service between Boston and Liverpool in 1844, just two years before the Irish potato famine first appeared. As the flow of immigrants swelled, Train's ships offered comparatively clean and comfortable passage to the United States for about $15, an eighth of the cabin fares aboard Cunard and Collins liners.[13]

The Inman and International Steamship Company would finally offer more relief, though not until the 1850s. William Inman saw a niche in the liner market when he became aware of the efficiency and reliability of screw propulsion compared with the side paddle wheels then dominating ocean liners. Building his ships at about two-thirds the cost of a Cunard vessel and fitting them with propellers, he offered service faster than the sailing packets and cheaper than the luxury liners. One of his partners, John Grubb Richardson, a Quaker, grieved for the Irish émigrés fleeing the potato famine and prevailed upon Inman to accept steerage passengers. The year after Irish emigration to the United States reached its peak of 219,000 in 1851, Inman Line inaugurated steerage passage for about $31, about one-quarter of the second-class fare on a Cunard or Collins ship. The conditions in steerage were less crowded and more sanitary than on other liners, and the passage took only about two weeks. Inman and Richardson did well by doing good.[14]

One other prominent figure also entered the North Atlantic liner trades. Cornelius Vanderbilt climaxed a remarkable career in shipping by challenging Cunard and Collins. He had begun his business career in 1810, at the age of sixteen, operating his own ferry between his native Staten Island and Manhattan. In 1818 he sold the several sailing vessels he had acquired to sign up as a steamboat captain for Thomas Gibbons (of *Gibbons v. Ogden* fame), who was already trying to break the Fulton-Livingston monopoly on steam ferry service in New York harbor. Vanderbilt launched his own steamboat service in 1829, growing wealthy in the coastal trade to Providence and Philadelphia. With the Accessory Steamship Company, he attempted to break into the trans-isthmian trade with California, before finally joining forces with the Pacific Mail Steamship Company and the United States Mail Steamship Company. The restless energy and ambition revealed in all these ventures naturally drew him to the most lucrative market of all, the North Atlantic liner trade.

Seizing upon the withdrawal of Cunard ships for service in the Crimean War, Vanderbilt announced in 1854 that he would inaugurate North Atlantic liner service in competition with the Collins Line, but at half the subsidy. The government offered no subsidy at all, but Vanderbilt bulled ahead without it, confident that his sound business practices could prevail over Collins's extravagance. Collins suffered the *Arctic* loss before Vanderbilt initiated service, but even in this environment, with his two major competitors hors de combat, Vanderbilt could not turn a profit. When Cunard returned its liners to North Atlantic service in 1856, he realized that he had misjudged the challenges of that most rewarding but demanding route. His modest intervention, just a few small ships, hastened the decline of the Collins Line without developing a viable American replacement. To recover his amour propre, he built and sailed a vessel to match his ego. The *Vanderbilt*, a liner of almost 5,000 tons and 355 feet in length, cost about $1 million.[15] It sailed for some years as the sole vessel of the Vanderbilt Line, a monument to the colossal conceit of its namesake and the failure of American business to find a sustainable, working business model for the North Atlantic. Cunard resumed its dominance of the North Atlantic, introducing the first all-metal, screw-propulsion steamship in 1860. When the Civil War broke out the following year, Vanderbilt offered his entire fleet, such as it was, to the federal government. *Vanderbilt*, the ship, served as a transport and then as a cruiser to help catch Confederate raiders. Vanderbilt, the man, withdrew from shipping, half a century after entering the field in which he earned the sobriquet "Commodore."[16]

Steamship liner service was at least possible on the North Atlantic, where vessels could make a crossing on one load of coal. But steamships could not compete in the full voyage around Cape Horn, nor yet in transpacific trade. On these longer routes coaling stations were required before regular service became practical. In 1859 the legendary British engineer Isambard Kingdom Brunel, having discovered that coal positioned at stations on the West African coast to support steamships sailing around the Cape of Good Hope would cost four times as much as at home, envisioned a great vessel that could carry enough for the whole trip. The resulting ship, the *Great Eastern*, was a commercial dud, useful only for laying the Atlantic cable. The clippers could not beat steamships on the North Atlantic route, but steamships could not yet compete with clippers over great distances.

Another realm of international shipping that experienced but little incursion from steamships before the Civil War was the notorious African slave trade. Initiated almost as soon as Europeans began their settlement of the Americas, it profited Americans and their colonial forebears from the time of the Massachusetts Bay Colony. Not only did it provide scarce labor for colonists from Maine to South Carolina and fuel the explosion of the cotton economy in the southern states of the new republic, it also stoked the economy of New England in the first half of the nineteenth century by returning enormous profits to those New England shipowners willing to transport their human cargo to ports all over the Americas. In three and a half centuries of African slave trade to the Americas, only 3.8 percent of the almost ten million Africans brought to the Americas came to the United States and its prior colonies, and less than 2.5 percent were borne by American ships.[17] And yet that small percentage of the Atlantic slave trade created some of the great commercial dynasties of early New England, such as the Browns and DeWolfs of Rhode Island. And it poured so much money into New England, especially Rhode Island, that it helped fund the region's textile industry, the foundation of America's industrial revolution. Furthermore, it sustained two triangular trades. The slave trade saw New England ships carry slaves from Africa to the Caribbean, whence molasses to New England, then rum to Africa. In an entirely different realm, the South of King Cotton, which the slave trade supported in the first half of the nineteenth century, sent cotton to the mills of New England, which shipped finished textiles to the western territories, while foodstuffs from those territories made their way back to the South, allowing southern planters to concentrate on their lucrative cash crop.[18] The slaves from Africa who continued to feed these systems of trade right up to the Civil War seldom traveled by steam vessel. By the time steamships began crossing the oceans, the slave trade had been largely—but not entirely—extinguished.

In their heyday from 1848 to 1857, the clippers made money for their investors, supported the boom in California, secured American markets in East Asia and elsewhere, and epitomized America's love affair with the wooden sailing ship. But when Samuel Cunard introduced his first all-metal, screw-propeller steamship on the North Atlantic in 1860, the future of shipping was clear. When the Civil War broke out, Cornelius

Vanderbilt transferred the ships from his Vanderbilt European Line to the Atlantic and Pacific Steamship Line to share the isthmian traffic with the Pacific Mail Steamship Company. By the time he got out of the shipping business altogether, he had already bought his first railroad, having joined Henry Shreve in envisioning the relative promise of that mode of transport.

On the eve of the Civil War, at the end of the transportation revolution, as Samuel Cunard ruled the North Atlantic liner business, several patterns were manifest. First, Americans had demonstrated a reckless infatuation with speed. Captains and engineers racing riverboats up and down the Mississippi tied down the safety valves on their boilers, producing higher pressure, more power, and often disastrous consequences. American clipper ships of all stripes, from the privateers of the War of 1812, to the coastal and oceanic packets of the 1820s and 1830s, to the legendary clippers of Donald McKay and his colleagues, sacrificed cargo capacity for speed. In some ways, this was simply a response to market demand; speed brought a premium. But in another way it became wrapped up in the North Atlantic's Blue Riband competition and in other unofficial speed records that often carried more prestige than profit. Cunard ships seldom held the Blue Riband, which went to the vessel that made the fastest North Atlantic crossing, but they won the commercial race. Alexis de Tocqueville might have had the likes of Samuel Cunard and Edward Collins in mind in 1835 when he wrote:

> The European navigator is prudent when venturing out to sea; he only does so when the weather is suitable; if any unexpected accident happens, he returns to port; at night he furls some of his sails; and when the whitening billows indicate the approach of land, he checks his course and takes an observation of the sun.
>
> The American, neglecting such precautions, braves these dangers; he sets sail while the storm is still rumbling by night as well as by day he spreads full sails to the wind; he repairs storm damage as he goes; and when at last he draws near the end of his voyage, he flies toward the coast as if he could already see the port.
>
> The American is often ship-wrecked, but no other sailor crosses the sea as fast.[19]

Edward Collins's *Arctic* went down running at full speed through a nighttime fog. It was only in his next observation that Tocqueville fell off the mark. He said of the American that, "doing what others do but in less time, he can do it at less expense." Not so on the North Atlantic. American shipping in this era captured the imagination, but it did not capture the market.

The American love affair with wood also retarded the development of America's merchant marine. While the American industrial revolution was under way in the 1850s, the country had not yet developed the iron and coal industries that would soon be demanded. Britain, because of its shortage of wood, opened up a substantial lead in iron-hulled steamships. The abundant supplies of wood in the United States disguised the urgency of this competition. The material demands of the Civil War and the trajectory of naval shipbuilding would accelerate the nation toward a competitive capability, but as late as the First World War the United States would still find itself arguing over the relative advantages of wood and metal ships, even of steam and sail vessels.

Perhaps most remarkable of all, oceanic shipping continued the relative decline that had begun in 1820. Even though the United States experienced an increase in oceanic shipping between the War of 1812 and the Civil War, even though it carried as much as 90 percent of its own trade, and even though it beat out the British in some markets at some times, still the volume of oceanic trade per capita was in decline by 1860. America was trading with itself more than with the rest of the world. Coastal traffic still carried the highest volume of all American shipping. And shipping on inland rivers, canals, and lakes continued to increase even when the railroad started to take a major share of domestic transportation in the 1850s. Speed remained the primary desideratum for transportation of passengers and fast freight. Ships became the conveyor of choice for bulk cargo. The oceans remained the one realm where ships could provide the speediest service, but the United States had not discovered a business model to make itself competitive in that arena. When the clipper ships went into decline after 1857, the golden age of American-flagged oceanic shipping was over. American investors and inventors would remain active in international shipping, but only fleetingly in the world wars would U.S. ships recapture the technological, commercial, and emotional pre-eminence of the clipper age.

19

MATTHEW FONTAINE MAURY AND THE GROWTH OF INFRASTRUCTURE

ANTEBELLUM AMERICA REALLY DID EXPERIENCE A GOLDEN AGE of shipping. But its shining icon, the clipper ship rushing to the gold fields of California, masked deeper transformations of the American maritime experience. Domestic shipping was displacing oceanic shipping in economic significance. Ocean-sailing vessels were losing out to steamships on the North Atlantic. And just as importantly, the United States was building a maritime infrastructure capable of supporting a virtually unlimited range of shipping activities. From a variety of sources appeared new charts and tables, shipyards, aids to navigation, harbor improvements, and countless other stimulants to more efficient navigation and safer shipping. The same forces that laid the groundwork for America's industrial revolution also wove a web of infrastructure to serve the shipping and shipbuilding industries.

In the storied seaport of Salem an improbable prodigy overcame adversity to produce the bible of American maritime navigation. Nathaniel Bowditch dropped out of school in 1783 to prop up his father's failing coopering business.[1] He proved a poor cooper but an exceptional autodidact, teaching himself languages, mathematics, and astronomy in his spare time, developing a local reputation and winning access to the holdings of the Salem Philosophical Library Company.

By the time he turned his hand to seamanship, he knew how to determine longitude at sea by lunar distance, a complex combination of observation and calculation that offered an alternative to the newly invented but prohibitively expensive marine chronometer of John Harrison. When young Bowditch sailed to Manila in 1796 as supercargo aboard Elias Derby's *Astrea*, he discovered for himself the errors of John Hamilton Moore's *The Practical Navigator*, the standard text of its day. He passed his time computing his own corrections, publishing a revision of Moore's book in 1799. As additional corrections accumulated in the ensuing years, he collected them in *The New American Practical Navigator* in 1802. An immediate hit with American seafarers, "Bowditch," as the book came to be called, was soon adopted by the U.S. Navy.

Bowditch produced nine more editions of his text before he died in 1838. His fame and talent won him a lucrative career in the marine insurance business, but he spent his spare time revising *The Practical Navigator* and translating and explaining Pierre-Simon LaPlace's *Mécanique Céleste*. He turned down faculty appointments at West Point, the University of Virginia, and Harvard, though he accepted from the last institution two honorary degrees and election as an overseer and member of the corporation. He was a member of, inter alia, the American Academy of Arts and Sciences, the Royal Society of London, the Royal Astronomical Society, and the Royal Academy of Berlin. His son Jonathan Ingersoll Bowditch oversaw twenty-five editions of his father's classic text between 1838 and 1867, and in 1868 the newly established U.S. Hydrographic Office bought the copyright and began government publication of "Bowditch" through more than seventy-five editions. By the time of the 2002 bicentennial edition, "Bowditch" editions were designated by the year of publication, not the serial number of the edition. In eulogy, the Salem Marine Society said in the year of his death that

> as long as ships shall sail, the needle point to the north, and the stars go through their wonted course in the heavens, the name of Dr. Bowditch will be revered as of one who helped his fellow-men in a time of need, who was and is a guide to them over the pathless ocean, and of one who forwarded the great interests of mankind.[2]

The transformation of America's ports, manifest in the decline of Bowditch's Salem and the rise of New Orleans, was mirrored by a transformation of dockyards in the first half of the nineteenth century. Two major trends marked the conversion. First, in this heyday of American shipbuilding, when brilliant designers such as Donald McKay and abundant resources of wood allowed America to challenge Britain's traditional dominance of international shipbuilding, American shipyards grew to meet the domestic and international demand. The nation built wooden steamships for its coastal and inland waters and oceanic vessels, such as the legendary clippers, in staggering numbers. The British ban on American-built vessels after the War of 1812 contributed to a modest output of 557 vessels and 51,394 tons in 1820. By 1855 these numbers had risen to 2,027 vessels totaling 583,450 tons.[3] The increasing size of these vessels, from an average of 93 tons in 1820 to 288 tons in 1850, meant that the small builders in shallow-water ports on the New England coast gave way to huge concerns in complex shipyards at the major harbors of Boston, Philadelphia, New York, and Norfolk. Portsmouth, New Hampshire, retained its position as a major naval shipyard, joined in the antebellum period by yards in Washington, D.C.; Norfolk, Virginia; Boston; New York; and Philadelphia.[4] But many small New England yards that had flourished in the colonial era withdrew from the high-end market.

This growth in the private sector was mirrored by the emergence of a new phenomenon in American maritime experience: naval shipyards as sites of design, construction, and repair. Beginning during the Quasi-War with France at the end of the eighteenth century, the new republic commissioned vessels built and maintained at its own facilities. The on-again, off-again naval policy of the first half of the nineteenth century meant that these yards pursued widely varying agendas, ranging from Jefferson's notorious gunboats in the early decades through Joshua Humphreys's unmatched frigates of the war with Britain. Though naval shipyards were modeled on commercial yards and purchased much of their material from commercial vendors, they nonetheless became instruments of a naval infrastructure that developed its own style and traditions. In 1842 the navy replaced its Board of Navy Commissioners, an administrative scheme inherited from the British, with five bureaus. The Bureau of Navy Yards and Docks—"Navy" was dropped from the title in 1862—took charge of the navy's eight existing shipyards and ran them until it was transformed into the Naval Facilities Engineering Command in 1966. During most of that time, naval architecture and business practices diverged significantly from commercial shipbuilding, though the federal government turned extensively to commercial shipyards during the Civil War.[5]

The decision of the United States to develop its own naval shipyards instead of relying on commercial facilities shaped American shipbuilding throughout the nineteenth century and contributed in its way to the eventual decline of the American maritime industry. The lack of cross-fertilization in the production and maintenance of commercial and naval vessels blocked a source of innovation and capital that the maritime industry dearly needed.

In other realms of shipping, government policy had a far more salutary effect. An attempt was made in 1843, in the administration of John Tyler, to bring under control of the central government the revenue cutter services that had served local customs collectors since the earliest days of the Republic. Though the experiment ended with the accession of the Whig Zachary Taylor, who succeeded the Democrat and Jacksonian James K. Polk, it would revive after the Civil War and lead to the creation of the Coast Guard.[6] Joseph Henry, the secretary of the Smithsonian Institution, was running a network of 150 stations that reported to him on local weather patterns. After the Civil War, this process would be taken over the by the U.S. Army Signal Corps and eventually the National Weather Service.[7] The government made ever-increasing appropriations for lighthouses and other aids to navigation, on the coasts and also on the Great Lakes, culminating in the appointment of a Lighthouse Board on October 9, 1852. In service until 1910, this arm of government oversaw the authorization, installation, and maintenance of a national system of lighthouses to assist both inland and international shipping in American waters.[8]

Even the navy's contributions spilled over into the commercial realm. In 1838 it dispatched a six-ship fleet of vessels under the command of Junior Lieutenant Charles Wilkes to explore the southern latitudes of the Atlantic and Pacific oceans. Wilkes, a strict disciplinarian, lost one ship and all its crew rounding Cape Horn and a second at the mouth of the Columbia River in what was then the Oregon Country. But on June 10, 1842, he returned the remaining vessels to New York, completing an 87,000-mile voyage with enormous implications for the future of American shipping. The Wilkes Expedition explored Antarctica, recommended San Francisco and Puget Sound for naval bases, emphasized the importance of Hawaii and the Pacific Ocean to America's future, and pushed the

United States into the confrontations with Britain and Mexico that led to its current western borders. After being court-martialed for harsh punishments meted out to crewmen on the voyage, Wilkes devoted most of the next two decades to publishing the results of his exploration—he personally wrote seven of the nineteen volumes—and lecturing on the riches and potential of the Pacific Ocean. The charts he published served the U.S. Navy in its Pacific campaigns in World War II.[9]

Wilkes had been primed for his expedition by eight years as officer in charge of the navy's new Depot of Instruments and Charts. Originally intended to simply maintain and issue commercial charts and instruments for naval vessels, the office soon revealed the inadequacy of existing products. The navy resolved to produce its own. One of Wilkes's successors at the depot, Matthew Fontaine Maury, so transformed the enterprise that he won the epithet "pathfinder of the seas."[10] After a crippling accident disabled him for sea service, Maury became a hydrographer of the navy in 1842. Starved for data, he issued logbooks to captains, in which they recorded the wind and sea conditions encountered in their voyages. Within five years, 26 million reports swamped the depot. Maury mined these to produce wind and current charts for the major shipping lanes of the world, in the process virtually inventing modern oceanography. His *Physical Geography of the Sea* (1855) was the first text in the field. What came to be called his *Sailing Directions* first appeared in 1851 and set a pattern like "Bowditch" that is still in print today.[11] The 1855 version recommended that commercial vessels sailing east and west across the Atlantic travel at different latitudes to avoid collisions. His work had as much impact on commercial sailing as on naval, for it allowed all captains to plot safe and expedient courses based on favorable wind and sea currents.

Nor was the navy the only military service to build maritime infrastructure in the first half of the nineteenth century. The U.S. Army Corps of Engineers proved as useful on coastal and inland waters as the navy did on the oceans. Thomas Jefferson had created West Point in 1802 specifically to produce engineers for both military and civilian roles. It graduates worked on all manner of internal improvement, from exploring the Louisiana Purchase to improving roads, railroads, and waterways.[12] By the time of the canal boom of the 1830s, the corps had developed a separate branch to handle hydrographic projects such as surveying for canals, clearing rivers and ports, and controlling floods.[13]

Matthew Fontaine Maury, the "pathfinder of the seas," alienated his base when he went over to the Confederacy during the Civil War. His portrait in the Salem Marine Society still hangs upside down and backward. This photo was found in 1988 in a drawer in a back basement of the Peabody Essex Museum, which holds the collection of the East India Marine Society.

The national Survey of the Coast, created by President Jefferson in 1807, struggled through its first thirty-six years, under the erudite but ineffective leadership of Ferdinand Rudolph Hassler, a Swiss geodesist. His successor, Alexander Dallas Bache, a great-grandson of Benjamin Franklin, matched Hassler's scholarly distinction but added political connections and skills to the superintendency. While making the survey "the dominant scientific institution in the United States," Bache also vastly extended its activities. After the Mexican War, he sent teams to survey the new U.S. coasts on the Gulf of Mexico and the Pacific Ocean. He and his colleagues improved measurement of the Earth's magnetic field, raised standards for tracking tidal data, and used the new telegraph to determine longitude with unprecedented accuracy. While raising the stature and visibility of science in the United States, Bache simultaneously made real and practical contributions to coastal navigation.[14]

The development of national infrastructure to support oceanic and brown-water shipping mirrored the general promotion of internal improvements that flowed from Secretary Gallatin's plan of 1808. Together they helped move the United States from a craft economy to large-scale manufacturing in such areas as textiles, clothing, iron, machinery, and leather goods.[15] Some of the techniques came from arms manufacture, which became such a central ingredient of the boom during the Civil War.[16] At the London Exposition of 1851, the United States shocked Britain and other European participants with such innovations as the Colt revolver, the McCormick harvester, and the yacht *America*, which bested all comers in a race around the Isle of Wight and gave its name to the America's Cup. The British were so struck by American achievement that they sent a delegation to the United States to study its industrial methods, coining the term "American System of Manufacture" and marking the maturity of the United States as an economic power. The transportation revolution leading up to the Civil War had contributed as much as any other factor to this economic transformation.[17] It remained to be seen what impact the war would have on American shipping, and what role shipping would play in the war.

PART III

MARITIME INDUSTRY AND LABOR IN THE GILDED AGE,
1861–1914

20

THE HINGE
OF WAR

THROUGHOUT THE TWENTIETH CENTURY, THE CIVIL WAR tended to be viewed as the fulcrum of American history. The American Revolution, of course, had created a new nation, but that nation was a federation of states divided regionally, economically, ideologically, and politically. Those divisions broke into open conflict in 1861, pitting a rural, agricultural, states' rights slavocracy against a more urban, increasingly industrial society. In the deadliest war in American history, the prevailing schisms were resolved in favor of the Northern model of "free labor, free soil, free men"—although the wounds of war ran deep and generations would pass before some of them healed. Still, modern America arose from the ashes of that war and launched itself onto a trajectory that would lead to world hegemony.

The history of American shipping was similarly represented as pivoting on the Civil War. But this was a story of declension. Whereas America as a nation had descended into war, whence it arose to union and world preeminence, the American merchant marine had entered the war from the apogee of its golden age and fallen into a downward spiral toward mediocrity, a victim of failed government policies and a lack of national will. Commerce raiding and the flight from the flag devastated the Northern merchant marine, while the Southern merchant marine was reduced to blockade-running in fast but inefficient vessels. After the war, Congress completed the disaster by denying the return of vessels that fled the flag in wartime.

The preceding chapters of this book have already suggested needed revisions to this canonical account, asserting that significant transformations of American shipping were under way before the Civil War, that the war itself was more of a catalyst than a turning point. Other dimensions of the traditional tale of declension also obscure key features of the nation's history. The decline of American-flagged international shipping, to cite one important example, was not tantamount to a decline of the American merchant marine: throughout the nineteenth century, the volume of waterborne commerce within the United States increased substantially, as did the number of ships involved in such commerce. Coastal traffic (restricted by law to American ships) increased, as did activity on the Great Lakes and the nation's rivers. In addition, many Americans owned interests in oceangoing ships that flew the flags of other nations.

More importantly, the conventional account, by emphasizing the failure of the federal government to adopt effective policies, has kept from view a theme of great significance: the collision between the market forces of late-nineteenth-century capitalism and the unusual, if traditional, quasi-public character of the maritime industry. The decades that followed the Civil War were, of course, witness to a great expansion of industrial (and agricultural) capitalism, as railroads crisscrossed the continent, manufacturing firms dramatically increased their size and reach, and relatively new industries—such as steel, oil, and petrochemicals—assumed dominant positions in the economy. These material changes stretched many traditional elements of economic and political life to their breaking point, spawning ideological shifts as well as powerful new interest groups.

This transformation—which had been building for much of the nineteenth century—bumped hard against the special relationship that had long existed between the state and the heart of the maritime world, the shipping and shipbuilding industries. Shipping and shipbuilding were private enterprises, controlled by individuals or partnerships, organized to produce profits for their owners. At the same time, however, ships were potential instruments of war and national defense, and by law America's merchant marine—like the merchant marines of other nations—could be pressed into service to carry supplies or troops, or even be converted for battle. For these reasons, it was widely believed that a nation like the United States had to maintain a shipbuilding industry—so that it could build military ships when the need arose—as well as a population of skilled mariners who stood at the ready to aid the navy. It was in recognition of this special (even if potential) role that the well-being of the maritime industry was regarded as a national priority and an appropriate goal of public policy. The protective tariffs of 1789 and the cabotage law of 1817 are simply two of the better-known protections that shipping enjoyed from the fledgling American state.[1]

For linked, yet somewhat different reasons, the men who labored on ships were also subject to unusual regulation by public authorities. Discipline in the isolated, floating workplace of a ship had to be maintained by a ship's captain, who was vested with the legal authority to maintain shipboard order. Sailors were treated as something of a breed apart among American workers: they were not "free labor," as Jacksonians or Whigs would have understood that phrase. Their relationships with ship captains and shipmasters were governed by a long-standing network of laws that both protected them and greatly restricted their freedom. A sailor in 1855—unlike a textile worker but not unlike a slave or, in earlier years, an indentured servant—could not walk away from his job at any time, sacrificing some wages, perhaps, but with no other penalties. He could in fact be compelled by the state, under threat of imprisonment, to carry out the original terms of any contract that he signed.

The upheaval of the Civil War exposed the tensions inherent in the maritime industry's ambivalent status as an assembly of private enterprises with an immensely significant yet only occasional public mission. The industry's two faces had coexisted without great stress during the antebellum years, as long as American-made ships could successfully compete in the world marketplace; shipowners could prosper by purchasing native vessels and legally registering them under the American flag. But that easy coexistence, already challenged in the 1840s and 1850s by international competition, did not survive Appomattox.

21

ANACONDA, ANYONE?

THE CIVIL WAR WAS A NAVAL WAR, AN ARTIFACT OF AMERICAN shipping infrastructure in 1861 and a reminder of the centrality of waterways to American economic and political life. The conflict, of course, was decided in land warfare, where most of the 234,000 combat deaths occurred. This unparalleled carnage gave the war its purchase on the American imagination and its salience in American memory. But fighting afloat circumscribed the land combat, carved out the theater of war, and regulated the logistics of the contending armies. Just as American shipping existed in two realms, domestic and oceanic, so too was the naval conflict within the Civil War fought in brown and blue waters. The North won the brown-water war, which set the stage for Union army victory. The Confederacy won the blue-water war, which helped to decide America's maritime future.

Ironically, the naval strategy ultimately pursued in the Civil War was first proposed by an army general. Winfield Scott, the hero of the Mexican War and the Union army's general-in-chief at the opening of the war, expected a long struggle with the Confederacy. He therefore recommended a strategy of surrounding the South east of the Mississippi River by blockading the ocean ports and by isolating Texas and the western territories from the heart of the Confederacy by seizing and occupying the Mississippi River. Derided in the press as Scott's "Anaconda Plan," the

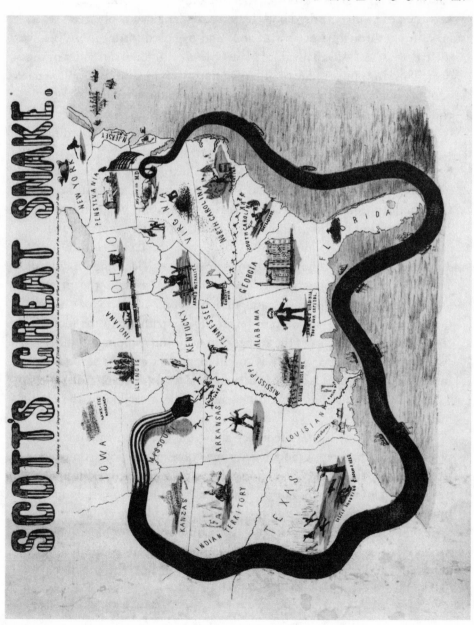

An 1861 cartoon mocked the Civil War strategy proposed by General Winfield Scott to use naval power to blockade the Confederacy and divide it along the line of the Mississippi River, calling it the "Anaconda Plan." While never formally adopted, Scott's proposal nonetheless guided Union strategy in the war.

concept nonetheless guided Northern strategy in the war. Scott himself resigned in 1861 at the age of seventy-five and died the following year, but his maritime strategy for the war survived him.[1]

The primary target of Union naval strategy at the outset of the war was New Orleans, the Confederacy's largest exporter of cotton and the nation's second largest exporter, behind only New York. Flag Officer David G. Farragut surprised both Union and Confederate observers when he stormed through river obstructions and bypassed fortifications below the city to work his way north of New Orleans and force surrender of the port. This stunning display of offensive spirit won him promotion to rear admiral, but it hardly offered a model for Union attacks on other Confederate ports. New Orleans would prove to be the only Southern port to fall to a solely naval attack. All other port conquests required coordinated amphibious assault by land and naval forces.

Still, Farragut exploited his coup to press north up the Mississippi with his steam warships, just as Winfield Scott had recommended. At the same time, his stepbrother, David Dixon Porter, worked his way south with a smaller flotilla of gunboats and mortar boats, ultimately coordinating his campaign with the land offensives of Ulysses S. Grant and William Tecumseh Sherman. The campaigns climaxed at Vicksburg in July of 1863. When that stronghold fell to amphibious assault, the primary artery of the Mississippi basin came under Union control.[2] Not only did this isolate Texas and the western territories sympathetic to the Confederacy, but it also completed the suspension of cotton shipping on the Mississippi and opened that waterway to international transport of foodstuffs from the West to the Gulf of Mexico and the world's ocean trade routes. The Anaconda squeezed the Confederacy while it facilitated the commerce of the Union.

The blockade of the Confederacy along the Gulf and Atlantic coasts proved more challenging and more time-consuming. The Confederate coastline stretched more than three thousand miles, from Virginia to Texas. The Union navy began the war with just forty-two vessels and no prospect that it could ever build enough to blockade the countless bays, inlets, and harbors the might accommodate Confederate blockade runners. It settled instead for a paper blockade—declared but not fully enforced—and a succession of attacks on the major ports. The paper blockade was unpalatable to the United States on two counts. First, it ran counter to the national position, long maintained, that blockades were illegal unless they were physically enforced by ships on station. Of course, this position reflected American experience in the wars of the French Revolution and Napoleon, when American ships prospered carrying passengers and goods to multiple belligerents. The Union also disliked blockade because it recognized the Confederacy's status as a belligerent; the government was trying to maintain that the Confederacy was simply a rebellious region of the United States.

Still, there was no help for it. The United States blockaded the South as best it could and attacked its major ports one by one. Some assaults were famously successful. Admiral Farragut's attack on Mobile Bay, for example, produced the memorable and apocryphal legend that he commanded his officers to "Damn the Torpedoes! Full steam ahead." Less colorful and less successful was the Union attack on the port it wanted most, Charleston, the heart of the Confederacy, where the war had begun with an artillery assault on Fort Sumter. Charleston fought off a joint army-navy siege for 567 days, withdrawing its defenders only in February 1865, when General Sherman approached on his march from Atlanta to the sea.[3] The blockade and capture of the major Confederate ports constricted the Confederacy, as Scott had recommended, but never achieved strangulation. High-speed blockade runners moved in and out of those ports throughout the war. The Confederate military suffered logistically, but it was not for want of matériel that the South lost the war.

Lacking a fleet to contest the Northern blockade, the Confederacy resorted to expedients, two of which would have lasting impacts on maritime history. Matthew Fontaine Maury, the "pathfinder of the seas" who had done so much to support American naval and commercial shipping in the years before the Civil War, resigned his commission in the U.S. Navy and threw in his lot with his native Virginia and the Confederacy. He led the Confederate development of "torpedo war," named for Robert Fulton's pioneering work in the field.[4] His Naval Submarine Battery Service institutionalized a method of war that had not yet achieved formal government recognition.[5] Primarily defensive weapons of the weak, mines and torpedoes proved effective both in land warfare and in protecting rivers and harbors from the advancing Union navy. By war's end, forty-three Union ships, including four monitors, had been sunk or damaged by underwater explosives.[6] Perhaps most famously, the Confederate submarine CSS *Hunley* sank the Union blockading sloop-of-war USS *Housatanic* in February 1864, though the *Hunley* was lost in the attack. The devices proved so effective that Union naval commanders simultaneously condemned them and imitated them, ensuring that other nations would take an interest as well. For his service to the Confederacy, Maury's honorary membership in the Salem Marine Society was revoked and his portrait hung upside down, face to the wall, with the word "traitor" inscribed on the back.[7] But another genie was out of its bottle. Underwater warfare would move in a direct line from the American Civil War to the unrestricted submarine warfare of the world wars in the North Atlantic.

The Confederacy also experimented with armoring its naval vessels. This innovation was a direct response to the blockade, an attempt to develop a ship that could attack blockading vessels in coastal waters and drive them farther offshore. For this purpose, the Confederacy redesigned the captured Union steam frigate *Merrimack*. The resulting CSS *Virginia* sported an iron casemate running the full length of the ship, pierced by 11 guns. An iron beak beneath the waterline at the bow allowed the warship to ram enemy vessels if the opportunity presented itself. As is often the case in civil wars, the enemy learned of the plans for the *Virginia* and offered its own innovation in return. The USS *Monitor*, the brainchild of the Swedish designer John Ericsson, featured armor plating on its hull and deck, an extremely low freeboard, and a single armored turret mounting two Dahlgren eleven-inch guns. The two ships fought famously and inconclusively in Hampton Roads on March 9, 1862.[8] The *Virginia* chastened the Union navy to be more cautious in its blockading policies, as the Confederacy's underwater warfare had done. And the *Monitor* convinced the Confederates that they could not hope to outduel the North in technological and industrial innovation. The confrontation between the two vessels baptized the new age of armored warships, which had really begun with the launch of Britain's HMS *Warrior* in 1859. This all-iron sail/steam vessel was, according to the naval historian Kenneth J. Hagan, "the first modern warship" and the harbinger of the next generation of naval architecture.[9]

Two other dimensions of the naval war between the states had such far-reaching consequences for American shipping that they warrant more detailed attention. Naval architecture and shipbuilding struck out on a new trajectory, with profound implications for commercial shipbuilding. And the blue-water contest within the Civil War inflicted lasting damage on the U.S. merchant marine.

22

BENJAMIN FRANKLIN ISHERWOOD AND THE INDUSTRIALIZATION OF SHIP PRODUCTION

THE ANACONDA PLAN RELIED ON SHIPS. OVER THE COURSE OF the war, the Union increased its fleet from about 42 vessels at the outset, to 264 by the end of 1861 (mostly by conversion of merchant vessels) to 671 by the end of the conflict.[1] To the man responsible for this expansion, quality was as important as quantity. Benjamin Franklin Isherwood introduced the U.S. Navy to the Industrial Revolution. While meeting the Union navy's needs in wartime, he simultaneously laid the groundwork for a modern navy in the future. He conducted research and development on steam propulsion, imitating in engineering science Matthew Fontaine Maury's contributions to oceanography. He designed and produced the world's fastest warship. He streamlined the manufacture of warships and moved the process away from the civilian shipbuilding yards that had built both naval and commercial vessels since colonial times. And he contributed significantly to a worldwide revolution in naval warfare. The twentieth century would dawn on an all-steel, steam-propelled,

189

screw-driven, armor-plated floating fortress that bore little resemblance to the commercial ships it was designed to protect.

Isherwood also revealed fault lines in American maritime development that would grow wider in the later decades of the twentieth century. The culture of sail died hard in America, in the navy as in the merchant marine. So too did America's love affair with wooden ships. The infatuation with speed that had once manifested itself in clipper ships migrated in the late nineteenth century to the navy, but not before the institution rejected the world's fastest vessel, mothballing a gift from Isherwood that the navy in its hidebound wisdom failed to appreciate. An evolving navy bureau system increasingly took unto itself chores of naval architecture and shipbuilding that it had heretofore shared with commercial firms, widening the gulf between naval and commercial practice and impeding the transfer of technology between the two realms. And the scientific engineering that Isherwood practiced and advocated met stiff resistance from the traditional lore that held the American navy and its merchant marine in a deadly grip.

Trained in science and civil engineering and experienced in railroads, aqueducts, lighthouses, and marine engines, Isherwood entered the navy in 1844 as an assistant engineer, because it was, he believed, a good place to practice engineering.[2] Finding his naval duties less than challenging, he devoted his ample free time to scientific study, developing a sufficient reputation by the late 1850s to get him appointed to technical boards for the service. The navy was just then converting its ships from sail to auxiliary steam propulsion. Since the technology of sail was well in hand, Isherwood naturally turned his attention to steam. In a series of experiments he conducted between 1856 and 1858, he learned that it was more efficient to leave the valve from the boiler open throughout the travel of the piston in the cylinder, letting the pressure work throughout the stroke, than to cut off the input of new steam partway through the stroke and let the natural expansive power of the steam do the remainder of the work. He learned, in short, the advantages of high-pressure steam engines. He positioned himself professionally as a "long cut-off man," who advocated admitting high-pressure steam into the engine cylinder for as much as 75 percent of the stroke. He rebutted the "short cut-off men" with a mountain of empirical data that he subsequently published as *Experimental Researches in Steam Engineering*.[3] This distinguished publication secured Isherwood's reputation around the world, but the effrontery of introducing scientific research into an American naval debate still dominated by rank amateurs won him enemies who would dog his career and finally drive him from the navy.

First, however, Abraham Lincoln, an astute judge of character, appointed Isherwood to be the engineer in chief of the navy. Controlling just ninety ships early in the war, only twenty-one of them steam-powered, he oversaw the design and construction of the power plants for the six hundred steamers added to the navy lists during that conflict. He improved boilers, introduced high-pressure steam engines, and established efficiency as the desideratum of ship propulsion. Throughout his tenure he championed the scientific method and empirical research as the standards of innovation. And he fought, and finally lost, the struggle to elevate engineers to the same status as the line officers who commanded ships. He promoted private contractors who could produce the special materials required by the navy, taking the service several steps closer to development of its own yards and away from the building and design that had hitherto been done by firms that also made commercial vessels. The gap that Isherwood thus helped open up would widen dramatically in the twentieth century and impede the technological transfer that might otherwise have taken place between naval and commercial shipbuilding and design.

Isherwood's contributions transcended the technical realm, reaching into grand strategy. Thirty years before Alfred Thayer Mahan articulated the theory of sea power that would undergird the development of a "new navy," Isherwood wrote:

> It is obviously cheaper, more effective, and more sustaining of the national honor to preserve our coasts from the presence of an enemy's naval force by keeping the *command of the open sea*, with all the power it gives of aggression upon his own shores and commerce, than to rely on any system of harbor defense which requires every point to be protected that may be assailed by any enemy, having, in that case, the choice of time and place, and the advantage of perfect security for his own ports and commerce.[4] (Italics added)

In other words, America should not rely on coastal defense to protect itself from foreign invasion. A battle fleet to intercept enemies far offshore offered far greater security.

For the duration of the Civil War, however, Isherwood had to curb his dreams of a blue-water navy and attend to the demands of blockade, commerce protection, riverine operations, and amphibious projections of power ashore. Blockade and commerce protection both revealed to the Union navy the growing importance of high-speed steam warships. The controversy over high-pressure steam engines that had embroiled Benjamin Franklin Isherwood even before the war resulted in an 1863 competition to test engine designs. Isherwood got to design and build two high-speed ships, while two advocates of the short-stroke philosophy received navy funding to build competing models. None of the vessels appeared in time for war service, but their development continued after the war as the navy contemplated its future.

Isherwood stood traditional practice on its head by designing his vessels around their respective power plants. As naval architects struggled with the technological revolution engulfing their practice, they tended to take existing hulls and fit them out with steam propulsion systems. Isherwood instead began with his power plant and designed a ship around it. The power plant design emphasized efficiency. The ship design emphasized a sleek hull, secure integration of the machinery, and an

During its sea trials in 1867, USS *Wampanoag* established speed records that were not broken for twenty years and vindicated the science-based empiricism of navy engineer in chief Benjamin Isherwood. Still, the navy withheld the *Wampanoag* from sea service and forced Isherwood into retirement.

efficient propeller suited to ease of handling. When sea trials finally took place in 1867, the competition's vessels, including one designed and built by John Ericsson, of *Monitor* fame, failed to come within two knots of their specified 15-knot goal. Isherwood's craft, the *Wampanoag*, averaged 16.6 knots over a twenty-four-hour period and 17.25 knots over a six-hour period. For one hour she maintained 17.75 knots, a world speed record that would stand for two decades.[5] Isherwood's style of science-based engineering and design to efficiency had been vindicated beyond question.

For his efforts, Isherwood was driven from office in 1869. The *Wampanoag* was laid up for a year, then converted to a receiving ship, and finally sold out of the navy in 1885, while she still held the world speed record. A board of officers appointed by the secretary of the navy in 1868 had concluded that the vessel was "a sad and signal failure, and utterly unfit to be retained in the service."[6] Driven partly by Washington politics and partly by navy conservatism, the board turned its back on the Industrial Revolution, on the lessons of the Civil War, and on the changing nature of warship design to embrace the familiar world of wood and sail in which its members had made their careers. Isherwood remained on active duty until 1884 and then retired to a prosperous civilian life, enjoying his international reputation as a steam engineer and leaving the navy to its warm embrace of the past.

In many ways, Isherwood and the *Wampanoag* symbolized the plight of the American maritime enterprise at the end of the Civil War. Undergoing its own Industrial Revolution, which was accelerated in the hothouse environment of war, the nation experienced firsthand many of the developments that would shape the coming decades: steam propulsion, mines and torpedoes, the new commerce warfare, government promotion of research and development, the flight from the flag. Some of these had the potential to make the United States a world shipping power. And some of them revealed the hazards of shipping in the machine age.[7] The coming years would reveal that the nation had ignored most of the warnings in this experience and turned its back on most of the opportunities. It was not for nothing that many historians came to see the Civil War as marking the beginning of the decline of the American merchant marine.

23

THE *ALABAMA* AND COMMERCE WAR

THE NAVAL WAR ON COMMERCE SPANNED BROWN AND BLUE water. On brown water, the conflict was fought to a draw. Of the 2,742 attempts made to penetrate the Union blockade during the war, 2,525 succeeded, 92 percent. The porosity of the blockade revealed the elusiveness of high-speed, specially built steam ships, the weaknesses of the combined sail/steam vessels assigned to blockade duties, and the failure of the blockade to starve the Confederacy. The Southern war machine suffered by comparison with that of the industrial North, but it fielded and equipped its armies to the very end. Many blockade runners brought consumer goods for the Southern aristocracy in holds that might have carried arms and ammunition. The more telling impact of the blockade was to strangle the cotton export trade that might have given the Confederacy more purchasing power on the world market. And of course the blockade did force the Confederacy to abandon high-volume shipping from its major ports in favor of small, speedy vessels with limited carrying capacity darting in and out of minor ports and harbors.

In blue water, the Confederacy clearly triumphed. American shipping had flourished during the decades preceding the Civil War. Between 1846 and the opening of hostilities, the nation's foreign commerce increased threefold, and more than two-thirds of these cargoes were carried in American ships—which meant, thanks to laws adopted at the nation's birth, ships built in the United States and wholly owned by American citizens. American ships had sailed back and forth across the North Atlantic to ports in Britain, the Baltic, and the Mediterranean; they had plied the Caribbean, crisscrossed the Pacific, and made the long journey from the East Coast around Cape Horn, often with stops in Brazil and Argentina. Domestic trade, up and down the East Coast and to the Gulf of Mexico, had also been substantial, while the fishing and more far-flung whaling industries prospered. In 1860 the registered tonnage of the United States had been roughly 2.5 million tons, only half a million less than that of Great Britain.[1]

After the outbreak of the Civil War, almost all of the nation's ships remained in the hands of the North: although obviously an economic boon for the Union, this asymmetry created a strategic vulnerability that was cleverly exploited by the small Confederate navy. Lacking a merchant

Dapper and cocky on the deck of the commerce raider *Alabama* in 1863, Captain Raphael Semmes poses with the executive officer Lieutenant John Kell and some of the armament that made his ship the bane of Northern shipowners through the Civil War. The *Alabama* prompted some of the flight from the flag that accelerated the decline of the American merchant marine.

marine itself, the South could attack Northern ships (a recognized form of combat among belligerents) without fear of reprisals, and the Northern merchant marine was far too large and dispersed to be adequately defended by the Union navy. The merchant marine, moreover, consisted largely of sailing ships that were easy prey for steam-driven vessels. The Confederacy seized this opportunity, deploying the *Alabama*, the *Florida*, and several other speedy steam-auxiliary cruisers (which also had a long range under sail) to destroy or capture roughly two hundred ships, many of them in the West Indies or in the Atlantic shipping lanes between the east coast of Brazil and the west coast of Africa. Trade was thus disrupted although, it should be noted, with minimal loss of life: crewmen on the ships were commonly spared and eventually conveyed to Confederate ports as prisoners of war. The *Alabama*, built in England and manned largely by British sailors who had been promised a bounty by the Confederate government, captured sixty-four merchantmen before being destroyed in 1864 by the Union ship *Kearsarge* outside the harbor of Cherbourg, France. The predations of the *Alabama* and other British-built Confederate cruisers gave rise to American demands for reparations from Britain after the war. These were partially (and symbolically) satisfied by Britain's agreement in the Treaty of Washington (1871) to pay the United States $15 million in damages.[2]

The most significant consequence of Confederate raiding, however, resided not in the number of ships destroyed but in the impact of such raids on the economic well-being of American-flagged shipping. The threat of hostile raids led to a significant increase in insurance rates for U.S. ships and their cargoes (as high as 4 percent of their value), thereby compelling shipowners to lower their freight rates in order to compete with neutral (predominantly British) ships. Yet even cutting freight rates did not solve the problem, because shippers, giving priority to the safety of their cargoes, fled in droves to neutral (again, predominantly British) ships. By 1863 three-quarters of the commerce in and out of New York was carried in non-American ships, compared to one-third in 1860. This in turn led American shipowners to sell their ships abroad or (through various maneuvers) to transfer them to foreign registry. By the end of the war, as many as one thousand American ships, easily one-quarter of the merchant marine, had come under foreign ownership. In direct or indirect result of the war, roughly half of the American merchant marine was lost to the American flag.[3]

The loss proved to be permanent. According to a law enacted in 1797 and still in effect in the 1860s, American ships that had been sold to foreign interests could not be repatriated. In 1866, moreover, Congress passed a law banning from American registry ships that had remained American-owned but had sailed under foreign flags: no ship of the United States "which has been recorded or registered as an American vessel . . . and which shall have been licensed or otherwise authorized to sail under a foreign flag, and to have the protection of any foreign government during the existence of the rebellion, shall be deemed or registered as an American vessel." Although East Coast and New England shippers, championed by the Maine senator James G. Blaine, tried to change the laws to permit once-American vessels to return, Congress resisted. Residents of the nation's interior, where maritime traffic was protected by cabotage laws, saw little immediate need for an oceangoing American-flagged fleet, as long as foreign ships were available for necessary trade; moreover, the owners who had expatriated their ships were widely regarded as profiteers, wanting to enjoy the benefits, but not pay the price, of being American.[4]

The American merchant marine thus entered the final third of the nineteenth century greatly diminished in size and capacity. Not only had ships been destroyed by raiders or sold abroad, but many others were harmed or worn out in extensive service to the Union, ferrying troops and supplies as well as being refitted for battle. (The largest steam vessels had all been requisitioned by the navy.) That four years of civil war had done such damage is not surprising: the cost of the nation's bloody internecine conflict was in nearly all respects incalculably greater than anyone had imagined when it began in 1861.

More startling and more notable was that the nation's oceangoing, international fleet failed to recover from the trauma of the war and to regain the prominence that it had held in 1850. American ships engaged in foreign trade numbered 1,388 in 1866, compared with 2,720 in the coastwise trade. The number in foreign trade actually increased in the ensuing years, until 1878, when a more or less steady decline began. By 1900 the United States had only 817 vessels engaged in the foreign trade, compared with 4,287 in coastwise service.[5] Those statistics are all the more remarkable given the immense growth in economic activity and international trade that took place during this period. The United States was becoming the foremost economic power in the world, but most of its exports and imports—including millions of immigrants—were being carried in foreign ships. In 1900 fewer than 10 percent of all international cargoes to and from the United States were carried in American ships, compared with more than 72 percent in 1850.[6]

There were numerous reasons for this failure to rebound from the war, yet in one way or another they all involved the triumph of capitalist values and interests in the United States, coupled with the increasing globalization of the world economy. (The late nineteenth century was the first modern period of economic "globalization."[7]) Technology, to be sure, played a role. The wooden sailing vessels that Americans were so adept at constructing had difficulty competing with the iron- and steel-hulled ships that Britain had been building since midcentury. By the 1870s the superiority of British-made ships was clear, and British shipyards had a head start in construction techniques that proved difficult for Americans to overcome. The 1870s and 1880s, moreover, witnessed the development of the triple-expansion, reciprocating steam engine, which made steam-powered ships even faster and more fuel-efficient. Wooden ships, powered by sails, could still profitably transport bulk cargoes when speed was not of the essence. But the future of passenger travel as well as rapid freight transport belonged to iron, steel, and steam and not to sailing ships made of wood.[8] The navy was moving in this direction, however haltingly, but America's commercial fleet lagged far behind.

This competitive advantage of foreign-built ships was significant because those Americans with cargoes to send abroad were more sensitive to price than to patriotic appeals for a native merchant marine: midwestern grain growers happily participated in the growing global market for the bountiful produce of their fields, choosing the cheapest and most reliable transportation, regardless of the flag under which it flew. Similarly, market forces doomed New England's whaling industry, already weakened by Confederate raiders. The discovery of petroleum led to the replacement of whale oil by kerosene as an illuminant. The New Bedford whaling fleet in 1860 had more than three hundred vessels, with a total of more than 100,000 tons; by 1900 only two dozen small vessels (with a total of less than 7,000 tons) remained from this once grand and profitable fleet.[9]

24

CORNELIUS VANDERBILT AND THE RISE OF THE RAILROAD

ANOTHER CIVIL WAR DEVELOPMENT RICH WITH IMPLICATIONS for future maritime development was the mobilization of railroads in the service of the state. Just as the geography of the United States offered the Union navy opportunities to isolate and strangle the Southern economy and to project military force ashore, so too did the geography of America's prewar railroads favor the Union cause and disadvantage the South. In general, railroads north of the Mason-Dixon line moved east and west, connecting the industrial North with the agricultural West, just as the canals had once done. The smaller and less robust railroad network of the South tended to connect the Southern heartland with ports on the rivers and coasts. Both networks favored the North. Union troops and matériel could move by rail between the eastern and western theaters of the war. And armies of invasion, such as General Sherman's, could follow the Southern rail lines to the heart of the Confederacy. Before the Prussian military demonstrated the power of railroads in modern war during the war of German unification, the United States exploited the infrastructure at hand to achieve the same end.[1]

Abraham Lincoln was among the first to appreciate the potential of the railroad system. He also quickly discerned that Union army officers tended to treat local rail assets as resources at their disposal, like soldiers and supplies. They would regularly commandeer railcars for use as warehouses and even bunkhouses and would reroute traffic within their theaters of war to suit their personal operational plans. If railroads were going to serve national purposes, they had to be run as a centrally coordinated system, in which national imperatives trumped local prerogatives. To impose this kind of order on the Union railroad system, Lincoln appointed Herman Haupt, a West Point graduate and civilian railroad executive, and gave him extraordinary powers. Though Haupt served only one year (1862–1863), due to his intolerance of army bureaucracy he transformed the Union railroad system. He designed and oversaw the construction of bridges and ad hoc feeder lines, established schedules and priorities for systemwide traffic, and initiated expedients to meet military emergencies, such as the battle of Gettysburg. He brought civilian standards of engineering and operation into military railroading, and he took his wartime experience back into the railroad industry at the end of the war.[2]

The American railroad boom in the last third of the nineteenth century hardly owed its vigor to the Civil War.[3] Haupt had made his fortune in railroading before the war, and as early as the 1840s, Henry Shreve, the man who cleared the Mississippi River, had withdrawn from shipping in favor of railroads. While they had been important to the nation's economy in the middle of the nineteenth century, railroads became its focal point after the Civil War. The first transcontinental line was completed in 1869; between 1870 and 1900 the number of miles of track in operation rose from 53,000 to nearly 200,000. Multiple railroad lines connected not only all major cities but also most minor ones, while even small towns competed to attract lines and stations. The nation's largest corporations were all railroad companies, and many of the great fortunes of the era were made in the railroad business.[4]

What this meant, of course, was that the United States was investing in an enormous transportation system—for people and goods—that, for the first time in its history, did not directly involve ships. America's capitalists and entrepreneurs turned their attention away from the sea and toward the development of the interior, particularly the trans-Mississippi West. Ambitious men seeking their fortunes had, of course, begun investing in manufacturing during the first half of the nineteenth century. Protected by tariffs, the nation aimed to produce goods that it once had imported, such as textiles. This was a goal that required capital (some of which came from the profits of the shipping industry) and that, if achieved, would lessen the need for ships to traverse the North Atlantic with imported goods. After the Civil War, investment in manufacturing—especially in iron and steel, as well as petrochemicals—accelerated dramatically, while the opening of the West expanded the domestic market for manufactured goods. Markets were opened up and extended, commerce and communication were quickened, and more and more freight was traveling from one locale to another—but not across the oceans. The Great Plains were settled, and migrants poured into the Far West, thanks to the railroads. Water transportation, of course, did not disappear (more on that later), but it had lost its uniqueness and preeminence.

A symbol of this shift can be found in the long and stunning career of Cornelius Vanderbilt, about the last person one would have expected to take an interest in railroads. The "Commodore" had built his vast fortune in shipping, from the modest ferry service he launched in 1810 to the foray into North Atlantic liner service that he tried in the 1850s. In fact, an early injury suffered in a train accident had instilled in him a personal hostility to railroads, which he valued throughout most of his career primarily as feeders to his steamships. Still, he became a director of the Long Island Railroad in 1844 and the New York and Harlem Railroad in 1857. In the 1850s he began investing in railroad stocks, taking the profits from his shipping empire and transferring them to railroads.

During the Civil War, Vanderbilt went another big step further, selling his shipping assets and investing the capital in railroads. As soon as the war broke out, he offered his large ships to the federal government for use in the conflict. His namesake, the *Vanderbilt*, the flagship of his once grandiose plans for North Atlantic liner service, served as a transport ship and was then outfitted as a cruiser to help catch Confederate raiders.[5] In the course of the war, he invested proceeds from the

Cornelius Vanderbilt's multifaceted maritime career began with ferry service in New York harbor, included intermodal shipping/railroad service across the Isthmus of Panama, and climaxed with a failed attempt to break into the lucrative North Atlantic liner trade. Then he turned from the sea to railroads.

sale of his steamships in the New York and Harlem Railroad, which he acquired in 1862–1863, and the Hudson River Railroad (1864). After acquiring the New York Central Railroad in 1867, he merged his holdings into the New York Central and Hudson River Railroad (later renamed just the New York Central). He led the partnership that built the terminal at East 42nd Street called originally the Grand Central Depot, later the Grand Central Terminal, the largest train station in the world by number of platforms and tracks.

Working with his son, William, Vanderbilt moved into the Midwest, where he came to control both the Lake Shore line and the Union Pacific railway. A major player in the railway financial battles of the late 1860s and 1870s, Vanderbilt had shrewdly concluded that the great business opportunities of the postwar era were on land rather than at sea. At his death in 1877, the Commodore was a railroad magnate worth approximately $100 million.[6] He left 96 percent of this fortune to his son and railroad partner, and to William's sons, with instructions to preserve both his dynasty and his rail empire.[7]

Vanderbilt was by no means the first American millionaire to transfer wealth from the shipping industry into other capital investments. The Browns of Providence, Rhode Island, built a diversified portfolio of manufacturing, retail, utilities, and more on the fortune amassed by the family patriarch Captain John Brown in the slave trade. Stephen Girard (1750–1831), the sixth richest man in American history, rose from cabin boy to shipowner, growing wealthy in the wars of the French Revolution and Napoleon and then shifting his focus to real estate, insurance, and banking. James J. Hill, a railroad magnate like Vanderbilt, began as a laborer for a steamboat company on his way to amassing a fleet that funded his dream of building up the Great Northern railroad to provide service to the Northwest.[8] About the only thing that separated Vanderbilt from these other former shipping magnates was that he changed industries when he was almost seventy.

The railroads that attracted so much capital in the years after the Civil War were not simply—or primarily—competitors with the maritime industry. They were also a growing, and dominant, feature of an "intermodal" transportation network that included both ships and railways. The nation's ports were also railway terminals, with rail lines commonly extending to the water's edge. The railroads transported freight and

Many railroad ventures in American history were funded by capital raised in the shipping industry. The luxury liner *Pennsylvania*, built in 1873 by William Cramp of Philadelphia, was part of a steamship line funded by the Pennsylvania Railroad to help attract cargo to its trains.

passengers to and from ships, while railway corporations purchased and owned their own vessels. In 1873, the great Philadelphia shipbuilding company of William Cramp and Sons launched a transatlantic passenger liner, the *Pennsylvania*, a large and luxurious vessel that Cramp considered the culminating achievement of his long career. The construction of the ship had been funded by the Pennsylvania Railroad.[9]

The Pennsylvania Railroad invested in far more than this one ship. Fearing that it could not compete with New York in attracting cargoes for its trains, it launched its own steamship line. From 1873 to 1884 the *Pennsylvania* and three other ships carried cargo and immigrants between Liverpool and Philadelphia. But the railroad insisted on sailing American ships, which could not compete with the lower construction and operating costs of foreign vessels. The experiment in railroad shipping coordination ended in 1884, when the line was sold to the Red Star Line of the International Navigation Company, finally to be absorbed by J. P. Morgan's International Mercantile Marine.[10] Intermodal transportation coordinating railroads and shipping would remain an alluring prospect for many entrepreneurs, but it would not realize its full potential until the middle of the twentieth century.

25

MARCUS HANNA AND THE GROWTH OF INLAND SHIPPING

IMMENSELY IMPORTANT AS THE RAILROADS SURELY WERE, THEY did not monopolize the transport of either goods or individuals within the United States. Indeed, the volume of domestic waterborne commerce increased throughout the last third of the nineteenth century, and the total tonnage of the American merchant marine (oceanic, coastal, and inland) actually ranked second in the world early in the twentieth century. The always important coastal trade grew steadily, not only among the ports of the East Coast but also in the Gulf and the Pacific. By the turn of the century, there were five times as many ships involved in the domestic trade than there were in international commerce, and the disparity was increasing—as was the size and speed of the vessels. Huge multimasted wooden schooners, reaching more than 3,000 tons, sailed up and down the Atlantic and Pacific coasts, aided, especially on the Pacific, by auxiliary steam or gasoline engines. Indeed, construction of multimasted schooners (out of wood or steel) peaked between 1898 and 1908.

Meanwhile, passenger and freight steamers, following regular schedules, moved back and forth between coastal cities. The Clyde Steamship Company, for example, owned twenty steamers that traveled regular routes between Boston, New York, Charleston, Jacksonville, Philadelphia, Wilmington, North Carolina, and several ports in Virginia. Proprietary shipping companies also appeared in industries such as coal and oil to

The 395-foot, 11,000-ton *Thomas W. Lawson* was built in 1902 at the Fore River Ship-building Company in Quincy, Massachusetts. The only seven-masted schooner ever built, the bulk carrier said more about America's continuing love affair with sailing vessels than it did about the future of shipping.

carry cargoes they produced and owned; John D. Rockefeller's Standard Oil of New Jersey owned the largest tanker fleet in the world before the company was broken up as an illegal monopoly in 1911.[1] Thanks to the acquisition of Alaska, Hawaii, and Puerto Rico, moreover, "coastal" shipping (restricted to American-flagged ships) was also extended south into the Caribbean and west in the Pacific.[2]

Traffic also swelled on the nation's rivers. The Mississippi remained the premier north-south waterway of the interior, as steamships and barges hauled heavy freight from northern cities like Minneapolis as far south as New Orleans. River steamers could push as many as thirty flat-bottomed scows, laden with coal, nearly the full length of the river or its many tributaries.[3] Although the relative significance of the Mississippi surely declined (due in part to a drop in lumber shipments), it remained vital to the nation's economy. River ports such as Memphis, St. Louis, and New Orleans prospered, providing critical links between railroads and the nation's central maritime artery.[4]

Even more striking was the growth of shipping on the Great Lakes. Open only eight months of the year, the lakes nonetheless became an extraordinarily busy waterway, lacing together the burgeoning industrial centers of the Midwest. Chicago, Gary, Milwaukee, Cleveland, Detroit, Buffalo: all of these cities were Great Lakes ports, as were Duluth, Waukegan, Toledo, and a dozen other locales. The waterway, which stretched roughly twelve hundred miles, was made more efficient by sizable governmental appropriations, for example, expanding the St. Mary's Falls Canal (first opened in 1855) connecting Lake Superior to Lakes Michigan and Huron. The federal government, which assumed definitive legal control of most of the lakes only in 1871, deepened the channels near Detroit as well as harbors throughout the lakes. By the turn of the century, the tonnage passing through the St. Mary's Falls (now Sault Ste. Marie) Canal surpassed that of its more famous counterpart in Suez, and cities like Cleveland and Buffalo had become major ports.[5]

Most of what moved across the lakes was heavy, bulk freight that could be transported more cheaply on water than on the railroads: lumber, millions of tons of iron ore from the Lake Superior region, coal (moving from east to west), and grain. To carry these cargoes, local builders constructed increasingly large, steam-driven, steel ships, designed both to tow barges and to permit the rapid loading of freight and fuel (coal). Fast turnarounds in port were essential if lake carriers were to complete twenty-two to twenty-five trips in a year before ice made the lakes impassable. By the turn of the century, one-quarter of the tonnage of the American merchant marine was involved in Great Lakes shipping, and roughly half of all shipbuilding was being done on and for these inland waterways. There was more American steel-hulled, steam-powered tonnage on the lakes than on the oceans.[6]

Shipping on the Great Lakes during these years (and for many years to come) was closely tied both to the railroads and to the iron, coal, grain, and lumber industries. The key ports on the lakes were also railway hubs, nodes in a complex transportation network that traversed the growing industrial heartland and, in so doing, linked the Northeast with the West. Buffalo exemplified this pattern. A thriving mid-nineteenth-century port thanks to the Erie Canal, the city's fortunes were potentially threatened by the canal's eclipse after the Civil War. Frozen in winter and with its traffic always slow, the canal was becoming obsolete. But the city acquired more than a dozen railway lines, which fed and revitalized its lake commerce. By the end of the century, its port boomed with shipments of grain, livestock, and iron ore. In 1910 it was the largest grain port in the world, its lakefront lined by a dozen steel grain elevators handling 2 million bushels a day. Convoys of specially designed "whaleback" barges entered and left the port as long as the lakes were open to traffic.[7]

Many of the ships that crisscrossed the lakes were owned by iron or coal companies or by partnerships of key players in those industries. The same was true of the lake shipbuilding industry, centered in Cleveland. Although the city was far from the world's great oceans, shipbuilding became its largest single industry in the late nineteenth century.[8]

One Cleveland businessman who made his fortune at the nexus of these industries was Marcus Alonzo Hanna, who later became an immensely influential senator from Ohio, William McKinley's presidential campaign manager, and a pioneer in the adept use of money to finance and manipulate election campaigns. The core of Hanna's business (originally his father-in-law's) was the mining of coal, as well as the distribution and commission sale of coal, iron ore, and pig iron across the Great Lakes region. Access to reliable transportation was essential to his business, which led him to purchase interests in both ships and railroads, including the Pennsylvania Railroad Company. As the iron ore and coal industries grew, in the 1870s and 1880s, Hanna, in partnership with his brother, Melville, also became a shipbuilder, purchasing the Globe Shipbuilding Company, in part to guarantee the availability of ships designed expressly to carry ore.[9] Melville's technical expertise in lake

Marcus Alonzo Hanna, the political operative behind the election of President William McKinley, made his fortune in his father-in-law's mining business, which led to shipping, shipbuilding, and railroad activity on and around the Great Lakes. This background shaped his promotion of government support for the maritime industry during his years in the U.S. Senate.

transportation contributed to the construction of new, and increasingly large, steel-hulled ships for transporting iron ore.[10] The wealth that Mark Hanna acquired in this commercial conglomerate funded his later ventures in banking, newspaper ownership, and politics. Not surprisingly, perhaps, he became a staunch advocate of federal government support for the shipping industry.[11]

The experience of Marcus Hanna also points to another key fact: despite its cries of distress, the shipbuilding industry in the United States did not disappear between the Civil War and the early twentieth century. The construction of ships for lake and river commerce flourished. By the early twentieth century, for example, the American Ship Building Company owned eleven huge yards along the Great Lakes, from Buffalo to Chicago to Duluth. Meanwhile shipbuilders on the East and West coasts continued to construct wooden and steel ships specially fitted to carry bulk cargoes on the oceans. In addition, the banks of the Delaware River in and near Philadelphia became the "American Clyde" (like the river Clyde in Scotland, the site of the industrial city of Glasgow), a center of innovative production of iron and steel ships and steam engines. As Benjamin Franklin Isherwood had discovered even before the Civil War, the construction of steel ships required an integration of hull and engine, demanding technological prowess particularly available in Philadelphia, home to a locomotive-building industry. Limited and beleaguered by foreign competition, builders like William and Charles Cramp and John Roach nonetheless turned out sizable numbers of modern, even luxurious, ships, including the passenger liner *St. Paul* and her sister ship, the *St. Louis* (launched in 1894 in the presence of President Grover Cleveland), which one historian has called the "single most sophisticated piece of engineering of the age." Shipbuilding in general was further buoyed by the federal government's decision in 1890 to create a "new Navy" appropriate to the nation's looming role as an imperial power, though the navy relied increasingly on its own architects and shipbuilders.[12]

In sum, the maritime industry did not die or disappear between the Civil War and World War I. It was, in effect, redirected to domestic trade while also becoming embedded in the heavy industries that flourished during this period. In part, this redirection was simply an expression of the sheer size of the United States. Voyages of five or six hundred or even a thousand miles that would have been international in Europe were domestic or coastal in the United States. The movement of freight from Lake Superior to Cleveland would, in many parts of the world, have crossed national boundaries. The economic growth of the nation in the late nineteenth century was grounded in an enormous expansion of domestic markets, and those markets were commonly served by American ships.

26

JOHN LYNCH AND THE QUEST FOR A NATIONAL MARITIME POLICY

DESPITE THE PREVIOUS CHAPTER'S MORE SANGUINE ASSESSMENT of the overall health of the maritime industry, it remains true that oceanic American-flagged shipping suffered a severe decline from 1860 through the early years of the twentieth century—relative both to other nations and to the buoyant decades that preceded the Civil War. While the decline relative to the volume and value of trade carried in foreign ships had begun in the 1840s, during America's maritime golden age, it accelerated markedly during and after the Civil War. It is also true that the condition of the maritime industry became a prominent national public policy issue in the last third of the nineteenth century. Shipowners and operators, as well as shipbuilders, were convinced that they could not solve their industry's problems without significant aid from the federal government, and they repeatedly pressed Congress to pass laws that would subsidize and stimulate the industry.

The first round of public debate in response to the industry's distress came in the politically overheated environment of the late 1860s. In March 1869 Congress, reacting to pressure from the industry, appointed a select committee to study (and presumably help remedy) the "causes of the reduction of American tonnage and the decline of navigation interests." Headed by a Maine Republican, Congressman John Lynch, the

committee held extensive hearings in Washington, New York, Philadelphia, Boston, and Portland, Maine. It received "statements of merchants,
shipbuilders, ship-owners, and insurance agents; gentlemen having practical knowledge and experience" of local conditions, and it sought the
opinions of American consuls "at the principal ports of foreign countries."
The committee reported back to Congress in 1870 with detailed statistics
that "mathematically demonstrated" the industry's decline. It also pressed
forcefully the claim that it was the War of the Rebellion and not "general
causes" that had so diminished American shipping. The committee
acknowledged that there had also been technological shifts and changes
"in naval architecture," but asserted that American business could readily
have coped with those changes had the war not intervened. The "decadence" of the industry "is attributable mainly, if not solely, to incidents of
the war."[1]

This argument about the "causes of the reduction of tonnage" was neither developed in detail nor compelling in its logic. Yet its purpose was
clear: to provide a justification for significant federal aid to the industry.
The preamble to the first piece of legislation introduced by Congressman
Lynch opened with the clause, "whereas the mercantile marine of the
country was nearly destroyed during the late rebellion in consequence of
the inability of the government to protect it." For a bit of extra rhetorical
zest, the committee's report pointed out that perfidious Great Britain had
been the primary beneficiary of the decline of the American fleet.[2] The
plight of the merchant marine was the fault of the government, and it was
thus up to the government to remedy an unacceptable situation. The
Lynch committee proposed that federal assistance take several different
forms, including a drawback (or refund) of any tariffs paid on materials
utilized in the construction of ships, or a payment "equivalent to the
drawback" for the use of American materials in the construction of iron
or composite vessels; the exemption of all tonnage from taxes other than
federal taxes; and the direct payment of subsidies (per ton) to all regularly
traveling lines, keyed to the carrying of mails.[3]

Notably, the Lynch committee did not endorse several other ideas that
had been proposed to Congress and were prominent in public debate.
Taking up once again the issue of American ships that had been registered
abroad during the Civil War, the committee concluded that those ships
should not be permitted to repatriate. "The readmission to American registry of vessels placed under foreign flags during the rebellion is against

sound public policy," the committee declared. It would set a "dangerous precedent." More significantly, at least in the long run, the Lynch committee rebuffed the request by some American shipowners to revise the nation's registry laws so that Americans could purchase ships abroad and register them in the United States. In the eyes of many shipowners, only such a policy of "free ships" would allow them to compete with foreign carriers, because foreign-built (particularly British) iron ships were cheaper and more efficient than any that could be built in the United States. The only "salvation for the shipping trade," testified Edward Hincken of the New York Ship-owners' Association, was for Congress to permit "the purchase of ships where they could be bought cheapest."[4]

Not surprisingly, given John Lynch's background as a congressman from the shipbuilding state of Maine, his committee's recommendations strongly favored the builders of ships, even at the expense of owners who wanted to rapidly replenish the American fleet. Changing the laws to allow foreign-built ships to acquire American registry would surely have provided a major shot in the arm to shipowners and shipping lines; but it just as surely would have devastated an already struggling shipbuilding industry, possibly destroying a way of life for thousands of families. Areas along the New England coast were already struggling with depressed economic conditions in the late 1860s. That said, there was a wishful, if not disingenuous, quality to the position taken by shipbuilders and their allies. Despite abundant evidence that Americans lagged significantly behind the British in the know-how needed to construct competitive iron ships, the builders insisted that the only real problem was that the United States imposed high tariffs on imported iron and other necessary materials. Free trade, rather than protection, they claimed, would save shipbuilding.[5]

This embrace of free trade, however, seemed more opportunistic than principled, a common occurrence in debates over tariffs during all historical epochs. American shipbuilders wanted to eliminate the tariffs on imported iron, but they wanted the shipbuilding industry itself to be protected against international competition through the registry laws. Advocates of "free ships" were only slightly more consistent, since they wanted "free trade" in ships but legal protection against competition in the coastal trade once they had purchased their ships from Britain or elsewhere in Europe. Edward Hincken of the New York Ship-owners' Association made the decidedly unsentimental declaration that shipowners "were for buying their tools where they could buy them cheapest, because a ship was but a tool, and it was the only tool that was prohibited from being imported." All of the interested parties, in effect, wanted free markets when it was to their advantage, while simultaneously asking for government protection—often on the grounds that it remained a national, military imperative for the United States to maintain both a shipping industry and the capacity to build ships.[6]

The nation's shipbuilders clearly gained the ascendancy in the Lynch committee, but they did not win the immediate post–Civil War policy battle. The legislation proposed by Lynch was never passed by Congress. Although the bills had significant (particularly Republican) support, they smacked heavily of special pleading for one industry at the expense of consumers, other producers, and the public treasury. The iron industry was also seen as a pet beneficiary of the laws, since shipbuilders could purchase iron at the high, protected domestic price and then be partially reimbursed by the government. To be sure, other industries, including the railroads, had succeeded in persuading or muscling the federal government into protecting or subsidizing their interests, but the maritime industry, beset by internal divisions, could not mobilize the clout to do so.[7]

Although the Lynch committee produced far more rhetoric than action, it set the terms of a debate about maritime policy that would continue for decades. The parties active in this debate agreed that it was imperative for the federal government to take steps to rescue the merchant marine. They also agreed that the failure of Congress to pass legislation in the early 1870s had contributed to the ongoing downward slide of the industry. But they disagreed, often sharply, about the deeper sources of the industry's "decadence" and about the remedies that needed to be adopted.

Those disagreements were voiced in a remarkable outpouring of books, pamphlets, and magazine articles from the early 1870s through the turn of the century. They found their way into congressional hearings, speeches, and drafts of numerous pieces of legislation. In 1882 Congress appointed another joint select committee "to inquire into the condition and wants of American ship-building and ship-owning interests."[8] In order to press their positions more effectively, diverse members of the maritime community organized themselves into an array of trade associations and lobbying groups, such as the American Shipping and Industrial League, the American Merchant Marine Association (headed by the Bath,

Maine, shipbuilder-banker-politician and 1896 Democratic vice presidential candidate Arthur Sewall), and the Merchant Marine League (sponsored by, among others, the Ohio senator Marcus Hanna.)[9] All of these organizations had, among their prime objectives, the shaping of maritime public policy.

The maritime community itself was divided into two broad camps. On one side stood those who continued to advocate "free ships." Prominent among them was John Codman, a former shipmaster who denounced the Lynch committee report as "infamously stupid" and spent years trying to have its conclusions reversed. Codman did not blame Lynch personally, since he thought that the Maine congressman was simply trying "to obtain a re-election," but he was scathing about other members of the committee. Along with his many allies in the shipping industry, Codman argued that American shipbuilders simply could not be made competitive with those of Britain, even if they received tariff drawbacks and gained experience with iron ships. Labor costs, he insisted, constituted a large proportion of the first costs of ships, and wages in the United States were inescapably higher than they were in Britain. "Free ship" advocates also maintained that it was hypocritical to defend the registry laws on the grounds that the laws protected American shipbuilding jobs and thus preserved vital skills that might be needed in wartime. By contributing to the shrinking of the merchant marine, the laws were also eliminating the jobs of American seamen, who were equally important to the national defense. "We find ourselves today almost literally without ships or sailors for the purposes of peace or of war," wrote Codman in the 1880s. The only solution was to give shipowners and merchants the same rights as all other capitalists and permit them to buy ships on the open market.[10] This argument had considerable appeal both to free traders and to those whose primary economic concern was reducing the cost of shipping. "Our merchant marine languishes for lack of liberty," concluded a minority of the joint select committee appointed in 1882, as it endorsed both "free ships" and the abolition of all tariffs on shipbuilding materials.[11]

Nor surprisingly, opposition to "free ships" remained strenuous and widespread, since changing the registry laws would have seriously hurt, if not doomed, the shipbuilding industry. Shipbuilders and their political allies attacked the idea of "free ships" on three grounds. First, it would not work; the savings in "first costs" alone were not sufficient to make American shipping lines competitive and to permanently resuscitate the maritime industry. Second, it was not an appropriate goal of public policy to simply "secure the profits of the foreign-carrying trade for American citizens." Americans who wanted to make money from shipping could (and often did) purchase interests in British ships and sail them under British or other foreign flags. The third and clearly most powerful argument was not economic at all, but rather the familiar trump card of national defense. In the words of Congressman Nelson Dingley Jr. of Maine, policy had to be guided by "the importance of preserving our commercial independence and securing safe transportation for our exports and imports in the event of wars between foreign nations, and from the necessity of maintaining a body of trained seamen who may be called upon to man our navy." The United States had to have "extensive shipyards" because "they are essential to maintain a strong merchant marine, and to build armed vessels and floating defenses in time of war." Such words were particularly resonant in the 1870s and 1880s when the poor and declining state of the American navy was increasingly evident and a growing source of concern.[12]

Opponents of the "free ships" policy were almost entirely successful in blocking initiatives for changing the registry laws to allow foreign-built ships to be registered in the United States. Congress in the 1890s did permit the American-owned Inman line, under unusual circumstances, to register two British-built ships in return for a commitment to purchase two domestically built ships. That same decade, it also allowed foreign-built ships that had been wrecked to be rebuilt in the United States and then registered under an American flag. The American lists added 350 ships before this act was repealed in 1906. But otherwise, the registry laws remained as they had been for a century.[13]

The primary alternative strategy put forward by maritime interests was to persuade Congress to subsidize shipping lines for carrying the mails. Rather than simply paying ships on an ad hoc basis for carrying particular quantities of mail, these proposals involved multiyear contracts for shipping lines to carry the mails between specified destinations at agreed-upon intervals. Precedents abounded. The nation had paid mail contracts for ships prior to the Civil War, discontinuing the practice only in 1858. Britain and most other European nations did the same, perhaps most famously in the case of Samuel Cunard's transatlantic service. It was British mail service to the west coast of South America that had prompted the development of the first trans-isthmian route in the 1840s. And

Washington was already paying the railroads to transport mail across the continent.[14] Indeed, the federal government, beginning in 1864, paid $150,000 per year for mail delivery on a monthly steamship service between Philadelphia and Rio de Janeiro. Later in the 1860s, Congress also authorized payments for mail steamship service to Japan, China, and Hawaii by the Pacific Mail Steamship Company, which operated four wooden, paddle-wheeled steamers with American officers and Chinese crews.[15]

As the debates over maritime policy heated up in the decade following the Civil War, the idea of generalizing this practice into a broad subsidy of the maritime industry gained popularity. Ostensibly at least, mail subsidies were not handouts but rather payments for a needed service. Restricted to American-built ships, they encouraged shipbuilding as well as shipping. And the subsidies could be tied to the size and speed of ships (the mails should travel safely and quickly), which would encourage the construction of faster, more modern, steam-powered, metal ships. "The plan of encouraging our own citizens to build steamships . . . by the grant of mail-contracts, is probably the best of those proposed," concluded the writer Henry Hall in 1880. "It will accomplish the end desired without sacrificing any other important national interest, and it is a simple and effective plan."[16]

Unfortunately, mail subsidies were also an obvious vehicle for corruption, in an era when it was rampant and not infrequently brought to light. That so many incidents of corruption, at all levels of government, became known to the public likely had less to do with effective policing than with the sheer brazenness of the schemes. There was no obvious way to calculate how large the payments to shipping lines should be, and acquiring a sizable, long-term mail contract was a potential gold mine for any shipping company. Inevitably, bribes were proffered to members of Congress and other public officials in return for their support of mail contracts, and—somewhat less inevitably—they were discovered. In 1874 it was disclosed that the Pacific Mail Steamship Company, which already held the contract for mail to China and Japan, had spent $1 million (a percentage of which went for bribes) in 1872 to successfully acquire another contract worth $500,000 per year. The disclosure led to the cancellation or nonrenewal of all mail contracts and tainted all discussions of shipping subsidies for more than a decade.[17]

27

JOHN ROACH AND THE NEW SHIPBUILDING

MANY OF THE KEY THEMES, SUCCESSES, DIFFICULTIES, AND failures of the maritime industry during this period were played out in the complex career of John Roach. Born in Ireland, Roach came to the United States as a penniless teenager in 1832. Unable to find work in New York, he made his way to Monmouth County, New Jersey, where he learned the trade of iron molding in the ironworks owned by James Allaire, a New York–based marine engine builder. He spent years working for Allaire and then, in the early 1850s, went into business for himself, purchasing a small ironworks on the east side of Manhattan.[1]

Roach made a success of his ironworks and, in 1862, recognizing the opportunities offered by the war, branched out into marine engine and boiler building. Aided by contracts with the Navy Department, his business boomed. With his yard employing five hundred workers, he became one of the leading engine builders in New York and a wealthy man by the late 1860s, despite several difficult contract disputes with the government.

In the aftermath of the war, Roach again saw opportunity, this time in the diminished state of the merchant marine. New ships would have to be built to restore American maritime power, and he correctly concluded that these would have to be iron ships, powered by compound steam engines with screw propellers. After carefully surveying production techniques and organization in Scotland, he decided in 1871 to purchase the site of a large (and troubled) shipyard on the Delaware River in Chester, Pennsylvania, just fifteen miles southwest of Philadelphia. This location, like the river Clyde in Scotland, had excellent access to the various raw materials needed for shipbuilding. In Chester, Roach set about building a large, vertically integrated yard for building modern, iron ships. Every element of production, from blast furnaces to rolling mills to the interior woodwork and the upholstery for the furnishings, would be under his control. Roach also intended to own shares in many of the ships that his yard produced. Sometimes called the "father of iron shipbuilding in the United States," he eventually launched more than a hundred iron vessels from his yard in Chester.

An Irish immigrant, John Roach became the "father of iron shipbuilding in the United States." Making his fortune manufacturing engines for the Union government during the Civil War, he spent the 1870s producing iron ships on the Delaware River southwest of Philadelphia, in a futile attempt to reverse the decline of American oceanic shipping.

From the outset, however, Roach needed buyers for his ships, and buyers were cautious, particularly in light of the possibility that the nation might change its navigation laws and embrace a "free ships" policy. His first orders, for combination passenger/cargo vessels, came from the Mallory Line, which operated between New York and ports on the Gulf Coast. Soon thereafter, Roach received orders for seven ships from the Pacific Mail Steamship Company, which had just received its mail subsidy from the federal government for monthly service between San Francisco, China, and Japan. These orders were an enormous potential boon to his new venture, but less than a year after production had begun, an embezzlement scandal at Pacific Mail left the firm unable to make its contractual payments to Roach. With half-built ships sitting in his yard, he had a considerable stake in saving the company. In a complex transaction, he effectively lent Pacific Mail a substantial sum of money, some of which ended up being used to bribe members of Congress.[2]

The faltering Pacific Mail then became a takeover target for the speculator Jay Gould, who hoped to gain control of the company while simultaneously purchasing shares in the Union Pacific railway, a set of moves that would leave Gould in control of major commercial transportation routes that would ultimately traverse almost every state in the western two-thirds of the country. To help drive down the price of Pacific Mail's stock, Gould and his allies used their influence in Washington to have the subsidy to Pacific Mail voided. The strategy worked. By 1875 Gould had come to control the company, while John Roach took heavy losses and found his reputation stained by the mail subsidy bribery scandal.

Bloodied but unbowed (and perhaps learning a thing or two from Gould), Roach regrouped and turned his attention to achieving his overarching goal of operating a massive steamship line that would travel from the northeastern United States to Europe and South America. One of his first steps was to establish cooperation with railway lines, including the Pennsylvania, in order to integrate international with domestic transportation. A second was to establish the United States and Brazil Mail Steamship Company, in order to demonstrate that an American line of iron ships could be run profitably. With the support of Brazil's emperor, Dom Pedro, a technology buff who had visited the Chester shipyards while on a trip that included his attendance at the opening of the nation's centennial exhibition in Philadelphia, Roach set about building two large and luxurious passenger/cargo vessels for his new line, the *City of Para* and the *City of Rio de Janeiro*, in 1877. President Rutherford B. Hayes himself attended the 1878 launching of the second of these ships, which began liner packet service late that spring, aided by a subsidy from the Brazilian government. Faced with fierce competition from British mail lines, however, Roach concluded that he also needed a subsidy from the U.S. government to survive. A subsidy was "available" in a sense, because the line that had been carrying mail between the United States and Brazil had discontinued service in 1875.

Roach and his agents descended upon Washington to lobby for a postal subsidy, quickly lining up the support of many influential Republicans, including Senators James G. Blaine of Maine and Roscoe Conkling of New York, as well as Congressman James Garfield of Ohio. Although his supporters depicted him as an exemplary entrepreneur whose energies could help rescue the shipping industry, Roach's campaign ran into significant opposition, most notably from other maritime interests. A competing American-owned firm, which regularly dispatched small cargo vessels to Brazil under the British flag, informed Congress that there was too little cargo available to warrant a line of large, luxurious ships. A collection of Baltimore merchants who operated a fleet of sailing ships to Brazil (mostly carrying flour) made a similar case, arguing that it was utterly unfair for Congress to subsidize one individual or corporation at the expense of others. Wilmington's shipbuilders opposed the subsidy bill because it would allegedly give Roach, as a shipbuilder, an unfair edge. And both "free ship" advocates and free traders, most of them Democrats, denounced the subsidy and Roach as corrupt. After intense jockeying over several sessions of Congress, the subsidy was dead. Faced with international competition and a withdrawal of the Brazilian subsidy, Roach discontinued service to Brazil in 1881, selling his luxurious ships to the Pacific Mail Steamship Company for one-third of their original cost. He was said to have lost a million dollars in the venture.

Roach's experiences revealed the difficulties and risks of engaging in the international maritime business during these years. Successfully building modern ships required not only capital and skill but also alliances with shipping lines, shippers, and even railroads. International competition was fierce, while domestic rivals fought one another bitterly for every conceivable advantage. Faced with these challenges, as well as relatively high costs for material and labor, entrepreneurs became convinced that the only sure route to predictable and stable profits ran through Washington and the provision of durable subsidies to the industry.

A decade after mail subsidies had disappeared under the taint of scandal, proposals to restore them resurfaced in Congress. After several years of jockeying, and with the Republican Party in control of the White House as well as one branch of Congress, Senator William Frye of Maine successfully negotiated the passage of the euphemistically named Postal Aid Law of 1891. (It was originally called the Ocean Mail Act.) The law authorized the postmaster general to make five- or ten-year contracts with American steamship companies to carry the mails between the United States and foreign countries. The steamships had to be American-built and substantially manned by American crews. The rate of compensation varied depending on the size and speed of the ship. Contracts were to be available for Atlantic, Pacific, and Gulf ports. There were, however, relatively few takers for these contracts, perhaps because the House insisted on cutting by one-third the subsidy for the swiftest ocean liners. Existing shipping lines, such as the Pacific Mail Steamship Company, did contract to carry the mails to several Caribbean ports and to the Pacific, and several American ships plied the lucrative North Atlantic route. But no new shipping lines were formed to take advantage of the postal subsidies.[3]

Faced with the ongoing decline of American international shipping and concluding that the subsidies offered by the Postal Aid Law were inadequate, key segments of the maritime industry began to press for a much stronger measure: a system of direct bounties for the construction and operation of American ships. The congressional champions of this idea were Senators Frye and Hanna, both Republican members of the Commerce Committee. Frye, of course, was from Maine and thus politically, if not genetically, obliged to actively promote shipbuilding interests. Like many Republicans, he also harbored a growing sense of the importance of international trade to the nation's well-being. The increasingly powerful Hanna not only had a background in Great Lakes shipping; he was also a critical exponent of a Republican vision that the state ought to be (and, in fact, long had been) an active sponsor of economic development. Unlike many of his contemporaries, he did not shrink from the prospect of utilizing public funds to promote a private industry. He was deeply certain that the strength of key industries was inseparable from the strength of the nation. Both Hanna and Frye, like many of their contemporaries, had imperial ambitions for the United States and were influenced by the naval theorist Alfred Thayer Mahan's emphasis on the importance of sea power in determining a nation's international status and clout.[4]

The Hanna-Frye Subsidy Bill was first introduced in 1898. Only in 1900 and 1901, however, did its backers, spurred on by the palpable importance and visible shortcomings of the merchant marine during the Spanish-American War, make the most strenuous efforts to get it passed. Hanna defended the measure as legislation "not aimed at any class or any particular industry" but as one "whose influence will permeate every industry and every class." Despite his immense clout, as a congressional leader and close ally of President McKinley, he was unable to get the bill through both houses of Congress. Democrats staunchly opposed it, as did many of Hanna's Republican colleagues from the Midwest, who saw little to be gained from government subsidies for international shipping.[5] "The professions of this bill are insincere and its principles are unsound," declared the Democratic minority of the House Committee on Merchant Marine and Fisheries.[6] The *New York Times* flatly opposed the measure, while endorsing, once again, the idea of "free ships."[7]

Hanna tried again after McKinley's assassination, with the support of President Theodore Roosevelt, who noted that he was "deeply concerned at the decline of our ocean fleet."[8] But the most that they could achieve, in 1904, was the congressional appointment of a new Merchant Marine Commission, empowered to conduct an extremely broad inquiry into the problem. After compiling a two-thousand-page report, the commission, headed by Harold Gallinger, in 1905 called for an extensive new system of subventions "to promote the national defense, to create a force of naval volunteers, to establish American ocean mail lines. . . , to promote commerce, and to provide revenue from tonnage." Some of these proposed subventions were tied to mail-carrying; others, including subventions for deep-sea fishing, were not.[9]

By the early years of the twentieth century, however, the maritime industry had developed a new political problem: monopolization. In 1901–1902, the United States Shipbuilding Company acquired Newport News Shipbuilding, the Bath Iron Works, the Union Iron Works, and several other major shipyards. At roughly the same time, J. P. Morgan launched his ultimately ill-fated effort to gain control of North Atlantic shipping by purchasing interests in various lines.[10] Both branches of the maritime industry, thus, were coming to appear less like small businesses or partnerships and more like corporate monoliths that hardly seemed to need or merit government subsidies. In part as a result, none of the proposals put forward by the Merchant Marine Commission was passed by Congress, despite repeated efforts in the years immediately following the issuance of its report.[11] It would take another decade, a decade of growing empire and approaching war, before the government enacted any significant changes in the navigation laws and public policy.

On the surface at least, the inaction of the federal government between the Civil War and the early years of the twentieth century is something of a puzzle. The decline of American international shipping was extraordinarily sharp and rapid; the industry had deep roots in American economic and political history, and one immediate cause of that decline was a war fought to preserve the nation. The maritime industry, moreover, had powerful political allies—Maine's congressional delegation alone was a pantheon of national leaders—and numerous industries were receiving government support in the form of protective tariffs. There was, moreover, a unique and compelling national defense argument for making sure that American shipping and shipbuilding remained strong.

Yet the case for an aggressive maritime policy inescapably became enmeshed in political and ideological conflicts over which the industry had little control. Protective tariffs, for example, may have been common, but they were hardly greeted with universal applause. Tariffs were one of the persistent, hot issues in late-nineteenth-century election campaigns, and the Democratic Party, with its rural and small-town base, stood for an end to high tariffs and the government protection of individual industries. There was a sectional dimension to these conflicts as well, with the South and the West squaring off against the more industrial Northeast, which was also the home of most advocates of public support for shipping and ship-building. Moreover, subsidies to shipping lines or shipbuilders seemed, in many respects, to be even more objectionable than high tariffs. The latter put money into the public coffers, while the maritime industry was, in effect, asking for cash directly from the public treasury. Most Americans, in the end, did not think that they had anything to gain from such expenditures. International trade may or may not have mattered to them, but the flag under which a ship sailed was of little direct consequence.[12]

The industry itself contributed mightily to its political failures. It was stained by its efforts to bribe public officials into supporting mail subsidies in the 1870s, and the increasing concentration of the industry in later decades undercut images of distressed towns and suffering workmen. Indeed, many Americans, especially in certain parts of the country, may have sensed that there was something disingenuous about portrayals of the maritime world as experiencing hardship. These citizens knew well that coastal and Great Lakes shipping were flourishing without any subsidy, although they benefited from cabotage protection. Finally, and perhaps most importantly, the divisions within the maritime industry made it extremely unlikely that the demands for financial aid would garner widespread public support. Shipowners who wanted free ships spent decades attacking and undercutting the claims of shipbuilders. Shipbuilders in turn savaged the arguments put forward by advocates of free ships. The participants in the policy wars acted like the self-interested businessmen that they were and not like the patriotic defenders of the national good that they claimed to be. In so doing, they repeatedly undermined the one argument—about the special role of the industry in wartime—that might plausibly have persuaded Congress to adopt more ample and supportive legislation.

28

West Coast Shipping and the Rise of Maritime Labor

In the second half of the nineteenth century, the shipping industry on the West Coast grew to match the economic development of the region. Leading the growth was California, whose population swelled from 35,000 (mostly forty-niners) in 1850 to more than a million inhabitants in 1890. By that time Washington had 350,000 residents and Oregon 313,000. San Francisco was both the major port on the West Coast and the hub of regional economic activity. Coastal sailing vessels brought lumber from Washington, Oregon, and even Canada to supply construction in the south, while return voyages carried oranges, wine, and other agricultural products. The dominant position of the Pacific Mail Steamship Company (PMSS), established during the gold rush, was overtaken in 1876, at least in the coastal trade, by the Pacific Coast Steamship Company, one of many shipping lines at the time to have deep ties to the railroad industry. The PMSS inaugurated steamer service to Asia in 1867, and Matson Line began serving Hawaii in 1882. By 1890 San Francisco ranked sixth among the country's forty customs districts, and the West Coast accounted for more than 5 percent of America's shipping.[1] This young, small, but thriving arena of shipping activity proved to be fertile ground for the birth of organized maritime labor.

Men who worked on the water enjoyed—more properly endured—a unique relationship to both their employers and to the state. The reasons for this were inherent in the enterprise itself. A ship at sea, whose next destination might well be a foreign port, was not a setting conducive to the operation of a conventional labor market. Workers could not quit and leave, they could not be fired and dispatched from the premises, they could not strike without endangering the ship and its crew. Moreover, the conventional instruments of state power, such as marshals, sheriffs, and courts, were unavailable to enforce order, adjudicate disputes, or respond to criminal acts committed by one seaman against another. From long experience, these special circumstances were addressed by vesting state power in a hierarchy of ships' officers while spelling out the terms of employment and behavior for seamen in detailed legal codes. The laws governing shipboard labor were designed both to maintain discipline and to varying degrees to protect seamen from the arbitrary or abusive exercise of the power granted to captains and masters.

A merchant seaman, thus, was a civilian whose working life resembled a series of short-term enlistments in the military. By signing the shipping articles for a particular voyage (many of the terms of which were dictated by statutes), a seaman agreed to surrender substantial freedoms, to accept the orders of officers, and to fulfill a variety of obligations. In turn, the ship's captain agreed not only to pay the seaman's wages but also to supply him with provisions and abide by a set of legal regulations regarding the welfare of the ship and the administration of discipline.[2]

The first acts of Congress dealing with seamen were passed in 1790, soon after the nation's creation. Modeled on British legislation of 1729, these acts outlined a shipboard penal code as well as regulations regarding the welfare of seamen, such as specifying the quantity of salted meat, water, and bread that had to be on board for a transatlantic voyage. More disciplinary than protective, the legislation was designed, above all, to prevent desertion and to formalize the traditional power of ship captains. Desertion was designated a criminal offense, which meant, in effect, that it was a crime for seamen, but not shipowners, to break their contracts. Although modified periodically—flogging was finally outlawed as a punishment in 1850—the basic structure of these maritime laws remained intact until after the Civil War. Notably, from the outset of American history, the laws governing the employment relations of seamen were the domain of the federal government, not the states. A major recodification of these laws was undertaken in the Shipping Commissioner's Act of 1872, which strengthened slightly the provisions protecting the welfare of seamen. The law also created the new office of shipping commissioner, a post to be filled in every major port. The commissioner was given the independence and authority to supervise the hiring and firing of all seamen, to regulate apprenticeships, and to settle disputes.[3]

There were, of course, many workers in the maritime industries who did not actually go to sea and whose terms of employment remained unregulated in the late nineteenth and early twentieth centuries. Skilled tradesmen who built ships negotiated their employment contracts, individually or collectively, much as skilled tradesmen did in other industries. Longshoremen were often indistinguishable from day laborers in hundreds of ports around the nation. They were casual laborers, working at irregular intervals for low wages and living in overcrowded, often unsanitary housing. No federal labor laws applied to these men, while state regulations were sporadic and generally feeble until after the turn of the century. Seamen constituted the only segment of the maritime labor world that received special attention from the state.[4]

Between the Civil War and World War I, most positions in the maritime labor force came to be filled by immigrants, their children, and African American males.[5] For white, native-born American men, the lure of seafaring diminished as the great sailing vessels were replaced by steam, corporate ownership came to dominate the industry, and opportunities for economic advancement and even adventure multiplied elsewhere in the economy. Their berths were filled by immigrants, particularly after 1884, when Congress passed legislation permitting American shipowners to sign up crew members in foreign ports at the wage rates prevailing in those ports. By the 1890s only a third of the men who signed articles in the presence of shipping commissioners were American citizens, a percentage that increased slightly after 1900. A detailed study by the Merchant Marine Commission in 1904 found that American citizens constituted "considerably less than 50 percent" of all seamen in the merchant marine, although the percentage of Americans, "native or naturalized," was substantially higher in the coastwise trade than in foreign commerce. Despite rampant discrimination and segregation, the number of African Americans in the merchant marine also rose, particularly in the South.[6]

Similarly, immigrants became increasingly prominent in many of the nation's fisheries, particularly as the class structure of fishing shifted and most fishermen became wage earners, rather than receiving "shares" of a catch. The traditional fishing towns of New England, for example, came to be dominated by Canadian and Portuguese immigrants.[7] Meanwhile, on land, occupations like longshoring underwent the same transformation that affected nearly all unskilled and semiskilled jobs. They became the domain of the foreign-born, their children, and, in some locales, African Americans. By 1910 roughly 60 percent of all longshoremen were immigrants, while another 20 percent were African American. In southern ports like New Orleans, blacks performed a great deal of the work done on the waterfront, but they did so in an increasingly segregated and racially tense environment.[8]

That Americans displayed less interest in going to sea was hardly surprising given the conditions of seaboard labor. Seamen lived in cramped, sometimes vile quarters aboard ship, often suffering from inadequate nutrition. A government report in the 1870s declared that conditions aboard American ships were worse than they were in prisons.[9] Common seamen had an arduous work schedule, generally sleeping only four hours at a time and working for an average of fourteen hours a day. Compelled to submit to the absolute authority of their officers, they were not infrequently abused or subjected to corporal punishment, and their jobs were inherently dangerous, especially on large sailing vessels in severe storms. In return, they were paid poorly. Although shipowners complained that American labor was more costly than labor on foreign-flagged ships, wages remained low, thanks in part to the competition of foreign sailors. In the 1890s able seamen on transoceanic voyages were paid $15 to $20 per month, while those in the unionized Pacific coastwise trades earned $25 to $30. These wages were roughly equivalent to those paid for semiskilled physical labor on land. Even without unionization, wages in the coastal trades were higher because of the absence of foreign competition. Officers, of course, were better paid and lived in more humane conditions. On the Great Lakes in 1904, according to statistics submitted to the Merchant Marine Commission, first mates on steel steamers were paid $115 per month, while firemen were paid $45 and ordinary seamen $25.[10]

The exploitation of seamen, moreover, was not limited to low wages for hard work, a common fate in the late-nineteenth-century working class. They were also vulnerable to petty entrepreneurs who preyed on merchant mariners in all of the nation's ports. Boardinghouse (or saloon) keepers, known as "crimps," often conspired with ship captains to control the labor market and fleece seamen of their wages. Crimps provided food, lodging, women, and alcohol, often driving men into debt. They then arranged new shipboard jobs for the seamen, pocketing an advance on their wages, which was paid directly from the captain to the boarding-house keeper. Crimps were also known to conspire with captains to put seamen in situations where they could be charged with desertion, making them liable to forfeiture of pay. Not unlike the padrones who controlled the markets for unskilled immigrant labor in some cities (and, in some respects, not unlike the merchants who utilized the crop-lien system to keep African Americans tied to the land through debt), the crimps prof-ited by controlling access to jobs and then taking advantage of the igno-rance and frailties of seamen. Complaints were widespread that merchant seamen, living on the margins of respectable society, were often ensnared in webs of exploitation that left them with little more freedom on shore than they had at sea. "From the day he arrives in port, until the day of his departure," the seaman "is never out of the hands of sharpers, who coax, wheedle, debauch and pander to his worst vices until his last dollar is gone," reported a government commission. "Not even then is he a free agent. As the price of release from their clutches, he must submit to have his future earnings mortgaged."[11]

Most accounts of maritime labor agree that conditions aboard Ameri-can ships were deteriorating in the late nineteenth century. Pressed by international competition, shipowners sought to cut expenses by hiring cheaper foreign workers and by reducing crew sizes, thereby increasing the workload of each man on board. Seamen also complained about abuse and cruelty aboard ship, by captains and officers all too accustomed to exercising nearly absolute authority over their crews. In the 1890s the Sailors' Union of the Pacific (SUP) collected examples of such abuse and published them first in the influential *Coast Seamen's Journal* and then as a widely distributed pamphlet known as *The Red Record*.[12] One entry noted:

LOUISIANA, Captain Oliver, arrived in San Francisco, August 1890. One seaman being sick begged to be permitted to stay on deck when there was work aloft. Second-mate Davis answered by striking him on the head with a belaying pin, then struck him several blows with his fist. Seaman appealed to the captain, who replied by striking him in the face. First-mate Oliver (son of the captain) beat the man with a block of wood till he sank to the deck.

Such incidents, no doubt, were extreme, but they nonetheless pointed to the unique hazards of the rough-cultured maritime world, to the precariousness of life, limb, and dignity in a workplace where employers, backed by the state, wielded extraordinary power over the men they commanded.[13] It was no coincidence that these abuses sparked the first organized resistance on the West Coast, where shipowners and operators were less entrenched than in the more established maritime regions of the United States.

29

ANDREW FURUSETH, THE UNIONS, AND THE LAW

EFFORTS TO IMPROVE THE LIVES AND WORKING CONDITIONS of seamen followed two distinct yet related paths during the late nineteenth century and thereafter. The first was unionization, a strategy common to almost all working-class occupations during the period. The second was to pressure the federal government for legislation to protect the interests of seamen. This latter strategy was virtually unique in American labor history and was rooted in the distinctive manner in which the nation had always superintended the relationship between shipmasters and seamen.

The first durable unions of seamen in the United States were formed on the West Coast.[1] The late 1860s and 1870s had witnessed several organizing efforts on the Great Lakes and in the ports of the Pacific, but these had faltered by 1880, a pattern mirrored in labor organizations in most occupations around the country. In 1885, however, just as the Knights of Labor were reaching peak strength and the American Federation of Labor was being founded, seamen on coastwise sailing schooners formed the Sailors' Union of the Pacific (SUP). A half dozen years later, they merged with an organization of sailors on steam schooners.[2]

A variety of factors made the West Coast more fertile ground for labor organizing than either the East or Gulf coasts or the Great Lakes. Until the building of the Panama Canal, the maritime industry in the Pacific was relatively isolated from major international competition, and the demand for seafaring labor was high. There were few ports along the Pacific coast compared to the Atlantic, the important coastwise lumber trade was not open to foreign ships, and the labor force was far more ethnically and racially homogeneous in the West than it was on the Atlantic, the Gulf, or the Great Lakes. Since the sailors of the Pacific were overwhelmingly of northern European origin, organizing efforts were not plagued by the racial conflicts so prevalent in the East and on the Gulf, where black and Hispanic workers were a significant constituency.[3]

The SUP, like all trade unions, sought to increase the wages and improve the working conditions of its members. Yet its leaders, most notably Walter Macarthur and the charismatic Andrew Furuseth, recognized from the outset that the union's distinctive challenge was to eliminate the control that crimps and ship captains wielded over maritime jobs. It was the crimp system that kept seamen so powerless and severely exploited, but the power of the crimps was rooted in the inescapably "casual" and decentralized structure of the market for maritime labor. Multiple, short-term employments subjected seamen to endless rounds of contracting for their services, compounding their vulnerability. Consequently, one of the central goals of the SUP was to take control of jobs away from the crimps by creating a union hiring hall where men would come to seek work and where captains would come to seek sailors. The union's first efforts to establish such a hiring hall, or shipping office, were met with ferocious resistance, both from shipowners' associations and from the benign-sounding Coasting Seamen's Shipping Association, an organization of boardinghouse keepers. That resistance was initially successful, largely because the SUP found it nearly impossible to win strikes during the prolonged depression of the 1890s. Yet after the turn of the century, when the depression had ended and key maritime laws had changed (as outlined below), the union did manage to rid the ports of crimps and bargain collectively with shipowners.[4]

Meanwhile, the SUP also tried to organize workers elsewhere in the country. In 1892 it sponsored a convention in Chicago attended by delegates from small maritime unions on the Atlantic and Gulf coasts and the Great Lakes. The convention announced the formation of the National (later International) Seamen's Union (ISU), an umbrella organization of local and regional groups that became affiliated with the American

Federation of Labor in 1893. At the convention, the SUP and the new seamen's union announced the creation of a fund to be utilized to increase organization and end the crimping system on the Atlantic coast. That effort, however, bore little fruit. In addition, the SUP sought to establish ties to unions of skilled maritime workers, including the marine firemen, although, as was common at the time, the different organizations did not merge into a single, industrial union.[5]

As was true for most American unions founded in the 1880s, the primary achievement of the SUP, from its creation until 1899, was to survive as an organization, despite bitter opposition from employers and adverse economic conditions. One ferocious opponent of maritime unions—indeed all unions—was Marcus Hanna, who was credited by the Cleveland Central Labor Union with having destroyed the seamen's union of the lower Great Lakes as well as an organization of street railway employees in Cleveland.[6] Having survived, the SUP was well positioned to take advantage of an improving economy to expand its membership and its clout after the turn of the century.

By 1905 the SUP and its affiliated West-Coast unions, such as the cooks, stewards, and firemen, had won recognition from many shipowners and had nearly seven thousand members, more than 80 percent of the men employed in that region's coastal and oceanic trades. The SUP's members paid dues, had access to jobs through union agreements, and received death, sickness, and shipwreck benefits. Additionally, members of affiliated unions could transfer their membership from one region to another without paying new initiation fees. The SUP also continued publishing the influential *Coast Seamen's Journal*, a widely read labor publication founded shortly after the union's birth. In addition, working with the AFL, it resolved several jurisdictional disputes with the longshoremen's union regarding the use of seamen to unload ships as well as the longshoremen's union's desire to organize some shipboard labor. On the East and Gulf coasts, there was also progress, although tensions surrounding the organization of African American sailors and Spanish-speaking firemen seriously checked the gains. On the Great Lakes, early in the twentieth century a contract between the Lake Carriers' Association and the Lake Seamen's Union provided that all steamers and barges would employ union labor, to be provided by the Lake Seamen's Union. By 1910 many, but not a majority, of seamen on the Atlantic and Gulf coasts, as well as the Great Lakes, were union members.[7]

The partial success of the SUP and other maritime unions was surely a credit to the energy and talents of Andrew Furuseth and other dedicated union activists. Yet the story of labor organizing in the maritime trades between the Civil War and World War I also mirrored developments throughout the nation's working class. Despite broad variations in the structure of labor markets and the social composition of occupations, many different trades witnessed the formation of their first durable unions in the wake of the long depression of the 1870s. Those commonly stumbled in the 1890s but survived to ride a wave of prosperity and sort out jurisdictional disputes after 1900. In the maritime industry, as in numerous others, the basic structures of labor organization erected by the first decade of the twentieth century remained in place until the late 1930s.

The story of labor organizing in the maritime trades may have been typical of the era, but the history of legal changes affecting the welfare of seamen was not. State governments passed very little legislation dealing with the rights of workers in the late nineteenth century, and federal statutes were even more rare. As discussed earlier, however, seamen had long been enmeshed in a significant network of federal laws, and they knew that improving their lot depended upon convincing Congress to pass new legislation. As quasi-wards of the state, seamen had no choice but to turn to it for help.

Two issues were paramount, both linked to the desire of seamen to escape the hold that captains and crimps had over their lives. One was putting an end to the long-standing use of imprisonment as a punishment for desertion. Laws making desertion a criminal offense put the state squarely in the service of employers, making it extremely difficult for seafaring workers to quit their jobs, no matter how poorly and abusively they were treated. The second issue (or cluster of issues) had to do with the timing of wage payments and the manner in which they were paid. Seamen wanted to eliminate the "allotment" system, which permitted captains to pay a portion of their wages directly to boardinghouse keepers or crimps, allegedly to pay off the seamen's debts. They also wanted to receive a percentage of their wages whenever they were in port, so that they did not have to become indebted to crimps during a midvoyage stopover. And they sought to prevent boardinghouse keepers from seizing the clothing of seamen who owed them money. Additionally, they desired higher wages, better provisions, more humane work schedules, and the ability to inspect ships to determine their safety. But the core of the seamen's legislative agenda was to dismantle the long-standing legal structures that kept them from the having the same economic freedom as other workers.

The Shipping Commissioner's Act of 1872 did little to achieve those goals, but the Dingley Act of 1884 struck a blow against the crimp system by making it illegal for shipmasters to advance wages or pay allotments to anyone other than a close relative of the seaman. At the same time, the legislation made concessions to shipowners by lessening their financial obligations to seamen who were discharged in foreign ports because of injury, violation of agreements, or the sale or lack of seaworthiness of their vessel. Unfortunately for seamen, the power of crimps and their allies was sufficient that they convinced Congress in 1886 to undo the good it had done by amending the Dingley Act to permit allotments to "original creditors" at a rate of ten dollars per month in settlement of debts for boarding or clothing. In 1890 Congress made things worse by passing a law that reinforced the penalties for desertion in the coastwise trades.[8]

In the early 1890s the SUP drew up a comprehensive set of legislative proposals that would become the centerpiece of reform efforts for the next twenty years. Labeled an "Appeal to Congress," this package of roughly thirty reforms was endorsed by the International Seamen's Union and the AFL and put forward tirelessly by Andrew Furuseth in Washington. It called, of course, for the abolition of the allotment system and of imprisonment for desertion. It also sought to limit employment on American-flagged ships to citizens or those having formally declared their intention to become citizens, a provision that would have, among other things, decisively eliminated the Chinese, who were not eligible for citizenship. The program further demanded guarantees regarding the right of seamen to receive a portion of their wages in any port upon demand, the content of shipboard provisions, the amount of crew living space, the regularity of working hours, and protections for seamen discharged in foreign ports.[9]

To promote this agenda, the SUP became involved in electoral politics, endorsing the congressional candidacy of the California Democrat James G. Maguire, an ex-judge who strenuously supported the seamen's program. Once elected, Maguire introduced into Congress a set of bills embodying the program. After several years of legislative jockeying, Congress passed the Maguire Act in February 1895. A partial and watered-down measure, the act terminated imprisonment for desertion and any use of allotments in the coastwise trade while also exempting a seaman's clothing from attachment. Although it had numerous gaps that were quickly exploited by shipowners, its passage was a significant political victory for the SUP.[10]

It was during this political campaign to seek legislative protections for seamen that Andrew Furuseth began his personal transformation from union organizer to maritime labor legend. A native of Norway, he had failed in his boyhood dream of becoming a military officer and turned instead to the sea.[11] Seven years after arriving in the United States, where he plied the coastal trade out of San Francisco, he came ashore permanently in 1886 to become the secretary of the Coast Seamen's Union (later the Sailors' Union of the Pacific) and devote the remainder of his eighty-three years to the cause of maritime labor. Self-taught in maritime law and tradition, he became a controversial but effective champion of the rights of American seamen. For his statesmanship, his selflessness, his crusade of speaking truth to power, and perhaps also for his angular features and soulful eyes, he became known in labor circles as the "Abe Lincoln of the Seas." Many public officials thought highly of him as well, but American shipowners saw him as a "foreign-born agitator" spreading "dissension and dissatisfaction among a class of men that were before his coming content, prosperous, and happy."[12] Maritime labor faced years of continuing adversity before Furuseth achieved victory.

One such setback came at the hands of the Supreme Court, in the famous *Arago* case. The shortcomings of the Maguire Act and other maritime labor laws still in effect became starkly apparent within months of its passage. In May 1895 Robert Robertson and three other seamen signed on to the barkentine *Arago* in San Francisco, for a voyage to Knappton, Washington, and then on to Valparaiso, Chile, and other foreign ports, returning eventually to the United States. When the ship stopped in Knappton, the sailors, unhappy with con-

Known as the "Abe Lincoln of the Seas," the Norwegian immigrant Andrew Furuseth converted from seaman to maritime labor advocate in the 1880s, finally achieving the Seamen's Act of 1915. By the 1930s, however, his strategy of working within the system gave way to more direct labor actions in the streets.

ditions aboard and aware (they thought) of their new rights under the Maguire Act, refused to continue the voyage, left the ship, and went to Astoria, Oregon. At the shipmaster's request, they were arrested in Oregon, held in jail for sixteen days, and then forcibly returned to the *Arago*. When Robertson and his allies failed to obey an order to "turn to" aboard ship, they were put in chains, brought to San Francisco, arrested, and placed in jail for desertion. There they remained for nine months, first awaiting trial and then awaiting the outcome of an appeal to the U.S. Supreme Court. The appeal, backed by the SUP and other maritime unions, claimed that the arrest of the men violated their constitutional rights under the Thirteenth Amendment, which prohibited involuntary servitude.[13]

In January 1897 the Supreme Court rejected the claims of the seamen and their allies, upholding their arrest and detention for desertion. The Court found ample legislative basis for such action, dating back to the original shipping laws of 1790, and the Shipping Commissioner's Act of 1872. The legislative sanction was not altered by the Maguire Act, the Court held, since the voyage of the *Arago* was international, not coastal, even if the ship had stopped at a domestic port. The Court also concluded that the use of state power to compel men to work did not constitute "involuntary servitude" since that term applied only to servitude that was "involuntary" at its outset, rather than service contractually agreed to that had become distasteful or unacceptable. That the Thirteenth Amendment prohibited not just "slavery" but "involuntary servitude," the Court stated, meant that its framers wanted to outlaw "the system of Mexican peonage and the Chinese coolie trade," not that they wanted to introduce any "novel doctrine with respect to certain descriptions of service which have always been treated as exceptional." The Court embraced the "ancient characterization of seamen as 'wards of admiralty,'" and observed that "the business of navigation could scarcely be carried on without some guaranty, beyond the ordinary civil remedies upon contract, that the sailor will not desert the ship at a critical moment."[14]

Justice John Harlan offered a ringing—and soon to be famous—dissent from the majority opinion. He dismissed the relevance of historical statutes, as well as the traditional treatment of desertion, claiming that ancient traditions dated from periods "when human life and human liberty were regarded as of little value." In any case, he said, the passage of the Thirteenth Amendment had provided new rights to all Americans. He challenged the analogy between seamen and soldiers (who also could not legally desert their posts) by pointing out that soldiers and sailors in the army and navy were "engaged in the performance of public, not private, duties." A seaman, on the other hand, had made a private contract and, although he could "be liable in damages for the non-performance of his agreement," he could not be "compelled against his will to continue" working for his employer. "The holding of any person in custody . . . against his will, for the purpose of compelling him to render personal service to another in a private business" did constitute "involuntary servitude forbidden by the Constitution of the United States." Denying that seamen constituted a unique group of employees, Harlan maintained that the same logic that made their desertion a criminal offense could be mobilized against the "employees upon railroads and steamboats."[15]

The *Arago* decision ignited a storm of protest from seamen, the labor movement more broadly, and social reformers around the nation. The *San Francisco Examiner* concluded that the Supreme Court had determined that "the difference between a deep-water sailor and a slave is $15 per month." In March 1897 a mass meeting in New York listened to Samuel Gompers and Andrew Furuseth denounce the decision, with Gompers claiming that the maritime laws of the United States were "more severe than . . . [those of] any other civilized nation on the globe." Furuseth, displaying his talent for the dramatic gesture, declined an invitation from the city of San Francisco for the seamen to participate in that year's Fourth of July parade, declaring that the "presence of bondsmen" would be "an imposition" on "the freemen who will on the Fourth of July celebrate their freedom." With the support of Gompers, as well as labor leaders throughout the country, Furuseth returned to Washington to lobby for passage of new legislation that would reverse the Supreme Court's decision.[16]

Congress reacted to the popular pressure and to Furuseth's indefatigable efforts by passing, in December 1898, a bill introduced in the Senate by California's Stephen S. White. It was sponsored in the House by James Maguire, among others. The White bill was something of a compromise, dotted with concessions to shipping interests, but it nonetheless constituted a significant advance in the rights of seamen. Most importantly, it provided for the abolition of imprisonment for desertion for any American seamen in American or nearby foreign ports, on coastal or international voyages. Americans could still be imprisoned, for a reduced term of

Savannah: First Transatlantic Steamship Leaving Port in May 1819. The United States conducted steamboat services on its coastal and inland waterways for two decades before the rest of the world caught on. It could not, however, transfer that capability to oceanic transport. The *Savannah* made just one passage to Europe and back. Successful oceanic steam navigation required more powerful engines and screw propellers. (From a painting by John Stobart.)

Salem: Derby Wharf and the Custom House, ca. 1825. The wharf and the custom house were symbols of Salem's eminence in worldwide shipping early in the nineteenth century. The shallow harbor, revealed here at low tide, explains why Salem was soon to be eclipsed by deeper-water ports. (From a painting by John Stobart.)

Santa Barbara: The Brig Pilgrim *Rounding Point Conception for Monterey.* Richard Henry Dana made the *Pilgrim* famous when he recounted his experiences as a crewman in 1835 in *Two Years before the Mast* (1840). This account of the abuses to which seamen were subjected by heartless shipowners and brutal officers contributed to the reform of the maritime industry. (From a painting by John Stobart.)

The Black Ball Packet Orpheus *Leaving New York in 1835*. A group of New York textile merchants initiated scheduled service to Liverpool in 1817, leaving New York on the fifth of each month and Liverpool on the first. The service came to be called the Black Ball Line for the distinctive insignia visible on *Orpheus*'s sail. (From a painting by John Stobart.)

Night Call at Bayou Sara. Mississippi riverboats in the 1800s had such shallow draft that they could be pulled close to shore for loading and unloading without elaborate docks. Here the *Belle Amour* is depicted taking on cotton by moonlight at a small settlement just south of Natchez, Mississippi. (From a painting by John Stobart.)

The Charles W. Morgan *Cutting In.* During its heyday in the first half of the nineteenth century, whaling was a mainstay of the American maritime industry supporting ship-building, training sailors, and even providing capital for other maritime ventures. The *Morgan*, depicted here in the latter part of the 1800s cutting up a carcass that was tied alongside, is preserved at Mystic Seaport in Connecticut. (From a painting by John Stobart.)

San Francisco: The Gold Rush Harbor in 1849. The steamship *California* is depicted aground and awaiting coal in the center of this painting, just one of the hundreds of ships abandoned in Yerba Buena Cove as crewmen fled to the gold fields. Telegraph Hill is visible to the left, through the early evening fog. (From a painting by John Stobart.)

San Francisco: The Flying Cloud *Entering Port After Her Record Passage from New York in 1851.* Ship captain Josiah P. Creesy drove John McKay's masterpiece on her maiden voyage from New York to San Francisco in less than ninety days, a record. Creesy brushed off broken spars and mutinous crewmen to complete the feat, then promptly set sail for China. (From a painting by John Stobart.)

a month, for desertion in a foreign port, and foreign seamen could still be imprisoned in the United States. It also abolished all corporal punishment aboard ship, and gave seamen in all ports the right to receive one-half of the wages they were due. Perhaps the most unpopular clause of the bill was one that still permitted one month's wages to be advanced as an allotment to an "original creditor" in the foreign trade.[17]

Furuseth and other union leaders were well aware that their victory was incomplete. Gompers himself noted that the White Act did not succeed in giving seamen "that full freedom to quit at will and move freely from place to place, which is the inalienable natural right of man." But significant progress had been made since 1890, both substantively and strategically, and the seamen, with growing union strength after 1900, were determined to continue the fight. The "navigation laws of the country," editorialized the *Coast Seamen's Journal* in 1904, "are antiquated and disgraceful, compared to American standards. . . . No American boy with any spunk in him will submit himself to the conditions created by the maritime law, except . . . as the alternative of a term in prison." Unions and their allies sought the complete abolition of imprisonment for debt for all seamen in all ports. They also demanded the end of all allotments, as well as improved wages, working conditions, and safety.

The changes in maritime labor law up to 1900 did not completely eliminate the "special" or hybrid status of men who worked aboard ship. Far more than in most trades, the terms of employment between seamen and shipmasters remained shaped by custom and law rather than the exigencies of the market, and the unusual circumstances of shipboard labor continued to warrant an umbrella of protection by the federal government. Yet what occurred between 1870 and 1900 was nonetheless a profound change, the cracking and stripping away of legal structures that did indeed date to "time immemorial," as the majority decision in *Robertson v. Baldwin* noted. This happened, in part, because of shifts in technology brought on by steam vessels with different schedules and staffing requirements and shifts in the social composition of the maritime labor force. Ship captains and sailors ceased to be relatives or men from the same town or region, with traditional and complex ties among them. By the late nineteenth century, they were strangers, employers and employees, brought together for brief and dangerous sojourns together on blue or brown water.

Yet there was another source as well. Deep and far-reaching shifts in economic, social, and political values were transforming the United States with the triumph of industrial capitalism in the nineteenth century. Throughout the nation, traditional and customary bonds were displaced by market relationships. Networks of obligation and constraints on individual behavior were overwhelmed by demands for economic liberty. During the first half of the nineteenth century, imprisonment for debt was abolished, and employers were increasingly required to pay wages weekly or monthly, rather than at the end of a season or the end of a year. Slavery, of course, was abolished in the 1860s, and the importation of immigrants for "contract labor," in which employers paid for the immigration journey in return for a kind of indenture, was made illegal in 1885. In the South, to be sure, a system of debt peonage was installed after the Civil War, dramatically limiting the actual freedom of rural African Americans. But elsewhere, the market was triumphing and with that triumph came the wholehearted ideological embrace of "that full freedom to quit at will and move freely from place to place" that both the economy and working people demanded. This was a force that even centuries of tradition could not resist.

30

SHIPS, STEEL, AND
MORE LABOR

THE NEXT GREAT ADVANCE FOR AMERICAN MARITIME LABOR took place in a dramatically changed political, technological, and economic environment. One icon of those technological and economic changes took float when the Great Lakes ore carrier *J. Pierpont Morgan* slid down the ways in 1906. Its launching heralded a twentieth-century revolution in commercial shipping just as significant in its way as another famous launching just two months earlier. When HMS *Dreadnought* slid into the waters off the Portsmouth Dockyard in February 1906, it initiated the age of the all-big-gun battleship, a design so compelling that it was said to have made all previous battleships obsolete. *J. Pierpont Morgan* likewise introduced a new era of shipping by raising the standard on the Great Lakes for ship size and efficiency. From the perspective of the twenty-first century, it also seems to have announced the age of the megaship, the bulk carrier that would dominate especially the late twentieth century.

Measuring 605 feet from bow to stern, the *J. Pierpont Morgan* became the largest ship on the lakes on the day of her launching. She and her sister ships to follow, the "standard 600-footers," were built from off-the-shelf plans in less than eight weeks for about $440,000. Her 1,800-horsepower triple-expansion engine allowed her to carry 14,000 tons of iron ore on about half an ounce of coal per ton-mile. At that rate, she

One of the first megaships of the twentieth century, the Great Lakes ore carrier *J. Pierpont Morgan* (1906) is seen here being serviced by new Hulett unloaders in Ashtabula, Ohio. The ship, named for the cofounder of United States Steel, sailed in that company's fleet.

could deliver her cargo from the rich iron mines around Lake Superior to transshipment points on the coast of Lake Erie for something like 0.7 mils per ton-mile (where 1 mil equals $0.001). At her destination, huge Hulett steam offloaders emptied the ship for one-tenth the cost of hand labor.[1]

It was no coincidence that the ship in the forefront of this transformation was named *J. Pierpont Morgan.* The financier and banking magnate dominated American capitalism at the turn of the twentieth century, just as the ship dwarfed its competitors. The ship remained in service for seventy-three years; Morgan lived for seventy-six. When Morgan, the scion of the New York banking family and mastermind of railroad consolidation, turned his attention and resources to steel in 1900, he transformed the industry. By the time the ship named for him entered service, he had done as much for shipping as well.[2] Unlike Cornelius Vanderbilt, who turned from shipping to railroads late in life, he turned from railroads to shipping late in life, though with far less happy results.

The canonical account of Morgan's conversion, first to steel and then to ships, begins on December 12, 1900. Two New York industrialists hosted a dinner that evening for Charles Michael "Charlie" Schwab, the thirty-eight-year-old president of Carnegie Steel. They invited Morgan and seated him next to the wunderkind who had moved so quickly up the corporate ladder. Morgan was both a colleague and a competitor of Schwab's mentor and benefactor, Andrew Carnegie. In spite of previous cooperation, the two tycoons seemed headed for a market war, pitting Morgan's recently created Federal Steel against the long-standing market dominance enjoyed by Carnegie. Schwab had a better idea.[3]

In his after-dinner remarks to Morgan and the other guests from the New York business establishment, Schwab spoke without text or notes. Energetic and exuberant as always, he projected in mental imagery a "super-trust of true verticality," a business combine burdened by "no wasteful competition, no unnecessary duplication among individual plants, no faulty planning in plant location, no inadequate transportation facilities."[4] He might have added, but did not need to, no costly price war between Carnegie and Federal Steel. Apparently captivated by the charismatic young executive, Morgan lingered after dinner and engaged Schwab in conversation. Within a year, Schwab's vision would become U.S. Steel, the product of what was then the largest business merger in U.S. history, a $1.4 billion deal. And Schwab would be its president, at the insistence of Morgan. Though Schwab would last only two years in that job, he had set the course that would draw Morgan and other capitalists back into shipping and make Schwab the czar of U.S. shipbuilding in World War I. More important, this infusion of new capital, the greatest since the U.S. merchant marine began its steady decline in the middle of the nineteenth century, would fuel both oceanic and domestic fleets. Once more the United States would challenge Britain for world shipping preeminence.

Schwab contributed to this outcome, just as much as Morgan. Carnegie called

The broker of the deal that created United States Steel, Charles Michael "Charlie" Schwab rose from the shop floor to the presidency of Carnegie Steel. The energetic and charismatic entrepreneur also served as the president of U.S. Steel and Bethlehem Steel and the director of the Emergency Fleet Corporation in World War I.

Schwab a "hustler."[5] In an age of robber barons, he stood out for his modest origins, his rocketing ascent to wealth and influence, and his charismatic ability to bend others to his own ambitions. Born during the Civil War in Loretto, Pennsylvania, two hundred miles from the Atlantic Ocean and almost as far from Lake Erie, he first set his sights on the steel industry; nothing in his youth suggested his future role in shipping. He signed on as a laborer at Andrew Carnegie's Edgar Thomson Steel Works at age seventeen. In two years he was assistant manager, then manager at age twenty-five. His personal charm and formidable persuasive skills recommended him to Carnegie to restore order at the Homestead plant after the bloody strike and lockout there in 1892. In spite of the hard line he took with labor throughout his career, he succeeded in restoring harmony to the plant and, characteristically, improving productivity. His mentor appointed him president of Carnegie Steel Company in 1897. Schwab was thirty-five years old.

His tireless pursuit of competitive advantage and production efficiency led him to recommend that Carnegie lease the Mesabi iron mines of John D. Rockefeller. Indeed, Rockefeller himself offered something of a model for Schwab's ambitions. Before he built his Standard Oil empire, Rockefeller owned iron mines in Minnesota, ore carriers on the Great Lakes, and a major share of the Great Lakes Towing Company.[6] The lease of his mining interests in Minnesota and Michigan drew Schwab's business ken to shipping on the Great Lakes. By the time Carnegie Steel was absorbed within U.S. Steel, it was operating a fleet of more than one hundred ore carriers on the Great Lakes. At first these ships brought their raw material to transfer ports on Lake Erie, where it was loaded on railway cars for the overland haul to the Pennsylvania steel mills. Later, steel mills would rise up at the shipping termini, such as Gary, Indiana, named for Elbert Gary, the chairman of the board of U.S. Steel.

Schwab's appreciation of the importance of transportation in general, and shipping in particular, to the production of steel helped him see that Carnegie's empire and Morgan's were better merged than pitted against each other. He applied his considerable persuasive skills to bring the two businessmen to terms. Shuttling the mile or so between their New York City mansions, he brokered the $1.4 billion deal to create the world's largest company. When in 1902 he built his own urban palace, it comprised seventy-seven rooms covering a full city block on Riverside Drive between 73rd and 74th streets, the largest private residence ever to rise in New York City.[7] He never grew quite as rich as Carnegie or Morgan, but he consumed more conspicuously. When asked once if he was going to engage in philanthropy like his benefactor, Carnegie, Schwab said that they harbored different notions of how to distribute their wealth. Carnegie gave his away; Schwab spent his.

Schwab resigned from U.S. Steel in 1903 because of a power struggle with Gary. The following year he assumed the presidency of Bethlehem Steel and launched a phase of his career that would have still greater impact on American maritime history. Meanwhile, the initiative he had launched with U.S. Steel ran its course and indelibly transformed shipping on the Great Lakes. The ore carrier *J. Pierpont Morgan* expressed several strands of that transformation, some of which reached into oceanic shipping as well. The *Morgan* embodied the belated migration of American shipping from wood to steel, both in its construction and in its cargo. It also represented the two most important business models for shipping in the twentieth century. First, it was a proprietary vessel serving a parent company outside the shipping industry. Companies such as Standard Oil of New Jersey, Ford Motor Company, and Weyerhaeuser, and even U.S. Steel, would successfully operate their own fleets in support of company strategies. Second, as a bulk carrier, the *J. Pierpont Morgan* represented the other great business model of twentieth-century American shipping, the megaship. The oil tankers, container ships, and even larger bulk carriers of the late twentieth century continued in the pattern of the giant ore carriers on the Great Lakes. Finally, the *Morgan* found itself enmeshed soon after its launching in a labor dispute that would permanently separate maritime labor on the Great Lakes from that on the coasts.

The nature of that separation can be understood only from a national perspective. By the turn of the twentieth century, the maritime labor movement nurtured by Andrew Furuseth and his colleagues on the West Coast was spreading to other regions. But maritime labor would struggle throughout the twentieth century to overcome the divisions bred by its inherent diversity.[8] Workers were divided geographically, with distinct camps on each coast, the Gulf of Mexico, and the Great Lakes. They were divided by carriers, establishing different relations with oceangoing vessels, coasters, and river shipping, for example. They were divided by craft among deckhands, engine-room workers, and other crew members, to say nothing of the deeper rift between seamen and longshoremen. And they were divided by race, with white West Coast workers hostile to Asians and Hispanics while their counterparts on the East Coast and the Gulf of Mexico were resistant to blacks, Hispanics, and various immigrants. Early attempts at labor organization tended to exacerbate these divisions instead of heal them.

By 1900 Furuseth and the West Coast seamen he represented had developed a legislative program that would define the Progressive Era of maritime history. Furuseth wanted American ships restricted to American seamen and those seamen protected from arbitrary imprisonment by shipmasters. He sought to have their wages freed of attachments, their working hours fixed, their right guaranteed to question the seaworthiness of vessels on which they served, and involuntary discharge in foreign ports proscribed. Wage equalization anchored his reform agenda. He argued that the comparatively high wages of American seamen flowed not from the ships but from the policies carried out in the ports. The way to restore the American merchant marine to international competitiveness was not to lower the wages of American seamen, as the shipowners insisted, but to raise the wages of seamen from other countries. Allow all seamen to leave their ship in any port, and qualified workers would flock ashore in American ports. Then foreign ships would have to pay American rates to get them back, or else forgo trade in the United States. Requiring that foreign ships trading in American ports meet American safety standards would also contribute to cost equalization. All of these reforms, he believed, would not only succor the forlorn American seaman, but also promote a healthy and competitive merchant marine. Furuseth won some of these reforms through collective bargaining on the West Coast, but he was unable to repeat the success on the East Coast or the Great Lakes. Some measures simply exceeded the reach of labor-management negotiation. For these he sought relief in federal legislation.

In virtually every session of Congress from 1900 onward, Furuseth's allies introduced what came to be called the Seamen's Bill, legislation designed to achieve his main objectives of wage equalization and freedom from imprisonment. A version of the bill actually passed both houses of Congress in 1911, only to die on the desk of lame-duck Republican president William H. Taft. Only in the full flood of Progressivism after 1912 did the legislation finally achieve passage. The congressional elections of

1910 gave Democrats control of the House of Representatives and put fifteen trade union members in office; William B. Wilson, the former secretary-treasurer of the United Mine Workers, assumed chairmanship of the House Labor Committee. The election of 1912 gave Democrats control of the Senate and placed Woodrow Wilson in the White House. Perhaps as importantly, the U.S.-owned but British-flagged luxury liner *Titanic* sank on the night of April 14–15, 1912, raising public alarm about the safety of modern shipping and contributing to platform planks from both parties promising reform legislation. Even at that, however, it took the legislative skills of the Progressive senator Robert "Fighting Bob" La Follette (R-WI) and almost two years of hearings and study to see the bill to passage. President Wilson signed the legislation only after personal audiences with Furuseth and La Follette.

Hailed by Furuseth as having "wiped out the last bondage existing under the American flag," the Seamen's Act of 1915 proved less effective in practice than he originally expected. Captain Robert Dollar, a leading Pacific shipper, threatened to sell his ships rather than subject them to the "humiliating" restrictions imposed on the shipping of a nation "that has practically no ships in the foreign trade."[9] Dollar was a successful maverick who had moved from coastal to oceanic trade by cynically ignoring requirements that the majority of his crew members be American. He was not about to allow labor reform and its attendant costs to further constrain his competitive position. Other shipowners blamed the "Furuseth–La Follette Folly" for all the subsequent problems besetting the industry. In the face of such opposition, the government proved unable to develop and enforce regulations to carry out all the provisions of the legislation. And the boom market brought on by World War I obviated some of the bill's provisions. The historian Joseph P. Goldberg concluded:

> The most that could be said for the Seamen's Act was that it had provided seamen with the same freedom to work or quit which was available to shore workers. In its effort to protect and entrench the seafaring crafts, and to equalize wages and working conditions nationally, and even internationally, it failed.[10]

Furuseth's long-term goals for seamen, to the extent that they were realized in his lifetime, were to flow from collective bargaining, not government decree.

Maritime labor, however, could not rise above its divisions. When workers on the Great Lakes faced a lockout in 1908, for example, not even Furuseth could unite East Coast and West Coast seamen in support of their brethren. Ore shipments on the Great Lakes had swollen with the growth of the American steel industry in the early years of the twentieth century, calling into existence ships like the *J. Pierpont Morgan*. At its creation in 1901, U.S. Steel controlled a lake ore-carrying fleet of 112 vessels, about a third of the total tonnage on the northern lakes.[11] Steel, therefore, dominated inland shipping at a time when U.S. domestic shipping outweighed oceanic shipping by two to one. It was only natural that corporate steel would apply the same benign despotism to labor on the Great Lakes as it had in its other industrial arms. The chosen instrument of corporate steel on the Great Lakes was the Lake Carriers' Association (LCA), led by Harry Coulby, the "Master of the Lakes."

Coulby offered a revealing counterpoint to Furuseth. Like the labor leader, he had escaped European poverty by shipping out as a teenager. Finding himself docked in Cuba with malaria, he stowed away on a ship bound for New York, determined to make his career in the United States. Recovering from his illness, he walked to Cleveland and found work as a stenographer with the Lake Shore and Michigan Southern Railway. By chance he met John Hay, the former secretary to Abraham Lincoln and future secretary of state, who was just then writing his twelve-volume biography of the Great Emancipator. Coulby became Hay's secretary and won a recommendation to Hay's brother-in-law, Samuel Mather, the director of Pickands Mather and Company, an iron-ore mining and shipping firm that managed four separate lake fleets. Coulby joined the company in 1886, specializing in fleet operations, and rose to senior partner by 1900. Then he was handpicked by U.S. Steel chairman Elbert Gary to be president of the Pittsburgh Steamship Company, one transportation arm of the huge U.S. Steel empire. Coulby affected a homespun style derived from his study of Lincoln,[12] but his English-tailored suits and expensive cigars bespoke his allegiance to corporate culture.[13] Like his masters, he fancied himself a benevolent despot, introducing safety reforms and wage benefits for lakes seamen. But he staunchly opposed trade unionism, choosing to dispense his largesse on his terms, not the seamen's.

The chosen instrument of corporate steel on the Great Lakes was Harry Coulby, a member of the Executive Committee of the Lake Carriers' Association (LCA) and the "Master of the Lakes."[14] It was a slow shipping season on the lakes and U.S. Steel had built up a reserve supply of iron ore. Shipowners recently had fenced their docks to protect strike-breakers. In April the association voted to establish an "open shop," effectively banning union members from LCA ships. In response, the union struck in May and turned immediately to its maritime brethren nationwide for a show of labor solidarity. They were quickly disabused of that faith. Indeed, the call for help provoked a split between seamen on the East and West coasts that soon spilled into other realms. The International Seamen's Union declined to vote strike funds, relying instead on voluntary contributions from members. These proved woefully inadequate. The strike dragged on until 1912, but the shippers found ample supplies of strikebreakers, especially among recent immigrants to the United States. In the end, Great Lakes sailors returned to work on terms dictated by the major shipping companies; they accepted the open shop. Maritime labor on the lakes existed for decades in the shadow of this strike. Working conditions improved steadily through the twentieth century, but the reforms had more to do with the shippers' perception of good business practice than with the power of the unions. Coulby's benign despotism prevailed, not Furuseth's labor solidarity.

Furuseth soldiered on until his death in 1938. He had much to be proud of, especially the Seamen's Act and the reforms he negotiated on the West Coast. But the divisions within maritime labor outweighed the common cause to which he tried to bend his members. Only with unification in truly national unions in the 1930s would many of his cherished reforms come to pass. Ironically, many observers perceived labor relations on the Great Lakes to be more harmonious and more advantageous to the worker than those on either coast, reflecting not only the successful union busting of 1908–1912 but also the peculiar features of shipping on inland waters, virtually free of foreign competition.

In the meantime, the return of capital to American shipping blossomed in the years before World War I. No venture illustrates the trend more grandiosely than J. Pierpont Morgan's International Mercantile Marine Company (IMM). Just one year after financing the U.S. Steel merger, Morgan formed IMM to corner the North Atlantic passenger business. In succession, the Morgan combine bought up Britain's Leyland Line, the White Star Line, the Dominion Line, the International Navigation Company (the holder of the American Line and other ships), and the Atlantic Transport Line, the holder of the National Line. By the end of

1902 the corporation controlled the largest private fleet in the world, 136 ships of 1,034,884 gross tons, about the same size as the entire French merchant marine. To escape restrictions imposed by American registry, Morgan placed 85 percent under the British flag and another 3 percent under the Belgian flag. The flight to foreign registry had begun in the nineteenth century, but the IMM experiment introduced a trend that would shape the American merchant marine throughout the twentieth century.[15]

Other shipping companies experienced similar, if less spectacular, growth. On the West Coast, Captain Robert Dollar, one of the most colorful figures in American shipping history, had nursed a small coastal line, the Dollar Steamship Company, into a Pacific powerhouse by assiduously cultivating markets in East Asia. James Farrell parlayed his international sales acumen into a business model for Isthmian Lines (1910–1956), a subsidiary of U.S. Steel that delivered its products around the world and found return cargoes to ensure profitability. The ever-resourceful Charles Schwab built up yet a third steel company, Bethlehem, by transporting ore to its mills in company ships.[16]

On the surface, at least, it appeared that the American shipping industry had staged a remarkable revival, just in time to serve the country's needs in World War I. But the sinking of the White Star Line's *Titanic* in 1912 revealed the fragility of this renaissance. "The 'unsinkable' *Titanic*" foundered on its maiden voyage, and at the same time J. P. Morgan's International Mercantile Marine was floundering on its own miscalculations. The company paid too much for the assets it purchased and never received the subsidies it expected from the government. Defeated by Britain's Cunard Line in its campaign to corner the North Atlantic passenger market, IMM could never raise fares high enough to pay down its debt. By 1914 IMM was bankrupt and unable to contribute much to the coming war effort.[17] Some shipping companies were in better financial condition, but they could not begin to fulfill the role that the United States would soon be called upon to play.

In spite of the great infusion of capital in the early years of the twentieth century, the United States was still not a great international trader. In 1913 it accounted for 23 percent of the world's wealth, but only 9 percent of its exports.[18] The stupendous growth of the U.S. economy since the Civil War, fed in part by the staggering industrial empires built up by entrepreneurs such as Andrew Carnegie, J. P. Morgan, Elbert Gary, and Charles Schwab, had outpaced the development of foreign trade, to say nothing of a merchant marine. America had become the world's arsenal, but it lacked the capacity to deliver its output overseas. When the crisis came, the country would turn to Charles Schwab and other captains of industry to do for shipping what they had done for railroads, steel, and the other mainstays of America's industrial revolution.

PART IV

THE WEIGHT OF WAR, 1905–1956

31

MAHAN, ROOSEVELT, AND THE SEABORNE EMPIRE

THEODORE ROOSEVELT SPENT HALF THE WEEKEND OF MAY 10–11, 1890, reading Alfred Thayer Mahan's *The Influence of Sea Power upon History*. Roosevelt was then a thirty-one-year-old civil service commissioner, an accomplished naval historian, and a passing acquaintance of Mahan's. He wrote to the author expressing his admiration for the book and confessing that he could hardly bring himself to put it down before finishing it. Roosevelt went on to write a glowing review for *Atlantic Monthly* and to draw Mahan into his inner circle of friends and associates.[1] They began what one historian has called an "ambiguous relationship."[2] The two navalists remained in close collaboration for the rest of Mahan's life, and Roosevelt's eulogy for his friend in January 1915 said that Mahan occupied a class by himself in educating the public on the importance of a strong navy. The ambiguity in their relationship stems not from any disagreements they might have had but from the question of who shaped whom. Was Roosevelt Mahan's cat's paw in the White House, as one historian has claimed, or did Roosevelt "use" Mahan, as other students of their relationship believe?[3] In either case, they collaborated in a transformation of American foreign policy that reverberated throughout the twentieth century.

The common cause binding Mahan and Roosevelt was the promotion of a modern navy befitting America's growing presence on the world stage.

255

In the last third of the nineteenth century, the navies of the world's industrialized states were converting from wooden sailing vessels and hybrid
sail/steam vessels to all-steel, steam-propelled, screw-driven, armored battleships with guns firing 1,100-pound, thirteen-inch projectiles up to four
miles.[4] In the 1880s a reluctant Congress had begun funding a "new
navy," but coastal defense and commerce raiding still dominated American naval strategy. The cruisers laid down in these years could not contend
with the battleships of Britain and other major powers. Only a new par-
adigm of sea power would convince an insular and largely self-sufficient
country to invest in a navy for empire.[5]

Rear Admiral Stephen B. Luce, another member of Roosevelt's inner
circle, laid the groundwork. Convinced that the technological revolution
then sweeping the world's navies required a more educated officer corps,
Luce persuaded his superiors to create a war college in Newport, Rhode
Island. Determined to produce officers who were broadly educated and
articulate spokesmen for their service, he recruited Captain Mahan to
teach a course on sea power. Mahan turned his lectures into the book that
hijacked Roosevelt's weekend in May 1890 and catapulted its author to
international renown. *The Influence of Sea Power upon History*, and a succession of histories and essays over the next two decades, secured Mahan's
reputation as the most influential strategic thinker in all of American history.[6] By studying the rise of British sea power, which dominated the
world's oceans in the nineteenth century, he laid the groundwork for
American sea power in the twentieth century. The key in both cases,
Mahan believed, lay in command of the sea, the maintenance of a battle
fleet that could meet and defeat the navy of any contender.

But Mahan's theories encompassed more than strategies of fleet engagement. He believed that navies existed to protect one's own commercial
shipping and threaten the shipping of one's enemies. "The necessity of a
navy," he wrote, "springs . . . from the existence of a peaceful shipping,
and disappears with it, except in the case of a nation which has aggressive
tendencies, and keeps up a navy merely as a branch of the military establishment."[7] This bold formulation discounted the ability of navies to protect their own coasts and project their power onto enemy shores,
functions that Mahan valued highly. Still, his priorities were clear. Navies
took their primary raison d'être from commerce protection, and by impli-
cation they derived one of their greatest advantages from being able to disrupt an enemy's commerce.

This last point generated endless confusion over Mahan's notions of sea power. Did not Admiral Mahan condemn *guerre de course*, commerce raiding, as a misuse of naval power? Did he not argue that the sole objective of a navy should be "command of the sea," which could be won only in decisive combat between main battle fleets? Yes, he did, but he saw no contradiction between the two positions. He drew a sharp line between commerce raiding on the one hand and what he called commerce destroying or blockading on the other.[8] He said:

> It is not the taking of individual ships or convoys . . . that strikes down the money power of a nation; it is the possession of that over-bearing power on the sea which drives the enemy's flag from it, or allows it to appear only as a fugitive; and which, by *controlling the great common*, closes the highways by which commerce moves to and from the enemy's shores.[9] (Italics added)

Navies, then, are instruments of the nation-state. They protect the state's interests on "the great common" of the sea. They ensure free passage to friendly communicants, and deny it those of the enemy. They do not seek to recover their costs by chasing individual travelers, or even convoys of travelers. Rather, they seek command of the common, so that friendly traffic may be assured safe passage and hostile traffic blocked. Mahan counseled the United States to keep in mind

> the difference between the *guerre-de-course*, which is inconclusive, and commerce-destroying (or commerce prevention) through strategic control of the sea by powerful navies. Some nations more than others, but all maritime nations more or less, depend for their prosperity upon maritime commerce, and probably upon it more than upon any other single factor. Either under their own flag or that of a neutral, either by foreign trade or coasting trade, the sea is the greatest of boons to such a state; and under every form its sea-borne trade is at the mercy of a foe decisively superior.[10]

"Blows at commerce," he continued, "are blows at the communications of the state; they intercept its nourishment, they starve its life, they cut the roots of its power, the sinews of its war." He went so far as to call "blows against commerce the most deadly that can be struck," concluding that the Northern blockade of the Confederacy in the Civil War was "decisive."[11] Historians today doubt that the blockade had so great an impact, but their quibbles would hardly have deterred Mahan.[12]

Mahan's crusade for a strong navy marched in time with his call for a revived American merchant marine. Writing in 1890, the same year as the publication of *The Influence of Sea Power upon History*, he lamented America's protectionist tariffs and the contraction of its shipbuilding and shipping industries. "Our self-imposed isolation in the matter of markets, and the decline of our shipping interest in the last thirty years," he observed, "have coincided singularly with an actual remoteness of this continent from the life of the rest of the world."[13] He believed that nations required foreign trade to prosper, a position reminiscent of Adam Smith. And he also believed that "it is the wish of every nation that this shipping business should be done by its own vessels."[14] He looked to a revival of American merchant shipping, in the sure expectation that a naval revival would follow. "When for any reason sea trade is again found to pay," he said, "a large enough shipping interest will reappear to compel the revival of the war fleet." This, for him, was "sea power in the broad sense."

Mahan and Roosevelt shared a number of related beliefs. Facing great oceans on either coast, the United States was destined to be a maritime state. To achieve this destiny, it needed a merchant marine and a powerful navy to protect it. The best protection, indeed the only real protection, came from command of the sea. Britain might be relied upon to police the Atlantic, but the United States had to attend to the Caribbean and the Pacific. The instrument of command was a fleet of modern battleships. To operate freely, especially in the Pacific, that fleet needed coal. Reliable, friendly coaling stations should be located strategically about the Pacific to support the fleet. The United States did not need colonies as much as outposts of empire, bases from which it could project power ashore when necessary and supply the fleet in its policing of the sea.

Roosevelt welcomed Mahan into a circle of like-minded expansionists who wished for the United States a place in the wave of imperialism then sweeping the globe. John Hay, the former secretary to Abraham Lincoln and the future secretary of state, the Massachusetts senator Henry Cabot Lodge, the brothers Henry and Brooks Adams, descendants of former presidents, and Elihu Root, the New York financier turned secretary of the army, were among the confidants who shared Roosevelt's ambitions for American empire.[15] Mahan's emphasis on the importance of coaling stations alerted them and other imperialists to the strategic significance of Hawaii.[16] When America's official representative helped overthrow Queen Liliuokalani early in 1893 and petitioned the United States for annexation, Republican expansionists rallied in support, only to have the treaty withdrawn when the newly elected Democrat Grover Cleveland assumed the presidency in March 1893.

Roosevelt's disappointment was temporary. In 1897 he began a breathtaking decade on the world stage, during which he would use all the powers allotted him by the American political system—and some that were not—to seize a two-ocean maritime empire to rival Britain's. A man of action and ideas, Roosevelt staked out a position as soon as he won appointment as assistant secretary of the navy in the new administration of William McKinley. Selected over the objections of Marcus Hanna, the Great Lakes shipping magnate turned U.S. senator and kingmaker, the activist Roosevelt found himself constrained by the high-tariff policies of the president and the lackadaisical, do-nothing behavior of his immediate boss, Secretary of the Navy John D. Long. In his first public address in office, a speech to the Naval War College in June 1897, he asserted that the growing crisis with Spain over the Cuban rebellion demonstrated the need for a world-class fleet. He told his audience that "we ask for a great navy partly because we feel that no national life is worth living if the nation is not willing, when the need shall arise, to stake everything on the supreme arbitrament of war, and to pour out its blood, its treasure and its taxes like water, rather than submit to the loss of honor and renown."[17]

Far from shirking the arbitrament of war, Roosevelt rushed out to embrace it. As the Cuban revolution brought Spanish-American relations to the breaking point in the early months of 1898, Assistant Secretary of the Navy Roosevelt prepared for war. He harangued the phlegmatic Secretary Long to ready the fleet, though he failed to instill in his boss the sense of urgency that consumed him. When the battleship *Maine* exploded on the night of February 15, Roosevelt immediately suspected "dirty treachery by the Spaniards."[18] He finally had what John Hay called their "splendid little war." He readied the Atlantic fleet for combat. He directed Admiral George Dewey to take on coal, position his fleet near the Spanish possessions in the western Pacific, and await orders. He probably convinced Long to recall America's most modern battleship, the *Oregon*, from its Pacific Ocean station, casting a spotlight on the strategic liability of a two-ocean navy divided by the sixteen thousand-mile passage around

South America.[19] He recalled Mahan from a European vacation to accept appointment on a Naval War Board to advise Secretary Long. Having positioned America's "new navy" to have its way with the premodern Spanish fleet, Roosevelt resigned his naval post and raised a regiment of Rough Riders for the assault on Cuba. At San Juan Hill, overlooking Santiago, he won fame enough to capture the governorship of New York in 1898 and the Republican Party's vice presidential nomination in 1900, on the McKinley reelection ticket. McKinley, the reluctant imperialist, had annexed not just Cuba, but also the Philippines, which had fallen like ripe fruit to the fleet of George Dewey. Marcus Hanna, the power behind the throne to McKinley, still mistrusted Roosevelt, but bowed to the Rough Riders' popular following. When McKinley fell to assassination early in his second term, Hanna lamented, "Now, look! That damned cowboy is president."[20]

Cowboy indeed. Roosevelt mounted the bully pulpit and rode it hard. Perhaps only in his enthusiasm for the environment was he more innovative and influential than in his promotion of the U.S. Navy and its new maritime empire. Mindful of the long and dangerous run of the *Oregon* on the eve of the Spanish-American War, he set his sights on an isthmian canal to connect America's two-ocean navy. Hoping to achieve for America what the Suez Canal did for Great Britain, he discounted the failed effort of the French to build one. With cavalier disregard for foreign sovereignty reminiscent of President Polk's provocation of war with Mexico, Roosevelt worked with rebels in Colombia to foment a revolution. When the rebels declared their independence in 1903, he sent American troops to protect the new state of Panama, with which he promptly signed a treaty for construction of an American canal. It would take more than ten years to realize the dream of California's 1849 gold rushers, but Roosevelt would live to see the opening of what the historian David McCullough has called a "path between the seas."[21] And Roosevelt would also live to boast that he took the Canal Zone and left Congress to debate.

Winning election to the presidency in his own right in 1904, Roosevelt went on to consolidate the maritime empire he had done so much to create. He won the Nobel Peace Prize in 1905 for helping to negotiate a settlement of the Russo-Japanese War, a conflict that seemed to confirm Mahan's theory of sea power. The Treaty of Portsmouth also validated the apparent lesson of the Sino-Japanese War of 1894: an Asian naval power was emerging to contest American command of the Pacific Ocean.

SS *Ancon* became the first ship to traverse the Panama Canal on August 15, 1914 (as shown here), just after World War I broke out in Europe. Like most American aids to navigation, from the sailing charts of Matthew Fontaine Maury to the construction of the St. Lawrence Seaway, the Panama Canal served both military and commercial interests.

Conceding the Atlantic to the British, U.S. strategy came to focus on the Pacific, the Caribbean, and the canal connecting them.[22] The Monroe Doctrine still spoke to the Caribbean and, after 1914, the canal.[23] The Open Door Policy of 1904 confirmed the importance of American access to Mahan's "great common" of the Pacific. Secretary of State John Hay, one of Roosevelt's inner circle, maneuvered the imperial states of Europe into accepting the principle of equal commercial access to their Asian colonies and thus ensured that the United States, the latecomer to turn-of-the-century imperialism, would partake of the markets of Asia.

As if to confirm America's new stature as a naval and commercial presence on the world's oceans, Roosevelt staged a global demonstration of America's naval power. In 1907 he sent the "Great White Fleet" on a fourteen-month, forty-five-thousand-mile tour of the world's principle maritime states, making twenty port calls on six continents. Originally intended simply to redeploy the Atlantic battleship fleet to the Pacific, the tour took on a life of its own, demonstrating America's new presence on the world stage, testing the ability of the navy to operate for extended periods at sea, promoting Roosevelt's plans to seek still more naval building, and generally showing the American flag for foreign and domestic consumption. Departing Hampton Roads on December 16, 1907, amid great fanfare and a presidential visit, the fleet sailed through the Caribbean, around South America, and into San Francisco Bay. Its second leg reached Puget Sound, an indication of the growing importance of the Pacific Northwest to American strategic and economic interests. A third leg included stops at Hawaii, New Zealand, the Philippines, Japan, and China. A final leg brought the fleet home via the Suez Canal. Roosevelt, in the last days of his presidency, welcomed the armada back to Hampton Roads on February 22, 1909.[24]

Three great ironies stalked the fleet as it paraded around the world. First, it traversed the Suez Canal, but Theodore Roosevelt's Panama Canal project was still wrestling with the challenges of engineering and disease that had defeated the French. Not until 1914 would the canal open to commercial and naval traffic. Second, coal supplies, the logistical and strategic challenge that so worried Mahan, remained a besetting problem. Not even the acquisition of Hawaii could guarantee sufficient fuel for the fleet to move freely about the Pacific. And the U.S. Navy still did not have sufficient coal ships to shadow the fleet for refueling. Just as the *California*, the first steamship to reach San Francisco in the gold rush of 1849, had to sit in port awaiting resupply by a British collier, the Great White Fleet had to purchase recoaling service from British vessels on its round-the-world tour. The United States was not yet the complete naval power that Roosevelt and Mahan envisioned. The more serious proof of that point, and the ultimate irony of the Great White fleet, is that its ships were already obsolescent as they circumnavigated the world. Indeed, one function of the white paint that gave the fleet its popular name was to cover up the corrosion that many of its vessels suffered. The British launch of HMS *Dreadnought* in 1906 had made all the Great White Fleet's ships obsolete. With its ten twelve-inch guns and 22,500-horsepower turbine engines, the *Dreadnought* and its sister ships could outdistance, outrace, and outgun any of the ships that Theodore Roosevelt displayed with such obvious pride. The first American *Dreadnought*-class ship, the *South Carolina*, was not completed until 1910.

Still, somewhere in this rush to empire, the American century had begun. Perhaps it started with the publication of Mahan's *The Influence of Sea Power upon History* in 1890, or the closing of the American frontier and the first attempt to annex Hawaii in 1893.[25] Maybe it was the Spanish-American War and the acquisition of overseas possessions in the Caribbean and Pacific. Maybe the building of the Panama Canal secured America's naval commitment to the Caribbean and Pacific. Perhaps by the time the Great White Fleet went on its symbolic global parade, the United States was already a world power. In any event, it seemed clear that the oceanic shipping that was the raison d'être of Mahan's new navy might be more important to the United States in the twentieth century than it had been in the nineteenth. Perhaps the American century, like the Pax Britannica that preceded it, would similarly flourish on Mahan's "great common."

32

WAR AND
WOODROW WILSON

ON MAY DAY 1915, THREE RELATED BUT SEPARATE EVENTS SET
America on a course that would test Mahan's theories of sea power and
transform the U.S. merchant marine. SS *Gulflight*, a 360-foot American
tanker on her maiden voyage carrying gas and oil to Rouen, France, was
torpedoed off Land's End, England, by the German submarine U-30.[1]
The *Gulflight* crew escaped the damaged vessel, though some were injured
and the master died of an apparent heart attack. Ironically, the German
ambassador to the United States chose that day to publish large ads in fifty
American newspapers, warning U.S. ships carrying cargo for the Allies to
stay out of British waters, which the Germans declared to be a war zone.
Ignoring the threat, the British Cunard liner *Lusitania* left New York on
the very same day, bound for London with 1,959 passengers and crew
(plus three stowaways) and 173 tons of ammunition. Six days later, the
German submarine U-20, heading home on low fuel with only two torpedoes, encountered the *Lusitania* steaming slowly off the coast of Ireland. U-20's torpedoes sent the *Lusitania* to the bottom in eighteen
minutes. Having conducted no lifeboat drills on its one-week passage
across the Atlantic, the *Lusitania* lost 1,198 of her passengers, including
128 of the 149 Americans aboard.[2]

The sinking of the *Lusitania* overshadowed the loss of the *Gulflight* and
the other American ships lost to German mines and submarines in the

first full year of World War I. It mocked the futile warnings of the German ambassador. And it sorely tested the neutrality policy that President Woodrow Wilson had declared when the war broke out in August 1914. Seeking to keep the United States out of an essentially European conflict, Wilson reinforced his formal statement of neutrality on behalf of the U.S. government with a personal plea to the American people to be neutral in both word and deed. His secretary of state, Robert Lansing, attempted to placate American outrage over the *Lusitania* while navigating the shallow waters between British and German interpretations of the law of the sea.

International law then required naval vessels involved in commerce-raiding to halt, board, and search commercial vessels suspected of transporting war materials. Vessels found trafficking in contraband could then be sunk, after the crew and passengers were removed and provided for. These rules were developed for surface raiders, warships of formidable mass and firepower. Such vessels could approach even armed merchantmen with impunity, for they occupied a comparatively high rung in the hierarchy of power that undergirded Mahan's theory of sea power.

Submarines were anathema to Mahan. They threatened the dominance of his beloved battleships and the security of commercial shipping. Furthermore, they fit poorly the model of commerce-raiding developed for surface ships. Fragile craft with scant firepower beyond their torpedoes, they could often be outdueled on the surface by large merchant ships mounting deck guns. The chances were even greater if the merchant vessel's armament was concealed and the submarine approached unawares. The United States had therefore supported Britain's arming of its merchant ships, though only for defensive purposes. Merchantmen, the United States reasoned, had a right to defend themselves against armed attack. They did not, however, have the right to abuse the traditional privileges of noncombatants on the high seas. Ignoring this latter sentiment, the British dispatched "Q-ships," armed decoys disguised as harmless merchant vessels, seeking to lure unsuspecting submarines to approach on the surface. Then the Q-ships would unveil their guns and take the submarine under fire. Secretary Lansing rejected these tactics, although the United States tried them later in the war and again in World War II, without much success.[3]

The more immediate problem for the United States appeared on its docks. American goods for export had backed up for lack of shipping as soon as war broke out. Though the nation owned the world's third largest fleet in terms of tonnage, most of those vessels plied inland and coastal waters. Less than 10 percent of America's exports were being carried in her own ships; after the collapse of J. P. Morgan's International Mercantile Marine , America accounted for only 2 percent of the world's oceangoing ships. The outbreak of war removed the world's two largest fleets, Britain's and Germany's, from routine commerce. The possibility of submarine attack only worsened a shipping shortage that drove down prices and closed off the export market for America's bumper harvest of 1914.[4]

The Wilson administration confronted the shipping dilemma as both a crisis and an opportunity. Long opposed to the protectionist tariffs and government neglect that had suppressed American oceanic shipping since the Civil War, Wilson had entered office in 1913 determined to promote the "arms of commerce" to enhance American influence in the world.[5] The Underwood Tariff of 1913 had lowered import duties and introduced an income tax to make up the lost revenue. Two months later the Federal Reserve Act had given the government unprecedented tools for controlling the country's money supply. Now the shipping shortage of 1914 provided another opening. "Without a great merchant marine," Wilson had said, "we cannot take our rightful place in the commerce of the world."[6] He intended to build one. If American business would not do it, the government would.

Quickly, the administration proposed legislation easing rules on foreign ship registry, established new terms for war risk insurance, and submitted a shipping bill allowing for government ownership of a merchant marine. The first two measures passed easily, but the prospect of government ownership and operation of a merchant fleet provoked strenuous opposition from the business community. The ensuing legislative struggle spilled into 1915 and climaxed with defeat of the Wilson plan for government ownership.[7] The administration created the Coast Guard in January of that year by merging the Revenue Cutter Service (1799) and the Life-saving Service (1878), but it made no further legislative progress until the German submarine campaign of 1915 began to shift public opinion.[8]

Not only did the contest for the Atlantic create a sympathetic environment for passage of Andrew Furuseth's Seamen's Act of 1915, it also emboldened the Wilson administration to renew its bid for a shipping act. This time Treasury Secretary William McAdoo and Secretary of State Lansing cast the argument for a merchant marine in terms of national security. "A merchant marine is just as essential to the effectiveness of the Navy . . . as the guns upon the decks of our battleships," McAdoo told the Indianapolis Chamber of Commerce in October 1915.[9] By the summer of 1916, when most Democrats and Progressives were endorsing preparedness in anticipation of the fall elections, the Shipping Act won the support necessary for passage. The legislation created a Shipping Board to oversee American maritime interests, and most importantly, to acquire and operate a $50 million merchant fleet.[10] When Germany declared unconditional submarine warfare in January of 1917, the Shipping Board created the Emergency Fleet Corporation (EFC).

The Shipping Board chairman William Denman, a San Francisco lawyer experienced in maritime labor, chose George E. Goethals, of Panama Canal fame, to be the general manager of the EFC. Quickly the two men slid into a series of crippling disputes that stalled creation of the government fleet. Most importantly, they differed over the relative merits of wooden and steel ships. Denman favored the construction of wooden vessels for the coastal and inland trade, freeing steel ships for oceanic service and exploiting the country's established assets. Goethals wanted to concentrate on steel vessels. After months of public wrangling, Denman, Goethals, and many of their supporters resigned.[11] The emergency fleet was nowhere in sight. The United States would have to charter foreign vessels to carry the American Expeditionary Force to Europe and to supply it once deployed.[12]

Wilson quickly appointed Edward N. Hurley chairman of the Shipping Board and president of the Emergency Fleet Corporation. A self-made millionaire, Hurley had served most recently as the chairman of the Federal Trade Commission. He quickly commandeered 97 German and Austrian vessels interned in American ports since the outbreak of war in 1914. Then he requisitioned all 431 vessels then under construction in American yards, including 246 for foreign countries, 163 for Britain alone. Finally, he appropriated to government service all American ocean-going steel vessels over 2,500 tons, adding another 657 ships to his emergency fleet.[13] Like the president, Hurley kept one eye on the postwar position of the United States. "We are building ships not alone for the war," he told the National Coal Association in 1918, "but for the future of world trade." "No nation can be great commercially," he said on another occasion, "unless it has its own manufacturing and its own shipping." The "bridge of ships" on which he planned to send American soldiers and equipment to Europe would also serve America in what he called the commercial "war after the war."[14]

On one front this entailed recruiting and training the seamen necessary to crew the ships he envisioned. Maritime labor viewed elements of the Shipping Board as hostile to unions, a suspicion aggravated by the large number of nonunion seamen brought into service during the war emergency. Another cause of union alarm was the large number of ships operated by navy personnel. Most vessels entering the war zone around Europe—36 percent of the U.S. deep-sea fleet—were crewed by naval personnel during the American phase of the war in 1917 and 1918.[15]

Hurley's aggressive action brought existing ships into the American fleet in short order. He was less successful, however, in producing new vessels. Rear Admiral Washington Lee Camps, General Goethals's successor as the general manager of the EFC, struggled beneath the burden of mobilizing America's shipbuilding capacity while navigating a labyrinthine, ad hoc wartime bureaucracy in Washington. Looking to replace Camps, Hurley tried Henry Ford in vain. Then he turned to Charles Schwab.

Schwab's qualifications for the position had been enhanced significantly since he introduced Andrew Carnegie to the economies of shipping ore on the Great Lakes. While still president of U.S. Steel, Schwab had twice bought and sold Bethlehem Steel, a major arms manufacturer located in the Lehigh Valley of Pennsylvania. Created at the behest of Secretary of the Navy W. C. Whitney in 1886, Bethlehem produced steel plate for naval vessels and artillery for both the army and the navy. In 1900 it introduced a new tungsten-chromium steel, coinvented by Frederick W. Taylor of "scientific management" fame, that became a standard for "high-speed" tool steel around the world. Schwab's repurchase of Bethlehem came at the importuning of the railroad magnate E. H. Harriman, who was orchestrating the creation of the United States Shipbuilding Company.[16] Harriman's idea had been to anchor a shipbuilding corporation to a steel company capable of producing metal plate. Given the worldwide transformation from wooden to steel vessels, in which the United States was lagging, the idea was a good one. The company, however, was not. It went into receivership in the summer of 1903, little more than a year after its creation. About the same time, Schwab resigned the presidency of U.S. Steel in a running dispute with board chairman Elbert Gary and briefly retired to Europe to seek relief from chronic neuritis. The following year, however, he assumed the presidency of a reorganized

Bethlehem Steel Corporation, complete with subsidiary shipbuilding companies that had been part of the Harriman concoction.[17]

Schwab quickly announced his intention to make Bethlehem "the greatest armor plate and gun factory in the world."[18] When World War I broke out, he personally sailed to Europe to negotiate tens of millions of dollars in arms contracts with the British and French governments. "It's a gigantic deal done in five minutes," First Sea Lord Sir John Fisher boasted to Admiral John Jellicoe after meeting with Schwab. "That's what I call war!"[19] It was also what the Wilson administration called war. Schwab returned home to find that Wilson considered his contracts to be in violation of America's neutrality pledge. Schwab ignored the president's concerns about selling guns and ammunition in Europe, which Bethlehem had been doing for years. He did, however, agree not to build the twenty submarines he had contracted to the British. Instead, he built submarine components at Bethlehem plants in the United States and shipped them to the Vickers plant in Montreal, which the British government had leased and made available to him. This circumvention of American neutrality, which Schwab personally negotiated on a return trip to Europe, won a 20 percent bonus for Bethlehem Steel and a $4 million windfall for Schwab personally.

With Bethlehem's coffers full and its order books overflowing, Schwab bought up Pennsylvania Steel in 1916. With it came Sparrows Point, a steel plant in Baltimore harbor that Schwab had been eyeing for twenty years. As he told an appreciative Baltimore audience feting him in November 1916, "the East is so located that by reason of our great water transportation facilities the great ore deposits of South America, Cuba, and other countries, of which there is a vast extent available, can be brought here. For 50, 100, nay 200 years to come the supply of steel will be practically undiminished."[20] Using the same insight that made ore shipping on the Great Lakes an integral part of the U.S. Steel empire, Schwab looked to cheap foreign ore, delivered directly to Sparrows Point by ship, to give Bethlehem a competitive advantage. In 1916 Schwab's Bethlehem Steel grew to be the largest arms manufacturer in the world, increasing its revenues over 1915 by 149 percent to $61,717,310. Earnings in that year doubled the company's stock capitalization.[21]

At that juncture, Schwab ceded the presidency of Bethlehem Steel to his protégé Eugene Grace. Elevated to the chairman of the company, Schwab presided over the creation of the Bethlehem Shipbuilding

Corporation and the greatest expansion of Sparrows Point in the site's history. The juxtaposition of a shipyard and a steel mill gave Bethlehem production efficiencies that it soon parlayed into $273 million in ship orders. Displaying the same rapacious ambition as his mentor and boss, President Grace negotiated with the EFC a "bonus for savings" clause in his contract that allowed the company to collect half of any savings on their contracts. He delivered the ships on his $140 million contract for $93 million, allowing him to collect $24 million in extra profits, above the 10 percent awarded by the contract. By their own lights, Schwab and Grace were doing well by doing good.

Hurley wanted such men and achievements for the EFC, but Schwab resisted Hurley's invitation to become the director general of the EFC.[22] Only when President Wilson personally guaranteed freedom from Washington red tape and the right to maintain his financial interests in Bethlehem Steel did Schwab finally accept the post. Immediately he moved the offices of the EFC to Philadelphia, partly to escape the suffocating politics and bureaucracy of Washington, and partly, perhaps, to get closer to Hog Island.

Hog Island shipyard was then under construction southwest of Philadelphia on the Delaware River, about three miles west of the Navy Yard. It mirrored what the journalist Mark Reuter has called "the psychology of hugeness," a hallmark of the Schwab/Bethlehem empire.[23] Located on more than nine hundred acres of marshy ground that now supports the south end of the Philadelphia airport, Hog Island finally encompassed fifty shipways and seven piers, each 1,000 feet long and 100 feet wide. It had 82 miles of railroad tracks, 36 warehouses, and 29 miles of water piping; 1.3 million gallons of water were filtered and chlorinated there daily. Crisscrossing the site were 26 miles of sewers and drains, 675 miles of electrical wiring, and 3,000 miles of telephone wiring serving 2,000 phones. Timber consumption reached 150 million board-feet. At one time the facility employed 41,000 workers, paying them $4 million a month. As Hurley himself had stated, "Hog Island was built . . . for the construction of vessels in accordance with the American system of doing big things in a big way."[24] Not surprisingly, the shipyard was owned by American International Corporation, a subsidiary of the banking empire of J. Pierpont Morgan Jr., the son of Schwab's erstwhile partner.

Hog Island appeared to be Schwab's kind of place. In scale, geography, and ambition it greatly resembled Bethlehem's Sparrows Point. But if

A crowd estimated at a hundred thousand gathers at Hog Island for the launching of SS *Quistconck*, the first ship to slide down the ways at the massive shipyard southwest of Philadelphia. *Quistconck*, the Delaware Indian name for Hog Island, was launched on August 5, 1918, less than eleven months after groundbreaking at Hog Island, but also slightly more than three months before the armistice ending World War I. Neither she nor her sister "Hog Islanders" saw service in the war, but the United States continued producing emergency cargo vessels at Hog Island until January 22, 1921.

Schwab protégé Eugene Grace can be credited, Schwab did not care for Hog Island.[25] In U.S. Steel and at Sparrows Point, he sought not gigantism for its own sake but rather efficiency. J. P. Morgan and his son seemed more attracted to size for market leverage than for economies of scale. While the Morgans sought to control markets with horizontal trusts, Schwab sought to undersell markets by reducing production costs in vertical trusts. Sparrows Point achieved economies by connecting production facilities at water's edge with ore mines overseas. His Bethlehem shipbuilding venture would realize efficiencies by juxtaposing the steel mill with the shipyard. Schwab believed that the United States had ample shipyard capacity; it only needed to be used more efficiently. He inherited Hog Island and made the best of it. His focus, however, fell equally on the other shipyards around the country working contracts for the EFC.

Schwab's techniques for boosting productivity were legendary. Touring his own steel plants, he would write a number on the shop floor, challenging the crew to meet that production goal. When they met it, he would dispense generous bonuses and raise the number. He believed in financial incentives, from the boardroom to the toolroom, raising workers through the ranks so long as they kept producing. He picked Gene Grace from the blue-collar ranks, the same way Andrew Carnegie had chosen him. And he distributed his largesse with such abandon that he created the highest-paid workforce in the steel industry. The bonus boys, they were called, pulling down fabulous compensation on modest salaries. In one year Grace took home more than $1 million in total compensation on a salary of $18,000.

Schwab ran the EFC not by managing Hog Island but by inspiring shipyard workers around the country and by getting them the resources they needed to do their job. As enormous as Hog Island was, it mustered only 50 of the 1,020 shipways that were finally devoted to steel ship construction during World War I.[26] Seattle, not Philadelphia, built the largest percentage of EFC ships, 26.5 percent. When the "Wobblies," members of the socialist Industrial Workers of the World, slowed construction at those Seattle shipyards, Schwab traveled there to rally labor to his cause. "I am a very rich man," he began his address to them, soon winning them over with his accustomed charm and candor. The workers had him to dinner and then returned to work, engaged by the openness and optimism of a manager who had begun his career on the shop floor.

But not even Charlie Schwab could wring the waste and inefficiency from Hog Island and the rest of the wartime shipbuilding program. Hog Island, for example, cost $66 million to build, compared to its estimate of $27 million, and it produced only 122 vessels, just four by the time of the armistice in November 1918.[27] The political cartoonist W. A. Rogers pilloried the government for its extravagance and waste. But cost overruns were hardly limited to the Philadelphia site. The EFC paid $145 a ton for ships that were being built in Britain at the time for $75 a ton. Its wartime average was $200 to $250 per deadweight ton.[28] The staggering cost of building Hog Island added to the government's bill $69 per deadweight ton for each of the ships constructed there, more than half a million dollars per ship

Nor could Schwab accelerate the production of new ships beyond the state of the art. The EFC delivered only 470 ships before November 1918, less than a third of the number of keels laid down.[29] The 600,000 tons of shipping delivered by the time of the Armistice constituted but a small fraction of the 17.4 million tons under contract. But the rate of production was naturally accelerating at war's end. In October 1918 about three hundred thousand workers at 150 yards around the country delivered 391,000 tons of shipping, more than the United States had ever produced in most full years.[30] Hog Island's first product, SS *Quistconck*, slid down the ways on August 5, 1918, the only Hog Islander launched during the war but still too late to be of service.[31] America's "bridge to France" finally carried 911,047 troops and 4.35 million tons of cargo. But more than half the American troops transported to France sailed on British ships.[32] And Britain suffered more than half the shipping losses to acts of war—3,146 vessels totaling 7,820,496 gross tons—with the remainder distributed between Allied and neutral vessels.[33] Most of the American ships came not from Schwab's EFC but from confiscation, purchase, and nationalization. By 1918, if not before, the real goal of the wartime shipbuilding program had become the construction of a merchant fleet to dominate the postwar world.

The United States fought World War I with a makeshift commercial fleet, and then produced most of its ships—72 percent—*after* the armistice. For an investment of $3.3 billion, more than sixty times what Congress had authorized in the Shipping Act of 1916, the nation created by 1922 the world's second largest merchant fleet.[34] Compared with the

2.7 million tons it had at sea when the war broke out, the United States ended up with 13.5 million tons, roughly 22 percent of the world's shipping. For the first time since America's golden age of shipping in the decades before the Civil War, the country had a merchant fleet proportional to its share of the world's economy.

Wilson and Hurley had continued the shipbuilding program past war's end, because both wanted to use it to increase American leverage at the Versailles peace conference. Wilson said he wanted "to go to the Peace Conference armed with as many weapons as my pockets will hold so as to compel justice," which he saw embodied in his Fourteen Points, and most especially in the League of Nations. Hurley had said during the war that "my whole thought is to get a fleet of large sized ships . . . so that we may be able to compete with Germany and England after the war."[35] Both would soon learn that a large fleet of ships, while valuable if used correctly, guaranteed neither international political power nor a successful merchant marine.

33

ROBERT DOLLAR AND THE BUSINESS OF SHIPPING, 1920–1929

SS *PRESIDENT HARRISON* SPRANG FROM THE WORLD WAR I ship-building program and succumbed, ironically, to an American submarine in World War II. In between it embodied the hopes of Wilson and Hurley to turn their emergency fleet into the foundation of a revived American merchant marine. The *Harrison* was a "502," a class of cargo/passenger steamers designated by their length. Launched in 1921 and sold to the Dollar Steamship Company in 1923, she helped carve out a niche in the Pacific trade long dominated by the Pacific Mail Steamship Company (PMSS) and most recently attracting competition from the Japanese.

Robert Dollar had entered the shipping business by the back door. The Scottish immigrant made his first fortune lumbering in the Northwest. Finding coastal shipping there unreliable, he started amassing his own fleet of West Coast "lumber schooners" in 1892. These ingenious adaptations to the steep coastline of America's Northwest could anchor just off-shore and load timber by chutes of wood and wire strung between the ship and the land.[1] Such vessels quickly turned a profit for Captain Dollar (as he came to be called) and drew him into steel steamers.

His fleet soon outgrew the needs of his lumber business. He delivered his lumber as far south as southern California and sought return cargoes of any type that could be delivered to ports on the route back north. In

"Captain" Robert Dollar, as he liked to be called, parlayed a small business running West Coast schooners in the lumber trade into a major Pacific shipping empire before his sons drove the company into bankruptcy. He worked hard, took risks, fought maritime labor, ignored the government as much as possible, and thrived on a business model that he could not transfer to his heirs.

1902 he expanded from the coastal trade to sample business opportunities in the Philippines. Finding ample demand for his lumber, he traveled personally to East Asia in search of return cargoes. He discovered prime oak timber in Japan and soon contracted with the Southern Pacific Railroad to supply ties for its railroad construction in Mexico. With that deal he undercut Southern Pacific's own subsidiary, Pacific Mail Steamship Company, and established Dollar Line as a major competitor. Soon he added iron ore from China, which he could deliver to the West Coast cheaper than ore originating in the heartland of the United States.

By World War I, Dollar had developed a successful business model based on his eye for markets, his deft balancing of costs, and a flexible combination of shipping modes. He engaged in proprietary shipping (owning the cargo) and tramp steaming (taking cargoes where he found them), with some limited passenger service on his passenger/cargo vessels. Until World War I, his oceanic vessels all sailed under the British flag, and he manned his vessels with Chinese crews. This last policy explains his vehement opposition to the Seamen's Act of 1915, which required that three-quarters of the crew in any department be able to speak English. PMSS, with mostly American-registered ships, withdrew from the Pacific trade when the act passed, but Dollar never carried out his threat to sell off his ships. He simply flouted the law. World War I further enriched his company and left it in a good position to become the dominant American shipping company in the Pacific during the 1920s and 1930s. This ambition prompted the purchase of five British steamers after the war, followed by seven "502s," including the *President Harrison*.[2]

By the time the *President Harrison* inaugurated Dollar's round-the-world liner service on January 5, 1924, Captain Dollar had turned over most of the company's operations to his son Robert Stanley Dollar. The younger ship-owner maintained his father's policies until succeeding him as president on his death in 1932. The family then diversified into various commercial ventures ashore and began to drain money from the firm to support an extravagant lifestyle. By acquiring control over the Admiral Line, a successful coastwise steamship company based in Tacoma, Washington, the Dollars developed experience with that company's five "535" liners, bought from the Shipping Board after World War I. They also acquired lucrative mail contracts authorized by the Merchant Marine Act of 1928, though these necessitated the purchase of newer, faster ships. The *President Hoover* (1930) and the *President Coolidge* (1931), purchased with only 25 percent cash, arrived just as the country sank into the Depression. Forced to choose between bankruptcy and government ownership, Dollar finally sold his stock to the government, which turned the venerable Dollar Line into the American President Lines.

The rise and fall of the Dollars mirrored the experience of many shipowners between the world wars. It also illuminates the consequences of strong government intervention in the shipping industry. The period between the wars witnessed the longest and most consistent attempt by the U.S. government to build up and sustain a merchant marine. The campaign achieved mixed results, many of which surfaced in the Dollar story.

The glut of ships produced by the EFC from 1918 to 1922 proved to be a two-edged sword. It allowed companies such as Dollar to purchase vessels like the *President Harrison* at bargain prices. Other companies got even better deals from the government. American Export Lines (AEL), for example, bought for $1 million a fleet of ships that had cost the government $33 million to build. But the ready availability of government-surplus ships depressed the shipbuilding industry through the 1920s and drove many builders out of business. No oceanic vessels were built in the United States between 1922 and 1928.[3] Furthermore, the compressed building program of World War I produced a huge cohort of vessels that would all move toward obsolescence at the same pace. A more rational building program would have replaced aging vessels with new ones to take advantage of evolving technology and to adjust to the changing needs of the marketplace. Many companies apprehended the growing obsolescence of their fleets only at the end of the 1920s, leading them to order new vessels, as Dollar had done, just at the onset of the Depression.

Follow-on government policies in the 1920s gave additional support to the shipping industry, but stopped well short of the ambitious vision of

Wilson and Hurley. Republican administrations through the decade leaned toward protectionism and business-friendly policies, neglecting the contributions to American economic development and national security that Progressives had hoped to realize. The Merchant Marine Act of 1920, for example, really aimed to get the government out of the shipping business. Sometimes called the Jones Act for Chairman Wesley Jones (R-WA) of the Senate Committee on Commerce, the legislation sustained some of the Wilson and Hurley goals while at the same time redirecting the American shipping program.[4] Its statement of policy remained a trope of government rhetoric through the remainder of the twentieth century:

> It is hereby declared the policy of the United States to do whatever may be necessary to develop and encourage the maintenance . . . of a merchant marine . . . sufficient to carry the greater portion of its commerce and serve as a naval or military auxiliary in time of war or national emergency.[5]

Legislators often embrace such sweeping declarations in part because they embody good intentions that do no harm. It is only when a price tag is attached to "whatever might be necessary" that the politics really start. More revealing than this general statement of principle was the clause that followed: the merchant marine was "ultimately to be owned and operated privately by citizens of the United States."[6] Many conservatives had resisted creation of the Emergency Fleet Corporation during the war; now, with Republicans about to recapture the White House and the Congress, they wanted the government to get out of the shipping business. By the mid-1920s the government owned only United States Lines (USL), created by the Shipping Board in 1921 to operate German liners confiscated during the war and retained as reparations at war's end, especially *Leviathan* (the former *Vaterland*), for many years the world's largest liner. A Wall Street speculator bought USL in 1929 but bankrupted it in the onset of the Depression. In 1931 the Shipping Board allowed the revived International Mercantile Marine and Dollar Line to buy USL, but Dollar soon withdrew to address its own collapsing business. For better or for worse, the government had relinquished ownership and operation of its merchant fleet before the full impact of the Depression fell on the shipping industry.[7]

The Merchant Marine Act of 1920 also sought to promote the American merchant marine in other ways. It tried to limit the power of conferences to set rates; to break the hold of Britain on marine insurance, thus encouraging the development of an American marine insurance industry; and to extend preferential inland railroad rates to cargoes carried on American ships. Its most durable and well-known provision reinforced long-standing cabotage laws governing domestic shipping, limiting this lucrative trade to vessels built, owned, and crewed by Americans. This policy unquestionably sustained a healthy domestic shipping industry, and shipbuilding to support it, but did nothing for the oceanic shipping that Wilson and Hurley desired. Indeed the act was so xenophobic in its provisions that Wilson finally signed it only after announcing that he would refuse to enforce the controversial section 28, which projected the coastal and inland restrictions to the Philippines. The brainchild of Admiral William S. Benson, Hurley's successor as chairman of the Shipping Board, this policy and others in the act sought to break the stranglehold that Britain, in Benson's view, was attempting to reimpose upon world shipping.

More legislation followed in the Harding and Coolidge administrations. The Shipping Board Loan Fund Act of 1924 modified a provision of the 1920 law by allowing the Shipping Board to use up to $25 million a year in proceeds from its activities to subsidize the construction of new vessels.[8] When these steps failed to produce the hoped-for revival of U.S. oceanic shipping, more government action seemed warranted. The catalyst appeared in 1928, when the British Cunard Line sent its highly competitive liners into the Caribbean for the winter months, interloping in an American preserve. Once more Senator Wesley Jones sprang into action, pushing through Congress a hastily drawn piece of legislation that gave generous mail contracts to shipping lines as a subterfuge for outright subsidy. To stimulate the construction of new, competitive vessels, the act created a Construction Loan Fund and offered the most lucrative mail contracts to the fastest—presumably the newest—vessels. Vagueness in the language of the bill and a growing coziness between the Shipping Board and the shipping industry led to abuses and outright corruption. Pursuit of these mail contracts and the generous construction allowance had lured Dollar Line to purchase the *President Hoover* and the *President Coolidge*, mistakes from which it never recovered. Other shipowners drawn into the profitable but risky liner business suffered similar reverses.

Henry Herbermann, for example, allowed early postwar success and generous government support to undermine his judgment. A successful businessman on the New Jersey waterfront, Herbermann won a commission from the Shipping Board in 1920 to rescue the failing Export Steamship Corporation. By 1924 he had, with a transfer of vessels from the Shipping Board and the purchase of more at generous terms, turned his renamed company, American Export Lines, into the main U.S. carrier to the Mediterranean. Electing to move into the passenger trade, Herbermann ordered the "Four Aces," combination cargo/passenger vessels (the *Excalibur, Exochorda, Exeter,* and *Excambion*), which came into service in 1931. To compound the bad timing of his expansion, the vessels proved slow and expensive to operate, suiting them to neither cargo nor passengers. Still, Herbermann's lucrative mail contracts masked the losing economics of his swollen company. He slid into a lavish lifestyle at company expense and sent his ships to ports where there was more prestige than business. In 1934 New York Shipbuilding Company, a creditor, stepped in to prevent the Shipping Board from foreclosing on AEL. A new president saved the company by selling off ships and rationalizing its route structure.[9]

Dollar Line and AEL revealed the difficulty that American firms experienced in the 1920s and 1930s finding a business model to achieve Wilson's dream of a strong merchant marine. They also suggest that the attempts by government to foster this activity often misfired. Three basic models presented themselves by the 1920s. One, tramp lines, had the greatest difficulty competing outside American waters, because the operating and construction costs of American ships were higher than those of the other tramp ships prowling the world's oceans for cargoes. When American shipowners used foreign construction, foreign registry, and foreign crews, as Captain Dollar had done at the turn of the century, they could succeed. But this was not the American merchant marine that Wilson and Hurley wanted.

The second model, the liner trade, operating on fixed, published schedules, was growing in importance around the world at the turn of the century, made possible in part by the increasing influence of shipping conferences. These conferences dated from the late nineteenth century, when improvements in marine technology, especially the introduction of triple-expansion steam engines in the 1880s, had raised speed and efficiency to levels that would prompt rate wars as the only means of competition between liner companies. Conferences sought to rationalize international shipping by establishing agreed-upon rates for trade on specified routes. Onto this generally accepted international practice,

Americans projected their own distrust of monopoly, born in the Progressive Era. The Shipping Act of 1916, therefore, attempted to limit the power of conferences by closing U.S. ports to ships that did not subscribe to fair pricing practices as defined by the United States. Soon agreements were reached that reconciled most conference rules with American stipulations, exempting from antitrust prosecution American shipping that operated in compliant conferences. In the 1920s more than a hundred conferences operated in American trade routes, though the Shipping Board never established as much control as the 1916 legislation had sought.

Even when conferences were open to American ships, competition was still intense. Cargo ships had to run efficiently to make money at the going rates, and passenger liners had to speed across their routes to attract passengers. Hybrid passenger/cargo vessels of the kind employed by Dollar and AEL had to be both fast and efficient. By the late 1920s, the World War I vessels that had built up the American merchant marine were losing out to newer, faster, more efficient vessels from other countries. The government lured American shipowners into new purchases in the late 1920s by offering construction subsidies and mail contracts, but the resulting expansion, some of it accompanied by extravagance and mismanagement, occurred just as the Depression provoked a worldwide decline in shipping. Many of the U.S. liner companies went the way of Dollar and AEL.[10] While some firms, such as Lykes Brothers Steamship Company and Waterman Steamship Corporation, built strong and lasting businesses based in the Gulf of Mexico, they proved to be exceptions to the general pattern of the interwar years.

In contrast to the troubled record of tramp and liner companies in the 1920s, bulk shippers and proprietary lines achieved sustained success, in both domestic and international trade. Often the two models were combined in a single fleet. Bulk carriers succeeded both in traditional cargoes, such as ore, coal, stone, grain, and wood products, and in the emerging marketplace for oil. Charles Schwab had introduced the concept to Carnegie, U.S. Steel, and Bethlehem Steel. Coulby's Interlake Steamship Company followed this lineage, as did Bethlehem's Ore Steamship Company. Henry Ford followed comparable practice, developing his own fleet on the Great Lakes to deliver raw materials to the giant River Rouge automobile factory he built in Dearborn, Michigan. The Aluminum Company of America created its own Alcoa Steamship

Company in 1919, and Weyerhaeuser, the forest products company, ran its own merchant ships starting in 1923.

The tanker trade enjoyed some of the advantages of the dry-bulk carriers, but suffered as well some of the problems that afflicted tramp and liner service between the wars. Emerging from the World War I building program with excess tonnage capacity, the oil companies such as Standard Oil of New Jersey, the owner of the largest fleet of tankers, allowed independents to take up to 15 percent of a market that the oil companies had completely controlled before the war. Fluctuations in the market could then be absorbed by idling the independents and keeping the proprietary vessels booked. But even this cynical calculus broke down in the early years of the Depression. For example, the largest independent, C.D. Mallory and Company, laid up all of its nineteen vessels from 1930 to 1934, but Standard of New Jersey had to lay up twenty-six of its vessels as well. In general, steady demand for oil on the East Coast, where it was displacing coal in a multitude of energy applications, kept the business stable enough to support a significant national tanker fleet.

Not all successful proprietary shipping lines carried bulk cargo. Even with break-bulk cargoes, proprietary lines could realize competitive advantages from vertical integration of business interests and freedom from the vagaries of conference pricing. In addition to the Ore Steamship Company, Bethlehem Steel also created the Calmar Steamship Company to carry its finished products. This paralleled the model of U.S. Steel, which matched Coulby's Interlake Steamship Company and Pittsburgh Steamship Company on the Great Lakes with perhaps the most successful proprietary line of the era. Isthmian Lines was organized in 1910 in London by U.S. Steel to carry the company's products around the world. The brainchild of James A. Farrell Sr., the head of U.S. Steel's export subsidiary and later president of the company, the line really operated as a tramp company, taking U.S. Steel's products wherever they needed to go and seeking return cargoes wherever they found themselves. When U.S. Steel's shipyards completed their work for the Shipping Board in World War I, they turned to construction of twenty-seven ships for their own fleet, further increasing the overall economy of the operation. So successful was Isthmian Lines in the 1920s that it operated without government subsidy, either for construction or mail carriage.[11]

The striking contrast between the successes of bulk and proprietary carriers on the one hand and the troubles of American tramp and liner companies on the other highlights the continuing dilemma of American shipping. While domestic shipping prospered between the wars, the Depression notwithstanding, oceanic shipping struggled. Higher operating expenses, driven primarily by labor costs, undermined the position of American-registered vessels. Many companies simply embraced foreign registry, while others struggled to find an accommodation with maritime labor. The 1930s, however, empowered labor to strike a still harder bargain.

34

A TALE OF TWO HARRYS: THE RADICALIZATION OF WEST COAST LABOR

THE EPIPHANY OF AMERICAN MARITIME LABOR OCCURRED IN the streets of San Francisco on "Bloody Thursday," July 5, 1934. Fifty-seven days into a waterfront strike that had all but closed the port, local shipowners determined to force scab cargo through the picket lines. Against the united seamen and longshoremen in the streets, the shipowners pitted strikebreakers and seven hundred local police. "A vast tangle of fighting men" struggled until, as the *San Francisco Chronicle* reported, "blood ran in the streets."[1] Before it was over, two men lay dead: Howard Sperry, a longshoreman, and Nicholas Counderakis, a strike sympathizer and a communist.[2] Maritime labor had its martyrs. Sympathy for the fallen protesters sparked a general strike in San Francisco, giving maritime labor more power than at any time since Andrew Furuseth's alliance with Robert La Follette to pass the Seamen's Act of 1915.

From the "Big Strike" emerged two rank-and-file leaders with the potential to unify maritime labor and realize the dream of "one big union." Harry Bridges, an Australian immigrant longshoreman of plebeian appearance and charismatic rhetoric, launched the strike from his position as the leader of the Pacific Coast District of the International Longshoremen's Association (ILA). Harry Lundeberg, a militant seaman of the Sailors' Union of the Pacific (SUP), left his ship in San Francisco

284

harbor to join the strike. He thereafter represented his local Seattle union, a subsidiary of Andrew Furuseth's International Seamen's Union (ISU), in the San Francisco strike. For a while the two Harrys made common cause, demonstrating on the West Coast the power of maritime labor when sailors and shore workers united. In the end, however, the factional divisions, jurisdictional disputes, and centrifugal forces that had plagued maritime labor for half a century overcame the marriage of convenience between Bridges and Lundeberg. The two Harrys became implacable foes and locked their respective constituencies into internecine conflict that mirrored the fracture of American labor in general.

The "Big Strike" of 1934 climaxed years of decline for maritime labor. The good times of World War I, when jobs were plentiful and wages high, proved short-lived. The prosperity was driven more by the exigencies of the war than by the reforms of the Seamen's Act of 1915. Maritime wages rose steadily from 1916 to 1919 in response to the worldwide demand for

A scene from the San Francisco strike of 1934, the closest American maritime labor ever came to the radical dream of "one great union." Seamen and longshoremen put aside their differences long enough to precipitate a general strike that won relief from the hated blue-book system of management control.

shipping and the shortages caused by wartime diversions of ships and losses to submarines, surface raiders, and mines. Andrew Furuseth's goal of wage equalization was virtually achieved in those years, as foreign shipping companies found themselves obliged to pay top dollar for scarce labor. The continuation of the U.S. shipbuilding program after the war promised to sustain the maritime prosperity.

Instead, the glut of American ships contributed to a downturn in the world economy early in the 1920s. Shipowners exploited the recession to regain control over terms of employment, roll back wages, and revise work rules. A national maritime strike in 1921 failed miserably. Andrew Furuseth blamed the "old reactionaries" such as Robert Dollar, but the Shipping Board bore equal responsibility. A political fluke had denied Admiral William Benson appointment as board chairman, allowing former ILA president Thomas O'Connor to maneuver himself into control. A staunch believer in free enterprise and a recent convert to the Republican Party, O'Connor, according to the historian René de la Pedraja, "did everything within his power to drain government funds, vessels, and resources in order to increase the profits of private companies."[3] In what the historian Joseph Goldberg called the "rout of the unions," wages fell 15 to 35 percent, overtime was eliminated, and watches aboard ship were changed from three to two: instead of four-hour watches twice a day, seamen served a single twelve-hour watch each day.[4]

Andrew Furuseth, the patriarch of American maritime labor, was bereft of miracles. Undeterred by the failure of the Seamen's Act of 1915 to protect labor in a declining economy, he sought relief in more legislation. With the government paying indirectly to operate the U.S. merchant fleet, Congress proved cool to reforms that would raise labor costs. Furuseth also turned to management, but he had no more success there than with Congress. Blaming the 1921 strike on Wobbly and syndicalist influence within the union, Furuseth promised to root out radicalism in return for post-strike reform. He convinced the ISU to end the strike, but his subsequent negotiations with the shipowners failed. They held the power. Reluctantly, Furuseth went along with the revival of the hated blue-book union, which essentially placed hiring power firmly in the hands of the owners. Furuseth spent much of the 1920s fighting in the courts the hiring practices to which he had reluctantly assented. His failure to support the 1921 strike alienated ISU members such as Harry

Bridges; membership fell from 115,000 to just 50,000 within months of the strike, and to 15,000 by 1926.[5]

Residing in Washington, the site of his greatest achievement and the focus of his tireless efforts on behalf of seamen, the incorruptible Furuseth distanced himself physically and experientially from his constituency. After 1921 he held on to power by the force of his personality and by the indebtedness people felt toward him because of his past contributions. Increasingly he found himself fighting a rearguard action against Wobblies and communists, radicals from the union rank and file who took exception to both his philosophy and his tactics. The Wobblies gained purchase in the seamen's unions, advocating direct action at the job site, labor solidarity in "one big union," and rejection of the kind of political activity that Furuseth pursued in Washington. In the late 1920s the communists targeted the waterfront and other economic sectors, advocating the industrial organization of workers and the use of concerted strikes to bring government and business to terms. Furuseth decried both movements as threats to maritime labor, and he promised business and government that he would root out such influences in return for their support. But he could deliver neither labor to the establishment nor improved working conditions to labor. As his stature and influence waned, the rank and file of maritime labor grew more radical.

The Depression finally ripped Furuseth's fingers from his fragile hold on power. The Republican administrations of the 1920s, with which Furuseth had negotiated, found themselves discredited by the 1929 collapse of the stock market. As the country and then the world slid into depression, President Herbert Hoover seemed unwilling or unable to help. Franklin Delano Roosevelt took office in 1933 on the strength of a new coalition of blue-collar voters and a program of reform.[6] Section 7(a) of the National Industrial Recovery Act (NIRA) of 1933 guaranteed to labor the right to collective bargaining.[7] West Coast longshoremen seized the opportunity to break the hiring power of the shipowners.

Their leader was Harry "the Nose" Bridges, one of the most remarkable personalities in the history of American labor. A Wobbly on the rebound from Furuseth's bungling of the 1921 strike, a fellow-traveler with communists, and a member of the communist-influenced Marine Workers Industrial Union (MWIU), he had developed his own brand of radicalism during the long period of shipowners' dominance from 1921 to 1933. He appealed directly to rank-and-file workers, calling them in plain language to a revolution rife with communist rhetoric. Woody Guthrie and Pete Seeger captured something of his style in their 1941 "Song of Bridges":

> Us workers got to get wise,
> Our wives and kids will starve to death if we don't organize.[8]

"He always had a snarl on his upper lip," recalled U.S. Maritime Commission chairman Emory Land, to go with the "hawk eyes and nose and long spidery arms" noted by *Fortune* magazine. Another contemporary reported that "he swaggers like a racetrack bookie." Frances Perkins, Franklin Roosevelt's secretary of labor, remembered Bridges as a "small, thin, haggard man in a much-worn overcoat," a striking contrast to dapper Joe Ryan, the president of the International Longshoremen's Association, headquartered in New York City, from which Bridges kept his Pacific Coast District at arm's length.[9] Schooled and hardened in the 1920s, Bridges preached the unity of labor, desegregation, job action when necessary, concerted action when possible, and fearless tenacity in the face of intimidation and violence. When his moment came in the spring of 1934, he seized it with a sureness and power that astonished the labor community as much as it surprised the shipowners. One veteran of the MWIU who had worked the San Francisco waterfront in 1931 and 1932 had to be reminded, "You know him, Australian Harry! He works on the Matson dock and plays the horses."[10] After the "Big Strike" propelled him from obscurity to preeminence in the West Coast maritime labor movement, no one had to be reminded of who Harry Bridges was.

Bridges called the "Big Strike" on May 9, 1934, after federal arbitration under the new NIRA failed to address labor's demand for a union hiring hall to replace the despised blue-book halls controlled by the shipowners. Quickly the longshoremen's strike spread from San Francisco to all Pacific coast ports. Though the ISU at first declined to join, many seamen made common cause with the shore workers. Thereupon, the ISU struck, in order to stay out in front of its membership. Their numbers were further swelled by Teamsters, who walked out in sympathy. President Roosevelt tried to mediate and failed. Joe Ryan, imported from the East Coast to impose ILA discipline, reached an agreement with management, only to have the West Coast workers reject it. Business stagnated in all West Coast ports except Los Angeles. Behind Bridges's passionate oratory and steadfast resolve, the strike defied all mediation and intimidation; only union recognition would do.

The patience of Robert Stanley Dollar and other San Francisco shipowners and businessmen ran out early in July. On the eve of Independence Day, seven hundred police and strikebreakers broke the picket lines to move "scab cargo." Violence resumed two days later on Bloody Thursday, leaving two strikers dead, thirty with bullet wounds, and forty-three seriously injured.[11] Brutality won the battle but lost the war. A mile-long funeral procession up Market Street on July 9 honoring the two fallen strikers attracted fifteen thousand marchers and even more spectators. On July 16 a general strike led a hundred thousand workers off the job in solidarity with their maritime brethren. Harry Bridges found himself at the head of the largest and most powerful maritime labor strike in American history.

But the center could not hold. Conservative forces within the labor movement made common cause with industry and government to divide and conquer. Force and intimidation moved from the streets into the labor halls and offices of the key unions. Bridges and other labor leaders, especially in the MWIU, were branded communists, and the strike was portrayed as a first step toward the overthrow of the government. Management made concessions to lure segments of the labor community into settlement. When labor in San Francisco called off the general strike and the Teamsters withdrew their support, resolve weakened. Ironically, the longshoremen gave in first, agreeing to arbitration. Harry Bridges thereupon met with the Sailors' Union of the Pacific on July 29 to try to explain the longshoremen's defection. But Andy Furuseth upstaged him. He called the seamen to a bonfire on the following day, at which all would dip their reviled blue books in oil and throw them to the flames. With this last act of defiance, the seamen gave up the strike on July 31, after eighty-three days that transformed American maritime labor.[12]

Among the transformations effected by the San Francisco strike was the radicalization of another labor leader who would come to challenge Bridges for control of the forces unleashed by the strike. Harald Olaf Lundeberg, better known in labor circles as Harry "Lunchbox" Lundeberg, came from his native Norway as Furuseth had done before him, shipping out as a youth and sailing the world's oceans to a landing on the American West Coast. Based in Seattle, he came to figure prominently in that city's branch of the SUP. When his ship was stranded in San Francisco by the Big Strike, he walked ashore and represented his local in the conflict.

Bridges found in him a kindred spirit, a militant seaman in refreshing contrast to the staid Uncle Tom that Bridges saw in Furuseth. Soon the two men hatched a plan to unite maritime labor, perhaps even to achieve the great Wobbly goal of "one big union."

Together Bridges and Lundeberg formed the Marine Federation of the Pacific (MFP). Bridges installed Lundeberg as the first president and set about expanding the reach and power of the rank-and-file movement launched in the Big Strike. The settlement of that strike had given the unions a hiring hall shared with management. Bridges wanted more. And he wanted to extend the maritime labor movement inland, embracing other labor allies. Denied the presidency of the Pacific Coast District of the ILA by the entrenched power of William "the Burglar" Lewis, Bridges poured his anger and his energy into the MFP. Though Lundeberg soon left the MFP to assume direction of the SUP in Seattle, he and Bridges cooperated through an even more successful strike in 1936 and 1937.

The big three West Coast shipping companies—Matson, Dollar, and American-Hawaiian—appear to have provoked the strike in an attempt to reverse their earlier concessions on union hiring halls. But this was the one issue on which Bridges would not budge. At midnight on October 29, 1936, forty thousand maritime workers walked off the job. The shipowners eschewed violence this time, prepared to wait out the strike. But to their surprise, it spread to the East Coast and the Gulf and gained strength as time went on. Shipowners on the West Coast remained true to their resolve to avoid violence, but twenty-seven seamen died on the other coasts and intimidation hung over the entire confrontation. Bridges used the strike to advocate maritime labor solidarity and a national union. In the end, the shipowners caved; the price of breaking the West Coast unions simply proved to be higher than the shipping companies could afford. For thirty-six years the sun had never set on the Dollar fleet, until the *President McKinley* joined the other vessels trapped in San Francisco on the fiftieth day of the strike. Even the combative and intransigent Robert Dollar had to admit defeat. When the strike ended after ninety days on February 4, 1937, the sailors had won real improvements in wages, hours, and overtime, and members of the Marine Federation of the Pacific (MFP) had held on to their cherished hiring halls. It was a sterling example of the power of solidarity.

Within months, however, the MFP dissolved, and its members divided once more into warring factions. Harry Bridges and the longshoremen, with their communist influences, squared off against Harry Lundeberg and the sailors, with their syndicalist leanings. Both groups advocated socialist alternatives to capitalism, but they differed strategically and organizationally. The greatest fault line was the age-old animosity between sailors and longshoremen. This was now exacerbated by the long-standing tension between Andrew Furuseth's belief in craft organization for the SUP and the ISU, which focused on the skills of workers such as deckhands and engine-room workers, versus the growing attraction of American labor to industrial organization, which tended to mirror the structure of businesses such as the steel or automobile industries. When the Congress of Industrial Organizations (CIO) broke with the AFL in 1936 to form an independent national union, Bridges took the longshoremen with it. Ironically, he had once tried to convince Lundeberg to rejoin the AFL, which he had left when Furuseth expelled his SUP from the ISU. But now Lundeberg reversed course and took the SUP back into the AFL.

The switching of sides and maneuvering for position marked a monumental struggle for control of maritime labor. The rhetoric was decidedly ideological. Lundeberg took up the shipowners' gambit of red baiting, and Bridges responded by castigating the SUP for racism and syndicalism. The vilification exchanged by Bridges and Lundeberg was personal and vicious, playing upon the cult of personality that had taken over the maritime labor movement, mirroring the same phenomenon in other labor organizations. The tension between the two camps exploded in violence in April 1938. When the Shepard Line freighter *Sea Thrush* docked in San Francisco, the SUP declared its cargo "hot" and untouchable because it had been loaded by workers not recognized by the SUP. The CIO longshoremen were unwilling to allow seamen in their union to be forced off the vessel. Lundeberg personally joined a picket line of five hundred sailors, arming some with baseball bats. A comparable army of longshoremen attacked. The ensuing bloody melee left casualties on both sides and the longshoremen in control of the pier and the unloading of *Sea Thrush*. The hopes of maritime labor solidarity washed with the workers' blood into the murky water of the Embarcadero.

The brief and fruitful alliance of seamen and longshoremen had demonstrated the power of concerted action. Real wages in the maritime industry began to rise in 1935, making up for the losses suffered from

1912 to 1933. These wage gains would continue until 1948. As had been true in World War I, however, they had more to do with world war than with labor activity. Just as the Seamen's Act of 1915 paled in importance relative to the market forces of wartime shortages and demand, so too did the golden epic of maritime labor in the mid-1930s carry less weight than the massive mobilization of the world's resources that was to be World War II. When labor resumed its claims in the postwar era, it would operate from a different base of power.

35

Hugo Black and Direct Subsidy, 1935–1941

The captain of the *Morro Castle* had died in his cabin of an apparent heart attack before the fire broke out. Whether he might have mitigated the tragedy that struck his ship in the early-morning hours of September 8, 1934, can only be guessed. But he could hardly have made it any worse. The Ward Line cruise ship, returning from Havana, was sailing slowly off the New Jersey coast, timing its arrival in New York for the following morning and allowing its passengers to sleep off the revelry of their last night aboard. At 2:45 a.m., a night watchman reported a fire in the writing room, near the midship passengers' lounge. One crewman tried to fight the flames with a fire extinguisher before recommending a general alarm. The acting captain waited another ten minutes before sounding the alarm. Meanwhile, smoke rose to the boat deck, where it was sucked into the ventilating system and delivered to the engine rooms. Fearing for their lives, the engine crews fled. The ship then lost fire-main water pressure, steering, and light and power belowdecks. Out of control, its bow turned into the strong winds, pushing the fire aft on the port side. The crew managed to launch only four of the ship's ten lifeboats. Rescue vessels arriving on the scene at dawn found the anchored, burning hulk surrounded in the water by many of the 413 survivors. Some had swum to the Jersey Shore. Ninety-four passengers and forty-three crewmen perished. Not done with its grisly business, the *Morro Castle* broke loose from a tow two days later and grounded on the beach at Asbury Park. At low tide, bathers could wade out and touch the still smoldering vessel.[1]

Blame for the disaster found many targets. The acting captain had responded slowly. Some crewmen had panicked and fled for their lives, jumping into lifeboats ahead of passengers. The passengers, many hungover from the previous evening's festivities, had added their own inertia and panic to the chaos. Safety equipment and procedures aboard ship proved inadequate, a sign of failed oversight and inspection. Opposition from Andrew Furuseth and the International Seamen's Union had blocked congressional ratification of the 1929 Safety of Life at Sea

SS *Morro Castle*, a cruise ship returning from Havana to New York City, caught fire on the night of September 7–8, 1934, off the New Jersey coast, killing 137 passengers and crew. Here the abandoned ship has drifted ashore at Asbury Park, New Jersey, where curious bathers could walk out and touch the still smoldering hulk. This tragedy contributed to national sentiment in favor of the Merchant Marine Act of 1936 and American adoption of the Safety of Life at Sea (SOLAS) convention of 1929, which was itself a consequence of the sinking of the *Titanic* in 1912.

(SOLAS) convention, a follow-on to the 1914 agreement prompted by the sinking of the *Titanic*. Once again, Congress would act after the fact, finally approving SOLAS in 1936.[2]

The *Morro Castle* disaster also spawned an even more important piece of legislation, the Merchant Marine Act of 1936. The smoking hulk beached like a dead whale on the Jersey Shore bore painful testimony to the sorry state of the American merchant marine in 1934. The huge fleet of commercial vessels built by the United States during and after World War I had mostly been sold off to private firms at bargain prices during the 1920s. Many of these firms had made significant profits operating the ships for the government or buying them at a fraction of replacement cost or market value. Few of the companies, however, had used these advantages to fund ongoing replacement programs. As the ships entered their second decade, they proved to be less and less competitive in the international marketplace, especially on the cutthroat Depression-era liner routes. Neither construction subsidies nor the generous mail contracts provided by the Merchant Marine Act of 1928 had succeeded in renewing America's commercial fleet.[3] When companies did use government funds to support new construction, they often chose the wrong designs. The *Morro Castle*, for example, was built in 1930 with Merchant Marine Act of 1928 funds, but its novel turboelectric drive proved uneconomical. The drive had been used successfully on some naval vessels and would be applied again in World War II to some cargo ships (an ironic instance of cross-fertilization between naval and commercial ship technology), but by the time it was installed on the *Morro Castle* and its sister ship the *Oriente*, improved reduction gears were more efficient.[4] The Depression, of course, compounded all of these problems. The demand for passenger transport fell precipitously, and imports and exports both declined steadily after 1929; the percentage coming and going on U.S. vessels failed to rise much above one-third of the total value of trade carried by ship.[5]

Congressional dissatisfaction with the merchant marine, sparked by the *Morro Castle*, found itself folded into the general scandal-hunting, blame-laying, and reform that marked the Democratic capture of Congress on the coattails of Franklin Roosevelt's presidential victory in 1932. Many of the country's problems were laid at the feet of the Republican presidents who had controlled the White House since World War I and their business cronies who had been shaping policies even during the war. Senator Gerald Nye's "Merchants of Death" hearings grabbed many of the headlines in the crusade to blame arms manufacturers for America's entry into World War I. But a more productive congressional investigation proceeded simultaneously and to greater effect. While Senator Nye never found the smoking gun of business malfeasance, not even in Charles Schwab's notorious profits at Bethlehem Steel, Senator Hugo Black's separate investigation of the U.S. merchant marine turned up scandal of epic proportions.

Black was an unlikely candidate for such a role. A native of Alabama, he took a law degree at the University of Alabama in 1906, practiced law, served as a county solicitor, joined the army artillery corps in 1917 without seeing action in Europe, and developed a reputation in Birmingham for political ambition. On September 13, 1923, he joined the Ku Klux Klan, whose members accounted for fifteen thousand of Birmingham's thirty-two thousand voters. Three years later, he was elected to the U.S. Senate, with a vote count about the same as the state membership of the Klan. In the Senate, however, and in his subsequent thirty-four years as an associate justice of the Supreme Court, Black displayed none of the elitism and bigotry of the Klan. He consistently championed civil rights and fought against the abuse of power and privilege.[6] When a Special Committee to Investigate Air Mail and Ocean Mail Contracts was created on February 25, 1933, Black took the chair. The case against the maritime industry had been laid out for his committee in a senate document entitled "The Truth about the Postal Contracts under Title VI, Merchant Marine Act of 1928 and its Application as a Subsidy to Shipping," written for the Senate by a former official of the U.S. Shipping Board.[7]

Senator Black and his colleagues found the scandal they were looking for. Their 1935 report revealed "a saturnalia of waste, inefficiency, unearned exorbitant salaries, and bonuses."[8] The devices of misappropriation amazed Black as much for their inventiveness as for their lack of scruple.

> Holding companies, subsidiaries, associates, affiliates, and whatnots have been used by shipping companies for the uniform purpose of siphoning the income of subsidized operating companies into the pockets of individuals. . . . When discovered, it was always found that these corporate devices concealed salaries, bonuses, secret expenses, and purloined revenues, which in equity and good conscience should have remained in the treasury of the subsidized

company. . . . Inexcusably heavy profits have been made by some ocean-mail contractors and excessive salaries, fees, commissions, and expense accounts have been paid to officers, agents, and high-powered "fixers" plying their art in Washington.[9]

The sorry state of American oceanic shipping, concluded Black, flowed from mismanagement by the shipping firms and abuse of government programs. The two causes reinforced one another. The ruin of Dollar Line has already been discussed. Bankruptcy hearings revealed that Dollar's son, Robert Stanley, had taken $2.5 million in salary between 1923 and 1934.[10] His brother walked off with another million. Henry Herbermann's American Export Lines had followed a similar path, though Hugo Black got to Herbermann before bankruptcy descended upon the company, forcing his resignation in April 1934.[11]

Not all of the personal malfeasance afflicting the shipping industry was as transparent. For example, the Ward Line, subsequently known as the New York and Cuba Mail Steamship Company, which operated the *Morro Castle*, was a wholly owned subsidiary of the Atlantic, Gulf & West Indies Steamship Lines (AGWI). So too was the Colombian Steamship Company, which sailed from East Coast ports to Colombia and the Caribbean. It was created for the sole purpose of qualifying for Shipping Board subsidies that had been denied AGWI. The parent company owned the vessels and leased them to its subsidiaries at exorbitant prices. Thus, while Ward struggled along with losses due to the *Morro Castle*, the owners of AGWI awarded themselves a $900,000 dividend on a $3 million investment. The profits that Ward Line should have been making with the help of government subsidies had been drained from the company in outrageous leasing fees and distributed to the owners of the parent firm.[12]

Senator Black's committee found that government malfeasance and corruption bore equal blame for the decline of the merchant marine, especially during the long reign (1924–1933) of Thomas V. O'Connor as chairman of the Shipping Board. As president of the International Longshoremen's Association (1908–1921), O'Connor had turned the organization into "little more than a company union," according to the historian René de la Pedraja.[13] After O'Connor and a clique of Republican appointees took control of the Shipping Board, ships built at public expense were sold off to American businessmen at a fraction of their construction costs. The government failed to enforce its own regulations about crews aboard American-flagged vessels. The Shipping Board consistently sided with management in labor disputes through the 1920s. Shipbuilding subsidies and mail contracts in the late 1920s were awarded at the highest allowable levels without competitive bidding, indeed without any independent verification of the petitioners' claims. Lobbyists and Washington "fixers" were able to deliver government contracts to firms that could pay their fees. The government accepted corporate losses, such as those by Ward Line, as proof that mail subsidies had to be raised. Too often the increased subsidies flowed through the corporation into profits without ever being used to improve service.

In contrast, Black found that the lines operated by the government had been comparatively efficient and honest. He favored a merchant marine owned and operated by the government, as Robert McAdoo and Woodrow Wilson had proposed in World War I, but he knew that a socialist solution could never win congressional approval, especially amid the furor being bred by Franklin Roosevelt's New Deal. Reluctantly, Black concluded that the United States would have to stay with a government-subsidized private merchant marine. But he and his committee joined President Roosevelt in proposing a startling new form for the subsidy.[14] In a message to Congress on March 4, 1935, little more than two months before the Black committee reported, Roosevelt had proposed direct differential subsidies of both shipbuilding and merchant ship operation. Rejecting the "subterfuge" of indirect subsidies, Roosevelt said that "if Congress decides that it will maintain a reasonably adequate American merchant marine I believe that it can well afford honestly to call a subsidy by its right name."[15]

The president and Senator Black came to their recommendations from slightly different positions, but their convergence on a program of direct subsidies marked a sea change in American policy toward the merchant marine. It also marked a sea change in the rationale for a merchant marine. Up to this point in the twentieth century, if not earlier, the United States had committed itself to sustain a robust merchant marine for two reasons: war and commerce.[16] Roosevelt now offered three: two were war and one was "fairness" in international commerce. In contrast, Black and his colleagues cited three "objectives": two were national security and the third was reliable transportation of American goods abroad "regardless of economic or war disturbances." Only in this last category, an apparent reference to the shipping dislocations experienced in 1914, was an economic argument being advanced. Perhaps because of the Depression, perhaps because of the ominous political developments in Europe, perhaps because of the "saturnalia of waste" uncovered in the past decade, the Roosevelt administration was clearly backing away from the economic justification for the merchant marine.[17]

The United States had turned a corner, embarking on a new road that would carry the maritime industry to the end of the twentieth century. The Merchant Marine Act of 1936 remained true to Woodrow Wilson's vision of a powerful national industry, but it downplayed Wilson's economic rationale. It adopted almost word for word the statement of purpose in the Merchant Marine Act of 1920, substituting only that the goal was a merchant marine to carry "a substantial portion" of the nation's shipping needs instead of "the greater portion." To achieve that end, it created differential subsidies to support both construction and operation of oceanic liners. The act did not support ships on coastal or inland routes, for these faced no foreign competition. Nor did it apply to tramp steamers or bulk carriers, which managed to compete internationally with varying degrees of success. It was liner service that was the most competitive, the most volatile, potentially the most lucrative, and in time of war the most useful to American military needs. The government therefore agreed to pay shipbuilders a construction subsidy equal to the difference between their costs and those of foreign firms building ships abroad, up to 50 percent of the price of a vessel. And it agreed to pay shipping firms for the difference between their operating costs and those of firms operating ships under foreign registry, up to 75 percent of yearly totals.

True to the principles of Hugo Black and Franklin Roosevelt and to the tenor of the New Deal, the primary rationale behind this legislation was to cover the higher cost of American labor while at the same time allowing the shipping industry to compete internationally. Other factors contributed to higher American costs—price of materials, safety restrictions, regulations, and so on. But labor costs contributed more than any other, and the Roosevelt administration could satisfy both labor and industry by simply picking up the tab. This appealing political compromise had enormous implications for the future, but concerns were drowned out in 1936 in a rush to pass a very popular and revolutionary piece of legislation.

The Merchant Marine Act of 1936 was one of the most important maritime laws in American history, second only to the cabotage laws of

1817 and 1920. It replaced the Shipping Board Bureau (an interim 1933 replacement for the discredited Shipping Board) with a United States Maritime Commission. The commission's most pressing business in 1936 was to negotiate an end to existing mail contracts in order to clear the way for the new subsidy program. President Roosevelt called upon Joseph Kennedy, an ambitious New York financier and New Dealer to chair it. Kennedy had served as a supervisor at the Fore River Shipyard in World War I, when Franklin Roosevelt was secretary of the navy, but that hardly prepared him for the task he took up in 1936. Many shipping firms held government contracts, over which they were prepared to go to court. To dissuade them, Kennedy had in hand the Black committee report and strong evidence of malfeasance by those same firms. In ten short months, he succeeded in clearing the decks, negotiating settlements in which companies generally traded their contractual hold on the government for immunity from prosecution. Then he accepted a post more to his liking, the U.S. ambassadorship to Great Britain, and left fellow commission member Emory S. Land to succeed him. Land, a retired navy rear admiral in the tradition of Edwin Benson, proved ideally suited for the role.

Land's nominal mission, to carry out the provisions of the 1936 act, paralleled that of Benson after World War I. Just as Woodrow Wilson had a grand plan to make the United States a world maritime power, so too did Franklin Roosevelt have a larger agenda for the merchant marine. He would bend it to the reversal of Republican isolationism. Sensing the growing danger from a Europe sliding into totalitarianism, he wanted the United States to engage more forcefully on the world stage. He orchestrated an amendment of the Smoot-Hawley Tariff in 1934 to abate the trade war that the 1930 legislation had provoked. He circumvented the Neutrality Act of 1935 by encouraging American shipping firms to register in Panama. And he pushed aggressively the construction and operating subsidies of the Merchant Marine Act to build up America's liners in the years before World War II. Just as he called for fifty thousand bombers a year in 1940, so too did he increase the Maritime Commission's original goal of fifty ships a year to two hundred by December 1940. As a result, the United States shipping industry was far better prepared for World War II than it had been for World War I.

Admiral Land also undertook an economic survey of the American merchant marine. The resulting report, published in 1937, confirmed President Roosevelt's appraisal and endorsed the route on which the nation had embarked.[18] Only commerce and war could justify government support of a national merchant marine; of these factors, war was the more important. In 1937 the United States exported more goods than any other nation, 10 percent of all it produced. Only Britain exported a greater percentage of its national product. In spite of that trade, however, the merchant marine was a comparatively small business, not very important to the American economy. Nor were the economic prospects for the industry bright. Historically it provided a poor return on investment. Labor conditions were chaotic. The United States remained a fundamentally protectionist nation, in spite of the reforms of the New Deal. The country had spent almost $4 billion since World War I to support the merchant marine, with little to show for it. Only national security provided a compelling argument for such support.

The report recommended some fine-tuning of the 1936 legislation to create a maritime labor board and to provide low-cost loans. Otherwise, the report affirmed President Roosevelt's position. An economic argument for a U.S. merchant marine had no merit. The country should subsidize as necessary to maintain maritime resources in support of national defense. Otherwise, it should let market forces take their course. There appeared to be viable business models for some proprietary vessels and bulk carriers, but the United States was not likely to find such a model for liner service. It was subsidies or nothing. On this policy platform, the nation sailed into World War II.

36

THE *HENRY BACON* AND THE WAR IN THE ATLANTIC, 1941–1945

THE SS *ROBIN MOOR* LINKED THE WORLD WARS. THE 5,000-TON, 400-foot cargo ship came to life at Hog Island in 1919, part of the World War I shipbuilding program that Woodrow Wilson and Edward Hurley extended into the postwar period in order to build up America's merchant fleet. Operated for years as part of the Shipping Board's fleet, the *Robin Moor* found herself doing tramp service for Robin Line between the United States and Africa on the eve of World War II. On May 21, 1941, about seven hundred miles off the coast of West Africa, en route from New York to Cape Town with general cargo, she was torpedoed and shelled by the German submarine U-69. The U-boat commander allowed the thirty-eight crewmen and eight passengers to disembark in safety, and offered them provisions and directions to shore. The *Robin Moor* achieved the dubious distinction of being the first American-flagged vessel sunk by a hostile act in the Atlantic Ocean in World War II. Six months earlier another American ship had succumbed in the Pacific. American shipping entered the Second World War long before Pearl Harbor.

The traditional narrative of World War II shipping features the Liberty ships, Victory ships, and tankers that gave the war's crash shipbuilding program its public face. These emergency vessels, so the story goes, issued from American shipyards in sufficient numbers to replenish the losses to

German submarines in the North Atlantic. There is more than a little truth in this picture. But most of America's shipping losses were not Liberties and Victories but stalwart veterans of the World War I shipbuilding program. Almost half of the American merchant vessels lost in World War II—306 ships—began life in the World War I Emergency Fleet. Another 11 percent either predated that conflict or came into the American fleet from other sources. Only 32 percent of the merchant ships lost in World War II were products of the war's shipbuilding program.[1]

One reason was timing. The United States began World War II with an old fleet, and 1942 was by far the most dangerous year of the war for merchant shipping. Half the American ships lost or damaged during the war succumbed before the end of 1942.[2] The U.S. Maritime Commission building program delivered 760 ships in 1942, and fewer than a thousand during the total prewar buildup beginning in 1937. In comparison, it produced almost five thousand vessels in the last three years of the war.[3] Older ships simply dominated the American fleet in the early, most dangerous years of the conflict for U.S. vessels. Furthermore, the newer ships entering service enjoyed higher speeds, the protection of increasing armament and Naval Armed Guards, and, most importantly, the protection of convoy. Incredibly, the United States was slow to organize convoys, which had proved themselves so effective in World War I.

Nowhere did the lack of convoys exact such a high toll as in the western Atlantic in the first six months of 1942. In late December 1941 Admiral Karl Dönitz, the commander of the German submarine fleet, launched Operation Drumbeat, or *Paukenschlag*, a campaign of Wagnerian conceit designed to crush American opposition to the hegemony of the Third Reich. Dönitz began by dispatching five of his Type VII boats to target American shipping along the East Coast of the United States and in adjacent waters. These 500-ton craft, 220 feet long, carried deck guns and fourteen torpedoes. Capable of 7.5 knots submerged and 17.5 knots on the surface, they could hide from faster warships and outrace most merchant vessels, especially the World War I relics then plying the coastal trade. Their greatest limitation was fuel, which confined them to six weeks of unsupported operations.[4] But they found in the western Atlantic such a target-rich environment that they tended to exhaust their ammunition before their fuel.

In the first six and a half months of America's participation in the war, German U-boats sank more than 360 Allied merchant ships, totaling

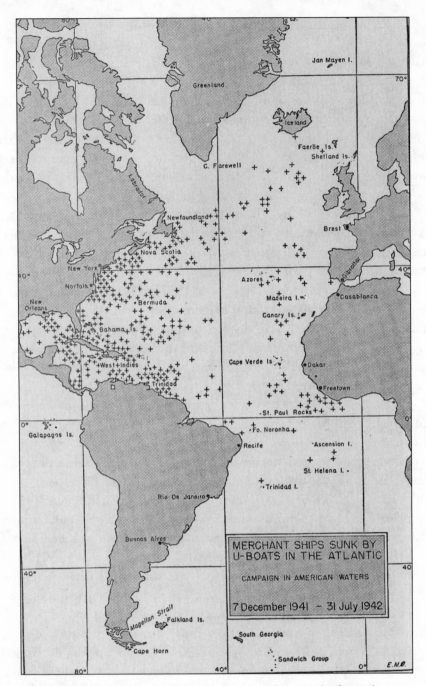

MERCHANT SHIPS SUNK BY
U-BOATS IN THE ATLANTIC

CAMPAIGN IN AMERICAN WATERS

7 December 1941 – 31 July 1942

This official U.S. Navy chart of commercial ship sinkings in the first eight months of America's participation in World War II shows the price of *Pauken-schlag*, the German campaign to attack shipping in the western North Atlantic. It is little wonder that the German submariners called this a "happy time" and that American merchant seamen denounced the navy for failing to protect them.

2,250,000 gross tons.[5] This represented the equivalent of half the American merchant fleet at the time. *Paukenschlag* accounted for most of these sinkings. From the Caribbean to Newfoundland, and all along the East Coast and the Gulf of Mexico, ships found themselves under attack.

Some Americans watched in impotent horror as ships burned and sank within sight of a shore that had been immune to hostile action since the War of 1812. Americans still knew virtually nothing of the Atlantic U-boat campaign in 1940 and 1941, which had claimed the *Robin Moor* and three other U.S. merchant ships in the North Atlantic in a warm-up for *Paukenschlag*.[6] Authorities covered this bad news with a security blanket, the same treatment they accorded intelligence reports that Drumbeat was coming. In place of reports on ship losses along the East Coast, the navy broadcast patently false claims of submarine sinkings. The famous declaration that an enlisted navy pilot had "sighted sub, sank same" was only half true. Navy public affairs personnel, who invented the phrase attributed to the pilot, simply equated sightings with sinkings. The real scandal of the campaign, however, from the American point of view, was not that it seemed to catch the nation unawares. The wonder was that the country took so long to respond.

Acrimonious controversy surrounds the failure of the United States to protect shipping along the East Coast in the first half of 1942. The naval historian and admiral Samuel Eliot Morison called the navy's response "pitifully inadequate."[7] Franklin Roosevelt told his secretary of the navy that the situation was a real disgrace. Edwin Hoyt, a historian of *Paukenschlag*, said the debacle revealed "the American high command at its worst."[8] The British historian Martin Middlebrook called the behavior of the American authorities "almost criminal."[9]

Critics focus on Admiral Ernest J. King, the accomplished, brilliant, imperious, abrasive, and universally disliked chief of naval operations.[10] The normally tolerant and diplomatic Dwight D. Eisenhower confided to his diary that the American war effort might be aided if someone would shoot King.[11] Merchant seamen had reason to agree. As shipping losses along the East Coast doubled in March compared to the previous two months, reaching one ship a day or an annual rate of 2 million tons a year, King continued to hold most of his aircraft and escort vessels in reserve. Ignoring American experience in World War I, and Britain's record in 1940 and 1941, he resisted convoys and limited countermeasures to arming some of the merchantmen. Placing the navy's priorities above the country's, King seems to have husbanded his resources in anticipation of some climactic Mahanian surface battle for command of the Atlantic Ocean. Awaiting that battle, which never came, he handed to the German submariners a hunting spree that they came to call their second "happy time," comparable to their early success against Britain in the summer and fall of 1940.

King's defenders claim that the admiral understood the importance of convoying but was trapped by the shortage of appropriate escort vessels and demands for higher-priority missions, such as escort of troop transports across the Atlantic.[12] These explanations not only ignore the navy's lack of foresight in procuring the vessels it would need for the war at hand, they also disregard steps that might have been taken to curb the carnage: arming the merchant vessels, blacking out coastal cities (whose lights allowed U-boats to spot their targets at night in clear silhouette), and providing air cover.[13] The navy held primary responsibility, but other arms of the Roosevelt administration might have intervened to good effect. In any event, King's grip on the levers of power, and his hold on Franklin Roosevelt's confidence, protected him from the consequences of his vile temperament and, in the case of *Paukenschlag*, the navy's inability or unwillingness to protect merchant shipping. Wherever responsibility lay, seamen blamed King, contributing to a hostility toward the navy that would continue through the war and hamper cooperation between the sea services.

The debacle along the East Coast in early 1942 proved to be an anomaly. The U.S. Navy finally rediscovered convoying and the shipping losses subsided. By May 1942 transatlantic passages were being escorted to a handoff in midocean, and coastal shipping was moving as well in protected packs. America's role in World War II was not to defend its shores against hostile action but to take the war to the enemy. That meant taking it around the world. And it meant taking matériel. Like its namesake, World War II was a war of industrial production. America was not just the arsenal of democracy, as President Roosevelt called it. The country was also the factory of democracy. Already the greatest industrial state in the world at the outbreak of war, the United States, alone among the major combatants, remained throughout the war virtually immune to enemy attack, its industrial infrastructure unimpaired. Also alone among the major combatants, it increased its gross domestic product steadily through the war, turning out arms and equipment at a rate unprecedented in world history.

Those arms and equipment, along with the men and women to use them, went to war by ship. Some went in support of U.S. operations in Africa, Europe, and the Pacific. In 1944, for example, 15 million tons of cargo went to the United Kingdom and continental Europe and 13 million tons to the Pacific, all in support of U.S. and Allied operations there. But 8 million tons went to the Mediterranean, 6 million to South America, 5 million to the Soviet Union, and 3 million to India and Ceylon. Between Pearl Harbor and the surrender of Japan, the United States shipped overseas 268,252,000 long tons of cargo and carried abroad 7,129,906 army personnel and 141,537 civilians. It also returned 4,060,883 soldiers (some former prisoners of war) and 169,626 civilians to the United States before November 30, 1945.[14]

The paths from the United States to these far-flung destinations led across the Atlantic and Pacific oceans. U.S. shipping experience on these two oceans in World War II could hardly have been more unlike. Most of the transatlantic shipping, especially across the North Atlantic, served two purposes. It supplied U.S. allies, Britain and the Soviet Union, with food, fuel, ammunition, and equipment, especially in the early years of the war, before the United States could make its military presence felt on the Continent. Second, it supported three great U.S. invasions: Africa in 1942, Italy in 1943, and France in 1944. Thereafter, it supplied the Allied armies that ground down Germany's military machine in the last year of the war in Europe. The challenge in the Atlantic was to deliver the people and matériel in the face of the most devastating commerce war at sea the world had ever seen, conducted by the Germans with mines, submarines, and land-based aircraft.

Shipping in the Pacific Ocean also supported allies and U.S. operations. American ships sailed to ports on the Indian Ocean and the Persian Gulf, delivering supplies both to the Soviet Union and to anti-Japanese resistance on the Asian mainland. Furthermore, they supported U.S. ground troops fighting their way from Australia north toward the Japanese homeland. And they supported the U.S. Navy and Marine Corps, as they fought their way west across the Pacific. Unlike the Atlantic, the greatest challenge to shipping in the Pacific was distance. The greatest risks were from aircraft and surface vessels, not submarines. They could operate over greater distances without convoys, but they were more likely to find themselves in direct support of combat operations. U.S. experience there was so different from that in the Atlantic that it requires a separate telling in the next chapter.

Priority went to the Atlantic. When the United States entered World War II in December 1941, German troops occupied the outskirts of Moscow and German submarines were tightening a noose around Britain that threatened to starve her into submission. Breaking of the German Enigma code had temporarily given the British the upper hand in the struggle with the submarine, but new boats coming online early in 1942 would have overwhelmed British antisubmarine warfare (ASW) capabilities had not many of those boats been diverted to the easy hunting along the East Coast of the United States.[15] Britain was to experience net losses in tonnage throughout 1942 and into 1943, mostly because the Germans were sinking their ships faster than they could build or acquire them.[16] As in World War I, the challenge for the United States on the Atlantic was to win this war of attrition.

Traditional Mahanian notions of command of the sea did not work against submarines and free-floating mines.[17] At least not at first. The ocean was too large. The U.S. ability to find and destroy submarines was inadequate, even when the United States gained the advantage of reading the secret radio traffic of the Germans. Britain and the United States enjoyed Mahanian command of the surface of the Atlantic, but not the depths. U.S. and British advances in ASW would be met by German advances in submarine technology and tactics. Airborne radar, improved sonar, and more effective depth charges, combined with tactics flowing from operations research, trumped the submarine's stealth and speed. But increased range in later German submarines extended the reach and duration of their patrols, and radio communications facilitated swarming wolfpack tactics to swamp the protection afforded by escorts. Not until the middle of 1943 did this seesaw balance tip in favor of the Allies.

Until the United States could defeat the submarine, it had to accept the grim calculus of attrition. It would not only have to build ships faster than the Germans could sink them, but also find competent crews to replace those lost at sea. Only about fifty-five thousand merchant seamen and officers were sailing in December 1941. Hundreds of thousands would be required to crew the ships that would carry the war to the enemy. By the spring of 1942, an average of forty-five ship sailings a month suffered delays from lack of crews. The War Shipping Administration (WSA) sought out and recruited experienced seamen engaged in other walks of life and set up training programs for new ones. The United States Merchant Marine Cadet Corps, authorized by the Merchant

Marine Act of 1936 and created in 1938, took up residence at the U.S. Merchant Marine Academy at Kings Point, New York, in January 1942. Other institutions around the country joined, finally producing, between 1938 and December 1945, 31,986 officers, 7,727 radio operators, 150,734 unlicensed seamen, 5,034 junior assistant purser-hospital corpsmen, 2,588 junior marine officers of the Army Transport Service, and 64,298 other graduates of specialized training programs who either learned anew or upgraded their maritime skills. In all, 262,474 graduates of these various programs qualified themselves to operate the country's merchant vessels.[18]

The maritime labor unions helped to supply the balance of the personnel needed. Jealous of the hard-won benefits achieved in the labor wars of the 1930s, and cognizant of the large profits being made by American shipping firms in the war years before Pearl Harbor, the unions nonetheless cooperated with government agencies to define working relationships during the war emergency. Mindful of World War I, when commercial ships were operated by the Shipping Board and more than a third were crewed by naval personnel, maritime labor sought to play a role in the war while also maintaining its autonomy and protecting its members from economic loss. The unions waived the right to strike for the duration, allowed enhanced authority to the shipmaster, and agreed to seek WSA approval for any changes in collective bargaining agreements. In return, they won significant increases in war risk compensation and insurance. By the end of 1943, war risk bonuses accounted for about half the pay of merchant seamen.[19] True to their word, the maritime unions did not strike once during the war; disputes were handled by negotiation, including such sensitive issues as sea risk insurance and compensation.[20]

Building the ships these men would sail around the world mobilized an entirely different set of resources. The enterprise began in 1938, when Congress appropriated funds for the commercial fleet envisioned by the Merchant Marine Act of 1936. Construction began in 1939. By the following year it was clear that more drastic steps were necessary. A second, emergency shipbuilding program then took shape to mass-produce a modified British design, officially designated EC2-S-C1 but more popularly known as the Liberty ship. After building sixty ships for the British, the United States went on to build thousands of Liberties and other commercial vessels in its emergency program. The War Shipping Administration classified these ships as shown in the table on the next page.

The U.S. Maritime Commission Wartime Shipbuilding Program, 1939–1945

Classification	Description	Numbers Produced
Major Types	Oceangoing merchant vessels	
Standard cargo	Long-range cargo and combination passenger/cargo types	530
Emergency cargo	All "Liberty" ships, except the ET1 tanker	2,648
Victory cargo	All cargo vessels of the VC2 or "Victory" design	414
Tankers	All liquid cargo vessels except navy oilers	620
Minor Types	Merchant vessels not designed for ocean service, such as coastal and lake vessels, tugs, barges, etc.	707
Military Types	Combatant and auxiliary vessels	682
Total		5,601

From Fischer, *Statistical Summary*, 17, 163.

The emergency ships were built at one hundred shipyards, most along the Atlantic and Pacific coasts and the Gulf of Mexico.[21] From the ten major private shipyards that existed in the United States in 1937, the numbers swelled to forty in 1941 and eighty by 1945.[22] Bethlehem Steel's Sparrows Point shipyard near Baltimore reprised its contribution of World War I, delivering ninety-eight ships of 1,345,000 deadweight tons in fifteen different categories. But Bethlehem also operated six other yards, from San Francisco to Quincy, Massachusetts. Its Fairfield Yard, across the Patapsco River from Sparrows Point, launched 508 vessels, mostly Liberty ships, totaling 5,233,000 deadweight tons.

The Maritime Commission sponsored expansion of existing yards and the building of new yards, sometimes as subsidiaries of established firms such as Bethlehem. The Newport News Shipbuilding and Drydock Company, one of the "Big Five" firms of the interwar period, at first resisted expansion of its capacity, having suffered painfully through the post–World War I downturn. By the end of 1940, however, swamped with orders from the navy, it sought a site for expansion. Unwilling to add capacity to the competition on the Chesapeake Bay, and anxious to block

Represented in this illustration are 1,080 of the ships built by Bethlehem Steel during World War II. A: 6 carriers, B: 1 battle-ship, C: 27 cruisers, D: 116 destroyers, E: 99 destroyer escorts, F: 23 naval transports, G: 6 minelayers, H: 94 Victory ships, I: 40 landing craft, J: 171 landing ships, K: 21 twin-screw tankers, L: 50 single-screw tankers, M: 8 troopships and 2 passenger liners, N: 10 transports, O: 384 Liberty ships, Q: 11 lighters, R: 3 fleet tugs, S: 4 harbor tugs, T: 4 trawlers.

Kaiser Corporation from establishing a yard in Wilmington, North Carolina, Newport News agreed late in 1940 to build a new yard at Wilmington. Thus was born the North Carolina Shipbuilding Company. Ground was broken for the yard on February 3, 1941. The first two keels were laid just 108 days later. The yard's first ship, a Liberty named for Civil War–era North Carolina governor Zebulon B. Vance, slid down the ways the day before Pearl Harbor. After fitting out, it was delivered on February 17, 1942, 271 days after keel laying and just over a year after groundbreaking. The yard's fortieth ship, the Liberty *Henry Bacon*, was delivered on November 24, 1942, just fifty-six days after its keel was laid. The United States was already building ships faster than the Germans could sink them, almost faster than crews could be found to man them.[23]

SS *Henry Bacon*, a typical World War II Liberty ship, is pictured here early in the war, before it received the full complement of deck guns that it carried on its final voyage. On February 23, 1945, returning from a run to Murmansk, the ship succumbed to attack by German airplanes in the Barents Sea after putting up what Admiral Samuel Eliot Morison called the finest "instance of merchant ship defense in the history of the North Russian convoys."

SS *Henry Bacon*'s career reveals what ships in general and Liberty ships in particular did in World War II. The *Bacon* slid into the Cape Fear River on November 11, 1942, less than a year after Pearl Harbor. Operated for the War Shipping Administration by the South Atlantic Steamship Line of Savannah, Georgia, the ship experienced the trials and triumphs that made Liberties the workhorses of World War II. On her first voyage, she carried "Russian aid" from Philadelphia to Karachi, India, via the Panama Canal. In Balboa, Canal Zone, on January 18, 1943, the flywheel on the starboard generator was "carried away," injuring the chief engineer and his assistant and delaying the ship for almost a month. In spite of a report that she was torpedoed and sunk en route, she arrived intact at Bushire (now Bushehr), Iran, on April 20, 1943. Through 1943 and into 1944, the *Henry Bacon* sailed to Fremantle, Australia; Durban and Cape Town, South Africa; Karachi, India; Plymouth, England; Molotovsk and Murmansk in the Soviet Union, in addition to her home port in Philadelphia. Along the way she experienced further mechanical and structural problems, ice damage, a "tradition of drunkenness in the galley," repeated cases of intoxication among crew and officers, and even the desertion of a steward who had been charged with "intoxication, inattention to duty, [and] fraud." But all the while she carried the sinews of war to Americans and their allies around the world.[24]

When the *Henry Bacon* went to Bethlehem's Fore River Shipyard in Quincy, Massachusetts, in October 1944 for her annual Coast Guard inspection, she was fitted with steel straps to strengthen the hull and prevent fractures that had been experienced on a number of Liberties, offering a clue to her next mission.[25] A still clearer indication of the ship's destination swung aboard the following month, as she took on cargo at Pier 60 in New York. The crates arrived marked "Destination Murmansk, USSR." Some of the crew debarked, unwilling to risk the most dangerous route east from America.

The hazards of the run to and from the Soviet port on the Barents Sea had been made notorious by the infamous convoy PQ-17. As this convoy came abreast of the northernmost reaches of Norway early in July 1942, it came under attack by German air, surface, and submarine forces. Concluding that its naval escort vessels were too far from base to provide adequate protection, the Allies recalled their British and American warships and told the merchant vessels to "scatter" as best they could. Twenty-five of the thirty-six merchant vessels in the convoy were lost.[26]

Throughout the war, German submarines combined with land-based aircraft in Norway to threaten even convoyed ships, and rough seas and cold water offered grim prospects for those who lost their vessels. Escorted convoys, improved air cover, and more effective ASW had lessened, though not eliminated, the dangers of crossing the North Atlantic. But the run up the coast of Norway remained perilous to war's end.

Captain Alfred Carini of the *Henry Bacon* replaced his departed crewmen and joined a convoy leaving New York on December 5. Carrying 7,500 tons of heating equipment, farm machinery, construction equipment, and locomotives, the *Bacon* crossed the Atlantic without incident, arriving at the famous convoy port of Gourock, Scotland, on December 19. When all his crew had been equipped with "one sheeplined coat, a fur hat, two suits of heavy underwear, two pairs of woolen stockings, and a pair of felt boots with rubber bottoms," Chief Engineer Donald Haviland wrote his wife, the *Bacon* joined convoy JW-63 on December 30 for the run to Murmansk. The ship fired at a German submarine that surfaced briefly in the middle of the convoy, but otherwise suffered no incident more serious than a galley fire before arriving in Kola Bay, off Murmansk, on January 8, 1945.[27]

The *Henry Bacon* unloaded her cargo and left Murmansk on February 17, 1945, one of twenty-eight ships in convoy RA-64. Assigned to an exposed "coffin corner" in the rear row of the convoy, the *Bacon* just missed being torpedoed by a waiting wolfpack outside the harbor. Though ships usually returned empty from Murmansk, the *Henry Bacon* carried a special cargo on this trip, nineteen refugees from Sørøya, a small island in the northernmost reaches of Norway recently subjected to German depredations in the face of Soviet forces moving west. A Beaufort Force 10 storm (on a scale of 12) struck the convoy on the night of its departure, creating waves of thirty to forty feet with winds of sixty knots. As the storm subsided on February 20 and the convoy reformed, German torpedo bombers struck. The *Bacon* escaped damage in the attack but began to suffer the effects of the previous days' storm. Her steering damaged, the ship struggled to keep up with the convoy. When a second and more powerful storm struck on February 22, the *Bacon*'s anemometer stuck at a reading of 112 mph in seas estimated at eighty to ninety feet. The air temperature of twenty-six degrees was just two below the water temperature, in which, the crew was told, they might expect to survive in rubber suits for less than half an hour. The *Bacon* lost contact with the convoy, experienced engine failure more than once, and reportedly rolled at one point to 57 degrees before managing to right herself. The remarkably resilient Liberty ship was actually making good progress toward rejoining the convoy in comparatively calm gale-force winds on February 23 when the Norway-based German airplanes struck again.

The twenty-three planes were He 111K and Ju 88 torpedo bombers. As they dove on the isolated and damaged ship, the Naval Armed Guard manned the 5-inch and 3-inch guns and the 20mm Oerlikon cannons. The crew claimed to have shot down five (some say seven) of the attacking planes while Captain Carini maneuvered the crippled vessel around dozens of torpedoes. Eventually, however, numbers overcame pluck, and a torpedo slammed into the port side at number five hold. The naval gunners shot down the plane that had torpedoed the ship, but the *Bacon* was fatally damaged. With one lifeboat wrecked in the storm and nineteen extra passengers aboard, Captain Carini and his chief mate elected to stay with the ship. Other crewmen gallantly relinquished their places in the lifeboats. Some remained aboard, hoping for rescue before she went down. Others jury-rigged crude rafts and took their chances in the cold sea. Two of the three lifeboats capsized. Still, all the refugees, twenty-six crewmen, and nineteen Armed Guards were rescued by British escort destroyers three hours after the sinking. Fifteen crewmen, including Captain Cariani, and seven Armed Guards were lost.[28] There is no doubt that some of those American seamen gave their lives to save the Norwegian passengers. The next of kin of the members of the Armed Guard received Purple Hearts and pensions. The next of kin of the merchant seamen received the Mariner's Medal and a lump-sum insurance settlement of $5,000. In his naval history of the Second World War, Samuel Eliot Morison said that there was "no finer instance of merchant ship defense in the history of the North Russian convoys."[29]

The world little noted nor long remembered the passing of the *Henry Bacon*. Like countless other tales of heroism and sacrifice in the merchant marine and the Army Transport Service, in which seamen faced dangers fully comparable to those experienced by the armed forces and displayed bravery and patriotism to compare with any of the services, the saga of the *Henry Bacon* had no ready audience, no public relations program, no institutional mechanism for recognizing heroic achievement. Merchant mariners died in World War II at rates comparable to the armed forces.[30] But at war's end, they found themselves overlooked. Despite promises and expectations to the contrary, they were denied veteran's status, cutting them off from the G.I. Bill and other postwar benefits. Not until 1988, after years of appeals, did the U.S. government conclude that members of the "American Merchant Marine in Oceangoing Service" during World War II were entitled to veteran's status after all.[31] This redemption came too late for the lost crew of the *Henry Bacon* and the thousands of other merchant mariners who had died in the war or in the ensuing thirty-three years of rejection and denial.

Of those merchant mariners who died during the war, more than 142 were merchant marine academy cadets and 68 were academy graduates. Built around the estate of Walter D. Chrysler in fifteen months, the academy had been designed to produce competent deck and engine officers to man the extraordinary growing World War II fleet of tankers and cargo ships supplying the Allied nations. As President Franklin D. Roosevelt wrote in a letter read on dedication day, September 20, 1943: "The Academy serves the merchant marine as West Point serves the Army and Annapolis serves the Navy." Wartime pressure cut the course to only eighteen months, with a maximum enrollment of 2,857 in 1944. By the war's end, 6,634 officers had graduated from the academy.

Finally, however, history seems to have caught up with the merchant seaman. As Williamson Murray and Allan R. Millett conclude in their study of World War II, "the courageous willingness of Allied merchant sailors to go down to the sea despite the appalling conditions of the North Atlantic and the terrifying losses on some convoy runs" won the battle of the Atlantic.[32] In doing so, they made possible Allied victory in Europe.

37

HENRY KAISER AND
THE WAR IN THE
PACIFIC, 1941–1945

AMERICAN SHIPPING PLAYED A VERY DIFFERENT ROLE IN THE
Pacific Ocean. This was an oceanic war. It targeted an island chain, Japan,
and it approached Japan by hopscotching islands, seizing some, bypassing
others. All the while it strangled the Japanese homeland with the same
kind of commerce war conducted by the Germans in the Atlantic. San
Francisco, the scene of intense labor strife in the 1930s, transformed itself
into a hub of both shipping and shipbuilding. The ships it sent to sea
traversed an ocean covering one-third of the earth's surface. Merchant
mariners did not win this war in the way they won the Battle of the
Atlantic. The navy won it, with significant help from army ground and air
forces. The role of shipping in the Pacific was to support American military operations and to supply American allies, principally the Soviet
Union and China.

The first American vessel lost to hostile action in the Pacific in World
War II, the American Pioneer Line freighter MS (motor ship) *City of
Rayville*, went down in the early evening hours of November 9, 1940, a
full year before Pearl Harbor.[1] Its sinking foreshadowed the great differences between the Pacific and Atlantic wars. It succumbed to a German
mine, not a submarine. It sank off Cape Ottway, Australia, not in the
major sea lanes of wartime commerce. And it carried ballast, not contraband, on its way to Melbourne to load wool and dried fruit. The third

engineer, Mark Burton Bryan, drowned abandoning ship, the first U.S. seaman to die in World War II. Merchant crews that fell victim to Japanese attacks fared less well than their mates in the Atlantic. Though the Japanese did not make American commerce a major target of their strategy, they treated their victims with far less humanity than their German or Italian allies. They were not above murdering captured merchant seamen in cold blood.[2]

The old Dollar Line stalwart SS *President Harrison* became the first U.S. commercial vessel to succumb to combat in the Pacific after Pearl Harbor when her captain intentionally grounded her at the mouth of the Yangtze River on December 8, 1941. The ironies of her fate were only beginning. Recently transferred to the newly created American President Lines, the *Harrison* was on a military mission to evacuate the U.S. legation guards at Beijing and Tientsin when the Japanese attacked Pearl Harbor. Coming under attack on the morning of December 8, the *Harrison*'s captain ran the ship hard aground on coral reefs, hoping to keep her out of enemy hands. Instead, the crew and passengers became POWs and the ship was salvaged and repaired by the Japanese. On September 12, 1944, the renamed vessel (*Kachidoki Maru*) was sunk by the USS *Pampanito* (SS-383) while carrying about nine hundred Allied POWs from Singapore to Tokyo. Almost half of the prisoners, many of them Americans, were lost.[3]

Most attacks on American shipping, like those on the *Rayville* and the *Harrison*, occurred in the western Pacific, though the West Coast of the United States did experience a brief submarine scare early in the war. SS *Emidio* was torpedoed by the Japanese submarine I-17 twenty-five miles west of Cape Mendocino, California, on December 20, 1941, less than two weeks after Pearl Harbor. The unarmed merchantman, en route from Seattle to San Pedro, California, in ballast, was first shelled by the submarine. When air support arrived from the mainland in response to a distress call, the boat submerged. But as the captain of the damaged but workable *Emidio* set about picking up the men he had ordered into lifeboats, the I-17 put a torpedo into the engine room. Three men died from the shelling, two more from the torpedo.[4] The attack might have foreshadowed a West Coast *Paukenschlag*.

But not much materialized. The real submarine story of the Pacific war was the American assault on Japanese commerce. Long-range American submarines penetrated the ring of island defenses that the Japanese had built out into the Pacific Ocean with their early conquests after Pearl Harbor. Moving directly to the critical supply line joining Japan to its raw materials in Southeast Asia, the submarines sank 63 percent of the Japanese commercial fleet by war's end, and 235 of its combat vessels.[5] One Japanese admiral concluded after the war that the American submarine assault had been sufficient to destroy the Greater East Asia Co-Prosperity Sphere all by itself.[6] American submariners were the great unrecognized heroes of the war in the Pacific.

The West Coast merchant marine supported the Pacific campaign from Pearl Harbor to Tokyo. It got its seamen by the same mechanisms feeding East Coast shipping. But its ships and ports were a different story. From 1940 through 1945, shipping from American ports on the North Atlantic increased by 240 percent, while that from South Atlantic and Gulf ports increased by 180 percent. But export freight from West Coast ports increased in the same period 1,487 percent, surpassing by almost 100 percent the volume of traffic out of the South Atlantic and Gulf ports and approaching that of the North Atlantic ports (see the table below).

The West Coast accounted for 7 percent of U.S. export freight shipping in 1940, 34.5 percent in 1945. World War II drove the creation of a Pacific merchant marine the way World War I had driven the Wilson/Hurley vision of an American bid for the North Atlantic market. This achievement taxed the entire U.S. transportation infrastructure, from inland and coastal shipping to railroads and rubber-wheeled vehicles (cars, trucks, buses). The nexus of overseas shipping, the ports, required a transformation of existing infrastructure and the creation of entirely new facilities where none had existed before.

CARLOAD VOLUME OF EXPORT FREIGHT

Area	1940	1941	1942	1943	1944	1945
North Atlantic	373,973	458,909	531,874	798,002	1,071,891	898,879
South Atlantic and Gulf	182,091	164,305	167,826	200,952	231,219	328,105
Pacific	43,504	57,525	216,235	451,613	602,059	647,021
Total U.S.	599,658	680,739	915,935	1,450,567	1,905,169	1,874,005

Rose, *American Wartime Transportation* (New York: Crowell, 1953), 75; based on Office of Defense Transportation, "A Review of Transportation during World War II" (unpublished). Coal is not included in the figures.

Shipbuilding on the West Coast experienced similarly explosive growth. In 1941 the West Coast was producing less than a third of the ships launched in the United States, hardly more than half as many as the East Coast. The following year, it was producing more than any other region. The year after that it built more than half the national total. By war's end, the West Coast had built 47 percent of the nation's new tonnage, more than that constructed in Wilmington and the other East Coast shipyards. (See the table below.)

Much of the credit for this transformation of West Coast shipbuilding belongs to Henry J. Kaiser. An ebullient, self-made tycoon cut in the mold of Charles Schwab, Kaiser had made several fortunes before becoming the "Paul Bunyan" of shipbuilding in World War II.[7] From his first construction company in 1913, he moved into road building and cement manufacture. He paired with Warren Bechtel to form the nucleus of a corporate conglomerate, Six Companies, to bid on the contract for Hoover Dam in 1931. They won the contract by coming in just under $50 million, and then topped their own achievement by landing as well the $400 million contract for Grand Coulee Dam. They built Bonneville and Shasta dams and the San Francisco–Oakland Bay Bridge. They built Boulder City, Nevada, a planned community to house the workers on the Hoover Dam. In 1939 Kaiser founded Permanente, the world's largest cement plant.[8] He was credited with saying, "When your work speaks for itself, don't interrupt."

Kaiser entered the maritime world by building not ships but shipyards. Six Companies worked for several shipbuilding firms before striking out on its own. The first contracts came from the Maritime Commission's 1937 building program, followed by British orders in 1940, and the Lib-

DISPLACEMENT TONNAGE OF SHIPS PRODUCED, BY REGION (THOUSANDS)

Area	1941	1942	1943	1944	1945	Total
East Coast	423	1,164	2,342	2,374	1,242	7,545
West Coast	250	1,673	3,648	3,121	1,614	10,306
Gulf	91	512	1,056	1,303	627	3,589
Great Lakes	18	121	124	122	78	463
Total	782	3,470	7,170	6,920	3,561	21,903

Gerald Fischer, *A Statistical Summary of Shipbuilding under the U.S. Maritime Commission during World War II* (Washington, DC: U.S. Maritime Commission, 1949), 48.

erty ship program, announced in January 1941. The famous Richmond Shipyard No. 1 arose first, in a small, blue-collar community on the eastern shore of San Francisco Bay. In its wake arose yards in Portland, Oregon; Vancouver, Washington; and three more yards (Nos. 2, 3, and 4) in Richmond. In all of the yards, Kaiser applied techniques of mass production to the building of ships. He divided ships into prefabricated components and distributed their manufacture around the American West. The massive components were gathered at the shipyards, hoisted by powerful cranes, and welded together in something like an assembly line. In lieu of the heavy equipment normally used to cut steel plate, he employed oxyacetylene torches. Welding replaced the more labor-intensive riveting. These were emergency ships with very limited life expectancies; quantity mattered more than quality. For publicity's sake, Richmond No. 2 actually built one Liberty ship from scratch in four days, fifteen hours, and twenty-six minutes. Kaiser was criticized for this grandstanding, but his yards nonetheless produced the Liberties faster than any other, about twice as fast as the industry average of two months.[9]

By the end of the war, Kaiser yards had produced 1,490 ships, 747 in the four Richmond yards and 743 in the Portland/Vancouver complex, accounting for 27 percent of total U.S. production. The output included thirteen different types of vessels, among them 821 Liberties, 219 Victories, and 107 warships. The total came to 15 million deadweight tons of shipping, at a price of just over $4 billion. A novice to the industry, Kaiser outpaced the East Coast giants that had dominated American shipbuilding through the twentieth century. For example, Bethlehem Steel's far-flung shipbuilding enterprises, pioneered by Charles Schwab in World War I, produced 614 commercial vessels of 6,900,000 deadweight tons in the U.S. Maritime Commission program, compared with 1,385 vessels of 15,005,000 deadweight tons for the Kaiser yards.[10] Reversing Schwab's experience, Kaiser found himself drawn into the steel industry by shipbuilding, creating his own steel mill in Fontana, California, to support his shipyards. Like Schwab, he found that his phenomenal wartime success brought postwar accusations of profiteering, painful but ultimately sterile.

Kaiser brought on some of his own problems. Success and fame bred a public relations program that portrayed him larger than life. A naturally shy man, he honed a public persona of ebullient optimism and self-confidence, a can-do entrepreneur cutting through red tape and forcing innovation on staid and conservative industries. Many business foes and

The relatively high percentages of women, African Americans, and older men in this work crew at the Kaiser Richmond Shipyard No. 4 reflect the labor shortages that afflicted the domestic U.S. economy during World War II. They also attest to the enlightened labor policies of Henry Kaiser in his West Coast shipyards, a significant factor in the production records established by his firm during the war.

even some of his business partners believed that he received personal credit for the achievements of others and that his mistakes were masked in a glare of publicity.

These criticisms have some merit, but they barely tarnish a remarkable and substantial record. His companies built more ships than any other. He maintained cordial relations with labor, employing blacks and women in exceptional percentages. He hired not only Rosie the Riveter but also Wendy the Welder. He provided day care facilities at his plants and worked to relieve the appalling housing shortages bred by wartime expansion. From the Hoover Dam project he transferred a health care program that would become in time the Kaiser Permanente Health Maintenance Organization, a pioneering program that went on to be the largest in the world. For all these reasons he escaped most of the labor problems that plagued East Coast and other shipyards. The North Carolina Shipbuilding Company, for example, experienced years of strife over attempts to unionize the yard, not ending until a settlement after the war.[11] Kaiser's labor practices, in contrast, were so benevolent as to allow him to resist unionization without threat or intimidation.[12] And he experienced little of the racial strife that plagued the Wilmington shipyard.

Though Kaiser made his maritime reputation building Liberty Ships, his yards, like most of the others, built a wide range of vessels for the Maritime Commission and partially switched to Victory ships in 1944. The Maritime Commission had developed its own standardized ships in 1937, and long resented the Liberty design, foisted upon them when the British brought their ship plans to the United States in 1940.[13] But the Liberty was cheap and quick to build, and the commission could not overcome the national attachment to it until late in 1943. Admiral Land advocated the Victory both because of its greater speed and capacity for the war effort but also because it would better serve the nation's merchant marine when the war was over. See the table below for a comparison of both ships.

The military services preferred the standard cargo types developed by the Maritime Commission before the war. Both the Naval Transportation Service and the Army Transport Service sailed C2s, C3s, and other Maritime Commission designs. These ships cost more to build and took longer, but they had compensating advantages in speed, carrying capacity, and strength. The politics that relegated Liberties and Victories to the merchant marine and higher-quality ships to the armed services also spilled into the realm of ship operations. The Army Transport Service, created in 1898 after the debacle of getting troops and their supplies to Cuba on short notice, controlled the nation's ports in wartime. On the theory that service responsibilities met at the shoreline, it was intended to turn its ships over to the navy for operation in an emergency, but it refused in World War II. Instead, both services supported their operations in the Pacific, carrying troops and supplies west and generally returning empty. In contrast, War Shipping Administration vessels took their loads west and returned with raw materials.[14]

LIBERTY/VICTORY COMPARISON

Type	Displacement (tons)	Length (feet)	Capacity (deadweight tons)	Propulsion	Speed (knots)
Liberty	3,479	442	10,419	Reciprocating	11
Victory	4,526	453	10,700	Turbine	17

While oceanic shipping swelled to meet the demand of carrying American matériel to the war, domestic shipping actually declined during World War II, from 331 billion ton-miles in 1939 to 260 billion in 1945. It reached its lowest point, less than 200 billion ton-miles, in 1943. More alarming still, the percent of total intercity freight traffic carried by water shrank from 41 percent in 1939 to 22 percent in 1945.[15] Economically speaking, domestic shipping retained its prewar advantage over land transport. But in the war emergency, when time was crucial, speed trumped cost. Intercoastal and coastwise traffic suffered most of all, but even the Mississippi River experienced losses in downstream traffic. Only the Great Lakes realized substantial increases during the war, thanks in large measure to vastly increased demand for bulk commodities such as iron, coal, grain, and limestone. It remained to be seen if these wartime dislocations in domestic shipping would prove transient.

38

EDWARD STETTINIUS
AND FLAGS OF
CONVENIENCE

THE UNITED STATES EMERGED FROM WORLD WAR II ATOP THE shipping world. In 1922, as the World War I shipbuilding program neared completion, it had controlled roughly 22 percent of the world's commercial tonnage, second only to Great Britain.[1] In 1939 it operated 14 percent of the world's ships and 15 percent of its tonnage, about half of Great Britain's share. In 1946 American dominance was transcendent. Having built 5,800 ships during the war at a cost of about $15 billion, the nation operated almost two-thirds of the world's shipping. It had 5,529 of the 10,175 total vessels at sea (54 percent), and 57 million of the world total of 92 million deadweight tonnage (62 percent). Britain, the next largest shipping power, controlled about one-third as much. Furthermore, the United States had the capacity to build 25 million new tons a year working three-shift days, and 15 million tons working regular shifts. By the estimate of the U.S. Maritime Commission, the country would need only 11 million tons to achieve the long-standing goal of carrying half of the commerce moving to and from the United States by ship. After scrapping over-age ships in the fleet, assigning some to military reserve, and selling abroad to restore the world market, the country was likely to be left with 30 million tons of excess shipping.[2] As was true after World War I, the United States faced an embarrassment of riches. Could it do better this time?

The relief and euphoria that settled over the nation following the surrender of Japan in August 1945 was muted by the tremendous dislocation of moving from war to peace. Millions of servicemen and servicewomen returned from overseas, while many stayed on for occupation duty. Rosie the Riveter and Wendy the Welder returned to more traditional walks of life. The vast industrial infrastructure built up to support the war effort had to be dismantled, scrapped, or converted to civilian purposes. Deferred maintenance and consumer spending absorbed some of the surplus and engaged the energies of a newly civilianized workforce. The United States boasted the world's largest economy, but its continued success would depend on the recovery of those parts of the world most devastated by the war. The resumption of international commerce loomed large in economic plans.

A Postwar Planning Committee within the U.S. Maritime Commission recommended in 1946 that the United States continue the "bald subsidies" established by the 1936 Merchant Marine Act, supporting both construction and operation. When combined with tax exemptions allowed to the maritime industry, these subsidies had accounted for $310 million between 1937 and 1945, or about $34 million a year. The committee estimated that a continuing subsidy of about $50 million a year could sustain the American merchant marine at the level anticipated by the 1936 act. The committee members interpreted this level as carrying half the passengers and cargo entering and leaving the country by ship. This model required that U.S. ships would "have to go into tramping," since "a third of the dry cargo entering and leaving American ports in 1938 [had been] carried by tramps."[3] Except for a brief period in the early 1920s, American ships had eschewed tramping for the previous seventy-five years. Yet for the security and economic prosperity of the nation, the committee argued, it was essential to maintain a fleet of these proportions.

It was not clear, however, that the model anticipated by the 1936 act still applied in the wake of World War II, for either domestic or international shipping. Reliance on tire-borne land transportation had blossomed during the war, compounding the gains made by the railroads since the late nineteenth century. The development of the interstate highway system, beginning in the 1950s, would only exacerbate this impact, affecting both passengers and cargo. The effect on the Great Lakes was already manifest. Though bulk shipping on the lakes remained healthy, the package-freight trade had "been pretty much wiped out by the war." Cargo handling in general was consuming 20 percent of all marine shipping costs, as much as 40 percent in the coastwise trade and 50 percent on the Great Lakes, a reflection of the wage concessions won by labor in the 1930s. This problem threatened to wipe out the increases in efficiency realized by faster oceangoing ships like the Victories, but its greatest impact appeared to be on domestic shipping, long the mainstay of the American merchant marine.[4]

Commercial airline service posed another threat to shipping. While the committee members anticipated little impact on cargo revenues, they did expect that airplanes would cut into passenger and mail revenues. It was partially for this reason that they recommended against the introduction of large passenger vessels of the kind run by European states in the first half of the twentieth century. When SS *United States* entered service in 1952, it was already obsolescent.

SS *United States*, still holder of the "Blue Riband" for the fastest crossing of the Atlantic ocean by a ship, in either direction. As a passenger liner, the *United States* was obsolescent when launched in 1952. But at 962 feet in length, she was a harbinger of the megaships that would come to dominate the second half of the twentieth century.

When the *United States* won the Blue Riband in July for crossing the Atlantic at an average speed of 35.59 knots, a record not likely to be broken by a conventional commercial vessel, it lent prestige to the American maritime industry and emergency troop-carrying capacity to the American government. It did not, however, reverse the trend in intercontinental passenger traffic.[5] Built and operated on government subsidies, the *United States* never found an economic model to make it competitive with airliners. When the Boeing 707 jetliner entered service in 1958, the *United States* and other superliners became instant dinosaurs.

The subsidies guaranteed by the 1936 act, and sustained in spite of the health of the maritime industry in 1946, contributed significantly to the economic disadvantage of the American merchant marine. The subsidies weakened the incentives of the industry to control wages and costs generally. The shipping industry enjoyed relative freedom from labor disputes during the war, thanks in large measure to the war risk bonuses paid to crews. While base pay was held in check, war risk bonuses doubled the gross pay earned by merchant seamen. Following the surrender of Germany, those bonuses were reduced. Expecting that they would soon be eliminated altogether, the maritime unions pressed at once for significant increases in base pay.[6]

Aware that American shipping and shipbuilding already competed at a disadvantage because of high salaries, maritime management at first resisted. In this instance and others, however, maritime subsidies worked against control of rising wages. Both shipbuilders and ship operators soon succumbed to the demands of labor, in part because the cost of higher-wage contracts would be borne by the government. The subsidy system paid for the differential between American and foreign costs, and it was that differential that would rise with increased wages. Furthermore, in the decade immediately after World War II, the United States enjoyed an exceptional percentage of the world's shipping assets and an increase in demand for shipping services, first to distribute postwar recovery aid and then to support the war in Korea. In such circumstances, many shipbuilders and ship operators accepted the short-term advantages of generous wage settlements and uninterrupted operations at the cost of exorbitant long-term labor costs. For their part, the maritime unions put aside their prewar toleration of communist infiltrators to take advantage of the generous terms being made available. Though corruption continued to shadow some maritime labor venues, especially New

York dockworkers, the chance to solidify in peacetime the gains made in the 1930s and through the war proved irresistible.[7]

None of these trends, however, had more impact on the American merchant marine than the flight from the flag. And no one contributed more to that flight than Edward R. Stettinius, Franklin Roosevelt's last secretary of state. Stettinius's role underscores the complexity of maritime commerce and its vulnerability to political influence.

Stettinius was born to privilege in 1900. His father was a partner of J.P. Morgan and Co. and had served as an assistant secretary of war in World War I. Nevertheless, the younger Stettinius, a college dropout who once considered entering the ministry, apparently rose on his own account. He was strikingly handsome, affable, charismatic, energetic, earnest, and genuinely altruistic. He turned an entry-level job at General Motors into a vice presidency in eight years. In 1934 he joined U.S. Steel, where he rose to chairman of the board in four years, a career trajectory that brings to mind Charles Schwab in the days of Stettinius père. Service on several New Deal advisory boards brought a personal invitation from Franklin Roosevelt to become commissioner for industrial materials in 1940. Stettinius immediately resigned from U.S. Steel and cut his other business ties. He took over the Lend-Lease program in 1940, gaining his first introduction to maritime issues. In all of these positions he impressed colleagues and associates with his organizational ability, interpersonal skills, and vigor. Thus, when Undersecretary of State Sumner Wells experienced a climactic falling-out with his boss, Roosevelt asked Stettinius to replace him. The younger man worked well with Secretary of State Cordell Hull and served him loyally until after the election of 1944, when the ailing Roosevelt confidant submitted his resignation. Stettinius's selection to succeed him was greeted favorably enough, though some wondered if he had the experience and gravitas for the assignment. But since Roosevelt acted largely as his own secretary of state, there was little opposition.[8] When Harry Truman acceded to the presidency, he accepted Stettinius's resignation, but appointed him to be the first American representative to the United Nations, a post he held for just six months before returning to private life.

Stettinius's lack of diplomatic experience and understanding were manifest at the Yalta conference of February 1945, where, many critics claimed, the failing Franklin Roosevelt was taken advantage of by Joseph Stalin. On his way home from that conference, Stettinius stopped in

Liberia to dedicate a new U.S.-built port there. Worried that Germany might try to use the West African country as a launching pad for intervention in Latin America, the United States had invested in it during World War II. From that visit Stettinius hatched the idea of developing Liberia after the war while at the same time making money. On leaving government the following year, he formed Stettinius Associates–Liberia Company with the cooperation of the Liberian president W. V. S. Tubman. Stettinius himself put up 20 percent of the initial $1 million capitalization. Profits would be distributed to Stettinius Associates (65 percent), the Liberian government (25 percent), and the nonprofit Liberia Foundation.[9]

Among the first projects undertaken was establishment of Liberian ship registry. Dissatisfaction with Panamanian registry and the consular fees and other forms of corruption associated with it were growing in the American shipping industry. Esso and other major oil companies operating their own tanker fleets expressed interest in the Liberian plan and reviewed the legislation drafted by Stettinius's colleagues for the Liberian government. Suggesting that he had State Department approval, Stettinius presented the legislation to Liberia, which passed it pretty much as drafted.[10] Esso became a partner of the company set up to administer the registry, allowing it to recover in profits the fees it would pay to register its ships there. To get U.S. government approval for his scheme, Stettinius had to do some backtracking. He worked with State Department reviewers to modify the plan and courted members of the national security establishment to convince them that the connection with Liberia would help build up African resistance to communist expansion. He hosted one meeting that brought together the secretaries of the army and the air force, an undersecretary of the navy, an assistant secretary of state, and the deputy director of the CIA, demonstrating the power of the connections bred by his years in Washington.

The capitalization ran out before revenue started to flow, sending Stettinius out to raise more money. His brother-in-law, Juan Trippe, the founder and president of Pan American World Airways, lent his stature and funds to the enterprise, but Stettinius intentionally kept the number of investors below seventy to avoid having to register with the Securities and Exchange Commission as a publicly owned corporation. Stettinius Associates developed an interlocking directorate with American Overseas Tanker Corporation (AOTC), which registered its ships in Liberia.[11] The first two ships were registered in 1948, the year before Stettinius's premature death. Liberian registry surpassed Panama's in tonnage in 1955 and number of ships registered in 1956.

By lending its belated approval to the Stettinius scheme, the U.S. government undermined the plans of the U.S. Maritime Commission. It may be argued that the Roosevelt administration had adhered to the letter but not the spirit of the Neutrality Act when it allowed registration of sixty-three American vessels in Panama between September 1939 and June 1941.[12] Roosevelt was prepared to sail very close to the legal wind to find ways to supply the British in their life-and-death struggle against the German submarines. But the creation of a Panamanian registry in the 1920s and the Liberian registry in the 1940s were primarily business expedients designed to resolve the ongoing dilemma of the American merchant marine. High labor costs and exceptional regulation made American-registered ships more expensive to operate than ships of other nations. Even the operational subsidies provided by the Merchant Marine Act of 1936 could not overcome all the relative disadvantages. Instead of resolving those problems, foreign registry simply allowed American shipping firms to escape them. Arguments were made that the registry mattered little because ownership by American firms would still ensure the availability of these ships to the United States in the event of national emergency. Ships in this category came to be called the "Effective United States Control Fleet" (EUSC). But no one could be sure if these ships could really be pressed into government service in time of national need.

When the next emergency came, in June 1950, with the North Korean invasion of South Korea, the question proved moot. America's shipping needs for the Korean War were readily met with existing resources and purchase on the international market. At no time during the war were American military operations jeopardized by a shortage of commercial shipping. That experience cast a still longer shadow over the nineteenth-century argument that a national merchant marine was essential to national security. It also framed the ongoing debate over the American merchant marine in the second half of the twentieth century.

PART V

MEGASHIP

The Rise of the Invisible,
Automated Bulk Carrier,
1956–2000

39

DANIEL K. LUDWIG
AND THE
GIANT SHIPS

THE EGYPTIAN PRESIDENT GAMAL ABDEL NASSER NATIONALIZED the Suez Canal on July 26, 1956, opening the age of the giant tanker. The "Suez Crisis" that flowed from Nasser's audacious gambit cast Egypt to the center of many of the most vexing conflicts of the second half of the twentieth century. The closing of the canal set off a tectonic shift in the cold war, altering the strategic balance between East and West. Secondarily, it inflamed the Arab-Israeli struggle for power and survival in the Middle East. It attacked the most important commodity coming out of the Middle East, oil, just when that oil-rich region was beginning its rise to preeminence in the world market. And by forcing oil tankers to sail around the Cape of Good Hope, it raised fuel costs in the West and helped to spawn the tanker wars, a struggle to control the worldwide distribution of oil.

The Suez Crisis exposed the vulnerability in the world's oil supply. In 1950, as the U.S. Marshall Plan took hold of the reconstruction of Europe, coal still accounted for most of the world's energy; oil provided only 25 percent. By 1965, however, oil was up to 37 percent, and by 1968, it had displaced coal as the main energy source for Europe. At the same time, the Middle East was becoming the world's dominant source of oil. Between 1948 and 1972, while world oil production grew from 8.7 million to 42 million barrels per day, an increase of 483 percent, Middle

Eastern production swelled from 1.1 million to 18.2 million barrels per day, 1,655 percent! In the same period, America's share of world production shrank from 64 percent to 22 percent.[1] By 1955, two-thirds of the traffic through the Suez Canal carried oil, and two-thirds of Europe's oil came by that route. France and Britain intervened in 1956 because they saw their vital national interests at stake.

But the Suez Crisis was just the first, and by no means the most important, of a series of international crises that emanated from the Middle East and threatened the world's growing dependence on cheap, reliable delivery of that region's oil. The formation of the Oil Producing and Exporting Countries (OPEC) in 1960 promised that none of the member states need stand alone against the major powers in future struggles. When war between the Arabs and Israelis came again in 1967, the Suez Canal closed once more. Worse still was the Yom Kippur War of 1973, which precipitated an Arab oil embargo against the United States and the Netherlands. By 1979 the Middle East accounted for almost three-fifths of world oil exports; when the American-Iranian crisis in that year brought on another oil embargo, quadrupling oil prices internationally, the United States was importing 35 percent of its oil from the Middle East.

The growing world demand for oil, the shifting center of supply from the United States to the Middle East, and the vulnerability of that region to military and political upheaval all placed a premium on shipping services. The diversion of shipping from the Suez Canal to the ocean route around Africa, adding forty-five hundred miles to the journey to Europe, suggested to some shipping firms that large, fast ships could meet demand better than traditional tankers of the kind that plied the Suez Canal. It is possible that tankers of any size would have profited in this environment, but competition drove the market to supertankers.

Three men led the shift to big ships. Two brothers-in-law, the Greek shipowners Aristotle Onassis and Stavros Niarchos, had prospered in the tanker business by buying up low-priced surplus U.S. T2 tankers after World War II, sailing them under flags of convenience, and serving Europe's and Japan's growing demand for oil. In the late 1940s an American entrepreneur, Daniel K. Ludwig, decided to challenge their dominance in the transport of Middle Eastern oil. He set off a three-way struggle for preeminence in the field, a contest that became a race for gigantism.

Ludwig was one of the most remarkable entrepreneurs in the history of American shipping. Descended from a family of ship captains and shipbuilders, he launched his own business in 1916 at the age of nineteen, running molasses from New York City north to Canada to be distilled into liquor. After an apparent brush with the law early in the Prohibition era, he turned to the tanker business. He formed the American Tanker Corporation in 1924, buying surplus World War I ships from the Shipping Board and later the Maritime Commission. Through clever and sometimes shady practices, he managed to use other people's money to buy, refit, and resell ships while building up his own fleet of tankers. Perhaps his greatest innovation in shipping was a technique called a "two-name paper." He first negotiated with an oil company to move petroleum, and then used the charter contract, not the ship, as his collateral to buy or build the necessary vessels.[2] In spite of the Depression, he made enough money to open his own Welding Shipyard near Norfolk, Virginia, in 1938. There he built T2 and T3 tankers for the government and emerged from World War II as the fifth largest independent tanker operator in the United States.

That was when he targeted the lucrative market hauling Middle Eastern oil. He bought surplus wartime vessels, as he had after World War I, and then convinced the Maritime Commission to let him register them in Panama. This allowed him to operate the ships with the same economies enjoyed by Onassis and Niarchos. He often outdid the two Greek operators in running his ships with even greater stinginess and economy. The vessels of all three magnates were models of business efficiency but nightmarish working environments. All three owners appreciated economies of scale.

Whichever of them first saw the relative efficiencies of larger tankers, Ludwig was the first to plunge into gigantism. Trapped by the limited space and infrastructure available in his Norfolk shipyard, he shut it down in 1951 and leased the Imperial Navy Shipyard in Kure, Japan. Here the Japanese had built the world's largest battleships in World War II, and here Ludwig intended to build the world's largest tankers. A pioneer in the introduction of welded vessels in World War II, he introduced these and other innovative designs and techniques to the production of a new generation of tankers. Onassis and Niarchos followed him to the shipyards of Japan. The T3s that all of them had bought after World War II had a capacity of 11,335 gross tons, equal to about 146,000 barrels of oil, roughly 20,000 tons.[3] Ludwig built 30,000-deadweight-ton tankers at Sewalls Point. All three shipowners were running vessels of 40,000 to 50,000 tons in 1955 when Ludwig ordered the *Universe Leader* from his Kure shipyard, at 85,515 tons. The race was on. The following year, after the Suez Crisis, Onassis ordered a 100,000-tonner. Niarchos followed with a 106,000-tonner, and Ludwig responded by ordering four 100,000-tonners.

The race did not stop for the rest of the twentieth century. Vessels of 200,000 tons, called Very Large Crude Carriers (VLCCs) first appeared in 1966. Ultra Large Crude Carriers (ULCCs) followed by 1969. While Ludwig's *Universe Leader* of 1956 displaced 85,515 gross deadweight tons and measured 855 feet in length, ULCCs carry more than 300,000 tons, more than 7 million barrels. These ships could displace 20,000 to 40,000 tons empty and measure almost a quarter of a mile in length. *Universe Leader* drew too much water to traverse the Suez Canal, and it was far too wide for the Panama Canal. By the end of the twentieth century, the largest of the vessels had difficulty navigating the Straits of Malacca on their way to East Asia.

The shipping magnate Daniel Ludwig moved his tanker shipbuilding operation to Japan's Kure shipyard to build the 85,515-deadweight-ton *Universe Leader*, pictured here, in 1956. This 855-foot vessel accelerated the race to gigantism in the tanker trade and contributed as well to the decline of shipbuilding in the United States.

Economies of scale drove this race to gigantism. Doubling the length, beam, and draft of a ship increases its carrying capacity eight times. Even without the automation that swept the shipping industry in the second half of the twentieth century, bigger ships meant smaller crews, and hence smaller costs, per ton of cargo carried. Additionally, power-plant weight and fuel consumption increase at a lesser rate than the increase in cargo. A 20,000-tonner might require a 10,000-horsepower engine to run at sixteen knots; a 100,000-tonner requires only a 21,000-horsepower engine to achieve the same speed.[4] Even the costs of construction and materials are proportionally less for large ships than for small. A kind of technological imperative took hold of the tanker industry in the 1950s and never let go. Bigger seemed better. By 1973 there were 366 supertankers—VLCCs and ULCCs—with another 525 under construction or on order. The orders represented 50 percent of the existing fleet in service.[5]

That was when the bottom fell out of the market for the first time. The Yom Kippur War of 1973 reignited the Arab-Israeli conflict and prompted the Arabs to play the oil card. In September, the Arab oil ministers announced a rolling embargo; in October they cut production by 5 percent.[6] Additional 5 percent cuts were to follow each month until the West's pro-Israeli policies changed. When this action failed to diminish U.S. support for Israel, the Arab oil-producing states imposed on the United States and several other countries a complete embargo. The ban lasted until the United States helped to broker a settlement of the Yom Kippur War in March of 1974. For the third time in less than two decades, the Arab-Israeli conflict had interrupted the flow of Middle Eastern oil to the developed world.

The turmoil that opened the door for supertankers also placed them at risk. The problem was capital investment. The supertankers were so expensive to build that they had to be kept sailing nearly continuously to service their debts. The enthusiasm for the vessels in the 1960s and 1970s had created an excess of carrying capacity that kept many shipping firms near the edge of bankruptcy, competing for customers with offers that maintained the thinnest of profit margins. The Yom Kippur War disrupted this fragile market as neither the Suez Crisis nor the 1967 Arab-Israeli War had done. While those conflicts disrupted the transportation of oil, they actually required more, not less, shipping, as reserves were moved about or shipped greater distances to meet demand. But the Arab oil embargo of 1973 and 1974 cut the supply of oil in play, calling for less, not more, transportation. Total world production of oil actually rose by almost 8 percent in 1973, before falling marginally (less than 1 percent) in 1974.[7]

But worse disruptions followed. The 1973 embargo helped to precipitate two other dislocations that had an even longer-term impact on the tanker market. First, the United States and other countries initiated conservation measures that curtailed the rapid growth in demand for oil that had characterized the post–World War II era. World production fell again in 1975 and resumed growth in 1976 at a pace considerably slower than that of the previous fifteen years. Many of the tankers produced in the 1960s and early 1970s had been ordered in anticipation of a rapidly growing market. Furthermore, the United States and other industrialized states took steps to insulate themselves from further shocks. They built up national reserves, explored alternative energy sources, accelerated the search for new oil reserves in such places as Alaska and the North Sea, and expanded pipeline capacity to speed and secure the flow of oil. Finally, the oil embargo of 1973, and the increase in oil prices that accompanied it, contributed to the worldwide recession of the 1970s, slowing economic growth and further dampening the demand for oil.

Worse was to come. In December 1978 Iran, the second largest oil exporter in the world, suspended all shipment of oil. The curtailment was part of a sequence of political events that would witness the end of the pro-American Pahlavi shahdom in Iran, the accession of a radical Islamist government under the Ayatollah Khomeini, war with Iraq, and a naval extension of that conflict into the Persian Gulf—the so-called tanker wars. The warring states attacked each other by attacking the ships carrying their oil to market. While the world supply of oil fell only 4 or 5 percent before Iran resumed exports in the fall of 1979, the price rose from $13 to $34 a barrel, an increase of 150 percent. This "Second Oil Shock," as Daniel Yergin called it, once more sent the world into a period of extreme economic dislocation. World oil consumption fell after 1979. Not until 1989 did it recover to 1979 levels, and by 2000 it had increased only 18 percent over 1979.[8] In the two intervening decades, the world economy had grown by 82 percent.[9]

Not least among the victims were the shipping companies that transported the world's oil. As with any economic dislocation, there was money to be made, especially for those nimble and clever enough to take advantage of spot markets and critical demands. But the volatility of the international oil market nonetheless took its toll. The tanker industry entered a period of contraction and consolidation. The oversupply of ships shrank through attrition and bankruptcy. Major oil companies reduced their proprietary fleets to avoid the losses sustained when shipments dropped off, allowing the independents to take the risks of volatility. Companies such as Overseas Shipholding Group (OSG) found that they could make money running tankers for charter by playing the market conservatively and avoiding the overexpansion of the golden age of oil shipping, when magnates such as Ludwig, Onassis, and Niarchos had become billionaires riding a wave of oil.[10]

By the time the *Exxon Valdez* grounded in Prince William Sound on March 24, 1989, the transformation of the oil shipping industry was all but complete. Spilling 11 million gallons of Alaska crude into Prince William Sound, the *Exxon Valdez* became the latest and worst in a series of tanker accidents that prompted the United States to pass the Oil Pollution Act of 1990. This legislation required double-hulled tankers and more attention to safety and training, setting a standard for worldwide reform of the industry.

All along, Ludwig had insulated himself against overexposure in any single market by diversifying his business interests in general and his shipping interests in particular. Even before World War II, he had begun a general move toward the development of large bulk carriers. These giant ships, in the tradition of the *J. Pierpont Morgan* and other megaships on the Great Lakes, carried coal, ore, stone, grain, and other unpackaged solids. Ludwig's gigantic tankers were really just part of that larger business plan. He formed National Bulk Carriers in 1936 and eventually turned it into a holding company for his far-flung maritime ventures and other businesses. Ever vigilant for efficiencies in ship design and operation, he pioneered OBOs, Oil/Bulk/Ore carriers that could accommodate multiple bulk cargoes, even grains. He initially sought a vessel that could make a complete round trip full. A tanker carrying oil from the United States to Chile could not bring oil back; in the 1930s it returned empty. With an OBO, however, it might return with guano. Additionally, a single ship that could hold different bulk cargo in different holds, both liquid and dry, might have a higher chance of sailing full by loading multiple cargoes for a single trip. The problems, of course, were technological. How might the tanks or holds be purged of one cargo to take on another without contamination? And what geometry of a hold might suit it to both liquid and solid cargoes and to their loading and unloading? Experiments with OBOs continued through the 1970s, though the ships never experienced in practice their theoretical potential. And they never grew in size as the tankers and the great dry bulk carriers did.

Oceanic shipping in the second half of the twentieth century was instead dominated by the megaships, the tankers, ore and grain carriers, and container vessels that thrived on economies of scale and the transformation of ports that countries and cities proved willing to effect. Specialty vessels such as LNG (Liquid Natural Gas) ships, car carriers, Ro/Ros (Roll-on/Roll-off vessels that allowed vehicles to embark and disembark under their own power), and ever larger ferries evolved to serve their growing markets. All of these larger ships took advantage of the technological refinement of shipbuilding and ship design that had been going on throughout the twentieth century: high-pressure boilers and steam turbines, diesel engines, welding in both construction and repair, structural fire protection, electronics (radio, radar, sonar, radio direction finding, global positioning satellites, satellite communication), air-conditioning, modern materials (aluminum, high-strength steels, stainless steels, fiberglass, plastics, sandwich panels), automation of ship operations, mechanization of loading and unloading, and more.[11] But the megaships remained the queens of the sea at century's end, pursuing a technological trajectory of gigantism that defined their era. Inexorably, they grew in size, capability, efficiency, and capital cost, fueling the globalization of commerce that they both spawned and accommodated.

40

MALCOM MCLEAN
AND THE
CONTAINER
REVOLUTION

THE MOST DRAMATIC AND CONSEQUENTIAL TRANSFORMATION of shipping in the second half of the twentieth century began exactly three months before President Nasser nationalized the Suez Canal. On April 26, 1956, the *Ideal X*, a converted World War II T2 tanker, departed New York harbor bound for Houston. On a reinforced spar deck it carried fifty-eight truck-trailer-size boxes with their wheels removed. In Houston, the trailers were joined to appropriate chassis and driven on their destinations. The container revolution was under way.

Like most industrial revolutions, containerization in the shipping industry was an idea whose time had come. The irony of containerization is that a trucker effected the transformation. While many shipping companies flirted with business and technological models for consolidating break-bulk cargo in secure, manipulable boxes, Malcom McLean, the owner of McLean Trucking Company, demonstrated to the shipping industry how to make it work. In doing so, he forever changed the face of shipping. Most importantly, he brought break-bulk cargo into the mainstream of bulk cargo, the transportation realm in which ships still outpaced ground and air transport. His great contribution was not a business model—his record as a businessman was decidedly mixed—but a technological model. Like Thomas Edison and Henry Ford, with whom he bears

The converted World War II T2 tanker *Ideal X* made history on April 26, 1956, when it departed Port Newark, New Jersey, bound for Houston, Texas, with fifty-eight containers attached to a special metal platform above the main decks. This picture shows the *Ideal X* on a subsequent voyage with fifty-six containers and two complete truck trailers on deck.

comparison, he was a "systems builder."[1] He saw containerization whole, from unitized or cellular cargo to intermodal transport to seamless transfer from ship to truck to train.[2]

Malcom McLean did not invent containerization. Many shipping companies were experimenting with packing break-bulk cargo in secure containers before he entered the field in 1954.[3] This was an idea that was in the air. Matson Line, for example, had experimented with what it called "unitized" cargo before World War II. Its "Jensen Boxes" were 6 by 6 by 4 feet, movable by forklift. They were introduced not to streamline the handling of break-bulk cargo, McLean's goal, but rather to address what the Matson executive R. F. McDonald called the "unholy trinity": loss, damage, and pilferage.[4] The naval architect Charles Cushing recalls his introduction to longshoreman culture when supervising the loading of scotch whisky for U.S. Lines in Glasgow, Scotland, after World War II. The crew handling the cargo came to work with buckets and asked him if it wasn't time for a "leaker," a damaged case from which they could collect the spillage. He refused, only to discover that a leaker appeared nonetheless. He could think of no way to prevent this kind of pilferage.[5] Matson solved the problem by sealing cargo in unitized boxes and locking them with aluminum seals. Similar technology had been developed by the U.S. military during and immediately after World War II. The CONEX boxes (288-cubic-foot steel containers) developed by the War Shipping Administration were thought of as "unitized packaging."[6]

Matson was not, however, able to convert its innovation into a universal system. Instead, it followed McLean's lead, converting the freighter *Hawaiian Merchant* to carry 24-foot containers on its run between Hawaii and the West Coast. In 1960, it introduced the first full container ship in Pacific service, the *Hawaiian Citizen*.[7] And it even attempted to extend container service to Asia. But cooperation with Asian partners foundered on the development of port facilities, and Matson's virtual monopoly on the California-Hawaii trade came under serious challenge as well. Because finished goods dominated its westbound cargo and bulk cargoes—mostly sugar and molasses—predominated on return trips, empty containers quickly piled up in Hawaii. Specialized barges were required to distribute containers to smaller ports in Hawaii, and the docks in San Francisco could not support the concentrated weight load of dense container storage, forcing three relocations before the business finally settled in Oakland. Matson was innovative and resourceful in addressing these growing pains, and it pioneered important innovations in containerization, but it never developed a complete system to compare with McLean's.[8]

Another precursor of McLean's innovation was Seatrain, a company formed in 1928 to move railroad cars by sea. Its founder, Graham M. Brush, a civil engineer, fitted his ships with rails, lashings, and loading equipment that allowed them to take on and discharge loaded railcars from dockside tracks. He could move this cargo in coastwise trade more cheaply than railroads and offshore to Cuba and other ports in the Caribbean more cheaply than competing break-bulk ships. He ran his service profitably for more than three decades until the Cuban revolution of 1959 idled many of his ships and left him financially vulnerable.

Declining an offer from McLean, Brush finally sold to new owners, who elected not to pursue containerization at that time.[9]

Malcom McLean at first planned to do for trucks what Seatrain had done for railroad cars. He was going to put complete trailers aboard ships and move them in the coastwise trade on the Atlantic Ocean and the Gulf of Mexico. Initially he planned to drive the trailers aboard "trailer ships" in an early version of Roll-on/Roll-off (Ro/Ro) technology, but he soon discovered that the space taken up by the chassis undercut the economics of the scheme. So he elected to remove the box from the trailer chassis, repeating the scheme with which others had already experimented. The difference with McLean was that the dimensions of his box, 35' by 8' by 8'6", was driven by trucking conventions and highway regulations

In 1955 he sold his shares in McLean Trucking Company, then the tenth largest in the United States, and bought Pan-Atlantic Steamship Corporation, a small coastwise ship company. Then, with borrowed money, he bought Pan-Atlantic's parent company, Waterman Steamship Corporation, the third largest ship firm in the United States, with diversified holdings in overseas shipping, shipbuilding, and real estate in its home base of Mobile, Alabama. The purchase gave him thirty-five World War II–vintage cargo ships, mostly World War II C2-type break-bulk ships. To these he added two T2 tankers, reinforcing their spar decks, which had been used to ferry aircraft in World War II. One of those ships was *Ideal X*, a vanguard of containerization.[10]

The challenge for McLean, as for his predecessors, was to bridge the chasm that separated the theory of containerization from its practical application. The greatest appeal for him was the potential to reduce delays and costs in handling break-bulk cargo. Two analysts estimated in 1959 that 60 to 75 percent of the cost of transporting break-bulk cargo by sea was incurred dockside. Another study calculated that a conventional ship might incur stevedoring expenses of $15,000 on a single port call, a charge that McLean's system could potentially reduce to $1,600.[11] And these direct savings in labor costs and lost steaming time took no account of the equally important economies in lower loss, pilferage, packaging costs, and cargo insurance. The problem was capitalization and infrastructure. McLean needed specialized ships and customized port facilities. Who would pay?

At first his new company, Sea-Land, hemorrhaged money. Because the Coast Guard would not allow him to ship oil and containers on the same vessels, the 1956 voyages using the T2s lost money. McLean converted six C2 cargo vessels to carry 226 containers in specially designed cells built into the holds. Each ship mounted its own cranes, meaning that it required no special port facilities. Docked beside any pier, it could put two of its containers on the ground in five minutes. No longshoreman would lift a finger, let alone touch the cargo inside the trailers. Once the container was placed on a chassis, the trailer could be driven away by any over-the-road tractor.[12] The concept clearly worked, but Sea-Land lost money throughout its first five years of operations.[13] McLean sold off Waterman assets and borrowed additional funds to stay in business.[14]

Through these tough times, however, he continued to refine the container *system*. The development of cellular frames in the cargo holds of the

Malcom McLean, the father of containerization, is pictured with icons of the system he developed. Two container ships dockside are being offloaded by teams of giant cranes, while a tractor hauls one of the boxes to its assigned place in the neat rows of the marshaling yard, perhaps for transfer to overland transport by truck or train.

C2 vessels placed a premium on standardization of the containers. Dimensions were finally set, largely on the basis of U.S. highway restrictions, at 40' by 8' (or 8'6") by 8', twice the "twenty-foot equivalent unit" (TEU) by which containers have been measured ever since.[15] On January 9, 1959, Matson Line pioneered moving the cranes from the ships to the pier, a reform than McLean and other ship operators followed.[16] Container design was standardized, providing strengthened vertical members at the corners and locking devices that allowed the containers to be stacked atop one another. These reforms opened the path to today's megaships, stacking nine containers high in the hold and five containers deep on deck. When McLean began, he needed no special port facilities, beyond an open pier and room for vehicles to move to and from shipside. Soon large parking areas were added for containers, followed by warehouse and maintenance facilities. By the mid-1960s McLean had designed a standardized container port, distinguishable by the acres of orderly container rows and the absence of the cargo sheds on wharves that dominated ports in the age of break-bulk cargo.

McLean developed his system in the coastal trade before taking it overseas. He experimented with domestic offshore shipping to Puerto Rico. In 1966 he entered the lucrative and competitive North Atlantic trade; in 1960 Europe still accounted for 29.1 percent of American imports and 40 percent of its exports.[17] For this venture, he built his own port facilities in Rotterdam, including shore cranes, large storage yards, and stevedoring tractors to shuttle the containers about the yard. European firms were already offering container service on the North Atlantic in 1966 when McLean's first ship to Europe, the *Fairland*, now sailing under the company name Sea-Land, carried a full load of 226 containers from New York to Rotterdam. The ship convinced many skeptical Europeans that containers were the shipping technology of the future.[18] But McLean's success came at a high price. He had borrowed heavily, sought government subsidies, sold large chunks of Sea-Land stock to Litton Industries, sold his rights to intercoastal shipping to the billionaire Daniel K. Ludwig, and sold off Waterman Steamship Corporation. Indeed, he entered the risky transatlantic trade because he found himself blocked from the coastwise shipping that had demonstrated his system. He had even sold his new ships to Litton Industries, leasing them back to operate them while escaping the debt burden they imposed.[19] He initiated service in the Pacific that profited from the increased demand created by the escalating war in

Vietnam. He introduced containerization to a skeptical U.S. Army, breaching the logistical logjam that kept break-bulk ships waiting at anchor in the river off Saigon. But still his system's demand for capital remained voracious. When he got the chance to sell his shares of Sea-Land to the cash-rich R.J. Reynolds Company, the tobacco giant looking to diversify, he took $160 million and a seat on the Reynolds board. The father of containerization completed his revolution in fourteen years and cashed in his chips. He had tripled his initial investment.

There were many keys to McLean's success. Rapid technical innovations in cranes, container design, locking mechanisms, lifting harnesses, and ship architecture followed one after another. Some came from McLean's team, some from other companies, such as Matson, that were experimenting with containerization. Fortunately, most agreed that standardization was in everyone's best interest. For example, in the late 1950s, McLean, Matson, and Grace Lines were all using different-size containers. The American Society of Mechanical Engineers convened a materials handling panel that standardized containers at ten-, twenty-, thirty-, and forty-foot lengths, with an 8- by 8.5-foot cross section. The twenty- and forty-foot standards caught on, leading to the twenty-foot equivalent unit (TEU) still used for containers today. Then the American Standards Association embraced the ASME metrics and convinced the International Standards Organization to adopt them.[20] The container revolution was going to proceed with American standards, even though the world was increasingly metric and the United States was not.

Another reason for McLean's success was salesmanship. He realized early on that he would have to sell his system to truckers, and also to railroaders. Though his initial intent had been to beat the trucking competition by short-sea shipping, that is, by coastwise delivery of truck trailers faster and more cheaply than they could be hauled overland, he pointed out that true intermodalism profited all forms of transportation. The container, originally a truck trailer,[21] was at the heart of his scheme. On any leg of a journey, it made the most sense to transport it by the carrier that worked most efficiently, be it ship, train, or truck. Short-sea shipping was likely to take away from the trucking industry some of its longest and thus most profitable routes, but McLean nonetheless succeeded in convincing the trucking industry to embrace the innovation. Truckers liked the system because they could participate with only a tractor, avoiding investment in a chassis and container.

Railroads were more difficult to enlist, as the railroad industry was just then engaged in a concerted campaign to reduce competition from coastwise shipping. Having experienced a boom in World War II when ships in the coasting trade were requisitioned by the War Shipping Administration to carry American troops and equipment overseas, the railroad industry then suffered through a postwar cutback in business in the late 1940s and 1950s. The U.S. Maritime Commission operated ships in the coastwise trade until 1948, attempting to restore the prewar shipping industry. Thereafter, however, the railroads were able to take business away from coastal shipping because of lower labor costs and favorable rulings from the Interstate Commerce Commission. Containerization had the potential to reverse that trend, stimulating short-sea shipping and strengthening the direct ties between shipping and trucking. Eventually the railroad industry embraced containers as an opportunity, seeing them as an extension of their earlier experiments with trailers on flatcars. They took to carrying containers not so much to complement coastal shipping as to forestall it.[22] But the full potential of intermodalism trumped their maneuvering, producing most famously the American President Lines' "land bridge," a coordinated system that moved containers seamlessly from Asia to Europe in Pacific Ocean ships, U.S. railroads, and back to Atlantic ships.[23]

McLean was also smart to target the coastal market first, in spite of the competition from railroads. He knew this market well and coastwise shipping offered him few rivals. Additionally, he found ports amenable to his system. In New York, for example, A. Lyle King, the executive director of the Port Authority of New York and New Jersey, actually approached McLean to propose that they work together. The liner terminals on Manhattan Island were traditional finger piers dominated by cargo sheds; they could not be made to serve McLean's system. Even if they could, Manhattan could not absorb the truck traffic that would be generated by large-scale container-ship operations. But King controlled enormous, undeveloped expanses of water frontage across the river in New Jersey that he was looking to develop. Soon plans were afoot to turn a 450-acre tract in Port Elizabeth, New Jersey, into the world's first container port, the largest port development ever undertaken in the United States.[24] Ports and harbors all over the world would soon follow suit, some riding the wave of the container revolution, some left behind in its wake. Designing a container port from scratch in Rotterdam helped turn that city into the world's largest container port and revealed the potential and scalability of McLean's system.

McLean was also lucky. Just when he began operations in the Pacific, American involvement in the Vietnam War created new demand for shipping. Taking a characteristic risk, he offered to set up complete container services—his whole system—including chassis, trucks, and terminals while charging a fixed price per ton.[25] He soon demonstrated that he could meet 10 percent of U.S. military demand for shipping to Vietnam with just 7 of his container ships, while other companies not yet containerized required 250 vessels to carry the other 90 percent.[26] This provided not only validation of his system but also desperately needed revenue. And it allowed the ever resourceful McLean to penetrate Asian markets in search of cargo for his empty ships returning from Vietnam. Because he avoided government subsidies to the greatest extent possible, he was free to move without government interference into evolving markets and trade routes in Asia.

McLean was both a hedgehog *and* a fox. His one big idea, which he pursued with dogged determination, was containerization as a *system* of intermodal transport.[27] He put the parts of his system together one piece at a time: technology, financing, ship design, port facilities, government regulation, trucking, railroading, labor, and shippers. To bring all those pieces together, he had to be a fox. He had to convince longshoremen to trade more jobs for better jobs and to relinquish their traditional patterns of pilferage and theft. He had to convince railroads to accept a system that directly competed with them. He had to convince ports to build entirely new docking facilities and in most cases abandon their old piers in the process. He had to convince bankers and investors to sink capital into an enterprise that lost money for years and gutted one of the nation's great shipping lines. He achieved all this by what one historian has called a remarkable feat of "financial and legal engineering."[28] Wealthy and powerful companies such as Matson and Grace Lines failed to achieve the system that McLean demonstrated with Sea-Land. Sea-Land was the world's largest container shipping company when McLean sold his shares, and it retained that title at the end of the twentieth century as part of Maersk Sealand.

But containerization went on to surpass even McLean's vision. At the end of the twentieth century, an apparel manufacturer in Asia could make dresses, mark them with the retail store's own price tags, hang them on racks, roll the racks into a container, and send that container efficiently, safely, and inexpensively to a department store in New York City, where the racks could be rolled out directly onto the showroom floor. The transportation revolution that made this possible was mostly invisible. It resulted from automation, economies of scale, and efficiencies of new technologies. The face of containerization was most apparent in three realms: ships, ports, and labor.

Several generations of Sea-Land container vessels illustrate the shift in cargo vessels from World War II to the twenty-first century. The first container ship, McLean's *Ideal X*, resembled other World War II tankers. It carried fifty-eight trailers (roughly equivalent to about 100 TEUs) on a 523-foot hull with a deadweight tonnage of 16,400. Its turboelectric engines produced 6,600 horsepower, allowing it to reach top speeds of 14.5 knots or cruise for 12,600 miles. The next generation of container ships saw the conversion of World War II cargo ships to cellular ships. Then came McLean's purpose-built SL-7s, launched in 1972, carrying 1096 containers at thirty-three knots. After acquiring United States Lines in 1977, McLean ordered a fleet of twelve "Jumbo Econships," then the largest container ships in the world, each with a capacity of 4,400 TEUs By comparison with the *Ideal X, Sea-Land Champion* (1995) is 958.5 feet long, has a gross tonnage of 49,985, is powered by a 49,600 brake (net) horsepower diesel engine, and carries 3,800 TEUs. By the year 2000, container ships of 6,600 TEUs were in service, delivering many of the 297 million TEUs that passed in and out of the world's 180 busiest ports.[29]

41

FAREWELL THE FINGER PIER: THE CHANGING FACE OF PORTS

WHEN MALCOM MCLEAN'S *IDEAL X* DEPARTED NEW YORK harbor in 1956 on the voyage that launched the container age, it pulled away from a then obscure wharf in Port Newark, New Jersey, across the Hudson River from the finger piers that were the face of shipping. Its departure marked not only the birth of containerization but also the transformation of the waterfront.

The row of piers that marched south down Manhattan's West Side, around the Battery, and back north up the East River hosted the communion between land and sea. Luxury Liner Row, from West 44th to West 52nd streets on the Hudson River, serviced the great luxury liners that still carried the bulk of transatlantic passenger traffic. Four hundred berths ringed Manhattan, nestled between piers 200 to 1,000 feet in length and 80 to 250 feet wide. Ships carrying break-bulk cargo took berths south of the luxury passenger ship terminals on the Hudson River, mixed in with ferries, coastal passenger vessels, barges, railcar floats, and the still pervasive cargo ships of the coasting trade. Vast cargo and transit sheds capped the piers, offering shelter and protection for the people and cargo embarking and debarking from the ships. Trucks and cars moved up and down the docks, into and out of the buildings, delivering and retrieving goods and passengers. Watching the majestic liners being eased into their berths by a bevy of tugboats, thence to be serviced by whole regiments of longshoremen, warehousemen, truckers, baggage handlers, coopers, gearmen, contractors, vendors, and agents, one would not doubt that this was the busiest port in America.

But New York harbor was always busier than the Manhattan waterfront suggested. Opposite the fifty-two piers on the Manhattan side of the Hudson River were fifteen more on the New Jersey side. Staten Island added eighteen more, plus seven on the Manhattan side of the East River and thirty-nine more on the Brooklyn side. In all, New York harbor had 470 miles of direct water frontage, much of it developed with piers, ferry slips, car-float bridges, bulkheads, shore wharves, grain silos, dry docks, and other facilities. Railroad terminals reached the waterfront at points all up and down the New Jersey shore of the harbor. Lloyd's of London reported that "port facilities cover every shipping requirement."[1]

In the second half of the twentieth century, containerization would transform New York harbor and others like it around the world. Many that could not transform themselves went into decline. New ports in hitherto obscure harbors rose to world prominence. In some cases, harbors were crafted virtually de novo. Some great ports emerged with no harbor at all, just a submarine pipeline stretching to an offshore platform or mooring buoy, where enormous tankers drawing as much as 45 feet discharged millions of gallons of oil per visit. Just as container ships grew inexorably in pursuit of economies of scale, so too did other bulk carriers, forcing ports to adapt or decline.

In New York, the change was actually embraced and accelerated by the Port Authority, a regional entity approved by the U.S. Congress under section 10 of Article I of the Constitution allowing that "when any river divides or flows through two or more States they may enter into compacts with each other to improve the navigation thereof." When they finally created the Port of New York Authority on April 30, 1921, New York and New Jersey had been in conflict over rights to the harbor going back at least to the days of Robert Fulton.[2] Modeled on the Port of London, the authority established a "Port District" of fifteen hundred square miles centered on the Statue of Liberty. In the 1930s it oversaw the construction of bridges and tunnels linking the harbor's islands to the mainland. After World War II, it leased from New York and New Jersey the three airports that continue to serve the region today: Idlewild (now Kennedy), LaGuardia, and Newark (now Newark Liberty). And in the 1950s, while continuing to expand the roadways serving the area, it initiated the world's first container ports at Port Newark and the Elizabeth–Port Authority Marine Terminal, whence the *Ideal X* departed.[3]

As with other container ports to follow, what was wanted was neither more waterfront nor more piers. Indeed containerization would *decrease* the overall demand for waterfront and obviate the need for finger piers and cargo sheds of the kind that rimmed Manhattan. More and bigger ships would load and unload from the docks, but they would do it in a fraction of the time required by conventional ships. While conventional break-bulk ships averaged a week or more in port, modern container vessels average only twenty-four hours.[4] Indeed, the economics of container ships and the other bulk megaships that came to dominate the world's oceans in the second half of the twentieth century put a premium on maximum time at sea, minimum time in port. The ships were capital-intensive in a way that not even the biggest freighters of the pre–World War II era could approach. As shipowners have always known, they could pay off their investment only by sailing, not by sitting dockside. What the container ship needed dockside was cranes, tractors, and an enormous marshaling yard, a parking lot for containers. In other words, it needed land, a commodity particularly dear in Manhattan.

So container terminals and other docks for bulk carriers sprang up in the harbor outside Manhattan. The table on the following page gives the results of a survey of container port capacity in the harbor in 2000.

In all, in 2000 New York harbor boasted 2,639 acres of container storage space, almost 25,000 feet of berthing space, and 51 cranes. Only a small percentage of this infrastructure was on Manhattan Island. In addition, many of these terminals offered enclosed "stuffing and stripping facilities" where cargo could be loaded and unloaded to and from containers.[5] A few piers remained on Manhattan Island, including mainly terminals for the cruise ships that now give most American citizens their taste of oceanic travel. But the Manhattan waterfront was barely recognizable from the great liner days. Some of the old piers had been converted to parking, amusement, and recreational facilities, but most had simply been abandoned.

New York City, especially the Department of Marine and Aviation, responded to the transformation of its waterfront with "Dolchstoss," a suspicion that it had been stabbed in the back by the Port Authority. But similar transformations were occurring around the world. London lost its

Capacity of Container Ports

Terminals	Container Storage (in acres)	Berthing Space and Cranes
Howland Hook Container Terminal	1,433	2,493 ft.; 3 cranes
South West Brooklyn Marine Terminal	111	1,535 ft.; 1 crane
Red Hook Container Terminal	50	2 container berths and 4 combination bulk/ container berths; 5 cranes
Global Marine Terminal	99	1,788 ft.; 9 cranes
Port Elizabeth Container Terminals	94	2,808 ft.; 4 cranes
Maher Fleet Street Terminal	200	4,898 ft.; 9 cranes
Maher Terminals	235	3,153 ft.; 7 cranes
Sea-Land Terminal	264	4,521 ft.; 7 cranes
Maersk Line Terminal	64	755 ft.; 3 cranes
Universal Terminal	89	3,041 ft.; 3 cranes
Total	2,639	24,992 ft.; 51 cranes

docks first to Tilbury and then to Felixstowe. Marseille's migrated across the bay to Fos-sur-Mer. Sydney, Australia, watched the new container port at Botany Bay absorb its maritime commerce.[6] The face of shipping had not only been transformed, it had been displaced. Citizens of the world's great port cities no longer strolled to the waterfront to gaze up at the great vessels transporting the world's goods and passengers.

In the United States, the city pier that had been so much a part of urban life in America since the days of Salem and Boston, Philadelphia and Baltimore, no longer pulsed with the tempo of oceanic shipping. Inevitably, that shipping receded further and further from public view and thus consciousness, even while the volume of traffic continued its inexorable rise, fueling the pace of American economic growth. Some ports, like New Orleans, simply could not adjust fully. Separated from the Gulf of Mexico by a hundred miles of winding and treacherous river channel, the city could no longer hope to accommodate the megaships that came to ply the world's oceans. Its 11.25 miles of river wharves could

When the U.S. Navy airship USS *Akron* flew over New York City in 1931, the island of Manhattan bristled with finger piers running down the East River on the right and up the Hudson River on the left. An aerial view of Manhattan in 2001 (top) reveals an island virtually denuded of finger piers, though cruise ships still come into the refurbished piers of the old luxury liner row, visible in the upper left corner of both photos.

handle barges and general cargo vessels, and the new France Road Container Terminal boasted four berths, 43.7 hectares of marshaling yards, and six cranes. To reach it from the Gulf, however, ships had to pass through the South West Pass or the Mississippi River Gulf Outlet, a shorter, artificial waterway. Both routes require annual dredging by the Corps of Engineers; by the end of the twentieth century neither could accommodate the largest container vessels. New Orleans instead claimed to be the main center of barge and LASH (Lighter Aboard SHip) shipping in the United States.[7] As before, it served primarily as a transshipment port, transferring cargo from rail and river craft to oceangoing ships. In 2001 it ranked twelfth among U.S. ports in the value of the cargo it handled, but third in tonnage.[8]

San Francisco was the New York of the West Coast. Since the time of the gold rush in 1849, it had been America's busiest port on the Pacific Ocean, hosting liners and tramps, tankers and ferries at a string of forty-two fingers piers jutting out from the curving Embarcadero Wharf. Lacking space at the city's edge to accommodate containers and their voracious demand for storage, San Francisco yielded container traffic to Oakland. That city, across the bay, claimed thirteen miles of berthing space in 1957 and 260 acres of covered space. The complex water frontage already accommodated the Oakland Army Base and the U.S. Naval Supply Center. But hundreds of acres remained free to expand into container storage.[9] By the year 2000, Oakland had twenty-eight cranes and 561 acres devoted exclusively or primarily to container handling, serving such lines as Maersk Sealand, Matson, CSX, and American President Lines. It stood seventh on the list of U.S. ports ranked by value of cargo in 2001, twenty-fourth by tonnage. San Francisco was not in the top twenty-five on either list.[10]

Oakland had not, however, become the busiest American port on the West Coast. That title went to a sprawling combination of port facilities in Los Angeles and Long Beach. The ranking of top American ports by value of cargo in 2001 placed Los Angeles first and Long Beach second. Between them they accounted for 27.7 percent of the value of all maritime cargo passing in and out of the United States in that year. New York–New Jersey was a distant third at 12 percent, the only other port in double digits. In the 2001 ranking by weight of cargo, Los Angeles ranked seventh, Long Beach ninth.[11] And the dominance of these two ports was especially pronounced in containers. Los Angeles passed an average of 9.4 million containers in 2001; Long Beach 8.8 million. Between them they accounted for 37 percent of the containers that entered or left the United States that year.[12]

This achievement contrasts sharply with the experience of the two ports in the 1950s. In 1954 Long Beach passed 8.6 million tons of cargo through 132 potential berthing spaces and thirty-five acres of covered working space. Los Angeles, already connected to Long Beach by a twenty-five-mile channel, was smaller, less busy, and less developed at the time. By the year 2000, however, the Port of Los Angeles spread across seventy-five hundred acres, offering twenty-nine terminals along twenty-eight miles of waterfront. Much of its capacity was in liquid and dry bulk cargo, but it also offered 596 acres of container storage space in six terminals served by 13,937 feet of berthing frontage and 24 cranes. Its cruise terminal served Carnival, Cunard, Kloster, Princess, and Royal Caribbean cruise lines. By comparison, Long Beach offered 680 acres of container storage space at eight terminals served by 17,320 feet of waterfront and 38 cranes. That port claimed storage capacity for 69,273 TEUs at these terminals, supplemented by an intermodal container transfer facility of 151 acres with a capacity of 264,000 TEUs. In 2000 Long Beach passed 110 million tons of cargo, almost thirteen times its achievement of 1954.[13]

Cities that had the available space, the financial resources, and the political will were able to capitalize on the transformation of shipping in the second half of the twentieth century. As shipping, especially international shipping, turned increasingly to megaships—container vessels carrying thousands of TEUs and tankers and other bulk carriers finally grown too large to pass through the Panama Canal—the old port facilities of Manhattan, Baltimore, Boston, Philadelphia, San Francisco, and other cities gave way to sprawling docks and yards served by massive cranes and acres of handling and storage space. Passenger liners that once docked at prestigious piers like those along New York's Luxury Liner Row disappeared in the 1970s and 1980s from the great cities. The cruise ships that replaced them for recreational voyaging grew in size to three thousand passengers, dwarfing SS *United States* and the other great passenger ships that marked the North Atlantic liner's last hurrah.[14] Like the tankers, bulk carriers, and container ships of the late twentieth century, the cruising megaships often had to embark and disembark their passengers not from city docks but from the sprawling new ports evolving to serve the ocean trade.[15]

But port capacity—cranes, acres, berthing space—does not fully explain the changing face of ports. It helps to explain the decline of New York and the rise of New Jersey, but it does not explain why Los Angeles and Long Beach displaced the New York–New Jersey combination in volume and value of cargo. New York harbor, after all, had more acres of container storage and almost as many cranes and feet of berthing space as Los Angeles and Long Beach combined. Not just American ports were changing in the late twentieth century, but the nature of shipping as well. After dominating American oceanic shipping traffic since 1600, the Atlantic found itself eclipsed in 1982 by the Pacific trade. For example, Atlantic container traffic outpaced Pacific by 10.7 to 5.8 million TEUs in 1975; twenty years later, 59.9 million TEUs crossed the Pacific, compared with 41.9 million on the Atlantic.[16] Globalization accounts for much of this change, the rise of rapidly expanding economies in East Asia. Japan was the United States' number-two trading partner through most of the last thirty years of the twentieth century. With Canada, Mexico, Germany, and Britain, it dominated the top five positions. By 2001, however, it was joined by China, South Korea, Taiwan, Singapore, and Malaysia in the top twelve. And much of the traffic coming to the United States from these countries was general merchandise in containers. Of the twelve busiest container ports in the world in 2000, ten were in Asia; only Los Angeles–Long Beach (#5) and Rotterdam (#7), the highly automated European container port pioneered by Malcom McLean, made the list.[17]

Another important trend shaping the development of American ports in the second half of the twentieth century was the relative decline of domestic shipping compared with international shipping. Continuing a trend that went all the way back to 1820, American domestic shipping outweighed oceanic shipping in both tonnage and value. Americans shipped mostly to other Americans. In 1924, for example, foreign shipping accounted for only 22 percent of the annual shipping tonnage of the United States. In 1934 it was 19 percent. Even during World War II, in 1944, it was 25 percent, about the same as in 1954. By 1964, however, it had risen to 34 percent, on its way to 43 percent in both 1974 and 1984. In 1994 foreign maritime commerce outweighed domestic shipping for the first time since the days of the early republic.[18]

Many factors contributed to the relative revival of American overseas shipping. The campaign of the railroads against coastal or short-sea shipping had some effect. More important was the interstate highway system and the rise of American trucking. Coastal passenger traffic suffered from the parallel expansion of automobile traffic, to say nothing of the rise of the domestic airline industry. Foreign trade patterns contributed as well. Canada remained America's largest trading partner through these decades, while Mexico grew from the fifth largest in 1970 to the second largest by 2001. Passage of the North American Free Trade Agreement (NAFTA) only accelerated a trading pattern that was long dominant. In 2001, 91 percent of merchandise trade with Canada moved by land, while only 2 percent moved by water; 6.5 percent moved by air. For Mexico, the comparable figures were 86 percent by land, 8.6 percent by ship, and 5 percent by air. Between them, Canada and Mexico accounted for almost one-third of America's international merchandise trade. More than twice as many containers entered the United States by truck from those two countries as entered by ship from all other countries in the world combined.[19]

But it was not just the relative decline of domestic shipping that altered the foreign/domestic balance in the late twentieth century. America's growing need for foreign oil drove a constant stream of tankers to American ports. And globalization generally increased the flow of goods on the world's oceans. As the world's largest trading nation, the United States participated in this burgeoning ocean traffic, importing far more than it exported as the century wore on. It especially increased its traffic in consumer merchandise moving by container. American ships and shipping companies carried an ever smaller percentage of that trade to and from the United States, but it came and went nonetheless, most of it in megaships, taxing American ports and further transforming the face of shipping.

42

THE SHRINKING
GIANT: MARITIME
LABOR IN AN AGE
OF MECHANIZATION

MALCOM MCLEAN'S CONTAINER REVOLUTION POSED A GREATER
threat to labor than to any other segment of the economy. On the waterfront, the container quickly became known as the "longshoreman's
coffin."[1] But the problem was not peculiar to dockworkers. Mechanization and automation swept the entire industry in the second half of the
twentieth century, challenging maritime unions to adapt or accelerate the
decline of American oceanic shipping. A shrinking labor force within a
shrinking industry offered few good options. While the share of U.S.
oceanic cargo carried on American ships shrank from 20.7 percent in
1956 to 2.6 percent in 2000, the number of seamen serving on American-
flagged vessels plummeted from 57,192 to 6,600.[2] The unions could hope
only to control this decline, not to prevent it. The reaction of the
longshoremen's unions to containerization offers a microcosm of the path
followed by all of maritime labor.

At the most fundamental level, containerization was always about
labor-saving; pilferage and damage to break-bulk cargo were secondary
considerations.[3] Malcom McLean often said that the idea for containerization came to him before World War II. In 1937 he spent the better part
of a day waiting to transfer his load in Jersey City, New Jersey, to a ship
bound for Istanbul, Turkey. He recalled in 2001:

I had to wait most of the day to deliver the bales, sitting in my truck, watching stevedores load other cargo. It struck me that I was looking at a lot of wasted time and money. I watched them take each crate out of a truck, slip it into a sling, and then lift it into the hold of a ship.

Once in the hold, every sling had to be unloaded, and the cargo stowed where it was to go. As I waited around that day, I had the thought that it would be easier to lift my trailer up, without any of the contents being touched, and put it on the ship.[4]

Whether or not McLean was driven by such visions of efficiency when he launched the container revolution in 1956, he surely understood the impact of his innovation on waterfront labor. Within a decade, his system permitted the loading of 20 to 25 tons of cargo in two and a half minutes. In break-bulk form, the same load would have required eighteen to twenty man-hours. Aboard ship, container vessels required two work gangs; conventional break-bulk vessels needed five to seven.[5] Foreseeing this impact, McLean targeted longshoremen as a critical constituency. He sought to portray containerization as a win-win proposition for both management and labor. The generous terms to which Sea-Land acceded in its early negotiations with labor helped smooth the way for the transformation of the docks. For example, when he initiated offshore service to Puerto Rico in 1958, he needed only nineteen workers per ship over a period of seventeen hours, rather than two hundred workers for three days. When the Puerto Rican shore workers struck in protest, Sea-Land negotiated a revenue-sharing system by which the company actually paid seventeen workers not to work. In contrast, Grace Lines failed to reach a comparable agreement with dockworkers in Venezuela to unload its experimental container vessels *Santa Eliana* and *Santa Leonor*. After negotiating from 1960 through 1962, Grace withdrew the vessels from service.[6]

Maritime labor confronted mechanization in the 1950s and 1960s from a position of weakness. Seamen and shore workers had suffered cutbacks in jobs and pay at the end of World War II. Mollified during the war by bonuses and plentiful hours, they tolerated the flat pay scales to which they had agreed in 1941. After the war, they needed significant pay increases to sustain their income levels, but they had little leverage amid the larger dislocations afflicting the American economy in the late 1940s and early 1950s.

To make matters worse, the maritime labor movement still split along the old fault lines. The larger schism within American labor between the AFL and CIO was mirrored in the divisions between competing labor factions. Joseph Curran's National Maritime Union (NMU) allied itself with the trade unionism of the Congress of Industrial Organizations (CIO), while the rival Sailors' Union of the Pacific (SUP), under the leadership of Harry Lundeberg, allowed itself to be absorbed into the Seafarers International Union of North America (SIU-NA or just SIU), an affiliate of the American Federation of Labor (AFL). The International Longshoremen's and Warehousemen's Union (ILWU) sided with the NMU, mostly on the West Coast, while the International Longshoremen's Association (ILA) made common cause with the SIU, most strongly on the East Coast. These alignments exacerbated regional differences in wage rates and labor practices; the East and Gulf coasts had similar conditions, but both differed from those on the West Coast and all differed from those on the Great Lakes. As had been true at the apogee of the maritime labor movement in the 1930s, the members could never speak with one voice nationally, not even when the AFL and the CIO joined forces in 1955. Maritime labor remained fractured, especially in the longshoring industry, where conditions and contracts tended to be negotiated locally.[7]

The Truman administration, though generally friendly to labor, provided little guidance. Truman embraced the New Deal and labor's role in the Roosevelt political coalition, but he could not escape his roots as a border-state Democrat susceptible to pressures from more conservative elements of his party. His dealings with union leaders in the United Mine Workers' strike of 1946 did nothing to nurture his sympathies for labor nor cultivate his standing within the labor movement. The general push of organized labor for wage increases after the flat rates of World War II endangered Truman's efforts to demobilize the country's war machine without provoking a recession. He vetoed the Taft-Hartley Act, but his ambivalence toward labor may well have contributed to the climate in which the act nonetheless became law.[8]

The Taft-Hartley Act cast a particularly revealing light on the dilemma of maritime labor. It prohibited, for example, union hiring halls that discriminated against nonunion members. Maritime dispatch or hiring halls had been a reform cherished by most seamen and some officers in the early decades of the twentieth century and still plays a large role in maritime labor practices throughout the United States. Their close associations with the maritime unions raised questions about their legality under the act and helped to bring on a maritime strike on the West Coast in 1948. The "shape-up" system for hiring casual workers on the waterfront attracted similar scrutiny. By the time maritime labor had to deal with mechanization, its power had been seriously undermined, and the power of the government to intervene in labor disputes greatly strengthened.[9] Maritime labor still had power, but negotiation made more sense than defiance.

Furthermore, mechanization had insinuated itself into the waterfront even before the crisis of containerization. Palletization of cargo and increasing reliance on forklifts became common in World War II, not just on the docks but in warehousing generally. Short-sea shipping was beginning to experiment with barges that could be loaded and unloaded without tying up ships. Mechanized conveyor belts proved more efficient than cargo nets for moving some break-bulk materials, such as bananas, for example, to and from ships' holds. Ships capable of side-port loading were particularly well adapted to conveyor belts. And, as mentioned earlier, some shipping firms, such as Matson, were already experimenting with unitized cargo to prevent damage and pilferage. Labor responded with a maritime version of featherbedding, insisting, for example, in some ports that palletized cargos be placed on the surface of the dock when passing to and from ships, that sling loads be unnecessarily limited in the name of "safety," and that work gangs include "witnesses"—observers who did no work.[10]

The first attempt in the container age to come to grips with the implications of mechanizing the waterfront arose on the West Coast. The Mechanization and Modernization Agreement (M and M Agreement), negotiated in 1960 and revised in 1966, established the pattern and principles that would ultimately be adopted by labor throughout the United States to ease the longshoring workforce into the container age. In essence, labor and management agreed to grandfather existing workers, while allowing the overall labor force to shrink by attrition as its work was mechanized. Existing workers would be paid higher wages, guaranteed generous pensions, and bought out into early retirement if they agreed to go quietly. West Coast ship operators paid $29 million between 1960 and 1966 into a special Mechanization Fund that provided longshoremen with early retirement incentives, disability pensions, and death benefits. The most important element of the fund consisted of individual lump-sum payments of $7,920 to encourage qualified longshoremen (those between the ages of sixty-two and sixty-five, and with a minimum of twenty-five years of service) to retire early, in addition to their regular Social Security and pension benefits. In addition, employers committed themselves to a guarantee of no layoffs for any of the fully registered work-force, and to a pledge of providing thirty-five hours of work or pay per week.[11] The gamble was that increased productivity would cover the cost of the plan. As it happened, all parties misjudged the speed with which containerization would sweep the shipping industry. Disputes over such issues as container stuffing and stripping, the analog of putting palletized cargo on the surface of the dock, arose during subsequent renegotiations of the agreement. But the fundamentals held. The unions agreed to downsize by attrition in return for generous payments to the existing workforce.[12]

Similar agreements followed on the Atlantic and Gulf Coast ports, though conditions there differed. They entailed a larger workforce, a multiplicity of employers' organizations, the ILA's more decentralized structure in comparison to the ILWU, and organizational turbulence within the ILU as a consequence of expulsion from the AFL between 1953 and 1958. Ultimately, however, the agreements reached by the parties revealed the same principles as the West Coast settlements: pay-ments to existing workers to allow attrition of the workforce and intro-duction of new work technologies and rules. New York set the standard with a 1959 agreement between the ILA and the New York Shipping Association (NYSA). The workers agreed to handle containers while the shipowners allowed continued gang size of twenty men, more than was necessary with the new technology. A follow-on agreement in 1964 guaranteed a minimum annual wage for longshoremen, gradual reduc-tion in gang size, and an increase in pensions.[13] Largely as a result of these agreements, the waterfront labor force in terminals overseen by the Port Authority shrank from thirty-one thousand in 1956 to barely a tenth of that number in 1998.[14]

The unions' particular methods of coming to terms with the effects of containerization and automation were criticized by representatives of both labor and employers. The former charged that the agreements, with their emphasis on benefits for veteran longshoremen, favored old union stalwarts, and amounted to a sellout of the rights and privileges the unions had gained in preceding decades.[15] The latter, by contrast,

The Empress of the Seas. Another creation of Donald McKay, this clipper famously raced *Surprise* from New York to San Francisco in 1853, raising the West Coast port in 119 days, two more than her rival. She burned at sea in 1860. (From a painting by John Stobart.)

Cincinnati: Morning Rush Hour. People board the *Queen City* ferry in Cincinnati for passage across the Ohio River to Covington, Kentucky, in this morning scene in 1859. This service would give way to the Roebling Suspension Bridge when it opened in December 1866. (From a painting by John Stobart.)

Sacramento: The Celebrated River Steamer Chrysopolis *Leaving in 1870.* This famous paddlewheeler of the California Steam Navigation Company was the preeminent vessel in the trade between San Francisco and the California capital. In the foreground a barge with its own pilot house carries farm produce under tow while sailing vessels that have tacked their way up river rest at shoreside. (From a painting by John Stobart.)

A Down-Easter Approaching Cape Horn. The fierce winds, high seas, and scattered islands at the southern tip of South America have challenged sailors ever since Ferdinand Magellan first navigated the course in 1520. Here a crewman seems to wonder if his late-nineteenth-century ship is carrying too much sail for the stormy conditions. (From a painting by John Stobart.)

St. Louis: View Through the Arches of the Eads Bridge in 1876. Pillars of the new Eads Bridge, the first iron span across the Mississippi, frame the row of steamboats tied up at the St. Louis pier. River traffic had made St. Louis a hub of western commerce, and the Eads Bridge helped make it one of the largest and fastest-growing cities in the United States. (From a painting by John Stobart.)

South Street by Gaslight in 1880. This scene from the East River captures the maritime presence that still surrounded New York City in the late nineteenth century. By the beginning of the twentieth century, these docks became increasingly denuded as sailing vessels disappeared and steamships moved to new facilities on the Hudson River and in New Jersey. The South Street Seaport Historic District has restored some of the maritime flavor depicted here. (From a painting by John Stobart.)

Pittsburgh: Moonlight over the Monongahela in 1885. The side-wheeler *Geneva,* Pittsburgh's excursion boat, disembarks passengers at the Smithfield Street Landing, illuminated by its own searchlight. The recently opened Smithfield Street Bridge over-looks the landing. (From a painting by John Stobart.)

New York City: The Henry B. Hyde *Leaving Pier 20, East River, in 1886.* John A. Roebling's Brooklyn Bridge looms in the background as a late American sailing vessel moves under tow into the ebb tide to begin its journey down the East River on a windless, sultry day. Scenes like this continued through the remainder of the nineteenth century, evidence of America's continuing infatuation with the wooden sailing vessel. Increasingly, however, the maritime action was across town at the steamship berths on the Hudson River. (From a painting by John Stobart.)

alleged that the West Coast "buyout"—and by analogy all of the agreements—was an egregious example of "featherbedding," and a stark demonstration of the power and influence of organized labor in the maritime sector.[16]

A more realistic appraisal might be that both sides, management and labor, faced inevitable change. Shipowners, port operators, and longshoremen realized that they were in this together. If they did not remain competitive, ships would simply go to other ports. The most attractive ports were going to be those that mechanized. Furthermore, the new economies of loading and unloading ships held out some promise of reviving the moribund costal shipping trade, creating a tide of business on which all boats would rise. Malcom McLean and other owners and managers even argued that the new technology could benefit labor by increasing the volume of shipping, and hence jobs. In spite of the clear featherbedding that the shipowners supported, the stunning economies realized by the new technologies more than covered the cost. On the Pacific Coast, for example, labor costs on the waterfront fell by $1 billion in the course of the 1960s alone.[17]

Of course the waterfront was not the only site of mechanization and automation in the shipping industry. Ship design, construction, and operation underwent their own revolutions in the second half of the twentieth century, bringing to seamen dislocations comparable to those experienced by longshoremen. While the waterfront was transformed primarily by mechanization, ships experienced both mechanization and automation. The former saved labor by assisting workers, the latter by replacing them. Most, though not all, of the changes came aboard megaships, the great bulk carriers that transported the world's grain, ore, oil, containers, and other cargoes sensitive to economies of scale. Over the course of five decades, ships grew ever larger, while their crews, both in absolute numbers and even more so in proportion to cargo, shrank dramatically.

On May 17, 2000, the Great Lakes ore carrier *Mesabi Miner* departed its berth at Lorain, Ohio, empty and unassisted (no tugs), to begin a 750-mile journey to Taconite Harbor, Minnesota, where it would take on low-grade iron pellets for delivery back to Lorain. At 1,004 feet in length and 105 feet wide, she represented the largest class of vessels that could navigate the winding Detroit and St. Clair rivers and squeeze through the locks (with five-foot clearance) at Sault Ste. Marie, joining

Lakes Huron and Superior. After sixty hours of continuous sailing, Captain Timothy Dayton used the ship's main propellers and bow thrusters to hold the vessel against the wind while nosing it into a berth beneath a huge dockside automated loader. His own crew jumped ashore to tie up the vessel, with no longshoremen required. Eighteen of the *Mesabi Miner's* thirty-six hatch covers were raised and shoreside conveyors started pouring about 57,000 tons of taconite into the hold. Three hours and twenty minutes later, with ballast water discharged to compensate for the cargo weight, the *Mesabi Miner* departed unaided from the loading pier to begin the return trip to Lorain. There, on the afternoon of May 22, captain and crew docked the vessel unaided and the ship's self-unloading mechanism began pouring its cargo onto the pier. Conveyor belts at the bottom of each hold fed the pellets to a giant offloader. As the ore piled up on the pier, the *Mesabi Miner's* crew slowly winched the huge vessel along its berth, leaving a ridgeline of taconite as long as the ship. Seven hours later, the empty *Mesabi Miner* departed again for Taconite Harbor.

With a total crew of twenty-six, the *Mesabi Miner* hauled dry bulk cargo with an efficiency unmatched by any other form of transportation. In 1999 it made a total of fifty-two trips across the Great Lakes, twelve carrying coal and forty carrying iron ore. It delivered 696,000 tons of coal and 2,280,000 tons of ore. On each trip it hauled the equivalent of six 100-car trainloads of coal or eight 100-car trainloads of ore. Trucks capable of carrying thirty net tons would have to make 2,182 trips to match one for the Mesabi Miner. Traveling the same distance, 750 miles, and getting four miles to the gallon, the trucks would use 400,000 gallons of fuel; the Mesabi Miner used 32,000 gallons. It achieved, in other words, about 1,500 ton-miles per gallon.[18]

This megaship, and others like it, relied on technology to attain such high efficiencies with such a small crew. Computerization had perhaps the greatest impact. In 1956 ships were run from the bridge, where the watch officer monitored the engine watch, the lookouts, the radio operator, and the helmsman. He (always a male) did his own navigating in the traditional way, aided on most ships by radar and perhaps even LORAN. By the end of the twentieth century, the most modern ships were controlled from a ship operation center (SOC) on the bridge. At sea, a rotation of single watch officers could operate the ship entirely from the bridge. Integrated navigation systems used signals from global positioning satellites,

The twentieth-century trend toward gigantism in bulk shipping began with the Great
Lakes 600-foot ore carriers, such as the *J. Pierpont Morgan*, pictured here. Descendants
of those unprecedented megaships are bulk carriers such as the 1,004-foot *Mesabi
Miner*, among the largest of vessels still able to navigate the Detroit River and the Sault
Ste. Marie locks between Lakes Superior and Huron.

electronic charts, and other automated navigation techniques to maintain
a constant reading of the ship's location, course, and speed. An autopilot
steered the ship along the chosen route. Radar detection of other vessels
or obstacles at sea could be enhanced by infrared detectors for poor
visibility and the spotting of small vessels that radar might miss. Though
many liner companies required two-person watches (male or female), the
Japanese actually researched the possibility of fully automated megaships
carrying no crew at all on the open sea.[19]

In addition to monitoring ship movement, the SOC also allowed the
watch officer to monitor and control the engines. Tank levels and engine
performance could be adjusted from the SOC, as could ballast. Within
the engine room itself, devices monitored engine revolutions, oil pressure,
fuel lines, and crankcase condition. Automatic sprinkler, or Halon, systems blanketed potentially dangerous spaces. A video display terminal

constantly scanned all aspects of machinery operation. By the end of the century, most vessels were driven by diesel engines, which needed less human intervention and maintenance in operation than the steam engines they replaced. Onboard cranes in the engineering spaces allowed removal of major engine parts when they required work. Computers also facilitated ship operations and management. Recordkeeping and reporting were increasingly computerized and information on the ship's condition and functioning could be digitally transmitted to shore to assist in planning future operations and maintenance stops.[20]

Even licensed officers aboard ship found their working conditions transformed by the new technology. Radio officers were eliminated on most modern ships, imposing upon the deck officer another duty and another training requirement. Improved mooring technology and self-docking capabilities allowed captains to dock their vessels without tugboats and with minimal crews, as Captain Dayton did aboard the *Mesabi Miner*. Monitoring of engine operations and other ship functions from the SOC placed a premium on cross-training for deck officers in engineering and other ship's systems. Increased responsibilities with smaller crews raised issues of fatigue and psychological stress that weighed most heavily on the licensed crew. At the same time, the pressure to keep ships at sea as long as possible meant that crews were in port usually for less than twenty-four hours, and even some maintenance was done at sea by riding crews that could board at one port and debark at another.

As a result of this automation and the shrinking American commercial fleet, the number of seamen serving aboard U.S.-flagged merchant ships fell dramatically in the second half of the twentieth century. Total U.S. seafaring jobs fell from 70,700 in 1952 to 7,500 in 1996. Nor was this exclusively an American phenomenon. By 2000 a worldwide shortage of licensed officers was arising in response to the changed life of the seaman: short turnaround times in port, remote terminals, low levels of crew competence, increased responsibilities, shipowners and managers driven by cost-cutting, and extended absences from home and family. Unlicensed seamen still outnumbered the jobs available on the world market, but the glut of seamen arose mostly from poorer countries in Asia, the Indian subcontinent, and eastern Europe. It reflected a disturbing trend away from merchant fleets operated by traditional, developed shipping countries with well-paid and highly trained crews toward large fleets operated by developing countries of open registry with poorly paid and poorly trained crews. Furthermore, the economics and regulation of international shipping actually provided incentives for some parties to operate substandard ships, compounding the problem of substandard crews. America's maritime labor problems were in reality a reflection of larger trends in the rapidly changing world shipping market.[21]

43

RICHARD NIXON AND THE QUEST FOR A NATIONAL MARITIME POLICY

THE VAST MERCHANT FLEET THAT THE UNITED STATES HAD acquired to meet the emergency of the Second World War posed a serious challenge to America's maritime policy once the conflict came to an end. With approximately forty-five hundred commercial vessels—roughly 60 percent of the world's commercial tonnage—America's merchant marine was then the largest in the world. These ships were operated by about 130 private companies with extensive experience in maritime operations, considerable financial resources, and a determination to stay in business. This expansion amounted to a threefold increase in the number of operators and a fourfold increase in the number of ships since 1939.[1] These attributes, combined with the sheer quantity of the merchant shipping under its control, presented the United States with what appeared to be an extraordinary opportunity to assert its dominance over the world's maritime carrying trade for years, if not decades, to come.

But America failed to sustain its position as the dominant commercial shipping power in the world. To begin with, the accumulation of a huge merchant fleet proved to be a mixed blessing. Immediately after the war, American merchant shipping could be used to assist in tasks related to postwar demobilization and reconstruction, such as ferrying American service personnel home and transporting Marshall Plan and UNRRA

(United Nations Reconstruction and Relief Agency) supplies to Europe. But these duties would not continue for long. Moreover, the devastation of much of the world's economy meant that in the initial years of peace international trade would be too anemic to sustain the American commercial fleet. At the same time, the existence of such a large fleet depressed the shipbuilding industry, as had happened after World War I. Compounding these influences were a traditional American distrust of state ownership of industry and a coolness to grand schemes of international economic hegemony.[2]

Still, the government took some steps to promote the American shipping industry. The Marshall Plan, for example, found its counterpart in the Merchant Ship Sales Act of 1946. The immediate aim of this legislation was to dispose of the wartime merchant fleet through sale of ships to American as well as foreign owners. Its greater purpose was to revitalize maritime trade, thus reviving international economic competition and providing the basis for the creation and distribution of wealth, as one advocate put it, "through the unfettered channels of trade rather than by imperial preferences, by conquest or by international brigandry."[3]

The act did not simply fulfill, but exceeded, the hopes invested in it. Competitive pricing attracted plenty of buyers, with U.S. operators acquiring 823 ships by 1950, when the authority to sell vessels to American citizens expired. Foreign owners bought over eleven hundred ships by 1948, when the act's authority to sell to aliens ended. The latter number replaced about half of the wartime shipping losses of the major foreign merchant fleets. By the time the last ships were sold abroad, the act's principal provisions had been met. The American merchant fleet had shed its excess wartime tonnage, and foreign fleets had acquired a nucleus of vessels to compensate for those they had lost during the war. The most remarkable consequence of these developments was the dramatic redistribution of the world's tonnage. In just two years, America's share dropped from 60 to 36.4 percent of the total. Great Britain completely made up for the shipping losses it had sustained during the war (although its share of the global fleet had decreased from 27 to 22 percent). The fleets of Norway, France, and Denmark were just 10 percent short of their prewar totals.[4]

In many respects, the Merchant Ship Sales Act actually worked too well. In the postwar years, American shipowners found themselves locked in a losing battle with foreign competitors—both private and state-owned—whose lower construction and operating costs allowed them to recapture their traditional markets, and placed their American counterparts at a distinct disadvantage.[5] American shipowners reacted to the revival of maritime competition by resorting to two traditional expedients. Some resorted to foreign registry. The flight to "flags of convenience" was nothing new, but the postwar years witnessed an unprecedented intensification of the phenomenon, fueled in part by Edward Stettinius's invention of Liberian registry. Between 1947 and 1963, approximately one thousand merchant ships of 1,000 or more gross tons were reported to have been constructed abroad for American shipowners operating under foreign registry. In addition, about seven hundred ships constructed in the United States were transferred to foreign registries by U.S. owners in the same period.[6]

What America's maritime labor leaders contemptuously referred to as the "runaway flag" problem received a particularly powerful stimulus in late 1949 and early 1950, when about fifty idle American-flagged tramp steamers were transferred to foreign registry to escape the fallout from the gradual decline in government contracts for war-relief and reconstruction shipments. In subsequent years, the Panamanian, Liberian, and Honduran registries (PanLibHon) proved among the principal—though by no means the only—beneficiaries of the "flight from the flag." Between 1950 and 1963, the deadweight tonnage under PanLibHon registry increased fourfold from 6.1 million to 24.2 million tons, representing a corresponding increase from 5.7 to 12.8 percent of its share of the active world fleet. Estimates placed the American ownership of the PanLibHon fleet at approximately 45 to 50 percent of its total tonnage by 1963.[7] In 1949 only fifteen ships totaling just 374,000 deadweight tons flew the Liberian flag.[8] Just over two decades later, the Liberian registry included 1,754 ships of 56,668,000 deadweight tons.[9]

A second strategy embraced by American shipowners was pursuit of U.S. government contracts. The post–World War II relief cargoes and shipments under the Marshall Plan filled many American holds in the late 1940s. The shipping requirements stimulated by the Korean War then increased private shipowners' reliance on government cargoes still further. The Agricultural Trade Development and Assistance Act of 1954—the Food for Peace Program—sent American agricultural surplus abroad in American ships, the so-called PL-480 cargoes. By 1962, government programs accounted for two-thirds of the total tonnage carried by ships in U.S.

registry. Meanwhile, the commercial business handled by American-flagged liners declined from 8.5 to 3.2 million tons a year between 1956 and 1962, and that carried by tramps plummeted from 2.1 to 0.2 million tons.[10]

The shipping industry's reliance on government business received a powerful stimulus from the government itself. The 1950s witnessed an expansion and elaboration of the preferential and protective provisions of Title IX of the Merchant Marine Act of 1936, which confirmed cargo-preference legislation passed in 1904 and 1934, favoring U.S.-flagged vessels in the carriage of government cargoes, especially those of a military nature.[11] In 1954 Congress enacted two pieces of legislation that strengthened Title IX even further. A coalition of shipowners and labor interests succeeded in persuading John M. Butler, the Republican chairman of the Senate Merchant Marine Subcommittee, to introduce legislation stipulating that all government shipments be carried exclusively in U.S. ships. The hostility of the Eisenhower administration to Butler's bill meant that in its final version the amendment would be significantly watered down. Still, the legislation proposed by Butler was passed in July and received Eisenhower's grudging presidential approval in late August of 1954. It took the form of two companion bills. Public Law 480, the Agricultural Trade Development and Assistance Act, facilitated the sales of agricultural surpluses, while Public Law 668, popularly known as the "Fifty-Fifty Act," amended Title IX by specifying that at least 50 percent of government cargoes—in this case the grain reserves slated to be shipped overseas—had to be transported in American ships.[12]

Congressional willingness to prop up an uncompetitive industry with preferences and subsidies may not have made much sense from the point of view of purely commercial considerations. But commercial utility was not the only influence on American maritime policy in the years after 1945. The crystalization of the cold war in the late 1940s reinforced the notion that national security alone could justify government support of the U.S. shipping industry, even if that industry lacked the ability to compete commercially in international trade.[13]

The salience of national security in U.S. maritime policy was manifest throughout the cold war. A 1945 study of shipping demobilization developed by the Harvard Business School for the U.S. Navy and the Maritime Commission set the tone. The study concluded that "the controlling factor in the determination of the characteristics of shipping and shipbuilding activities in the United States in peacetime as well as in wartime is the national security." While never codified in law, this affirmation of the conclusion reached by Hugo Black in his 1930 report and affirmed by Franklin Roosevelt was rising to the status of informed consensus by midcentury. Economic considerations remained subordinate to the extent that they had any impact at all.[14] Reinforcing this consensus was a 1961 study conducted by the Transportation Center at Northwestern University. It found "little net economic contribution to the United States by the subsidized liner firms or deriving from the subsidy program."[15]

These security concerns also gave rise to the National Defense Reserve Fleet (NDRF), composed of ships not sold by the act's 1951 expiration date of the Merchant Ship Sales Act of 1946. Though its size diminished over the years, the NDRF was repeatedly activated throughout the cold war, most notably during the Korean War (1950–1953), the crises in the Suez and Lebanon (1956–1958), the Cuban blockade (1962), and the Vietnam War (1965–1973). So too did national security spur government efforts to establish "Effective United States Control" (EUSC) over American-owned ships flying flags of necessity.[16]

Legislative assistance to the maritime industry of the kind undertaken in the 1940s and 1950s, even when cloaked with justifications of national security, was no substitute, however, for a comprehensive national maritime policy. At best, the legislation represented piecemeal interventions that failed to produce lasting solutions to the shipping industry's most pressing problems. Indications of a grim future for the American maritime sector continued to mount throughout the late 1950s and 1960s, suggesting the need for a thorough overhaul of maritime policy. Between 1950 and 1960, total world merchant tonnage grew from 85 million to 130 million gross tons, while the American-flagged share of the figure declined from 28 million (32.5 percent of the total) to 25 million (19 percent).[17] The majority of vessels serving in the U.S. merchant marine were veterans of the Second World War, approaching obsolescence by the early 1960s. A ship replacement program targeted about three hundred vessels operated by fifteen subsidized lines for a period of fifteen years. The results were disappointing. The subsidized operators contracted for only 182 new ships. Of this number, only 156 had been delivered by 1970, mostly obsolescent break-bulk vessels.[18]

The industry's problems were not confined to an aging fleet. The emergence of the Japanese, West German, and South Korean economies as viable shipbuilding and ship-operating competitors in the international marketplace coincided with American involvement in the Vietnam War, a conflict whose costs precluded additional capital investment in commercial tonnage. At the same time, in keeping with the historical precedents established during the world wars and the Korean War, Vietnam stimulated a significant expansion of the U.S. merchant marine. This growth temporarily masked the shipping industry's troubles, but also prompted serious anxiety among more perceptive observers about the effects on the U.S. merchant marine of the inevitable postwar contraction of shipping requirements.[19]

The search for a coherent national maritime policy began in earnest following a 1963 union boycott of grain shipments destined for the Soviet Union. Dismayed by the exemptions from the "Fifty-Fifty Act" granted by the Department of Commerce to a number of exporters, the Maritime Trades Department of the AFL-CIO ordered the picketing of offending grain ships. President Lyndon Johnson appointed a Marine Advisory Committee (MAC) that quickly shifted its focus from the immediate labor crisis to the need for a new maritime policy.

Composed of representatives of government, labor, management, and the public, the MAC split into two factions. The majority of the MAC membership endorsed the recommendations drafted by labor lawyer Theodore Kheel. Titled "Maritime Policy and Program of the United States," it suggested continuing the policy status quo: a combination of existing construction differential subsidies (CDSs), operating differential subsidies (ODSs), and cargo preference laws. In addition, it recommended requiring that all ship construction and repair take place in American shipyards. In contrast, a small faction of the MAC headed by Alan S. Boyd, the undersecretary of commerce for transportation, and Nicholas Johnson, the maritime administrator, voiced the position of the government. Their "Merchant Marine in National Defense and Trade: A Policy and a Program" (also known as the Boyd Report and the Interagency Task Force Report) proposed eliminating all cargo preference practices, allowing U.S. shipowners to build vessels in foreign shipyards, and permitting foreign-built ships in subsidized foreign trade. In the end, neither of the two reports spawned legislative action. The cautious character of the MAC report did not seem to impress the Johnson administration. The more radical proposals of the Boyd Report, on the other hand, especially those concerning foreign ship construction, threatened the established interests of the U.S. shipbuilding industry, American maritime labor, and the nonsubsidized shipping companies represented by the American Maritime Association (AMA). Incapable of generating the kind of broad support necessary to give it a fighting chance in Congress, the Boyd Report was never submitted for consideration by that body. As had often been true in American history, a comprehensive national maritime policy was blocked by the inability or unwillingness of the maritime industry to speak with one voice.

In 1967 Boyd, newly appointed as the first secretary of the new Department of Transportation, unveiled before the Senate Commerce Committee another set of proposals. Among the most important was a plan to transfer the Maritime Administration (MARAD) from the Department of Commerce to the Department of Transportation. Boyd also tried to placate the maritime industry by agreeing to retain cargo preferences, but remained adamant on allowing foreign construction, a centerpiece of his vision of maritime policy. His unrelenting attitude on the latter issue once again made it practically impossible for him to overcome the traditional opposition of shipbuilding, labor, and operator interests. Without their support, the Johnson administration did not dare to formally propose Boyd's still controversial recommendations to Congress. By the time Lyndon B. Johnson left office in 1969, national maritime policy had become a thicket into which politicians and bureaucrats ventured at considerable risk.

Still, the contenders for the presidency in 1968 felt obliged to stake out positions. At the nominating conventions that preceded the presidential race of that year, both political parties vowed to sponsor a vigorous ship replacement initiative.[20] It was, however, the Republican presidential candidate, Richard Nixon, who articulated the most intriguing maritime policy. He promised to adopt toward the maritime industry "remedial measures far more constructive than those of his predecessor."[21] This relatively modest goal masked Nixon's vision of a holistic national maritime philosophy that would fuse the American merchant marine's role as a vital pivot of national security with its increasingly dubious contribution to national prosperity. At the intersection of these two themes stood Nixon's avowed anticommunism. In his view, the Soviet Union was expanding its merchant marine in order to become a major maritime and naval power.[22]

Following his election, Nixon took concrete steps to fulfill his campaign pledge, directing his newly appointed maritime administrator, Andrew Gibson, to develop policy proposals reflecting his vision.[23] In May 1969 Gibson and his staff presented their recommendations to the key executive departments. The reception was cool. In contrast, Nixon himself, as well as ship-operating and shipbuilding industry groups, gave Gibson strong support. In spite of his own cabinet's opposition to Gibson's proposals, Nixon decided to send them to Congress. After the obligatory hearings, which lasted until the fall of 1970, the maritime program was passed by both the House and the Senate with only one dissenting voice in each. Nixon's campaign pledge had been fulfilled, or so it seemed.

At the heart of the Merchant Marine Act of 1970 was a program for a ship construction and replacement that would reverse the growing obsolescence of the American commercial fleet and create jobs in U.S. shipyards. The act authorized the construction of more than three hundred ships over a ten-year period beginning in 1971. Among the greatest beneficiaries of this initiative were the nonsubsidized carriers, who lacked capital to build high-cost ships in the United States and lacked the right to buy cheaper, foreign-built vessels. The 1970 act extended construction differential subsidies to these nonsubsidized carriers and to owners of additional ship types, including bulk carriers and tankers. In order to lower the construction subsidy closer to the 33.5 percent level specified by the Merchant Marine Act of 1936, the 1970 law specified a gradual reduction of the construction differential from the 50 percent that was often the norm by the late 1960s to just 35 percent by fiscal year 1976. Subsidies were to be paid directly to shipyards, instead of being channeled through shipowners. Once more the United States embarked upon an ambitious national program to reverse the decline of its ailing merchant marine.

The results were "mixed." Some companies, such as Waterman Steamship Corporation and Delta Line, used the program's provisions to fund pioneering work in LASH technology, which turned out to have a limited future in the United States. The Yom Kippur War of 1973 brought in its wake oil embargoes and a collapse of the shipbuilding of tankers. Continuing labor disputes over the loading of grain for shipment to the Soviet Union further curtailed American shipping operations. And continued jockeying for advantage among various factions of the maritime industry through the 1970s undermined the fleeting political consensus that Richard Nixon had briefly patched together. When Ronald Reagan took office in 1980, he was committed to reinvigorating the U.S. Navy, but he distrusted the system of subsidies keeping the American oceanic merchant marine afloat. Through the remainder of the twentieth century, he and his successors either suspended or limited funding of the operating and construction differential subsidies called for by the 1936 act. As Gibson concluded woefully about his failed efforts, "economically, U.S.-flag shipping was a marginal activity at best."[24]

44

HOT WARS
AND COLD

THE NORTH KOREAN INVASION OF SOUTH KOREA ON JUNE 25, 1950, challenged U.S. maritime resources in a most unexpected way. Within days, General Douglas MacArthur, the Supreme Commander for Allied Powers (SCAP) and commander of the U.S. Far East Command (FEC) flew Task Force Smith, a small artillery unit, into Korea to help the South Korean army resist the North Korean assault. The rest of the 24th Division followed by ship. Lacking combat experience and adequate arms and equipment, these forces fell back into a perimeter around Pusan, South Korea's largest port and the country's lifeline to MacArthur's meager resources in Japan. MacArthur's appointment on July 7 as commander in chief, United Nations Command, did not give him the troops, supplies, and ships he needed to push back the North Korean assault.[1] The army's Second Division was able to depart Fort Lewis, Washington, for Korea in late July and early August, followed by the Third Division in late August and early September.[2] Not until September, however, did ships from Hawaii and the United States bring the men and matériel MacArthur needed to secure the Pusan perimeter and to fashion a counteroffensive. His amphibious assault at the port of Inchon on September 15, 1950, halfway up the west coast of the Korean peninsula, turned the tide of the war.

This crisis in the early days of the Korean War reversed once again the canonical Mahanian notion that navies exist to protect oceanic commerce. In this emergency, oceanic shipping was needed to save the army. After September 1950 the Korean War turned into a seesaw stalemate that moved up and down the Korean peninsula before finally settling near the original border between North and South Korea. This unexpected, conventional war challenged the United States to revive some of the military-industrial infrastructure that had been demobilized following World War II and also to find the shipping necessary to carry men and matériel nearly five thousand miles from the West Coast to Pusan. Airlift had already demonstrated its power to help, both in the Berlin Crisis of 1948 and again in sending Task Force Smith into the maw of the North Korean invasion. But the vast majority of the troops and the 31.5 million tons of cargo that would eventually travel to Korea went by ship.

Those ships sailed under the direction of the navy's Military Sea Transportation Service (MSTS). Created in 1949 to provide ocean transport for all the military services, MSTS reflected the unification of the armed services in the new Department of Defense. When the war broke out, MSTS had 174 ships, with 115 more being transferred from the army between March and November of 1950.[3] These included fifty troop transports, forty-eight tankers, twenty-five cargo vessels, and fifty-one miscellaneous vessels, virtually all them of World War II vintage. To supplement this fleet, MSTS chartered eighty-seven U.S. commercial vessels and thirteen foreign commercial ships. It also began reconditioning and activating vessels from the National Defense Reserve Fleet, beginning immediately with a group of fifteen and adding more than a hundred additional vessels in the ensuing months. By the fall of 1950, MSTS commanded 404 ships, of which about 350 were oceanic vessels, virtually all of them committed to Far East Command. Early in 1951 the Maritime Commission, in conjunction with the navy, let contracts for construction of thirty-five new high-speed "Mariner" cargo vessels.

But by this time, the shipping crisis had passed. Almost 100,000 military personnel and 2 million tons of cargo had been shipped to FEC by the time of the Inchon landing,[4] most of it from San Francisco and Seattle. By 1952 Allied forces in Korea numbered around 700,000, about half UN and half South Korean. Of the UN forces, about 90 percent were American. Another 450,000 Korean and Allied personnel were also supported in whole or in part by American logistics.[5] Ammunition supplies remained a problem in Korea until late 1952, but that was a production, not a shipping, problem. In general, shipping had proved adequate to the crisis. It could not be mobilized as quickly as air transport in the first critical month of the war, but it made possible the dramatic reversal of fortune in September and it carried the great bulk of men and material that fought through the duration. In the thirty-seven months of the war, leading up to the armistice in July 1953, the United States shipped 31.5 million measurement tons to Korea, almost twice again as much as it shipped to General MacArthur's command in the southwest Pacific in the comparable period of World War II from August 1942 to August 1945.[6] Approximately 65 percent of that cargo was petroleum, oil, and lubricants (POL).[7] The transportation infrastructure in Korea posed a greater problem to the supply chain than American shipping did, and local longshoring labor created bottlenecks in the ports that could be alleviated only partially by the extensive use of CONEX boxes.

At the end of the war, however, it was possible to conclude that American shipping had been equal to the demands of a military crisis that came almost entirely without warning. Cargo did not pile up on the docks, as it had done in the summer of 1914, but then again this was not a world war. It was a police action, the first of a series of brushfire wars that would tax American military resourcefulness in the cold war and pose a new set of challenges for the shipping industry. Partly in response to the Korean experience, the MSTS system was reformed in 1954, not to enhance its capability, but to reduce it. The Cargo Preference Act of 1954, passed under pressure from the shipping industry, required that half of all military cargoes going overseas had to move on privately owned U.S.-flagged vessels. A related agreement actually cut the size of the MSTS fleet, even though these vessels, manned by civil service crews, operated more efficiently than the commercial vessels hired to replace them.[8]

The country appeared to agree that military sealift, like airlift, should be provided by a combination of core military assets supplemented in national emergency by commercial resources. The great question, which would loom over military transportation throughout the cold war and beyond, was how to balance those military and commercial assets. The core military fleets should be as small as possible, so as not to consume unnecessary funding in peacetime and not to compete unfairly with commercial operations, but they should also be sufficiently robust to respond immediately in an emergency and to have the special characteristics necessary for military missions. The proper balance would prove controversial and elusive.

When the next military crisis arose in 1965, MSTS concluded that it had the wrong ships and too few of them. It required special authorization to expand its fleet. The role of shipping in the Vietnam War paralleled in many ways the experience in Korea, with some important differences. The demand for shipping arose gradually, as the United States assumed a larger and larger supporting role, first for the French in the late 1940s and early 1950s and then, after the Geneva accords of 1954, for the newly created government of the Republic of Vietnam. By the time President Lyndon Johnson committed American ground forces in March 1965, patterns of supply were well established and infrastructure had been installed in Vietnam. But no one at the time imagined that the American commitment would swell to more than half a million men at the peak in 1969 and that the logistic tail behind this force would total 81 million measurement tons of cargo and 97 million long tons of fuel over the course of American involvement.[9] Nor was it clear in 1965 that Malcom McLean's nascent system of containerization would play a leading role in supplying the war effort while giving his financially strapped experiment some much-needed revenue.

As in Korea, the vast majority of cargo traveling to Vietnam from the United States moved by ship. Unlike Korea, most of the military personnel serving in country came and went by airplane. The United States had established a Civil Reserve Air Fleet (CRAF) in 1952. In return for annual payments, participating commercial airlines agreed to modify their aircraft to make them suitable for and available to the military in time of national need.[10] These assets complemented military cargo and passenger planes in the Vietnam War, carrying the bulk of U.S. personnel to and from the war zone and obviating the need to find passenger vessels for their transport. But this hardly diminished the demand on shipping, for the shrinking tooth-to-tail ratio of the American military in the late 1960s meant that servicemen in Vietnam would be supported with an unprecedented volume of matériel. Estimates of the ratio of fighters (teeth) to support personnel (tail) in Vietnam ranged from 1:3 to 1:10.[11] Whatever the number, American servicemen in Vietnam had at their disposal resources undreamed of by any other army in history, everything from swimming pools and air-conditioned clubs to personal sound systems and private refrigerators. And Americans consumed oil, ammunition, and equipment as fast they consumed beer and soda. In-country consumption of oil swelled from 2.7 million barrels in 1964 to 36.5 million in 1970.[12] From 1964 to 1973, the United States dropped more than 7.6 million tons of ordnance on North and South Vietnam, more than three times the munitions expended by the United States in all of World War II, more than fourteen times that employed in Korea.[13] By some calculations, Americans fired fifty thousand bullets for every enemy soldier they killed. This leant a whole new meaning to the term "bulk cargo." Only ships could deliver such mass the seven thousand miles from the West Coast of the United States to Vietnam. Though MSTS carried only about forty thousand allied and American personnel to Vietnam—3.4 million Americans served in the Southeast Asia Theater during the Vietnam War period—its 527 ships carried 99 percent of the ammunition and fuel and 95 percent of the other supplies and equipment.[14] The transformation of MSTS to the Military Sealift Command (MSC) in 1970 was a political and rhetorical gambit in the continuing turf struggle with commercial shippers, not a fundamental alteration of the service's function.[15]

Shipping in support of the Vietnam War appeared successful to all parties.[16] The shipping companies thrived on the extra business and appear not to have been greatly inconvenienced or taxed by the added demand on resources. The military services found sealift adequate for their needs, though they did identify areas in which support could be improved. Vietnam lacked adequate storage facilities for arriving cargo. Palletized loads could be discharged faster than they could be assimilated ashore. Too few lighters were available to unload anchored vessels. And port authority was confused.[17] Commercial vessels chartered to supplement MSTS and MSC resources were ill-equipped to handle heavy or outsized cargo, to operate in restricted waters, or to handle fuel.[18] And ships in the National Defense Reserve Fleet were obsolescent. The military recommended that the American merchant fleet be built up with modern vessels suited to military needs.[19] This was tantamount to a call for a maritime CRAF. The services also expressed an interest in pursuing containerization but showed an appreciation for the infrastructure issues involved; the container ports being developed around the world were not in the places that the U.S. military would likely deploy. There were no easy answers to making commercial shipping fit military needs. Both the Military Airlift Command and the MSC made major investments in the 1980s to build up their own assets and to strengthen the commercial resources they could call upon in time of emergency. In both cases, however, they were dealing with shrinking industries.[20]

The next large-scale American deployment of armed forces to make significant demands on shipping assets arose when Iraq invaded Kuwait in the summer of 1990. As far from American shores as Vietnam, the Tigris-Euphrates river valley posed important logistical challenges for the American military, most especially the need to transport the increasingly sophisticated equipment and support services required for armored warfare in the desert. As with the Vietnam War, the military had the luxury of building up forces slowly before the actual fighting began; Operation Desert Shield extended from August 7, 1990, five days after the Iraqi invasion of Kuwait, until Operation Desert Storm began on January 17, 1991. Furthermore, an even greater proportion of the required men and matériel could be airlifted to the region. By one account, 15 percent of all dry cargo and 501,000 passengers flew to the war zone, while 95 percent of all cargo and POL and 3,000 passengers went by sea.[21]

The Sealift Readiness Program, established in response to the Vietnam experience, provided the framework for mobilizing the necessary shipping. Companies bidding on Department of Defense (DOD) cargo had to agree to contract 50 percent of their fleets to the MSC in time of emergency, half of that within thirty days and the other half within sixty days. MSC could also requisition ships in the Effective United States Control Fleet, American-owned ships flying PanLibHon or Bahamian flags. The Ready Reserve Fleet (RRF), established in 1976, offered ninety-six ships maintained by the Maritime Administration and available in five to twenty days. Finally, the National Defense Reserve Fleet preserved two hundred to three hundred older ships requiring more time for activation. By August 20, 1990, MSC had committed all eight of its fast sealift ships (high-speed container vessels bought from Sea-Land in the early 1980s and converted to Ro/Ros)[22] and most of the twenty-three cargo ships it had predeployed around the world. Within seven more days DOD ordered forty ships activated from the RRF, the first time this resource had ever been called upon. Then MSC began chartering vessels, both American ships and foreign-flagged ships. By mid-January, when combat operations began in Operation Desert Storm, 70 of the 96 RRF vessels had been activated, and 199 ships, including 10 tankers, had been chartered. The government had also suggested that it might invoke the Sealift Readiness Program, though this never proved necessary.[23]

In 1972 Malcom McLean gambled on a new generation of container ships, the large, fast SL-7s, comparable in speed and size to SS *United States*. When the oil embargo of 1973 doomed the experiment, the ships ended up in the U.S. Navy, rebuilt as fast supply ships. Pictured is USS *Capella*, formerly SS *Sea-Land McLean*.

Because of the long lead time afforded by Desert Shield before combat operations began in January 1991, the military's lift requirements were met with only minimal disruptions of commercial shipping. Excess shipping capacity worldwide helped; the sealift used only about a hundred cargo vessels of the three thousand estimated to be available. Bunker fuel prices doubled in August and insurance rates rose, but neither development proved critical to the market as a whole. Tanker costs spiked in response to market forces unrelated to the war—a worldwide oversupply of crude oil had some charters using tankers for storage—but the supply of shipping was always adequate.[24] Of the 165 vessels chartered for the purpose, most came from foreign companies, usually at a high premium. The seventy-two vessels brought out of the RRF were old and slow and it proved difficult to find qualified crews to man them.[25] War-related shipments to the Middle East and a recession at home created a temporary container shortage in the United States, and some foreign crews refused to enter the war zone in the Persian Gulf, recalling, no doubt, the tanker wars of the Iran-Iraq War of the 1980s.[26]

One student of transportation policy called the sealift "military logistics at its best."[27] The chief of public affairs for the Army's Military Traffic Management Command said in March 1991 that "the whole thing has been so smooth it is almost as if there isn't a war going on."[28] For sealift, the war experience confirmed the impression of some observers that commercial backup of military shipping resources was growing less important over time, both because shipping was now more efficient and because air transportation was picking up a greater share of the burden.[29] But ships still carried 95 percent of the cargo for Desert Shield/Desert Storm, 86 percent of the dry cargo, and all POL. Commercial vessels from outside the MSC and reserve fleets had carried 47 percent of all dry cargo to Saudi Arabia. After the war, the military services looked for improvements that might be made in sealift, and there was even some political discussion of reform.[30] But the administrations of neither George H. W. Bush nor William Clinton sought any major policy changes.[31] Indeed the Gulf War appears to have confirmed the impression created by Korea and Vietnam. The system of a core fleet of military transports supplemented by commercial resources in time of emergency was adequate to meet the oceanic transportation needs of the U.S. military.

In 1996 sealift underwent another institutional transformation. Most of its functions were absorbed within the U.S. Transportation Command, one of the major unified commands into which the armed services divided following the landmark Goldwater-Nichols Department of Defense Reorganization Act of 1986. At one level, this change reflected the desire to overcome interservice rivalry and achieve truly unified operation of the armed services. At a more functional level, it represented the military face of intermodal transportation, a reflection of the increasingly seamless transition from air to sea to land transportation. It extended the general principles of containerization to all facets of cargo movement.

American military sealift was not seriously challenged again in the twentieth century.[32] Aside from the Arab-Israeli wars, the U.S.-Soviet confrontation in the cold war probably had as much impact on U.S. shipping as anything other than Korea, Vietnam, and the Gulf War. The Soviet Union made a concerted effort to build up a subsidized commercial fleet that could capture a share of the world shipping market and exploit the perceived weaknesses of U.S. oceanic shipping. As it happened, however, the Soviets were less successful in this venture than other countries such as China, South Korea, and Singapore that adopted similar industrial policies in support of their commercial fleets. When the Soviet Union collapsed in 1991, its challenge to American oceanic shipping disappeared, but by then the American oceanic merchant marine was a shadow of its former self.

45

TED ARISON AND THE FUN CRUISE FOR THOUSANDS

JUST AS MALCOM MCLEAN CAME TO SHIPPING FROM ANOTHER transport sector—trucking—so too did Ted Arison, entering from air transport. Born in Tel Aviv, Palestine, in 1924, Arison inherited a small shipping business, M. Disengoff, from his father but abandoned it in the early 1950s to move to the United States. After starting and losing two air cargo companies, he found himself "retired" in Miami in 1966 looking for a new venture. Briefly he ran two ferries as cruise ships, but the Israeli company that owned the ships went bankrupt and the Israeli government foreclosed on the vessels and returned them to Israel on the eve of the 1967 Arab-Israeli War. Then he learned that the Norwegian shipowner Knut Kloster had a new vessel, the *Sunward*, that was failing in European cruise/ferry trade. Arison offered to operate the ship in the Caribbean trade, guaranteeing Kloster a profit. The resulting Norwegian Caribbean Line prospered, adding three more ships by 1971 and launching the modern cruise industry in Florida.[1]

Falling out with his partner in 1972, Arison set out once again on his own. First he tried to purchase two retired Cunard vessels. Failing that, he turned to an old Israeli schoolmate, Meshulam Riklis. Now a successful and wealthy businessman, Riklis held the principal shares of Boston-based American International Travel Service (AITS), which ran tours in Europe and the Americas under the name Carnival. Using $1 million in assets appropriated during his withdrawal from the Norwegian Caribbean Line, Arison launched Carnival Cruise Lines as a subsidiary of AITS, which purchased a laid-up Canadian cruise ship and renamed it the *Mardi Gras*. On its maiden voyage for Arison in March 1972, the flagship of Carnival Lines ran hard aground at the end of Miami Beach. In spite of this ominous beginning, the line began to make money, promoting the *Mardi Gras* as the "fun ship," and targeting the middle class.[2] By 1975, Arison was able to buy the company from AITS and begin investing profits in new ships. He was on his way to building the largest cruise line in the world.

The American cruise industry had been around since the days of the *Morro Castle* and her sister ship the *Oriente*, when passenger ships carried middle- and upper-class Americans from ports like New York on recreational tours through the Caribbean.[3] At that time, cruising was a form of casual wandering, far less significant economically than other forms of passenger shipping. Scheduled ocean liners carried travelers between countries and continents, and ferries moved them about port cities and between waterside urban centers. For Americans, cruising represented a middle realm between the coastal shipping that ferried passenger traffic from city to city through the nineteenth and early twentieth centuries and the oceanic shipping that brought many of America's immigrants to the New World and carried the passengers who could afford ocean travel for business and pleasure. Cabotage guaranteed American ships a monopoly on the service moving from one American port to another, but passage between the United States and Caribbean destinations that were not American possessions were open to international traffic. The Cunard Line, for example, gave American companies fits by sending its liners into the Caribbean in the winter months, when the North Atlantic was uninviting.[4]

But cruising had a spotty history before Ted Arison. Discounting the ill-conceived 1867 voyage that Mark Twain recorded in *The Innocents Abroad*, commercial oceanic cruising really began with the 1891 voyage of Hamburg-Amerika's *Augusta Victoria*. This two-month tour of the Mediterranean, like the oceanic cruises that followed in the ensuing decades, was for "millionaires, or facsimiles thereof," as the historian John Malcolm Brinnin has put it. Only in the lean years of the Depression, when ships like the *Morro Castle* and the *Oriente* offered "short cruises by long ships," did cruising for the middle class attract a significant following. Interrupted by World War II, cruise shipping resumed in the 1960s in a very different economic environment. The introduction of jet airlines in the 1950s had spelled the beginning of the end for scheduled luxury liners on the North Atlantic and other formerly prosperous routes. For a brief period, liner companies such as Cunard began to see "the cruise as a stopgap—an employment of resources not to make money but to carry the overhead."[5] This was the losing business model that Ted Arison overturned with the "fun ship."

Aided by the popular television series *The Love Boat* (1977–1986), Arison began to shift the focus of cruising from the destination to the ship. "Getting there was at least half the fun."[6] The great North Atlantic liners had similarly stressed the opulence and comfort of their accommodations,

The passenger ship *Oriente*, pictured here on a pre–World War II postcard, served the American cruise industry in the 1930s, along with her sister ship, the ill-fated *Morro Castle*. The *Oriente* served as an army troopship, the *Thomas H. Barry*, in World War II and never returned to the cruise industry.

but first-class passage on such ships was beyond the means of most Americans. Arison sought to bring at least an aura of luxury and entertainment to the middle class. Working in his favor was the largest cruise port in the world, Miami, Florida; the most sought-after cruise destination, the Caribbean; and an American economy that was growing steadily in spite of the economic woes of the 1970s. The rest was marketing.

As the cruise industry blossomed in America in the last third of the twentieth century, two major trends shaped its development. Carnival led the way in both. Mergers consolidated the industry, much as they had done in many other fields such as aircraft manufacturing and operation. By the end of the twentieth century, three conglomerates dominated the world cruise industry: Carnival Lines, Princess Lines, and Royal Caribbean. Carnival, for example, used acquisition as a corporate strategy not only to dominate the Caribbean cruise industry but also to diversify its client base and market penetration. Expansion began in 1989 with Holland America Lines, complementing the mass-market appeal of the Carnival ships with Holland America's upscale vessels. Later Carnival added the Seabourn Line to tap the ultra-luxury market and Windstar for worldwide adventure/sail cruising. A string of six cruise-line acquisitions was capped by the Cunard Line in 1998.[7] Since the introduction of regular passenger jetliners across the Atlantic, the once proud Cunard had been experiencing declining revenues, fleet shrinkage, and serial ownership, just barely keeping its flagship *Queen Elizabeth II* in service by replacing her obsolete oil-fueled steam turbines with modern diesels in 1987. But with Carnival's ambitions and assets behind it, Cunard began planning the *Queen Mary II*, a megaliner that would "cruise" as well.[8]

The *Queen Mary II* illustrated the other major trend in the cruise industry in the last third of the twentieth century, the wholesale rush toward megaships. Just as tankers, bulk carriers, and container ships exploded in size in the 1980s and 1990s, so too did cruise ships turn into monster vessels of unprecedented size, expense, and efficiency. When Ted Arison launched Carnival Lines in 1972, he squeezed 950 passengers aboard the *Mardi Gras*, whose previous owner, Canadian Pacific Lines, had cruised with 650.[9] When the *Carnival Destiny* entered service in 1996 as the first 100,000-ton cruise ship, she carried 2,758 passengers with a maximum capacity of 3,360. Five megaships over 100,000 tons were in service by the end of the twentieth century, with thirteen more to follow in the first five years of the twenty-first century.[10] Economies of scale drove this race to gigantism, mostly the logic of propulsion. Fuel and labor were the two great operating expenses of cruise shipping.[11] A 100,000-ton vessel consumed little more fuel than a 50,000-ton vessel, but it could accommodate more than twice the passengers. Before 1990, few cruise ships exceeded 50,000 tons or carried more than a thousand passengers. By the end of the 1990s, new ships regularly exceeded 100,000 tons and carried up to three thousand passengers.[12] Furthermore, larger ships incorporated more bars, shops, and paid entertainments that could generate revenue beyond the fixed room and board that all passengers paid up front. Even labor could be stretched on the megaships, lowering the crew-to-passenger ratio by imposing long hours and assigning crews to multiple tasks.

While small ships—the American Canadian Caribbean Line called itself the "Small Cruise Line"—continued to serve niche markets and restricted seas, megaships dominated mass-market cruising in the Caribbean, the Mediterranean, the Baltic, and other premier venues, as well as the historic North Atlantic and other long-distance routes. The big three Caribbean lines and Star Cruises of Asia combined to control 90 percent of the industry's total passenger capacity.[13] This trend brought in its wake concentration and specialization similar to that bred by containerization. Some smaller ports with shallow or narrow waterways dropped out of contention. Ports that wanted to compete for this business made huge capital investments in infrastructure to serve the new vessels. And the cruise industry targeted ports like New Orleans that had the potential to attract and support passenger transfers.[14] The Walt Disney Company added a new dimension to the business model when it developed its own cruise line to partner with Disney World. Customers were offered package vacations that included days at Disney properties in Orlando, Florida, followed by transportation to Port Canaveral, where customers would board the *Disney Magic* or the *Disney Wonder* for a Caribbean tour.[15] Soon Carnival was developing its own version of the land-sea vacation.

Finally, it seemed, the American shipping industry had found a segment of the oceanic shipping business in which it could not only compete but thrive. The geography of the Caribbean, the world's most popular cruise destination, paired with the wealth of the United States, made the American cruise industry a world-beater. Americans cruised more than all the rest of the world combined. Symbolic of that dominance was Micky

When the Walt Disney Company decided to enter the megaship cruise business, it selected a slightly retro design, complete with red smokestacks reminiscent of the great North Atlantic liners. Like most of the high rollers in the cruise industry, Disney built and registered its ships abroad. *Disney Wonder*, pictured here in July 2006 flying the civil ensign of the Bahamas, was built in Europe and registered in the Bahamas.

Arison, who assumed leadership of Carnival Lines when his father, Ted, retired in 1990. Described in 1999 as "the most powerful influence in the cruise industry," Micky Arison then sat atop an empire of forty-three cruise ships that grossed more than $3 billion in 1998. *Forbes* magazine ranked him thirty-sixth on its list of wealthiest Americans. This was a pinnacle to rival those achieved by Elias Haskett Derby, Robert Fulton, Cornelius Vanderbilt, Robert Dollar, and other American shipping barons.

Beneath the surface, however, lurked the paradox and ambiguity that afflict all American maritime activity. First, Carnival was incorporated in Panama and its ships were flagged abroad, primarily in Panama and the Bahamas.[16] From 1986 to 1998, it paid only 1.4 percent in U.S. corporate taxes on $4.7 billion in gross profits. Second, Carnival itself, while still primarily a family-owned, American-directed company, went public in 1987, and Micky Arison sold off a significant chunk of his stock in 2003. The crews aboard Carnival ships were recruited overseas and paid well below American standards, as little as $1.50 an hour according to one source. The Arison family, father and son, were generous philanthropists, but they also contributed heavily to political candidates who would protect their business interests and countenance what critics saw as tax evasion. Arison père renounced his American citizenship when he retired and moved to Israel in 1990, reportedly to escape the estate tax that would otherwise have claimed a significant percentage of the billions he had earned in his shipping career in the Untied States.[17] In the globalized world of 2000, Carnival Lines was based in America and controlled by an American family, but it was far more international, far less American, than the shipping empires of previous American magnates. Little wonder that Representative Duncan Hunter (R-CA) asked his colleagues on the floor of Congress in 1999 how it was that Carnival Cruise Lines, home ported in the United States and carrying 90 percent American passengers, could earn $652 million in 1998 and pay no U.S. taxes.[18]

The largest fully American cruise shipping company carrying passengers on American-built ships with American crews was American Classic Voyages Company (AMCV). With only seven small ships in 2000, it was not in the same league with Carnival, Princess, and Caribbean.[19] Still, AMCV hoped to capitalize on the cruise craze sweeping America in the 1990s. Relying on a government subsidy and a thirty-year monopoly in Hawaii guaranteed by the U.S.-flagged Cruise Ship Pilot Project Statute of 1997, AMCV ordered two 1,900-passenger cruise ships from Litton Ingalls Shipbuilding in Pascagoula, Mississippi, intended for Hawaiian service. They were the first large cruise ships ordered from an American shipbuilder since SS *Brasil* and SS *Argentina* were built by Ingalls for Moore McCormack Lines in 1958. At a ceremony to cut the initial steel plates for the first vessel, John E. Graykowski, the acting administrator of the U.S. Maritime Administration (MARAD), invoked rhetoric that resonated with speeches going far back into the nineteenth century. "No government," he said, "no country which considers itself part of the world community as a trading nation can live and exist and hope to be part of that community without a shipbuilding industry and a maritime industry." Philip C. Calian, the chief executive officer of AMCV, went even further: "This is not just any passenger ship," he said. "This is America's passenger ship. This is not just any cruise line. This is America's cruise line. Finally, this is not just any shipyard. This is America's shipyard."[20]

Barely fifteen months later, however, in the wake of the terrorist attacks of September 11, 2001, AMCV declared bankruptcy; too many of its passengers had ceased flying from the mainland to the Hawaiian Islands for the cruises. Shortly thereafter it canceled both ships, citing lack of loan guarantees from MARAD.[21] One hull was 40 percent complete, the other 55 percent, and 90 percent of the production material had been committed to the joint project. The hulls were later sold to Norwegian Cruise Line (NCL)—formerly Norwegian Caribbean Line—and towed ignominiously and symbolically across the Atlantic to a German shipyard to be finished. Europe was then, and apparently would continue for some time to be, the center of cruise shipbuilding in the world. NCL—owned by Malaysia's Genting Group and operated from Hong Kong and Miami—would later register three ships in the United States and staff them with American crews, also for service in Hawaii, but all the ships had been built abroad.[22]

The inability of American ships and shipbuilding to penetrate the cruise industry did not, however, mean that the United States was without influence and market share. The dominance of American passengers and American ports meant that cruise ships that wanted to tap this market would have to pay port fees and comply with port regulations in Miami, Fort Lauderdale, Port Canaveral, New York, San Francisco, New Orleans, Seattle, and the other hubs of the American cruise industry. Ports could demand that ships meet minimum standards of safety and comply with local environmental regulations, thus imposing criteria that foreign flags might not otherwise observe. And the United States could exert legal jurisdiction over vessels that sailed from home ports in America, regardless of their national registry.

In this way, the United States could recoup some of the leverage that it was seen to have lost to the International Maritime Organization (IMO). This arm of the United Nations was nominally committed "to encourage the adoption of the highest practicable standards in matters concerning maritime safety, efficiency of navigation and prevention and control of maritime pollution from ships."[23] In practice, however, it was widely perceived as "a weak regulatory body, the poorest specialized agency within the United Nations."[24] Even the IMO's official literature notes that while the organization "has plenty of teeth some of them don't bite."[25] It was no secret that the United States imposed upon its own ships higher standards of pay, safety, work conditions, professional qualifications, and environmental practice than did many other nations. Countries such as Liberia and Panama had captured much of the world's registry in the twentieth century by offering low registration fees and low levels of enforcement. In the latter decades of the twentieth century, however, the IMO found itself under increasing pressure to police those states that operated loose registries; indeed, it found itself pulling world standards up to approach the American level.[26]

Nowhere was this more true than in the cruise industry. Of particular concern to the industry was the issue of safety aboard ships. The IMO administered the series of Safety of Life at Sea (SOLAS) conventions that had begun in response to the sinking of the *Titanic* in 1912. SOLAS 60 was the first of these conventions negotiated under the aegis of the United Nations Inter-Governmental Maritime Consultative Organization, predecessor of the IMO. The last formal agreement, SOLAS 74, concentrated on fire hazards, part of a continuing SOLAS pattern of reacting to past mishaps instead of trying to anticipate future dangers. Late in the twentieth century, the IMO's Maritime Safety Committee began cooperating with industry to explore the safety of large passenger ships, again concentrating on fire hazards.

In the escalating scale of maritime disasters, the loss of a huge ore carrier with a crew of two or three dozen would be a major blow to a shipping firm and its maritime insurer, but it would not likely attract great public attention. Nor would it necessarily damage the industry as a whole. Spilling of the ship's fuel might concern the public more than the ship itself. But a serious accident aboard a megaliner with thousands of passengers on board could send the cruise industry into a downward economic spiral. Even the outbreak of disease aboard cruise ships attracted significant press attention in the 1990s and raised alarms within the industry. The major cruise lines attended to such issues assiduously, as matters of enlightened self-interest, resulting in an admirable safety record in the last third of the twentieth century. Of course, accidents still happened. The 1987 sinking of the Ro/Ro–passenger ferry *Herald of Free Enterprise* in the North Sea off Zeebrugge, Belgium, which claimed 187 lives, brought criminal indictments of the captain and two crew members for unlawful killing and introduced the principle that even corporate leadership could face criminal charges for what one judge called a "disease of sloppiness" in operating the vessel.[27] On April 7, 1990, a relatively minor fire aboard the Bahamian-registered passenger/car ferry *Scandinavian Star*, sailing from Frederikshaven, Denmark, to Oslo, Norway, claimed 156 passengers and 2 crew, of the 483 people aboard.[28] The Baltic ferry *Estonia* sank in strong seas on September 28, 2004, killing 840 of the 1,049 passengers aboard.[29] Though large luxury ferries such as the *Estonia* were akin to cruise ships, no modern catastrophe to compare with the *Titanic* or the *Morro Castle*, or even the 1956 sinking of the Italian passenger liner *Andrea Doria* after its collision with the Swedish passenger liner *Stockholm* off Nantucket, afflicted the cruise industry in the last third of the twentieth century.

Barring a crisis of confidence in the safety of cruise ships, industry executives expected the cruise business to continue growing into the twenty-first century. Though Carnival backed out of an early agreement with Star Cruises, another line owned by the Genting Group of Malaysia, feeling that the Asian market was not yet ready, it looked to expand into growing venues, such as Europe.[30] From 1995 to 1999, Caribbean and Bahamian cruises combined fell from 51 percent of the world market to 41.5 percent while Europe grew from 14 percent to 20 percent.[31] Cruise industry executives spoke in terms of "market penetration" as they viewed future development. The cruise industry accounted for only 2 percent of American recreational and vacation spending, not much more for Europeans. The key to increasing that number, they felt, was marketing. The bigger, more efficient megaships offered increasing bargains even while they taxed the ability of ports and destinations to service them. As plans for even larger ships escalated at the end of the twentieth century, some observers began to wonder if the trajectory laid out by Ted Arison in the 1970s might not end with the ship itself becoming the destination. Perhaps ships would become so large and all-encompassing that they would stay in port and let passengers come and go like visitors to a theme park. To some skeptics, this reduced the cruise ship to a city and robbed it of its essential quality—the ability to sail the seas. But no one knew where the trends would climax.

CONCLUSION

LATE IN THE TWENTIETH CENTURY, OTHER AMERICANS, OUTSIDE the cruise industry, continued to seek business models that could flourish in the volatile marketplace of oceanic international shipping. For example, Malcom McLean, the father of containerization, came out of retirement in 1977 to try his hand again at cargo liner service. Gaining control of United States Lines (USL), once the "largest and most prestigious shipping company" in America, he gambled all on twelve huge vessels with which he planned to inaugurate round-the-world liner service. His "Jumbo Econships" were Panamax vessels (able to traverse the Panama Canal) of 57,800 deadweight tons, 950 feet long, carrying 4,380 containers of twenty-foot equivalent units.[1] Rejecting modern turbines for propulsion, McLean chose more economical diesel engines, believing that he would gain in efficiency what he sacrificed in speed. He guessed wrong, opting for economy when fuel costs were dropping, mirroring the mistake he made in the early 1970s when he ordered speedy SL-7s on the eve of the oil embargo. Unable to attract the 50 percent loading required to break even, the ships ran up annual losses that drove USL into bankruptcy in 1986. McLean lost a significant portion of his personal fortune in the failure. Nevertheless, in 1991 he launched one last maritime venture, introducing "Trailer Bridge" short-sea service to Puerto Rico, a variation on his initial containerization scheme. At the end of the twentieth century, Trailer Bridge was still providing integrated trucking and shipping services between the United States and Puerto Rico, though it paled beside the heights to which Sea-Land had risen in its prime. Not even a genius such as Malcom McLean could reprise his greatest success in the volatile marketplace of oceanic shipping.[2]

Raphael Recanati had a better plan, more like Ted Arison's than McLean's. Born in Greece of Italian and Spanish extraction, Recanati inherited his father's Israeli banking business, from which he funded his shipping ventures. In 1969, he founded Overseas Shipholding Group (OSG) in the United States to compete in the tanker and bulk cargo markets. Realizing that many oil companies wanted to divest their own fleets of tankers, he took OSG public, raising money to build new tankers, which he leased to the oil companies. Then he guessed correctly that the opening of the Alaska oil fields would create a market for American tankers sailing under cabotage protection. So OSG built and registered American ships for protected trade carrying oil from Alaska to other American ports. By careful management of its growing fleet and agile anticipation of market fluctuations, OSG grew steadily through the last quarter of the twentieth century. By the year 2000, it operated a fleet of fifty ships—tankers, supertankers, bulk carriers, product carriers, and even a car carrier—reporting revenues in excess of $467 million on assets approaching $2 billion.[3]

Like Ted Arison, however, Raphael Recanati turned his attention increasingly to a financial empire in Israel, where the Recanati family shared control of the country's largest capital group, built around a controlling interest in the Israel Discount Bank. From that vantage point he was able to arbitrate the competition for Celebrity Cruise Lines, when Carnival and Royal Caribbean both sought to purchase the line in 1997. With OSG controlling 50 percent of Celebrity, Recanati tipped the scales toward Royal Caribbean, which was controlled by the Ofer brothers, the second largest capital group in Israel. The loser in the deal was Arison, who still owned 47 percent of Carnival and headed the fifth largest capital group in Israel. Raphael Recanati oversaw this financial empire in Israel in spite of his expulsion from the Israel Discount Bank and his conviction on multiple felony counts surrounding the collapse of the bank in 1983.[4] These problems did, however, divide the Recanati family and diminish their role in OSG. In a pattern that repeated itself around the world, historic shipping families were disappearing from the maritime scene, to be replaced by corporate ownership, often with little shipping heritage.[5] OSG continued to thrive, in part by embracing the trend toward foreign registry that had so depleted the U.S. merchant marine. In 2001 the company reduced its New York staff by 62 percent and moved its administrative functions and technical management to Newcastle, England.[6] In hardly more than three decades, this shipping company had gone from a small American start-up to a powerful international conglomerate, whose ownership, management, focus, and fleet were increasingly international.

Not all American shipping firms found themselves in the same web of corporate, transnational ownership and operation as OSG and Carnival. Crowley Maritime Corporation, for example, built a strong, diversified shipping business on a solid base of domestic business. Begun in 1892 as a San Francisco tug and barge operation, Crowley expanded first into the Alaska trade, and then Puerto Rico, both protected by cabotage. In 1986 it initiated service to Central and South America, competing successfully in the international market. The business model included family ownership and operation, modern technology, and nimble adaptation to shifting markets.[7] Matson Line of Hawaii perfected a different model to sustain a near monopoly of California-Hawaii shipping through most of the twentieth century, introducing new technologies such as containerization and Ro/Ro vessels and fighting off attempts by other companies to break into the trade.[8]

But a handful of exceptions could not alter the general pattern of American shipping in the late twentieth century. The successful companies in international trade built, registered, and staffed their ships abroad. Even the Walt Disney Company, an iconic American film, built its cruise ships in Europe and registered them in the Bahamas. Targeted legislation might allow Norwegian Cruise Line to place foreign-built ships in the Hawaiian trade, or provide exemptions to allow American-owned but foreign-registered vessels to carry oil from Alaska, but not even the concerted effort by President Nixon to develop a national policy in support of an American merchant marine could stem the tide. No U.S. policy after World War II could do for the American maritime industry what countries like Japan, Korea, Taiwan, and China did for their shipbuilding and operating industries.[9]

Nor was the decline of the merchant marine peculiar to the United States. Around the world, traditional maritime states lost ships and jobs to developing and newly industrialized states.[10] Even proud Britain watched its once paramount commercial fleet slide into foreign registry. In 2004 the United States ranked sixth on the list of countries owning vessels, behind Greece, Japan, Germany, China, and Norway; the United States had 931 self-propelled oceangoing vessels over 1,000 gross tons (3 percent of the world's fleet) and 39,574,000 deadweight tons (5 percent of the world total). And this happened while the nation was the world's largest importer and exporter in dollar volume, generating 15.7 percent of the world's trade in 2000.[11] At the same time Britain ranked ninth, owning only 2 percent of the world fleet, just 1.5 percent of the deadweight tonnage.[12] Registry was worse. In 2004 the United States ranked twelfth, registering just 1.4 percent of the world's self-propelled oceangoing vessels over 1,000 gross tons and just 1.5 percent of the tonnage.[13] Britain ranked sixteenth, with 0.8 percent and 0.6 percent respectively. The registry list was topped by Panama, Liberia, Greece, the Bahamas, Hong Kong, and Malta, an island one-tenth the size of Rhode Island. While the U.S.-flagged merchant fleet had peaked after each world war—27 percent of the world fleet in 1920 and 36 percent in 1948—it accounted for just 2 percent of the world fleet in 2000. In fact, the U.S. merchant fleet in 2000 was physically smaller than its fleet in 1920.[14] The dominant countries were those of open registry, like Panama and Liberia, which the United States had helped to create.

Regardless of where the world's ships were registered, however, they participated in the globalization that spurred world trade in the last third of the twentieth century. While the world's economy grew by 648 percent between 1950 and 2000, world exports grew by 1,968 percent from 1950 to 1998.[15] As the second half of the century wore on, an increasing percentage of that trade was in services, a decreasing amount in goods, so that by 2002, 68 percent of the world's gross domestic product came from services: transportation, entertainment, consulting, management, lodging, dining. Only 28 percent came from industry and a paltry 4 percent from agriculture, the sectors of the economy that hire shipping.[16] The distribution in the United States was even more stark, with 80 percent of the economy in services by 1999.[17]

Globalization in the last third of the twentieth century sparked an outpouring of interpretive literature. Most students of the topic fall into one of two camps: those who attribute this globalization to technology, and those who attribute it to politics or policy. In the former category are

those who credit efficiencies in transportation and communication, interpretations that verge on technological determinism.[18] Critics of this
approach note that the world economy was less integrated in 1950 than
it was in 1913, in spite of the fact that the intervening years witnessed significant improvements in the efficiency of transportation and communication. Analysts in the latter category identify at least four factors that
contributed to increased integration: (1) intra-trade of manufactured
goods between states that produce similar products (e.g., Japanese driving
BMWs and Germans driving Toyotas); (2) slice-up of the value chain, or
distribution of manufacturing roles among widespread producers of component parts (e.g., automobile parts and subassemblies produced in different countries and brought together for final construction of the end
product); (3) supertrader countries such as Singapore and Hong Kong
that add services in this value chain without producing final products
themselves; and (4) manufacturing by low-wage countries (e.g., China)
for export to high-wage countries. When these phenomena are combined
with lowered barriers to trade brought about by a decline in protectionism and the rise of regional trade communities such as the European
Economic Community (EEC) and the North American Free Trade Agreement (NAFTA), the result is an acceleration of trade unlike any seen since
the Pax Britannica of the nineteenth century.[19] Many observers see this
wave of globalization as a consequence of the Pax Americana following
World War II.[20]

Other observers find more complicated forces at work. For example,
Shashi Kumar and Jan Hoffmann argue that globalization is built on four
cornerstones: transportation, telecommunications, trade liberalization,
and international standardization. Shipping carries two-thirds of world
trade by weight, but air transport takes a larger share of high-value cargo.
In an empirical study of seven Latin American nations in 2000, for example, they find that for six of the countries 92 percent of the trade moved
by ship, just 0.4 percent by air; but in dollar value, the same trade was
68.4 percent by ship and 16.7 percent by air. Mexico, because of its overland trade with the United States, evinced an entirely different pattern.
Almost 82 percent of its international trade by weight moved by land,
while only 18.3 percent moved by water and 0.1 percent by air. Not surprisingly, the dollar value of Mexican waterborne commerce accounted
for 15.6 percent of the total, with 76.2 percent going by land; the rest was
taken up by air traffic, which accounted for 8.1 percent of the total. As

with U.S. trade, and world trade in general, dollar value follows the airplane and the container; in Mexico truck traffic in containers outweighs and outvalues all other forms of transport.[21]

Still, at the end of the twentieth century, world trade in manufactured and unprocessed goods was growing faster than world gross domestic product (GDP), as was demand for shipping.[22] Within this realm, market demand and evolving ship technology dramatically changed the face of world shipping. The relative size of the world tanker fleet actually declined in the last quarter of the twentieth century, from 44 percent of the world fleet in 1977 to 28 percent in 1999. Meanwhile, dry bulk carriers increased their percentage of the world fleet from 26 percent to 29 percent, and other vessels, including container ships, moved from 30 percent to 42 percent of fleet size.[23] Thus, while tankers carried 61 percent of the world's oceanic ton-miles in 1970, they carried only 45 percent in 2000. This was still the largest single commodity to move across the world's oceans, but its relative dominance declined in the closing decades of the twentieth century. Meanwhile iron ore, coal, grain, bauxite, alumina, and phosphate accounted for 19 percent of ton-miles in 1970; they moved up to 29 percent in 2000. And other dry cargoes moved from 20 percent in 1970 to 26 percent in 2000.[24] Efficiencies in all these realms brought freight payments down to 5.39 percent of total import value in 1999, an even smaller percent of retail value of those commodities. These increased shipping efficiencies contributed to a general integration of the world's economy. Real merchandise trade expanded at an annual rate of 6.1 percent from 1948 to 2000. In the same period, the value of world merchandise exports grew from $58 billion to $6.19 trillion, more than two orders of magnitude.[25] These were measures of globalization that could be directly attributed to shipping efficiencies.

The growth of tankers and bulk carriers into megaships changed not only the scale and economics of shipping but also its patterns. New port facilities emerged, sometimes in the shadow of the old ports they supplanted, sometimes in entirely new locations. Many bulk carriers required specialized loading equipment dockside; some carried their own equipment. Container vessels called forth ever larger and more efficient cranes, towering dockside instruments that might work round the clock to offload and load thousands of containers a day. Tankers, with similar operational imperatives, had their own unique requirements for loading and unloading. At some ports, they did not go to shore at all, but tied up at huge pumping stations erected on artificial platforms offshore. The capital costs of these megaships drove their operational costs to tens of thousands of dollars a day; by 2004 VLCCs shipping oil charged $86,000 a day.[26] Amortizing those costs meant the ships had to be working at sea to survive.

In the 1980s these megaships started to exceed the handling capability of not only ports and harbors but also historic international waterways. The Suez Canal could not take ships with drafts greater than fifty feet, and the locks of the Panama Canal limited ships to 1,050 feet in length and 110 feet in width. Perhaps most ironically, the St. Lawrence Seaway entered service and passed into obsolescence in a single generation. Built jointly by Canada and the United States in the 1950s, the connection between the Great Lakes and the North Atlantic achieved a long ambition of the Canadians and a cold war imperative for the Americans. But by the end of the century, traffic on the seaway was in decline, driven in large measure by its inability to accommodate the new megaships. The enormous cost of enlarging the locks, combined with the end of the cold war, diminished the prospects that the waterway would ever accommodate the megaships. Such vessels ply the Great Lakes, but they are landlocked.

Globalization and the gigantization of shipping had a very complicated impact on the United States. Just as the world economy became more integrated in the second half of the twentieth century, so too did the U.S. economy integrate in the world economy. Beginning in 1994, international shipping tonnage to and from the United States surpassed domestic shipping tonnage.[27] This marked the first time since 1820—not counting the world wars—when the United States exchanged waterborne trade with the rest of the world more than it did with itself. And once the tipping point was reached, the gap between international and domestic shipping continued to widen during the remaining years of the twentieth century.

This sea change did not arise from a decline in domestic shipping. Rather, domestic shipping in the second half of the twentieth century grew at a slower pace than international shipping. Different sectors of the domestic market fared differently. Shipping on the Great Lakes leveled off late in the twentieth century, in part because of the increase in size of oceanic vessels, which precluded them from using the St. Lawrence Seaway.[28] The Mississippi River remained the backbone of American domestic shipping, sending and receiving grains, fuel, cement, chemicals, stone, scrap metal, steel products, rice, vegetable oils, wood chips, and sundry other products through New Orleans to and from ports all over the world.[29] On the Mississippi and elsewhere, increasing loads of domestic traffic were carried on barges, pulled or pushed by tugs. Coastwise and intercoastal trade migrated to cheaper and faster trains and trucks, lowering the demand for new vessels, even though shipbuilding yards serving the rivers and inland waterways remained strong. The completion of building programs for the navy's prepositioned vessels and Ready Reserve Fleet vessels further depressed the shipbuilding industry, leaving it largely dependent on fleet replacement orders.[30]

But the shifting balance between American domestic and international shipping had more to do with globalization than with the decelerating growth of brown-water shipping. The American consumer economy demanded more oil than its continental resources and even the Alaskan oil fields could supply. Petroleum and petroleum products accounted for 38.9 percent of American waterborne foreign commerce in 1988 and 51 percent in 2000, even though world trade in oil leveled off late in the twentieth century.[31] Oil also accounted for much, if not all, of the tonnage passing through America's leading international ports; seven of the ten busiest ports in tonnage were on the Gulf Coast, where most oil enters the country.[32] From there it spread through pipelines to the East Coast and up the Mississippi River to the American heartland. Container ships shaped the other great American ports. The three largest non-oil ports among the world's top ten—Los Angeles, Long Beach, and New York (including Elizabeth, New Jersey)—became the major American termini for containers on the Atlantic and Pacific Oceans, collectively passing through 8.6 million containers in the year 2000.[33] Though Japan remained the major shipping partner of the United States in dollar value and weight of cargo, China became the major container shipping partner. While China's exceptional economic growth at the end of the twentieth century removed it from the ranks of the developing countries, it nonetheless represented a larger pattern of world trade: developing countries were doing more of the world's manufacturing, gaining market share from cheap labor and the absence of labor regulation, environmental protection, product liability, and consumer protection. And more and more of those manufactured goods traveled by container, accounting for 38.4 percent of the dollar value of American imports by the end of the twentieth century even though containers still represented only 7.1

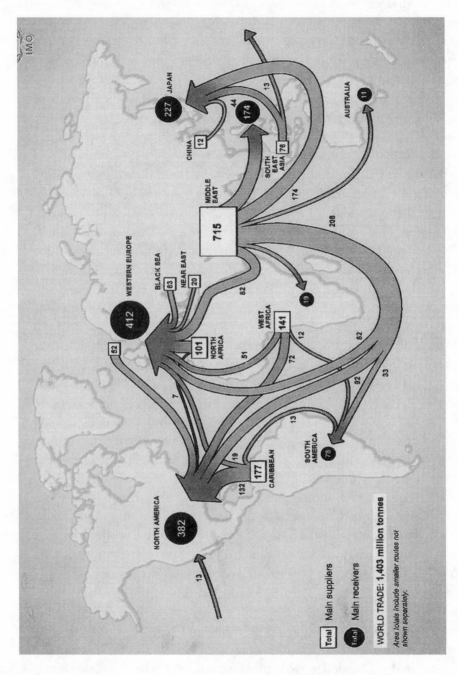

Crude oil seaborne trade, 1994. Most oil enters the United States through the Gulf of Mexico, whence it is transferred by ship and pipeline around the country. Only a small percentage comes into the West Coast.

percent by weight of American imports. The relative revival of American international shipping in the late twentieth century depended more on imports than exports. Perhaps the most telling icon of America's alarming balance of trade in the late twentieth century was the accumulation of empty containers in American ports.[34] Americans no longer exported manufactured goods to balance the riot of consumer goods the nation imported from abroad.

Still, globalization had less impact on the United States than it did on the world at large. America was *more* integrated in the world economy in the last decade of the twentieth century than it had been in 170 years, but it was still *less* integrated than the world at large. While U.S. exports as a percentage of GDP were 5 percent in 1950 and 8 percent in 1992, world exports as a percentage of world GDP were 11 percent in 1950 and 13 percent in 1992. In 1990, six countries had exports exceeding 50 percent of GDP; Singapore's exports totaled 174 percent of GDP and Hong Kong's 144 percent.[35] In imports, the United States was certainly closer to the world average, but it still traded with the world at a lower rate than the rest of the world traded with itself. While the U.S. GDP was 27 percent of world GDP in 1950 and 20 percent in 1992, its exports in those years were only 10 percent and 12 percent of world exports respectively.[36] Indeed, the United States in the middle of the 1990s still had the lowest share of world trade of any advanced nation; surprisingly, Japan had the second lowest share.[37]

The United States had even less of a relative impact on world shipping, and vice versa. While the world economy in 2000 was based on 68 percent services and only 32 percent materials that could be shipped, the U.S. economy was 75 percent services, 23 percent industrial, and only 2 percent agriculture.[38] Furthermore, America's leading trade partner was Canada, and most of that material trade moved overland, not by ship. Mexico was America's fifth leading trading partner in 1970 and third in 1980. (Japan was second in both years.) In 2000, 76.2 percent of Mexico's foreign trade traveled by land (principally with the United States), only 15.6 percent by water.[39] And, as had been true throughout most of the nineteenth and twentieth centuries, in 2000 the United States still traded primarily with itself, and most of that trade moved by truck. As Paul Krugman notes for the world at large, "although it has become easier and cheaper to trade whatever can be traded, a declining share of the economy consists of tradable goods and services."[40]

So shipping at the end of the twentieth century continued a trajectory that had been manifest throughout American history. In the colonial period and into the new republic, shipping carried people, news, and cargo more quickly and more efficiently over long distances than any other means of transportation or communication. The steamboat and the clipper ship were revealing icons of American innovation and preeminence. Beginning around 1820, when domestic shipping superseded oceanic shipping for the first time, the role of the ship in American history, as in world history generally, began to change. Trains started to draw news, passengers, and some high-value cargo from domestic shipping. For a while, oceanic shipping was immune to this trend; the age of the great liners would emerge and flourish until the arrival of the commercial jet airplane at the middle of the twentieth century. Within little more than fifty years, this new means of transportation would doom the great passenger liners and start taking market share from cargo carriage as well. In the 1840s the telegraph began the electromagnetic transmission of information, though the mail would continue to travel overseas by ship until airmail gained purchase in the twentieth century. Also in the twentieth century, trucks began to compete with trains and ships in the carriage of high-value cargo, further diminishing the realm of shipping. Throughout the last two centuries, the way of the ship has been steadily narrowing to a concentration on bulk cargoes: containers, liquids, loose solids, and finally cruise passengers.

The transformation of shipping in the second half of the twentieth century only accelerated these patterns. The rise of gigantism increased the relative advantage of the ship over all other means of transporting bulk cargoes. Ships carried those cargoes more efficiently, more cheaply, and more safely than ever before, contributing their share to the global integration of world markets so manifest at the end of the twentieth century. It is simply an irony that megaships performing these services are increasingly invisible to the American population. Only those Americans vacationing on the giant cruise ships are likely to see the tankers, container ships, and other leviathans of the sea that import and export the material base of America's unprecedented economy.

In spite of its invisibility, shipping remains an essential aspect of American life, just as America remains the most influential force in world

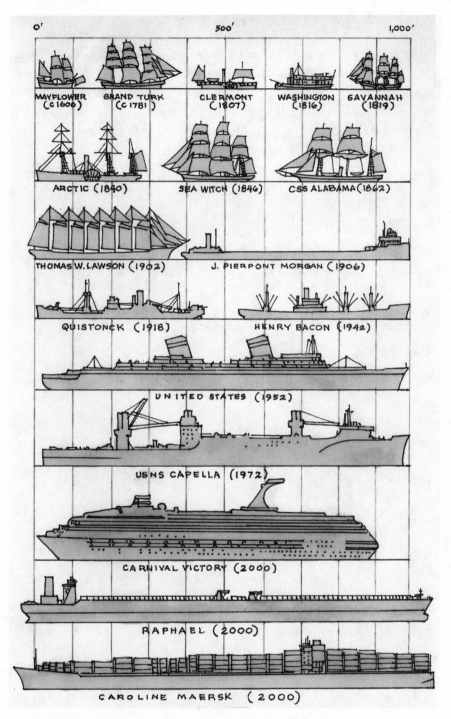

The historic ships on the first two lines served American maritime interests through the colonial era and the nineteenth century. All the rest are twentieth-century vessels, megaships that represent the trend toward gigantism and bulk carriage.

shipping. As Kumar and Hoffmann have put it, "today most carriers earn their income transporting other countries' trade, and the trade of most countries is largely moved by foreign companies."[41] As the world's largest trader, the United States is thoroughly integrated in that system, just as shipping is thoroughly integrated in the American economy.

EPILOGUE

ON THE SURFACE, THIS BOOK APPEARS TO HAVE REPLACED ONE story of decline with another. The canonical account of American maritime history describes the rise and fall of the American merchant marine, usually pivoting on the Civil War. By taking a global perspective and adding domestic shipping, this study has revealed that shipping contributed steadily to American history, from the first days of the colonial period to the end of the twentieth century. The contribution became less apparent in the nineteenth and twentieth centuries, but it was nonetheless real. In the new version of American maritime history, this post–Civil War decline arises not from the diminished size of the merchant marine but from the shrunken realm of shipping. Shipping used to carry news, people, and cargo. Americans lived near the sea and depended upon it. Over the course of the nineteenth and twentieth centuries, however, news moved to electromagnetic means of travel; people and high-value cargo moved to trains, motor vehicles, and airplanes. Shipping was left with bulk cargo, and even some of that moved by alternate means, such as pipelines. At the end of the twentieth century, shipping remained critical to the American economy and way of life, but its realm of activity was greatly reduced and still shrinking. Its visibility was a shadow of the golden age when clippers raced between New York and San Francisco.

This broad characterization is true, but simplistic. Beneath the surface, the continuing impact of shipping on American life, and the trajectory of shipping in the future, are much more complicated. In at least nine areas, the influence of shipping on American history now appears at once stronger and more vulnerable than it does when viewed from a distance.

The United States functions in an increasingly globalized world, which is unimaginable without modern shipping. Whatever definition of globalization one adopts, and however many waves of globalization the world may have experienced before the end of the twentieth century, the phenomenon in which the world then found itself depended in large part on a greatly expanded trade in material cargo—both bulk materials such as oil and grain, and "merchandise" or manufactured goods. Ships still carry most of that cargo in international trade, both in weight and value. Air and land transport are growing faster than shipping, and they may soon carry more of the dollar value of international trade than shipping does. They will not, however, in any foreseeable future, carry more of the bulk.

Furthermore, the fastest-growing segment of the shipping industry is containerization, which also dominates the high-value cargoes. Here too the story is decidedly mixed. Sixty percent of the value of oceanborne trade now comes and goes from the United States in containers. On the other hand, more containers enter and leave the country every year by truck to and from Mexico than arrive or depart by ship. In this realm of transportation, the historical pattern of American shipping seems to hold. As the value of cargo increases, market forces tend to push it toward ever faster means of transportation. It remains to be seen where the tipping point will be reached with containers. They themselves are too heavy for most commercial airplanes, but the United States and other developed countries increasingly use trains and trucks where ships might do the job more efficiently though more slowly.

Of course, the global economy is a service economy. At the end of the twentieth century, two-thirds of the world economy was services, as was anywhere from three-quarters to four-fifths of the American economy. Services contribute far less to international trade than goods, but globalization would not work without material trade. Indeed, one of the great transformations wrought by shipping in the late twentieth century was the transfer of manufacturing from the developed to the developing world. As transportation costs fell, goods manufactured in remote parts of the world far from the largest markets could compete. This was a two-edged sword for the United States. One the one hand it diminished the gap between the haves and have-nots of the world. On the other hand, it promoted the migration of American manufacturing jobs offshore.

A second development challenging the past record of shipping in American history is the growth of all world trade. At many times in history, as at the end of the twentieth century, world trade was growing faster than the world economy, as measured by world GDP. Such patterns, of course, cannot last indefinitely, but they happen. Less common was the fact that U.S. international trade was growing faster than the U.S. economy. Throughout most of American history, the economy grew faster than overseas trade. Americans simply traded more often with themselves than with others. But slowly across the twentieth century, the pattern reversed. U.S. exports rose from 2 percent of GDP in 1820 to 3 percent in 1929 to 8 percent in 1992.[1] The value of both imports and exports rose from 18 percent of GDP in 1975 to 30 percent in 1999.[2] The downside to this dramatic reversal of historical patterns is that the United States also became a net importer in the late twentieth century, after being a net exporter for most of its history. Its favorable balance of trade in services partially offsets the trade imbalance in material goods, but it remains to be seen how long the United States can continue to send its wealth overseas. But for as long as those Chinese consumer goods keep crossing the Pacific Ocean to fill the shelves at Wal-Mart, shipping will be a mainstay of the American economy.

A third variable at work on American shipping is the size of the American commercial fleet. It is often noted that only 2.6 percent of the commerce moving to and from the United States by sea travels on American ships. This is really an argument about the American merchant marine, more than it is about shipping in general. But even then, it masks more than it reveals. As this book has attempted to show, the American domestic fleet, protected by cabotage, continues to flourish in American waters. Its growth has been slowed by competition from planes, trains, and motor vehicles, but it has grown nonetheless. When the oceanic and domestic fleets are combined, the United States ranks twelfth in the world in total tonnage. Perhaps this is less than the world's leading economy should deploy, but it is part of a much larger story to which the United States contributed seminally. Most of the world's large ships are registered under flags of convenience. A handful of states flag a majority of the world's shipping tonnage; Panama, Liberia, Greece, and the

Bahamas accounted for half in 2004.[3] America set up two of those registries—Panama and Liberia—and contributed significantly to a third, the Marshall Islands. Furthermore, the flight of American ships to these flags of convenience mirrors the experience of Britain and other developed states that saw their flagged fleets shrink in the last decades of the twentieth century. Opinions vary on the significance of the phenomenon. It is estimated that American investors "own" three times as many ships in total as are actually registered in the country. In fact, in 2005 the United States ranked fifth in the world in owned tonnage, with a fleet of 739 vessels of 43.6 million deadweight tons.[4] The U.S. Maritime Administration keeps track of those vessels, identifying all that are subject to U.S. control in time of need, the so-called Effective United States Control (EUSC) vessels.

Fourth, what used to be called the flight from the flag, the movement of American ships to foreign flags of convenience, may be seen not so much as a peculiarly American loss traceable to the Civil War, but rather an international dimension of globalization. In patterns that Adam Smith would have welcomed, maritime services have spread around the globe in an economic diaspora leading from the "traditionally developed maritime countries" (TDMCs) to developing countries in Asia, Africa, and Latin America. The building of megaships is concentrated in Japan, Korea, and other Asian states. More seamen come from the Philippines than any other country. The dominant registries are in Liberia, Panama, Greece, and so on. Seven of the world's largest container ports are in Asia. The only major niches dominated by the developed nations is cruise ship building, which is concentrated in Europe, and cruise ship sailing, which is concentrated in the United States. These shipping activities have not only brought wealth directly to the developing nations that promote (and often subsidize) them, they have also spawned manufacturing in those countries with ready access to this shipping. Containers allow modest production facilities with access to intermodal transportation to compete globally for markets.

A fifth reason to believe that shipping will remain an important part of America's future is the sheer volume of U.S. trade. Though the United States still trades at a lower rate than the rest of the world, it nonetheless imports and exports more goods than any other country. Because it has the world's largest economy by far, it has the highest volume of trade. And since 1994, the United States has been shipping more cargo to the rest of the world than it ships to itself. That volume of trade means that most nations want access to U.S. imports and exports, giving the United States enormous leverage through its port system to set international standards for the shipping industry.

Sixth, the steadily increasing efficiency of the megaships continues to lower barriers to trade, independent of international diplomacy and politics. These ships achieve their efficiencies in three ways. As tankers, bulk carriers, container ships, and even cruise ships grow ever larger, they experience economies of scale that lower the cost of moving goods and people. As technology improves aboard ships, fewer crew members per ton of cargo (or hundreds of passengers) are required to operate the ships safely and efficiently. This is especially important to American ship operators, whose labor costs per capita are so high. Finally, improved technologies aboard ship—engines, hull design, navigation, auxiliary systems, maneuvering aids, and so on—bring operating costs still lower. All of these factors drive up the capital costs of new ships and accelerate the obsolescence of existing ships, but it is not clear that the upper limits of any of these trends has been reached.

Seventh, short-sea shipping—the kind of coastal and riverine shipping that fueled the American economy from colonial times to the end of World War II—may be poised for a comeback. It was really coastal shipping that Malcom McLean had in mind when he launched the container age in 1956 with the voyage of the *Ideal X* from New York to Houston. This is an idea whose time may come again. Because shipping is the most efficient way to move cargo over long distances, it could be revived domestically to eliminate some of the congestion on America's highways and reduce the air pollution caused by motor vehicles. The practicality of this technique depends on many variables, from local and national politics on the one hand to the development of alternative fuels for motor vehicles. But coastal shipping may well be in America's future.

Eighth, the cruise industry continues to expand in the early twenty-first century, with no leveling off in sight. Americans cruise more than any other people, and the Caribbean is the world's most popular cruise destination. Most of the major cruise lines are at least partially foreign-owned and almost exclusively foreign-flagged; even the iconically American Disney line runs Bahamas-flagged vessels. These companies pay only a small fraction of the U.S. taxes that American firms would face. But the ships sail primarily from American ports. This brings income to those ports as tourists embark and disembark, and it increases American leverage over maritime practice aboard the ships using those ports. Barring a terrorist scare or a serious accident, there seems to be no immediate limit to the growth of this industry.

Finally, many American companies successfully pursue niche markets. Domestic shipping, still protected by cabotage, thrives in many quarters, in spite of stiff competition from trucks and trains. Containerization has proved to be a boon to all three modes of transportation. Short-sea shipping is already under way, and may grow significantly in the future. Small lines serve local and regional markets, both domestically and internationally. And some specialty shipping, such as LNG (Liquid Natural Gas) ships, appear to have strong prospects.

This study looked in vain for a sustainable American business model, one that would work longer than a generation or two. There are only a handful in all of American history. But neither are there examples from other countries of multigenerational formulas for successful shipping or shipbuilding businesses. Rather individuals, companies, and sometimes countries have from time to time fashioned models that thrive in the international marketplace of shipping for some years or even decades. Shipping and shipbuilding are volatile industries that respond to a complex array of market forces. While that was the case since the colonial era, never before had those forces been as global and fast-moving as they were at the end of the twentieth century. Shipping in the twenty-first century will be determined by the individuals and companies that find successful business models responsive to market forces. There is no way to predict who those innovators will be or what models they will divine. But it seems likely that the way of the ship will continue to be a critical part of America's future.

APPENDIX A

World and U.S. Commercial Vessels

WORLD AND SELECT NATIONAL COMMERCIAL FLEETS, 1850–2000

Year	World Total	U.S.	U.K.	Liberia	Panama	Source
1850	9,031	3,484	4,237	n/a	n/a	1
1860	13,294	5,298	5,800	n/a	n/a	1
1870	16,761	4,193	7,149	n/a	n/a	1
1880	19,991	4,067	8,447	n/a	n/a	1
1884	22,880	2,700	11,191	n/a	n/a	2
1890	22,265	4,423	9,687	n/a	n/a	1
1900	22,369	1,455	11,514	n/a	n/a	3
1901	24,009	1,704	12,053	n/a	n/a	3
1902	25,860	1,954	12,898	n/a	n/a	3
1903	27,183	2,222	13,411	n/a	n/a	3
1904	28,633	2,441	13,999	n/a	n/a	3
1905	29,963	2,559	14,497	n/a	n/a	3
1906	31,745	2,785	15,207	n/a	n/a	3
1907	33,970	3,122	15,930	n/a	n/a	3
1908	35,723	3,511	16,337	n/a	n/a	3
1909	36,473	3,624	16,473	n/a	n/a	3
1910	37,291	3,789	16,768	n/a	n/a	3
1911	38,782	3,918	17,293	n/a	n/a	3
1912	40,518	4,060	17,731	n/a	n/a	3
1913	43,079	4,258	18,274	n/a	n/a	3
1914*	45,404	4,287	18,892	n/a	n/a	3
1919	47,897	11,933	16,345	n/a	n/a	3
1920	53,905	14,525	18,111	n/a	n/a	3
1921	58,846	15,674	19,320	n/a	n/a	3
1922	61,343	15,733	19,089	n/a	n/a	3
1923	62,335	15,623	19,115	n/a	n/a	3
1924	61,514	14,707	18,954	n/a	84	3
1925	62,380	14,208	19,305	n/a	98	3
1926	62,672	13,740	19,264	n/a	101	3
1927	63,267	13,606	19,179	n/a	47	3
1928	65,159	13,607	19,754	n/a	71	3
1929	66,407	13,487	20,046	n/a	62	3
1930	68,024	13,103	20,322	n/a	75	3
1931	68,723	12,794	20,194	n/a	131	3
1932	68,368	12,716	19,562	n/a	138	3
1933	66,628	12,563	18,592	n/a	287	3

(*continued*)

WORLD AND SELECT NATIONAL COMMERCIAL FLEETS, 1850–2000 (*continued*)

Year	World Total	U.S.	U.K.	Liberia	Panama	Source
1934	64,358	12,303	17,630	n/a	271	3
1935	63,727	12,145	17,298	n/a	137	3
1936	64,005	11,905	17,183	n/a	429	3
1937	65,271	11,788	17,436	n/a	512	3
1938	66,870	11,404	17,675	n/a	611	3
1939	68,509	11,362	17,891	374	718	3
1946	99,220	50,389	24,010	n/a	1,329	4
1947	n/a	44,203	20,135	n/a	2,931	5
1948	98,990	38,072	21,399	n/a	4,140	6
1949†	102,007	37,417	21,622	127	4,459	6
1949†	103,461	36,619	21,697	374	4,613	7
1950	107,215	36,448	22,394	710	4,998	7
1951	110,655	36,267	21,917	1,167	5,386	7
1952	114,946	36,138	21,905	1,836	5,633	7
1953	119,427	36,376	22,179	2,816	5,931	7
1954	124,754	35,107	22,876	5,452	5,425	7
1955	129,975	34,754	22,984	7,203	5,856	9
1956	136,880	33,674	23,314	10,365	6,124	9
1957	147,316	33,278	23,724	14,774	6,462	9
1958	158,047	33,652	24,372	17,790	6,609	9
1959	166,014	33,293	24,996	19,092	6,584	9
1960	171,890	32,568	25,189	17,435	6,076	9
1961	177,290	30,975	25,685	16,693	5,870	9
1962	185,843	31,106	26,246	17,230	5,759	9
1963	194,274	30,509	26,510	20,705	6,054	9
1964	204,154	29,632	26,170	25,568	6,737	9
1965	217,229	28,283	26,385	30,906	7,228	9
1966	232,197	27,225	26,759	35,276	7,120	9
1967	250,403	26,079	27,536	39,599	7,232	9
1968	273,210	25,464	29,917	45,141	8,009	9
1969	297,523	24,560	33,133	52,119	8,657	9
1970	326,999	21,346	37,065	60,992	9,140	8
1971	361,739	19,634	40,673	71,156	9,838	8
1972	399,552	17,949	43,495	83,208	12,348	8
1973	446,370	17,294	47,783	95,315	15,246	9
1974	472,020	17,334	50,723	103,386	16,838	8
1975	556,572	17,694	54,913	132,694	22,112	9
1976	578,749	18,350	54,812	141,172	22,969	8
1977	626,715	19,469	56,012	154,292	26,385	8
1978	644,300	21,253	46,752	153,792	32,529	8
1980	650,902	22,997	41,937	158,702	32,257	8
1981	654,909	23,979	42,302	153,342	38,011	8

Year	World Total	U.S.	U.K.	Liberia	Panama	Source
1982	665,753	24,477	37,146	146,124	45,820	8
1983	671,093	24,108	32,067	140,293	56,288	8
1984	666,404	24,737	27,251	131,545	57,781	9
1985	656,255	24,439	21,043	121,250	65,638	8
1986	616,667	24,499	19,557	113,856	70,379	8
1987	593,229	24,612	11,759	96,406	66,119	8
1988	588,557	25,677	n/a	93,537	68,884	8
1989	601,919	25,576	5,766	89,200	72,977	9
1990	604,489	24,457	n/a	88,275	70,537	8
1991	637,493	24,262	n/a	92,057	67,938	8
1992	652,025	23,286	n/a	93,522	74,905	8
1993	656,591	22,980	n/a	97,173	79,414	8
1994	665,911	21,658	n/a	87,755	91,687	8
1995	691,903	18,792	n/a	96,729	102,904	8
1996	717,617	18,021	n/a	97,405	119,150	8
1997	738,822	16,820	n/a	94,816	133,577	8
1998†	744,284	16,828	n/a	96,627	136,536	10
1998†	752,482	16,853	n/a	97,946	144,120	8
1999	780,361	n/a	n/a	96,365	152,308	8
2000	770,894	16,137	n/a	77,242	165,028	8
2001	777,315	15,769	n/a	78,743	167,850	11
2002	793,836	n/a	n/a	78,490	180,170	12

* No data available for 1915–1918.

† These years have values for each six-month period.

Sources

1. William A. Lovett, "Maritime Rivalries and World Markets," in Lovett, *U.S. Shipping Policies and the World Market*, 1976, 8 (thousands of net tons; his source: P. N. Davies, "British Shipping and World Trade," pp. 48–49, in Tsuneheko Yui and Keiichiro Nakagawa, *Business History of Shipping: Strategy and Structure* (Tokyo, 1985).

2. "Total seagoing merchant fleet sailing & steam tonnage," *Annual Report of the Commissioner of Navigation*, 1884.

3. Lloyd's Register of Shipping *Statistical Tables* 1964 and 1976 (gross tonnage of steam and motor vessels of 100 gross tons and over, as of July 1 annually; sailing and nonpropelled craft not included).

4. U.S. Maritime Administration, *Merchant Fleets of the World, September 1, 1939–December 31, 1951* (1953).

5. U.S. Maritime Commission, *Ocean Shipping: Facts and Figures* (1947).

6. U.S. Maritime Commission, *Report to Congress*, 1948–1950.

7. U.S. Maritime Administration, *Handbook of Merchant Shipping Statistics Through 1958* (1959).

8. U.S. Maritime Administration, *Annual Report*, 1951–2000.

9. U.S. Maritime Administration, *Merchant Fleets of the World*, 1955–1989.

10. U.S. Department of Transportation, Bureau of Transportation Statistics, *Maritime Trade & Transportation 1999*, 6.

11. *World Almanac and Book of Facts 2002* (their source: MARAD).

12. U.S. Maritime Administration Web site (www.marad.gov), "Top 20 Merchant Fleets of the World," March 28, 2002 (source: Lloyd's Register Fairplay).

U.S. Commercial Vessels, 1934–1997

Year	Total Vessels		Total Active Vessels		Active Foreign-Trade Vessels		Active Domestic-Trade Vessels		Foreign-Flagged Merchant Ships Owned by U.S. Parent Companies Total	National Defense Reserve Fleet Total
	Total	Thousand tons	Number	Thousand tons	Number	Thousand tons	Number	Thousand tons		
1934	1,673	12,986	1,097	8,767	438	3,753	657	4,993	n/a	n/a
1935	1,637	12,809	1,145	9,194	434	3,748	709	5,425	n/a	n/a
1936	1,563	12,323	1,208	9,697	430	8,714	776	5,958	n/a	n/a
1937	1,517	12,335	1,231	10,251	426	3,643	805	6,608	n/a	n/a
1938	1,422	11,814	1,060	9,019	366	3,301	694	5,718	n/a	n/a
1939	1,398	11,699	1,092	9,808	319	2,804	772	6,499	n/a	n/a
1940	1,300	11,019	1,119	9,653	425	3,749	693	5,893	n/a	n/a
1941	1,168	10,096	1,137	9,919	471	4,052	663	5,836	n/a	n/a
1945	n/a	n/a	n/a	n/a	n/a	n/a	n/a	n/a	n/a	5
1946	4,852	50,263	2,762	29,127	1,890	20,592	442	4,807	n/a	1,421
1947	3,696	38,882	2,114	23,651	1,603	17,238	511	6,413	n/a	1,204
1948	3,490	36,774	1,723	19,552	1,246	13,767	477	5,785	n/a	1,675
1949	3,379	36,228	1,386	16,044	1,004	11,416	382	4,628	n/a	1,934
1950	3,408	86,526	1,145	13,828	711	8,353	434	5,474	n/a	2,277
1951	3,386	36,336	1,654	19,284	988	11,425	426	5,333	n/a	1,767
1952	3,350	36,081	1,447	16,976	782	9,052	395	5,190	n/a	1,853
1953	3,349	36,255	1,415	16,738	629	7,390	437	5,725	n/a	1,932
1954	3,333	35,860	1,123	13,645	623	7,299	398	5,324	n/a	2,067
1955	3,235	35,017	1,163	14,232	601	6,992	425	5,880	n/a	2,068
1956	3,150	34,052	1,127	13,988	644	7,538	402	5,639	422	2,061
1957	3,032	32,900	1,199	14,874	721	8,406	399	5,595	n/a	1,889

Year										
1958	3,047	38,316	970	12,358	551	6,208	356	5,369	n/a	2,074
1959	3,047	33,565	963	12,636	533	5,935	375	5,912	n/a	2,060
1960	2,934	82,601	951	12,922	558	6,541	372	5,926	n/a	2,000
1961	2,810	31,525	644	8,837	415	5,066	182	3,107	n/a	1,923
1962	2,716	30,954	940	13,473	543	6,616	340	5,951	n/a	1,862
1963	2,691	30,753	946	13,812	587	7,344	299	5,479	n/a	1,819
1964	2,598	30,084	940	13,868	584	7,271	295	5,504	n/a	1,739
1965	2,425	28,755	779	11,821	512	6,877	217	3,953	429	1,594
1966	2,292	27,393	1043	15,388	494	6,576	248	4,825	436	1,327
1967	2,209	26,560	1107	16,273	460	6,037	233	4,654	452	1,152
1968	2,101	25,699	1104	16,416	481	6,332	242	4,934	467	1,062
1969	2,013	25,079	1013	15,180	447	6,021	199	4,062	n/a	1,017
1970	1,780	23,280	819	14,073	386	5,775	245	5,368	552	1,027
1971	1,478	20,474	690	12,971	321	5,273	236	5,418	n/a	860
1972	1,233	18,412	632	12,813	262	4,683	201	4,881	706	673
1973	1,051	17,297	595	12,847	312	6,618	196	4,725	739	541
1974	965	17,334	588	13,619	305	6,909	202	5,169	677	487
1975	891	17,608	532	13,105	267	6,204	205	5,687	687	419
1976	843	17,989	548	14,088	294	7,770	194	5,136	641	348
1977	841	19,468	564	15,542	281	6,817	214	7,442	n/a	333
1978	841	21,253	554	17,649	266	8,484	221	7,721	n/a	306
1979	871	22,997	552	18,948	276	10,109	208	7,629	n/a	317

(continued)

U.S. COMMERCIAL VESSELS, 1934–1997 (continued)

Year	Total Vessels		Total Active Vessels		Active Foreign-Trade Vessels		Active Domestic-Trade Vessels		Foreign-Flagged Merchant Ships Owned by U.S. Parent Companies Total	National Defense Reserve Fleet Total
	Total	Thousand tons	Number	Thousand tons	Number	Thousand tons	Number	Thousand tons		
1980	863	23,979	551	19,099	227	6,619	257	11,259	639	303
1981	863	24,477	539	18,561	216	5,141	235	10,951	602	317
1982	828	24,108	496	18,423	197	5,141	224	11,308	525	303
1983	819	24,737	420	17,553	184	5,700	204	10,335	485	304
1984	749	23,965	367	16,459	160	5,432	183	9,606	420	386
1985	748	24,439	403	16,695	161	5,448	171	9,568	394	300
1986	738	18,146	391	16,554	156	5,475	168	9,474	361	299
1987	724	31,467	367	15,823	135	4,702	170	9,581	336	326
1988	683	25,677	403	19,182	170	7,356	177	10,339	330	320
1989	661	24,457	383	17,720	164	7,251	158	8,967	332	312
1990	635	24,267	397	17,590	156	7,222	158	8,624	n/a	329
1991	636	24,266	449	19,038	149	7,068	160	8,804	n/a	316
1992	619	23,254	411	18,286	134	7,080	161	8,741	n/a	306
1993	603	22,461	365	16,765	158	7,367	143	7,695	n/a	302
1994	564	21,126	359	16,358	162	7,232	134	7,727	542	286
1995	543	19,968	343	15,279	154	6,605	129	7,318	n/a	296
1996	509	18,585	303	13,543	123	5,297	127	7,017	n/a	303
1997	495	17,511	291	13,076	114	4,926	130	7,058	n/a	307
1998	n/a	n/a	n/a	n/a	n/a	n/a	n/a	n/a	n/a	307
1999	n/a	n/a	n/a	n/a	n/a	n/a	n/a	n/a	n/a	312
2000	n/a	n/a	n/a	n/a	n/a	n/a	n/a	n/a	n/a	325

Oceangoing vessels of 1,000 gross tons and over engaged in foreign and domestic trade and vessels employed on the Great Lakes. This excludes special types and inactive vessels. Source: *Historical Statistics of the United States, Earliest Times to the Present: Millennial Edition*, edited by Susan B. Carter et al. (New York: Cambridge University Press, 2006), Table Df 758-821.

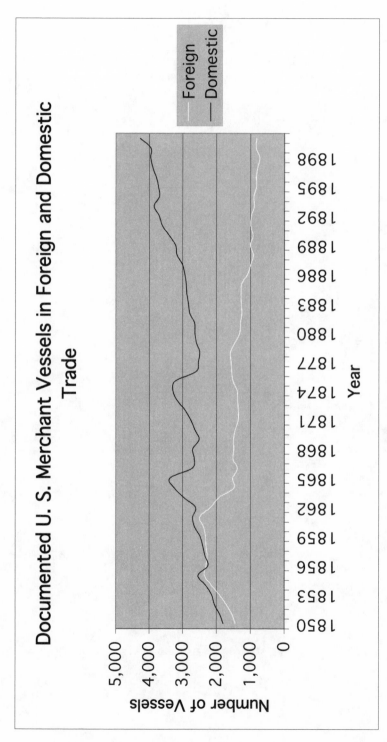

Documented U. S. Merchant Vessels in Foreign and Domestic Trade

Number of Vessels (5,000 / 4,000 / 3,000 / 2,000 / 1,000 / 0)

Year (1850, 1853, 1856, 1859, 1862, 1865, 1868, 1871, 1874, 1877, 1880, 1883, 1886, 1889, 1892, 1895, 1898)

— Foreign
— Domestic

Source: U.S. Bureau of the Census, *Historical Statistics of the United States, Colonial Times to 1957* (Washington, DC: Government Printing Office, 1960), Series Q 165, 166.

APPENDIX B

Values of U.S. Waterborne Cargo 1790–1994 (in millions of dollars)

Year*	Imports			Exports			Exports/Imports			
	Total	U.S. Vessels	Foreign Vessels	Total	U.S. Vessels	Foreign Vessels	Total	U.S. Vessels	Foreign Vessels	Percent Carried on U.S. Vessels
1790	23	9	14	20	8	12	43	17	26	39.5
1791	29	17	12	19	10	9	48	27	21	56.3
1792	32	21	10	21	13	8	53	34	18	64.2
1793	31	26	6	26	20	6	57	46	12	80.7
1794	35	31	3	33	28	5	68	59	8	86.8
1795	70	64	6	48	42	6	118	106	12	89.8
1796	81	77	5	59	53	6	140	130	11	92.9
1797	75	69	6	51	45	6	126	114	12	90.5
1798	69	62	6	61	53	8	130	115	14	88.5
1799	79	71	8	79	68	10	158	139	18	87.9
1800	91	83	8	71	62	9	162	145	17	89.5
1801	111	101	10	93	81	12	204	182	22	89.2
1802	76	67	9	72	61	11	148	128	20	86.5
1803	65	56	9	56	46	9	121	102	18	84.3
1804	85	77	8	78	67	11	163	144	19	88.3
1805	121	112	8	96	85	11	217	197	19	90.8
1806	129	120	9	102	90	11	231	210	20	90.9
1807	139	130	8	108	98	11	247	228	19	92.3
1808	57	53	4	22	20	3	79	73	7	92.4

(continued)

Values of U.S. Waterborne Cargo 1790–1994 (in millions of dollars) (continued)

Year*	Imports			Exports			Exports/Imports			
	Total	U.S. Vessels	Foreign Vessels	Total	U.S. Vessels	Foreign Vessels	Total	U.S. Vessels	Foreign Vessels	Percent Carried on U.S. Vessels
1809	59	52	7	52	44	8	111	96	15	86.5
1810	85	79	6	67	60	7	152	139	13	91.4
1811	53	48	5	61	53	9	114	101	14	88.6
1812	77	65	12	39	31	8	116	96	20	82.8
1813	22	16	6	28	18	10	50	34	16	68
1814	13	8	5	7	4	3	20	12	8	60
1815	113	87	26	53	37	15	166	124	41	74.7
1816	147	107	40	82	56	26	229	163	66	71.2
1817	99	78	21	88	65	23	187	143	44	76.5
1818	122	103	18	93	75	19	215	178	37	82.8
1819	87	67	20	70	58	13	157	125	33	79.6
1820	74	67	7	70	62	8	144	129	15	89.6
1821	63	58	5	65	55	10	128	113	15	88.3
1822	83	77	6	72	61	11	155	138	17	89
1823	78	72	6	75	65	9	153	137	15	89.5
1824	81	75	5	76	67	9	157	142	14	90.4
1825	96	92	4	100	89	11	196	181	15	92.3
1826	85	81	4	78	70	8	163	151	12	92.6
1827	79	75	5	82	72	10	161	147	15	91.3
1828	89	82	7	72	61	11	161	143	18	88.8
1829	74	69	5	72	62	10	146	131	15	89.7
1830	71	66	4	74	64	10	145	130	14	89.7

1831	103	94	9	81	66	16	184	160	25	86.9
1832	101	90	11	87	66	21	188	156	32	82.9
1833	108	98	10	90	68	22	198	166	32	83.8
1834	127	114	13	104	78	27	231	192	40	83.1
1835	150	135	15	122	94	28	272	229	43	84.2
1836	189	171	18	129	97	32	318	268	50	84.3
1837	141	122	19	117	91	26	258	213	45	82.6
1838	115	104	11	108	89	19	223	193	30	86.5
1839	162	144	18	121	95	26	283	239	44	84.5
1840	107	93	14	132	106	26	239	199	40	83.3
1841	128	113	15	122	95	27	250	208	42	83.2
1842	100	89	11	105	80	25	205	169	36	82.4
1843	65	50	15	84	65	19	149	115	34	77.2
1844	108	94	14	111	78	33	219	172	47	78.5
1845	117	102	15	115	87	28	232	189	43	81.5
1846	122	106	16	113	87	27	235	193	43	82.1
1847	147	113	33	154	100	54	301	213	87	70.8
1848	155	129	26	154	110	44	309	239	70	77.3
1849	148	120	27	146	101	45	294	221	72	75.2
1850	178	140	38	152	100	52	330	240	90	72.7
1851	216	164	53	218	152	66	434	316	119	72.8
1852	208	155	53	210	139	70	418	294	123	70.3

(continued)

Values of U.S. Waterborne Cargo 1790–1994 (in millions of dollars) *(continued)*

Year*	Imports			Exports			Exports/Imports			
	Total	U.S. Vessels	Foreign Vessels	Total	U.S. Vessels	Foreign Vessels	Total	U.S. Vessels	Foreign Vessels	Percent Carried on U.S. Vessels
1853	268	192	76	231	155	76	499	347	152	69.6
1854	301	215	86	276	191	84	577	406	170	70.4
1855	261	202	59	275	203	72	536	405	131	75.6
1856	315	250	65	327	232	95	642	482	160	75.1
1857	361	259	102	363	251	112	724	510	214	70.4
1858	283	204	79	325	243	81	608	447	160	73.5
1859	339	216	123	357	250	107	696	466	230	66.9
1860	362	228	134	400	279	121	762	507	255	66.5
1861	336	202	134	249	180	69	585	382	203	65.3
1862	206	92	113	230	125	105	436	217	218	49.8
1863	253	110	143	332	132	200	585	242	343	41.4
1864	330	81	248	340	103	237	670	184	485	27.5
1865	249	74	174	356	93	263	605	167	437	27.6
1866	446	112	333	565	214	352	1,011	326	685	32.2
1867	418	117	301	461	181	281	879	298	582	33.9
1868	372	123	249	477	175	302	849	298	551	35.1
1869	437	137	301	439	153	286	876	290	587	33.1
1870	462	153	309	530	200	330	992	353	639	35.6
1871	526	163	363	583	190	393	1,109	353	756	31.8
1872	623	177	445	562	168	394	1,185	345	839	29.1
1873	647	175	472	666	172	495	1,313	347	967	26.4
1874	581	176	405	708	174	534	1,289	350	939	27.2

1875	541	158	383	658	156	502	1,199	314	885	26.2
1876	465	143	321	660	168	492	1,125	311	813	27.6
1877	481	152	330	695	165	530	1,176	317	860	26.9
1878	454	146	307	736	167	570	1,190	313	877	26.3
1879	454	144	310	729	128	601	1,183	272	911	22.9
1880	653	149	503	830	109	721	1,483	258	1,224	17.4
1881	625	134	492	894	117	777	1,519	251	1,269	16.5
1882	702	130	572	738	97	641	1,440	227	1,213	15.8
1883	700	136	564	799	104	694	1,499	240	1,258	16
1884	648	135	513	714	99	615	1,362	234	1,128	17.2
1885	556	113	444	718	82	636	1,274	195	1,080	15.3
1886	611	119	492	660	78	582	1,271	197	1,074	15.5
1887	665	121	543	695	73	622	1,360	194	1,165	14.3
1888	692	124	568	674	67	606	1,366	191	1,174	13.9
1889	707	121	586	714	83	631	1,421	204	1,217	14.4
1890	749	125	624	825	78	747	1,574	203	1,371	12.9
1891	804	127	677	853	79	774	1,657	206	1,451	12.4
1892	788	139	649	997	81	916	1,785	220	1,565	12.3
1893	822	127	695	804	71	733	1,626	198	1,428	12.2
1894	625	122	504	843	74	769	1,468	196	1,273	13.4
1895	699	108	591	758	62	695	1,457	170	1,286	11.7
1896	744	117	627	821	70	751	1,565	187	1,378	11.9

(continued)

Values of U.S. Waterborne Cargo 1790–1994 (in millions of dollars) (continued)

Year*	Imports			Exports			Exports/Imports			
	Total	U.S. Vessels	Foreign Vessels	Total	U.S. Vessels	Foreign Vessels	Total	U.S. Vessels	Foreign Vessels	Percent Carried on U.S. Vessels
1897	729	109	620	986	80	906	1,715	189	1,526	11
1898	586	94	492	1,158	68	1,090	1,744	162	1,582	9.3
1899	664	82	582	1,143	79	1,065	1,807	161	1,647	8.9
1900	806	104	701	1,284	91	1,193	2,090	195	1,894	9.3
1901	776	93	683	1,376	84	1,292	2,152	177	1,975	8.2
1902	847	102	745	1,258	84	1,174	2,105	186	1,919	8.8
1903	960	124	836	1,281	91	1,190	2,241	215	2,026	9.6
1904	923	132	791	1,308	97	1,211	2,231	229	2,002	10.3
1905	1,039	161	878	1,355	130	1,225	2,394	291	2,103	12.2
1906	1,140	168	971	1,550	154	1,396	2,690	322	2,367	11.9
1907	1,340	177	1,164	1,662	142	1,521	3,002	319	2,685	10.6
1908	1,123	152	971	1,670	121	1,550	2,793	273	2,521	9.8
1909	1,241	151	1,090	1,481	108	1,373	2,722	259	2,463	9.5
1910	1,467	147	1,319	1,516	114	1,403	2,983	261	2,722	8.7
1911	1,436	147	1,290	1,774	134	1,641	3,210	281	2,931	8.8
1912	1,551	171	1,380	1,880	152	1,729	3,431	323	3,109	9.4
1913	1,698	193	1,505	2,075	188	1,887	3,773	381	3,392	10.1
1914	1,738	199	1,539	2,048	170	1,878	3,786	369	3,417	9.7
1915	1,526	281	1,245	2,466	291	2,176	3,992	572	3,421	14.3
1916	2,157	532	1,625	4,820	665	4,155	6,977	1,197	5,780	17.2
1917	2,590	733	1,857	5,403	946	4,457	7,993	1,679	6,314	21
1918	2,577	717	1,860	5,226	986	4,240	7,803	1,703	6,100	21.8

Year										
1919	3,414	1,228	2,186	7,090	2,596	4,494	10,504	3,824	6,680	36.4
1920	4,731	1,988	2,743	7,252	3,165	4,087	11,983	5,153	6,830	43
1921	2,187	765	1,422	3,888	1,402	2,486	6,075	2,167	3,908	35.7
1922	2,704	921	1,783	3,281	1,261	2,020	5,985	2,182	3,803	36.5
1923	3,312	1,040	2,272	3,539	1,358	2,181	6,851	2,398	4,453	35
1924	3,145	1,012	2,133	4,010	1,532	2,478	7,155	2,544	4,611	35.6
1925	3,716	1,151	2,565	4,224	1,473	2,751	7,940	2,624	5,316	33.0
1926	3,891	1,195	2,696	4,050	1,401	2,649	7,941	2,596	5,345	32.7
1927	3,662	1,215	2,447	4,097	1,434	2,663	7,759	2,649	5,110	34.1
1928	3,550	1,133	2,418	4,277	1,472	2,804	7,827	2,605	5,222	33.3
1929	3,807	1,205	2,602	4,322	1,487	2,835	8,129	2,692	5,437	33.1
1930	2,635	898	1,737	3,168	1,117	2,051	5,803	2,015	3,788	34.7
1931	1,829	619	1,210	2,043	732	1,311	3,872	1,351	2,521	34.9
1932	1,164	431	734	1,385	476	909	2,549	907	1,643	35.6
1933	1,287	461	826	1,471	515	956	2,758	976	1,782	35.4
1934	1,446	528	917	1,837	658	1,179	3,283	1,186	2,096	36.1
1935	1,813	649	1,164	1,973	705	1,268	3,786	1,354	2,432	35.8
1936	n/a	n/a	n/a	n/a	n/a	n/a	n/a	n/a	n/a	n/a
1937	n/a	n/a	n/a	n/a	n/a	n/a	n/a	n/a	n/a	n/a
1938	n/a	n/a	n/a	n/a	n/a	n/a	n/a	n/a	n/a	n/a
1939	n/a	n/a	n/a	n/a	n/a	n/a	n/a	n/a	n/a	n/a
1940	n/a	n/a	n/a	n/a	n/a	n/a	n/a	n/a	n/a	n/a

(continued)

Values of U.S. Waterborne Cargo 1790–1994 (in millions of dollars) (continued)

Year*	Imports			Exports			Exports/Imports			
	Total	U.S. Vessels	Foreign Vessels	Total	U.S. Vessels	Foreign Vessels	Total	U.S. Vessels	Foreign Vessels	Percent Carried on U.S. Vessels
1941	n/a	n/a	n/a	n/a	n/a	n/a	n/a	n/a	n/a	n/a
1942	n/a	n/a	n/a	n/a	n/a	n/a	n/a	n/a	n/a	n/a
1943	n/a	n/a	n/a	10,275	4,828	5,447	n/a	n/a	n/a	n/a
1944	n/a	n/a	n/a	11,382	5,582	5,800	n/a	n/a	n/a	n/a
1945	n/a	n/a	n/a	7,860	4,052	3,808	n/a	n/a	n/a	n/a
1946	3,691	2,239	1,452	7,705	4,692	3,013	11,396	6,931	4,465	60.8
1947	4,368	n/a	n/a	11,026	n/a	n/a	15,394	n/a	n/a	n/a
1948	5,197	n/a	n/a	8,877	n/a	n/a	14,074	n/a	n/a	n/a
1949	4,965	n/a	n/a	8,475	n/a	n/a	13,440	n/a	n/a	n/a
1950	6,754	n/a	n/a	7,097	n/a	n/a	13,851	n/a	n/a	n/a
1951	8,441	n/a	n/a	10,109	n/a	n/a	18,550	n/a	n/a	n/a
1952	8,118	n/a	n/a	9,031	n/a	n/a	17,149	n/a	n/a	n/a
1953	8,292	n/a	n/a	7,852	n/a	n/a	16,144	n/a	n/a	n/a
1954	7,334	n/a	n/a	8,286	n/a	n/a	15,620	n/a	n/a	n/a
1955	8,073	n/a	n/a	9,227	n/a	n/a	17,300	n/a	n/a	n/a
1956	8,899	n/a	n/a	11,045	n/a	n/a	20,600	7,000	n/a	39.6
1957	9,244	n/a	n/a	12,948	n/a	n/a	22,800	7,300	n/a	39.1
1958	9,700	n/a	n/a	10,664	n/a	n/a	20,900	6,000	n/a	35.3
1959	11,633	n/a	n/a	10,618	n/a	n/a	22,800	6,000	n/a	32.5
1960	11,140	n/a	n/a	13,164	n/a	n/a	24,700	6,500	n/a	32.1
1961	10,644	n/a	n/a	13,635	n/a	n/a	24,700	6,300	n/a	31.4
1962	11,805	n/a	n/a	13,705	n/a	n/a	25,900	6,500	n/a	30.1

1963	12,382	n/a	n/a	14,793	n/a	n/a	27,500	6,900	n/a	31.5
1964	13,441	n/a	n/a	17,089	n/a	n/a	30,000	7,700	n/a	32.8
1965	14,943	n/a	n/a	16,926	n/a	n/a	32,400	6,900	n/a	27.8
1966	17,319	n/a	n/a	18,520	n/a	n/a	36,400	8,200	n/a	30.4
1967	17,434	n/a	n/a	18,636	n/a	n/a	36,600	7,900	n/a	29.8
1968	21,139	n/a	n/a	19,359	n/a	n/a	41,100	8,500	n/a	29
1969	21,570	n/a	n/a	19,915	n/a	n/a	41,900	8,100	n/a	27.6
1970	24,728	n/a	n/a	24,394	n/a	n/a	49,700	10,300	n/a	28.8
1971	26,793	n/a	n/a	22,610	n/a	n/a	50,400	9,900	n/a	28.4
1972	33,617	n/a	n/a	25,520	n/a	n/a	60,500	11,100	n/a	27.7
1973	42,742	n/a	n/a	39,642	n/a	n/a	84,000	15,900	n/a	29.1
1974	67,148	n/a	n/a	55,506	n/a	n/a	124,200	22,000	n/a	30.6
1975	63,469	n/a	n/a	61,408	n/a	n/a	127,500	22,400	n/a	31.2
1976	81,171	n/a	n/a	64,712	n/a	n/a	148,400	26,400	n/a	31.6
1977	103,037	n/a	n/a	65,376	n/a	n/a	171,200	28,000	n/a	30.7
1978	135,480	n/a	n/a	77,338	n/a	n/a	195,800	30,700	n/a	28.6
1979	140,091	n/a	n/a	97,579	n/a	n/a	242,100	35,700	n/a	27.6
1980	164,924	n/a	n/a	118,835	n/a	n/a	294,300	42,300	n/a	28.7
1981	177,059	n/a	n/a	123,495	n/a	n/a	315,400	47,000	n/a	28.1
1982	155,493	n/a	n/a	115,885	n/a	n/a	281,200	43,500	n/a	27.8
1983	195,311	n/a	n/a	100,651	n/a	n/a	267,400	43,000	n/a	27.2
1984	191,113	n/a	n/a	101,803	n/a	n/a	302,700	44,600	n/a	25.1

(continued)

Values of U.S. Waterborne Cargo 1790–1994 (in millions of dollars) (continued)

Year*	Imports			Exports			Exports/Imports			
	Total	U.S. Vessels	Foreign Vessels	Total	U.S. Vessels	Foreign Vessels	Total	U.S. Vessels	Foreign Vessels	Percent Carried on U.S. Vessels
1985	205,605	n/a	n/a	91,680	n/a	n/a	311,000	46,400	n/a	24
1986	217,776	n/a	n/a	87,946	n/a	n/a	320,500	49,000	n/a	23.3
1987	245,028	n/a	n/a	99,009	n/a	n/a	359,400	44,800	n/a	18.8
1988	254,766	n/a	n/a	126,192	n/a	n/a	397,700	57,700	n/a	21
1989	270,621	n/a	n/a	143,184	n/a	n/a	437,000	71,300	n/a	23.3
1990	283,412	n/a	n/a	150,739	n/a	n/a	451,500	69,800	n/a	21.5
1991	272,287	n/a	n/a	162,354	n/a	n/a	458,300	70,700	n/a	20.7
1992	293,099	n/a	n/a	170,313	n/a	n/a	487,300	73,600	n/a	20.1
1993	310,282	n/a	n/a	166,689	n/a	n/a	501,400	74,100	n/a	18.6
1994	338,809	n/a	n/a	177,333	n/a	n/a	564,600	76,800	n/a	16.6

Amounts are in then-year dollars.

*Year-end date changes over time.

Data include reexports of merchandise, gold and silver coin bullion through 1879, imports and exports by land prior to 1871, and all waterborne foreign commerce of ports on the Great Lakes. Source: *Historical Statistics of the United States, Earliest Times to the Present: Millennial Edition*, edited by Susan B. Carter et al. (New York: Cambridge University Press, 2006), Table Df 606–611.

Maritime Labor, 1925–2000

Date or Year	Employment	Seafaring Shipboard Jobs	Shipyard Production	Longshore Total
6/30/1925	56,750	n/a	n/a	n/a
6/30/1926	58,630	n/a	n/a	n/a
6/30/1927	61,430	n/a	n/a	n/a
6/30/1928	61,100	n/a	n/a	n/a
6/30/1929	64,480	n/a	n/a	n/a
6/30/1930	64,250	n/a	n/a	n/a
6/30/1931	58,780	n/a	n/a	n/a
6/30/1932	54,000	n/a	n/a	n/a
6/30/1933	54,380	n/a	n/a	n/a
6/30/1934	55,100	n/a	n/a	n/a
6/30/1935	56,150	n/a	n/a	n/a
6/30/1936	57,200	n/a	n/a	n/a
6/30/1937	59,150	n/a	n/a	n/a
6/30/1938	49,800	n/a	n/a	n/a
6/30/1939	52,000	n/a	n/a	n/a
6/30/1940	49,810	n/a	n/a	n/a
6/30/1941	51,280	n/a	n/a	n/a
6/30/1942	47,410	n/a	n/a	n/a
6/20/1943	75,000	n/a	n/a	n/a
12/20/1943	100,070	n/a	n/a	n/a
6/20/1944	125,290	n/a	n/a	n/a
12/20/1944	143,980	n/a	n/a	n/a
6/20/1945	158,860	n/a	n/a	n/a
9/20/1945	168,070	n/a	n/a	n/a
2/20/1946	166,220	n/a	n/a	n/a
6/20/1946	120,050	n/a	n/a	n/a
12/20/1947	110,820	n/a	n/a	n/a
6/30/1948	82,100	n/a	n/a	n/a
12/31/1948	72,985	n/a	n/a	n/a
6/30/1949	71,970	n/a	n/a	n/a
12/31/1949	62,115	69,300	63,608	n/a
6/30/1950	61,550	n/a	n/a	n/a
12/31/1950	68,050	57,250	42,538	n/a
6/30/1951	84,300	n/a	n/a	n/a
12/31/1951	97,630	n/a	70,137	n/a
6/30/1952	76,650	n/a	n/a	n/a
12/31/1952	70,850	n/a	n/a	n/a
6/30/1953	72,750	72,700	127,100	n/a
6/30/1954	63,850	63,850	106,000	n/a

(continued)

Date or Year	Employment	Seafaring Shipboard Jobs	Shipyard Production	Longshore Total
6/30/1955	57,507	57,500	38,200	n/a
6/30/1956	57,192	57,200	40,900	n/a
6/30/1957	61,059	60,700	53,300	n/a
6/30/1958	51,515	51,500	55,500	n/a
6/30/1959	50,223	50,200	55,250	n/a
6/30/1960	49,153	49,200	56,965	n/a
6/30/1961	30,900	48,800	54,000	est. 70,000
6/30/1962	47,300	47,650	52,200	est. 70,000
6/30/1963	48,000	46,900	50,100	est. 70,000
6/30/1964	48,000	47,500	45,900	est. 70,000
6/30/1965	39,100	47,160	54,100	est. 70,000
6/30/1966	51,900	50,660	57,300	est. 70,000
6/30/1967	54,600	54,790	58,753	est. 70,000
6/30/1968	54,200	53,880	60,940	est. 70,000
6/30/1969	47,500	49,534	64,290	68,700
6/30/1970	37,600	41,731	61,731	66,120
6/30/1975	20,500	31,179	72,668	63,725
9/30/1980	19,600	25,915	94,925	48,747
9/30/1981	18,300	25,184	96,648	46,245
9/30/1982	16,700	22,861	89,968	42,380
9/30/1983	15,300	20,695	84,713	34,727
9/30/1984	13,700	19,193	82,976	32,116
9/30/1985	13,100	17,887	81,752	29,759
9/30/1986	11,500	16,182	72,866	28,421
9/30/1987	10,400	14,639	65,277	26,904
9/30/1988	10,700	14,470	64,143	28,503
9/30/1989	9,900	14,268	62,328	28,339
9/30/1990	11,100	14,168	63,632	27,997
9/30/1991	11,700	16,308	63,885	26,698
9/30/1992	9,200	14,446	61,620	25,220
9/30/1993	9,300	12,266	55,279	24,745
9/30/1994	9,100	12,696	52,843	23,538
9/30/1995	7,900	12,204	48,796	22,427
9/30/1996	7,500	11,205	44,190	22,829
9/30/1997	8,600	10,843	34,591	22,743
9/30/1998	7,900	10,324	34,591	22,743
9/30/1999	7,300	10,458	34,591	23,562
9/30/2000	6,600	n/a	n/a	n/a

Sources: U.S. Maritime Administration, *Handbook of Merchant Shipping Statistics through 1958* (Washington, DC: Government Printing Office, 1959), 177; U.S. Department of Commerce, Bureau of the Census, *Historical Statistics of the United States, Colonial Times to 1970* (Washington, DC: U.S. Department of Commerce, Bureau of the Census, 1975), Part 2, Series Q414; U.S. Bureau of the Census, *Statistical Abstract of the United States* (Washington, DC: Government Printing Office, 1955, 1961, 1991, 1996, 1998, 2001); U.S. Maritime Commission Annual Report (1947–1950); U.S. Maritime Administration, Annual Report (1951–1999).

APPENDIX D

U.S. Shipbuilding, 1769–1969

	U.S. Vessels Built				World Vessels Built*	
	5 Gross Tons or More		100 Gross Tons or More		100 Gross Tons or More	
Year	Number	Gross Tons	Number	Gross Tons	Number	Gross Tons
1769†	390	20,081	n/a	n/a	n/a	n/a
1770†	401	20,620	n/a	n/a	n/a	n/a
1771†	421	24,092	n/a	n/a	n/a	n/a
1797	n/a	56,679	n/a	n/a	n/a	n/a
1798	635	49,435	n/a	n/a	n/a	n/a
1799	767	77,921	n/a	n/a	n/a	n/a
1800	995	106,261	n/a	n/a	n/a	n/a
1801	n/a	124,755	n/a	n/a	n/a	n/a
1802	n/a	n/a	n/a	n/a	n/a	n/a
1803	n/a	88,448	n/a	n/a	n/a	n/a
1804	n/a	103,753	n/a	n/a	n/a	n/a
1805	n/a	128,507	n/a	n/a	n/a	n/a
1806	n/a	126,093	n/a	n/a	n/a	n/a
1807	n/a	99,783	n/a	n/a	n/a	n/a
1808	n/a	31,755	n/a	n/a	n/a	n/a
1809	n/a	91,397	n/a	n/a	n/a	n/a
1810	n/a	127,575	n/a	n/a	n/a	n/a
1811	n/a	146,691	n/a	n/a	n/a	n/a
1812	n/a	85,148	n/a	n/a	n/a	n/a
1813	371	32,583	n/a	n/a	n/a	n/a
1814	490	29,751	n/a	n/a	n/a	n/a
1815	1,329	155,579	n/a	n/a	n/a	n/a
1816	1,431	135,186	n/a	n/a	n/a	n/a
1817	1,087	87,626	n/a	n/a	n/a	n/a
1818	923	87,346	n/a	n/a	n/a	n/a
1819	876	86,670	n/a	n/a	n/a	n/a
1820	557	51,394	n/a	n/a	n/a	n/a
1821	519	57,275	n/a	n/a	n/a	n/a
1822	639	77,569	n/a	n/a	n/a	n/a
1823	630	75,857	n/a	n/a	n/a	n/a
1824	793	92,798	n/a	n/a	n/a	n/a
1825	1,000	116,464	n/a	n/a	n/a	n/a
1826	1,033	130,373	n/a	n/a	n/a	n/a
1827	951	106,456	n/a	n/a	n/a	n/a

(continued)

U.S. Shipbuilding, 1769–1969 (*continued*)

	U.S. Vessels Built				World Vessels Built*	
	5 Gross Tons or More		100 Gross Tons or More		100 Gross Tons or More	
Year	Number	Gross Tons	Number	Gross Tons	Number	Gross Tons
1828	886	98,964	n/a	n/a	n/a	n/a
1829	796	79,408	n/a	n/a	n/a	n/a
1830	648	58,560	n/a	n/a	n/a	n/a
1831	712	85,556	n/a	n/a	n/a	n/a
1832	1,065	144,544	n/a	n/a	n/a	n/a
1833	1,187	161,492	n/a	n/a	n/a	n/a
1834	957	118,389	n/a	n/a	n/a	n/a
1835	725	75,107	n/a	n/a	n/a	n/a
1836	911	116,230	n/a	n/a	n/a	n/a
1837	972	115,905	n/a	n/a	n/a	n/a
1838	913	125,913	n/a	n/a	n/a	n/a
1839	899	125,260	n/a	n/a	n/a	n/a
1840	895	121,203	n/a	n/a	n/a	n/a
1841	793	123,660	n/a	n/a	n/a	n/a
1842	1,027	129,806	n/a	n/a	n/a	n/a
1843	483	63,888	n/a	n/a	n/a	n/a
1844	766	103,537	n/a	n/a	n/a	n/a
1845	1,038	146,042	n/a	n/a	n/a	n/a
1846	1,420	188,203	n/a	n/a	n/a	n/a
1847	1,597	243,633	n/a	n/a	n/a	n/a
1848	1,851	318,075	n/a	n/a	n/a	n/a
1849	1,554	256,988	n/a	n/a	n/a	n/a
1850	1,422	279,255	n/a	n/a	n/a	n/a
1851	1,368	299,472	n/a	n/a	n/a	n/a
1852	1452	355,356	n/a	n/a	n/a	n/a
1853	1,717	427,494	n/a	n/a	n/a	n/a
1854	1,777	536,046	n/a	n/a	n/a	n/a
1855	2,027	583,450	n/a	n/a	n/a	n/a
1856	1,714	469,293	n/a	n/a	n/a	n/a
1857	1,434	378,804	n/a	n/a	n/a	n/a
1858	1,225	244,712	n/a	n/a	n/a	n/a
1859	870	156,602	n/a	n/a	n/a	n/a
1860	1,071	214,797	n/a	n/a	n/a	n/a
1861	1,143	233,194	n/a	n/a	n/a	n/a
1862	864	175,075	n/a	n/a	n/a	n/a
1863	1,823	311,045	n/a	n/a	n/a	n/a
1864	2,366	415,740	n/a	n/a	n/a	n/a
1865	1,788	383,805	n/a	n/a	n/a	n/a
1866	1,888	336,146	n/a	n/a	n/a	n/a
1867	1,519	303,528	n/a	n/a	n/a	n/a
1868	1,802	283,304	n/a	n/a	n/a	n/a

| | U.S. Vessels Built | | | | World Vessels Built* | |
| | 5 Gross Tons or More | | 100 Gross Tons or More | | 100 Gross Tons or More | |
Year	Number	Gross Tons	Number	Gross Tons	Number	Gross Tons
1869	1,726	275,230	n/a	n/a	n/a	n/a
1870	1,618	276,953	n/a	n/a	n/a	n/a
1871	1,755	273,226	n/a	n/a	n/a	n/a
1872	1,643	209,052	n/a	n/a	n/a	n/a
1873	2,271	359,245	n/a	n/a	n/a	n/a
1874	2,147	432,725	n/a	n/a	n/a	n/a
1875	1,301	297,638	n/a	n/a	n/a	n/a
1876	1,112	203,585	n/a	n/a	n/a	n/a
1877	1,029	176,591	n/a	n/a	n/a	n/a
1878	1,258	235,503	n/a	n/a	n/a	n/a
1879	1,132	193,030	n/a	n/a	n/a	n/a
1880	902	157,409	n/a	n/a	n/a	n/a
1881	1,108	280,458	n/a	n/a	n/a	n/a
1882	1,371	282,269	n/a	n/a	n/a	n/a
1883	1,268	265,429	n/a	n/a	n/a	n/a
1884	1,190	225,514	n/a	n/a	n/a	n/a
1885	920	159,056	n/a	n/a	n/a	n/a
1886	715	195,453	n/a	n/a	n/a	n/a
1887	844	150,450	n/a	n/a	n/a	n/a
1888	1,014	218,086	n/a	n/a	n/a	n/a
1889	1,077	231,134	n/a	n/a	n/a	n/a
1890	1,051	294,122	n/a	n/a	n/a	n/a
1891	1,384	369,302	n/a	n/a	n/a	n/a
1892	1,395	199,633	n/a	n/a	n/a	n/a
1893	956	211,639	n/a	n/a	n/a	n/a
1894	838	131,195	n/a	n/a	n/a	n/a
1895	694	111,602	n/a	n/a	n/a	n/a
1896	723	227,096	n/a	n/a	n/a	n/a
1897	891	232,232	n/a	n/a	n/a	n/a
1898	952	180,458	n/a	n/a	n/a	n/a
1899	1,273	300,038	n/a	n/a	n/a	n/a
1900	1,447	393,790	n/a	n/a	n/a	n/a
1901	1,580	483,489	n/a	n/a	n/a	n/a
1902	1,491	468,831	n/a	n/a	n/a	n/a
1903	1,311	436,152	n/a	n/a	n/a	n/a
1904	1,184	378,542	n/a	n/a	n/a	n/a
1905	1,102	330,316	n/a	n/a	n/a	n/a
1906	1,221	418,745	n/a	n/a	n/a	n/a
1907	1,157	471,332	n/a	n/a	n/a	n/a
1908	1,457	614,216	n/a	n/a	n/a	n/a
1909	1,247	238,090	n/a	n/a	n/a	n/a
1910	1,361	342,068	n/a	n/a	n/a	n/a

(*continued*)

U.S. Shipbuilding, 1769–1969 (*continued*)

| | U.S. Vessels Built | | | | World Vessels Built* | |
| | 5 Gross Tons or More | | 100 Gross Tons or More | | 100 Gross Tons or More | |
Year	Number	Gross Tons	Number	Gross Tons	Number	Gross Tons
1911	1,422	291,162	n/a	n/a	n/a	n/a
1912	1,505	232,669	n/a	n/a	n/a	n/a
1913	1,475	346,155	n/a	n/a	n/a	n/a
1914	1,151	316,250	n/a	n/a	n/a	n/a
1915	1,157	225,122	n/a	n/a	n/a	n/a
1916	937	325,413	n/a	n/a	n/a	n/a
1917	1,297	664,479	n/a	n/a	n/a	n/a
1918	1,528	1,300,868	n/a	n/a	n/a	n/a
1919	1,953	3,326,621	n/a	n/a	n/a	n/a
1920	2,067	3,880,639	n/a	n/a	n/a	n/a
1921	1,361	2,265,115	n/a	n/a	n/a	n/a
1922	845	661,232	n/a	n/a	n/a	n/a
1923	770	335,791	n/a	n/a	n/a	n/a
1924	1,049	223,968	n/a	n/a	n/a	n/a
1925	967	199,846	n/a	n/a	n/a	n/a
1926	924	224,673	n/a	n/a	n/a	n/a
1927	917	245,144	n/a	n/a	n/a	n/a
1928	969	257,180	n/a	n/a	n/a	n/a
1929	808	128,976	n/a	n/a	n/a	n/a
1930	1,020	254,296	n/a	n/a	n/a	n/a
1931	1,302	386,906	n/a	n/a	n/a	n/a
1932	722	212,892	n/a	n/a	n/a	n/a
1933	642	190,803	n/a	n/a	n/a	n/a
1934	724	66,649	n/a	n/a	n/a	n/a
1935	748	62,919	n/a	n/a	n/a	n/a
1936	1,207	224,084	n/a	n/a	n/a	n/a
1937	1,939	471,364	n/a	n/a	n/a	n/a
1938	753	237,374	n/a	n/a	n/a	n/a
1939	673	339,899	n/a	n/a	n/a	n/a
1940	705	446,894	n/a	n/a	n/a	n/a
1941	703	647,097	n/a	n/a	n/a	n/a
1942	1,108	4,543,946	n/a	n/a	n/a	n/a
1943	1,901	10,431,734	n/a	n/a	n/a	n/a
1944	1,723	8,032,009	n/a	n/a	n/a	n/a
1945	1,744	6,313,977	n/a	n/a	n/a	n/a
1946	1,275	548,262	n/a	n/a	n/a	n/a
1947	1,259	267,331	72	258,167	691	1,180,111
1948	1,118	200,290	64	183,501	879	2,481,779
1949	978	195,190	52	573,298	896	3,113,836
1950	861	194,370	45	392,813	953	3,524,029
1951	992	308,825	40	153,208	984	3,557,269
1952	990	437,378	46	397,017	1,046	4,210,690

| | U.S. Vessels Built | | | | World Vessels Built* | |
| | 5 Gross Tons or More | | 100 Gross Tons or More | | 100 Gross Tons or More | |
Year	Number	Gross Tons	Number	Gross Tons	Number	Gross Tons
1953	1,190	633,966	72	600,043	1,148	4,937,755
1954	1,186	589,317	52	568,450	1,219	5,450,219
1955	1,116	400,076	21	100,189	1,365	4,966,755
1956	1,385	445,617	42	126,379	1,687	6,291,021
1957	1,582	585,048	52	306,231	1,964	8,117,091
1958	1,390	836,799	49	553,339	1,920	9,059,267
1959	1,180	791,640	54	769,362	1,798	8,696,601
1960	949	629,295	49	378,725	2,005	8,382,342
1961	877	620,287	61	402,169	1,973	8,057,542
1962	1,175	821,431	66	397,519	1,882	8,182,306
1963	1,365	942,809	90	428,567	2,038	9,028,210
1964	1,551	867,910	68	249,826	2,032	9,723,825
1965	n/a	n/a	116	218,345	2,202	11,763,251
1966	n/a	n/a	187	191,914	2,484	14,105,450
1967	n/a	n/a	233	208,841	2,766	15,156,857
1968	n/a	n/a	166	367,617	2,740	16,844,962
1969	n/a	n/a	179	463,682	2,912	18,738,741
1970	n/a	n/a	156	374,907	2,814	20,979,977
1971	n/a	n/a	235	489,876	2,917	24,387,691
1972	n/a	n/a	292	481,747	2,776	26,748,822
1973	n/a	n/a	277	964,165	2,999	30,408,930
1974	n/a	n/a	233	733,422	2,949	33,541,289
1975	n/a	n/a	127	475,521	2,730	34,202,514
1976	n/a	n/a	143	814,530	2,723	33,922,193
1977	n/a	n/a	129	1,012,354	2,796	27,531,824
1978	n/a	n/a	151	1,033,142	2,618	18,194,120
1979	n/a	n/a	182	1,352,370	2,466	14,289,369
1980	n/a	n/a	205	555,262	2,412	13,101,104
1981	n/a	n/a	223	360,136	2,269	16,931,719
1982	n/a	n/a	204	215,746	2,312	16,820,101
1983	n/a	n/a	159	380,899	2,276	15,911,143
1984	n/a	n/a	73	83,738	2,210	18,334,061
1985	n/a	n/a	66	179,735	1,964	18,156,526
1986	n/a	n/a	36	223,396	1,634	16,844,909
1987	n/a	n/a	29	164,326	1,528	12,259,419
1988	n/a	n/a	60	10,765	1,575	10,909,340
1989	n/a	n/a	10	4,078	1,593	13,236,169

*Excludes U.S.S.R. and People's Republic of China.

†1769–1771: topsails, sloops, and schooners built in the thirteen colonies and West Florida.

Sources: Bureau of the Census, *Historical Statistics of the United States, Colonial Times to 1970* (Washington, DC: Government Printing Office, 1975), Part 2, Series Z 516 and Q 433–434; *Lloyd's Register of Shipping: Statistical Tables* (1964, 1976, 1990).

GLOSSARY

AEL: American Export Lines

AFL: American Federation of Labor

AGWI: Atlantic, Gulf & West Indies Steamship Lines

AITS: American International Travel Service

AMA: American Maritime Association

AMCV: American Classic Voyages Company

AOTC: American Overseas Tanker Corporation

ASW: antisubmarine warfare

blockade: a declaration by a belligerent in warfare prohibiting waterborne commerce with an enemy state. If the declaring state enforces the declaration, third-party ships are liable to interdiction.

blue books: the membership certificates of the San Francisco Bay area Blue Book Union, a management-controlled longshoremen's union that continued the *shape-up system* (see entry) of controlling labor. Workers destroyed their blue books in the Big Strike of 1933–1934.

Blue Riband: a traditional award, dating to the nineteenth century, for the passenger liner making the fastest crossing of the North Atlantic

blue water: the ocean, in contrast to the brown water of coastal and inland shipping

break-bulk cargo: general cargo stored in packages in the holds or on the decks of ships

brown water: coastal and inland waters, including lakes, rivers, and canals. It contrasts with blue water, international seas and oceans.

bulk cargo: homogeneous commodities, liquid or solid, such as coal, oil, ore, and stone that are carried unpackaged in the holds of specially designed vessels

bunker: a shipboard compartment for the stowage of fuel, either coal or oil

burthen: burden, the carrying capacity of a ship, expressed in tons (see *tonnage*)

cabotage: Originally coastwise shipping, the term has come to describe the restriction that many maritime states place up their coastal and inland shipping, limiting it to their own vessels and excluding foreign ships.

carrying trade: the business of transporting goods by land or sea

CDS: construction differential subsidy

CIO: Congress of Industrial Organizations

clipper ship: Clippers generally were fast sailing ships of the nineteenth century, noted for sharp-raked stems. The famous clipper ships of midcentury combined speedy hull forms with three-masted, square rigging.

coaster: a ship engaged in coastal trade

coastwise: along the coast. It is sometimes used to describe trade between the mainland United States and Puerto Rico in the Atlantic Ocean and Alaska and Hawaii in the Pacific. These latter trades are more accurately termed "offshore domestic."

collier: a tender to provide coal to a steamship

CONEX boxes: 288-cubic-foot steel containers developed by the U.S. military in World War II. They are the forerunners of modern containers.

conferences: trade associations among liner companies dating to the late nineteenth century, to establish conditions and rates of shipping service on certain routes. Beginning with the Shipping Act of 1916, the United States regulated the terms under which ships in its registry could participate.

container ship: a vessel that carries its cargo primarily or exclusively in standardized containers. Since the 1960s, these containers have been primarily 8' by 8'6" in cross section and 20 or 40 feet long.

convoy: the organization of a fleet of vessels with armed escorts in order to move them together through contested waters

CRAF: Civil Reserve Air Fleet

crimps: boardinghouse or saloon keepers who conspired with shipowners and captains to deliver crews for their vessels. They provided services for seamen ashore and then sold their debts to unscrupulous shipping executives.

deadweight tons: the weight in long tons (2,240 pounds) of a ship's cargo as determined by displacement (see *tonnage*)

dock: in the United States a wharf or pier where ships tie up to load and unload. In Britain, the dock refers to the water between the piers or wharves or the land on which a boat or ship may be beached.

domestic shipping: internal shipping within a country, moving people and cargo from one port to another within the same country. This shipping may be coastal or inland.

draft: the depth of water a ship draws, especially when fully loaded

EFC: Emergency Fleet Corporation

embargo: a temporary restraint on the arrival or departure of ships in time of war or anticipation of war. Embargoes may be general or applied only to the ships of one or more countries.

EUSC: Effective United States Control

FEC: U.S. Far East Command

flags of convenience: the registry of ships in countries of which the ship's owners are not nationals. American critics of the practice sometimes called them "runaway flags," while defenders referred to them as "flags of necessity."

free ships: a political term used around the turn of the twentieth century to advocate the right to register in the United States ships built abroad

freighter: the preferred term in shipping circles is cargo vessel, which avoids confusion with anyone who loads or handles freight

GDP: gross domestic product

gross tons: the volume of a ship's enclosed spaces measured in hundreds of cubic feet (see *tonnage*) *guerre de course*: privateering, the authorization in wartime for commercial ships to be armed and to conduct attacks on enemy commercial shipping

hiring hall: a union-run labor office that replaced the hated *shape-up system* (see entry) for maritime labor in the days before the Big Strike of 1934. The halls provided seamen and longshoremen with information about work opportunities and a rational system for assigning applicants.

ILA: International Longshoremen's Association

ILWU: International Longshoremen's and Warehousemen's Union

IMM: International Mercantile Marine Company

IMO: International Maritime Organization

impressment: the British practice of conscripting their own nationals for service at sea

inland waters: navigable rivers, canals, and lakes beyond coastal waters

intercoastal: trade between the East and West coasts of the United States

ISU: International (formerly National) Seamen's Union

Jones Act: The Merchant Marine Act of 1920, especially the provision reaffirming cabotage as U.S. policy

knots: a ship's speed as measured in nautical miles per hour. One nautical mile equals 1.151 statute miles.

LASH: Lighter Aboard SHip, a vessel design offering an alternative to container ships. Barges or lighters could be lifted aboard LASH vessels for long-distance travel and then discharged to operate in shallow waters.

LCA: Lake Carriers' Association

liner: a kind of merchant ship service providing regular carriage between two ports on a published schedule. In passenger shipping, the term also applies to the vessel itself.

LNG: Liquid Natural Gas

longshoreman: a worker involved in loading and unloading cargoes from ships

MAC: Marine Advisory Committee, under President Lyndon Johnson

mail subsidy: an annual subsidy paid by a government to a shipping company or airline to carry all mails along certain routes at specified intervals

MARAD: Maritime Administration

marshaling yard: the dockside parking lot in which containers are placed to await carriage by truck, train, or ship

megaships: the large tankers and bulk-cargo, container, and cruise ships of the twentieth century that achieved economies of scale by approaching and sometimes exceeding 1,000 feet in length

merchant marine: the commercial vessels carried on a country's registry. Called the merchant navy in Britain and the mercantile marine in some other parts of the world.

merchant mariner: a crew member on a merchant ship; historically a seaman or sailor below the rank of officer

MFP: Marine Federation of the Pacific

M and M Agreement: Mechanization and Modernization Agreement

MSC: Military Sealift Command

MSTS: Military Sea Transportation Service

MWIU: Marine Workers Industrial Union

NAFTA: North American Free Trade Agreement

NIRA: National Industrial Recovery Act

naval: originally of or relating to seafaring or shipping; now of or related to the navy

naval architecture: the design of any craft used on water, both naval and commercial

Naval Armed Guard: U.S. Navy gun crews serving on merchant ships in World War II. Small numbers of navy gun crews had also served on merchant ships in World War I.

Navigation Acts: a series of English/British laws beginning in 1651 that restricted foreign shipping through taxation and limitations on trade with Britain or her colonies

NCL: Norwegian Cruise Lines

NDRF: National Defense Reserve Fleet

NMU: National Maritime Union

NYSA: New York Shipping Association

OBO: Oil/Bulk/Ore carrier

oceanic (ocean, oceangoing): of or related to shipping on the world's seas and oceans, as opposed to coastal or inland shipping

ODS: operating differential subsidy

OPEC: Oil Producing and Exporting Countries

OSG: Overseas Shipholding Group

packet: originally a ship or boat traveling on a regular schedule between two ports to carry "packets," an early English name for mail. These vessels sometimes carried passengers and cargo as well. In time the term came to be applied to regularly scheduled shipping service, until these vessels were replaced in the nineteenth century by commercial liners carrying mail under subsidy.

Panamax: a vessel of the maximum size capable of passing through the Panama Canal, the locks of which are 1,000 feet long and 110 feet wide

PanLibHon: The trio of states—Panama, Liberia, and Honduras—that registered many American-owned ships in the twentieth century

Paukenschlag: "Drumbeat," the German submarine campaign in the first half of 1942 to attack Allied commercial shipping in the western Atlantic Ocean, the Caribbean, and the Gulf of Mexico

pier: a structure built from shore out into the water on pilings to provide a landing place for ships or a site for recreation

pirates: those who take vessels on the high seas, without state authority or sanction, from those who lawfully own them. They are distinct from *privateers* (see entry) who had letters of marque from their country to seize enemy vessels.

PMSS: Pacific Mail Steamship Company

privateers: privately owned vessels and their crews who operated with letters of marque to seize enemy commercial vessels in time of war

POL: petroleum, oil, and lubricants, a category of commodities employed by the U.S. military

proprietary shipping companies: companies that maintained a fleet of ships to support their manufacturing or distribution operations

reexporting: the transshipment of goods, which arrive in port only to be transferred to another ship for transportation to another port

registry: the system by which a ship is allowed to fly the flag of a country in return for paying fees and taxes and adhering to the country's regulations governing the ownership and operation of ships

Ro-Ro: Roll-on/Roll-off vessel, a cargo ship with special ramps that allow vehicles to be driven directly onto and off the ship at dockside

RRF: Ready Reserve Fleet

sailor: generally a seaman or mariner; one who is involved in navigation, usually of shipboard rank below an officer or petty officer. It formerly applied to both naval and commercial mariners, but now is reserved in the United States primarily for naval mariners. Commercial sailors in the United States are usually seamen, mariners, or merchant mariners.

scab cargo: cargo subject to boycott by union maritime workers because it has been handled by nonunion longshoremen or carried on a ship with nonunion seamen

seaman: see *sailor*

shape-up system: a method of hiring maritime workers on the American waterfront in the days before the union hiring halls. Would-be workers would "shape up" in a circle around the representative of management, who would often choose favorites or those who offered a kickback.

shipbuilder: a shipwright or a naval architect; one who designs or builds ships

shipper: one who has cargo to transport; the shipper is not necessarily the shipowner or ship operator, unless it is a *proprietary* company (see entry).

shipping: the act of transporting goods or passengers by water; also, the collective assets available to move goods and passengers by water, as in "the shipping available within the U.S. merchant marine in 1917 was inadequate."

shipowner: the person or organization that owns a vessel; this may or may not be the ship operator.

SOC: ship operation center

SOLAS: Safety of Life at Sea

SS: steamship

steerage: that portion of a passenger-carrying vessel, originally near the steering mechanism, reserved for passengers paying the lowest fare. Later it came to apply to all ship's spaces, often wretched, allotted to such passengers.

stevedore: one who loads and unloads cargo from commercial vessels. In the United States, the term is often reserved to supervisors.

Suezmax: Vessels of the maximum size capable of passing through the Suez Canal. Since the Suez Canal has no locks, the defining limitation is draft, currently fifty-three feet. The restriction applies almost exclusively to tankers.

SUP: Sailors' Union of the Pacific (formerly Coast Seamen's Union)

supercargo: originally the superintendent of cargo, an officer aboard ship who supervised management of the cargo and all commercial transactions abroad; also an agent of the owner of the cargo when this was not the shipowner

syndicalism: an industrial labor movement to transfer the means of production and

distribution from current owners to labor unions; a trans-union movement that
favored general strikes

tanker: a vessel specially designed to carry unpackaged liquid cargo, especially oil

TEU: twenty-foot equivalent unit. The standard measure of shipping container size:
8' by 8'6" by 20'.

tonnage: originally a measure of how many tuns (barrels) of wine a ship could carry,
it came to be a general volumetric measure of a ship's carrying capacity, that is,
the size of its enclosed spaces. Over time, various formulae have been adopted to
calculate the cubic feet of space below the main deck, which is now converted to
gross tons on the basis of 100 cubic feet per ton. The same dimension minus the
shipboard spaces devoted to crew quarters, stores, engine space, fuel, and so on,
is net tonnage. *Deadweight tons* is the total weight of cargo as determined by
measuring the displacement of the vessel fully loaded and subtracting the displacement with crew, fuel, and stores, but no cargo, aboard. Deadweight tons are
equal to 2,240 pounds, with 35 cubic feet of water equal to one ton.

tramp shipping: moving from port to port in search of cargoes. Usually the realm of
older, slower ships, tramping responded to market conditions in ways that *packets* (see entry) and *liners* (see entry) could not.

triangular trade: shipping along routes with three legs. Some such voyages actually
visited all three ports sequentially. More often cargoes from port A and C were
sent to port B for *reexporting* (see entry)

ULCC: Ultra Large Crude Carrier

unitized cargo: break-bulk cargo that has been placed in some container for shipment. Modern containers are a form of unitized cargo.

UNRRA: United Nations Reconstruction and Relief Agency

USL: United States Lines

USMC: United States Maritime Commission

USS: United States ship

VLCC: Very Large Crude Carrier

"witnesses": union dockworkers who were paid (featherbedded) to observe the loading and unloading of ships

WSA: War Shipping Administration

Wobblies: members of the Industrial Workers of the World, advocates of a single
world labor union and the abolition of the wage system of labor, that is, of
capitalism

BIBLIOGRAPHIC
ESSAY

This study relies primarily on secondary sources. This strategy was designed both to allow for the completion of such a wide-ranging work in a reasonable amount of time and also to conduct something of a survey of the existing literature on American maritime history. The authors have concluded that the literature is extensive and of generally good quality. The greatest weakness, both in the secondary literature and in the primary data on the topic, is the spottiness of coverage in some areas that have yet to attract the scholarly attention they deserve. For example, there is no thorough and reliable history of the American merchant marine in World War II, and the data on American domestic shipping is inconsistent and irregular.

What follows is a brief account of the most important works consulted for this study. Detailed citations and documentation are provided in the notes. The goal here is to give a sense of the source material, its strengths and weaknesses, and the critical studies that should serve as the basis for further research. This is also something of a catalog of the works that had the greatest impact on our thinking.

Sources of Data

The U.S. Maritime Administration (MARAD) within the Department of Transportation maintains historical data on American maritime activity. Some of the historical materials can be found only by visiting MARAD in Washington, D.C., but much is available online at www.marad.dot.gov. MARAD has a historical bias toward oceanic shipping, which may be balanced by consulting the records of the U.S. Army Corps of Engineers. Many of these records are available only in government print publications of the nineteenth and twentieth centuries, but the U.S. Army Corps of Engineers Institute for Water Resources in Alexandria, Virginia, maintains publications going back to the 1960s, some of which are available online at www.iwr.usace.army.mil/index.cfm. Earlier material on the work of the Corps of Engineers may be found in the corps' library system, which is accessible at www.usace.army.mil/library/contact.html.

The corps' Waterborne Commerce Statistic Center in New Orleans, Louisiana, is accessible at www.ndc.iwr.usace.army.mil/wcsc/wcsc.htm.

Merchant Marine Statistics were published annually from 1924 to 1944 by the Bureau of Navigation and its successor agencies, variously within the Treasury Department or the Department of Commerce. The *Annual Report of the Commissioner of Navigation* (1884–1932) was likewise published by agencies within the Treasury Department or the Department of Commerce. The *Annual Report of the Lake Carriers' Association* has appeared since 1885.

Historical Statistics of the United States (various editions, 1957–2006) and the *Statistical Abstract of the United States*, publications of the U.S. Bureau of the Census, have significant information on shipping, as well as related data on transportation, the economy, labor, and population. Online versions of the latest editions of both are available at the Bureau of the Census Web site, www.census.gov. The gold standard for comparative international data has been set by Angus Maddison's magisterial studies for the United Nations Organisation for Economic Co-operation and Development, especially *Monitoring the World Economy* (1992) and *The World Economy: A Millennial Perspective* (2001). For a comparable survey with more maritime data, see B. R. Mitchell, *International Historical Statistics*. The fifth edition of this three-volume set, which appeared in 2003, covers 1750 to 2000. Most data on the world's commercial ships derives from *Lloyd's Register of Shipping*, which has been published annually since 1760 and in occasional compendia. Many sources provide information on the world's ports since the Second World War, but data on ports before that time is scattered and inconsistent.

The most consulted reference work in the preparation of this study was undoubtedly René de la Pedraja, *A Historical Dictionary of the U.S. Merchant Marine and Shipping Industry since the Introduction of Steam* (Westport, CT: Greenwood Press, 1994). *The Oxford Companion to Ships and the Sea*, edited by I. C. B. Dear and Peter Kemp, 2nd ed. (Oxford: Oxford University Press, 2005), is more recent and focuses on the entire world from a British perspective. Martin Stopford, *Maritime Economics*, 2nd ed. (London: Routledge, 1999), explains its topic with clarity and thoroughness.

Something of an encyclopedia of American maritime experience may be found in Benjamin W. Labaree et al., *America and the Sea: A Maritime History* (Mystic, CT: Mystic Seaport Museum, 1998). This large-format, sumptuously illustrated survey features anecdotes, pictures, vignettes, and profiles from American maritime experience, stitched together with a loose narrative thread. In the same vein are a number of reliable picture books that visually explore world or American maritime experience. Among the most useful have been John and Alice Durant, *Pictorial History of American Ships* (New York: A.S. Barnes, 1953); Peter Kemp, ed., *Encyclopedia of Ships and Seafaring* (New York: Crown, 1980); Chris Marshall, ed., *The Encyclopedia of Ships: The History and Specifications of Over 1200 Ships* (New York: Barnes and Noble, 1995); *The Lore of Ships* (New York: Crescent Books, 1975); and Lincoln Paine, *Ships of the World: An Historical Encyclopedia* (Boston: Houghton Mifflin, 1997).

Synthetic Works

A number of important histories cover more than one of the chronological parts into which *The Way of the Ship* has been divided. The historian K. Jack Bauer came closest to a synthetic analysis in *A Maritime History of the United States: The Role of America's Seas and Waterways* (Columbia: University of South Carolina Press, 1988). A number of stimulating essays were brought together in Robert A. Kilmarx, ed., *America's Maritime Legacy: A History of the U.S. Merchant Marine and Shipbuilding Industry since Colonial Times* (Boulder, CO: Westview Press, 1979). Still, none of the modern studies that we found compare with John G. B. Hutchins, *The American Maritime Industries and Public Policy, 1789–1914: An Economic History*, Harvard Economic Studies, vol. 71 (Cambridge, MA: Harvard University Press, 1941). Hutchins's work not only organizes an enormous amount of primary evidence in a thorough and thoughtful analysis of the American maritime industries broadly conceived, it also sets the standard for historical investigation of the impact of public policy on the American merchant marine. The latest installment in this scholarly tradition, Andrew Gibson and Arthur Donovan, *The Abandoned Ocean: A History of United States Maritime Policy* (Columbia: University of South Carolina Press, 2000), carries the story through the end of the twentieth century. Most such studies attempt to explain the failure of the United States to maintain a competitive merchant marine, in the tradition of Winthrop L. Marvin, *The American Merchant Marine: Its History and Romance from 1620 to 1902* (New York: Charles Scribner's Sons, 1902). Samuel L. Lawrence, *United States Merchant Shipping Policies and Politics* (Washington, DC: Brookings Institution, 1966) is a distinguished contribution to this tradition. Clinton H. Whitehurst Jr. posed a similar question in *The U.S. Shipbuilding Industry: Past, Present, and Future* (Annapolis, MD: Naval Institute Press, 1986), though the study focuses far more on contemporary policy than on its history. His study may be profitably supplemented by F. G. Bassett Jr., *The Shipbuilding Business in the United States*, vol. 1 (New York: Society of Naval Architects and Marine Engineers, 1948), which contains a surprising amount of historical information. On one of the most important policy questions in American maritime history, see Rodney Carlisle, *Sovereignty for Sale: The Origins and Evolution of the Panamanian and Liberian Flags of Convenience* (Annapolis, MD: Naval Institute Press, 1981), and George Dalzell, *Flight from the Flag: The Continuing Effect of the Civil War upon the American Carrying Trade* (Chapel Hill: University of North Carolina Press, 1940).

General Monographs

A number of noteworthy studies cross chronological boundaries but focus more narrowly on special topics. They deserve special mention because they are models of scholarship and they shaped the interpretations that permeate this study. Though the work of Douglass C. North on the development of the American economy has fallen out of favor with many economic historians, we found it enormously stimulating, especially on the period of the early republic. We relied particularly on *The Economic Growth of the United States, 1790–1860* (Englewood Cliffs, NJ: Prentice Hall, 1961). We also turned often to one of North's students, Gary M. Walton. Among his many works, we found particularly useful Gary M. Walton and Ross M. Patterson, *History of the American Economy*, 5th ed. (New York: Harcourt Brace Jovanovich, 1983); Gary M. Walton and James F. Shepherd, *The Economic Rise of Early America* (New York: Cambridge University Press, 1979); and James F. Shepherd and Gary M. Walton, *Shipping, Maritime Trade, and the Economic Development of Colonial North America* (Cambridge: Cambridge University Press, 1972).

René de la Pedraja, *The Rise and Decline of U.S. Merchant Shipping in the Twentieth Century* (New York: Twayne, 1992), has all the archival mastery of his

Historical Dictionary combined with a critical deconstruction of the American maritime establishment. Shipowners come in for especially withering analysis. Joseph P.
Goldberg's *The Maritime Story: A Study in Labor-Management Relations* (Cambridge,
MA: Harvard University Press, 1958) tells the seamen's story from the late nineteenth
century to the mid-1950s, touching on the history of longshore labor when it inter-
sects. Thomas R. Heinrich, *Ships for the Seven Seas: Philadelphia Shipbuilding in the
Age of Industrial Capitalism* (Baltimore: Johns Hopkins University Press, 1997),
moves from the colonial era to the period between the world wars, doing for shipbuilding on the Delaware River what Goldberg did for labor. Still useful on the relationship between commercial shipping and naval activity is Robert Greenhalgh
Albion's *Sea Lanes in Wartime: The American Experience, 1775–1942* (New York:
Norton, 1942). A somewhat narrower study that nonetheless addresses an important
civil-military issue that has spanned the centuries is Charles Dance Gibson, *Mer-
chantman? Or Ship of War: A Synopsis of Laws; U.S. State Department Positions; and
Practices Which Alter the Peaceful Character of U.S. Merchant Vessels in Time of War*
(Camden, ME: Ensign Press, 1986). The best overview of the U.S. Navy is Kenneth
J. Hagan, *This People's Navy: The Making of American Sea Power* (New York: Free
Press, 1991). Peter Neill, ed., *American Sea Writing: A Literary Anthology* (New York:
Library of America, 2000), captures the lore of the sea from the colonial period to the
late twentieth century.

Temporal Monographs

Within each part of this study, a number of sources proved to be especially influen-
tial or exemplary. In Part I, the works of Gary M. Walton were supplemented with
John J. McCusker and Russell R. Menard, *The Economy of British America,
1607–1789* (Chapel Hill: University of North Carolina Press, for the Institute of
Early American History and Culture, 1985). Joseph A. Goldenberg, *Shipbuilding in
Colonial America* (Charlottesville: University Press of Virginia, 1976), provides the
best treatment of this critical topic, while Cathy Matson, *Merchants and Empire:
Trading in Colonial New York* (Baltimore: Johns Hopkins University Press, 1998),
illuminates colonial commerce far more broadly than its title suggests. Maritime
labor has been captured with stunning historical verisimilitude in a number of
important works, including Daniel Vickers, *Farmers and Fishermen: Two Centuries of
Work in Essex County, Massachusetts, 1630–1850* (Chapel Hill: University of North
Carolina Press, 1994); Daniel Vickers with Vince Walsh, *Young Men and the Sea:
Maritime Society in Salem, Massachusetts, 1630–1850* (New Haven, CT: Yale Univer-
sity Press, 2005); Marcus Rediker, *Between the Devil and the Deep Blue Sea: Merchant
Seamen, Pirates, and the Anglo-American Maritime World, 1700–1750* (Cambridge:
Cambridge University Press, 1987); Paul Gilje, *Liberty on the Waterfront: American
Maritime Culture in the Age of Revolution* (Philadelphia: University of Pennsylvania
Press, 2004); and W. Jeffrey Bolster, *Black Jacks: African American Seamen in the Age
of Sail* (Cambridge, MA: Harvard University Press, 1997).

The central interpretation of Part II relies heavily on George Rogers Taylor, *The
Transportation Revolution, 1815–1860*, vol. 4 of *The Economic History of the United*

States (New York: Rinehart, 1951). This was profitably complemented by yet another Walton collaboration, Erik F. Haites, James Mak, and Gary M. Walton, *Western River Transportation: The Early Era of Internal Development, 1810–1860* (Baltimore: Johns Hopkins University Press, 1975). James Thomas Flexner's *Steamboats Come True: American Inventors in Action* (New York: Fordham University Press, [1944] 1992), proved to be still the most useful guide to this pivotal story, complemented on the western rivers by Louis C. Hunter, *Steamboats of the Western Rivers: An Economic and Technological History* (New York: Dover, [1949] 1993). Of the many excellent works on the California gold rush, the most useful proved to be H. W. Brands, *The Age of Gold: The California Gold Rush* (New York: Doubleday, 2002).

In Part III, Hans Keiler, *American Shipping: Its History and Economic Conditions* (Jena, Germany: G. Fischer, 1913), provided a useful perspective on American experience and policy. Several works on maritime labor revealed how thoroughly this topic had changed since the colonial period and the early republic: Elmo P. Hohman, *History of American Merchant Seamen* (Hamden, CT: Shoe String Press, 1956); Paul S. Taylor, *The Sailors' Union of the Pacific* (New York, Ronald Press, 1923); and Hyman Weintraub, *Andrew Furuseth: Emancipator of the Seamen* (Berkeley: University of California Press, 1959).

Part IV framed World War I in the context of Jeffrey J. Safford's *Wilsonian Maritime Diplomacy, 1913–1921* (New Brunswick, NJ: Rutgers University Press, 1978). Joseph Goldberg's *The Maritime Story* was complemented with Bruce Nelson, *Workers on the Waterfront: Seamen, Longshoremen, and Unionism in the 1930s* (Urbana: University of Illinois Press, 1988). The definitive work on American merchant marine losses in World War II is Arthur A. Moore's exhaustive, meticulous *A Careless Word . . . A Needless Sinking* (n.p.: Dennis A. Roland Chapter of New Jersey of the American Merchant Marine Veterans, 1998). For certain information, it may be profitably supplemented by Robert M. Browning Jr., *U.S. Merchant Vessel War Casualties of World War II* (Annapolis, MD: Naval Institute Press, 1996). Michael Gannon, a noted authority on the battle of the Atlantic, wrote the most useful book on *Paukenschlag*: *Operation Drumbeat: The Dramatic True Story of Germany's First U-Boat Attacks Along the American Coast in World War II* (New York: Harper and Row, 1990). The best source on the Liberty ship program is still Frederick C. Lane, *Ships for Victory: A History of Shipbuilding under the U.S. Maritime Commission in World War II* (Baltimore, MD: Johns Hopkins University Press, [1951] 2001).

In addition to the works already cited, Part V relied upon Marc Levinson, *The Box: How the Shipping Container Made the World Smaller and the World Economy Bigger* (Princeton, NJ: Princeton University Press, 2006); Brian J. Cudahy, *The Cruise Ship Phenomenon in North America* (Centreville, MD: Cornell Maritime Press, 2001); and Shashi Kumar and Jan Hoffmann, "Globalisation: The Maritime Nexus," in *The Handbook of Maritime Economics and Business*, ed. Costas Th. Grammenos (London: Informa, 2002), 35–62, http://bell.mma.edu/~skumar/IAMEBook.pdf (accessed July 1, 2006).

NOTES

1. The Colonies and the Sea

1. Cynthia J. Van Zandt, "The Dutch Connection: Isaac Allerton and the Dynamics of English Cultural Anxiety in the *Gouden Eeuw*," in *Connecting Cultures: The Netherlands in Five Centuries of Transatlantic Exchange,* ed. Rosemarijn Hoefte and Johanna Kardux (Amsterdam: European Contributions to American Studies, 1994), 51–76.

2. Josiah Child quoted in Joseph A. Goldenberg, *Shipbuilding in Colonial America* (Charlottesville: University Press of Virginia, 1976), 23.

3. John J. McCusker, "Measuring Colonial Gross Domestic Product: An Introduction," *William and Mary Quarterly,* 3d Ser., vol. 56 (Jan. 1999): 3–8; John J. McCusker and Russell R. Menard, *The Economy of British America, 1607–1789* (Chapel Hill: University of North Carolina Press, for the Institute of Early American History and Culture, 1985), 5; Bernard Bailyn, "The Idea of Atlantic History" *Itinerario* 20 (1996): 19–44.

4. Stanley Lebergott, *Manpower in Economic Growth: The American Record Since 1800* (New York: McGraw-Hill, 1964); Elaine Forman Crane, *Ebb Tide in New England: Women, Seaports, and Social Change, 1630–1800* (Boston: Northeastern University Press, 1998); Lisa Norling, *Captain Ahab Had a Wife: New England Women and the Whalefishery, 1720–1870* (Chapel Hill: University of North Carolina Press, 2000).

2. Richard Hakluyt's Maritime Plantations

1. Robert Brenner, *Merchants and Revolution: Commercial Change, Political Conflict and London's Overseas Traders, 1550–1653* (Princeton, NJ: Princeton University Press, 1993).

2. Brenner, *Merchants and Revolution,* 48; Kenneth R. Andrews, *Trade, Plunder and Settlement: Maritime Enterprise and the Genesis of the British Empire, 1480–1630* (Cambridge: Cambridge University Press, 1984).

3. Jonathan I. Israel, *Dutch Primacy in World Trade, 1585–1740* (Oxford: Clarendon Press, 1989), 1–11; K. G. Davies, *The North Atlantic World in the Seventeenth Century* (Minneapolis: University of Minnesota Press, 1974), 313; Andrews, *Trade, Plunder and Settlement,* 362.

4. Jack P. Greene, *The Intellectual Construction of America: Exceptionalism and Identity from 1492 to 1800* (Chapel Hill: University of North Carolina Press, 1993), 36–45.

5. Samuel Eliot Morison, *The European Discovery of America: The Northern Voyages, A.D. 500–1600* (New York: Oxford University Press, 1971), 494–650; Andrews, *Trade, Plunder and Settlement*, 304–340; Carole Shammas, "English Commercial Development and American Colonization, 1560–1620," in *The Westward Enterprise: English Activities in Ireland, the Atlantic and America, 1480–1650*, ed. K. R. Andrews, N. P. Canny, and P. E. H. Hair (Detroit: Wayne State University Press, 1979), 159; David Beers Quinn, *England and the Discovery of America*, 1481–1620 (New York: Knopf, 1974).

6. Bernard Bailyn, *The New England Merchants in the Seventeenth Century* (Cambridge, MA: Harvard University Press, 1955), 13–15, 24, 26, 29.

7. Pring quoted in Charles Herbert Levermore, ed., *Forerunners and Competitors of the Pilgrims and Puritans*, 2 vols. (Brooklyn, NY: New England Society of Brooklyn, 1912), vol. I, 64; Horace P. Beck, *The American Indian as a Sea-Fighter in Colonial Times* (Mystic, CT: Marine Historical Association, 1959), 10–11.

8. Beck, *American Indian as a Sea-Fighter*, 5.

9. Ibid. 16–22; Brereton quoted in Levermore, *Forerunners and Competitors*, vol. I, 32.

10. Beck, *American Indian as a Sea-Fighter*, 22.

11. Hicks quoted in Beck, *American Indian as a Sea-Fighter*, 63–64.

3. John Winthrop's Godly Society by the Sea

1. Shammas, "English Commercial Development and American Colonization, 1560–1620," 163.

2. Joyce Appleby, *Capitalism and a New Social Order: The Republican Vision of the 1790s* (New York: New York University Press, 1984), 28.

3. Hall quoted in Quinn, *England and the Discovery of America*, 208; Darrett B. Rutman, *Winthrop's Boston: Portrait of a Puritan Town, 1630–1649* (Chapel Hill: University of North Carolina Press, for the Institute of Early American History and Culture, 1965), 8.

4. Shammas, "English Commercial Development and American Colonization, 1560–1620," 164–167.

5. Goldenberg, *Shipbuilding in Colonial America*, 8.

6. Rutman, *Winthrop's Boston*, 3–8, 21–22.

7. Goldenberg, *Shipbuilding in Colonial America*, 7–8; Bailyn, *New England Merchants*, 23–26.

8. Bailyn, *New England Merchants*, 25.

9. *Calendar of State Papers, Colonial Series* (London: Kraus Reprint of HM Stationer's Office, 1860–1964), vol. I, 275, cited in William Burgess Leavenworth, "The Ship in the Forest: New England Maritime Industries and Coastal Environment, 1630–1850" (Ph.D. dissertation, University of New Hampshire, 1999), 46–47.

10. William Avery Baker, "Some Seventeenth-Century Vessels and the Sparrow-Hawk," *Pilgrim Society Notes*, Ser. 1, no. 28 (Nov. 28, 1980).

11. Leavenworth, "Ship in the Forest," 24–25, 34–38, 42–47, 66–69, 78–80. Winthrop quote on 80.

12. John G. B. Hutchins, *The American Maritime Industries and Public Policy, 1789–1914* (Cambridge, MA: Harvard University Press, 1941), 123–124, 144–157; Leavenworth, "The Ship in the Forest," 58–78.

13. McCusker and Menard, *Economy of British America*, 65; Margaret Ellen Newell, *From Dependency to Independence: Economic Revolution in Colonial New England* (Ithaca, NY: Cornell University Press, 1998), 52–55.

14. *Winthrop's Journal*, vol. II, 23 (Feb. 1641), quoted in Leavenworth, "Ship in the Forest," 63.

15. Rutman, *Winthrop's Boston*, 180–189; Bailyn, *New England Merchants*, 75–86. Quotation from William Wood, *New England's Prospect* (London, 1634), ed. Alden T. Vaughn (Amherst: University of Massachusetts Press, 1977), 59.

16. Rutman, *Winthrop's Boston*, 184–193; Bailyn, *New England Merchants*, 88–98. John Eliot quoted in Rutman, *Winthrop's Boston*, 188.

17. Bailyn, *New England Merchants*, 95–98, quotation on 96.

4. Codfish, Timber, and Profit

1. Ralph Davis, *The Rise of the English Shipping Industry in the Seventeenth and Eighteenth Centuries* (London: Macmillan, 1962), 267–298, quotation on 268.

2. McCusker and Menard, *Economy of British America*, 108, 130, 174, 199; Daniel Vickers, *Farmers and Fishermen: Two Centuries of Work in Essex County, Massachusetts, 1630–1850* (Chapel Hill: University of North Carolina Press, for the Institute of Early American History and Culture, 1994), 98.

3. Vickers, *Farmers and Fishermen*, 85–100.

4. Neill DePaoli, "Life on the Edge: Community and Trade on the Anglo-American Periphery, Pemaquid, Maine, 1610–1689" (Ph.D. dissertation, University of New Hampshire, 2001); Vickers, *Farmers and Fishermen*, 91–98, quotation on 98.

5. Vickers, *Farmers and Fishermen*, 98.

6. Ibid., 91–98, quotation on 144.

7. McCusker and Menard, *Economy of British America*, 100–101, quotation on 101.

8. Goldenberg, *Shipbuilding in Colonial America*, 26; Israel, *Dutch Primacy in World Trade*, 324; Oliver Rink, *Holland on the Hudson: An Economic and Social History of Dutch New York* (Ithaca, NY: Cornell University Press, 1986), 158.

9. Philip D. Curtin, *The Rise and Fall of the Plantation Complex: Essays in Atlantic History* (Cambridge: Cambridge University Press, 1990), 11–13; Davis, *Rise of the English Shipping Industry*, 267–299.

10. Goldenberg, *Shipbuilding in Colonial America*, 6–7.

5. An Infant Industry

1. Newell, *From Dependency to Independence*, 14.
2. Vickers, *Farmers and Fishermen*, 13–29; Newell, *From Dependency to Independence*, 36–71.
3. Newell, *From Dependency to Independence*, 49–59, quotes on 57 and 55. Leavenworth, "Ship in the Forest," 87, 92–93.
4. Davis, *Rise of the English Shipping Industry*, 300–308, quotation on 303.
5. Nuala Zahedieh, "Overseas Expansion and Trade in the Seventeenth Century," in *The Origins of Empire: British Overseas Enterprise to the Close of the Seventeenth Century*, ed. Nicholas Canny (Oxford: Oxford University Press, 1998), 398–422, esp. 408.
6. Zahedieh, "Overseas Expansion and Trade," 406; McCusker and Menard, *Economy of British America*, 47.
7. Compare McCusker and Menard, *Economy of British America*, 35-39 with W. A. Speck, "The International and Imperial Context," in *Colonial British America: Essays in the New History of the Early Modern Era*, ed. Jack P. Greene and J. R. Pole (Baltimore: Johns Hopkins University Press, 1984), 384–407. See also Joyce Appleby, *Economic Thought and Ideology in Seventeenth-Century England* (Princeton, NJ: Princeton University Press, 1978).
8. Speck, "The International and Imperial Context," 392–393; McCusker and Menard, *Economy of British America*, 48–49.
9. McCusker and Menard, *Economy of British America*, 354.
10. Robert C. Ritchie, *Captain Kidd and the War against the Pirates* (Cambridge, MA: Harvard University Press, 1986); Douglass C. North, "Sources of Productivity Change in Ocean Shipping, 1600–1850," *Journal of Political Economy* 76 (1968): 953–970, quotations on 959, 960.
11. Gary B. Nash, *The Urban Crucible: Social Change, Political Consciousness, and the Origins of the American Revolution* (Cambridge, MA: Harvard University Press, 1979), 66–68; Cathy Matson, *Merchants and Empire: Trading in Colonial New York* (Baltimore: Johns Hopkins University Press, 1998), 63.
12. Quotations in Nash, *Urban Crucible*, 68, and Matson, *Merchants and Empire*, 63.
13. Ritchie, *Captain Kidd*, 228–238. Viola F. Barnes, "Richard Wharton, A Seventeenth Century New England Colonial," *Publications of the Colonial Society of Massachusetts, Transactions*, ed. Kenneth Ballard Murdock (Boston, 1927), 238–270, quotation on 241.

6. The Shipping Business in 1700

1. Bernard Bailyn and Lotte Bailyn, *Massachusetts Shipping, 1697–1714: A Statistical Study* (Cambridge, MA: Harvard University Press, 1959), 56–73.
2. Ibid., 5, 15, 21, 24, 25, 81, quotation on 21.
3. Ibid., 21; McCusker and Menard, *Economy of British America*, 190–193; Matson, *Merchants and Empire*, 50–51.

4. McCusker and Menard, *Economy of British America*, 202–204, quotation on 204.

5. Converse D. Clowse, *Economic Beginnings in Colonial South Carolina, 1670–1730* (Columbia: University of South Carolina Press, 1971), 90–91, 136–137, 225–226, 236; W. Jeffrey Bolster, *Black Jacks: African American Seamen in the Age of Sail* (Cambridge, MA: Harvard University Press, 1997), 21–24.

6. Jacob M. Price, "Summation: The American Panorama of Atlantic Port Cities," in *Atlantic Port Cities: Economy, Culture and Society in the Atlantic World, 1650–1850* (Knoxville: University of Tennessee Press, 1991), 262–276, quotation on 269. Bailyn and Bailyn, *Massachusetts Shipping*, 22.

7. Paul Hoffman, *Florida's Frontiers* (Bloomington: Indiana University Press, 2002), population figures on 202; John Jay TePaske, *The Governorship of Spanish Florida* (Durham, NC: Duke University Press, 1964); J. Leitch Wright Jr., *Anglo-Spanish Rivalry in North America* (Athens: University of Georgia Press, 1971).

8. Marcel Giraud, *A History of French Louisiana: The Reign of Louis XIV, 1698–1715* (Baton Rouge: Louisiana State University Press, 1974); Daniel H. Thomas, *Fort Toulouse: The French Outpost at the Alabamas on the Coosa* (Tuscaloosa: University of Alabama Press, 1989); John G. Clark, *New Orleans, 1718–1812* (Baton Rouge: Louisiana State University Press, 1970).

9. Bailyn and Bailyn, *Massachusetts Shipping*, 18–19.

10. Ibid., 27–29.

11. Ibid., 15–38, quotation on 35.

12. Ibid., 31–32.

13. Nash, *Urban Crucible*, 23, 424.

14. Byron Fairchild, *Messrs. William Pepperrell: Merchants at Piscataqua* (Ithaca, NY: Cornell University Press, 1954), 19–20.

15. Ibid., 31–37.

16. Fairchild, *Messrs. William Pepperrell*, 165–166; William M. Sargent, *York Deeds* (Portland: Brown Thurston and Company, 1889), vi, folios 58, 59, 129, 137, 138, 139, 163; *York Deeds* (Portland: Brown Thurston and Company, 1894), x, folios 263, 264, 123.

17. Fairchild, *Messrs. William Pepperrell*, 165; Neal W. Allen Jr., ed. *Province and Court Records of Maine: The Court Records of York County, Maine, 1692–1711* (Portland: Anthoensen Press, 1958), iv, 32–33, 39, 41, 45, 67, 121, 206, 245–247, 268, 385; Neal W. Allen, Jr., ed. *Province and Court Records of Maine: The Court Records of York County, Maine, 1711–1718* (Portland: Anthoensen Press, 1964), v, xxii, 3, 26, 52, 75, 86, 121, 133, 160, 175, 196.

18. Bailyn and Bailyn, *Massachusetts Shipping*, 68–71; Nash, *Urban Crucible*, 56–57.

19. Fairchild, *Messrs. William Pepperrell*, 48–50, 54–65.

20. Ibid., 73–77.

21. Ibid., 93–98, 122–123, 127–129.

7. The Eclipse of Boston

1. On demographic growth, see Greene, *Intellectual Construction of America*, 78–79.

2. T. H. Breen, *The Marketplace of Revolution: How Consumer Politics Shaped American Independence* (New York: Oxford University Press, 2004).

3. Two prominent studies conveying the sense that the business of shipping did not change much are K. Jack Bauer, *A Maritime History of the United States: The Role of America's Seas and Waterways* (Columbia: University of South Carolina Press, 1988); and Benjamin W. Labaree et al., *America and the Sea: A Maritime History* (Mystic, CT: Mystic Seaport Museum, 1998). For emphasis on the diversification of mercantile activity, see Thomas M. Doerflinger, *A Vigorous Spirit of Enterprise: Merchants and Economic Development in Revolutionary Philadelphia* (Chapel Hill: University of North Carolina Press, for the Institute of Early American History and Culture, 1986).

4. Doerflinger, *Vigorous Spirit of Enterprise*, 85; Matson, *Merchants and Empire*; John W. Tyler, "The First Revolution: Boston Merchants and the Acts of Trade, 1760–1774" (Ph.D. dissertation, Princeton University, 1980).

5. Greene, *Intellectual Construction of America*, 81.

6. Nash, *Urban Crucible*, 54–75, quotations on 61.

7. Ibid., 72–75; Doerflinger, *Vigorous Spirit*, 5.

8. Nash, *Urban Crucible*, 65–66; Matson, *Merchants and Empire*, 130.

9. Matson, *Merchants and Empire*, 130, 142.

10. Ibid., 141–142, 170–171.

11. Ibid., 142–143, 150–151.

12. Tyler, "First Revolution," 10.

13. W. T. Baxter, *The House of Hancock: Business in Boston, 1724–1775* (New York: Russell and Russell, 1965, reprinted from Harvard Studies in Business History, 1945), 58–107, quotations on 61–62.

14. Matson, *Merchants and Empire*, 203–214; Tyler, "First Revolution," 28–90, 116–118.

15. Carl E. Swanson, *Predators and Prizes: American Privateering and Imperial Warfare, 1739-1748* (Columbia: University of South Carolina Press, 1991), 3, 118, 139–140, 181–182.

16. Ibid., 218–219; Doerflinger, *Vigorous Spirit*, 157–164.

17. Christine Leigh Heyrman, *Commerce and Culture: The Maritime Communities of Colonial Massachusetts, 1690-1750* (New York: W. W. Norton & Co., 1984), 52.

18. Paul G. E. Clemens, *The Atlantic Economy and Colonial Maryland's Eastern Shore: From Tobacco to Grain* (Ithaca, NY: Cornell University Press, 1980), 198–205; McCusker and Menard, *Economy of British America*, 128–133.

19. McCusker and Menard, *Economy of British America*, 133.

20. Gary M. Walton and James F. Shepherd, *The Economic Rise of Early America* (Cambridge: Cambridge University Press, 1979) 91–93, quotation on 93; Doerflinger, *Vigorous Spirit of Enterprise*, 116–119.

21. Jay Coughtry, *The Notorious Triangle: Rhode Island and the African Slave Trade, 1700–1807* (Philadelphia: Temple University Press, 1981); Walton and Shepherd, *Economic Rise of Early America*, 91.

22. Coughtry, *Notorious Triangle*, 6–7.

23. The emigration figures come from Aaron Spencer Fogelman, *Hopeful Journeys: German Immigration, Settlement and Political Culture in Colonial America* (Philadelphia: University of Pennsylvania Press, 1996), 2. On the slave trade, see David Eltis, "The Volume and Structure of the Transatlantic Slave Trade: A Reassessment," *William and Mary Quarterly*, 3d Ser., vol. 58 (Jan. 2001): 17–46. That issue of *William and Mary Quarterly*, devoted to "New Perspectives on the Transatlantic Slave Trade," includes other valuable essays. See also Philip D. Curtin, *The Atlantic Slave Trade: A Census* (Madison: University of Wisconsin Press, 1969); Herbert S. Klein, "Economic Aspects of the Eighteenth-Century Slave Trade," in *The Rise of the Merchant Empires*, ed. James D. Tracy (Cambridge: Cambridge University Press, 1990); and David Eltis and David Richardson, "The 'Numbers Game' and Routes to Slavery," *Slavery and Abolition* 18 (1997): 1–15.

24. Marianne S. Wokeck, *Trade in Strangers: The Beginnings of Mass Migration to North America* (University Park: Pennsylvania State University Press, 1999), 59–77, quotation on 68.

25. Wokeck, *Trade in Strangers*, 95–97.

26. Doerflinger, *Vigorous Spirit*, 157–158.

8. Coastal Commerce in Colonial America

1. Emory R. Johnson et al., *History of Domestic and Foreign Commerce of the United States* (Washington, DC: Carnegie Institute of Washington, 1915), 162–163; McCusker and Menard, *Economy of British America*, 86; Andros quoted in Matson, *Merchants and Empire*, 73; Jefferson to Albert Gallatin, May 6, 1808, in Louis Martin Sears, *Jefferson and the Embargo* (New York: Octagon Books, 1966), 75–76.

2. Rutman, *Winthrop's Boston*, 35–36.

3. *Thomas Lechford Notebook, 1638–1641* (Cambridge, MA: John Wilson and Son, 1885), 223.

4. Daniel Vickers, *Young Men and the Sea: Maritime Society in Salem, Massachusetts, 1630–1850* (New Haven, CT: Yale University Press, 2005), 29–41.

5. Manuscript Account Book of Col. William Pepperrell, 1716–1720, Portsmouth Athenaeum, Portsmouth, NH.

6. Piscataqua Naval Officer's report "clearings for coasting sloops and other small open vessels loaden with lumber, &c," 1695, Public Record Office, CO 5, North America and the West Indies, original correspondence, etc., 1606–1807 (Nendeln, Lichtenstein: Kraus Thomson Organization, 1972), microfilm 968.

7. Naval Office Shipping Lists for New Hampshire, 1723–1769, Public Records Office, CO 5 (East Ardsley, England: Micro Methods, 1966), microfilm 967; Doerflinger, *Vigorous Spirit*, 116.

8. James F. Shepherd and Samuel H. Williamson, "The Coastal Trade of the British North American Colonies, 1768–1772," *Journal of Economic History* 32 (Dec. 1972): 783–810; McCusker and Menard, *Economy of British America*, 17–88.

9. Naval Office Shipping Lists for New Hampshire, 1744, Public Records Office, CO 5 (East Ardsley, England: Micro Methods, 1966), microfilm 967.

10. Goldenberg, *Shipbuilding in Colonial America*, table 34, 217–218.

11. Naval Office Shipping Lists for New Hampshire, 1746, Public Records Office, CO 5 (East Ardsley, England: Micro Methods, 1966), microfilm 967.

12. Vickers, *Young Men and the Sea*, quotations on 71.

13. David C. Klingaman, "The Coastwise Trade of Colonial Massachusetts," Essex Institute (Salem, MA), *Historical Collections*, CVIII (1972), esp. 217–234, 221–222; Matson, *Merchants and Empire*, 196–202.

14. Doerflinger, *Vigorous Spirit*, 106.

15. Ibid., 107.

16. Shepherd and Williamson, "The Coastal Trade of the British North American Colonies, 1768–1772," 783–810, esp. 796.

17. McCusker and Menard, *Economy of British America*, 111–116.

18. David C. Klingaman, *Colonial Virginia's Coastwise and Grain Trade* (New York: Arno Press, 1975), 73–76, 120–123, quotation on 122.

19. Shepherd and Williamson, "Coastal Trade of the British North American Colonies, 1768–1772," 799.

20. *NH Provincial Papers* (Manchester: New Hampshire Historical Society, 1868), vol. 2, 1686–1722, part 1, 77–81.

21. Carl Bridenbaugh, *Cities in Revolt: Urban Life in America, 1743–1776* (New York: Oxford University Press, 1955), 25–26, 232–235.

22. Alan Taylor, *Liberty Men and Great Proprietors: The Revolutionary Settlement on the Maine Frontier, 1760–1820* (Chapel Hill: University of North Carolina Press, for the Institute of Early American History and Culture, 1990), 62–63.

23. "A Description of Orleans, in the County of Barnstable. September, 1802," *Collections of the Massachusetts Historical Society*, vol. VIII (Boston: 1802), 186–195, quotation on 195; "A Description of Chatham, in the County of Barnstable. September, 1802," ibid., 142–154, esp. 148.

24. This paragraph summarizes McCusker and Menard, *Economy of British America*, 108–110. See also Shepherd and Williamson, "Coastal Trade of the British North American Colonies," 801–804.

25. Shepherd and Williamson, "Coastal Trade of the British North American Colonies," 800–801.

26. McCusker and Menard, *Economy of British America*, table 9.2, 196.

27. Lt. Governor Wentworth to the Council of Trade and Plantations, Dec. 26, 1720, in *Calendar of State Papers, Colonial Series, America and the West Indies, March, 1720 to December, 1721*, ed. Cecil Headlam (London: His Majesty's

Stationery Office, 1933, reprinted Vaduz: Kraus Reprint, Ltd., 1964), vol. 32, 222–223.

28. Matson, *Merchants and Empire*, 95–105.

29. Ibid., 315.

30. Charles E. Clark, *The Public Prints: The Newspaper in Anglo-American Culture, 1665–1740* (New York: Oxford University Press, 1994), 7–10, 251–257, quotation on 253.

9. The Sailor's Life

1. Nash, *Urban Crucible*, 63, 64, quotation on 451, note 93.

2. James F. Shepherd and Gary M. Walton, *Shipping, Maritime Trade, and the Economic Development of Colonial North America* (Cambridge: Cambridge University Press, 1972), 63–73.

3. Nash, *Urban Crucible*, 183, 322–323.

4. Billy G. Smith, *The "Lower Sort": Philadelphia's Laboring People, 1750–1800* (Ithaca, NY: Cornell University Press, 1990), 64, 125, 142–143, 213–215, quotation on 215.

5. Vickers, *Young Men and the Sea*, 96–130, quotation on 123.

6. Jesse Lemisch, "Jack Tar in the Streets: Merchant Seamen in the Politics of Revolutionary America," *William and Mary Quarterly* 3d. Ser., vol. 25 (1968): 371–407; Marcus Rediker, *Between the Devil and the Deep Blue Sea: Merchant Seamen, Pirates, and the Anglo-American Maritime World, 1700–1750* (Cambridge: Cambridge University Press, 1987). For a recent alternative, see Paul Gilje, *Liberty on the Waterfront: American Maritime Culture in the Age of Revolution* (Philadelphia: University of Pennsylvania Press, 2004).

7. Vickers, *Young Men and the Sea*, 129.

8. Bolster, *Black Jacks*, 5.

9. Ibid., 4–5.

10. War and Transformation

1. Shepherd and Walton, *Shipping, Maritime Trade, and the Economic Development of Colonial North America*, 135.

2. Ibid., 3.

3. Ibid., 49–90, quotations on 78, 72, 80.

4. McCusker and Menard, *Economy of British America*, 82.

5. This paragraph closely follows McCusker and Menard, *Economy of British America*, 82.

6. Ibid., 85–86.

7. Ibid., 79–80, 191; Edward C. Papenfuse, *In Pursuit of Profit: The Annapolis Merchants in the Era of the American Revolution, 1763–1805* (Baltimore: Johns Hopkins University Press, 1975), 53–75.

8. Doerflinger, *Vigorous Spirit of Enterprise*, 179–180.

9. Ian R. Christie and Benjamin W. Labaree, *Empire or Independence,*

1760–1776: A British American Dialogue on the Coming of the American Revolution (New York: W. W. Norton, 1976), 25–45; McCusker and Menard, *Economy of British America,* 190.

10. Tyler, *The First Revolution,* 17–19, 407–408, quotation on 18; Doerflinger, *Vigorous Spirit of Enterprise,* 168, 218; Benjamin W. Labaree, *Patriots and Partisans: The Merchants of Newburyport, 1764–1815* (Cambridge, MA: Harvard University Press, 1962), 16–17; Papenfuse, *In Pursuit of Profit,* 72–78.

11. Papenfuse, *In Pursuit of Profit,* 82.

12. Labaree, *Patriots and Partisans,* quotation on vii.

13. Doerflinger, *Vigorous Spirit of Enterprise,* 204.

14. Ibid., 236–242, quotation on 238.

15. Ibid., 242–250, quotation on 249; Edward Countryman, *The American Revolution* (New York: Hill and Wang, 1985).

11. A Tale of Two Ports

1. Frank Haigh Dixon, *A Traffic History of the Mississippi River System* (Washington, DC: Government Printing Office, 1909), 16; Erik F. Haites, James Mak, and Gary M. Walton, *Western River Transportation: The Early Era of Internal Development, 1810–1860* (Baltimore: Johns Hopkins University Press, 1975).

2. Gary M. Walton and Ross M. Robertson, *History of the American Economy,* 5th ed. (New York: Harcourt Brace Jovanovich, 1983), 157–158.

3. James D. Philips, *Salem in the Eighteenth Century* (Boston: Houghton Mifflin, 1937), 133; Robert E. Peabody, *Merchant Venturers of Old Salem: A History of the Commercial Voyages of a New England Family to the Indies and Elsewhere in the XVIII Century* (Boston: Houghton Mifflin, 1912), 4–5.

4. National Park Service, Division of Publications for Salem Maritime National Historic Site, *Salem: Maritime Salem in the Age of Sail* (Washington, DC: Department of the Interior, 1987), 39, 46.

5. G. Bhagat, *Americans in India, 1784–1860* (New York: New York University Press, 1970).

6. Ibid., 10–20.

7. *Maritime Salem,* 118; Samuel Eliot Morison, *The Maritime History of Massachusetts, 1783–1860* (Boston: Houghton Mifflin, 1941), 84.

8. Bhagat, *Americans in India,* 26.

9. K. Jack Bauer, *A Maritime History of the United States: The Role of America's Seas and Waterways* (Columbia: University of South Carolina Press, 1988), 53. Daniel Vickers presents slightly different figures, but the pattern is similar. See Daniel Vickers with Vince Walsh, *Young Men and the Sea: Yankee Seafarers in the Age of Sail* (New Haven, CT: Yale University Press, 2005), 170.

10. *Maritime Salem,* 87.

11. John G. B. Hutchins, *The American Maritime Industries and Public Policy, 1789–1914: An Economic History* (Cambridge, MA: Harvard University Press, 1941), 221–56.

12. Bauer, *Maritime History*, 54.
13. W. J. Eccles, *The French in North America, 1500–1763* (East Lansing: Michigan State University Press, 1998), 114, 122; John G. Clark, *New Orleans, 1718–1812: An Economic History* (Baton Rouge: Louisiana State University Press, 1970), 5, 7; Marcel Giraud, *A History of French Louisiana*, vol. I: *The Reign of Louis XIV, 1698–1715* (Baton Rouge: Louisiana State University Press, 1974), 9–15.
14. N. M. Miller Surrey, "The Development of Industries in Louisiana during the French Regime, 1673–1763," *Mississippi Valley Historical Review* 9, no. 3 (Dec. 1922): 231–232.
15. Thomas N. Ingersoll, *Mammom and Manon in Early New Orleans: The First Slave Society in the Deep South, 1718–1819* (Knoxville: University of Tennessee Press, 1999), 26.
16. Daniel H. Usner, *Indians, Settlers, and Slaves in a Frontier Exchange Economy: The Lower Mississippi Valley before 1783* (Chapel Hill: University of North Carolina Press, 1992), 105–106.
17. Jon Kukla, *A Wilderness So Immense: The Louisiana Purchase and the Destiny of America* (New York: Knopf, 2003)
18. Clark, *New Orleans*, 167.
19. Ibid., 161–162.
20. Arthur P. Whitaker, *The Spanish-American Frontier, 1783–1795: The Westward Movement and the Spanish Retreat in the Mississippi Valley* (Lincoln: University of Nebraska Press, 1927), 101–102, 209–216.
21. Arthur P. Whitaker, *The Mississippi Question, 1795–1803: A Study in Trade, Politics, and Diplomacy* (New York: D. Appleton, 1934), 189–196; Clark, *New Orleans*, 89.
22. Douglass C. North, *The Economic Growth of the United States, 1790–1860* (Englewood Cliffs, NJ: Prentice Hall, 1961), 35; Clark, *New Orleans*, 302; W. F. Galpin, "The Grain Trade in New Orleans, 1804–1814," *Mississippi Valley Historical Review* 14 (March 1928): 501; James E. Winston, "Notes on the Economic History of New Orleans, 1803–1836," *Mississippi Valley Historical Review* 11 (Sept. 1924): 201.

12. Robert Livingston and the Art of the Deal

1. North, *Economic Growth*, 41.
2. U.S. Department of Commerce, Bureau of Navigation, *Annual Report of the Commissioner of Navigation to the Secretary of Commerce for the Fiscal Year Ended June 30, 1921* (Washington, DC: Government Printing Office, 1921); idem., *Merchant Marine Statistics* (Washington, DC: Government Printing Office, 1937).
3. Emory R. Johnson et al., *History of Domestic and Foreign Commerce of the United States* (Washington, DC: Carnegie Institution, 1915), table 12, 209.
4. Quoted in James Thomas Flexner, *Steamboats Come True: American Inventors in Action* (New York: Fordham University Press, [1944] 1992), 235.

Flexner gives no source. It was probably Benjamin Latrobe. See Kirkpatrick Sale, *The Fire of His Genius: Robert Fulton and the American Dream* (New York: Free Press, 2001), 30.

5. Ibid., 7.

6. Ibid.

7. George Dangerfield, *Chancellor Robert R. Livingston of New York, 1746–1813* (New York: Harcourt, Brace, 1960), 307–394.

8. Interest payments finally brought the price to $27,267,622, still little more than five cents an acre. *Encyclopaedia Britannica*, 15th ed. (Chicago: Encyclopaedia Britannica, 1986), vii, 512.

9. The American Bureau of Shipping, *The American Merchant Marine* ([New York?]: American Bureau of Shipping, 1933), 97.

10. Flexner, *Steamboats Come True*, 247.

11. Alex Roland, *Underwater Warfare in the Age of Sail* (Bloomington: Indiana University Press, 1978), ch. 7.

12. Flexner, *Steamboats Come True*, 286.

13. Robert Fulton and the Art of Steaming

1. *Ibid.*, 318–325. The full name of Fulton's craft was *The North River Steamboat of Clermont.* Fulton referred to it as both the *North River Steamboat* and the *North River*, though the name *Clermont* would finally become most popular.

2. Sale, *Fire of His Genius*, 120–122.

3. Ibid., 90–91.

4. Flexner believes this is why Fulton succeeded while Fitch failed. Flexner, *Steamboats*, 372–78

5. Ibid., 328.

6. Flexner, *Steamboats Come True*, 346.

7. Fulton quoted in Sale, *Fire of His Genius*, 14.

8. Quote from Hunter, *Steamboats of the Western Rivers*, 4.

9. Sale, *Fire of His Genius*, 112–13.

10. Fulton and Livingston appear to have created two companies for business on the western rivers, the Ohio Steamboat Navigation Company and an unincorporated company based in New Orleans to handle business below Louisville and St. Louis. Hunter, *Steamboats on the Western Rivers*, 309–310.

11. Ibid., 125.

12. Flexner, *Steamboats Come True*, 337–338.

13. Ibid., 347.

14. Quoted in Hunter, *Steamboats on the Western Rivers*, 21.

14. The War of 1812

1. E. B. Potter and Chester W. Nimitz, eds., *Sea Power: A Naval History* (Englewood Cliffs, NJ: Prentice Hall, 1960), 189.

2. North, *Economic Growth*, 28.

3. W. Jeffrey Bolster, "The Impact of Jefferson's Embargo on Coastal Commerce," *The Log of Mystic Seaport* 37 (Winter 1986): 111–123.

4. John A. Butler, *Sailing on Friday: The Perilous Voyage of America's Merchant Marine* (Washington, DC: Brassey's, 1997), 20–21; Bauer, *Maritime History*, 54.

5. Potter and Nimitz, *Sea Power*, 208.

6. Donald Hickey, *The War of 1812: A Forgotten Conflict* (Urbana: University of Illinois Press, 1990), 46.

7. John K. Mahon, *The War of 1812* (New York: Da Capo, 1991), 54–55.

8. Rodney Carlisle, *Sovereignty for Sale: The Origins and Evolution of the Panamanian and Liberian Flags of Convenience* (Annapolis, MD: Naval Institute Press, 1981), 1 and passim.

9. North, *Economic Growth*, 249.

10. American Bureau of Shipping, *American Merchant Marine*, 97.

11. Haites et al., *Western River Transportation*, 124.

12. *Maritime Salem*, 129.

13. Morison, *Maritime History of Massachusetts*, 214.

14. Hutchins, *American Maritime Industries*, 228–230.

15. Henry Shreve and the Taming of the River

1. George Rogers Taylor, *The Transportation Revolution, 1815–1860*, vol. 4 of *The Economic History of the United States* (New York: Rinehart, 1951); Walton and Robertson, *History of the American Economy*, 233–235.

2. Florence L. Dorsey, *Master of the Mississippi: Henry Shreve and the Conquest of the Mississippi* (Boston: Houghton Mifflin, 1941), 8; Edith McCall, *Conquering the Rivers: Henry Miller Shreve and the Navigation of America's Inland Waterways* (Baton Rouge: Louisiana State University Press, 1984), 9.

3. Ibid., 9–16.

4. Leland D. Baldwin, *The Keelboat Age on Western Waters* (Pittsburgh: University of Pittsburgh Press, 1941), 57–61.

5. Dorsey, *Master of the Mississippi*, 68.

6. McCall, *Conquering the Rivers*, 133. Louis C. Hunter disagrees. He believes that the existing flood conditions would have made the voyage of the *Enterprise* more difficult "due to the great swiftness of the current and the presence of great quantities of driftwood." Louis C. Hunter, "The Invention of the Western Steamboat," *Journal of Economic History* 3 (Nov. 1943): 206n.

7. Hunter, *Steamboats on the Western Rivers*, 17–20, 75–76.

8. John G. Burke, "Bursting Boilers and Federal Power," *Technology and Culture* 7 (1966): 1–23.

9. Haites et al., *Western River Transportation*, 11, 21, 61, 81, 111–22, 124, 162.

16. DeWitt Clinton and the Canal Craze

1. Carol Sheriff, *The Artificial River: The Erie Canal and the Paradox of Progress, 1817–1862* (New York: Hill and Wang, 1996), 19; Evan Cornog, *The Birth*

of Empire: DeWitt Clinton and the American Experience, 1769–1828 (New York: Oxford University Press, 1998), 112.

2. Hunter, *Steamboats on the Western Rivers*, 309n.
3. Quote from Sale, *Fire of His Genius*, 161.
4. Albert Gallatin, *Report of the Secretary of the Treasury, on the Subject of Public Roads and Canals: Made in Pursuance of a Resolution of Senate, of March 2, 1807* (Washington, DC: Senate, 1808).
5. U.S. Congress, House, *Laws of the United States Relating to the Improvements of Rivers and Harbors from August 11, 1790, to January 2, 1939*, House Doc. No. 379, 76th Cong., 1st Sess., 3 vols., 1940, III, 4–11. See also John Majewski, "Who Financed the Transportation Revolution? Regional Divergence and Internal Improvements in Antebellum Pennsylvania and Virginia," *Journal of Economic History* 56 (Dec. 1996): 763–788; Collen M. Callahan and William K. Hutchinson, "Antebellum Interregional Trade in Agricultural Goods: Preliminary Results," *Journal of Economic History* 40 (March 1980): 25–31. Most of Gallatin's 1808 plan was completed by the time of the Civil War; Carter Goodrich, "The Gallatin Plan after One Hundred and Fifty Years," *Proceedings of the American Philosophical Society* 102 (Oct. 20, 1958): 436–441.
6. North, *Economic Growth*, 251.
7. Ibid., 196.
8. Taylor, *Transportation Revolution*, 47.
9. William Cronon, *Nature's Metropolis: Chicago and the Great West* (New York: W. W. Norton, 1991), 63–65.
10. Walton and Robertson, *History of the American Economy*, 212.
11. Taylor, *Transportation Revolution*, 39.
12. Walton and Robertson, *History of the American Economy*, 211.
13. North, *Economic Growth*, 143,154, 196.
14. Louis Bernard Schmidt, "Internal Commerce and the Development of National Economy before 1860," *Journal of Political Economy* 47 (Dec. 1939): 812.
15. Taylor, *Transportation Revolution*, 173.
16. Ibid., 164.
17. Ibid., 52–53.
18. Walton and Robertson, *History of the American Economy*, 212, 228.
19. Schmidt, "Internal Commerce," 809.
20. Taylor, *Transportation Revolution*, 52.
21. Ibid., 173–74.
22. Walton and Robertson, *History of the American Economy*, 263.
23. Schmidt, "Internal Commerce," 798, 818.
24. Gordon S. Wood, *The Radicalism of the American Revolution* (New York: Vintage, 1993), ch. 17.
25. Angus Maddison, *The World Economy: A Millennial Perspective* (Paris: Development Centre for the Organisation of Economic Development and Co-operation, 2001), 241, 243, 261, 263; and *Monitoring the World Economy,*

1820–1992 (Paris: Development Centre for the Organisation for Economic Development and Co-operation, 1995), 38, 227, 236, 239.

26. North, *Economic Growth*, 122–76.

17. Rushing to San Francisco

1. This exceeded the 892,000 square miles of the original thirteen colonies and the 827,987 square miles of the Louisiana Purchase. The Louisiana Purchase had practically doubled the size of the United States; Polk increased the total by another 70 percent. Congress actually approved annexation of the independent Republic of Texas on February 28, 1845, four days before Polk's inauguration, but Texas did not become the twenty-eighth state until December 29, 1845.

2. H. W. Brands, *The Age of Gold: The California Gold Rush* (New York: Doubleday, 2002), 27–31, quote at 29–30

3. William Tecumseh Sherman, *Memoirs of General W. T. Sherman: Early Recollections of California–1846–1848*, ch. 2, 34, www.sonofthesouth.net/union-generals/sherman/memoirs/general-sherman-california.htm (accessed May 25, 2006); Brands, *Age of Gold*, 46–47; James P. Delgado, *To California by Sea: A Maritime History of the California Gold Rush* (Columbia: University of South Carolina Press, 1990), 16; James K. Polk, "Fourth Annual Message," December 5, 1848, www.presidency.ucsb.edu/ws/index.php?pid' 29489 (accessed May 25, 2006). Naval Lieutenant Edward Beale had carried comparable documents and a smaller gold sample on a two-and-a-half-month voyage that delivered him to Washington on September 16, but many newspapers discounted his news. J. S. Holliday, *Rush for Riches: Gold Fever and the Making of California* (Berkeley and Los Angeles: Oakland Museum of California and California University Press, 1990), 87.

4. Brands, *Age of Gold*, 128–130.

5. Ibid., 144–189, 411. By the time Mark Twain traveled from St. Louis to San Francisco in 1861, the stagecoach moved at 100 miles per day.

6. Ibid., 104.

7. Ibid., 105–110, 115–121.

8. Gladys Hansen, *San Francisco Almanac: Everything You Want to Know about Everyone's Favorite City*, revised and expanded (San Francisco: Chronicle Books, 1995), 255.

9. John Haskell Kemble, *The Panama Route, 1848–1869*, University of California Publications in History, vol. 29 (Berkeley: University of California Press, 1943), 37.

10. Brands, *Age of Gold*, 114–115; Delgado, *To California by Sea*, 18. The first of Maury's revolutionary wind and current charts appeared in 1846, the complementary sailing instructions the following year. Steven J. Dick, *Sky and Ocean Joined: The U.S. Naval Observatory, 1830–2000* (Cambridge: Cambridge University Press, 2003), 73–74, 95–96.

11. Delgado, *California by Sea*, 47. A more complete account of the complex negotiations behind the creation of the PMSC may be found in Kemble, *The Panama Route*, 1–30.

12. Brands, *Age of Gold*, 72; Duncan S. Somerville, *The Aspinwall Empire* (Mystic, CT: Mystic Seaport Museum, 1983).

13. Brands, *Age of Gold*, 73–92, 202–204.

14. Ibid., 82; Holliday, *Rush to Riches*, 101.

15. Kemble, *The Panama Route*, 253–255.

16. Brands, *Age of Gold*, 404.

17. Kemble, *The Panama Route*, 58–94.

18. Hansen, *San Francisco Almanac*, 254; Holliday, *Rush to Riches*, 94, counts 782 ships from all countries entering San Francisco from May through December of 1849.

19. James H. Hitchman, *A Maritime History of the Pacific Coast, 1540–1980* (Lanham, MD: University Press of America, 1990), 17.

20. William Kooiman, "S.S. California: First Steamer through the Golden Gate," *Sea Classics* (Sept. 1990): 20.

21. Holliday, *Rush to Riches*, 114.

22. Hitchman, *Maritime History of the Pacific Coast*, 22.

23. Brands, *Age of Gold*, 85.

24. Ships brought 17,000 argonauts in 1849 and another 25,000 the following year, matched by the 42,000 who arrived overland in 1850 alone. Holliday, *Rush to Riches*, 83.

25. Brands, *Age of Gold*, 254–258.

26. The passenger list comes from J. F. Cleaveland, "Journal of a Voyage to the N.W. Coast of America in the Ship Niantic of Warren" [RI] (Sept. 16, 1848–July 12, 1849), J. Porter Shaw Library, San Francisco Maritime National Historical Park, F865.3 C55.

27. Delgado, *To California by Sea*, 25, 88–89; Holliday, *Rush for Riches*, 126.

18. Steam, Speed, Schedule

1. Butler, *Sailing on Friday*, 51.

2. Robert Greenhalgh Albion, *Square-Riggers on Schedule: The New York Sailing Packets to England, France, and the Cotton Ports* (Princeton, NJ: Princeton University Press, 1938), 20–31.

3. On flattening the keel, see Frank. W. Geels, "Technological Transitions as Evolutionary Reconfiguration Processes: A Multi-level Perspective and a Case-study," paper presented at Nelson and Winter Conference, June 12–15, 2001, Aalborg, Denmark, www.druid.dk/conferences/nw/paper1/geels.pdf#search'%22flatten%20keel%20baltimore%20clipper%22 (accessed Sept. 1, 2006).

4. Ibid., 36.

5. Stephen Fox, *Transatlantic: Samuel Cunard, Isambard Brunel, and the Great Atlantic Steamships* (New York: HarperCollins, 2003), 50–54.

6. Fox, *Transatlantic*, 92.

7. Ibid., 89.

8. Ibid., xii–xviii.

9. Quoted in ibid., 112.

10. Quoted in John A. Butler, *Atlantic Kingdom: America's Contest with Cunard in the Age of Sail and Steam* (Washington, DC: Brassey's, 2001), 211.

11. Fox, *Transatlantic*, 122–23, 133.

12. Ibid., 139.

13. Butler, *Atlantic Kingdom*, 114–119; Fox, *Transatlantic*, 171–172.

14. Fox, *Transatlantic* 177–187.

15. John Malcolm Brinnin, *Sway of the Grand Saloon: A Social History of the North Atlantic* (New York: Barnes and Noble, 1986), 205–207.

16. Wheaton J. Lane, *Commodore Vanderbilt* (New York: Knopf, 1942), 13–14, 18–31, 44–45, 50–73, 87, 94, 102–105, 118–48, 150–79.

17. David Etis et al., eds., *The Trans-Atlantic Slave Trade: A Database on CD-ROM* (Cambridge: Cambridge University Press,1999), cited in David Etis, "The Volume and Structure of the Transatlantic Slave Trade: A Reassessment," *William and Mary Quarterly* 58 (Jan. 2001), www.history cooperative.org/journals/wm/58.1/eltis.html (accessed July 10, 2006).

18. Ronald Bailey, "The Slave(ry) Trade and the Development of Capitalism in the United States: The Textile Industry in New England," *Social Science History* 14 (Autumn 1990): 373–414.

19. Alexis de Tocqueville, *Democracy in America* (1835), quoted in Benjamin W. Labaree et al., *America and the Sea: A Maritime History* (Mystic, CT: Mystic Seaport Museum, 1998), 239.

19. Matthew Fontaine Maury and the Growth of Infrastructure

1. Unless otherwise indicated, the following account of Nathaniel Bowditch's career is taken from *The American Practical Navigator: An Epitome of Navigation*, originally by Nathaniel Bowditch, LL.D., 1995 Edition (Bethesda, MD: National Imagery and Mapping Agency, 1995), i–viii.

2. Quoted in ibid., v.

3. "Vessels Built in the U.S. and Documented, 1769–1771 and 1797–1964 (sailing & steam vessels, canal boats & barges, of 5 gross tons and over)," U.S. Bureau of the Census, *Historical Statistics of the United States, Colonial Times to 1970* (1975), Part 2, Series Z 516 and Q 433–434.

4. Aaron L. Friedberg, *In the Shadow of the Garrison State: America's Anti-Statism and the Cold War Grand Strategy* (Princeton, NJ: Princeton University Press, 2000), 250. Other naval shipyards followed in Florida and California; Thomas R. Heinrich, *Ships for the Seven Seas: Philadelphia Shipbuilding in the Age of Industrial Capitalism* (Baltimore: Johns Hopkins University Press, 1997), 23.

5. Friedberg, *Shadow of the Garrison State*, 250.

6. Donald R. Whitnah, ed., *Government Agencies* (Westport, CT: Greenwood Press, 1983), 523–524.

7. Ibid., 384–390.

8. *Laws of the United States Relating to the Improvement of Rivers and Harbors from August 11, 1790 to June 29, 1938* (Washington, DC: Government Printing Office, 1940), 8–11. Truman R. Strobridge, "Chronology of Aids

to Navigation and the United States Lighthouse Service, 1716–1939," www.uscg.mil/history/h_USLHSchron.html (accessed July 9, 2006).

9. Kenneth J. Hagan, *This People's Navy: The Making of American Sea Power* (New York: Free Press, 1991), 112–115.

10. John Walter Wayland, *The Pathfinder of the Seas: The Life of Matthew Fontaine Maury* (Richmond: Garrett and Massie, 1930); Charles Lee Lewis, *Matthew Fontaine Maury: The Pathfinder of the Seas* (New York: AMS Press, 1969).

11. M. F. Maury, *Notice to Mariners* (Washington, DC: C. Alexander, 1850); [Matthew Fontaine Maury,] *Explanations and Sailing Directions to Accompany the Wind and Current Charts . . .* (Washington, DC: C. Alexander, 1851).

12. Forest G. Hill, *Roads, Rails, and Waterways: The Army Engineers and Early Transportation* (Norman: University of Oklahoma Press, 1957).

13. Todd A. Shallatt, *Structures in the Stream: Water, Science, and the Rise of the U.S. Army Corps of Engineers* (Austin: University of Texas Press, 1994).

14. Whitnah, *Government Agencies*, 343–347.

15. Walton and Robertson, *History of the American Economy*, 253.

16. David A. Hounshell, *From the American System to Mass Production, 1800–1932: The Development of Manufacturing Technology in the United States* (Baltimore: John Hopkins University Press, 1984).

17. Walton and Robertson, *History of the American Economy*, 237.

20. The Hinge of War

1. Craig J. Forsyth, *The American Merchant Seaman and His Industry: Struggle and Stigma* (New York: Taylor and Francis, 1989), 4–6.

21. Anaconda, Anyone?

1. Theodore Ropp, "Anaconda, Anyone?" *Military Affairs* 27 (Summer 1963): 71–76. Fittingly, the first shots of the Civil War were fired on January 9, 1861, when cadet gunners from the South Carolina Military Academy (now the Citadel) fired on SS *Star of the West*, a civilian merchant vessel attempting to resupply the federal garrison at Fort Sumter. The war began in earnest in April, when Confederate forces fired directly at Fort Sumter to force its capitulation before the arrival of civilian supply ships dispatched by newly inaugurated President Abraham Lincoln.

2. Kenneth J. Hagan, *This People's Navy: The Making of American Sea Power* (New York: Free Press, 1991), 167–169.

3. Ibid., 162–165, 169–170.

4. Robert Fulton, *Torpedo War, and Submarine Explosions* (New York: W. Elliott, 1810).

5. Alex Roland, *Underwater Warfare in the Age of Sail* (Bloomington: Indiana University Press, 1978), 150–165.

6. Milton F. Perry, *Infernal Machines: The Story of Confederate Submarine and Mine Warfare* (Baton Rouge: Louisiana State University Press, 1985 [1965]), 4.

7. Robert A. Albion, review of *The East India Marine Society and the Peabody Museum of Salem: A Sesquicentennial History*, in *New England Quarterly* 24 (June 1951): 277; Dan Finamore, email to Alex Roland, Feb. 2, 2007.
8. Hagan, *This People's Navy*, 159–160, 165–167.
9. Ibid., 160.

22. Benjamin Franklin Isherwood and the Industrialization of Ship Production

1. Hagan, *This People's Navy*, 163–164, 176.
2. Edward William Sloan III, *Benjamin Franklin Isherwood, Naval Engineer: The Years as Engineer in Chief, 1861–1869* (Annapolis, MD: U.S. Naval Institute Press, 1965), 5–11.
3. B. F. Isherwood, *Experimental Researches in Steam Engineering*, 2 vols. (Philadelphia: W. Hamilton, 1863–1865). See also Elting E. Morison, "Men and Machinery," in *Men, Machines, and Modern Times* (Cambridge, MA: MIT Press, 1966), 101–102.
4. "Light-Draught Monitors" (1864), quoted in Sloan, *Isherwood*, 53.
5. Elting E. Morison, "Men and Machinery," 98–122.
6. Quoted in ibid., 115. The majority report of the board argued that the *Wampanoag* design sacrificed traditional ship characteristics, such as storage space and maneuvering characteristics, on the altar of speed. See Lance C. Buhl, "Mariners and Machines: Resistance to Technological Change in the American Navy, 1865–1869," *The Journal of American History* 61 (Dec. 1974): 703–727, esp. 710n.
7. Bernard Brodie, *Sea Power in the Machine Age* (Princeton, NJ: Princeton University Press, 1941).

23. The *Alabama* and Commerce War

1. George W. Dalzell, *The Flight from the Flag: The Continuing Effect of the Civil War upon the American Carrying Trade* (Chapel Hill: Univeristy of North Carolina Press, 1940), 1–7; U.S. Congress, House, *Causes of the Reduction of American Tonnage and the Decline of Navigation Interests, Being the Report of the Select Committee*, Report No. 28, 41st Cong., 2d. Sess. (Washington, DC, 1870), ii.
2. Dalzell, *The Flight from the Flag*, 4, 5, 9, 24–7; Winthrop L. Marvin, *The American Merchant Marine: Its History and Romance from 1620 to 1902* (New York: Charles Scribner's Sons, 1902), 319–352; Andrew Gibson and Arthur Donovan, *The Abandoned Ocean: A History of United States Maritime Policy* (Columbia: University of South Carolina Press, 2000), 67.
3. Dalzell, *The Flight from the Flag*, 237–47.
4. Ibid., 248–249; Gibson and Donovan, *Abandoned Ocean*, 73.
5. U.S. Bureau of the Census, *Historical Statistics of the United States: Colonial Times to 1957* (Washington, DC: Government Printing Office, 1961), Series Q 153–168, 444–445.

6. See Appendix B.

7. O'Rourke and Williamson argue that the late nineteenth century was the first modern period of globalization. Kevin H. O'Rourke and Jeffrey G. *Williamson, Globalization and History: The Evolution of a Nineteenth-Century Atlantic Economy* (Cambridge, MA: MIT Press, 2001).

8. For a summary of these developments, see Lawrence C. Allin, "The Civil War and the Period of Decline: 1861–1913," in Robert A. Kilmarx, ed., *America's Maritime Legacy: A History of the U.S. Merchant Marine and Shipbuilding Industry since Colonial Times* (Boulder, CO: Westview Press, 1979), 68, 75–78.

9. Gibson and Donovan, *Abandoned Ocean,* 73; Lance E. Davis, Robert E. Gallman, and Karin Gleiter, *In Pursuit of Leviathan: Technology, Institutions, Productivity, and Profits in American Whaling, 1816–1906* (Chicago: University of Chicago Press, 1997), 217–218.

24. Cornelius Vanderbilt and the Rise of the Railroad

1. Dennis Showalter, *Railroads and Rifles: Soldiers, Technology, and the Unification of Germany* (Hamden, CT: Archon Books, 1975).

2. James A. Ward, *That Man Haupt: A Biography of Herman Haupt* (Baton Rouge: Louisiana State University Press, 1973).

3. Robert A. Angevine, *The Railroad and the State: War, Politics, and Technology in Nineteenth-Century America* (Stanford, CA: Stanford University Press, 2004).

4. Keiler, *American Shipping,* 95; and see also Pauline Maier et al., *Inventing America: A History of the United States* (New York: W. W. Norton, 2006).

5. Wheaton J. Lane, *Commodore Vanderbilt* (New York: Knopf, 1942), 13–14, 18–31, 44–45, 50–73, 87, 94, 102–105, 118–148, 150–179.

6. Lane, *Commodore Vanderbilt,* 174, 185–188, 192–194, 202–212, 218–240, 263–271, 291–299, 323. See also Edwin Hoyt, *The Vanderbilts and Their Fortunes* (New York: Doubleday, 1962); and Wayne Andrews, *The Vanderbilt Legend* (New York: Harcourt, Brace, 1941).

7. Lane, *Commodore Vanderbilt,* 319–325.

8. Michael Klepper et al., "The American Heritage 40: A Ranking of the Forty Wealthiest Americans of All Time," *American Heritage,* October 1998, 56–74. Elias Haskett Derby is on the list (#39), but he never moved his wealth out of shipping.

9. Thomas R. Heinrich, *Ships for the Seven Seas: Philadelphia Shipbuilding in the Age of Industrial Capitalism* (Baltimore: Johns Hopkins University Press, 1997), 49, 55, 79.

10. René de la Pedraja, *A Historical Dictionary of the U.S. Merchant Marine and Shipping Industry since the Introduction of Steam* (Westport, CT: Greenwood Press, 1994), 34; "S/S Pennsylvania, American Line," at www.norway heritage.com/p_ship.asp?sh=pennt (accessed July 15, 2006).

25. Marcus Hanna and the Growth of Inland Shipping

1. De la Pedraja, *Historical Dictionary*, 498–99, 579.
2. Keiler, *American Shipping*, 107–113; Marvin, *American Merchant Marine*, 365–380. The Philippines, acquired in the Spanish-American War, were never brought under the U.S. cabotage umbrella. De la Pedraja, *Historical Dictionary*, 108.
3. In chapter 28 of *Life on the Mississippi*, Mark Twain recalled when "there used to be four thousand steamboats and ten thousand acres of coal-barges, and rafts and trading scows, there wasn't a lantern from St. Paul to New Orleans, and the snags were thicker than bristles on a hog's back," www.online-literature.com/view.php/life_mississippi/28 (accessed July 12, 2006).
4. Keiler, *American Shipping*, 114–115; U.S. Army Corps of Engineers and U.S. Shipping Board, *Transportation in the Mississippi and Ohio Valleys* (Washington, DC: Government Printing Office, 1929), 184–188. The Corps of Engineers report indicates that data on river shipping can be difficult to aggregate and gauge with precision.
5. Marvin, *American Merchant Marine*, 395, 400–412; James C. Mills, *Our Inland Seas: Their Shipping and Commerce for Three Centuries* (Chicago: McClurg, 1910), 293, 310, 347–359; Jay Ehle, *Cleveland's Harbor* (Kent, Ohio: Kent State University Press, 1996), 27–30; U.S. Shipping Board, *The Port of Buffalo, New York* (Washington, DC: Government Printing Office, 1931).
6. Marvin, *American Merchant Marine*, 395, 402–412; George G. Tunell, Report to the Bureau of Statistics, *Statistics of Lakes Commerce* (Washington, DC: Government Printing Office, 1898), 3–8, 24–27.
7. Mark Goldman, *High Hopes: The Rise and Decline of Buffalo, New York* (Albany: State University of New York Press, 1983), 125, 129, 143–52; J. N. Larned, *A History of Buffalo Delineating the Evolution of the City*, 2 vols. (New York: Progress of the Empire State Company, 1911), vol. I, 118–132.
8. Herbert Croly, *Marcus Alonzo Hanna: His Life and Work* (New York: Macmillan, 1912), 56.
9. Ibid., 60–61.
10. The Hanna brothers were, in several ways, precursors to Charles Schwab, whose career is discussed in chapter 30.
11. Croly, *Marcus Alonzo Hanna*, 40, 41, 49, 55–67,
12. Heinrich, *Ships*, 1–2, 49–68, 70–84, 122–140, quote on 1. William D. Walters, "American Naval Shipbuilding, 1890-1989," *Geographical Review* 90, no. 3 (July 2000); James O. Curwood, *The Great Lakes: The Vessels that Plough Them, their Owners, their Sailors, and their Cargoes* (New York: Putnam, 1909), 15; for statistics regarding shipbuilding, see Ernest G. Frankel, *Regulation and Policies of American Shipping* (Boston: Auburn House, 1982), 22–25.

26. John Lynch and the Quest for a National Maritime Policy

1. U.S. House, *Causes of the Reduction*, i, ix–xi.
2. Ibid., ii, xix.
3. Ibid., xi–xx; Gibson and Donovan, *Abandoned Ocean*, 77.
4. U.S. House, *Causes of the Reduction*, ix; 1, see also 4, 8; Gibson and Donovan, *Abandoned Ocean*, 74–75; see also Captain John Codman, *Letter to the Honorable John Lynch on the Navigation Interest* (Boston, 1869).
5. For examples of the shipbuilders' arguments, see *Causes of the Reduction*, 11, 15–17, 21, 23, 144. See also John Hutchins, "The Declining American Maritime Industries: An Unsolved Problem, 1860–1940," *Journal of Economic History*, 6 (May 1946): 112.
6. U.S. House, *Causes of the Reduction*, 1, 11, 13, 23, 31, 52, 79, 99, 107, 167; for an example of a more extreme free trade position, from a New York banker, see 57; Gibson and Donovan, *Abandoned Ocean*, 73–77.
7. Gibson and Donovan, *Abandoned Ocean* 78.
8. U.S. Congress, House of Representatives, Rpt. 1827, 47th Congress, 2d ses., 1.
9. Allin, "The Civil War and the Period of Decline: 1861–1913," in Kilmarx, ed., *America's Maritime Legacy*, 73–74.
10. John Codman, "The Decline of American Shipping," *North American Review*, CCCXXIX (April, 1894), 324–335; the same themes appear later in Codman, "The Case of a Few Ship-Builders vs. The American People," a speech to and pamphlet then issued by the New England Free Trade League in 1895.
11. U.S. Congress, House, Rpt. 1827, 47th Congress, 2d ses. 15–23. The minority members were George Vest, Robert McLane, and S. S. Cox; Gibson and Donovan, *Abandoned Ocean*, 5; see also *The Question of Ships: I. The Decay of Our Ocean Mercantile Marine Its Cause and Cure*, by David A. Wells; *II. Shipping Subsidies and Bounties*, by Captain John Codman (New York: G. P. Putnam's, 1890).
12. Codman, "Decline," 313–324; Henry Hall, *American Navigation* (New York: Appleton, 1880), 74–75.
13. Allin, "Civil War," 91–93; According to Marvin, *American Merchant Marine* (418–419), the American-owned International Navigation Company had purchased the Inman line and ordered the construction in Britain of two mail ships, only to have their contract canceled by the British government. Congress then consented to permit the owners to register those ships in the United States.
14. Edwin M. Bacon, *Manual of Ship Subsidies: An Historical Summary of the Systems of All Nations* (Chicago: McClurg, 1911), 69–89, www.gutenberg.org/files/13718/13718.txt (accessed July 13, 2006).
15. Bacon, *Manual of Ship Subsidies*, 79–80; Allin, "Civil War," 70.
16. Hall, *American Navigation*, 65–69, 77–87.
17. Bacon, *Manual of Ship Subsidies*, 82–83; Allin, "Civil War," 71–72.

27. John Roach and the New Shipbuilding

1. This account of Roach's career is based upon Leonard A. Swann Jr., *John Roach: Maritime Entrepreneur* (Annapolis, MD: Naval Institute Press, 1965).
2. Roach was accused of having participated in the bribery, a charge that he vehemently disputed and that his biographer thinks is untrue.
3. Bacon, *Manual of Ship Subsidies*, 83–86; Marvin, *American Merchant Marine*, 413–425.
4. Croly, *Hanna*, 344–346; Allin, "Civil War," 89–90. On Mahan, see pp. 255–258 herein.
5. Croly, *Hanna*, 346–349; Allin, "Civil War," 85. For various reports on the progress of this bill, see the *New York Times*, December 26, 1899; January 14, 1900; February 19, 1900; February 27, March 2, 9, 26, 30, April 8, 13, 15, 23, May 14, December 2, 1900; January 10, 16, 17, 26, February 1, 6, 16, 1901.
6. *New York Times*, May 14, 1900
7. Ibid., May 16, 1900.
8. Theodore Roosevelt, annual message to Congress, Dec. 7, 1903, quoted in Bacon, *Manual of Ship Subsidies*, 47.
9. See the *Report of the Merchant Marine Commission*, 3 vols. (Washington, DC: Government Printing Office, 1905).
10. See pp. 249–250 herein.
11. Bacon, *Manual of Ship Subsidies*, 86–96; Allin, "Civil War," 76–77, 93–95.
12. On the politics, see: Samuel A. Lawrence, *United States Merchant Shipping Policies and Politics* (Washington, DC: Brookings Institution, 1966), 33–37; Paul M. Zeis, *American Shipping Policy* (Princeton, NJ: Princeton University Press, 1938), 16–19, 66–69.

28. West Coast Shipping and the Rise of Maritime Labor

1. James H. Hitchman, *A Maritime History of the Pacific Coast, 1540–1980* (Lanham, MD: University Press of America, 1990), 17–33.
2. Elmo P. Hohman, *History of American Merchant Seamen* (Hamden, CT: Shoe String Press, 1956), 20.
3. Walter Macarthur, *The Seaman's Contract, 1790–1918: A Complete Reprint of the Laws Relating to American Seamen* (San Francisco: [James H. Barry, Co.,] 1919), 35, 39, 68, 190–196; Hohman, *History of American Merchant Seamen*, 20–24; Bruce Nelson, *Workers on the Waterfront: Seamen, Longshoremen, and Unionism in the 1930s* (Urbana: University of Illinois Press, 1988), 12; James Baker Farr, *Black Odyssey: The Seafaring Traditions of Afro-Americans* (New York: Peter Lang, 1989), 4–5. In 1874, this law was modified to exempt seamen on coastwise voyages from the hiring and discharge supervision of shipping commissioners.
4. For an excellent examination of work in the shipbuilding industry, see Heinrich, *Ships*, 84–98, 140–151; see also Josef Konvitz, "The Crisis of Atlantic Port Cities, 1880-1920," *Comparative Studies in Society and Social History* 36, no. 2 (April 1994): 305–308.

5. *Ninth Census of the United States*, vol. 3: *Statistics of Wealth and Industry* (Washington, DC: Bureau of the Census, Department of Commerce, 1872), Table XX, 832–839; *Thirteenth Census of the United States*, vol. 4: *Population: Occupation Statistics* (Washington, DC: Bureau of the Census, Department of Commerce, 1914), table VI, 410–411.

6. Joseph H. Goldberg, *The Maritime Story: A Study in Labor-Management Relations* (Cambridge, MA: Harvard University Press, 1958), 10–11; Farr, *Black Odyssey*, 238–248; Lawrence, *United States Shipping Policies*, 37; *Report of the Merchant Marine Commission*, II, 1266. Regarding African Americans in the mid-nineteenth century, see W. Jeffrey Bolster, *Black Jacks: African American Seamen in the Age of Sail* (Cambridge, MA: Harvard University Press, 1997), 215–230.

7. Wayne M. O'Leary, *Maine Sea Fisheries: The Rise and Fall of a Native Industry, 1830–1890* (Boston: Northeastern University Press, 1996), 197–247; Andrew W. German, *Down on T Wharf: The Boston Fisheries as Seen through the Photographs of Henry D. Fisher* (Mystic, CT: Mystic Seaport Museum, 1982), 35, 74, 63, 115–116. In some other locales, Norwegians dominated; Knut Gjerset, *Norwegian Sailors in American Waters* (Northfield, MN: Norwegian-American Historical Association, 1933), 72–73, 131.

8. *Population: Occupation Statistics*, Table VI, 410–411; Goldberg, *The Maritime Story*, 1. The percentage of native-born rose some the after 1890s, but those figures included men who were native-born of foreign parents. Regarding New Orleans labor, black and white, see Eric Arnesen, *Waterfront Workers of New Orleans: Race, Class, and Politics, 1863–1923* (New York: Oxford University Press, 1991).

9. Forsyth, *American Merchant Seaman*, 9.

10. Goldberg, *The Maritime Story*, 11–12; Hohman, *History of American Merchant Seamen*, p. 25; Farr, *Black Odyssey*, 243; *Report of the Merchant Marine Commission*, II, 746–747.

11. Forsyth, *American Merchant Seaman*, 6; Hohman, *History of American Merchant Seamen*, 24–25; Gjerset, *Norwegian Sailors*, 166–170; quote in Goldberg, *Maritime Story*, 12–13; Paul S. Taylor, *The Sailors' Union of the Pacific* (New York: Ronald Press, 1923), 26–29; Nelson, *Workers*, 16.

12. *The Red Record: A Brief Résumé of Some of the Cruelties Perpetrated upon American Seamen at the Present Time* (San Francisco: Coast Seamen's Journal Print, 1895).

13. See also Taylor, *Sailors' Union of the Pacific*, 21–23. Excerpts from *The Red Record* are from this text.

29. Andrew Furuseth, the Unions, and the Law

1. The Marine Engineers Beneficial Association was formed on the Mississippi in 1875, but it is an officer's union.

2. Goldberg, *Maritime Story*, 16; Taylor, *Sailors' Union of the Pacific*, 35–45; Hohman, *History of American Merchant Seamen*, 25–26.

3. Goldberg, *Maritime Story*, 16; Taylor, *Sailors' Union of the Pacific*, 35–74; Nelson, *Workers*, 32.

4. Goldberg, *Maritime Story*, 16–28, 45–74.

5. Ibid., 18–20; *New York Times*, April 24, 1892. Regarding efforts to build a more industrial union of maritime workers on land and at sea (and regarding the presence of a strong syndicalist impulse among maritime workers), see Nelson, *Workers*, 39–74.

6. *New York Times*, September 7, 1896

7. Goldberg, *Maritime Story*, 25–38; Taylor, *Sailors' Union of the Pacific*, 55, 65–74, 94–109; *Report of the Merchant Marine Commission*, II, 747–753.

8. Hyman Weintraub, *Andrew Furuseth: Emancipator of the Seamen* (Berkeley: University of California Press, 1959), 30; Macarthur, *Seaman's Contract*, 218–219; Hohman, *History of American Merchant Seamen*, 24–25.

9. Goldberg, *Maritime Story*, 20–21; Weintraub, *Andrew Furuseth*, 30–31.

10. Weintraub, *Andrew Furuseth*, 32–36; Goldberg, *Maritime Story*, 21–22; Macarthur, *Seaman's Contract*, 219–21.

11. Weintraub, *Andrew Furuseth*, 2.

12. Goldberg, *Maritime Story*, 21.

13. Taylor, *Sailors' Union of the Pacific*, 87–89; Weintraub, *Andrew Furuseth*, 35; Hohman, *History of American Merchant Seamen*, 28.

14. *Robertson v. Baldwin*, 165 U.S. 275-88; 17 S. Ct. 326. Justice Harlan's was the lone dissent; Justice Horace Gray was absent.

15. *Robertson v. Baldwin*, 292–303; *New York Times*, January 26, 1897.

16. Weintraub, *Andrew Furuseth*, 35–36, 39–43; *New York Times*, March 26, 1897; Taylor, *Sailors' Union of the Pacific*, 89–91.

17. Taylor, *Sailors' Union of the Pacific*, 91–93; Macarthur, *Seaman's Contract*, 221; Hohman, *History of American Merchant Seamen*, 28–30; Weintraub, *Andrew Furuseth*, 36–44.

30. Ships, Steel, and More Labor

1. Mark L. Thompson, *Queen of the Lakes* (Detroit: Wayne State University Press, 1994), 101–102; idem, *Steamboats and Sailors of the Great Lakes* (Detroit: Wayne State University Press, 1991), 48; "History of the Iron Ore Trade," from 1910 annual report of the Lake Carriers' Association, http://web.ulib.csuohio.edu/SpecColl/glihc/articles/carrhist.html (accessed Aug. 30, 2001), 8.

2. Benjamin W. Labaree et al., *America and the Sea: A Maritime History* (Mystic, CT: Mystic Seaport Museum, 1998), 376.

3. Jean Strouse, *Morgan: American Financier* (New York: Random House, 1999), 396–409.

4. Thomas Misa, *A Nation of Steel: The Making of Modern America, 1865–1925* (Baltimore: Johns Hopkins University Press, 1995), 165.

5. Charles Hessen, *Steel Titan: The Life of Charles M. Schwab* (New York: Oxford University Press, 1975), 74.

6. George J. Ryan to Alex Roland, Nov. 16, 2006.

7. Of course the address overlooked the railroad yards strung along the east bank of the Hudson River, so far north of the Carnegie and Morgan residences downtown as to be practically in the country. But it made up in scale what it lacked in location. I am indebted to Barbara Hahn for instructing me in turn-of-the-century urban geography.

8. Goldberg, *The Maritime Story*, viii and passim. Unless otherwise indicated, the following account is drawn from this study, especially chapters 1 and 2.

9. Ibid., 63.

10. Ibid., 71.

11. Abraham Berglund, *The United States Steel Corporation: A Study of the Growth and Influence of Combination in the Iron and Steel Industry*, Columbia University Studies in the Social Sciences (New York: Columbia University Press, 1907), 78.

12. Given Furuseth's reputation as the "Lincoln of the Seas," one is reminded of David Donald's insightful essay about "Getting Right with Lincoln." Donald argued that aligning oneself with Abraham Lincoln became a staple of American politics, among both Democrats and Republicans. Such is Lincoln's stature in American history that politicians of all stripes are inclined to invoke him in Fourth of July speeches and in other patriotic venues, sensing that his appeal transcends party boundaries. So too did he appear to cross the boundaries separating management and labor. The essay first appeared in the *Atlantic Monthly* in 1956. It is reprinted in David Herbert Donald, *Lincoln Reconsidered: Essays on the Civil War Era*, 3d ed. (New York: Vintage, 2001), ch. 1.

13. Al Miller, *Tin Stackers: The History of the Pittsburgh Steamship Company* (Detroit: Wayne State University Press, 1999), 51–54.

14. Henry Hoagland, *Wage Bargaining on the Vessels of the Great Lakes* (Urbana: University of Illinois Press, 1917), 84–102.

15. John G. B. Hutchins, *The American Maritime Industries and Public Policy, 1789–1914: An Economic History*, Harvard Economic Studies, vol. LXXI (Cambridge, MA: Harvard University Press, 1941), 537–539. Hutchins reports that in 1894, American firms owned more foreign-flagged iron and steel steamships than American-flagged; important owners included the Chesapeake and Ohio Railroad and Anglo-American Oil Company.

16. See pp. 268–270 herein.

17. Labaree et al., *America and the Sea*, 383.

18. Angus Maddison, *Monitoring the World Economy, 1820–1992*, tables I-2, I-4, G-2.

31. Mahan, Roosevelt, and the Seaborne Empire

1. Alfred Thayer Mahan, *The Influence of Sea Power upon History, 1660–1783* (New York: Hill and Wang, [1890] 1957); *Atlantic Monthly*, Oct. 1890, 563–567.

2. Richard W. Turk, *The Ambiguous Relationship: Theodore Roosevelt and Alfred Thayer Mahan*, Contributions in Military Studies, no. 63 (New York: Greenwood Press, 1987), 1–5.

3. The historian Kenneth Hagan has said that "Roosevelt was Mahan distilled." *This People's Navy: The Making of American Sea Power* (New York: Free Press, 1991), 210.

4. Bernard Brodie, *Sea Power in the Machine Age* (Princeton, NJ: Princeton University Press, 1941). These gun characteristics apply to the USS *Oregon*, commissioned in 1896; Frank Uhlig Jr., "The Constants of Naval Warfare," *Naval War College Review* 50 (Spring 1997), www.usnwc.edu/press/Review/ 1997/spring/art5sp97.htm (accessed June 7, 2006).

5. Hagan, *This People's Navy*, 179–187.

6. Robert Seager II, *Alfred Thayer Mahan: The Man and His Letters* (Annapolis, MD: Naval Institute Press, 1977).

7. Mahan, *The Influence of Sea Power*, 23.

8. Alfred Thayer Mahan, *Sea Power and Its Relations to the War of 1812*, 2 vols. (Boston: Little, Brown, 1905), I, 284–290.

9. Mahan, *The Influence of Sea Power*, 121.

10. Alfred Thayer Mahan, "Possibilities of an Anglo-American Reunion," *North American Review* (Nov. 1894): 551–564, quote on 561.

11. Ibid., 563.

12. See, for example, Robert M. Browning Jr., *Success Is All that Was Expected: The South Atlantic Blockading Squadron during the Civil War* (Washington, DC: Brassey's, 2002), for a critique of a unit in which Mahan served.

13. Alfred Thayer Mahan, "The United States Looks Outward," *Atlantic Monthly* (Dec. 1890): 816–824, quote on 821.

14. Mahan, *The Influence of Sea Power*, 23.

15. Warren Zimmermann, *First Great Triumph: How Five Americans Made their Country a World Power* (New York: Farrar, Straus and Giroux, 2002). Zimmermann argues for Roosevelt, Mahan, Lodge, Hay, and Root. John A. Corry, *1898: Prelude to a Century* (New York: John A. Corry, 1998), 20, adds the Adams brothers.

16. Corry, *1898*, 119–120.

17. Ibid., 20.

18. David Traxel, *1898: The Birth of the American Century* (New York: Knopf, 1998), 109. A naval review board concluded that accidental detonation of coal dust sank the *Maine*, but Roosevelt was determined to have what John Hay called their "splendid little war." Frank Freidel, *The Splendid Little War* (Boston: Little, Brown, 1958). Modern research has confirmed the judgment of the naval board; see H. G. Rickover, *How the Battleship Maine Was Destroyed* (Washington, DC: Naval History Division, Department of the Navy, 1976).

19. Traxel, *1898*, 117.

20. Library of Congress, "American Memory," http://rs6.loc.gov/papr/ mckpanex.html (accessed June 6, 2006).

21. David G. McCullough, *The Path between the Seas: The Creation of the Panama Canal, 1879–1914* (New York: Simon and Schuster, 1977).

22. Craig C. Felker, *Testing American Sea Power: U.S. Navy Strategic Exercises, 1923–1940* (College Station: Texas A&M University Press, 2007).

23. James P. Isenhower, "Protean Policy: Understanding the Monroe Doctrine's Regular Recurrence within the American Foreign Policy Debate" (Ph.D. dissertation, Duke University, 2004).

24. James R. Reckner, *Teddy Roosevelt's Great White Fleet* (Annapolis, MD: Naval Institute Press, 1988), 1–18, and passim.

25. The historian Frederick Jackson Turner introduced his famous thesis on the closing of the American frontier at the annual meeting of the American Historical Association in 1893. See Frederick Jackson Turner, *The Frontier in American History* (New York: H. Holt and Company, 1920).

32. War and Woodrow Wilson

1. Bruce L. Felknor, ed., *The U.S. Merchant Marine at War, 1775–1945* (Annapolis, MD: Naval Institute Press, 1998), 114–117.

2. Stephen Fox, *Transatlantic: Samuel Cunard, Isambard Brunel, and the Great Atlantic Steamships* (New York: HarperCollins, 2003), 405–407. Fox notes that this tragedy ended the seventy-five-year Cunard record of no passenger fatalities.

3. Charles Dana Gibson, *Merchantman? Or Ship of War: A Synopsis of Laws; U.S. State Department Positions; and Practices Which Alter the Peaceful Character of U.S. Merchant Vessels in Time of War* (Camden, ME: Ensign Press, 1986), 38–66, esp. 50–52.

4. Jeffrey J. Safford, *Wilsonian Maritime Diplomacy, 1913–1921* (New Brunswick, NJ: Rutgers University Press, 1978), 35–40.

5. Quoted in Jeffrey J. Safford, "World War I Maritime Policy and the National Security: 1914–1919," in *America's Maritime Legacy: A History of the U.S. Merchant Marine and Shipbuilding Industry since Colonial Times*, ed. Robert A. Kilmarx (Boulder, CO: Westview Press, 1979), 111–148, quote on 115.

6. Ibid.

7. Ibid., 40–65.

8. Donald R. Whitnah, ed., *Government Agencies* (Westport, CT: Greenwood Press, 1983), 523–530. In 1936 the Bureau of Navigation and Steamboat Inspection became the Bureau of Marine Inspection and Navigation. Its functions were divided between the Coast Guard and the Customs Service in 1942.

9. Quoted in Safford, *Wilsonian Maritime Policy*, 71.

10. Shipping Act, 1916, Sept. 7, 1916, *United States Statutes at Large*, 64th Cong., 1st sess., ch. 451.

11. Stafford, *Wilsonian Maritime Policy*, 95–104.

12. René de la Pedraja, *The Rise and Decline of U.S. Merchant Shipping in the Twentieth Century* (New York: Twayne, 1992), 47–58.

13. De la Pedraja, *Rise and Decline of U.S. Merchant Shipping*, 56–57; Stafford, *Wilsonian Maritime Policy*, 104–108.

14. Stafford, *Wilsonian Maritime Policy*, 142–43; see also Edward N. Hurley, *The Bridge to France* (Philadelphia: J. B. Lippincott, 1927).

15. Joseph P. Goldberg, *The Maritime Story: A Study in Labor-Management Relations* (Cambridge, MA: Harvard University Press, 1958), 77–78; Hurley, *The Bridge to France*, 209. Memories of this experience would shape maritime labor policies on the eve of World War II. They may even shape modern efforts by maritime unions to place merchant mariners on naval auxiliaries. Donald R. Yearwood to Alex Roland, December 1, 2006.

16. This short-lived company should not be confused with the American Ship Building Company, which long dominated construction on the Great Lakes. K. Jack Bauer, *A Maritime History of the United States: The Role of America's Seas and Waterways* (Columbia: University of South Carolina Press, 1988), 294.

17. Arundel Cotter, *The Story of Bethlehem Steel* (New York: Moody Magazine and Book Company, 1916), 7–13.

18. Mark Reutter, *Sparrows Point: Making Steel—The Rise and Ruin of American Industrial Might* (New York: Summit Books, 1988), 91.

19. Ibid., 95–96.

20. Quoted in ibid., 113.

21. Ibid., 115, 119.

22. Ibid., 129–155.

23. Ibid., 265.

24. Edward N. Hurley, *The New Merchant Marine* (New York: Century Company, 1920), pp. 74–83, quote on 75.

25. E. G. Grace, *Charles M. Schwab* (n.p., 1947), 45.

26. Bauer, *Maritime History*, 299301.

27. Mark H. Goldberg, *The "Hog Islanders": The Story of 122 American Ships*, American Merchant Marine History Series, vol. 1 (Kings Point, NY: American Merchant Marine Museum, 1991), 244–247.

28. Andrew Gibson and Arthur Donovan, *The Abandoned Ocean: A History of United States Maritime Policy* (Columbia: University of South Carolina Press, 2000), 114. Goldberg, *The "Hog Islanders,"* 3–17. Gibson and Donovan do not specify what kinds of tons are used in the British-American comparison, but presumably these are also deadweight tons, the most commonly used measure in the American shipbuilding program.

29. De la Pedraja, *Rise and Decline of U.S. Merchant Shipping*, 59.

30. Clinton F. Whitehurst Jr., *The U.S. Shipbuilding Industry: Past, Present, Future* (Annapolis, MD: Naval Institute Press, 1986), 25. Whitehurst does not say if this means gross or deadweight tonnage. The shipbuilding community often spoke of deadweight tons while the operational community spoke of gross tons.

31. Benjamin W. Labaree et al., *America and the Sea: A Maritime History* (Mystic, CT: Mystic Seaport Museum, 1998), 505.

32. Ibid., 493.

33. *Lloyd's War Losses: The First World War: Casualties to Shipping through Enemy Causes, 1914–1918* (London: Lloyd's of London Press, 1990), 315.

34. Bauer says that the United States had the world's largest merchant fleet in 1922; *Maritime History*, 299–301. In his careful compilation of data on ships registered, B. R. Mitchell confirms that judgment; see *International Historical Statistics: Europe, 1750–1993*, 4th ed. (New York: Stockton Press, 1998), 720; and *International Historical Statistics: The Americas, 1750–1993*, 4th ed. (New York: Stockton Press, 1998), 573. But *Lloyd's Register of Shipping: Statistical Tables* (London: Lloyd's, 1970), 55, 59, lists the combined fleet of Great Britain and Northern Ireland as being larger than that of the United States.

35. Both are quoted in Safford, "World War I Maritime Policy and National Security," 130, 126.

33. Robert Dollar and the Business of Shipping

1. Jevne Hangan, "Dog Holes and Wire Chutes: From Sailing to Steaming in the Lumber Trade," *Maritime Life and Traditions* 29 (Winter 2005): 20–29.

2. René de la Pedraja, *Rise and Decline of U.S. Merchant Shipping*, 20–22; idem, *A Historical Dictionary of the U.S. Merchant Marine and Shipping Industry since the Introduction of Steam* (Westport, CT: Greenwood Press, 1994), 174–180.

3. Gibson and Donovan, *Abandoned Ocean*, 121.

4. Merchant Marine Act, 1920, June 5, 1920, United States Statutes at Large, 66th Cong., 2d sess., ch. 250 (46 U.S.C. 861–889). The cabotage provision, generally associated with Senator Jones, is § 27. Warren G. Leback and John W. McConnell Jr., "The Jones Act: Foreign-Built Vessels and the Domestic Shipping Industry," Society of Naval Architects and Marine Engineers *Transactions* 91 (1983): 169–194; and U.S. Department of Transportation, Maritime Administration, "The Jones Act: A 72 Year Old Cabotage Law and a 203 Year Old Tradition," (Washington, DC: 1992); copy provided by Warren Leback.

5. Ibid., 988.

6. Donald R. Yearwood notes the contrast between this provision and conditions at the end of the twentieth century, when the U.S.-government-owned and effectively owned merchant fleet was the largest in the nation, perhaps eclipsing the aggregate holdings of all commercial owners.

7. De la Pedraja, *Historical Dictionary*, 624–627.

8. An Act To amend sections 11 and 12 of the Merchant Marine Act, 1920, June 6, 1924, United States Statutes at Large, 68th Cong., 1st sess., ch. 273.

9. De la Pedraja, *Historical Dictionary*, 25–27.

10. Both companies actually survived, after a fashion. The U.S. government took over the Dollar Line and renamed it American President Lines, which became "the largest U.S. merchant shipping company in the transpacific

trade." On the brink of foreclosure, AEL was rescued in 1934, sold to new owners, and returned to profitability by the end of World War II. De la Pedraja, *Historical Dictionary*, 41–46, 176–80, 25–30, quote on 41.

11. Ibid., 277–278.

34. A Tale of Two Harrys

1. Bruce Nelson, *Workers on the Waterfront: Seamen, Longshoremen, and Unionism in the 1930s* (Urbana: University of Illinois Press, 1988), 128–132, quote on 128.

2. Counderakis is normally identified as Nick Bordoise, the name by which he was known within the Communist Party. Charles P. Larrowe, *Harry Bridges: The Rise and Fall of Radical Labor in the United States* (New York: Lawrence Hill, 1972), 69.

3. De la Pedraja, *Historical Dictionary*, 403–405, quote on 404.

4. Goldberg, *Maritime Story*, 97–112, quotes on 103 and 97.

5. Ibid., 121.

6. Roosevelt was descended on his mother's side from Amasa Delano (1763–1823), a Revolutionary-era Massachusetts sea captain and privateer. FDR was related on his father's side to Nicholas Roosevelt of steamship fame and cousin Theodore, the twenty-sixth president.

7. This section found its way into the National Labor Relations Act of 1935, the Wagner Act, which guaranteed to maritime and many other workers (though not all) the right to organize in unions, bargain collectively, and strike.

8. Millard Lampell, Lee Hays, and Pete Seeger, "Song for Bridges," recorded with Woody Guthrie, June 1941, www.geocities.com/Nashville/3448/bridges.html (accessed on Nov. 28, 2001). This song was recorded while these four artists, the Almanac Singers, were producing their famous "Talking Union," with Seeger's oft-repeated closing line, "take it easy, but take it!"

9. Quoted in Nelson, *Workers on the Waterfront*, 139–142.

10. Ibid., 139.

11. De la Pedraja, *Historical Dictionary*, 76–77.

12. Nelson, *Workers on the Waterfront*, 152–155.

35. Hugo Black and Direct Subsidy, 1935–1941

1. Hal Burton, *The Morro Castle* (New York: Viking, 1973); De la Pedraja, *Historical Dictionary*, 416–418.

2. Ibid., 521–522.

3. The historians John H. Kemble and Lane C. Kendall argue that the ship construction subsidized by the Merchant Marine Act of 1928 produced good ships that competed successfully and served America well in World War II. See their "The Years between the Wars, 1919–1939" in *America's Maritime Legacy: A History of the U.S. Merchant Marine and Shipbuilding*

Industry since Colonial Times, ed. Robert A. Kilmarx (Boulder, CO: West-view Press, 1979), 160–161.

4. William M. McBride, "Strategic Determinism in Technology Selection: The Electric Battleship and U.S. Naval-Industrial Relations," *Technology and Culture* 33 (April 1992): 248–277.

5. "Value of Waterborne Imports and Exports (Including Reexports) of Merchandise: 1790–1946," *Historical Statistics of the United States: Colonial Times to 1957* (Washington, DC: Department of Commerce, Bureau of the Census, 1961), 452–53.

6. Roger K. Newman, *Hugo Black: A Biography* (New York: Pantheon, 1994), 3–121.

7. U.S. Congress, Senate, Senate Doc. 210, 71st Cong., 2d sess.

8. U.S. Congress, Senate, Special Committee to Investigate Air Mail and Ocean Mail Contracts, *Preliminary Report*, Rpt. 898, 74th Cong., 1st sess., May 13, 1935, 39.

9. Ibid., 22–23.

10. Economic History Services, www.eh.net/ehresources/howmuch/dollar_question.php (accessed on Dec. 14, 2001).

11. De la Pedraja, *Historical Dictionary*, 246–247.

12. Gibson and Donovan, *Abandoned Ocean*, 129.

13. De la Pedraja, *Historical Dictionary*, 453, 565–566.

14. One of the three members of the Black committee, Senator William H. King (D-UT), signed the report but advocated revised tariffs to support the merchant marine instead of subsides of any kind.

15. Franklin Delano Roosevelt, "President's Message on Government Aid to Merchant Shipping," March 4, 1935, in U.S. Congress, House, Committee on Merchant Marine and Fisheries, *To Develop an American Merchant Marine*, Hearings on H.R. 7521, 74th Cong., 1st sess., 1935, 1093–1095.

16. Gibson and Donovan, *Abandoned Ocean*, 2–3.

17. Ellis Wayne Hawley, *The New Deal and the Problem of Monopoly: A Study in Economic Ambivalence* (New York: Fordham University Press, 1995), 234, 236.

18. United States Maritime Commission, *Economic Survey of the American Merchant Marine* (Washington, DC: Government Printing Office, 1937).

36. The *Henry Bacon* and the War in the Atlantic, 1941–1945

1. James E. Valle, "United States Merchant Marine Casualties," in *To Die Gallantly: The Battle of the Atlantic*, ed. Timothy J. Runyan and Jan M. Copes (Boulder, CO: Westview Press, 1994), 263.

2. Ibid.

3. Gerald J. Fischer, *A Statistical Summary of Shipbuilding under the U.S. Maritime Commission during World War II*, Historical Reports of War Administration, United States Maritime Commission, No. 2 ([Washington, DC: Government Printing Office,] 1949), 39.

4. Edwin P. Hoyt, *U-Boats Offshore: When Hitler Struck America* (New York: Stein and Day, 1978), 25.

5. Samuel Eliot Morison, *The Battle of the Atlantic, September 1939–May 1943*, vol. 1 of *History of the United States Naval Operations in World War II* (Boston: Little, Brown, 1947), 157.

6. Robert M. Browning Jr., *U.S. Merchant Vessel War Casualties in World War II* (Annapolis, MD: Naval Institute Press, 1996), 1–14.

7. Morison, *The Battle of the Atlantic*, 131.

8. Hoyt, *U-Boats Offshore*, 7–8.

9. Martin Middlebrook, *Convoy* (New York: William Morrow, 1976), 24.

10. See the merciless bill of particulars in Michael Gannon, *Operation Drumbeat: The Dramatic True Story of Germany's First U-Boat Attacks Along the American Coast in World War II* (New York: Harper and Row, 1990), 414. He concluded that "one individual person must be assigned final responsibility for the U.S. Navy's failure to prevent America's worst-ever defeat at sea: Admiral King" (415).

11. Quoted in Felknor, ed., *The U.S. Merchant Marine at War*, 222.

12. Robert W. Love Jr., "The U.S. Navy and Operation *Roll of Drums*, 1942," in *To Die Gallantly*, ed. Runyan and Copes, 95–120.

13. Felknor, ed., *The U.S. Merchant Marine at War*, 215–218.

14. War Shipping Administrator, *The United States Merchant Marine at War* (Washington, DC: [Government Printing Office], January 14, 1946), 9.

15. J. David Brown, "The Battle of the Atlantic, 1941–1943: Peaks and Troughs," in *To Die Gallantly*, ed. Runyon and Copes, 145.

16. C. B. A Behrens, *Merchant Shipping and the Demands of War*, rev. ed. (London: HMSO and Kraus Reprint, 1978), 293.

17. R. A. Bowling, "Mahan's Principles and the Battle of the Atlantic," in *To Die Gallantly*, ed. Runyan and Copes, 231–250.

18. War Shipping Administrator, *Merchant Marine at War*, 54–64.

19. Goldberg, *Maritime Story*, 214.

20. Ibid., 64–65. Surviving beneficiaries of seamen lost at sea received $5,000, half of what was allowed to members of the armed forces. Charles Dana Gibson, *Merchantman? Or Ship of War*, 139.

21. Ibid., 18, 57. This includes all yards contributing ships to the U.S. Maritime Commission shipbuilding program between 1939 and 1945.

22. Whitehurst, *U.S. Shipbuilding Industry*, 143.

23. Robert Lee Scott, "Welding the Sinews of War: A History of the North Carolina Shipbuilding Corporation [sic]," unpublished master's thesis, East Carolina University, 1979, 1–29, www.coltoncompany.com/shipbldg/us...hant%20Shipbuilders/North%20Carolina.htm (accessed May 20, 2002).

24. Donald R. Foxvog and Robert I. Alotta, *The Last Voyage of the SS Henry Bacon* (St. Paul, MN: Paragon House, 2001), 26–35; John Bunker, *Heroes in Dungarees: The Story of the American Merchant Marine in World War II* (Annapolis, MD: Naval Institute Press, 1995), 319–325. The account of the *Henry*

Bacon's last voyage is taken from Foxvog and Alotta, unless otherwise noted.

25. Warren Leback to Alex Roland, Nov. 13, 2006.

26. Robert Carse, *A Cold Corner of Hell: The Story of the Murmansk Convoys, 1941–45* (New York: Doubleday, 1969); Bunker, *Heroes in Dungarees*, 92–103; Valle, "Merchant Marine Casualties," 270. As with the North Atlantic, losses on this route were greatest in 1942 and 1943. By March 14, 1943, 46 of 143 American merchant ships sailing to Murmansk were lost; thereafter, for the remainder of the war, 10 of more than 200 succumbed. Department of the Navy, Naval Historical Center, "Naval Armed Guard Service: Convoys to Northern Russia—An Overview and a Bibliography," www.history.nav.mil/faqs/faq104-2.htm (accessed Aug. 2, 2006).

27. Foxvog and Alotta, *Last Voyage*, 41–55.

28. Arthur R. Moore, *A Careless Word . . . A Needless Sinking* (n.p.: Dennis A. Roland Chapter of New Jersey of the American Merchant Marine Veterans, 1998), 125–126; Foxvog and Alotta, *Last Voyage*, 195.

29. Samuel Eliot Morison, *The Atlantic Battle Won—May 1943-May 1945*, vol. 10 of *History of United States Naval Operations in World War II* (Boston: Little, Brown, 1956).

30. Total deaths and death rates defy precise calculation, due in large part to definitional problems surrounding merchant marine service and statistical problems surrounding the total number of people who served in the "oceangoing service" in World War II. The most judicious appraisal of this issue and its surrounding context is by Charles Dana Gibson. See his undated manuscripts, "U.S. Merchant Marine and Army Transport Service Casualties, World War II," and "Total Force: U.S. Merchant Marine, Oceangoing Service, World War II" (typescripts provided by the author). On the larger context, see Gibson's "United States Merchant Shipping under Arms: A Historical Perspective," *American Neptune* 58 (Winter 1998): 37–48; and his *Merchantman? Or Ship of War: A Synopsis of the Laws; U.S. State Department Positions; and Practices Which Alter the Peaceful Character of U.S. Merchant Vessels in Time of War* (Camden, ME: Ensign Press, 1986). Gibson puts the total number of merchant seaman deaths (Nov. 1, 1940, through Dec. 31, 1946) at 5,607, very close to the number 5,616 recorded by the Coast Guard; letter to Alex Roland, June 18, 2003. Arthur Moore, supplementing the Coast Guard records with research in MARAD insurance files, counts 6,847 deaths, including 98 U.S. seamen serving on foreign-flagged ships; "Arthur Moore, "U.S. Merchant Seamen Lost—World War II," undated typescript in possession of Roland. See also Moore to Roland, September 26, 2003.

31. On January 19, 1988, the secretary of the air force made an administrative finding that oceangoing seamen in World War II qualified as "active duty" under the provisions of the "GI Bill Improvement Act of 1977," P.L. 95-202, approved November 23, 1977 (91 Stat. 1433).

32. Williamson Murray and Allan R. Millett, *A War To Be Won: Fighting the Second World War* (Cambridge, MA: Belknap Press of Harvard University Press, 2000), 261.

37. Henry Kaiser and the War in the Pacific, 1941–1945

1. Arthur Moore lists this ship as being operated by "American Pioneer Lines"; *A Careless Word*, 58. Robert Browning says it was owned by the U.S. Maritime Commission and operated by U.S. Lines; *Merchant Vessel War Casualties*, 1.

2. One particularly harrowing account of an American merchant seaman in the hands of the Japanese is Gerald Reminick, *Death's Railway: A Merchant Mariner on the River Kwai* (Palo Alto, CA: Glencannon Press, 2002).

3. De la Pedraja, *Historical Dictionary*, 491–492; Moore, *A Careless Word*, 227.

4. Moore, *A Careless Word*, 88–89.

5. Japanese merchant seamen suffered 79 percent fatalities. Valle, "Merchant Marine Casualties," 267.

6. Michel Thomas Poirer has estimated that the American submarine campaign against Japanese shipping cost the Japanese, in defenses and losses, forty-two times what the United States spent on its submarine force. Michel Thomas Poirer, "Results of the American Pacific Submarine Campaign of World War II," www.navy.mil/navydata/con/n87/history/pac-campaign.html (accessed June 10, 2007).

7. Mark S. Foster, EH-NET book review of Stephen B. Adams, *Mr. Kaiser Goes to Washington*, www.eh.net/bookreviews/library/0057.shtm (accessed June 12, 2002); John H. Leinhard, "Liberty Ships," at www.uh.edu/engines/epi1525.htm (accessed June 12, 2002).

8. Mark S. Foster, *Henry J. Kaiser: Builder in the Modern American West* (Austin: University of Texas Press, 1989), 6–67; "Kaiser, Henry John," *Columbia Encyclopedia*, 5th ed. (New York: Columbia University Press, 1993), 1443.

9. Foster, *Kaiser*, 84.

10. Fischer, *Statistical Summary*, 58–75. The production of the California Shipbuilding Corporation yard in Los Angeles, which was managed by Kaiser during the war, is included in the Kaiser totals.

11. Scott, "Welding the Sinews of War," 74–126.

12. Foster, *Kaiser*, 76–82.

13. Frederick C. Lane, *Ships for Victory: A History of Shipbuilding under the U.S. Maritime Commission in World War II* (Baltimore: Johns Hopkins University Press, [1951] 2001), 42–46.

14. De la Pedraja, *Rise and Decline of U.S. Merchant Shipping*, 140–147; Richard M. Leighton and Robert W. Coakley, *Global Logistics and Strategy, 1940–1943*, United States Army in World War II (Washington, DC: Office of the Chief of Military History, 195), 616–617.

15. Rose, *American Wartime Transportation*, 250.

38. Edward Stettinius and Flags of Convenience

1. See chapter. 33, note 34.

2. *The Postwar Outlook for American Shipping*, A Report Submitted to the

United States Maritime Commission by the Postwar Planning Committee (Washington, DC: Government Printing Office, June 15, 1946), 95, 98, 107, 109.

3. Ibid., 40.

4. Ibid., 41–48, 87–90, quotes on 47. Containerization was proposed as one promising way to address this problem.

5. Robert Gardner, ed., *The Golden Age of Shipping, Conway's History of the Ship* (Edison, NJ: Chartwell Books, [1994] 2000), 156–157.

6. Goldberg, *The Maritime Story*, 214–218.

7. K. Jack Bauer, *A Maritime History of the United States: The Role of America's Seas and Waterways* (Columbia: University of South Carolina Press, 1988), 311–325; John A. Butler, *Sailing on Friday: The Perilous Voyage of America's Merchant Marine* (Washington: Brassey's, 1997), 195–213; De la Pedraja, *Rise and Decline*, 115–116.

8. Richard L. Walker, *E. R. Stettinius, Jr.*, vol. 14 of *The American Secretaries of State and their Diplomacy*, ed. Robert E. Ferrell (New York: Cooper Square, 1965), 1–26.

9. This account of the creation of Liberian registry is drawn from Rodney Carlisle, *Sovereignty for Sale: The Origins and Evolution of the Panamanian and Liberian Flags of Convenience* (Annapolis, MD: Naval Institute Press, 1981), 110–133.

10. For reservations to Carlisle's account on this point and others, see oral history interview of Guy E. C. Maitland, conducted by Eliot Lumbard, Kings Point, NY, July 23–24, 2003.

11. Because Stettinius Associates were technically in a different business than AOTC, their interlocking directorates escaped the legal prohibitions in existing antitrust laws.

12. De la Pedraja, *Rise and Decline*, 134–135.

39. Daniel K. Ludwig and the Giant Ships

1. Daniel Yergin, *The Prize: The Epic Quest for Oil, Money, and Power* (New York: Free Press, 2003), 499–500.

2. Steven Mark Adelson, "The Art of Creative Financing," *Financial History* (Fall 2005): 12–15.

3. Ludwig ignited a building race in tankers that developed a language of its own to denote liquid carrying capacity. In the era of World War II, tankers were still rated as other ships by gross tonnage, deadweight tonnage, and displacement. Gross tonnage indicated the total volume of a ship measured in tons equal to 100 cubic feet of volume. Deadweight tons measured the weight of everything the ship carried—cargo, crew, passengers, water, fuel, stores—by subtracting the empty weight of the vessel from its loaded displacement, expressed in long tons or metric tons. Displacement is simply the total weight of the loaded ship, also measured in long tons or metric tons. Because one metric ton equals .982 long tons, the two measures are often used interchangeably, as they will be here. In the account of tanker develop-

ment in this chapter, tons refer to deadweight tons unless otherwise indicated. *Glossary of Shipping Terms* (Washington, DC: Department of Transportation, Maritime Administration, April 2005), www.marad .dot.gov/Publications/05%20reports/Glossary.final.pdf (accessed Sept. 29, 2006).

4. Noël Mostert, *Supership* (New York: Knopf, 1974), 73.
5. Donald R. Yearwood to Alex Roland, Dec. 1, 2006.
6. Unless otherwise stated, the account of the 1973 embargo and later Middle Eastern events relies on Yergin, *The Prize*, 606–612.
7. Energy Information Agency, Department of Energy, "World Petroleum Consumption, 1960–2002," www.eia.doe.gov/emeu/aer/txt/ptb1110.html (accessed July 26, 2005).
8. Ibid.
9. Angus Maddison, *The World Economy: Historical Statistics* (Paris: Organisation for Economic Co-operation and Development, 2003), 235.
10. On OSG, see pp. 401–402 herein.
11. Charles R. Cushing to Alex Roland, February 4, 2003.

40. Malcom McLean and the Container Revolution

1. Thomas P. Hughes, *Rescuing Prometheus* (New York: Pantheon, 1998).
2. The following account relies heavily on four recent studies of containerization: Marc Levinson, *The Box: How the Shipping Container Made the World Smaller and the World Economy Bigger* (Princeton, NJ: Princeton University Press, 2006), esp. ch. 4; Brian J. Cudahy, *Box Boats: How Container Ships Changed the World* (New York: Fordham University Press, 2006); Arthur Donovan and Joseph Bonney, *The Box That Changed the World: Fifty Years of Container Shipping—An Illustrated History* (East Windsor, NJ: Commonwealth Business Media, 2006); and Frank Broeze, *The Globalization of the Oceans: Containerization from the 1950s to the Present*, Research in Maritime History, No. 23 (St. John's, Newfoundland: International Maritime Economic History Association, 2002).
3. Donovan and Bonney, *The Box That Changed the World*, 1–49.
4. Adner, "Containers—Revolutionizing Global Transport," June 9, 2002, http://faculty.insead.fr/adner/PREVIOUS/Projects%20May/Container%20Project.pdf (accessed June 28, 2005), 22.
5. Interview of Charles Cushing by David Sicilia, New York, NY, Oct. 3, 2003, 84–85.
6. Levinson, *The Box*, 177 (quote); Donovan and Bonney, *The Box That Changed the World*, 118; Cudahy, *Box Boats*, 107.
7. De la Pedraja, *Historical Dictionary*, 380.
8. Donovan and Bonney, *The Box That Changed the World*, 73–84.
9. De la Pedraja, *Historical Dictionary*, 547–549; Donovan and Bonney, *The Box That Changed the World*, 5–9, 12–14, 30–32.
10. McLean divested himself of McLean Trucking to avoid the requirement

that the Interstate Commerce Commission approve any joint ownership of shipping and trucking firms. Levinson, *The Box*, 44–48.

11. Ibid., 21; Cudahy, *Box Boats*, 35.

12. Ron Adner, "Containers," 17. Charles Cushing says that the ships could put four containers on the dock in five minutes. Cushing to Alex Roland, Dec. 1, 2006.

13. Levinson, *The Box*, 70–75.

14. McLean sold Waterman outright in 1965. The company survived as a subsidiary of International Holding Company. De la Pedraja, *Historical Dictionary*, 653–655.

15. These dimensions have been modified slightly over the years, with some containers up to forty-eight and even fifty-three feet long and as much as nine and a half feet high.

16. Levinson, *The Box*, 65.

17. William A. Lovett, Alfred E. Eckes Jr., and Richard Brinkman, *U.S. Trade Policy: History, Theory, and the WTO* (Armonk, NY: M. E. Sharpe, 2004), 39.

18. Cudahy, *Box Boats*, 87–88. When A.P. Moller-Maersk Group took over Sea-Land Corporation in 1998, it changed the name, creating Maersk Sealand Corporation in 1999. In 2006 Maersk dropped the name "Sealand" from its title.

19. The ships were actually bought by Litton Leasing, a subsidiary of Litton Industries created to conduct this business. Levinson, *The Box*, 163.

20. Cushing interview, 42–45. Formerly the American Engineering Standards Committee, the American Standards Association became in 1966 the USA Standards Institute, which in turn became the American National Standards Institute in 1969.

21. For the most part, these were semi-trailers, whose chassis were supported by wheels at the rear and the tractor at the front.

22. De la Pedraja, *Rise and Decline of U.S. Merchant Shipping*, 154–158.

23. Cudahy, *Box Boats*, 163–167.

24. Levinson, *The Box*, 44, 85–86.

25. Ibid., 176–183.

26. Adner, "Containers," 20. Warren Leback says that McLean actually used eleven ships, nine for the transpacific haul and two operating coastwise in Vietnam. Leback to Alex Roland, Nov. 13, 2006.

27. Levinson, *The Box*, ch. 4.

28. Ibid., 45.

29. By 2005, this figure had risen to more than 8,000 TEUs, eighty times the capacity of the *Ideal X*. The volume of container traffic is from Institute of Shipping Economics and Logistics, SSMR, Market Analysis No. 6, 2001, Executive Summary.

41. Farewell the Finger Pier

1. Archibald Hurd, ed., *Ports of the World*, 11th ed. (London: Shipping World Limited, 1957).

2. "History of the Port Authority," www.panynj.gov/AboutthePortAuthority/ HistoryofthePortAuthority (accessed July 11, 2005). In 1972 it became the more accurately named the Port Authority of New York and New Jersey.
3. The decision to support Malcom McLean's experiment in containerization came not easily to the Port Authority. After World War II, it had decided to invest in the harbor infrastructure supporting oceanic shipping. Its initial plan was to revitalize the municipally owned piers on Manhattan, but the city refused, seeing it as an intrusion of the Port Authority into local business. Only then did the authority accept McLean's importunings to invest in a container port across the river. Mitchell Moss, "New York v. New Jersey: A New Perspective," *Portfolio* 1 (Summer 1988), www.mitchellmoss.com/ articles/nynj.html (accessed July 15, 2005), 2.
4. "Shipping Shows a Way to Manage the Use of the Sea," *Economist*, May 21, 1998, www.economist.com/surveys/displayStory.cfm?Story_id=371975 (accessed July 15, 2005).
5. *Lloyd's Ports of the World 2000* (Colchester, Essex: Lloyd's of London Press, 2000), 148.
6. Stephen G. Marshall, "Containerization's First 'Tipping Point': The Fall of the New York Port, 1965–1975," at www.gothamcenter.org/festival/ 2001/confpapers/marshall.pdf (accessed July 15, 2005).
7. The lighter is a barge that may be towed or pushed by tugboat around inland and coastal waters and then lifted aboard specialized ships for oceanic transport.
8. U.S. Department of Transportation, Bureau of Transportation Statistics, *U.S. International Trade and Freight Transportation Trends* (Washington, DC: U.S. Department of Transportation, [2003]), 31.
9. Hurd, ed., *Ports of the World*, 170, 146.
10. *Lloyd's Ports of the World 2000*, 150.
11. *U.S. International Trade and Freight Transportation Trends*, 31.
12. Ibid., 32.
13. *Lloyd's Ports of the World 2000*, 140–143.
14. The exception that proves the rule is the *Queen Mary II*, which docks in Brooklyn in the twenty-first century.
15. See pp. 393–395, 399 herein.
16. Brian Slack, "Across the Pond: Container Shipping on the North Atlantic in the Era of Globalisation," *GeoJournal* 48 (1999): 10.
17. *U.S. International Trade and Freight Transportation Trends*, 18, 38.
18. U.S. Waterborne Commerce, Total Imports and Exports, 1923–2000; see Appendix B.
19. *U.S. International Trade and Freight Transportation Trends*, 1, 18, 20.

42. The Shrinking Giant

1. "Shipping Shows a Way," 1.
2. "U.S. Oceanborne Foreign Trade/Commercial Cargo Carried 1947–2000," table prepared for this study from U.S. Maritime Administration Annual

Reports, 1970, 1975, 1990, 1996, 1997, 2000 (data include trans–Great Lakes shipping); Bureau of the Census, *Historical Statistics of the United States, Colonial Times to 1970* (1975), Part 2, Series Q 414; Bureau of the Census, *Statistical Abstract of the United States, 2001.*

3. Charles R. Cushing says that the most important advantage of container ships is "greater utilization of the capital investment, i.e., more efficiency." Cushing to Alex Roland, Dec. 1, 2006. Because ships spent less time loading and unloading, they spent more time earning revenue at sea.

4. Robert Motley, "The Gentleman from Maxton: A Trucker at Heart, Malcom McLean's Containerization of Cargo Revolutionized the Shipping Industry," *American Shipper* 43 (July 2001): 22–28, quote on 22. Several versions of McLean's epiphany exist. See, for example, Donovan and Bonney, *The Box That Changed the World,* 4.

5. Joseph P. Goldberg, "Containerization as a Force for Change on the Waterfront," *Monthly Labor Review* 91 (January 1968): 9. Charles Cushing says that the cargo could be moved in two minutes, not two and a half. Cushing to Alex Roland, Dec. 1, 2006. Donald Yearwood says that having two work gangs aboard container ships was unnecessary, a compromise arrived at in labor negotiations. Yearwood to Alex Roland, Dec. 1, 2006.

6. Adner, "Containers," 18; Ralph E. Holthausen, "Whitey's Grace Log," www.islandnet.com/~reh/gracelog.htm (accessed July 18, 2005).

7. Joseph P. Goldberg, *The Maritime Story: A Study in Labor Management Relations* (Cambridge, MA: Harvard University Press, 1958), 152–174.

8. Nelson Lichtenstein, "Labor in the Truman Era: Origins of the 'Private Welfare State,'" in *The Truman Presidency,* ed. Michael J. Lacey (Cambridge: Cambridge University Press, 1989), 135–139; Mark S. Byrnes, *The Truman Years, 1945–1953* (New York: Longman, 2000), 26–27; Barton Bernstein, "The Truman Administration and Its Reconversion Wage Policy," *Labor History* 4 (1965); 216–225; R. Alton Lee, *Truman and Taft-Hartley: A Question of Mandate* (Lexington: University of Kentucky Press, 1966), 22–48.

9. Steven Wagner, "How Did the Taft-Hartley Act Come About?," http://hnn.us/articles/1036.html (accessed July 19, 2005), 1–2; Joseph P. Goldberg, "Longshoremen and the Modernization of Cargo Handling in the United States," *International Labour Review* 107 (March 1973): 253–257.

10. Goldberg, "Longshoremen," 257.

11. Joseph H. Ball, *The Government-Subsidized Union Monopoly: A Study of Labor Practices in the Shipping Industry* (Washington, DC: Labor Policy Association, 1966), 191–196; Goldberg, "Containerization," 10; Philip Ross, "Waterfront Labor Response to Technological Change: A Tale of Two Unions," *Labor Law Journal,* July 1970, 412–414.

12. Goldberg, "Longshoremen," 257–259. It is estimated that members of the Pacific Maritime Association of West Coast shipowners realized $200 million in savings on their $9 million investment in the M and M Agreement. Donovan and Bonney, *The Box That Changed the World,* 83.

13. Goldberg, "Containerization," 12–13.
14. "Shipping Shows a Way," 1–2.
15. Harvey Swados, "West-Coast Waterfront: The End of an Era," *Dissent* 8 (1961): 455.
16. Ball, *The Government-Subsidized Union Monopoly*, 233–234.
17. Goldberg, "Longshoremen," 264.
18. Notes by Alex Roland, who accompanied the *Mesabi Miner* on this trip, supplemented by notes of a conversation between Eliot Lumbard and Timothy Dayton, Kings Point, NY, July 25, 2000.
19. Bureau of Labor Statistics, U.S. Department of Labor, *Technology and Labor in Copper Ore Mining, Household Appliances, and Water Transportation Industries*, Bulletin 2420 (Washington, DC: Government Printing Office, May 1993), ch. 3, 28–30.
20. Ibid., 31.
21. Valentina Carbone, "Developments in the Labour Market," in *International Maritime Transport: Perspectives*, ed. Heather Leggate, James McConville, and Alfonso Morvillo (London: Routledge, 2005), 67–82; BIMCO (Baltic and International Maritime Council)/ISF (International Shipping Federation), *BIMCO/ISF 2000 Manpower Update, Summary Report* (April 2000), www.marisec.org/resources/2000Manpowerupdate.htm (accessed July 24, 2005); Organisation for Economic Co-operation and Development, Directorate for Science, Technology and Industry, *The Cost to Users of Substandard Shipping* (Jan. 2001), www.oecd.org/dataoecd/27/18/1827388.pdf (accessed July 24, 2005).

43. Richard Nixon and the Quest for a National Maritime Policy

1. Samuel A. Lawrence, *United States Merchant Shipping Policies and Politics* (Washington, DC: Brookings Institution, 1966), 84; K. Jack Bauer, *A Maritime History of the United States: The Role of America's Seas and Waterways* (Columbia: University of South Carolina Press, 1988), 311.
2. Andrew Gibson and Arthur Donovan, *The Abandoned Ocean: A History of United States Maritime Policy* (Columbia: University of South Carolina Press, 2000), 169.
3. Robert Earle Anderson, *The Merchant Marine and World Frontiers* (Cambridge, MD: Cornell Maritime Press, 1945), 180, as quoted in Clark G. Reynolds, "American Maritime Power since World War II," in Robert A. Kilmarx, ed., *America's Maritime Legacy: A History of the U.S. Merchant Marine and Shipbuilding Industry since Colonial Times* (Boulder, CO: Westview Press, 1979), 216; Daniel Marx Jr., "The Merchant Ship Sales Act of 1946," *Journal of the University of Chicago* 21 (Jan. 1948): 12–28.
4. Lawrence, *United States Merchant Shipping*, 84; S. G. Sturmey, *British Shipping and World Competition* (London: Athlone Press, 1962), 139.
5. Bauer, *Maritime History*, 311.
6. Lawrence, *United States Merchant Shipping*, 182–183.

7. Ibid., 102.

8. United States Department of Commerce, Maritime Administration, *The Handbook of Economic Merchant Shipping Statistics through 1958* (Washington, DC: Government Printing Office, 1959), 31.

9. United States Department of Commerce, Maritime Administration, *MARAD 1970: Year of Transition* (Washington, DC: Government Printing Office, 1971), Appendix II, 63.

10. Lawrence, *United States Merchant Shipping*, 88–89, 179.

11. Ibid., 166–167n; Whitehurst, "Government Support of Merchant Shipping, 1845–1983," 23.

12. Lawrence, *United States Merchant Shipping*, 169–170; Gibson and Donovan, *Abandoned Ocean*, 174–175. A subsequent amendment of the Merchant Marine Act of 1936 raised the requirement to 75 percent of certain foreign food aid.

13. Reynolds, "American Maritime Power since World War II," 218; Gibson and Donovan, *Abandoned Ocean*, 170, 181.

14. Harvard Graduate School of Business Administration, *The Use and Disposition of Ships at the End of World War II* (Washington, DC: Government Printing Office, July 1945), 5, 13–14, quoted in Reynolds, "American Maritime Power since World War II," 218.

15. The report continued: "The operation of the reserve fleet in mitigating shipping crises [e.g., Korea and Suez] is the only major exception to these gloomy conclusions." Allen R. Ferguson et al., *The Economic Value of the United States Merchant Marine* (Evanston, IL: The Transportation Center at Northwestern University, 1961), 470.

16. Among the incentives offered by the U.S. government to American shipowners operating under foreign registry was an interim war insurance program that would be extended to any owner willing to enter into a contractual agreement with the Maritime Administration to make vessels available to the nation in time of war or national emergency. By 1970 the EUSC program covered 394 ships of 18.4 million deadweight tons, but the actual availability of these vessels to the U.S. government has always been fraught with unresolved legal and practical questions. See John G. Kilgour, *The U.S. Merchant Marine: National Maritime Policy and Industrial Relations* (New York: Praeger, 1975), 70; and Clinton H. Whitehurst Jr., "U.S.-Owned, Foreign-Flag Shipping," in Whitehurst, ed., *The U.S. Merchant Marine* (Annapolis, MD: Naval Institute Press, 1983), 226–228.

17. By 1970 the figures had increased to 228 million tons worldwide, of which U.S. shipping accounted for 13 million tons (6 percent of the total). Reynolds, "American Maritime Power since World War II," 227.

18. Ibid., 228; Henry S. Morgan, *Planning Ship Replacement in the Containerization Era* (Lexington, MA: D. C. Heath, 1974), 7–8, 11–13, 45; Kilgour, *The U.S. Merchant Marine*, 81.

19. Lawrence J. O'Brian, "The Making of Maritime Policy," 45, in Whitehurst, ed., *The U.S. Merchant Marine*, 45; Kilgour, *The U.S. Merchant Marine*, 204–205.

20. Kilgour, *The U.S. Merchant Marine*, 183.
21. *Traffic World*, February 1, 1969, 24, as quoted in Kilgour, *The U.S. Merchant Marine*, 183.
22. Gibson and Donovan, *Abandoned Ocean*, 197–198.
23. In 1950 President Truman had attempted to separate the regulatory and administrative functions of President Roosevelt's Maritime Commission by dividing it into a Maritime Administration and a Federal Maritime Board. Both bodies were placed in the Department of Commerce and the maritime administrator served as chairman of the Maritime Board. President Kennedy separated the two functions, making the Federal Maritime Commission an independent office reporting directly to the president. In 1981 the Maritime Administration was transferred to the Department of Transportation. Lane C. Kendall, "Federal Maritime Commission," in *Government Agencies*, ed. Donald R. Whitnah (Westport, CT: Greenwood Press, 1983), 229–233.
24. Gibson and Donovan, *Abandoned Ocean*, 202–207, quotes on 202, 207.

44. Hot Wars and Cold

1. Vincent J. Esposito, ed., *The West Point Atlas of American Wars*, 2 vols. (New York: Praeger, 1967), II, maps 2, 3.
2. James A. Huston, *Guns and Butter, Powder and Rice: U.S. Army Logistics in the Korean War* (Selinsgrove, PA: Susquehanna University Press, 1989), 67–74, 97–98.
3. Ibid., 213. Earlier in the book, Huston reported that MSTS had at its disposal at the outbreak of the war 147 ships totaling 1,539,333 deadweight tons (p. 76). The discrepancy seems to arise from the ongoing transfer of army ships.
4. Robert D. Paulus, "Logistics and the 'Forgotten War,'" *Army Logistician* 35 (Nov.–Dec. 2003): 38–41.
5. Huston, *Guns and Butter*, 123–124.
6. Ibid., 370.
7. Paulus, "Logistics," 6.
8. De la Pedraja, *Historical Dictionary*, 402. This experience comports with Hugo Black's findings in 1936 on the operation of government-owned ships between the world wars. See pp. 296–299 herein.
9. These numbers include materials shipped to Vietnam between July 1, 1964, and March 31, 1973. Salvatore R. Mercogliano, "Sealift: The Evolution of American Military Sea Transportation" (Ph.D. dissertation, University of Alabama, 2004), 286.
10. David Graham, *Sustaining the Civil Reserve Air Fleet (CRAF) Program*, Institute for Defense Analyses Study ([Alexandria, VA]: IDA, May 1, 2003), 75–77, www.acq.osd.mil/log/tp/new_airlift_policies/craf_study_final_%20may12003.pdf (accessed Aug. 6, 2005).
11. James William Gibson, *The Perfect War: Technowar in Vietnam* (New York: Atlantic Monthly Press, [1986] 2000), 189–191.

12. Ibid., 240.

13. Edward Miguel and Gérard Roland, "The Long Run Impact of Bombing Vietnam," first draft, January 2005, http://emlab.berkeley.edu/users/webfac/emiguel/e271_s05/long.pdf (accessed Aug. 6, 2005).

14. Edward J. Moralda, *By Sea, Land, and Air: An Illustrated History of the U.S. Navy and the War in Southeast Asia* (Washington, DC: Naval Historical Center, 1994), 233–238.

15. De la Pedraja, *Historical Dictionary*, 400–401.

16. Many admirers of Malcom McLean believed that shipping would have been inadequate without his contribution. See, for example, Levinson, *The Box*, ch. 9.

17. Salvatore R. Mercogliano, "Sealift: American Military Sea Transportation," paper presented at the "World Out of Containers Workshop," Buies Creek, NC, June 18, 2005, 11.

18. Donald Yearwood says that the government chartered many commercial vessels to transport fuel. Yearwood to Roland, Dec. 1, 2006.

19. Joint Logistics Review Board, *Logistic Support in the Vietnam Era, Vol. 3, Monograph Summaries and Recommendations* (n.p., n.d.), Record #253794, Virtual Vietnam Archive, The Vietnam Project, Texas Tech University, www.vietnam.ttu.edu/virtualarchive/index.htm (accessed Aug. 6, 2005).

20. Kent Gourdin and Richard L. Clarke, "Winning Transportation Partnerships: Learning from the Desert Storm Experience," *Transportation Journal* 32 (Fall 1992): 30–37, www.cofc.edu/sobe/vitaes/GourdinKent_March2005.pdf (accessed July 17, 2006).

21. "Airlift-Sealift Performed Well in War/Some Shortcomings Noted," *Defense Daily* 172 (Aug. 13, 1991): 246.

22. These were Malcom McLean's ill-fated SL-7s. See pp. 401–402 herein.

23. Unless otherwise noted, the following account is based on Evelyn Thomchick, "The 1991 Persian Gulf War: Short-term Impacts on Ocean and Air Transportation," *Transportation Journal* 33 (Winter 1993): 40–53, http://proquest.umi.com/pqdweb?index=1&did=1339497&SrchMode=1&sid=1&Fmt=3&VInst=PROD&VType=PQD&RQT=309&VName=PQD&TS=1123428334&clientId=15020 (accessed Aug. 6, 2005).

24. Janet Porter, "War Creates Bonanza for Tanker Owners," *Journal of Commerce and Commercial* 387 (Feb. 21, 1991): 1A; Daniel Machalaba, "Oil Tanker Firms' Earnings Surge amid Gulf War," *Wall Street Journal*, Feb. 25, 1991, p. A3, reported that about 10 percent of the world's tankers were being used for storage.

25. Gourdan and Clarke, "Winning Transportation Partnerships," 6–7.

26. Richard Knee, "Foreign Crews Shun Gulf," *American Shipper* 33 (March 1991): 14.

27. Thomchick, "1991 Persian Gulf War," 1; see also Larry Hall, "Mideast Deployment: A Logistical Success," *Journal of Commerce and Commercial* 388 (June 27, 1991): 15.

28. Quoted in "In Support of Our Troops in the Gulf," *Chilton's Distribution* 90 (March 1991): 1.

29. John Hazard, "A Competitive U.S. Maritime Policy," *Transportation Journal* 22 (1982): 32–62.

30. Bruce Vail, "Pentagon Transport Chief Calls for Better Use of Boxes," *Journal of Commerce and Commercial* 387 (Feb. 19, 1991): 1; idem, "Military Learned Big Lessons in Persian Gulf Sealift," ibid., 387 (Feb. 22, 1991): 12; "[Marine Corps Commandant General Alfred] Gray Sees Less Emphasis on Sealift Speed," *Defense Daily* 171 (May 20, 1991): 285; "Airlift-Sealift Performed Well in War/Some Shortcomings Noted," ibid. 172 (Aug. 13, 1991): 246; "Official [Lt. Gen. Edward Honor] Calls for Help for Merchant Marine," *Journal of Commerce and Commercial* 388 (June 27, 1991): 20; William J. Warren, "Lessons of War," *American Shipper* 33 (April 1991): 31; Bruce Vail, "U.S. Sealift Needs More Ships, War Showed," *Journal of Commerce and Commercial* 387 (March 6, 1991): 1; William DiBenedetto, "Seminar Participants Debate Impact of Gulf War on Maritime Policy," ibid. 388 (1 May 1991): 8; David A. Menachoff and Karl B. Manrodt, "Four Steps to Maritime Reform," ibid. 387 (Feb. 19, 1991): 8.

31. Thomchick, "1991 Persian Gulf War," 7.

32. For example, the American intervention in Bosnia in 1995 and 1996 required only four hundred container shipments per week, compared with the forty thousand deployed to the Middle East for the Gulf War. Rip Watson, "Supply Movements in Bosnia Fail to Disrupt Boxed Transport Network," *Journal of Commerce and Commercial* 407 (Feb. 20, 1996): 6.

45. Ted Arison and the Fun Cruise for Thousands

1. This account of Ted Arison's early career is derived from Samuel Bichler and Jonathan Nitzan, "New Economy or Transnational Ownership? The Global Political Economy of Israel," paper presented at the international conference sponsored by the Canadian Centre for German and European Studies at York University, Toronto, May 3–4, 2002, pp. 6–7, 28–31; Adam Hanieh, "From State-Led Growth to Globalization: The Evolution of Israeli Capitalism," *Journal of Palestine Studies* 32, no. 4 (Summer 2003): 12, 19; Bob Dickinson, *Selling the Sea: An Inside Look at the Cruise Industry* (New York: John Wiley and Sons, 1997), 23–24, 30–34; "In Memory of Ted Arison," www.arison.co.il/in_memory.htm (accessed June 8, 2006); Simon Jones, "Micky and Carnival Setting Dynamic Standards," *International Cruise and Ferry Review* [hereafter *ICFR*] (Spring 1999): 13–16.

2. The first "fun ships" were the *Yarmouth* and *Yarmouth Castle*, vessels run by Eastern Steamship Lines from Miami to the Bahamas in the 1930s. Brian J. Cudahy, *The Cruise Ship Phenomenon in North America* (Centreville, MD: Cornell Maritime Press, 2001), 14. In 1965, while being operated by Yarmouth Cruise Lines, the *Yarmouth Castle* burned and sank on its way to Nassau, claiming eighty lives.

3. See pp. 293–295 herein.

4. John Maxtone-Graham, *Queen Mary II: The Greatest Ocean Liner of Our Time* (New York: Bullfinch Press, 2004), 120. For an evocative comparison of late-twentieth-century cruising with mid-twentieth-century liner travel, see Maxtone-Graham's *Liners to the Sun* (New York: Macmillan, 1985), esp. ch. 1.

5. John Malcom Brinnin, *The Sway of the Grand Saloon: A Social History of the North Atlantic* (New York: Barnes and Noble, [1971] 2000), 491–504, quotes on 498, 502, 503.

6. This slogan appears to have been introduced by the Cunard Line after World War II. Cudahy, *Cruise Ship Phenomenon*, xv.

7. Jones, "Micky and Carnival Setting Dynamic Standards." By the year 2000, Carnival had also acquired Seabourn, Windstar, and Costa Cruises of Italy. In 2003 it added P&O Princess Cruises.

8. When the *Queen Mary II* entered operations in 2004, it briefly reclaimed for Cunard the record of the world's largest cruise ship, weighing in at 150,000 gross tons and carrying 2,600 passengers. Maxtone-Graham, *Queen Mary II*. It was soon eclipsed, however, by the 160,000-ton *Freedom of the Seas*, a Royal Caribbean ship that entered service in 2006. "Cruise Critic," www.crusiecritic.com/reviews/cruiseline.cfm?CruiselineID=13 (accessed June 9, 2006).

9. www.simplonpc.co.uk/EmpressOfCanadaPCs.html (accessed June 20, 2006).

10. http://members.aol.com/CruiseAZ/largest.htm (accessed June 20, 2006).

11. David Mott, "Are Big Ships the Way Forward for the Cruise Industry?" *ICFR* (Spring 2004): 94–95.

12. Edwin McDowell, "Huge Cruise Ships Are Coming," *New York Times*, Jan. 12, 1997, http://query.nytimes.com/gst/fullpage.html?sec=travel&res=9906E2D91739F931A25752C0A961958260 (accessed June 19, 2006); Carolyn Spencer Brown, "Is Big Better: Sailing Destiny, the World's Largest Cruise Ship," *Washington Post*, Feb. 1, 1998, www.washingtonpost.com/wp-srv/travel/index/stories/brown02011998.htm (accessed June 19, 2006).

13. Ross A. Klein, *Cruise Ship Blues: The Underside of the Cruise Industry* (Gabriola, BC: New Society Publishers, 2002), 4.

14. Angie Wright, "Expanding for the Booming Cruise Industry," *ICFR* (Autumn 2005): 119.

15. Simon Jones, "Disney Magic–The Building of a Masterpiece," *ICFR* (Spring 1998): 41; Art Rodney, "Magic of Disney Opens New Markets," *ICFR* (August 1998): 17; Mac McLouth, "Port Canaveral Evolves and Grows," *ICFR* (Spring 1999): 170–171.

16. "Carnival Cruise Lines," www.taxpayer.net/budget/katrinaspending/contracts/carnival.htm (accessed June 19, 2006).

17. Bichler and Nitzan, "New Economy or Transnational Ownership?" 28–29; Jim DeFede, "The Real Micky Arison," *Miami New Times*, Feb. 3, 2000, www.miaminewtimes.com/issues/2000-02-03/defede.html (accessed June

8, 2006); Kirk Nielson, "The Perfect Scam," www.miaminewtimes.com/Issues/2000-02-03/news/feature_print.html (accessed June 8, 2003); "Carnival Cruise Lines," www.taxpayers.net/budget/katrinaspending/contracts/carnival.htm (accessed June 19, 2006).

18. Comments of Duncan Hunter on "The All American Cruise Act of 1999," November 16, 1999, *Congressional Record—Extensions*, 106th Cong., 1st sess. (Nov. 17, 1999), 145 Cong Rec E 2432.

19. Philip C. Calian, "Make No Little Plans . . . Make Big Plans," *ICFR* (Autumn 1999): 43.

20. "US Cruiseship Building Restarts after 40 Years," *ICFR* (Autumn 200): 121.

21. "Northrup Grumman Suspends Work on US-Flag Cruise Ships," *Bridgedeck*, www.bridgedeck.org/mmp_news_archive/2001/mmp_news_011026.html#anchor613366 (accessed June 8, 2006). Northrup Grumman owned Litton Ingalls. Also contributing was a steep decline after 9/11 in tourist air travel to Hawaii; those tourists formed the customer pool for cruising in the islands.

22. Following passage of special legislation in February 2003, NCL put the first of the three American-flagged and American-crewed vessels, the *Pride of Aloha*, into service on the Fourth of July 2004. www.cruisemates.com/articles/reviews/ncl/index.cfm (accessed June 20, 20006). See also M. T. Schwartzman, "A Great Day for the USA: Delivery Report: Pride of America," *ICFR* (Autumn 2005): 74–75.

23. "Convention on the International Maritime Organization," March 6, 1948, www.imo.org/Conventions/mainframe.asp?topic_id=771 (accessed Aug. 13, 2006).

24. Alan W. Cafruny, *Ruling the Waves: The Political Economy of International Shipping* (Berkeley: University of California Press, 1987), 84.

25. International Maritime Organization, "Legal," www.imo.org/home.asp (accessed Feb. 12, 2006).

26. Sarah Leipciger, "IMO Drives up Safety Standards," *ICFR* (Spring 2004): 103–104.

27. "1987: Zeebrugge Disaster Was No Accident," BBC, "On This Day," http://news.bbc.co.uk/onthisday/hi/dates/stories/October/8/newsid_2626000/2626265.stm (accessed June 20, 2006).

28. Alan Robinson, "The Scandinavian Star Incident: A Case Study," www.fire.org.uk/marine/papers/scanstar.htm (accessed June 12, 2006).

29. Eve Tarm and Michael Tarm, "The Sinking of the MS Estonia: A Chronology of the Disaster," http://balticsww.com/news/features/msestonia.htm (accessed June 12, 2006).

30. "Outlook for the European Market," *ICFR* (Spring 2000): 213.

31. Cudahy, *Cruise Ship Phenomenon*, 35. Asia was poised to challenge North America and Europe, boasting 14 percent of the world's cruise passenger capacity by 1998. Ibid., 18. The Genting Group's Star Cruises assumed dominance in this emerging market.

Conclusion

1. Charles R. Cushing coined the term "Econship," which stands for economical container ship. He developed this inexpensive and austere but reliable and habitable class of ship and built a number of them in France, Spain, South Korea, China, and elsewhere. Malcom McLean ordered twelve of a "Jumbo" version. Cushing to Roland, Dec. 1, 2006

2. Not even when he accepted government subsidy. He had declined to build Sea-Land with government subsidy, but accepted it for his United States Lines Econships. The quotation above and this account of McLean's post-Sea-Land adventures is derived from René de la Pedraja, *Historical Dictionary*, 188–189, 387–389, 624–627, quote on 624. See also de la Pedraja, *Rise and Decline of U.S. Merchant Shipping*, 274–280.

3. Overseas Shipholding Group, Inc., *2001 Annual Report*; De la Pedraja, *Historical Dictionary*, 460–461.

4. Bichler and Nitzan, "New Economy or Transnational Ownership?" 6, 31–35, 80, 86.

5. Shashi Kumar and Jan Hoffmann, "Globalisation: The Maritime Nexus," in *The Handbook of Maritime Economics and Business*, ed. Costas Th. Grammenos (London: Informa, 2002), 35–62, http://bell.mma.edu/~skumar/IAMEBook.pdf (accessed July 1, 2006), 54. Kumar and Hoffmann believe that this movement toward corporate ownership contributed to a "certain loss of identity and respectability for the industry."

6. OSG, *2001 Annual Report*, 2. On the family and legal problems that drew the Recanati family away from OSG from the point of view of an alienated brother who left the family business, see "Harry Recanati," http://harryrecanati.org (accessed June 10, 2006).

7. De la Pedraja, *Historical Dictionary*, 160–161.

8. Ibid., 379–382.

9. William A. Lovett, "U.S. Shipping Policies," in *United States Shipping Policies and the World Market*, ed. William A. Lovett (Westport, CT: Quorum Books, 1996), 41–65, esp. 57–62.

10. Kumar and Hoffmann, "Globalisation," 58. Valentina Carbone calls these TDSCs, "traditional developed shipping countries,": "Developments in the Labour Market," in *International Maritime Transport*, 67–82.

11. Kumar and Hoffman, "Globalisation," 51–52.

12. U.S. Maritime Administration, "Top 20 Merchant Fleets of the World by Country of Owner," http://marad.dot.gov/MARAD_statistics/Country-MEW-7-04.pdf (accessed June 21, 2006).

13. U.S. Maritime Administration, "Top 20 Merchant Fleet [sic] of the World," http://marad.dot.gov/MARAD_statistics/Flag-MFW-7-04.pdf (accessed June 21, 2004).

14. www.coltoncompany.com/shipping/statistics/wldflt.htm (accessed June 21, 2006).

15. Angus Maddison, *The World Economy: Historical Statistics* (Paris: Development Centre of the Organisation for Economic Co-operation and

Development, 2003), 233; idem, *The World Economy: A Millennial Perspective* (Paris: Development Centre of the Organisation for Economic Co-operation and Development, 2001), 362.

16. World Bank, United Nations Conference on Trade and Development, "Economics and Financial Flows," www.grida.no/wrr/pdf/wrr05_dt5.pdf (accessed June 24, 2006).

17. Douglas B. Cleveland, "The Role of Services in the Modern U.S. Economy," www.ita.doc.gov/td/sif/pdf/rolserv199.pdf (accessed Aug. 12, 2006).

18. Numo Limao and Anthony J. Venables, for example, found in an empirical study for the World Bank that "halving transport costs increases the volume of trade by a factor of five." "Infrastructure, Geographical Disadvantage, and Transport Costs," World Bank Working Paper 2257 (Dec. 2000), quoted in Kumar and Hoffmann, "Globalisation," 42.

19. Some analysts also feel that the hegemonic role of the United States promotes trade, just as Britain did in the nineteenth century. See Cafruny, *Ruling the Waves*; and Christopher Chase-Dunn, Yukio Kawano, and Benjamin Brewer, "Economic Globalization since 1795: Structures and Cycles in the Modern World-System," http://wsarch.ucr.edu/archive/papers/c-d&hall/isa99b/isa99b.htm (accessed June 4, 2001).

20. Paul Krugman, Richard N. Cooper, and T. N. Srinivasan, "Growing World Trade: Causes and Consequences," *Brookings Papers on Economic Activity* 1995 (1995): 327–377, esp. 327–337.

21. Kumar and Hoffmann, "Globalisation," 39.

22. Ibid., 35.

23. OECD figures, based on Lloyd's Register *World Fleet Statistics Tables*, www.oecd.org/dataoecd/39/20/2751848.pdf (accessed June 22, 2006). Percentages based on gross tonnage.

24. United Nations Conference on Trade and Development, *Review of Maritime Transport, 2001* (New York: United Nations, 2001), 15.

25. World Trade Organization, *Statistics on Globalization, 2001*, 7.

26. "Boom and Bust at Sea," *Economist*, August 20, 2005, 47.

27. U.S. Army Corps of Engineers, *Waterborne Commerce of the United States.* Part 5 *National Summaries* (Fort Belvoir, VA: Department of the Army, Corps of Engineers, 1989, 2000).

28. George Ryan says that the decline in tonnage on the Great Lakes was driven by the switch from iron ore to taconite pellets, which contain up to 97 percent iron, thus decreasing demand for iron ore, and the contraction of the American steel industry. George Ryan to Alex Roland, email attachment, Nov. 16, 2006.

29. U.S. Army Corps of Engineers, *Mississippi River Ports below and above New Orleans, Louisiana*, Port Series No. 20A, NDC-03-P-1 (Washington, DC: Government Printing Office, 2003), 34–45.

30. Leback to Alex Roland, Nov. 13, 2006.

31. U.S. Army Corps of Engineers, *Waterborne Commerce of the United States:*

Part 5, National Summaries, 1955–1968, 1970–1986, 1988–1989, 1990–2000.

32. The ten leading ports by tonnage in 2000 were Houston; South Louisiana; New Orleans; New York; Corpus Christi, TX; Beaumont, TX; Morgan City, LA; Long Beach, CA; Los Angeles; and Philadelphia. By 2003, Lake Charles, LA, had displaced Philadelphia at number ten. In dollar value, however, Houston was the only Gulf port in the top ten in 2000. U.S. Maritime Administration, *Waterborne Databank*, www.marad.dot.gov/ MARAD_statistics/index.html#Official%20U.S.%20Waterborne%20 Transportation%20Statistics (accessed Aug. 14, 2006).

33. Bureau of Transportation Statistics, *U.S. International Trade and Freight Transportation Trends*, 32.

34. Shmuel Z. Yahalom and Chang Q. Guan, "Trade Imbalance and Empty Container Surplus: The Case of Northern New Jersey," Proceedings of the Annual Conference, International Association of Maritime Economists, Izmir, Turkey, July 2, 2004.

35. Krugman et al., "Growing World Trade," 334–335.

36. Angus Maddison, *Monitoring the World Economy, 1820–1992* (Paris: OECD Development Centre of the Organisation for Economic Co-operation and Development, 1995), 227, 236, 239.

37. Krugman et al., "Growing World Trade," 335.

38. Speaking in January 1999, Douglas B. Cleveland of the Office of Service Industries, International Trade Administration in the Department of Commerce reported that the service sector's share of the U.S. economy was "roughly 80 percent." Douglas B. Cleveland, "The Role of Services in the Modern U.S. Economy," www.ita.doc.gov/td/sif/pdf/rolserv199.pdf (accessed Aug. 12, 2006).

39. Kumar and Hoffmann, "Globalisation," 39.

40. Krugman et al., "Growing World Trade," 342–343.

41. Kumar and Hoffman, "Globalisation," 59.

Epilogue

1. Angus Maddison, *Monitoring the World Economy, 1820–1992* (Paris: Development Centre of the Organisation for Economic Co-operation and Development, 1995), table 2-4, 38.

2. U.S. Department of Commerce, Bureau of Economic Analysis, International Transactions Account, www.bea.doc.gov/bea/dil.htm (accessed May 5, 2000).

3. U.S. Maritime Administration, "Top 20 Merchant Fleet [*sic*] of the World," http://marad.dot.gov (accessed Sept. 29, 2004).

4. U.S. Department of Transportation, Maritime Administration, *World Merchant Fleet 2005*, http://marad.dot.gov (accessed Feb. 13, 2006).

ART
CREDITS

Interior Art Credits

Page 192:	U.S. Naval Historical Center
Page 195:	U.S. Naval Historical Center
Page 201:	Library of Congress
Page 203:	Richard Henry Stoddard, ed., *A Century After: Picturesque Glimpses of Philadelphia and Pennsylvania* (Philadelphia: Allen, Lane & Scott and J. W. Lauderbach, 1876)
Page 206:	Copyright © by Mystic Seaport, Photographer Collection, Mystic, CT #83.23.1
Page 208:	Library of Congress
Page 219:	The Mariners' Museum, Newport News, VA
Page 236:	Copyright © by the Dorothea Lange Collection, the Oakland Museum of California, City of Oakland, gift of Paul S. Taylor
Page 242:	Great Lakes Marine Collection of the Milwaukee Public Library/Wisconsin Marine Historical Society
Page 243:	Bethlehem Area Public Library, Bethlehem, PA
Page 261:	Library of Congress
Page 271:	The Mariners' Museum, Newport News, VA
Page 276:	The Bancroft Library, University of California, Berkeley
Page 285:	The Bancroft Library, University of California, Berkeley
Page 294:	The Mariners' Museum, Newport News, VA
Page 304:	Samuel Eliot Morison, *The Battle of the Atlantic, September 1939 - May 1943* (Boston: Little, Brown, 1947), 124
Page 311:	National Canal Museum, Easton, PA
Page 312:	U.S. Maritime Administration
Page 322:	Point Reyes National Seashore, Point Reyes Station, CA
Page 327:	Eliot Lumbard
Page 338:	Børre Ludvigsen
Page 344:	Keith Tantlinger
Page 347:	Maersk Line
Page 357 (top):	U.S. Naval Historical Center
Page 357 (bottom):	Bob Vergara, All Photographic Services
Page 369:	Don Coles
Page 387:	Military Sealift Command
Page 392:	The Mariners' Museum, Newport News, VA
Page 395:	Shorelander
Page 408:	International Maritime Organization
Page 411:	John Lane

Insert Art Credits

John Stobart painting images courtesy of Maritime Heritage Prints

INDEX

Page numbers in italics refer to illustrations or photos.